THE

ANCIENT WORLD

FROM THE EARLIEST TIMES TO 800 A.D.

BY

FRANCIS S. BETTEN, S.J.

TEACHER OF HISTORY AT ST. IGNATIUS COLLEGE, CLEVELAND, OHIO
AND AT CREIGHTON UNIVERSITY SUMMER SCHOOL
OMAHA, NEBRASKA

—◦◦❧◦◦—

ALLYN AND BACON

Boston   New York   Chicago

A DI

Norwood Press
J. S. Cushing Co. — Berwick & Smith Co.
Norwood, Mass., U.S.A.

PREFACE

Sincere thanks are due both to Professor Willis M. West and to Messrs. Allyn and Bacon for the complete liberty they have granted in utilizing and altering the *Ancient World*. The author of the revision is alone responsible for all the changes introduced into the new book. It contains rather too much than too little matter, and the teacher will accordingly select what he thinks should be studied and what should be omitted or, perhaps, made the subject of cursory reading. The principles guiding the selection of books recommended for reading are laid down in the note preceding the booklist at the end of the volume.

May the book, presented in so attractive a shape by the publishers, be found helpful in promoting the great cause of Catholic education.

FRANCIS S. BETTEN, S.J.

St. Ignatius College, Cleveland, O.

TABLE OF CONTENTS

		PAGE
LIST OF ILLUSTRATIONS	. . . .	v
LIST OF MAPS AND PLANS	. . . .	xi
INTRODUCTION	. . . .	xiii

PART I—THE ORIENT

CHAPTER
I.	A. Mankind Undivided	1
	B. Nations of the Orient—General	11
II.	Egypt	15
III.	The Tigris-Euphrates States	50
IV.	The Middle States—Phoenicians and Hebrews . .	72
V.	The Persian Empire	86
VI.	Summary of Oriental Civilization	96

PART II—THE GREEKS

VII.	The Influence of Geography	99
VIII.	How we know about Prehistoric Hellas . . .	105
IX.	The First (Cretan) Civilization	111
X.	The Homeric Age	120
XI.	From the Achaeans to the Persian Wars . . .	130
XII.	The Persian Wars	167
XIII.	Athenian Leadership : The Age of Pericles . .	191
XIV.	Life in the Age of Pericles	234
XV.	The Peloponnesian War	246
XVI.	From the Fall of Athens to the Fall of Hellas, 404–338	254

PART III—THE GRAECO-ORIENTAL WORLD

XVII.	Mingling of East and West—Alexander and his Conquests	267
XVIII.	The Widespread Hellenistic World	277

PART IV — ROME

CHAPTER		PAGE
XIX.	The Place of Rome in History	303
XX.	The Land and the Peoples	306
XXI.	Legendary History	313
XXII.	Conclusions about Rome under the Kings	316
XXIII.	Class Struggles in the Republic, 510–367 B.C.	329
XXIV.	The Unification of Italy, 367–266 B.C.	339
XXV.	United Italy under Roman Rule	345
XXVI.	Government of the Republic	353
XXVII.	The Army	359
XXVIII.	Roman Society, 367–200 B.C.	363
XXIX.	The Winning of the West, 264–146 B.C.	369
XXX.	The West from 200 to 146 B.C.	388
XXXI.	The Winning of the East, 201–146 B.C.	393
XXXII.	New Strife of Classes, 146–49 B.C.	405
XXXIII.	The Gracchi	425
XXXIV.	Military Rule : Marius and Sulla	434
XXXV.	Pompey and Caesar	443

PART V — THE ROMAN EMPIRE

XXXVI.	Founding the Empire : Julius and Augustus	451
	JESUS CHRIST AND HIS WORK	471
XXXVII.	The Empire of the First Two Centuries : Story of the Emperors	476
XXXVIII.	The Empire of the First Two Centuries : Topical Survey	491
XXXIX.	The Decline in the Third Century	532
XL.	The Rise of Christianity	539
XLI.	Fourth Century : Story of the Emperors	551
XLII.	Fourth Century : Topical Survey	566

PART VI — ROMANO-TEUTONIC EUROPE

XLIII.	The Teutons	582
XLIV.	The Wandering of the Peoples, 376–565 A.D.	588
XLV.	Western Europe, 400–600 A.D.	608
XLVI.	Western Europe, 600–768 A.D.	621
XLVII.	The Empire of Charlemagne	637

APPENDIX : A Classified List of Selected Books for a High School Library in History 653

INDEX, PRONOUNCING VOCABULARY, AND MAP REFERENCES . . 659

ILLUSTRATIONS

PAGE

Prehistoric Stone Daggers xiii

Facsimile from Latin Bible xiv

Series of Axes, Stone and Bronze xvii

Reindeer, drawn by Cave-men in France and in Switzerland . . xviii

Some Stages in Fire-making. From Tylor 7

Portion of the Rosetta Stone, containing the hieroglyphs first deciphered 12

Part of the Rosetta Inscription, on a larger scale 12

Photograph of Modern Egyptian sitting by a Sculptured Head of an
Ancient King ; to show likeness of feature 17

Boatmen fighting on the Nile. Egyptian relief 19

A Capital from Karnak. From Lübke 20

Portrait Statue of Amten, a self-made noble of 3200 B.C. . . 22

Egyptian Noble hunting Waterfowl on the Nile. After Maspero . 23

Temple at Luxor 25

Egyptian Plow. From Rawlinson 28

Market Scene. An Egyptian relief 29

Shoemakers. Egyptian relief, from Maspero 30

Sphinx and Pyramids. From a photograph 31

Restoration of an Egyptian Temple 33

Ra-Hotep ; perhaps the oldest portrait statue in existence . . 34

Princess Nefert ; a portrait statue 5000 years old 34

Temple of Edfu 35

A Relief from the Temple of Hathor at Dendera 36

Egyptian Numerals 37

Isis and Horus 38

Sculptured Funeral Couch ; picturing the soul crouching by the
mummy 39

A Tomb Painting ; showing offerings to the dead 40

	PAGE
Weighing the Soul before the Judges of the Dead. Egyptian relief	41
Cheops (Khufu). A portrait statue	43
Sculptors at Work. An Egyptian relief	44
Thutmosis III	46
Rameses II	47
Psammetichus in Hieroglyphs	48
Neco in Hieroglyphs	48
Nebuchadnezzar in Cuneiform Characters	58
Colossal Man-beast, from the Palace of Sargon	59
Assyrian Contract Tablet in Duplicate	60
Assyrian Tablets; showing the older hieroglyphs and the later cuneiform equivalents in parallel columns	61
An Assyrian " Book "	63
An Assyrian Dog. A relief on a clay tablet	64
Assyrian " Deluge Tablet "	65
Assyrian Cylinder Seals	66
Impression from a Royal Seal	67
A Lion Hunt. An Assyrian relief	68
Section of the Temple of the Seven Spheres ; according to a " restoration " by Rawlinson	69
Parts of Alphabets	74
Growth of the Letter A	74
Temple of Solomon	79
Jerusalem To-Day, with the road to Bethlehem	83
Impression from a Persian Cylinder Seal	89
Persian Queen. A fragment of a bronze statue	91
Persian Bronze Lion, at Susa	93
Persian Jewelry	96
Scene in the Vale of Tempe. From a photograph	103
Bronze Dagger from Mycenae, inlaid with gold	108
The Gate of the Lions at Mycenae	109
Mouth of the Palace Sewer at Knossos, 2200 B.C., with terra-cotta drain pipes. From Baikie	110
Head of a Bull. From a relief at Knossos	111
The Vaphio Cups, of 1800 or 2000 B.C.	112

PAGE

Scroll from the Vaphio Cups, showing stages in netting and taming wild bulls. From Perrot and Chipiez 113

Vase from Knossos (about 2200 B.C.), with sea-life ornament . . 114

Cretan Writing 115

"Throne of Minos." From Baikie 116

Cooking Utensils ; found in one tomb at Knossos . . . 117

Cretan Vase of Late Period (1600 B.C.), with conventionalized ornament 118

Ruins of the Entrance to the Stadium at Olympia . . . 133

Ruins of Athletic Field at Delphi 137

Greek Soldier 148

Ground Plan of Temple of Theseus at Athens 158

Doric Column, with explanations. From the Temple of Theseus . 159

Ionic Column 159

Corinthian Column 159

A Doric Capital. From a photograph of a detail of the Parthenon 160

West Front of the Parthenon To-day ; to illustrate Doric style . 162

West Front of Temple of Victory at Athens ; to illustrate Ionic style 163

Marathon To-day. From a photograph 175

Thermopylae. From a photograph 182

The Bay of Salamis. From a photograph 185

Pericles. A portrait bust ; now in the Vatican . . . 200

Side View of a Trireme. From an Athenian relief . . . 201

The Acropolis To-day 214

Propylaea of the Acropolis To-day 215

Erechtheum and Parthenon 216

Figures from the Parthenon Frieze 217

Sophocles. A portrait statue, now in the Lateran . . . 218

Theater of Dionysus at Athens 219

Thucydides. A portrait bust ; now in the Capitoline Museum . 221

The Acropolis as "restored" by Lambert 225

Women at their Toilet. Two parts of a vase painting . . 228

Greek Women at their Music. From a vase painting . . 229

Plan of a Fifth-century Delos House. After Gardiner and Jevons . 235

	PAGE
Greek Girls at Play. From a vase painting	237
A Vase Painting showing Paris enticing away Helen	239
Greek Women, in various activities. A vase painting	240
A Barber in Terra-cotta. From Blümner	241
Athene	242
School Scenes. A bowl painting	244
Route of the Long Walls of Athens. From a recent photograph	252
The Hermes of Praxiteles	258
Philip II of Macedon. From a gold medallion struck by Alexander	264
Alexander. From a gold medallion of Tarsus	268
Alexander in a Lion-hunt. Reverse side of the above	268
Alexander. The Copenhagen head	269
Alexander as Apollo. Now in the Capitoline	273
Pylon of Ptolemy III at Karnak	280
Julius Caesar. The British Museum bust	300
Remains of an Etruscan Wall and Arch at Sutri	308
Etruscan Tombs at Orvieto	309
So-called Wall of Servius	318
Cloaca Maxima	319
An Early Roman Coin (Janus and a ship's prow)	321
Bridge over the Anio	332
A Coin showing the City Seal of Syracuse	340
A Coin of Syracuse about 400 B.C.	340
A Coin of Pyrrhus	343
A Coin of Pyrrhus, struck in Sicily	343
The Appian Way, with the Aqueduct of Claudius in the Background	350
Head of a Javelin	359
A Roman Boxing Match	367
A Coin of Hiero II of Syracuse	372
Ruins at Corinth	399
The House of M. Olconius at Pompeii	410
A Court in a Pompeian House (House of the Vettii)	413
An Excavated Street in Pompeii	418
Temple of Apollo at Pompeii	431

PAGE

A Theater at Pompeii 436
A Coin of Mithridates VI 439
Sulla. A portrait bust 440
Cicero. A portrait bust 446
Pompey. The Copenhagen bust 454
Julius Caesar. The Naples bust 455
The Forum at Pompeii 456
The Roman Forum, looking south 459
The Roman Forum, looking north 460
Marcus Brutus. A bust now in the Capitoline Museum . . . 461
Octavius Caesar as a Boy 464
Augustus. The Vatican statue 467
Bridge at Rimini built by Augustus 468
Church of the Nativity 471
A Gold Coin of Augustus 476
Ruins of the Claudian Aqueduct. From a photograph . . . 478
A Bronze Coin of Nero 479
Agrippina, Mother of Nero 480
The Coliseum To-day 481
Detail from the Arch of Titus 482
A Coin of Domitian 484
Temple of Zeus at Athens, built by Hadrian 486
The Tomb of Hadrian 487
Marcus Aurelius. An equestrian statue 488
Head of Commodus. From a coin 489
Interior of the Coliseum To-day 493
A German Bodyguard : a detail from the column of Marcus Aurelius 497
Part of the Aqueduct of Claudius, built into a modern wall . . 500
Aqueduct near Nîmes, built by Antoninus Pius 503
A City Gate at Pompeii 505
Palace of the Roman Emperors at Trier 514
The Black Gate at Trier 515
The Pantheon 518
A Section of the Pantheon 518

	PAGE
The Coliseum, seen through the Arch of Titus	519
Trajan's Column	520
General Plan of Basilicas	521
Trajan's Basilica, "restored" by Canina	521
The Arch of Titus	524
Trajan's Arch at Beneventum	525
The Way of Tombs at Pompeii	528
Detail from Trajan's Column, showing the famous bridge over the Danube	530
Crypt of St. Cecilia in the Catacombs of St. Callixtus	549
Ruins of the Baths of Diocletian	552
Hall of the Baths of Diocletian: now the Church of St. Mary of the Angels	557
The Milvian Bridge To-day	559
The Arch of Constantine	562
The Lateran Basilica, Rome	570
Frontispiece of the "Golden Gospel"	585
Church of San Vitale at Ravenna	599
A Gold Coin of Theodosius II, showing Byzantine characteristics	600
The Tomb of Theodoric at Ravenna	611
Monastery of St. Benedict at Subiaco	613
The "Monogram Page" of the Book of Kells	614
The Mosque of Omar at Jerusalem	625
The Damascus Gate at Jerusalem	628
Outer View of St. Paul's Gate, Rome	633
A Silver Coin of Charlemagne	638
Medallion of Sts. Peter and Paul	642
Throne of Charlemagne at Aachen	647
Cathedral of Aachen; the "Carolingian part"	648
Ancient Monograms of Jesus Christ	652

MAPS AND PLANS

	PAGE
The Field of Ancient History	9
The First Homes of Civilization. Full page, colored . *after*	12
Ancient Egypt	16
Egyptian Empire at its Greatest Extent	45
Assyrian and Babylonian Empire	55
Northern Egypt and Southern Palestine	76
Syria, showing Dominion of Solomon and Other Features of Hebrew History	77
Lydia, Media, Egypt, and Babylonia, about 560 B.C. Full page, colored . . . . *after*	86
The Persian Empire. Full page, colored . . . . *after*	88
Greece and the Adjoining Coasts. Double page, colored . *after*	98
The Greek Peninsula. Double page, colored . . . *after*	102
The Greek World. (For general reference.) Double page, colored . . . . *after*	136
Peloponnesian League	169
Plan of Marathon	174
Attica, with reference to Marathon and Salamis . . .	184
Athens and its Ports, showing the "Long Walls" . . .	193
Athenian Empire. Full page, colored . . . . *after*	202
Plan of Athens	206
The Acropolis at Athens	213
Greece at the Beginning of the Peloponnesian War. Full page, colored . . . . *after*	250
Plan of the Battle of Leuctra	260
Greece under Theban Supremacy. Full page, colored . *after*	262
The Growth of Macedonia	265

PAGE

Campaigns and Empire of Alexander the Great. Full page,
    colored . . . . *after* 270

The East about 300 B.C. Full page, colored . . . *after* 282

The Achaean and Aetolian Leagues 287

The World according to Eratosthenes 297

Italy. (For general reference.) Full page, colored . *after* 308

The Peoples of Italy 310

Rome and Vicinity 311

Rome under the Kings 317

Italy about 200 B.C. ; Roads and Colonies 354

Plan of a Roman Camp 367

Rome and Carthage at the Opening of the First Punic War . . 370

The Mediterranean Lands at the Opening of the Second Punic War.
    Double page, colored . . . . *after* 378

Roman Dominions and Dependencies in 146 B.C. 401

The Roman Empire at its Greatest Extent, showing States of Growth.
    Double page, colored . . . . *after* 498

Rome under the Empire 535

The Roman Empire divided into Prefectures and Dioceses. Double
    page, colored . . . . *after* 554

The Rhine-Danube Frontier before the Great Migrations. Full
    page 584

The Migrations. Double page, colored . . . . *after* 588

Europe in the Reign of Theodoric (500 A.D.). Full page,
    colored . . . . *after* 598

Europe at the Death of Justinian (565 A.D.). Full page, colored
                                            after 602

Germanic Kingdoms on Roman Soil at the Close of the Sixth Cen-
    tury. Double page, colored . . . . . *after* 606

Kingdom of the Merovingians. Full page, colored . . *after* 622

Europe at the End of the Seventh Century. Full page, colored
                                            after 632

The Four Great Powers in 800 A.D. Double page, colored *after* 640

THE ANCIENT WORLD

INTRODUCTION

Historical Sources. — The student learns of the many events and facts which make up the history of mankind from the historical books written and published in our own time. But how do the authors of these books know what happened centuries ago? They consult what we call the *sources of history.* There are three kinds of such sources:

(1) *Oral Traditions.* — The stories of happenings of the past if handed down and propagated by word of mouth only, are called oral traditions. These stories tell of the deeds of prominent men, both good and bad, or of the beginnings and vicissitudes of nations, and frequently they relate to matters of relig-

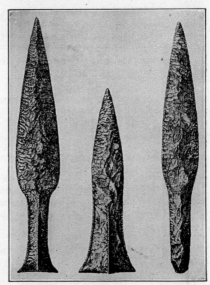

PREHISTORIC STONE DAGGERS.

ion. Many, perhaps the greatest part of them, have undergone changes in the course of time and have become more or less fabulous. But historians often discover even in these a certain amount of truth, though it may be obscured by legendary fictions.

(2) *Relics.* — By relics we understand the weapons, tools, household things, articles of ornament, etc., which were used by men of former ages; also their works of art, the ruins of their buildings, the very remains of their dead buried in simple

FACSIMILE FROM THE CODEX AMIATINUS OF THE LATIN BIBLE.

ET FACTUS EST PAVOR IN OMNIBUS ET COLLOQUEBANTUR AD INVICEM DICENTES QUOD EST HOC VERBUM QUIA IN POTESTATE ET VIRTUTE IMPERAT SPIRITIBUS IMMUNDIS ET EXEUNT

And there came fear upon all, and they talked among themselves, saying: What word is this, for with authority and power he commandeth the unclean spirits, and they go out? Luke iv. 36.

Ancient manuscript copies of important books, such as the Bible, are called Codices. The Codex Amiatinus was originally preserved in the Italian monastery of Amiatæ, but is now in a library of Florence, Italy. It was written, about the year A.D. 541, by the Abbot Servandus, disciple of St. Benedict.

graves or elaborate mausoleums; finally the pictorial representations in painting and sculpture.

(3) *Written Records,* inscriptions and especially manuscript or printed books, coming from persons who are both able and willing to tell the truth. It does not matter whether or not the author lived at the time the events he describes took place, provided it is known that he used reliable sources.

The Bible. — The noblest of all the written records concerning the history of mankind is the Bible. God himself is the author of this Book of Books; those whom we call the authors of its various parts acted, as it were, only as God's secretaries. They wrote down what God "inspired" them to write; the knowledge of the various facts and truths they obtained partly through direct revelation from God, partly as a result of their own efforts; but God put the seal of His authorship upon whatever they actually embodied in their work.

The purpose of this divine condescension was man's eternal salvation by a supernatural life; no error, therefore, regarding faith and morals could ever find its way into the Bible. God did not intend, however, to furnish the world with a handbook of geology or astronomy or history, or to advance man directly in any of these or other sciences; hence the sacred writers when touching upon such matters simply reflected the views, scientific or popular, of their own time and surroundings. Their books, if judged by this standard, were in the beginning free from any error. It is not absolutely impossible, however, that errors concerning secular matters, figures, for instance, should have crept in later through the fault of copyists. Pope Leo XIII warns us not to be hasty in presuming such errors; the scrupulous care always taken for the preservation of this most important document of revealed religion does not make it likely that they are numerous.

"The Bible is not the oldest book in the world. No writing, however, no document on stone or clay, no hieroglyphic or cuneiform inscription takes us back to the primitive history of mankind, as told on the first pages of the Bible. The sacred writer drew his information primarily from Divine Revelation, but an unbroken tradition and ancient documents were also at his disposal." (*Outlines of Bible Knowledge*, Edited by Archbishop Messmer, p. 11.)

After briefly acquainting us with the general history of the first times of mankind, Holy Writ confines itself to the development, successes and failures of the chosen people of God, the Hebrews, but it is full of references to other nations and their rulers.[1]

Great care must be exercised when assigning dates to remote events. Relics, and not only the ruder ones, frequently leave us without the slightest clew as to the time when they were in actual use. Much of the idle conjectures in so-called popular histories is due to rash conclusions which ignore this fact.

Evolution.[2] — It has been observed that some plants as well as animals undergo changes when they are acted upon in various ways by their surroundings. There are many interesting instances of such adaptations. But they are not so numerous as people are often led to think. So-called popular scientific works often enlarge upon them in a manner which is entirely unwarranted by facts. They maintain without the slightest proof, that lifeless matter, under the influence of heat, pressure or electricity, may " evolve " into a plant, and a plant, large or small, into an animal. Nothing has ever been discovered or observed to substantiate such a preposterous statement.

But it is the height of folly to maintain that man himself, body and soul, has " evolved " from some beast. The human soul can only come directly from God. Not even man's body has " evolved " from that of a beast. Holy Scripture tells us how the first men were created.

Hence the supposition that rational man is a mere product of natural evolution and that his first stages were spent in the lowest savagery is without foundation and directly contrary to our Faith. It is an error of many modern histories which seek to explain human development, intellectual, political, and religious, as independent of God the Creator and His Providence. Human development in as far as it is natural depends upon the exercise of man's natural faculties and not upon some inanimate or fatalistic force which has its origin in the mere powers of matter.

---

[1] For editions of the Bible, see Appendix.

[2] The teacher may postpone the study of this section and the following to some time later in the year, that is, if he sees fit to make it an object of recitation at all. He may explain the matter orally or refer to these pages as occasion requires.

Civilization. — We live in a civilized country. We have good houses, build beautiful churches and schools, and splendid cities, and a good government preserves order in the land. A farming class tills the soil and thereby provides food for the whole population. Other peoples live a different life. Their dwellings are the rudest kind of huts or tents or even caverns in the ground. Such peoples we say are not civilized at all, or at any rate, they are on the lowest level of civilization.

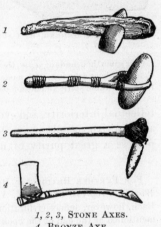

We speak of *material* civilization, by which we mean the control and employment of nature, its treasures and its forces, as the fruits of the earth, the metals, wind, fire, water, electricity. *Intellectual* civilization stands higher; it shows itself in the pursuit of learning and all kinds of art. There is also a *social* civilization; it consists in good government, in a cer-

1, 2, 3, STONE AXES.
4, BRONZE AXE.

tain refinement of manners, and above all in the integrity of family life, which is the natural foundation of society. But higher than all this is *religious and moral* civilization. Individual man as well as the whole race must pay due respect to the Creator and observe the laws which God has given. A nation which is wanting in this lacks the most necessary element in true civilization. These sundry elements, however, are not separated from one another by hard and fast lines. Many features in a nation's life may be classed under several of them.

The terms "savagery" and "barbarism" are often used to denote the lowest and a somewhat higher degree of civilization. But care is required in using them. They are frequently meant to denote not only rude material conditions, but also in-

REINDEER, BY CAVE-DWELLERS (STONE AGE).

On slate, in France.   *On horn, in Switzerland.*

(For some thousands of years, the reindeer has been extinct in these countries. Compare these drawings with modern pictures for accuracy of detail; and note the remarkable spirit and action depicted by the prehistoric artists.)

tellectual inferiority, and even a low standing of morality. Yet a primitive people may display a keen mental acumen or possess a great purity of morals and correct religious ideas.

FOR FURTHER READING IF DESIRED. — Charles S. Devas, *Key to the World's Progress*, Part I; E. A. Hull, S.J., *Civilization and Culture*. Each, however, defines civilization somewhat differently. Also the works mentioned at the end of the book under Evolution.

PART I. — THE ORIENT

CHAPTER I

A. MANKIND UNDIVIDED

1. From the Creation to the Deluge. — "In the beginning God created heaven and earth." In six periods of uncertain duration called "days," the dwelling place of intellectual man was prepared. Then "God formed man of the slime of the earth and breathed into his face the breath of life, and man became a living soul." Man thus came directly from the hands of his Creator, endowed with perfect faculties of body and soul, and with a wonderful knowledge of the natural things which surrounded him. To make Adam the true fountainhead of mankind, the first woman, Eve, was created from his body. She was to be his "helpmate" in the occupations of his earthly existence, but his perfect equal in the vocation to eternal life. Thus God established matrimony.

God had raised man from the beginning to an essentially higher level by endowing him with Sanctifying Grace which elevated him to a supernatural order. He had besides bestowed upon him preternatural gifts, as the immortality of the body and freedom from tribulations and diseases. But unfortunately Adam did not stand the test of fidelity and lost Sanctifying Grace together with these gifts for himself as well as his entire posterity. In his mercy, however, God promised a Redeemer who was to atone for the offences against his Divine Majesty and regain for mankind the possibility of entering into Heaven.

Soon there must have been a kind of patriarchal community, consisting of the children and children's children of Adam who was its head. The descendants of Adam's first-born son, Cain, excelled in material progress. They were masters in the use of musical instruments and possessed great skill in the working of bronze and iron. But also the relaxation of the marriage tie is on their short record in Holy Writ. The descendants of Seth, another son of Adam, devoted themselves more to a life of piety. Both these clans found their sympathizers and adherents. But intermarriages finally brought about a general decline of morals. " The wickedness upon earth was great." Only Noe and several of his family " walked with the Lord."

The Deluge. — God now resolved to destroy all mankind by a vast inundation which we call the Deluge. Noe alone with seven other souls was saved in the Ark, a huge craft built by him at God's command. It is difficult for us to form an adequate idea of the terrible catastrophe, the result of which was a wholesale destruction of the entire human race. The Ark finally landed somewhere in Armenia. From here the rapidly increasing population began to spread over the whole earth. The inhabitants of a plain called Senaar, the later Babylonia, resolved in sinful pride to erect a city with a colossal tower as a lasting monument of their own power. But their language became " confounded." We may presume that God's inter ference accelerated the differentiation of the languages, which is otherwise a natural process. The locality of this unfinished " Tower of Babel " was probably the city of Babylon or its environs.

Chronologists following the Vulgate, the official Latin Bible of the Church, assign 2350 B.C. as the date of the Deluge, while the figures in the Greek Bible which is also acknowledged by the Church would point to 3134 B.C. Hence, the Church does not hold us to either number. All we know with certainty is that the Deluge must antedate by many years the beginnings of the earliest distinct nations. And probably one or two thousand years had elapsed between the Creation and the Flood. Those who give to man an existence of 200,000 years or more have never proved their assertion. There is no reason to go beyond eight or at the most ten thousand years before Christ. As to the extent of the Deluge, we may, if we choose, hold that the water covered not the entire earth but only the entire " land " where mankind lived. But the opinion that other human beings beside those saved in the Ark survived the Flood is not favored by the Church and lacks scientific proof.

2. The New Nations. — After relating the story of the Tower of Babel, Holy Writ still gives us the names of Noe's next descendants with some short hints as to their dwelling places. These valuable notes connect as it were by a thin thread many of the great nations of the earth with the eight persons in the Ark. The three sons of Noe became the ancestors of three families of nations. The descendants of Sem (Shem) are called the Semites ; to them belong the Assyrians, Arabs, and Jews. Cham (Ham) was the father of the Hamites, among whom are the Chanaanites (the original inhabitants of Palestine), the Babylonians, Egyptians and the Negroes of Africa. The Aryans or Indo-Europeans, comprising the Hindoos, the Medes and Persians, the Greeks, Italians, Celts, Germans and Slavs, were the offspring of Japhet. Mixture of race, however, and the influence of climate and country produced an infinitely greater variety than this plain enumeration would lead one to believe. There is in fact hardly any people in the world which represents an unmixed stock. It ought not to surprise us, if many a people, the Chinese for instance, does not fit neatly into our simple classification.

Sameness of language as a rule argues sameness of origin. Yet some few nations have exchanged their own idiom for that of a neighbor. On the other hand, learned men assure us that the diversities among the inhabitants of the globe, such as color and language, are no reason to doubt the unity of the human race. The languages, in spite of their variety, positively point to one common origin.

Religious Decay. — Unfortunately this extension of mankind over the earth was, on the whole, accompanied by a decay in religion and morals. In the course of time much of the supernatural truth revealed to Adam and by him transmitted to his children, became obscured. The worship of the One True God gave way to idolatry. Even the natural knowledge of man's various duties was very generally disregarded or overlaid with gross superstitions and errors.

In the beginning this deterioration probably did not proceed very rapidly. Much that makes on us the impression of polytheism may have been the adoration of the same God under different names. Little by little, too, a people may have come to look upon many violations of the moral law as less blameworthy than they really are. This of course somewhat lessened personal guilt, but became an immense calamity for a nation at large. Every human soul, however, is created immediately by God. On arriving at the full development of its faculties it is able to realize its essential duties, and the transgressions of the natural law are recognized as sinful and deserving of punishment. Hence we should not be surprised if we notice among pagans instances of true natural virtue and even meet with with an honest endeavor to rescue religion and morality from complete ruin. But we also understand the severe verdict of St. Paul who declares of the pagans that "they are inexcusable." (Rom. I, 20.)

But the Almighty forgot not the promise given to the first parents. While idolatry threatened to enslave all mankind, He took care that at least one nation still worshipped the God "Who made heaven and earth," and hoped and waited for the appearance of the "light for the revelation of the Gentiles."

Civilization after the Flood. — By the time of the flood mankind must have been on a very high level of civilization. Arts were practised, metal instruments were in use. The construction of a vessel of the dimensions and character of the Ark, and the planning and partial erection of the Tower of Babel, suppose an astounding proficiency in mathematical knowledge and technical ability. This precious heirloom was not suddenly lost. The various tribes took it along to their new domiciles. It could, however, avail them only where there was a large number of people together and where nature supplied the necessary material. If thrown into less favored regions and deprived of connection with the stream of original civilization, they could forget or fail to practise much of what they or their fathers had seen in their ancient homes. Their civilization sank to a lower level and was likely to sink still lower with every new generation. The natural sources of history disclose the fact that nations living at the same time but in different countries often show a remarkable difference in civilization. Far from being surprising, this is but the consequence of the dispersion of the human race.

Such tribes, rendered helpless by isolation and the miserly character of their soil would frequently resort to a very primitive mode of life. Stone, wood or bone is the only material they know how to work into implements for household use or into weapons for the chase. Similarly, intellectual civilization, the taste for arts of all kinds, theoretical knowledge of nature and its secrets, could be wholly or in part forgotten.

God's Providence, however, watched over the greatest natural possession of mankind. Some nations always kept the torch of material and intellectual civilization burning and in their turn spread its light abroad. They added to it by their own inventions, by devising better methods of the government of cities and empires, or by increasing the knowledge of nature, and by building up systems of every kind of science. Each people did this according to its own character, thus giving to its civilization a peculiar national type. As a matter of fact, just those peoples whose traces we can with some degree of certainty follow back the farthest into remote antiquity, at once appear with a rather full-grown civilization. But the only efficient way of reclaiming fallen races is vigorous contact with one more highly civilized. There is no genuine case known of auto-development of any savage people.

Some Terms Relating to Early History. — With the information obtained from natural sources we are able to reconstruct with varying accuracy the story of the most important nations. Of some nations we have no written records at all. We call them *prehistoric* — which, however, is by no means synonymous with savage. Often the traces of prehistoric nations are discovered in localities which later on became the homes of highly civilized peoples. These may or may not have been the descendants of the former. We also speak of *Stone Age*, *Bronze*[1] *Age*, *Iron Age*, according to the principal material used for implements. But all these terms must be used carefully There has been no general stone

---

[1] Bronze is an amalgamation of copper and tin. It is harder than either of its components, but not by far so hard as iron.

period for all mankind. Many peoples were satisfied with ruder implements while others show a high degree of civilization. Columbus found
the natives of America using stone very largely. Nor did stone tools and
weapons disappear directly after the introduction of iron. It would be
rash to conclude that the " stone men " themselves re-invented the working
of metals, because this art may have been imported. Rasher still would
be the verdict that they were inferior in intellect. (See p. xvii.) As to
their religion and morals we have hardly any clew except that they bestowed much care upon the burial of their dead.

We do not apply these terms to pre-diluvian times. Whether there was
a pre-diluvian stone age, that is, a period during which the first men were
ignorant of the metals, we do not know. Maybe their knowledge was
included in the extraordinary science of natural things which God granted
to our first parents.

Nor is the age before the Flood prehistoric. We know of it from a
written document, the Bible, the author of which is an infallible eye witness, God Himself.

3. Elementary Features of Civilization. — The civilization of
many nations in their earliest period was indeed low. Yet·
with few if any exceptions all appear to have saved certain
elements of pre-diluvian inheritance. Prehistoric civilization,
no matter when and where encountered, is in possession of at
least three achievements. The historic nations come under our
view equipped with the same achievements. The very oldest,
however, stand higher than this alone would indicate. These
three elements are : —

(a) *The use of fire*, which perhaps more than any other
material advantage shows man superior to the beasts. While
the animal flees from it, fire is man's most powerful friend.
Charred fragments of bone and wood are common among the
earliest human deposits. One of the oldest tools in the world
is the " fire borer," a hard stick of wood with which man started
a fire by boring into a more inflammable wood. The methods
of making fire which are pictured on the next page are all used
by prehistoric nations.

(b) *The use of domestic animals.* — They are not the same nor
equally numerous with all peoples and in all countries. Those
familiar to us in the barnyard or on the farm have come from

Asia. The western hemisphere is considerably poorer, and those found there are not so excellently fitted for domestic purposes. This fact partly accounts for the backwardness of America before the discovery. Nations that retained little of

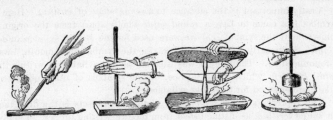

SOME STAGES IN FIREMAKING. — From Tylor.

the original civilization have few domestic beasts, but there are hardly any that have none at all.

(c) *The use of agricultural plants*, in the first place the food-grains, as wheat, barley, rice, and the vegetables. Those who were nearer the stream of original civilization in the Asiatic countries enjoyed a great advantage. Out of the myriads of wild plants all our marvelous progress in science has failed to reveal even one other in the Old World so useful as those which man has already actually cultivated. Their only successful rivals are the potato and maize (Indian corn) contributed by the New World. All the prehistoric nations knew the cultivation of some agricultural plants.

(d) To call a nation "historic" we must have written information about it, records composed by its own chroniclers or by others who knew about it. This presupposes the *art of writing*. It is impossible to tell when and in what way man obtained this most important accomplishment.

It is certainly interesting to learn about the various kinds of writing which our historical sources disclose to us.

Many early peoples used a *picture writing* such as is common still among North American Indians. In this kind of writing, a picture represents either an object or some idea connected with that object. A drawing of an animal with wings may stand for a *bird* or for *flying;* or a character like this ☉ stands for either the *sun* or for *light.* At first such pictures are true drawings : later they are simplified into forms agreed upon. Thus in ancient Chinese, *man* was represented by 大, and in modern Chinese by 人 .

Vastly important is the advance to a *rebus stage of writing.* Here a symbol has come to have a *sound value* wholly apart from the original object, as if the symbol ☉ above were used for the second syllable in *delight.* So in early Egyptian writing, ◯, the symbol for "mouth," was pronounced *rû.* Therefore it was used as the last syllable in writing the word *khopirû,* which meant " to be," while symbols of other objects in like manner stood for the other syllables.

This representation of *syllables* by pictures of objects is the first stage in *sound writing,* as distinguished from picture writing proper. Finally, some of these characters are used to represent not whole syllables, but *single sounds.* One of Kipling's *Just So* stories illustrates how such a change might come about. Then, if these characters are kept and all others dropped, we have a *true alphabet.* Picture writing, such as that of the Chinese, requires many thousand symbols. Several hundred characters are necessary for even simple syllabic writing. But a score or so of letters are enough for an alphabet. Several primitive peoples developed their writing to the syllabic stage; and about 1000 B.C., in various districts about the eastern Mediterranean, alphabetic writing appeared.

4. Our Field of History. — It is the historical nations, then, to which we confine ourselves. Prehistoric civilization will be alluded to in so far only as it may throw light upon the conditions in historic times. Yet a further limitation is necessary.

Soon after the Deluge numerous tribes must have turned toward the East, where we now find the multiform populations of China, Japan, and the Indies, with their distinct civilizations. With this large fraction of humanity the present book can not deal. We care most to know of those peoples whose life has borne fruit for our own life. *We shall study that part of the recorded past which explains our present.* Thus we bound our study in space.

We have to limit it in time as well. Until after Columbus, our interest centres in Europe. And when we look for those early peoples to which we must ascribe the greatest influence upon the life of Europe, we find two eminent, — *the Greeks* and *the Romans*. A third ancient people, the insignificant nation of *the Hebrews*, had the great mission of keeping the road open for the most important factor in the life of mankind, Christianity. Under the guidance of Christianity *newer races* were to take up the work. By A.D. 800 all these various influences

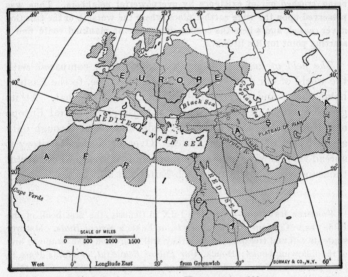

THE FIELD OF ANCIENT HISTORY, TO 800 A.D.

had merged in one, and the result was the beginning of modern Europe. *Ancient History*, then will carry us to this date, the turning point in European history. This book will deal with *Ancient History* only.

Of the historic peoples of ancient Europe the Greeks were the first to rise to highly civilized life. But the civilization of the Greeks was not wholly their own. Its germs were received from the older civilizations outside Europe, near the eastern shores of the Mediterranean. The history of these Oriental peoples covered thousands of years; but we shall view only fragments of it, and we do that merely by way of introduction to Greek history. Oriental history is a sort of anteroom through which we pass to European history.

The Hebrews indeed contributed very little to material civilization. But their importance for our religious and moral culture is paramount. A special Providence watched over this little nation and kept it from being crushed out of existence by overpowerful neighbors. Thus was preserved upon the wide earth a place where the worship of the true God never ceased, and where the coming Redeemer of mankind could find a starting point for His lifework.

The field of ancient history, then, is small, compared with the world of our day. It was limited, of course, to the Eastern hemisphere, and covered only a small part of that. At its greatest extent, it reached north only through Central Europe east through less than a third of Asia, and south through only a small part of Northern Africa. Over even this territory it spread very slowly, from much more limited areas. For several thousand years, it did not reach Europe at all.

FURTHER READING. — Chapters I–IX in Genesis (the first book of the Bible) as in Coppens' *Choice Morsels*, or Ecker's *School Bible*. Maturer students will find treatments which they will enjoy and understand in any of the following books : Houck, *Our Palace Beautiful,* or *Man's Place in the Visible Creation.* Keary, *Dawn of History ;* Starr, *Some First Steps in Human Progress ;* also the books quoted after the Introduction, p. xviii.

The textbook will confine its special suggestions for library work in Greek history (up to the period of Alexander) to William Sterns Davis' *Readings in Ancient History* and to one other single-volume work, — J. B. Bury's *History of Greece,* — with occasional *alternatives* suggested for the latter.

In like manner, for Rome (to the Empire), the *Readings* and either Pelham's *Outlines of History* or How and Leigh's *History* afford satisfactory material. For Oriental history, there is no one satisfactory volume to go with the *Readings ;* but library work is less important for that period.

The giant ruins of Egyptian glory and the mummies and mummy cases of our museums provoke serious and gloomy reflections. They recall an ancient long vanished world, a buried world peering with the craggy remnants of its walls through the sands of the desert, a world finally winnowed out of the sepulchral dust of millenniums. And yet it existed some time, radiant with sunlight and pleasure, alive with gay and brilliant crowds and ever stirring activity. — A. BAUMGARTNER, S.J.

5. The Rediscovery of Early History. — Until about a hundred years ago the early history of the East was almost unknown. The precious information contained in the Bible and the notes of ancient Greek travelers disclosed too little about the lands and peoples in the Nile valley and on the banks of the Euphrates and Tigris. Yet there were the extensive remains of temples, palaces, and tombs with inscriptions in mysterious characters. A buried world was awaiting its resurrection. The strange writings found in the Euphrates lands were at first set down as some peculiar form of Hebrew or Chinese, or as mere ornamentations or the effect of the weather. But in A.D. 1802, the German scholar Grotefend was able to identify several royal names. Others by patient labor corrected and completed the result of his studies. About 1850 Rawlinson, one of the greatest investigators, read and translated a gigantic rock inscription, which in three languages celebrated the deeds of Darius I (§§ 75, 76). The kind of writing thus discovered is called " cuneiform " (§ 47), and it was found to have been adapted to a great many Eastern languages. Good luck furnished a clue to the Egyptian kind of writing. About 1800 A.D., some soldiers of Napoleon in Egypt, while laying foundations for a fort at the Rosetta mouth of the Nile (map, page 16), found a curious slab of black rock. This " Rosetta Stone " bore three inscriptions : one of these was in Greek ; one, in the ancient hieroglyphs of the pyramids (§ 22) ; and the third, in a later Egyptian writing, which had likewise been forgotten. A French scholar, Champollion, guessed shrewdly that the three inscriptions all told the same story and used many of the same words; and in 1822 he proved this to be true. Then, by means of the Greek, he found the meaning of the other characters, and so learned to read the long-

PORTION OF ROSETTA STONE, containing the hieroglyphs first deciphered.
From Erman's *Life in Ancient Egypt.*

forgotten language of old Egypt. A key to the language of the inscriptions had been found.

At first there was little to read; but a new interest had been aroused, and, about 1850, scholars began extensive explorations in the East. Sites of forgotten cites, buried beneath

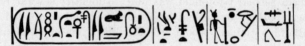

PART OF THE ABOVE INSCRIPTION, on a larger scale.

desert sands, were rediscovered. Many of them contained great libraries on papyrus,[1] or on stone and brick. A part of these have been translated; and since 1880 the results have begun to appear in our books. The explorations are still going on; and very recent years have been the most fruitful of all in discoveries.

---

[1] The papyrus was a reed which grew abundantly in the Nile and the Euphrates rivers. From slices of its stem a kind of " paper " was prepared by laying them together crosswise and pressing them into a smooth sheet. Our word " paper " comes from " papyrus."

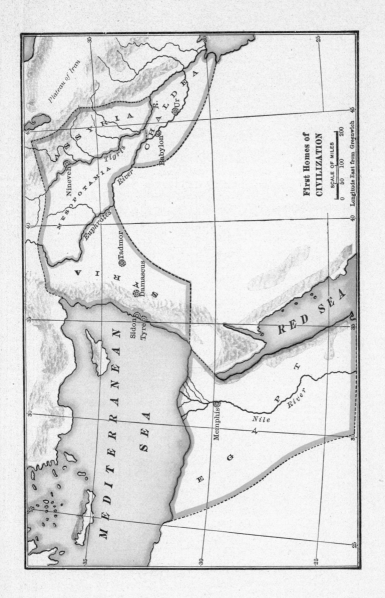

First Homes of
CIVILIZATION

SCALE OF MILES
0   50   100   200

Longitude East from Greenwich

RED SEA

MEDITERRANEAN
SEA

Plateau of Iran

SYRIA

ASSYRIA

CHALDEA

MESOPOTAMIA

Tigris River

Euphrates River

Nineveh

Babylon

Ur

Tadmor

Damascus

Sidon

Tyre

Memphis

EGYPT

Nile River

6. The Two Centers. — The first homes of civilization were Egypt and Chaldea, — the lower valleys of the Nile and the Euphrates. In the Euphrates valley the wild wheat and barley afforded abundant food, with little effort on the part of man. The Nile valley had the marvelous date palm and various grains. In each of these lands we very early find a dense population, and so part of the people were able to give attention to other matters than getting food from day to day.

In a straight line, Egypt and Chaldea were some eight hundred miles apart. Practically, the distance was greater. The only route fit for travel ran along two sides of a triangle, — north from Egypt, between the mountain ranges of western Syria, to the upper waters of the Euphrates, and then down the course of that river.

Except upon this Syrian side, Egypt and Chaldea were shut off from other desirable countries. In Asia, civilizations rose at an early date in China and in India (§ 4); but they were separated from Chaldea by vast deserts and lofty mountains. In Africa, until Roman days, there was no great civilization except the Egyptian, unless we count the Abyssinian on the south (map on page 16). The Abyssinians were brave and warlike, and they seem to have drawn some culture from Egypt. But a desert extended between Abyssinia and Egypt, a twelve-day march; and intercourse by the river was cut off by long series of cataracts and rocky gorges. It was hard for trade caravans to travel from one country to the other, and extremely hard for armies to do so. To the west of Egypt lay the Sahara, stretching across the continent, — an immense, inhospitable tract. On the north and east lay the Mediterranean and the Red Sea; and these broad moats were bridged only at one point by the isthmus.

7. Syria a Third Center.[1] — Thus, with sides and rear protected, Egypt faced Asia across the narrow Isthmus of Suez.

---

[1] The term "Syria" is used with a varying meaning. In a narrow sense, as in this passage, it means only the coast region. In a broader use, it applies to all the country between the Mediterranean and the Euphrates.

Here, too, the region bordering Egypt was largely desert; but farther north, between the desert and the sea, lay a strip of habitable land. This Syrian region became the trade exchange and battle-ground of the two great states, and drew civilization from them.

Syria was itself a nursery of warlike peoples. Here dwelt the Phoenicians, Philistines, Canaanites, Hebrews, Hittites, and other nations, whom we hear of in the Bible. But they do not all appear at the same time in history. Not before 1500 did the Hebrews settle in that part which we now call Palestine. And we hear of their existence much later than of the peoples on the Nile and the Euphrates. Usually all these nations were tributary [1] to Egypt or Chaldea.

Despite Syria's perilous position on the road from Africa to Asia, its inhabitants might have kept their independence, if they could have united against their common foes. But rivers and ranges of mountains broke the country up into five or six districts, all small, and each hostile to the others. At times, however, when both the great powers were weak, there did arise independent Syrian kingdoms, like that of the Jews under David.

---

[1] A tributary country is one which is subject to some other country, without being absolutely joined to it. The "tributary" pays "tribute" and recognizes the authority of the superior country, but for most purposes it keeps its own government.

CHAPTER II

EGYPT

GEOGRAPHY

Egypt as a geographical expression is two things — the Desert and the Nile. As a habitable country, it is only one thing — the Nile.
— ALFRED MILNER.

8. The Land. — Ancient Egypt, by the map, included about as much land as Colorado or Italy; but seven eighths of it was only a sandy border to the real Egypt. The real Egypt is the valley and delta of the Nile — from the cataracts to the sea. It is smaller than Maryland, and falls into two natural parts.

Upper Egypt is the valley proper. It is a strip of rich soil about six hundred miles long and usually about ten miles wide — a slim oasis between parallel ranges of desolate hills (map, page 16). For the remaining hundred miles, the valley broadens suddenly into the delta. This *Lower Egypt* is a squat triangle, resting on a two-hundred-mile base of curving coast where marshy lakes meet the sea.

9. The Nile. — The ranges of hills that bound the "valley" were originally the banks of a mightier Nile, which, in early ages, cut out a gorge from the solid limestone for the future "valley." The "delta" has been built up out of the mud which the stream has carried out and deposited on the old sea bottom.

And what the river has made, it sustains. This was what the Greeks meant when they called Egypt "the gift of the Nile." Rain rarely falls in the valley; and toward the close of the eight cloudless months before the annual overflow, there is a brief period when the land seems gasping for moisture, — "only half alive, waiting the new Nile." The river begins to rise in July, swollen by tropical rains at its upper course in distant Abyssinia; and it does not fully recede into its regular channel until November. During the days while the flood is at its height, Egypt is a sheet of turbid water, spreading be-

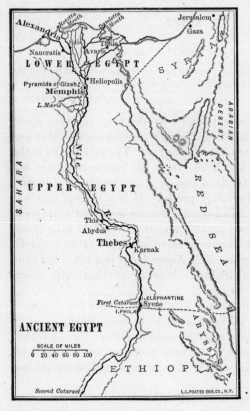

tween two lines of rock and sand. The waters are dotted with towns and villages, and marked off into compartments by raised roads, running from town to town; while from a sandy plateau, at a distance, the pyramids look down upon the scene, as they have done each season for five thousand years. As the water retires, the rich loam dressing, brought down from the hills of Ethiopia, is left spread over the fields, renewing their wonderful fertility from year to year;

while the long soaking supplies moisture to the soil for the dry months to come.

10. The Inhabitants. — Egypt is far away from those places where the new mankind must have originated. Barriers of desert and water separate it from the cradle lands of the human race.

Yet our natural sources carry us back as far into the history of
Egypt as is the case with any of the oldest nations of the world.
For the period they cover they furnish more definite information. Very conservative Catholic historians allow the time of
about 3200 b.c. but they do not find fault with those who think
they can go as far as 5000 as the beginning of Egyptian history. It is certainly safe to say that there lived a rather

PHOTOGRAPH OF A MODERN EGYPTIAN WOMAN SITTING BY A SCULPTURED
HEAD OF AN ANCIENT KING. — From Maspero's *Dawn of Civilization*.
Notice the likeness of feature. The skulls of the modern peasants and of
the ancient nobles are remarkably alike in form.

highly civilized people on the banks of the Nile several thousand years before the coming of the Redeemer.

The population of historical Egypt is said to have replaced
an older one. It will probably never be found out by what
route the first settlers reached Egypt, nor whether the Nile
valley or rather the surrounding countries were inhabited first.
Ethnologists say that there are points of relationship between
the Egyptians and the Abyssinians, Arabs, Negroes, and other

peoples. The historical Egyptians, at any rate, exhibit one type which has remained to the present day. They were evidently Hamites (See § 4), a sturdy race, and from their very first appearance in history well versed in many features of civilized life, including the working of bronze.

11. Growth of a Kingdom. — Our sources do not give us any certain information as to the actual causes which brought about political unification among the small communities of the Nile valley. Hostile inroads of desert tribes may have led to alliances of the petty chiefs or kings. Or one more powerful than his neighbors may have conquered a whole region. In fact the engravings on early monuments show the people of different villages waging bloody conflicts along the dikes or in rude boats on the canals. Voluntary agreements, no doubt were formed to carry out by coöperation projects of wider proportion than one little community could undertake; for instance to drain marshes, to create systems of canals and reservoirs for a more profitable distribution of the water of the Nile. For, to control the yearly overflow to the best advantage was certainly one of the most obvious common interests of all the people. And once a larger state was established, these evident benefits of unified action must have tended greatly to give it stability and permanence. Thus the Nile which had made the country played a part in making Egypt into one state.[1]

At any rate, before history begins, the multitudes of villages had combined into about forty petty states. Each one extended from side to side of the valley and a few miles up and down the river; and each was ruled by a "king." In order to secure prompt action against enemies to the dikes, and to direct all the forces of the state at the necessary moment, the ruler had to have unlimited power. So these kings became

---

[1] The word "state" is commonly used in history not in the sense in which we call Massachusetts a state, but rather in that sense in which we call England or the whole United States a state. That is, the word means *a people, living in some definite place, with a supreme government of its own.*

absolute despots, and the mass of the people became little better than slaves. Then the same forces which had worked to unite villages into states tended to combine the many small states into a few larger ones. Memphis, in the lower valley, and Thebes, 350 miles farther up the river, were the greatest of many rival cities. *Menes*, prince of Memphis, united the petty principalities around him into the kingdom of Lower

BOATMEN FIGHTING ON THE NILE. — Egyptian relief; [1] from Maspero.

Egypt. In like manner Thebes became the capital of a kingdom of Upper Egypt. About the year 3400 before Christ, the two kingdoms were united into one. Later Egyptians thought of Menes as the first king of the whole country.

GOVERNMENT AND PEOPLE

12. Social Classes. — *The king* was worshiped as a god by the mass of the people. His title, *Pharaoh*, means The Great House, — as the title of government of Turkey in modern times has been the Sublime Porte (Gate). The title implies that the ruler was to be a refuge for his people.

The pharaoh was the absolute owner of the soil. Probably the kings had taken most of it for their own from the first, in return for protecting it by their dikes and reservoirs. At all events, this ownership helped to make the pharaoh absolute master of the

---

[1] A relief is a piece of sculpture in which the figures are only partly cut away from the solid rock.

inhabitants, — though in practice his authority was somewhat limited by the power of the priests and by the necessity of keeping ambitious nobles friendly.[1] Part of the land he kept in his own hands, to be cultivated by peasants under the direction of royal stewards; but the greater portion he parceled out among the nobles and temples.

In return for the land granted to him, a *noble* was bound to pay certain amounts of produce, and to lead a certain number of soldiers to war.   Within his domain, the noble was a petty monarch: he executed justice, levied his own taxes, kept up his own army.   Like the king, he held part of his land in his own hands, while other parts he let out to smaller nobles. These men were

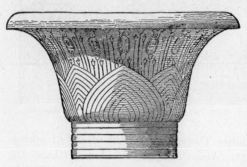

A CAPITAL FROM KARNAK. — From Lübke.

dependent upon him, much as he was dependent upon the king.

About a third of the land was turned over by the king to the temples to support the worship of the gods.   This land became the property of the *priests*.   The priests were also the scholars of Egypt, and they took an active part in the government.   The pharaoh took most of his high officials from them, and their influence far exceeded that of the nobles.

The *peasants* tilled the soil.   They were not unlike the peasants of modern Egypt.   They rented small "farms," — hardly more than garden plots, — for which they paid at least a third of the produce to the landlord.   This left too little for a family; and they eked out a livelihood by day labor on the land of the nobles and priests.   For this work they were paid by a small part of the produce.   The peasant, too, had to

---

[1] See Davis' *Readings*, Vol. I, No. 2.

remain under the protection of some powerful landlord, or he might become the prey of any one whom he chanced to offend.

Still, in quarrels with the rich, the poor were perhaps as safe as they have been in most countries. The oldest written "story" in the world (surviving in a papyrus of about 2700 B.C.) gives an interesting illustration. A peasant, robbed through a legal trick by the favorite of a royal officer, appeals to the judges and finally to the king. The king commands redress, urging his officer to do justice "like a praiseworthy man praised by the praiseworthy." The passage in quotation marks shows that there was a strong public opinion against injustice. Probably such appeals by the poor were no more difficult to make than they were in Germany or France until a hundred years ago. And we have not yet learned how to give the poor man an absolutely equal chance with the rich in our law courts.

In the towns there was a large *middle class*, — merchants, shopkeepers, physicians, lawyers,[1] builders, artisans (§ 20).

Below these were the *unskilled laborers*. This class was sometimes driven to a strike by hunger.

Maspero, a famous French scholar in Egyptian history, makes the following statement (*Struggle of the Nations*, 539): —

"Rations were allowed each workman at the end of every month; but, from the usual Egyptian lack of forethought, these were often consumed long before the next assignment. Such an event was usually followed by a strike. On one occasion we are shown the workmen turning to the overseer, saying: 'We are perishing of hunger, and there are still eighteen days before the next month.' The latter makes profuse promises; but, when nothing comes of them, the workmen will not listen to him longer. They leave their work and gather in a public meeting. The overseer hastens after them, and the police commissioners of the locality and the scribes mingle with them, urging upon the leaders a return. But the workmen only say: 'We will not return. Make it clear to your superiors down below there.' The official who reports the matter to the authorities seems to think the complaints well founded, for he says, 'We went to hear them, and they spoke true words to us.'"

Throughout Egyptian society, the son usually followed the father's occupation; but there was no law (as in some Oriental countries) to prevent his passing into a different class. Some-

---

[1] These were mainly *notaries*, — to draw up business papers, record transfers of property, and so on.

times the son of a poor herdsman rose to wealth and power. Such advance was most easily open to the *scribes*. This learned profession was recruited from the brightest boys of the middle and lower classes. Most of the scribes found clerical work only; but from the ablest ones the nobles chose confidential secretaries and stewards, and some of these, who showed special ability, were promoted by the pharaohs to the highest dignities in the land. Such men founded new families and reinforced the ranks of the nobility.

The *soldiers* formed an important profession. Campaigns were so deadly that it was hard to find soldiers enough. Accordingly recruits were tempted by offers of special privileges. Each soldier held a farm of some eight acres,[1] free from taxes; and he was kept under arms only when his services were needed. Besides this regular soldiery, the peasantry were called out upon occasion, for war or for garrisons.

PORTRAIT STATUE OF AMTEN, a "self-made" noble of 3200 B.C.

There was also a large body of *officials*, organized in many grades like the officers of an army. Every despotic government has to have such a class, to act as eyes, hands, and feet; but

---

[1] For Egypt this was a large farm. See page 20.

in ancient Egypt the royal servants were particularly numerous
and important. Until the seventh century B.C. the Egyptians
had no money. Thus the immense royal revenues, as well as all
debts between private men, had to be collected "in kind."
The tax-collectors and treasurers had to receive geese, ducks,
cattle, grain, wine, oil, metals, jewels, — "all that the heavens

EGYPTIAN NOBLE HUNTING WATERFOWL ON THE NILE with the "throw-
stick" (a boomerang). The birds rise from a group of papyrus reeds. —
Egyptian relief; after Maspero.

give, all that the earth produces, all that the Nile brings from
its mysterious sources," as one king puts it in an inscription.
To do this called for an army of royal officials. For a like
reason, the great nobles needed a large class of trustworthy
servants.

13. Summary of Social Classes. — Thus, in Egyptian society,
we have at the top an *aristocracy,* of several elements: (1) the
nobles; (2) the powerful and learned priesthood, whose influence almost equaled that of the pharaoh himself; (3) scribes

and physicians; (4) a privileged soldiery; and (5) a mass of privileged officials of many grades, from the greatest rulers next to the pharaoh, down to petty tax collectors and the stewards of private estates. Lower down there was *the middle class*, of shopkeepers and artisans, whose life ranged from comfort to a grinding misery; while at *the base of society* was a large mass of toilers on the land, weighted down by all the other classes. It is not strange that, in time, upper and lower classes came to differ in physical appearance. The later monuments represent the nobles tall and lithe, with imperious bearing; while the laborer is pictured heavy of feature and dumpy in build.

14. Life of the Wealthy. — For most of the well-to-do, life was a very delightful thing, filled with active employment and varied with many pleasures.[1] Their homes were roomy houses with a wooden frame plastered over with sun-dried clay. Light and air entered at the many latticed windows, where, however, curtains of brilliant hues shut out the occasional sand storms from the desert. About the house stretched a large garden with artificial fish-ponds gleaming among the palm trees.[2]

15. The Life of the Poor. — There were few *slaves* in Egypt; but the condition of the great mass of the people fell little short of practical slavery. Toilers on the canals, and on the pyramids and other vast works that have made Egypt famous, were kept to their labor by the whip. "Man has a back," was a favorite Egyptian proverb. The monuments always picture the overseers with a stick, and often show it in use. The people thought of a beating as a natural incident in their daily work.

The peasants did not live in the country, as our farmers do. They were crowded into the villages and poorer quarters of the

---

[1] The student who has access to Maspero's *Dawn of Civilization* (or to various other illustrated works on Early Egypt) can make an interesting report upon these recreations from what he can see in the pictures from the monuments.

[2] A full description of a noble's house is given in Davis' *Readings*, Vol. I, No. 5.

towns, with the other poorer classes.   Many of them lived in
mud hovels of only one room.   Such huts were separated from
one another merely by one mud partition, and were built in
long rows, facing upon narrow crooked alleys filled with filth.
Only the extremely dry air kept down pestilences.   Hours of

TEMPLE AT LUXOR.

toil were from dawn to dark.   Taxes were exacted harshly,
so that an Egyptian writer of about 1400 B.C. exclaims in
pity :—

"Dost thou not recall the picture of the farmer, when the tenth of his
grain is levied ?   Worms have destroyed half of the wheat.   There are
swarms of rats in the fields ; the grasshoppers alight there ; the cattle
devour ; the little birds pilfer ; and if the farmer lose sight for an instant
of what remains upon the ground, it is carried off by robbers.   It is then
that the scribe steps out of the boat at the landing place to levy the tithe,
and there come the keepers of the doors of the granary with cudgels and
the Negroes with ribs of palm-leaves [very effective whips], crying:
'Come now, corn !'

Yet other writers blame an utter lack of provision on the
part of many farmers for the occurrence of such scenes of
distress.

Still, judging from Egyptian literature, the peasants seem to have been careless and gay, petting the cattle and singing at their work. Probably they were as well off as the like class has been during the past century in Egypt or in Russia.

16. The position of women was better than it was to be in the Greek civilization, and much better than in modern Oriental countries. The poor man's wife spun and wove, and ground grain into meal in a stone bowl with another stone. Among the upper classes, the wife was the companion of the man. She was not shut up in a harem or confined strictly to household duties: she appeared in company and at public ceremonies. She possessed equal rights at law; and sometimes great queens ruled upon the throne. In no other ancient country, except that of the Jews, do pictures of happy home life play so large a part.

INDUSTRY AND LEARNING

17. The Irrigation System. — Before the year 2000 B.C., the Egyptians had learned to supplement the yearly overflow of the Nile by an elaborate irrigation system. Even earlier, they had built dikes to keep the floods from the towns and gardens; and the care of these embankments remained a special duty of the government through all Egyptian history. But between 2400 and 2000 B.C. the pharaohs created a wonderful reservoir system. On the one hand, tens of thousands of acres of marsh were drained and made fit for rich cultivation : on the other hand, artificial lakes were built at various places, to collect and hold the surplus water of the yearly inundation. Then, by an intricate network of ditches and "gates" (much like the irrigation ditches of some of our western States to-day), the water was distributed during the dry months as it was needed. The government opened and closed the main ditches, as seemed best to it ; and its officers oversaw the more minute distribution of the water, by which each farm in the vast irrigated districts was given its share. Then, from the main ditch of each farm, the farmer himself carried the water in smaller water courses

to one part or another of his acres, — these small ditches
gradually growing smaller and smaller, until, by moving a
little mud with the foot, he could turn the water one way or
another at his will. Ground so cultivated was divided into
square beds, surrounded by raised borders of earth, so that the
water could be kept in or out of each bed.

The most important single work of this system of irrigation was the
artificial *Lake Moeris* (map, page 16). This was constructed by improving a natural basin in the desert. To this depression, a canal was dug
from the Nile through a gorge in the hills for a distance of eight miles.
At the Nile side, a huge dam, with gates, made it possible to carry off
through the canal the surplus water at flood periods. The canal was
30 feet deep and 160 feet wide ; and from the "lake," smaller canals
distributed the water over a large district which had before been perfectly
barren. This useful work was still in perfect condition two thousand
years after its creation, and was praised highly by a Roman geographer
who visited it then.

So extensive were these irrigation works in very early times
that more soil was cultivated, and more wealth produced, and
a larger population maintained, than in any modern period
until English control was established in the country a short
time ago. Herodotus (§ 21) says that in his day Egypt had
twenty thousand "towns" (villages).

18. Agriculture. — Wheat and barley had been introduced at
an early time from the Euphrates region, and some less important grains (like sesame) were also grown. Besides the
grain, the chief food crops were beans, peas, lettuce, radishes,
melons, cucumbers, and onions. Clover was raised for cattle,
and flax for the linen cloth which was the main material for
clothing.[1] Grapes, too, were grown in great quantities, for the
manufacture of a light wine.

Herodotus says that seed was merely scattered broadcast on
the moist soil as the water receded each November, and then
trampled in by cattle and goats and pigs. But the pictures on

---

[1] There was also some cotton raised, and the abundant flocks of sheep
furnished wool.

the monuments show that, in parts of Egypt anyway, a light
wooden plow was used to stir the ground. This plow was
drawn by two cows. Even the large farms were treated
almost like gardens; and the yield was enormous, — reaching

the rate of a hun-
dred fold for
grain. Long after
her greatness had
departed, Egypt
remained "the
granary of the
Mediterranean
lands."

EGYPTIAN PLOW. — After Rawlinson.

The various crops matured at different seasons, and so
kept the farmer busy through most of the year. Besides the
plow, his only tools were a short, crooked hoe (the use of
which bent him almost double) and the sickle. The grain was
cut with this last implement; then carried in baskets to a
threshing floor, — and trodden out by cattle, which were driven
round and round, while the drivers sang, —

"Tread, tread, tread out the grain.
Tread for yourselves, for yourselves.
Measures for the master ; measures for yourselves."

An Egyptian barnyard contained many animals familiar to
us (cows, sheep, goats, scrawny pigs much like the wild hog,
geese, ducks, and pigeons), and also a number of others like
antelopes, gazelles, and storks. Some of these it proved impossible to tame profitably. We must remember that men,
though aided by original traditions, learned by experiment
which animals could be domesticated both successfully and
usefully. The hen was not known. Nor was the horse present in Egypt until a late period (§ 29); even then he was never
common enough to use in agriculture or as a draft animal.

During the flood periods cattle were fed in stalls upon clover
and wheat straw. The monuments picture some exciting

scenes when a rapid rise of the Nile forced the peasants to remove their flocks and herds hurriedly, through the surging waters, from usual grazing grounds to the flood-time quarters. Veal, mutton, and antelope flesh were the common meats of the rich. The poor lived mainly on vegetables and goats' milk.

19. Trade. — Until about 650 B.C., the Egyptians had no true money. For some centuries before that date, they had used rings of gold and silver, to some extent, somewhat as we use money; but these rings had no fixed weight, and had to be

MARKET SCENE. — Egyptian relief from the monuments.

placed on the scales each time they changed hands. During most of Egypt's three thousand years of greatness, indeed, exchange in her market places was by *barter*. A peasant with wheat or onions to sell squatted by his basket, while would-be customers offered him earthenware, vases, fans, or other objects with which they had come to buy, but which perhaps he did not want. (The student will be interested in an admirable description of a market scene in Davis' *Readings*, Vol. I, No. 7. The picture above, from an Egyptian monument, is one of those used as the basis of that account.)

We hardly know whether to be most amazed at the wonderful progress of the Egyptians in some lines, or at their failure to invent money and an alphabet, when they needed those things so sorely and approached them so closely.

In spite of this serious handicap, by 2000 B.C. the Egyptians carried on extensive trade. One inscription of that period describes a ship bringing from the coast of Arabia "fragrant woods, heaps of myrrh, ebony and pure ivory, green gold, cinnamon, incense, cosmetics, apes, monkeys, dogs, and panther skins." Some of these things must have been gathered from distant parts of Eastern Asia.

20. The Industrial Arts. — The skilled artisans included brickworkers, weavers, blacksmiths, goldsmiths, coppersmiths,

SHOEMAKERS. — Egyptian relief from the monuments; from Maspero.

upholsterers, glass blowers, potters, shoemakers, tailors, armorers, and almost as many other trades as are to be found among us to-day. In many of these occupations, the workers possessed a marvelous dexterity, and were masters of processes that are now unknown. The weavers in particular produced delicate and exquisite linen, almost as fine as silk, and the workers in glass and gold and bronze were famous for their skill. Jewels were imitated in colored glass so artfully that only an expert to-day can detect the fraud by the appearance. Though iron was used by men long before the Deluge, it does not occur in the ruins of Egypt before 800 B.C. This useful metal evidently did not find its way into the Nile valley — Egypt has no mines — in sufficient quantity to allow of the formation of an iron workers' craft before that date.

The Chief Fine Arts. — In conformity with the strong belief of the Egyptians in a life after death and their general religious character, the principal works of *architecture* were tombs and temples. The palaces of the kings, at times grand, were on the whole of less importance.

In the oldest times of the kingdom the richer people built for themselves **tombs** called *Mastabas*, which were flat-topped massive stone chapels, containing several rooms above ground. A vertical shaft led down to the cavity in the rocky soil, in which the mummy — the carefully embalmed body (see note page 40) — was deposited. The earliest kings, however, erected the majestic *Pyramids*, artificial hills of stone, for their resting

PYRAMIDS AND SPHINX. From the group of Gizeh, near the site of ancient Memphis (see map, page 16), where the most known of the pyramids are found. This sphinx is about seventy feet high.

places. There are about seventy pyramids of various sizes still extant in Egypt. The highest, which is said to have been built by Cheops about 3000 B.C., rises to 481 feet above its base. More than two million stones went to make it. No mortar is used in these structures, but the edges of the huge blocks are so nicely fitted together that in many places it is even now difficult to detect the joints. They disclose a remarkable knowledge of mathematics and physics. The king's mummy was placed in a chamber near its center. Sometimes a later ruler cast out the mummy of a predecessor and took possession of the pyramid for himself.

Herodotus, a Greek historian of the fifth century B.C., traveled in Egypt and learned all that the priests of his day could tell him regarding these wonders. He tells us that it took thirty years to build the Great Pyramid, — ten of those years going to piling the vast mounds of earth, up which the mighty stones were to be dragged into place, — which mounds had afterwards to be removed. During that thirty years, relays of a hundred thousand men were kept at the toil, each relay for three months at a stretch. Other thousands, of course, had to toil through a lifetime of labor to feed these workers on a monument to a monarch's vanity. All the labor was performed by mere human strength : the Egyptians of that day had no beasts of burden, and no machinery, such as we have, for moving great weights with ease.

When, in the Middle Kingdom (§ 28), Thebes became the capital, the kings and nobility preferred *graves hewn into the rocks*. They were regular underground dwellings, sumptuously and artificially furnished. As in the Mastabas, there was a vertical shaft to receive the mummy. The pharaohs added large temples in front of their rock chambers. In these tombs are found many of the papyrus rolls which like the inscriptions and paintings tell us of ancient Egyptian life.

Temples were erected from the oldest times. The larger ones among them contained several smaller rooms and also wide halls arranged around courts. Columns of massive dimensions supported the heavy stone ceiling and were placed in long rows so as to give the effect of an indescribable grandeur. The capitals of the columns often imitated the sacred lotus flower. (See illustrations on pages 25, 35, 20, 280.)

Statues, ranging in size from diminutive to gigantic, were very frequent, both in and near the tombs and temples. Remarkable are the numerous portrait statues, destined to retain the features of deceased persons. To characterize the gods, their statues often have the heads of such animals as excel in certain qualities. The *Sphinxes*, sometimes of colossal size, were combinations of a lion's body and a human head, and are thought to symbolize the union of intellect with great physical strength. Rows of them flank the avenues to temples and palaces. The *Obelisks*, often placed in front of the temples, are square, pointed columns, sometimes of enormous height, and made of a single piece of stone. They combine elegance with solidity. (See figure on back of this volume.)

The walls of the temples and tombs, the surface of the huge columns, and the sides of obelisks and other monuments are commonly covered

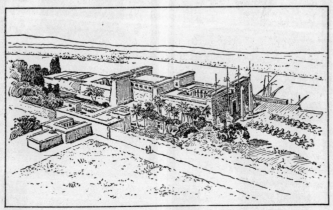

RESTORATION OF AN EGYPTIAN TEMPLE.

with *inscriptions*, which in turn are illustrated by *paintings* and colored reliefs (p. 19, note). Often both run belt-like around the walls of the buildings. They are of secular or sacred nature and make the ruins of Egypt veritable libraries in stone. In the closed tombs the brilliant painting lasted with perfect freshness during all the centuries, but it fades quickly upon exposure to the air.

The Egyptian art was architecture, to which nearly all other arts were made subservient. The Egyptians had the will, the skill, and the material to build for ages. Their work possesses grandeur and majesty, but has not quite the grace and attractiveness which we ourselves would desire. In their sculpture we generally miss naturalness and ease in posture. The arms, for instance, are commonly placed upon the knees or held close to the body. (See illustrations on pages 34, 43, 47.) The Egyptian painter completely neglected shading and perspective.

22. Literature and the Hieroglyphs. — The Egyptians wrote religious books, poems, histories, travels, novels, orations, treatises upon morals, scientific works, geographies, cook-books,

RA-HOTEP, a noble of about 3200 B.C. Portrait statue. Now in the Cairo Museum.

PRINCESS NEFERT, a portrait statue 5000 years old. Now in the Cairo Museum.

catalogues, and collections of fairy stories, — among the last a tale of an Egyptian Cinderella, with her fairy glass slipper. On the first monuments, writing had advanced from mere pictures to a rebus stage (cf. § 3 e). This early writing was used mainly by the priests in connection with the worship of the gods, and so the characters were called *hieroglyphs* (" priest's writing "). The pictures, though shrunken, compose " a delightful assemblage of birds, snakes, men, tools, stars, and beasts." Some of these signs grew into real letters, or *signs of single*

TEMPLE AT EDFU, a village between Thebes and the First Cataract. This is one of the best preserved Egyptian temples, and the finest example of ancient Egyptian religious buildings. It was begun by Ptolemy III in 237 B.C. (See pictures on pages 20, 25, 280. Note the difference in the capitals.)

sounds. If the Egyptians could have kept these last and have dropped all the rest, they would have had a true alphabet. But this final step they never took. Their writing remained to the last a curious mixture of *thousands* of signs of things, of ideas, of syllables, and of a few single sounds.[1] This was what made the position of the scribes so honorable and profitable. To master such a system of writing required long schooling,

---

[1] A good account of the hieroglyphs is given in Keary's *Dawn of History*, 298–303. Another may be found in Maspero's *Dawn of Civilization*, 221–224, and there is a pleasant longer account in Clodd's *Story of the Alphabet*.

and any one who could write was sure of well-paid employment.

When these characters were formed rapidly upon papyrus or pottery (instead of upon stone), the strokes were run together, and the characters were gradually modified into a running script, which was written with a reed in black or red ink. The dry air of the Egyptian tombs has preserved to our day great numbers of buried papyrus rolls.

RELIEF FROM THE TEMPLE OF HATHOR (goddess of the sky and of love), at Dendera, 28 miles north of Thebes. This temple belongs to a late period. Notice the "conventionalized" wings, and the royal "cartouches." In Egyptian inscriptions, the name of a king is surrounded by a line, as in the upper right-hand corner of this relief. Such a figure is called a "cartouch." See the Rosetta stone, on page 12.

23. Science. — The Nile has been called the father of Egyptian science. The frequent need of surveying the land after an inundation had to do with the skill of the early Egyptians in *geometry*. The need of fixing in advance the exact time of the inundation directed attention to the true "year," and so to *astronomy*.

Great progress was made in both these studies. We moderns, who learn glibly from books and diagrams the results of this early labor, can hardly understand how difficult was the task of these first scientific observers.

Uncivilized peoples count time by " moons " or by " winters " ; but to fix the exact length of the year (the time in which the sun apparently passes from a given point in the heavens, through its path, back again to that point) requires patient and skillful observation, and no little knowledge. Indeed, to find out that there is such a thing as a " year " is no simple matter. If the student will go out into the night, and look upon the heavens, with its myriads of twinkling points of light, and then try to imagine how the first scientists learned to map out the paths of the heavenly bodies, he will better appreciate their work.

Long before the unification of the kingdom, the Egyptians counted by years. Later on they fixed the year at $365\frac{1}{4}$ days and invented a leap year arrangement. Their "year," together with their calendar of months, we get from them through Julius Caesar (improved, in 1582, by Pope Gregory XIII). In *arithmetic* the Egyptians dealt readily in numbers to millions, with the aid of a notation similar to that used later by the Romans. Thus, 3423 was represented by the Romans : M M M C C C C XX III and by the Egyptians :

All this learning is older than the Greek by almost twice as long a time as the Greek is older than ours of to-day. No wonder, then, that (according to a Greek story) in the last days of Egyptian greatness, a priest of Saïs exclaimed to a traveler from little Athens : " O Solon, Solon ! You Greeks are mere children. There is no old opinion handed down among you by ancient tradition, nor any science hoary with age ! " (§ 140.) It must be remembered, however, that this science was the possession only of the priests, and perhaps of a few others.

24. Religion. — It is not impossible that some of the first settlers in the Nile valley had already lost the idea of one God. The Egyptians, however, undoubtedly admitted the dependency of man on superior beings. But there existed, especially among the common people, a curious mixture of religions. Each family worshiped its *ancestors*. Beasts also, such as cats, dogs, bulls, crocodiles, were sacred. To injure one of these " gods," even by accident, was to incur the fury of the people. Probably this worship was a degraded kind of ancestor worship known as *totemism*, which is found among many peoples. North American Indians of a wolf clan or a bear clan — with a fabled wolf or bear for an ancestor — must on no account injure the ancestral animal, or "totem."[1] In Egypt, however, the worship of animals became more widely spread, and took on grosser features than has ever been the case elsewhere.

Isis, goddess of the sky, holding her son, Horus, the rising sun.

Above all this, there was a worship of countless deities and demigods representing sun, moon, river, wind, storm, trees, and stones. Each town had its special god to protect it; and the gods of the capitals became national deities.

Among the more educated classes many had a higher and purer concept of God. Some passages in their books speak in a language which closely resembles and in some isolated cases equals the words of the Bible. This is especially so about 1500 B.C., the time when the Israelites were in Egypt. "God," say some of the inscriptions, "is a spirit; no man knoweth his form," and again, "He is the creator of the heavens and the earth and all that is therein."

The substance of such truths was no doubt inherited, but they were not at all times expressed with equal clearness. In the later centuries the gross popular beliefs alone remained. The following hymn to Aten (the Sundisk), symbol of Light and Life, was written by an Egyptian king of the fifteenth century B.C. Some of its lines seem to indicate that it is addressed to the true creator of the world.

---

[1] Cooper's *Last of the Mohicans* contains an illustration of totemism.

"Thy appearing is beautiful in the horizon of heaven,
    O living Aten, the beginning of life! . . .
    Thy beams encompass all lands which thou hast made.
    Thou bindest them with thy love. . . .
    The birds fly in their haunts —
    Their wings adoring thee. . . .
    How many are the things which thou hast made !
    Thou createst the land by thy will, thou alone,
    With peoples, herds, and flocks. . . .
    Thou givest to every man his place, thou framest his life."

25. The idea of a future life. From the earliest times the
Egyptians believed that man is survived in death by a certain
principle of life corresponding to what we call the soul. But

SCULPTURED FUNERAL COUCH: the soul is represented crouching by the
mummy. — From Maspero.

this idea was very much obscured. They generally thought
that either the body remains the home of the soul, or at least
that the soul lives on in a pale shadowy existence near the
tomb.[1] If the body be not preserved, or if it be not given
proper burial, then, it was thought, the soul becomes a wandering ghost, restless and harmful to men. The universal

---

[1] The poor endeavored to give their dead a resting place which at least was
not reached by the waters of the Nile.

Egyptian practice of embalming[1] the body before burial was
connected with it.   They wished to preserve the body as the
home for the soul.   In the early tombs, too, there are always
found dishes in which had been placed food and drink, which
were in later times replaced by painted food.   These practices continued through
all ancient Egyptian
history.

A TOMB PAINTING, showing offerings to the
dead.

There existed however,
especially among the
higher classes, the con-
viction of a truer immor-
tality for those who de-
served it.   After death
the soul had to undergo a
severe trial by forty-two
"judges of the dead."   If
found guiltless it entered
a kind of heaven, where
it enjoyed all the pleas-
ures of life without any
pain.   The other souls
might be obliged to re-
turn to the world for a
second probation, or they would finally perish.

Unfortunately this imperfect idea of a future retribution
was very much weakened by the rankest superstition.   The
people thought that certain formulas or articles would serve
to deceive the judges.   But even so it could not fail to
exercise a great and wholesome influence upon the moral
conduct of men.

The following noble extract comes from the " Repudiation of Sins."
This was a statement which the Egyptian believed he ought to be able to

---

[1] " Embalming " is a process of preparing a dead body with drugs and
spices, so as to prevent decay.

say truthfully before the "Judges of the Dead." It shows a keen sense of duty to one's fellow men, which would be highly honorable to any religion.

"Hail unto you, ye lords of Truth! hail to thee, great god, lord of Truth and Justice! ... I have not committed iniquity against men! I have not oppressed the poor! . . . I have not laid labor upon any free man beyond that which he wrought for himself! . . . I have not caused the slave to be ill-treated of his master! I have not starved any man, I have not made any to weep, . . . *I have not pulled down the scale of the*

WEIGHING THE SOUL in the scales of truth before the gods of the dead. — Egyptian relief; after Maspero. (The figures with animal heads are gods and their messengers. The human forms represent the dead who are being led to judgment.)

balance! I have not falsified the beam of the balance! I have not taken away the milk from the mouths of sucklings. . . .

"Grant that he may come unto you — he that hath not lied nor borne false witness, . . . *he that hath given bread to the hungry and drink to him that was athirst, and that hath clothed the naked with garments.*"

Some other declarations in this statement run: "I have not blasphemed;" "I have not stolen;" "I have not slain any man treacherously;" "I have not made false accusation;" "I have not eaten my heart with envy." These five contain the substance of half of the Ten Commandments, — hundreds of years before Moses gave to the Children of Israel by divine inspiration that admirably worded code of the natural law.

26. Moral Character. — The ideal of character, indicated above, is contained in many other Egyptian inscriptions. Thus, some three thousand years before Christ, a noble declares in his epitaph : " I have caused no child of tender years to mourn ; I have despoiled no widow; I have driven away no toiler of the soil [who asked for help] . . . None about me have been unfortunate or starving in my time." [1] Of course, like other people, the Egyptian fell short of his ideal. On the other hand, it is not fair to expect him to come up to our modern standard in all ways. The modesty and refinement which we value were lacking among the Egyptians; but they were a kindly people. The sympathy expressed by their writers for the poor (§ 15) is a note not often heard in ancient literature. Scholars agree in giving the Egyptians high praise as " more moral, sympathetic, and conscientious than any other ancient people," with exception of course of the Hebrews and most probably the Persians. Professor Petrie sums up the matter thus : " The Egyptian, without our Christian sense of sin or self-reproach, sought out a fair and noble life. . . . His aim was to be an easy, good-natured, quiet gentleman, and to make life as agreeable as he could to all about him."

THE STORY

27. The Old and Middle Kingdoms. — It is convenient to mark off seven periods in the history of Egypt (§§ 27–33). For more than a thousand years after Menes (3400–2400 B.C.), the capital remained at Memphis in Lower Egypt. This period is known as the Old Kingdom. It is marked by the complete consolidation of the country under the pharaohs, by the building of the pyramids and sphinxes, and by the rapid development of the civilization which we have been studying. The only names we care much for in this age are Menes and Cheops (§ 21).

28. The Middle Kingdom. — Toward 2400 B.C., the power of the pharaohs declined; but the glory of the monarchy was re-

---

[1] The same ideas of duty are set forth more at length in extracts given in Davis' *Readings*, Vol. I, Nos. 9 and 10.

stored by a new line of kings at *Thebes* in the upper valley.
Probably this was the result of civil war between Upper and
Lower Egypt. The Theban line of pharaohs are known as
the Middle Kingdom. Their rule lasted some four hundred
years (2400–2000 B.C.), and makes the second period. The two
features of this period are *foreign conquest* and a new *development of resources at home.*

Ethiopia, on the south,
was subdued, with many
Negro tribes; and parts
of Syria were conquered;
but the chief glory of this
age, and of all Egyptian
history, was the development of the marvelous
system of irrigation that
has been described in § 17
above. The pharaohs of
this period, in happy contrast with the vain and
cruel pyramid-builders,
cared most to encourage
trade, explore unknown
regions, improve roads,
establish wells and reservoirs. A king of 2200 B.C.
boasts in his epitaph —
probably with reason —

CHEOPS (more properly called Khufu),
builder of the Great Pyramid: a portrait-
statue discovered in 1902 by Flinders
Petrie. As Professor Petrie says, "The
first thing that strikes us is the enormous
driving power of the man."

that all his commands had "ever increased the love" of his
subjects toward him. Egyptian commerce now reached to
Crete on the north, and probably to other islands and coasts
of the Mediterranean, and to distant parts of Ethiopia on the
south. One of the greatest works of the time was the opening
of a canal from a mouth of the Nile to the Red Sea, so that
ships might pass from that sea to the Mediterranean. This
gave a great impulse to trade with Arabia (§ 19).

29. The Hyksos. — This outburst of glory was followed by a strange decay (2000–1600 B.C. — the "third period"), during which Egypt became the prey of roving tribes from Arabia. From the title of their chiefs, these conquerors were called *Hyksos,* or *Shepherd Kings.* They maintained themselves in Egypt about two hundred years. For a time they harried the land cruelly, as invaders; then, from a capital in the lower Delta, they ruled the country through tributary Egyptian

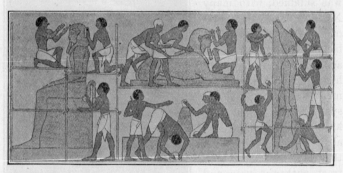

SCULPTORS at work on colossal figures. — From an Egyptian relief.

kings; and finally they acquired the civilization of the country and became themselves Egyptian sovereigns. It was this Arabian conquest that first brought the horse into Egypt (§ 18). After this period, kings and nobles are represented in war chariots and in pleasure carriages.

30. The New Empire. — A line of native monarchs had remained in power at Thebes, as under-kings. About 1600 B.C., after a long struggle, these princes expelled the Hyksos. During this "fourth period," 1600–1330, Egypt reached its highest pitch of military grandeur. The long struggle with the Hyksos had turned the attention of the people from industry to war; and the horse made long marches easier for the leaders. A series of mighty kings recovered Ethiopia, conquered all western Syria, and at last reached the Euphrates, ruling for a brief time even over Babylonia.

Here, on the banks of a mighty river, strangely like their own Nile, they found the home of another civilization, equal to their own, but different. For some thousand years, these two

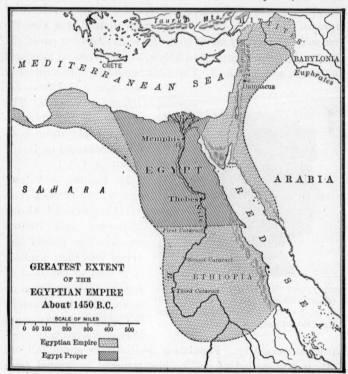

GREATEST EXTENT
OF THE
EGYPTIAN EMPIRE
About 1450 B.C.

SCALE OF MILES
0 50 100   200   300   400   500

Egyptian Empire
Egypt Proper

early civilizations had been existing without much intercommunication with each other [1] (§ 19). Now a new era opened. The long ages of isolation gave way to an age of intercourse.[2]

---

[1] The Egyptians did know something of the Euphrates culture, because it had, long before, extended into Syria (§ 38), which Egyptian armies and traders had visited occasionally, for some centuries; but now first they saw it in its full magnificence.

[2] Egypt did not admit foreigners into her own Nile district, except the official representatives of other governments. But the Syrian lands were the middle ground where the two civilizations held intercourse.

The vast districts between the Euphrates and the Nile became covered with a network of roads. These were garrisoned here and there by fortresses; and over them, for centuries, there passed hurrying streams of officials, couriers, and merchants. The brief supremacy of Egypt over the Euphrates district was also the *first political union of the Orient.* In some degree it paved the way for the greater empires to follow, — of Assyria, of Persia, of Alexander, and of Rome. The most famous Egyptian rulers of this age are *Thûtmosis*[1] *III*, and *Rameses II.* The student will find interesting passages about both these monarchs in Davis' *Readings,* Vol. I.

SCULPTURED HEAD OF THÛTMOSIS III (about 1470 B.C.), who in twelve great campaigns first carried Egyptian arms from the isthmus to Nineveh.

31. Decline. — A long age of weakness (the "fifth period," about 1330–640) soon invited attack. The priests had drawn into their hands a large part of the land of Egypt. This land paid no taxes, and the pharaohs felt obliged to tax more heavily the already overburdened peasantry. Population declined; revenues fell off. Early in this period of decline, the Hebrews emigrated from Egypt. Their ancestors had come from Syria during the rule of the Arabian Hyksos, who were friendly to them. In Egypt they grew into a populous nation, but the great monarchs of the New Empire reduced them to serfdom. They now left Egypt to settle in the " promised land" (§ 59).

The government was no longer strong enough in armies for the defense of the frontiers. Dominion in both Africa and

---

[1] All difficult proper names have the pronunciation shown in the index.

Asia shrank, until Egypt was driven back within her ancient bounds. The Hittites (§ 7), descending from the slopes of the Taurus Mountains (map, page 45), overthrew Egyptian power in Syria; and the tribes of the Sahara, aided by "strange peoples of the sea" (Greeks among them), threatened to seize even the Delta itself. In 730 B.C. the Ethiopians overran the country; and, in 672, *Egypt finally became subject to Assyria* (§ 40).

Dates are not fixed *exactly* in Egyptian history until about this time. For all earlier periods, a margin of a century or two must be allowed for errors in calculation.

This vagueness is due to the fact that ancient peoples did not reckon historical or political periods from a common fixed point of time as we do: instead, they reckoned from the building of a city, or from the beginning of the reigns of their kings. An in-

RAMESES II, a conquering pharaoh of about 1375 B.C. This colossal statue stands in the ruins of the palace at Luxor.

scription may tell us that a certain event took place in the tenth year of the reign of Rameses ; but we do not know positively in just what year Rameses began to reign.

32. The Sixth Period, 653–525. — After twenty years of Assyrian rule, *Psammetichus* restored Egyptian independence and became the pharaoh. He had been a military adventurer, apparently of foreign blood; and had been employed by the Assyrians as a tributary prince. During her former greatness, although her own traders visited other lands, Egypt had kept herself jealously closed against strangers. But Psammetichus *threw open the doors to foreigners.* In particular, he welcomed

the Greeks, who were just coming into notice as soldiers and
sailors. Not only did individual Greek travelers (§§ 21, 23,
156) visit the country, but a Greek colony, *Naucratis*, was established there, and large numbers of Greek soldiers served in
the army. Indeed *Sais*, the new capital of Psammetichus
and his son, thronged with Greek adventurers. This was the
time, accordingly, when Egypt "fulfilled her mission among
the nations." She had received the heirloom of civilization
ages before; now she passed it on to the western world through
this younger race.

Neco, the second monarch of this new line of kings, ruled
about 600 B.C. He was greatly interested in reviving the old

PSAMMETICHUS.

Egyptian commerce. His
efforts to restore Egyptian
influence in Syria and Arabia were foiled by the rise
of a new empire in the Eu-

NECO.

phrates valley (§ 42); and he failed also in a noble attempt
to reopen the ancient canal connecting the Red Sea with
the Mediterranean (§ 28). But, in searching for another
route for vessels between those waters, he did succeed in a remarkable attempt. *One of his ships sailed around Africa*,
starting from the Red Sea and returning, three years later, by
the Mediterranean. Herodotus (§ 21), who tells us the story,
adds: "On their return the sailors reported (others may believe them but I will not) that in sailing from east to west
around Africa they had the sun on their right hand." This
report, which Herodotus could not believe, is good proof to us
that the story of the sailors was true.

33. Egyptian History merges in Greek and Roman History. —
The last age of Egyptian independence lasted only 128 years.
Then followed the "seventh period," — one of long dependence
upon foreign powers. Persia conquered the country in 525 B.C.
(§ 72), and ruled it for two centuries under Persian governors.
Then Alexander the Great established Greek sway over all the
Persian world (§§ 278 ff.). At his death Egypt became again a

separate state; but it was ruled by the *Greek Ptolemies* from their new Greek capital at Alexandria. Cleopatra, the last of this line of monarchs, fell before Augustus Caesar in 30 B.C., and Egypt became a Roman province. Native rule has never been restored.

EXERCISES. — 1. Make a summary of the things we owe to Egypt. 2. What can you learn from those extracts upon Egypt in Davis' *Readings*, which have not been referred to in this chapter? (If the class have enough of those valuable little books in their hands, this topic may make all or part of a day's lesson : if only a copy or two is in the library, one student may well make a short report to the class, with brief readings.) 3. Do you regard the first pyramid or Lake Moeris or the canal from the Nile to the Red Sea as the truest monument to Egyptian greatness? 4. Students who wish to read further upon ancient Egypt will find the titles of three or four of the best books for their purpose in the Appendix.

CHAPTER III

THE TIGRIS-EUPHRATES STATES

GEOGRAPHY

34. The Two Rivers. — Across Asia, from the Red to the Yellow Sea, stretches a mighty desert. Its smaller and western part, a series of low, sandy plains, is really a continuation of the African desert. The eastern portion (which lies almost wholly beyond the field of *our* ancient history, § 4) consists of lofty plateaus broken up by rugged mountains. The two parts are separated from each other by a patch of luxuriant vegetation, reaching away from the Persian Gulf to the northwest.

This oasis is the work of the Tigris and Euphrates. (In this connection see map facing p. 12.) These twin rivers have never interested men so much as the more mysterious Nile has; but they have played a hardly less important part in history. Rising on opposite sides of the snow-capped mountains of Armenia, they approach each other by great sweeps until they form a common valley; then they flow in parallel channels for the greater part of their course, uniting just before they reach the Gulf. The land between them has always been named from them. The Jews called it " Syria of the Two Rivers "; the Greeks, *Mesopotamia*, or " Between the Rivers "; the modern Arabs, " The Island."

35. Divisions of the Valley. — The valley had three distinct parts, two of which were of special importance. The first of these was *Chaldea*,[1] the district near the mouth of the rivers.

---

[1] This is the name that has been used for many centuries. It seems best to keep it, though we know now that it is inaccurate for the early period. The Chaldeans proper did not enter the valley until long after its civilization began.

Like the delta of the Nile, Chaldea consisted of deposits of soil carried out in the course of ages into the sea. In area it equaled modern Denmark, and was twice the size of the real Egypt. As with Egypt, its fertility in ancient times was maintained by an annual overflow of the river, regulated by dikes, canals, and reservoirs. Wheat and barley are believed to have been native there. Certainly it was from Chaldea that they spread west to Europe.

The Euphrates district is more dependent upon artificial aids for irrigation than the Nile valley is; and in modern times Chaldea has lost its ancient fertility. During the past thousand years, under Turkish rule, the last vestiges of the ancient engineering works have gone to ruin. The myriads of canals are choked with sand; and, as a result, in this early home of civilization, the *uncontrolled* overflow of the river turns the eastern districts into a dreary marsh; while on the west the desert has drifted in, to cover the most fertile soil in the world; — and the sites of scores of mighty cities are only shapeless mounds, where sometimes nomad Arabs camp for a night.

To the north of Chaldea, the rich plain gives way to a rugged table-land. The more fertile portion lies on the Tigris side, and is the second important part of the valley. It was finally to take the name *Assyria*.

The western half of the upper valley is sometimes called *Mesopotamia Proper*. This third district was less fertile than the others, and never became the seat of a powerful state. It opened, however, upon the northern parts of Syria, and so made part of the great roadway between the Euphrates and the Nile.

THE STORY

36. The People. — The rich Euphrates valley with its fertile plains was one of the first places where men settled after the Flood (§ 1). Here the Tower of Babel was projected and partly built. The inhabitants that remained after the confusion of languages appear to have been Hamites (§ 2). But this valley was much less walled up than that of the Nile. Hence it invited longer to peaceful immigration and was at the same time less protected against hostile inroads. Thus it was that successive waves of tribes from the Arabian desert were able to greatly affect the original population. In the southern part, Chaldea, the Hamitic language by and by yielded before the Semitic and became a "dead language." But the bulk of the inhabitants always remained Hamitic in appearance and blood. They preserved in large measure the characteristics of the older generations who had been the first bearers of civilization in the valley. The change was much greater in the North. The Assyrians not only adopted the language of the invaders but became mainly Semitic in blood — akin to the Arabs.

There was a great difference between the populations of the two countries. The men of the South (Chaldeans, or Babylonians) were quick-witted, industrious, gentle, pleasure-loving, fond of literature and of peaceful pursuits. The hook-nosed, larger-framed, fiercer Assyrians cared mainly for war and the gains of commerce, and had only such arts and learning as they could borrow from their neighbors. They delighted in cruelty and gore and their kings boasted of deeds which would shame a modern ruler. In the old inscriptions, they brag incessantly of torturing, flaying alive, and impaling thousands of captives. Numerous are the pictorial representations which perpetuate in stone the memory of these royal brutalities.

37. The Early City-States. — As in Egypt, so in this double valley there clustered many cities at an early time, perhaps before 5000 B.C. Each such city was a "state" (§ 11, note) by itself, under its own king, and it controlled the surrounding hamlets and farming territory. These little states often waged war with one another and with outside invaders; but they also managed to develop the culture which was to characterize the country in its historic age. Each city, indeed, had a literature of its own, written in libraries of brick (§ 48), and our scholars are learning more of this ancient period every day from the study of the remains recently discovered. Only four cities, out of scores, will be mentioned in this book, — four leading cities, whose names, too, are familiar from the Old Testament, — *Accad* (Agade), *Ur, Babylon,* and *Nineveh.* The first three are in the southern Euphrates district : Nineveh is in Assyria, on the Tigris.

Gradually, war united the rival states into larger ones ; and then contests for power among these, with outside conquests, gave rise to *three great empires,* whose story we shall survey rapidly. Two of these empires were in the south, with their chief center at Babylon (First and Second Babylonian Empires). Between their two periods there arose the still mightier Assyrian Empire, with Nineveh for its capital.

An *empire* is a state containing many sub-states and one ruling state. Egypt was called a *kingdom* while it was confined to the Nile valley, but an *empire* when its sway extended over Ethiopia and Syria (§ 30).

38. Early Attempts at Empire. — About 2800 B.C., *Sargon,*[1] king of Accad, made himself ruler of all Chaldea. Then in a series of victorious campaigns, he carried his authority over the northern part of the river valley, and even to the distant Mediterranean coast. His empire fell to pieces with his death, from lack of organization ; *but his campaigns had transplanted the Euphrates culture into Syria to take lasting root there.* Chaldean traders spread the seed more widely. For more than two thousand years, the fashions of Chaldea were copied in the cities of Syria ; and her cuneiform[2] script was used, and her literature was read, by great numbers of people all over western Asia.

Ur succeeded Accad as mistress of the land. But the cities of the valley were soon overrun by new barbarians from the Arabian desert. These conquerors finally adopted thoroughly the civilization of the country, and took *Babylon* for their chief city.

---

[1] The Babylonians of about 600 B.C. rediscovered a certain inscription of the son of Sargon, long buried even in that day, and fixed his date from it at 3200 years before their own time. Very recent discoveries, however, prove that they placed him a thousand years too early. Davis' *Readings,* Vol. I, No. 17, gives the Babylonian story.

[2] See § 47 for explanation of this term.

39. **The First Babylonian Empire** begins strictly with the rule of *Hammurabi,* who lived about as many years before the birth of Christ as we do after it. In 1917 B.C. he completed the consolidation of the states of the Euphrates valley into one empire. Later, he extended the rule of Babylon to the bounds of Sargon's conquests — and with more lasting results. Ever since, the name Babylon has remained a symbol for magnificence and power.

During the fourth century of this empire (about 1500 B.C.), it came in contact with the " New Empire" of Egypt to which for a time it lost most of its dominions (§ 30).

40. **The Assyrian Empire.** — Assyria first comes to notice in the nineteenth century B.C. It was then a dependent province, belonging to the Babylonian Empire. Six hundred years later it had become a rival ; but its supremacy begins two centuries later still, about 1100 B.C. New invaders from Arabia were harrying the Euphrates country ; and this made it easier for *Tiglath-Pileser I,* king of Assyria, to master Babylonia. This king ruled from the Persian Gulf to the Mediterranean; but after his death his dominions fell apart. The real Assyrian Empire dates from 745 B.C.

In that year, the adventurer *Pul* seized the throne. He had been a gardener. Now he took the name of the first great conqueror, *Tiglath-Pileser* (II), and soon established the most powerful empire the world had so far seen. It was larger than any that had gone before it (map opposite), and *it was better organized.* In the case of each of the earlier empires, the subject kingdoms had been left under the native rulers, as tributary kings. Such princes could never lose a natural ambition to become again independent sovereigns ; and if they attempted revolt, the people were sure to rally loyally to them as to their proper rulers. Thus this loose organization tempted constantly to rebellion. It now gave way to a stronger one. The subject kingdoms were made more completely into parts of one state and *were ruled by Assyrian lieutenants (satraps).* We call such subordinate parts of an empire by the name *provinces.* This new invention in government *was Assyria's chief bequest to the later world.*

The next great Assyrian king was *Sargon II*, who carried away the Ten Tribes of Israel into captivity (722 B.C.). This transplanting of a rebellious people, or at least of the better classes among them, to prevent rebellion, was a favorite device

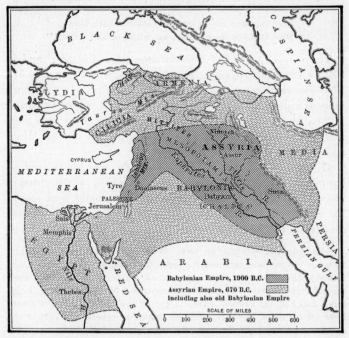

of the Assyrians. Sargon's son, *Sennacherib*, is the most famous Assyrian monarch. He attacked the king of Judah,[2]

---

[1] The Bible attributes the conquest of the Ten Tribes to Salmanassar (Shalmanezer), Sargon's predecessor, under whom the siege of Israel's capital, Samaria, was begun. As to the difference in the spelling of oriental names by Catholics and Protestants see Pope, *The Catholic Student's Aid to the Bible*, p. 418 ff.

[2] Kings xix, 20–37. For the Assyrian story see Davis' *Readings*, Vol. I, No. 12.

but he will be better remembered from the Bible account of a mysterious destruction of his army, perhaps in another expedition, — smitten by " the angel of the Lord." This is the incident commemorated by Byron's lines: —

> " The Assyrian came down like a wolf on the fold,
>   And his cohorts were gleaming with purple and gold.
>
>   .   .   .   .
>
>   Like leaves of the forest when autumn hath blown,
>   That host, on the morrow, lay withered and strown."

The empire recovered quickly from this disaster; and in 672 B.C. Sennacherib's son, *Esarhaddon*, subdued Egypt (§ 31). *This was the second political union of the East.* It was much more complete than the first one of several centuries earlier (§ 30); and the territory was larger, for the Assyrians were reaching out west and east into the new regions of Asia Minor and of Media on the Plateau of Iran.

41. Fall of Assyria. — This wide rule was short-lived, — happily so, for no other great empire has ever so delighted in blood. Disagreeable as it is, the student should read one of the records in which an Assyrian king exults over his fiendish cruelties. The following one is by Assur-Natsir-Pul, 850 B.C.: —

" They did not embrace my feet. With combat and with slaughter I attacked the city and captured it ; three thousand of their fighting men I slew with the sword. Their spoil, their goods, their oxen, and their sheep I carried away. The numerous captives I burned with fire. I captured many of the soldiers alive. I cut off the hands and feet of some ; I cut off the noses, the ears, and the fingers of others ; the eyes of the numerous soldiers I put out. I built up a pyramid of the living and a pyramid of heads. In the middle of them I suspended their heads on vine stems in the neighborhood of their city. Their young men and their maidens I burned as a holocaust. The city I overthrew, dug up, and burned with fire. I annihilated it."

Of another city : " The nobles, as many as had revolted, I flayed ; with their skins I covered the pyramid. Some of them I immured in the midst of the pyramid ; others above the pyramid I impaled on stakes ; others round about the pyramid I planted on stakes."

See also Sennacherib's boast, at the close of No. 12 in Davis' *Readings*, Vol. I.

Against such cruelty and against the crushing Assyrian taxation, there rankled a passionate hatred in the hearts of the oppressed peoples.[1] After twenty years of subjection, Egypt broke away. Twenty years later, Babylon followed. Scythian hordes poured in repeatedly from the north, to devastate the empire; and in 606 the new power of the *Medes* (§ 72), aided by Babylonia, captured Nineveh itself. The Assyrian Empire disappeared, and the proud " city of blood," which had razed so many other cities, was given over to sack and pillage. Two hundred years later the Greek Xenophon could not even learn the name of the crumbling ruins, when he came upon them, in the " Retreat of the Ten Thousand " (§ 257). All signs of human habitation vanished, and the very site was forgotten, until its rediscovery in recent times.

Ancient and modern judgments upon Assyria are at one. Nahum closed his passionate exultation, — " All that hear the news of thy fate shall clap their hands over thee; for whom hath not thy wickedness afflicted continually." And says Dr. Davis (Introduction to No. 14 of his *Readings*, Vol. I): " Its luxuries and refinements were all borrowed from other lands: its insatiable love of conquest and slaughter was its own."

42. The New Babylonian Empire. — Babylon had risen in many a fierce revolt during the five centuries of Assyrian rule. Sennacherib declares, with great exaggeration certainly, that on one occasion he razed it to the ground in punishment: " I laid the houses waste from foundation to roof with fire. Temple and tower I tore down and threw into the canal. I dug ditches through the city, and laid waste its site. Greater than the deluge was its annihilation."

In 625 came a successful rebellion. Then (as noticed in § 41) Babylonia and Media soon shared between them the old Assyrian Empire. The Second Babylonian Empire lasted less than a century. The middle half of the period — the most glorious

---

[1] The student should read the terrible denunciation of Nineveh by the Hebrew prophet in the year of its fall (Book of Nahum, iii, 1–19). Cf. also Isaias xiii, 16–22, and Jeremias l and li.

part, 604–561 B.C. — falls to the reign of *Nabuchodonosor*. The reviving Egyptian power, under Neco, was checked in its effort to extend its sway into Asia (§ 32). Rebellious Jerusalem was sacked, and the Jews were carried away into the Babylonian captivity. The ancient limits of the First Empire were restored, with some additions. Babylon was rebuilt on a more magnificent scale, and the ancient engineering works were renewed.[1] But in 538, soon after this reign,

NABUCHODONOSOR.

Babylon fell before the rising power of the Persians (§ 72), and her independent history came to an end.

SOCIETY, INDUSTRY, CULTURE

43. **The king** was surrounded with everything that could awe and charm the masses. Extraordinary magnificence and splendor removed him from the common people. He gave audience, seated on a golden throne covered with a purple canopy which was supported by pillars glittering with precious stones. All who came into his presence prostrated themselves in the dust until bidden to rise. His rule was absolute; but he worked through a large body of trusted officials, largely taken from the priests.

44. **Classes of Society.** — Chaldea had no class like the nobles of Egypt. Wealth counted for more, and birth for less, than in that country. There were really only two classes, — rich and poor, with a mass of slaves.

The *peasants* tilled the rich land in misery. As in Egypt they paid for their holdings with half of the produce. In a poor year, this left them in debt for seed and living. The creditor could charge exorbitant interest; and, if not paid, he could levy not only upon the debtor's small goods, but also upon wife or child, or upon the person of the farmer himself, for

---

[1] Nebuchadnezzar's own account is given in Davis' *Readings*, Vol. I, No. 13.

slavery.   As early as the time of Hammurabi (§§ 39, 45), however, the law ordered that such slavery should last only three
years.

The *wealthy class* included landowners, officials, professional
men, money lenders, and merchants.   The merchant in particular was a prominent figure.   The position of Chaldea, at the

COLOSSAL MAN-BEAST IN ALABASTER. — From the Palace of Sargon (now in
the Louvre).

head of the Persian Gulf, made its cities the natural mart of
exchange between India and Syria; and for centuries, Babylon
was the great commercial center of the ancient world, far more
truly than London has been of our modern world.   Even the
extensive wars of Assyria, cruel as they were, were not merely
for love of conquest: *they were largely commercial in purpose,* —
to secure the trade of Syria and Phoenicia, and to ruin in

those lands the trade centers[1] that were competing with Nineveh.

45. Law and Property. — In 1902 A.D., a French explorer found a valuable set of Babylonian inscriptions containing a collection of 280 laws. This "code" asserts that it was enacted by Hammurabi (§ 39). It is the oldest known code of laws in the world; and it shows that the men for whom it was made were already far advanced in civilization, with many

ASSYRIAN CONTRACT TABLET IN DUPLICATE. — The outer tablet is broken and shows part of the inner original, which could always be consulted if the outside was thought to have been tampered with.

complex relations with one another. It tries to guard against bribery of judges and witnesses, against careless medical practice, against ignorant or dishonest building contractors. (About a tenth of the code is reproduced in Davis' *Readings*, Vol. I, No. 20.)

Other discoveries prove that rights of property were carefully guarded. Deeds, wills, marriage settlements, legal contracts of all kinds, survive by tens of thousands. The numerous signatures of witnesses, in a variety of " hand writings," testify to a widespread ability to write the difficult cuneiform text.

---

[1] Damascus, Jerusalem, Tyre, and others whose names have less meaning to us to-day. Tyre, often besieged and reduced to a tributary state, was not actually captured, owing to her mastery of the sea.

From the contracts we learn that a woman could control property and carry on business independently of her husband.

46. Law and Men. — Criminal law is the term applied to that portion of a code which relates, not to property, but to the personal relations of men to one another. Here the code

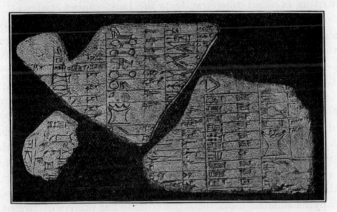

ASSYRIAN TABLETS, showing the older hieroglyphics and the later cuneiform equivalents (apparently for the purpose of instruction).

of Hammurabi in many provisions reminds us of the stern Jewish law of an eye for an eye and a tooth for a tooth.

" If a man has caused a man of rank to lose an eye, one of his own eyes must be struck out. If he has shattered the limb of a man of rank, let his own limb be broken. If he has knocked out the tooth of a man of rank, his tooth must be knocked out."

Injuries to a poor man, however, could be atoned for in money.

" If he has caused a poor man to lose an eye, or has shattered a limb, let him pay one maneh of silver " (about $32.00 in our values).

47. Cuneiform Writing. — The early inhabitants of Chaldea had a system of hieroglyphs not unlike the Egyptian. At first they painted these on the papyrus, which grew in the Euphrates as well as in the Nile. At a later time they came to press the characters with a sharp metal instrument into clay tablets (which were then baked to preserve them). This change of material led to a change in the written characters. The pictures shriveled and flattened into wedge-shaped symbols, which look like scattered nails with curiously battered heads. (This writing is called *cuneiform*, from the Latin *cuneus*, wedge.)

The Semitic conquerors adopted this writing and used it in such minute characters — six lines to an inch sometimes — that some authorities believe magnifying glasses must have been used. This surmise was strengthened when the explorer Layard found a lens among the ruins of the Nineveh library.

48. Literature. — The remains of Chaldean literature are abundant. Each of the numerous cities that studded the valley of the twin rivers had its library, sometimes several of them. A library was a collection of clay tablets or bricks covered with cuneiform writing. In Babylon the ruins of one library contained over thirty thousand tablets, of about the date 2700 B.C., all neatly arranged in order. Originally the libraries contained papyrus rolls also, but these the climate has utterly destroyed.

A tablet, with its condensed writing, corresponds fairly well to a chapter in one of our books. Each tablet had its library number stamped upon it, and the collections were carefully catalogued. The kings prided themselves on keeping libraries open to the public; and Professor Sayce is sure that "a considerable portion of the inhabitants (including many women) could read and write."[1]

The literary class studied the "dead" language of the pre-Semitic period, as we study Latin; and the merchants were obliged to know the languages spoken in Syria in that day. The libraries contained dictionaries and grammars of these languages, and also many translations of foreign books, in columns parallel with the originals. Scribes were constantly employed in copying and editing ancient texts, and they seem

---

[1] The evidence he collects in his *Social Life among the Babylonians*, 41–43. "The ancient civilized East was almost as full of literary activity as is the world of to-day," adds the same eminent scholar, in an extreme statement.

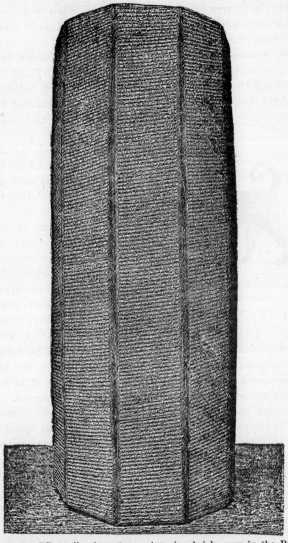

AN ASSYRIAN "BOOK."—An octagon Assyrian brick, now in the British Museum; after Sayce. This representation is about one third the real size.

to have been very careful in their work : when they could not make out a word in an ancient copy, they tell us so and leave the space blank.

49. Science. — In *Geometry* the Chaldeans made as much advance as the Egyptians ; in *Arithmetic* more. Their notation combined the decimal and duodecimal systems. Sixty was a favorite unit, because it is divisible by both ten and twelve : it was used as the hundred is by us.

Scientific *Medicine* was hindered by a belief in charms and magic ; and even *Astronomy* was studied largely as a means of fortune-telling by the stars.[1] Some of our boyish forms for " counting out " — " eeny, meeny, mīny, moe," etc. — are remarkably like the solemn forms of divination used by Chaldean magicians.

AN ASSYRIAN DOG. — Relief on a clay tablet; after Rawlinson.

Still, in spite of such superstition, important progress was made. As in Egypt, the level plains and clear skies invited to an early study of the heavenly bodies. The Chaldeans foretold eclipses, made star maps, and marked out on the heavens the apparent yearly path of the sun. The " signs of the zodiac " in our almanacs come from these early astronomers. Every great city had its lofty observatory and its royal astronomer ; and in Babylon, in 331 B.C., Alexander the Great found an unbroken series of observations running back nineteen hundred years. As we get from the Egyptians our year and months, so through the Chaldeans we get the *week* (with its " seventh day of

---

[1] For hundreds of years the stars were believed to have influence upon human life, and a class of fortune tellers claimed to be able to discover this influence, and to foretell the future, by studying the heavens. This pretended science is called *astrology*, to distinguish it from real astronomy. It lasted in England as late as the days of Queen Elizabeth ; and all through the middle ages in Europe astrologers were often called " Chaldeans."

rest for the soul ") and the division of the day into *hours,* with the subdivision into *minutes.* Their notation, by 12 and 60, we still keep on the face of every clock. The *sundial* and the *water clock* were Assyrian inventions to measure time.

FRAGMENT OF ASSYRIAN "DELUGE-TABLET," with part of the story of a deluge.

50. Chaldean Legends. — Besides this scientific and scholarly literature, the Babylonians had many stories, including an ancient collection of legends which claimed to carry their history back seven hundred thousand years, to the creation of the world. Their story of the creation resembled, in many features, the account in the Bible; and one of their legends concerned a "deluge," from which only one man — favorite of the gods — was saved in an ark, with his family and with one pair of every sort of beasts. These stories, however, have an exaggerated style, and lack the noble simplicity of the Bible narrative.

51. Industries and their Arts. — More than the other ancient peoples, the men of the Euphrates made practical use of their science. They understood the *lever* and *pulley,* and used the *arch* in making vaulted drains and aqueducts. They invented

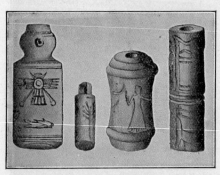

ASSYRIAN CYLINDER SEALS.

the *potter's wheel* and an excellent *system of weights and measures.* Their measures were based on the length of the finger, breadth of the hand, and length of the arm; and, with the system of weights, they have come down to us through the Greeks. The symbols in the "Apothecaries' Table" in our arithmetics are Babylonian in origin. Books upon *agriculture* passed on the Babylonian knowledge of that subject to the Greeks and Arabs. They had surpassing skill in *cutting gems,* enameling, inlaying. Every well-to-do person had his seal with which to sign letters and legal papers. The cheaper sort were of baked clay, but the richer men used engraved precious stones, in the form of cylinders, arranged to revolve on an axis of metal. Thousands of these have been found. Some of them, made of jasper or chalcedony or onyx, are works of art which it would be hard to surpass to-day. Assyrian looms, too, produced the finest of *muslins* and of fleecy *woolens,* to which the *dyer* gave the most brilliant colors. The rich wore long robes of those cloths, decorated with embroideries. Tapestries and carpets, also, wonderfully colored, were woven, for walls and floors and beds. In many such industries, little advance has been made since, so far as the products are concerned.

52. Architecture and Sculpture. — The Euphrates valley had no stone and little wood. Brick making, therefore, was, next to agriculture, the most important industry. Ordinary houses

IMPRESSION FROM A KING'S CYLINDER SEAL. — The figure in the air represents the god who protects the king in his perils.

were built of cheap *sun-dried* bricks. The same material was used for all but the outer courses of the walls of the palaces and temples[1]; but for these outside faces, a kiln-baked brick was used, much like our own. With only these imperfect materials, the Babylonians constructed marvelous tower-temples and elevated gardens, in imitation of mountain scenery. The "Hanging Gardens," built by Nebuchadnezzar to please his wife (from the Median mountains), rose, one terrace upon another, to a height of one hundred and fifty feet. They were counted by the Greeks among the "seven wonders of the

---

[1] The extensive use of sun-dried brick in Chaldean cities explains their complete decay. In the course of ages, after being abandoned, they sank into shapeless mounds, indistinguishable from the surrounding plain.

world." The Babylonian *palaces* were usually one story only in height, resting upon a raised platform of earth. But the *temples* rose stage upon stage, as the drawing opposite shows, with a different color for each story.

Assyria abounded in excellent stone. Still for centuries her builders slavishly used brick, like the people from whom they borrowed their art. Finally, however, they came to make use of the better material about them for sculpture and for at least the facings of their public buildings. Thus in architec-

A LION HUNT. — Assyrian relief; from Rawlinson.

ture and sculpture, though in no other art, Assyria, land of stone, excelled Babylonia, land of brick. In the royal palaces, especially, the almost unlimited power of the monarchs, and their Oriental passion for splendor and color, produced a sumptuous magnificence which the more self-restrained modern world never equals.

The following description of a palace of ancient Nineveh is taken from Dr. J. K. Hosmer's *The Jews*. The passage is partly condensed.

"Upon a huge, wide-spreading, artificial hill, faced with masonry, for a platform, rose cliff-like fortress walls a hundred feet more, wide enough for three chariots abreast and with frequent towers shooting up to a still loftier height. Sculptured portals, by which stood silent guardians, colossal figures in white alabaster, the forms of men and beasts, winged and of majestic mien, admitted to the magnificence within. . . . Upward, tier above tier, into the blue heavens, ran lines of colonnades, pillars of costly cedar, cornices glittering with gold, capitals blazing with vermilion, and, between them, voluminous curtains of silk, purple, and scarlet, interwoven with threads of gold. . . . In the interior, stretching for miles, literally for miles, the builder of the palace ranged the illustrated record of his exploits. . . . The mind grows dizzy with the thought of the splendor — the processions of satraps and eunuchs and tributary kings, winding up the stairs, and passing in a radiant stream through the halls — the gold and embroidery, the ivory and the sumptuous furniture, the pearls and the hangings."

A description with more precise details and less "color" is given in Davis' *Readings*, Vol. I, No. 19. See also No. 18, " An Assyrian City."

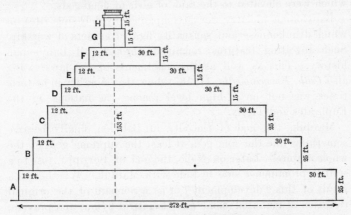

SECTION OF THE TEMPLE OF THE SEVEN SPHERES, according to a "restoration." — From Rawlinson.

H is a sacred shrine. The seven stages below it were colored in order from the bottom as follows : black, orange, red, golden, yellow, blue, silver.

53. Religion and Morals. — It cannot now be ascertained at what exact date and in what way polytheism began to strike root in this cradle of mankind. Whether there were still many adorers of the true God in Chaldea at the time when Abraham left this country for the west, that is, about 2000 B.C., is disputed. The idolaters certainly formed an overwhelming majority.

It is possible that each of the many little city-states (see § 37) originally worshiped the true God, but each under a different name; and that these names by and by came to signify many gods, each of whom was the local deity of the respective tribe. When the small communities, by peaceful means or otherwise, combined more and more politically, the "gods" of each found worshipers in all the tribes thus united, perhaps by being officially recognized. (Hull, S. J., *Archaic Religions*, pp. 108 ff.) Like all those nations with whom the original idea of God is obscured, the Chaldeans worshiped the powers of nature, the sun and the moon, thunder, the day, etc., which were elevated to the rank of gods or demi-gods.

Babylonian idolatry was accompanied by debasing rites, in which drunkenness and sensuality figured as acts of worship. Such revolting features remained through all Babylonian history. This as well as the enactments of the laws (§ 46 ; also *Cath. Encyclopædia*, II, 187) show that morality in historic times was not on a high level among the nations on the Euphrates and Tigris.

Marduk, the god of the city of Babylon, finally became something like the sole god, at least the supreme god, of the whole empire. Later on Nebo, the god of Borsippa, rose to a similar prominence side by side with Marduk. Whether as a result of this "development" or as a remnant of the original tradition of mankind, some most beautiful hymns and prayers, discovered amid the wild chaotic vagaries of Chaldean polytheism, reveal a sublime idea of a Supreme Being, which, however, was not shared by the masses. (See extracts below.)

The Life after Death. — The Chaldeans did not bestow so much care upon their dead as did the Egyptians. However, each tomb had an altar for offerings of food. A man was buried with his arms, a girl with her scent bottles and ornaments. The condition of the soul after death seems to have been considered as a disagreeable, gloomy state, in or near the tomb. Yet, as in the case of Egypt (see § 25), there were not wanting those who believed in a more perfect retribution : some souls were to suffer in a hell of tortures, others who knew how to secure the divine favor were to dwell amid varied pleasures in the distant Isles of the Blest.

From a Chaldean hymn, composed in the city of Ur, before the time of Abraham.

"Father, long suffering and full of forgiveness, whose hand upholds the
     life of all mankind ! . . .
First-born, omnipotent, whose heart is immensity, and there is none
     who may fathom it ! . . .
In heaven, who is supreme ?   Thou alone, thou art supreme !
On earth, who is supreme ?   Thou alone, thou art supreme !
As for thee, thy will is made known in heaven, and the angels bow
     their faces.
As for thee, thy will is made known upon earth, and the spirits below
     kiss the ground."

From an Assyrian prayer for remission of sins.   (Note the
sense of sin and hope of forgiveness.)

"O my god, my sins are many ! . . .   O my goddess, . . . great are
my misdeeds !   I have committed faults and I knew them not.   I have
fed upon misdeeds and I knew them not. . . .   I weep and no one comes
to me; I cry aloud and no one hears me ; . . . I sink under affliction.   I
turn to my merciful god and I groan, Lord, reject not thy servant, — and
if he is hurled into the roaring waters, stretch to him thy hand !   The sins
I have committed, have mercy upon them ! my faults, tear them to pieces
like a garment ! "

(See also Davis' *Readings,* Vol. I, Nos. 22 and 24.)

NOTE. — *Articles found buried* with the dead do not necessarily imply
that they were thought useful to the deceased person.   We bury our priests
in their vestments, our officers with their swords.   Well-to-do persons of
both sexes are laid to rest in costly robes and sometimes with precious
jewelry.   Yet nobody imagines that these things will be needed ; they refer
not to the future life but to that which was ended, or simply express affection.
Therefore the presence of such articles in the tombs of ancient nations
alone does not prove that the nations held erroneous opinions regarding
the life after death ; to make such a statement we must have other indications, as inscriptions, or the literature of the time.   Even the fact that
food and drink were placed in the tombs allows of a correct interpretation ;
this may have been considered as a token of love, or in a time when
material sacrifices were customary, may even have been an offering to the
true God.

CHAPTER IV

THE MIDDLE STATES

The two Syrian peoples that demand notice in a book of this kind are the Phoenicians and the Hebrews. Each of these was an important factor in history.

THE PHOENICIANS

54. Early Sailors. — Before 1000 B.C. the Phoenicians had become *the traders of the world*. Their vessels carried most of the commerce of Babylonia and Egypt. Phoenician sailors manned the ship that Neco sent to circumnavigate Africa. Indeed the fame of these people as sailors so eclipsed that of earlier peoples that it has been customary to speak of them as "the first men who went down to the sea in ships."

The Phoenicians dwelt on a little strip of broken coast, shut off from the rest of the continent by the Lebanon Mountains (map, page 77). The many harbors of their coast invited them seaward, and the "cedar of Lebanon" furnished the best of masts and ship timber. When history first reveals the Mediterranean, about 1600 B.C., it is dotted with the adventurous sails of the Phoenician navigators, and for centuries more they are the only real sailor folk. Half traders, half pirates, their crews crept from island to island, to barter with the natives or to sweep them off for slaves, as chance might best offer.

Farther and farther their merchants daringly sought wealth on the sea, until they passed even the Pillars of Hercules,[1] into

---

[1] The Greeks gave this name to two lofty, rocky hills, one on each side of the Strait of Gibraltar. They were generally believed by the ancients to be the limit of even the most daring voyage. Beyond them lay inconceivable dangers. (See map after page 132.)

the open Atlantic. And at last we see them exchanging the
precious tin of Britain, the yellow amber of the Baltic, and the
slaves and ivory of West Africa, for the spices, gold, scented
wood, and precious stones of India.

55. The chief Phoenician cities were *Tyre* and *Sidon.* For
many centuries, until the attacks by Assyria in the eighth
century B.C., these cities were among the most splendid and
wealthy in the world. Ezechiel (xxvi, xxvii) describes the
grandeur of Tyre in noble poetry that teaches us much regarding Phoenician trade and life : —

" O thou that dwellest at the entry of the sea, which art the merchant
of the peoples unto many isles, . . . thou, O Tyre, hast said, I am perfect in beauty. *Thy borders are in the heart of the seas ;* thy builders
have perfected thy beauty. They have made all thy planks of fir trees.
. . . They have taken cedars from Lebanon to be masts for thee ; they
have made thy benches of ivory inlaid in boxwood from the isles of Kit-
tim [Kition in Cyprus]. Of fine linen with broidered work from Egypt
was thy sail, . . . blue and purple from the isles of Elishah [North
Africa] was thy awning. . . . All the ships of the sea were in thee
to exchange thy merchandise. . . . Tarshish [Tartessus, southwestern
Spain] was thy merchant by reason of the multitude of all kinds of riches.
With silver, iron, tin, and lead they traded for thy wares. Javan [Greek
Ionia], Tubal, and Mesheck [the lands of the Black and Caspian seas],
they were thy traffickers. . . . They of the house of Togarmah [Arme-
nia] traded for thy wares with horses and mules. . . . Many isles were
the mart of thy hands. They brought thee bones of ivory and of ebony."
Ezechiel names also, among the articles of exchange, emeralds, coral,
rubies, wheat, honey, oil, balm, wine, wool, yarn, spices, lambs, and
goats.

56. Place in History. — *The Phoenicians were the first colo-*
nizers of the sea, — the forerunners of the Greeks, Spaniards,
Portuguese, and English. They fringed the Mediterranean with
trading stations, many of which grew into cities ; but these
" colonies " never depended on their mother cities politically.
Chief among them was Carthage in northern Africa, founded
about 800 B.C. Later on this city was to engage in a long struggle with the Greeks and the Romans. (See map after page 132.)

Phoenician articles are found in great abundance in the ancient tombs of the Greek and Italian peninsulas — the earliest European homes of civilization. In a selfish but effective way, the Phoenicians became the "missionaries" to Europe of the culture that Asia and Africa had developed. *It was their function, not to create civilization, but to spread it.* Especially did they teach the Greeks, who were to teach the rest of Europe.

The chief export of the Phoenicians, some one has said, was *the alphabet.* They were only one of several early peoples (as we have recently discovered) to develop a true alphabet; but it is theirs which has come down to us through the Greeks and Romans. When the Egyptians conquered Syria about 1500 B.C. (§ 30), the Phoenicians were using the cuneiform script of Babylon, with its hundreds of difficult characters. It was natural that, for the needs of their commerce, they should seek a simpler means of communication: and about 1100 B.C., after a gap of some centuries in our knowledge of their writing, we find them with a true alphabet of twenty-two letters. They seem to have taken these from the symbols for sounds among the Egyptian hieroglyphs (§ 22), though some scholars think they got them from Crete (§ 96).

Phoenician.	Old Greek.	Roman.
⊀	A	A
⟨	B	B
⟩	C	⟨C
△	▷D	D
⅂	Ɛ	E
BH	EH	H
⅄	K	K
I	∟	∟L
W	M	M
Ⅎ	N	N
O	O	O
ⵁ	ⵁ	ⵁQ
⫾	PR	R
W	⧑⧑	⧑S
⟙	T	T

PARTS OF ALPHABET.

Egyptian Hieroglyph.

Egyptian Script.

Phoenician.

Ancient Greek.

Ancient Latin.

A
Later Latin.

GROWTH OF THE LETTER A.

57. Society. — The Phoenicians in themselves do not interest us particularly. They spoke a Semitic tongue (§ 36); but their religion was revolting, especially for the cruel sacrifice of the firstborn to Baal, the sun god, and for the licentious worship of Astarte, the moon goddess.

" Syria was the confluence and the sink of the nations.   The
result was an extreme degree of degradation, low conceptions
of the gods, wild forms of worship dissociated from morality
and vitiated by licentious extravagance." (Hull, S. J., *Arch. Rel.*)

Several cities were grouped loosely about Sidon and Tyre :
but they never formed a united state.   Satisfied with the profit
of trade, they submitted easily, as a rule, to any powerful
neighbor — Assyria or Egypt.   As tributaries, they sent workmen to construct the magnificent buildings of Assyria or to
develop the mines of Egypt, and they furnished the fleets of
either empire in turn.

About 730 B.C. Tyre was reduced in power, by attacks from
Assyria ; but it remained a great mercantile center until its
capture by Alexander the Great (332 B.C.).   From this downfall the city never fully recovered, and fishermen now spread
their nets to dry in the sun on the bare rock where once its
proud towers rose.   (Ezechiel xxvi, 5.)

THE HEBREWS

58. The Patriarchs. — As the Phoenicians were men of the
sea, so the Hebrews were to carry out their mission, the greatest any nation has ever had, in the interior of the continent.
They are also called Israelites or Jews.   No nation has such
accurate records of its origin and history as they.   God Himself called their ancestor, Abraham, a descendant of Sem, away
from his home, the ancient city of Ur (§ 37), where idolatry
had become general.   God ordered him to settle in what is
now Palestine, and promised to make him the father of a great
people which was to occupy this very land.   In him "all the
nations of the world should be blessed," that is to say, the Redeemer of the world, promised to Adam after the fall, was to
come from his descendants.   Abraham " believed the Lord."
It must have been about 2000 B.C. that he emigrated from Ur.
But for a short stay in Egypt caused by a famine, he as well as
his son and grandson, Isaac and Jacob, lived a nomadic life in

the "Promised Land," for two centuries. God repeated to Isaac and Jacob the pledges given to Abraham.

59. Sojourn in Egypt. — Jealousy arising between Jacob's twelve sons, one of them, Joseph, was sold by his heartless brothers as a slave, but he eventually became the prime minister

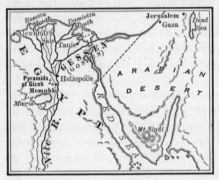

of the king of Egypt. Soon again a famine broke out. Jacob sent his sons to Egypt to find relief. Here they were recognized by Joseph. He invited his father Jacob to come with his whole offspring and settle in Europe. "Seventy souls" they arrived and found in the northeast corner, the region of Gessen (Goshen), a congenial dwelling place. All this happened under the Hyksos kings. In Gessen the Children of Israel grew into a large people.

But the time came when the Hyksos rulers were dislodged by the native princes of Thebes. "There arose a new king who knew not Joseph." Might not the numerous Israelites, in the case of a new attack of nomads from the northeast, side with the invaders? So a systematic persecution began. The king "made their life bitter with hard work in clay and brick and with all manner of service." (Exodus i, 14.) Finally he ordered killed all the male infants born of Israelite mothers.

60. The Exodus. — Among those saved from royal brutality was Moses, whom God eventually chose to lead His people out of the "house of bondage" into the land which He had promised to their forefathers, Abraham, Isaac, and Jacob. But the "ten plagues of Egypt" had to come, before Pharaoh was inclined to do the bidding of the God of Israel.

The people first turned to the fastnesses of Mount Sinai, where God renewed with them the *covenant* He had made with their patriarchal ancestors. Under thunder and lightning He gave to them the Ten Commandments, which are chiefly a wonderfully concise and yet complete code of the natural law.

They promised to observe it faithfully, together with all the ceremonial and other laws which Moses would make known to them. God in return promised them a special care, such as He did not bestow on any other nation. *" They shall be My people and I will be their God."* He added pledges of temporal prosperity and of an independent national existence. But the greatest was the renewal of the promise given to Abraham, that the Redeemer of the world would be born from among their number. They were to have the honor of keeping ready for Him a place where the worship of the true God would be actually practiced.

Then began the forty years' wandering in the desert, during which they were miraculously fed by the manna. During this period Moses perfected the "Law," consisting of detailed ceremonial, civil and political regulations. After Moses' death a new generation entered the "Promised Land" and undertook its conquest under the leadership of Josue. The corrupt population of Palestine had long provoked the wrath of the Almighty. The land was now divided among the Children of Israel according to their twelve tribes. Contrary to the injunction of God, they did not destroy all the former settlers, and the survivors of the latter, though subject to Israel, proved a very disastrous neighborhood. Chiefly by mixed marriages, they frequently seduced numerous Israelites to idolatry and the gross immorality connected therewith.

61. The Judges. — In their new abodes, the people at first were without any political central authority. Each community had local government, but there was no common bond to unite the whole Hebrew population. It was during this period that on account of their many violations of the covenant, chiefly by idolatry, God allowed portions of the people to be oppressed by the surrounding races, especially by the powerful Philistines. When they returned to Him in sorrow and contrition, He often raised up among them men of great bravery and capability, who freed them from their enemies. These men retained their influence even after peace was restored and acted as rulers and *judges*. Hence this period is called the time of the JUDGES. They were, however, no stable institution and none of them controlled the whole people. The only strong bond of Unity during this time of political weakness was their religion. Unity of belief, a centralized priestly organization, and yearly pilgrimages to the Holy Tabernacle which had accompanied their fathers through the desert, prevented the nation from falling apart or disappearing among their neighbors who were so often their conquerors.

62. Kingship. — The last of the judges and at the same time the greatest of the prophets was Samuel (§ 68). To him the ancients of the people signified repeatedly that the nation wished to have a king like the races around them. Finally, inspired by God, he anointed *Saul* king of His people.　Saul, however, although he won great victories over their enemies, was ultimately rejected, because he arrogated to himself priestly privileges.

God now selected *David*, the shepherd boy, who became the most powerful king of Israel.　He succeeded in completely unifying the nation and in extending its boundaries from the Red Sea to the Euphrates.　He fortified and beautified the

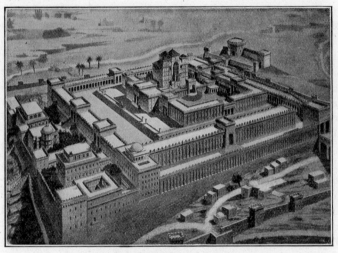

THE TEMPLE OF SOLOMON (Restoration).
(From Herder's Konvers.-Lexikon.)

city of Jerusalem, which he made his capital, perfected the organization of the priesthood, and enriched the Hebrew literature with the Psalms, the greatest lyric poems of the world.　As a reward for his zeal in the service of God he received the solemn promise, that the Redeemer of the world would come from his family, and that, if his descendants remained faithful to God, they would be forever preserved in their royal power.

David was succeeded by his son *Solomon*, famous for his wisdom, who with the aid of Phoenician workmen built the splendid temple of Jerusalem, which was to be the center of Divine worship for the nation. He also erected a magnificent royal palace, and by his commercial connections with foreign countries enriched the whole people. The first part of his reign is the most glorious period of the history of Israel. But at length the heavy taxes made necessary by his extravagance and luxury embittered his subjects and made them ripe for revolt. Moreover, while polygamy was not forbidden by the Mosaic law, Solomon, contrary to the law, took wives from pagan nations, who eventually perverted his heart, so much so that he even built temples to their gods and took part in their sacrifices. Consequently a prophet announced to him that he had forfeited God's favor. But for the sake of David his father, the destruction was not to come in his own days, nor would the house of David be deprived of the dominion over the entire nation.

63. Division of the People. — After Solomon's death, ten of the tribes separated themselves from Roboam his son. Juda alone, with the insignificant tribe of Benjamin, remained faithful to the hereditary ruler. Jeroboam, a commander of the army, who had fled the country under Solomon, was proclaimed king by the ten tribes. Thus, after 975 B.C., the nation was divided into the northern kingdom of *Israel*, with Samaria as capital, and the southern kingdom of *Juda*, with Jerusalem as capital.

64. Kingdom of Israel. — In the kingdom of Israel idolatry became very general, so that many pious Israelites, ancients and priests emigrated to Juda and Jerusalem. Jeroboam, the first king to alienate the people from Jerusalem and the temple, erected golden calves at Dan and Bethel, the northern and southern points of his kingdom, and invited his subjects to worship them. The fiery zeal of the prophet Elias alone prevented Israel from bending the knee to Baal, the Phoenician sun-god. The kingdom lasted 252 years. It had in all nine-

teen kings, belonging to nine different dynasties ; seven of these
dynasties were entirely rooted out by those who succeeded
them.   One king reigned but a few months, another a few days.
Only a single king, Jehu, showed true zeal for the Law, and
even he tolerated the worship of the golden calves, although he
abolished that of Baal.

At the time when the Hebrew nation thus weakened itself,
the great empires on the Euphrates and the Nile also were in
a state of decline and showed little aggressiveness.   The wars
of the two Israelitic kingdoms recorded in Holy Scripture were
waged between themselves and with the small nations around
them.   But after Assyria had recovered under the usurper
Pul (§ 40), it at once began a policy of extension and soon its
boundaries reached as far as the confines of Israel.   In 722
B.C. Salmanassar and his successor Sargon II conquered
Samaria and led the king Osee with almost the whole people
into captivity.   The captives were settled in the most distant
districts of the Assyrian Empire.   These, " the lost ten tribes,"
never returned to the land of their fathers.   Colonists were
sent to repeople the deserted land ; they fused with the remaining Israelites, and thus produced the half-pagan population of
the Samaritans.

65. The Kingdom of Juda, though much smaller, enjoyed
greater advantages in possessing the national temple and with
it the center of the priesthood, and in having the family of the
greatest kings as their rulers.   It lasted nearly four hundred
years, and in this time had twenty kings, all of the house of
David.   Only for five years a woman, the pagan Athalia, a
cruel tyrant, held the reins of government.   She destroyed the
whole royal family with the sole exception of one child, Joas,
who was for some time concealed in the temple.   Not all of
the twenty kings were truly religious.   The four last ones
practiced paganism openly and showed a supreme contempt
for the religion of David their great ancestor.

66. Destruction. — Nabuchodonosor, king of the second Babylonian Empire (§ 42), destroyed Jerusalem and the kingdom.

He first made Juda tributary. Several times it rose against him, and as early as 606 B.C. he led away the foremost men into captivity. Finally, he appeared with a strong army before the walls of Jerusalem and took it after a siege of several years in 586 B.C. King Sedecias saw his own sons slain before him; then his eyes were put out, and laden with chains he was carried to Babylon, where he died in prison. The Babylonians utterly destroyed the splendid city; the king's palace and the magnificent temple sank in ashes; the people, save some poor vinedressers and husbandmen, were forced to emigrate to the Euphrates.

The prophet Jeremias had foretold this catastrophe and warned king and priests and people for years. Persecution was his reward. He was now permitted to stay with the miserable remnant of the population. It was then that he sang over the ruined city those touching lamentations which resound in our churches every year during Holy Week.

> " How doeth the city sit solitary that was full of people !
> How is the mistress of the nations become a widow !
> How is the queen of provinces become tributary !
> The ways of Sion mourn, because none come to her solemnities,
> All her gates are broken,
> Her priests sigh,
> Her virgins are in affliction,
> And she herself is oppressed with bitterness.
> All ye that pass by the way attend and see,
> If there be any sorrow like to my sorrow."

67. Restoration. — This severe chastisement had a lasting effect. In their captivity the people again turned to God. Their greatest desire was to go back to the land of their fathers, and to rebuild the temple and the Holy City. After fifty years this desire was fulfilled. As soon as Cyrus, king of Persia, had made himself master of Babylon, he allowed the Jews to return. A large number availed themselves of his permission, and city and temple rose from their ruins. Their land was now ruled by Persian governors. The Persian rule, however,

JERUSALEM TO-DAY, from the southwest, with the road to Bethlehem.

was mild; and many privileges distinguished this province from the rest of the empire (§ 72).

By constant and most flagrant violation of God's law, kings and people had lost the claim to that independent national existence which had been promised to their ancestors. But in view of their sincere repentance God did not take away from them their spiritual mission with regard to the future Redeemer of mankind. The temple was once more the most hallowed spot on earth. The land of Juda and the new little nation were the only place on earth where "Wisdom dwelt." Nor did the people ever again fall away from the God of Abraham, Isaac, and Jacob. But the house of David did not reascend the throne. It disappeared in obscurity until the time of "Joseph, the husband of Mary, from whom was born Jesus, who is called the Christ."

68. The priesthood of the Hebrews was not conferred by any kind of ordination like the Christian sacrament of Holy Orders. According to the will of God, Moses made his brother Aaron high priest, which dignity was always to descend from the actual high priest to his eldest son. In like manner all the other descendants of Aaron were to be the priests of the nation. They and they alone could perform the priestly functions in

the temple. Nobody else could "become" priest. Moses and Aaron were of the tribe of Levi; all the other male members of this tribe, called the *levites*, were to be the servants and assistants of the priests in their sacred office. Crippled persons, however, or such as were affected with diseases or found guilty of immoral life were not permitted to act as either priests or levites. Unlike the other tribes (§ 60) the tribe of Levi had no territory assigned to it but lived in cities scattered over the whole land. To the support of the priests and levites the whole nation contributed the tithe — one-tenth of the agricultural products of the soil.

An important part in Hebrew history is played by the **prophets**. Each prophet represents a special act of God's providence towards His people, because each one was called and sent individually. Each prophet, therefore, had to prove his mission by some kind of miracle. The prophets were somewhat like the missionaries of our own times. They reminded the people of its duties and did not hesitate to rebuke the powerful, even the kings. To give force to their preaching, they frequently foretold the chastisements which the wrath of God would inflict in case of continued unfaithfulness. To encourage the people in times of distress, they pointed to the wonders of Divine mercy and kindness, and announced many particular circumstances of the life and death of the Redeemer and the greatness of his spiritual empire. Their title — prophet = one who foretells — expresses only one part of their important office.

The Hebrews have not contributed any invention or discovery or other advancement to the material civilization of the world. Theirs was an infinitely higher mission. Of their literature we know beside some other comparatively unimportant productions only the sacred books of the Bible.[1] They are for us an infallible source of faith. But even from the merely secular point of view, they not only contain a great amount of historical and philosophic truth, but have furnished the world with the most sublime works of lyric poetry ever produced.

For Further Reading. — Pages 13–168 in Ecker's *School Bible* treat of the matter condensed on the above few pages; nearly every section will engage the interest of young minds. — Coppens' *Choice Morsels*, pp. 12–300, offers a selection of the most important chapters of the Bible which refer to this subject. It leaves the original scriptural language entirely intact. — Let the student always keep before his eyes the systematic arrangement as outlined above.

---

[1] The *Talmud* was not written before the second century after Christ. It is a voluminous collection of laws with their interpretations. It claims to be based on the Bible, but with many Jews it is practically taking its place.

EXERCISE. — 1. Locate on the map four centers of civilization for 1500 B.C.; and note when they would naturally come into touch with one another.   (One more center for this same age — Crete — is yet to be treated §§ 93–97.)   2. What new center of civilization appeared between 1500 and 1000 B.C. ?

CHAPTER V

THE PERSIAN EMPIRE

69. The Map grows. — So far, we have had to do only with the first homes of civilization — the Nile and Euphrates valleys — and with the middle land, Syria. Assyria did reach out somewhat, east and west (see map, page 55); but her new regions had no special importance in her day, and made no contributions to civilized life. But shortly before the overthrow of Babylon, two new centers of power appeared, one on either side of the older field. These were Persia and Lydia.

70. Expansion on the West. — *Lydia* was a kingdom in western Asia Minor. Somewhat before 550 B.C. its sovereign, *Croesus,* united all Asia Minor west of the Halys River under his sway. This made the Lydian Empire for a time one of the great world-powers (see map following). The region was rich, especially in metals; and the wealth of the monarch so impressed the Greeks that " rich as Croesus " became a by-word. Croesus counted among his subjects the Greek cities that fringed the western coast of Asia Minor. We have noticed that, shortly before, Greeks had been brought into close touch with Egypt. *From this time, history has to do with Europe as well as with Asia and Egypt;* and soon that new field was to become the center of interest.

Lydia's own gift to the world was the invention of *coinage.* As early as 650 B.C., a Lydian king stamped upon pieces of silver a statement of their weight and purity, with his name and picture as guarantee of the truth of the statement. Until this time, little advance had been made over the old Egyptian method of trade, except that the use of silver rings and bars had become more common. The Babylonians, along with their

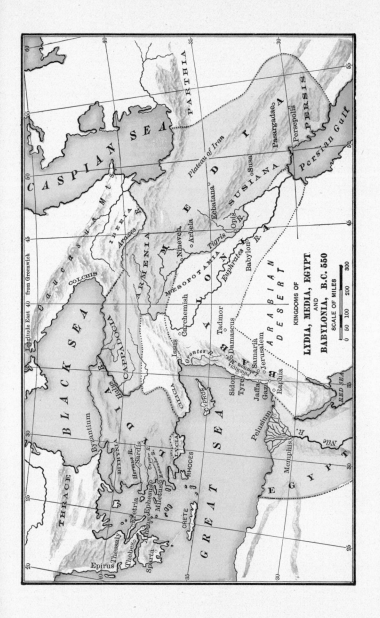

KINGDOMS OF
LYDIA, MEDIA, EGYPT
AND
BABYLONIA, B.C. 550

SCALE OF MILES
0 50 100 200 300

other weights and measures, had taught the world to count riches in *shekels*, — a certain weight of silver, — but there were no *coined* shekels.   The ring and bar "money" had to be weighed each time it passed from hand to hand; and even then there was little security against cheaper metals being mixed with the silver.[1] The true money of Lydia could be received anywhere at once at a fixed rate. This made all forms of trade and commerce vastly easier. Other states began to adopt systems of coinage of their own.   Ever since, the coinage of money has been one of the important duties of governments.

We must not suppose, however, that the old sort of " barter " vanished at once. It remained the common method of exchange in all but the great markets of the world for centuries; and in new countries it has appeared, in the lack of coined money, in very modern times. In our early New England colonies there were times when people paid taxes and debts "in kind," much after the old Egyptian fashion. One student at Harvard college, who afterward became its president, is recorded as paying his tuition with " an old cow."

71. Expansion in the East. — On the farther side of the Euphrates and Tigris lay the lofty and somewhat arid Plateau of Iran. This was the home of the *Medes and Persians.* These peoples appeared first about 850 B.C., as fierce barbarians, whom Assyria found it needful to subdue repeatedly.   Gradually they adopted the civilization of their neighbors; then, about 625 B.C., a chieftain of the Medes united the western tribes of the plateau into a firm monarchy; and in 606, as we have seen, this new power conquered Assyria.

We are now ready to take up again the story of the growth of the great Oriental empires, where we left it at the close of Chapter III. Chapter IV, dealing with the small Syrian states, was a necessary interruption to that story.

72. Rise of the Persian Empire. — The destruction of Assyrian rule, which we noted toward the close of § 41, took place some

---

[1] In all this ancient period, silver was more valuable than gold, and so was taken for the standard of value.

years before 600 B.C. Then the civilized world was divided, for three generations,[1] between four great powers, — Babylon, Egypt, Lydia, and Media. Most of that time, these kingdoms were bound together in a friendly alliance; and the civilized world had a rare rest from internal war. Media, it is true, busied herself in extending her dominions by war with barbarous tribes on the east. By such means she added to her territory all the Plateau of Iran and the northern portion of the old Assyrian Empire. This made her far the largest of the four states. But in 558 B.C., *Cyrus*, a tributary prince of the Persian tribes, threw off the yoke of the Medes and set up an independent Persian monarchy.[2]

Then Persia quickly became the largest and most powerful empire the world had known. The war with Media resulted in the rapid conquest of that state. This victory led Cyrus into war with Lydia and Babylon, which were allies of Media. Again he was overwhelmingly victorious. He conquered Croesus of Lydia and seized upon all Asia Minor. Then he captured Babylon, and so was left without a rival in the Euphrates and Syrian districts. A few years later his son subdued Egypt. *Thus the new empire included all the former empires, together with the new districts of Iran and Asia Minor.*

With the Greeks Persia came into conflict, about thirty years after the death of Cyrus. The story belongs to European history (§§ 158 ff.). It is enough here to note that the Persians were finally defeated. Their empire lasted, however, a century and a half more, until Alexander the Great conquered it and united it with the Greek world (§§ 276 ff.).

---

[1] It is time for the student to have a definite understanding of this term, which is used constantly in measuring time. A *generation* means the average interval that separates a father from his son. This corresponds in length, also, in a rough way, to the active years of adult life, — the period between early manhood and old age. *It is reckoned at twenty-five or thirty years.*

[2] This prince is known in history as *Cyrus the Great.* He is the earliest sovereign whose name we distinguish in that way. A student may well make a special report to the class upon the stories connected with his life. Any large history of ancient times gives some of these stories ; and they may be found, in the original form in which they have come down to us, in a translation of Herodotus. See also Davis' *Readings*, Vol. I, Nos. 25 and 26.

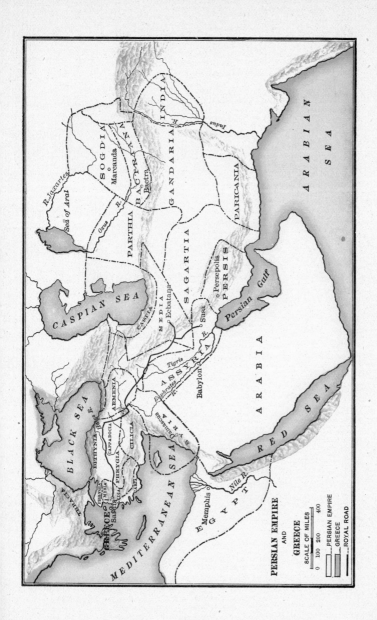

PERSIAN EMPIRE
AND
GREECE

SCALE OF MILES

0   100 200   400

....PERSIAN EMPIRE
.....GREECE
....ROYAL ROAD

ARABIAN
SEA

SOGDIA

Marcanda

Bactra

PARTHIA

BACTRIA

INDIA

GANDARIA

PARICANIA

R. Iaxartes

Sea of Aral

Oxus R.

CASPIAN SEA

SAGARTIA

PERSIS

Persian Gulf

CASPIA

MEDIA

Ecbatana

Persepolis

Susa

Persian Gulf

Tigris

ASSYRIA

Babylon

Euphrates R.

ARABIA

BLACK SEA

ARMENIA

CAPPADOCIA

BITHYNIA

Halys R.

CILICIA

SYRIA

Damascus

THRACE

GREECE

PHRYGIA

MYSIA

LYDIA

Sardis

RED SEA

MEDITERRANEAN SEA

Memphis

Nile R.

EGYPT

73. Extent of the Empire. — *The field of history now widened again.* The next three Persian kings (after Cyrus and his son) added vast districts to the empire: on the east, modern Afghanistan and northwestern India, with wide regions to the northeast beyond the Caspian Sea; and on the west, the European coast from the Black Sea to the Greek peninsula and the islands of the Ægean.

This huge empire contained about seventy-five million people. Its only civilized neighbors were India and Greece. Else-

IMPRESSION FROM PERSIAN CYLINDER SEAL.

where, indeed, it was bounded by seas and deserts. The eastern and western frontiers were farther apart than Washington and San Francisco. The territory included some two million square miles. It was four times as large as the Assyrian Empire, and equaled more than half modern Europe.

74. Industry and Art. — Originally, the Persians were lowly shepherds. Later, they were soldiers and rulers. After their sudden conquests, the small population had to furnish garrisons for all the chief cities of the empire, while the nobles were busied as officers in the vast organization of the government. Accordingly, Persian art and literature were wholly borrowed, — mainly from Babylonia. The cuneiform writing

was adopted from that land; and even the noble palaces,
which have been rediscovered at Persepolis, were only copies
of Assyrian palaces, built in stone instead of in clay. *Persia's
services to the world* were three:[1] the immense *expansion of
the map* already discussed; *the repulse of Scythian savages*
(§ 75); and *a better organization of government* (§§ 76, 77).
The religion of the Persians, too, was remarkable (78).

75. Persia and the Scythians. — About 630 B.C., shortly before the downfall of Nineveh, the frozen steppes of the North
had poured hordes of savages into western Asia (§ 40). By
the Greeks these nomads were called Scythians, and their inroads were like those of the Huns, Turks, and Tartars, in later
history. They plundered as far as Egypt; and they were a
real danger to all the culture the world had been building up
so painfully for four thousand years. Assyria and Lydia both
proved helpless to hold them back; but the Medes and Persians
saved civilization. The Medes drove the ruthless ravagers
back to their own deserts; and the early Persian kings made
repeated expeditions into the Scythian country. By these
means the barbarians were awed, and for centuries the danger
of their attacks was averted.

Darius, the greatest of the successors of Cyrus, seems to
have justified his conquests on the ground of this service to
civilization. In a famous inscription enumerating his conquests, he says : " Ahura-Mazda [the God of Light] delivered
unto me these countries when he saw them in uproar. . . .
By the grace of Ahura-Mazda I have brought them to order
again."

The lengthy inscription from which this passage is taken is cut into
a rock cliff, 300 feet from the base, in three parallel columns, in different
languages, — Persian, Babylonian, and Tartar. It served as the " Rosetta
Stone " of the cuneiform writing (§ 5). Enough of the Persian was
known so that from it scholars learned how to read the Babylonian.
Davis' *Readings*, Vol. I, No. 27, gives a large part of this inscription,

---

[1] Observe that these services were connected with political history, — as
we might expect with a people like the Persians.

which is one of the most important documents of early history, throwing much light upon Persian life and ideals.

76. The Imperial Government. — The empires which came before the Assyrian had very simple machinery for their government. The tributary states kept their old kings and their separate languages, religions, laws, and customs. Two subject kingdoms might even make war upon each other, without interference from the head king. Indeed, the different kingdoms within an empire remained almost as separate as before they became parts of the conquering state, except in three respects: they had to pay tribute; they had to assist in war; and their kings were expected, from time to time, to attend the court of the imperial master.[1]

Plainly, such an empire would fall to pieces easily. If any disaster happened to the ruling state, — if a

PERSIAN QUEEN: fragment of a bronze statue. The dress seems very "modern."

foreign invasion or the unexpected death of a sovereign occurred, — the whole fabric might be shattered at a moment. Each of the original kingdoms would become independent

---

[1] The brief empire of the Jews, for instance, had been of this nature. Solomon, the Book of Kings tells us, "reigned over *all the kingdoms* . . . unto the border of Egypt; they brought presents and served Solomon."

again; and then would follow years of bloody war, until some king built up the empire once more. Peace and security could not exist under such a system.

Assyria, it is true, had begun to reform this system. The great Assyrian rulers of the eighth century were not simply conquerors. They were also organizers. They left the subject peoples their own laws and customs, as before; but they broke up some of the old kingdoms into *satrapies*, or provinces, ruled by appointed officers (§ 40).

The system, however, was still unsatisfactory. In theory the *satraps* were wholly dependent upon the will of the imperial king; but in practice they were very nearly kings themselves, and they were under constant temptation to try to become independent rulers, by rebellion.

This was the plan of imperial government as the Persians found it. They adopted and extended the system of satraps; and *Darius*, the fourth Persian king (521–485 B.C.), introduced *three checks upon rebellion.* In each of the twenty provinces, power was divided between the satrap himself and the commander of the standing army. In each province was placed a royal secretary (the "King's Ear") to communicate constantly with the Great King. And, most important of all, a special royal commissioner (the "King's Eye"), backed with military forces, appeared at intervals in each satrapy to inquire into the government, and, if necessary, to arrest the satrap.

Darius is well called "*the Organizer.*" Political organization advanced no farther until Roman times. Not much had been done to promote a *spirit of unity* among the diverse peoples of the empire. Each still kept its separate language and customs. Still, for the age, the organization of Darius was a marvelous work. It was the most satisfactory ever devised by Orientals; and indeed it was nearer to the later Roman imperial government than to the older and looser Asiatic system of kingdom-empires. The modern Turkish empire, in its best days, has used this system.

77. Post Roads. — The Persians, too, were more thoughtful of the welfare of their subjects than the Assyrians had been. To draw the distant parts of the empire closer, Darius built a magnificent system of post roads, with milestones and excellent inns, with ferries and bridges, and with relays of horses for the royal couriers. The chief road, from Susa to Sardis (map, after page 84), was over fifteen hundred miles

PERSIAN BRONZE LION, at Susa.

long; and it is said that dispatches were sometimes carried its whole length in six days, although ordinary travel required three months. Benjamin Ide Wheeler writes of this great highway (*Alexander the Great*, 196–197) : —

" All the diverse life of the countries it traversed was drawn into its paths. Carians and Cilicians, Phrygians and Cappadocians, staid Lydians, sociable Greeks, crafty Armenians, rude traders from the Euxine shores, nabobs of Babylon, Medes and Persians, galloping couriers mounted on their Bokhara ponies or fine Arab steeds, envoys with train and state, peasants driving their donkeys laden with skins of oil or wine or sacks of grain, stately caravans bearing the wares and fabrics of the south to exchange for the metals, slaves, and grain of the north, travelers and traders seeking to know and exploit the world, — all were there, and all were safe under the protection of an empire the road-way of which pierced the strata of many tribes and many cultures, *and helped set the world a-mixing.*"

78. Religion and Morals. — We know little about the kind of religion which the Persians practiced before they came into the limelight of history. When they appear they had adopted the teachings of Zoroaster (about 1000 B.C.[1]), which are laid down in the *Avesta*, the Persian Bible. According to the Avesta there is one good god, called Ahura Mazda, or Ormuzd, who created all good things, and another god, called Ahriman, who is bad and created all evil things. A continuous struggle is going on between these two gods, in which man by his free actions must necessarily take part. Those who observe the commandments of Ahura Mazda will be rewarded in the next world; if any one sins, the door is open for repentance and forgiveness. But those whose evil deeds outweigh the good will suffer in a terrible hell of fire.

In the end Ahura Mazda will conquer. There will be a general resurrection from death, the whole earth will be cleansed by fire, the bad god, Ahriman, will be destroyed, and all, even those that are in hell, will enter upon a state of eternal happiness. Each god is surrounded by spirits, which, however, are his creatures. The outward sign of Ahura Mazda, and as it were his robe, is the light; hence their veneration for the sun and the fire.

The moral system, as far as we know, was nobler and purer than that of any ancient nation except the Hebrews. Virtues and vices are enumerated much as in Christian ethics. Special stress is laid on purity, material cleanliness included, on charity and kindness, and on truthfulness. Lying is one of the greatest evils; "may Ahura Mazda protect this land from the hostile inroad, from the bad harvests and from lying." The youths of the Persian nobility were trained to ride, to shoot with the bow, and to tell the truth. Agriculture and farming were raised to the dignity of religious duties.

---

[1] Date is uncertain. Some scholars put Zoroaster as late as 600 B.C.

The kings of Persia, while referring to Ahura Mazda frequently and ascribing to him all their successes, never mention the evil god Ahriman. Did they perhaps see that this part of the doctrine contained a very gross error? The evil spirit is a creature and of course lacks the power of creating. Nor will he and his "angels" be annihilated on the last day, nor will hell come to an end, because Our Lord says, "their worm dieth not and the fire is not extinguished." On the whole, however, we may agree with E. R. Hull, S.J., who considers "the religion of the ancient Persians to have preserved the primitive revelation in a form most closely approximating to its pristine purity; the main ideas being retained intact, and the erroneous accretions being of a secondary and not very bizarre nature." (*Archaic Religions*, p. 126.) It is justly presumed that the favor shown by Cyrus and his successors to the Hebrews was greatly due to the similarity between the Persian and Jewish religions.

Conquest and dominion corrupted in some measure the early simplicity of the Persians. If they afterwards were conquered by the Greeks, it was not for the superiority of Greek religion, nor for lack of bravery, but because of improved weapons and better generalship.

In India some 90,000 persons called Parsees, the descendants of those who took refuge there when Persia was forced into Mohamedanism, still profess the religion of Zoroaster.

FOR FURTHER READING. — There is a good twenty-page treatment of the Persian Empire in Benjamin Ide Wheeler's *Alexander the Great* (pp. 187-207). On Persian religion see *History of Religions*, Vol. II, Sections 1 and 2.

EXERCISE. — Would you have expected the Persians to adopt the Egyptian hieroglyphs or the cuneiform writing? Why? In what ways was the organization of the Persian Empire an improvement upon that of the Assyrian? In what way did Assyrian organization improve upon Egyptian?

CHAPTER VI

A SUMMARY OF ORIENTAL CIVILIZATION

A compact summary, like the following, is best suited for reading in class with comment or questions.

79. The Bright Side. — At a very early date, in the valleys of the Nile and Euphrates, men developed a remarkable civilization.

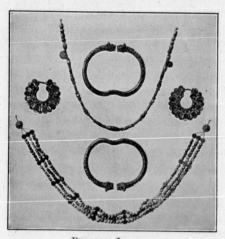

PERSIAN JEWELRY.

They invented excellent tools of bronze (and later of iron), and practised many arts and crafts with a skill of hand that has never been surpassed. They built great cities, with pleasant homes for the wealthy, and with splendid palaces for their princes. They learned how to record their thoughts and doings and inventions in writing, for one another and for their descendants. They built roads and canals; and with ships and caravans, they sought out the treasures of distant regions. At home they found out rather efficient methods of government. Though only the little nation of Israel fully preserved the religion of original mankind, yet much of it was saved everywhere and found dignified expression in literature and buildings. Some thinkers rose above their surroundings in emphasizing moral truth and in teaching justice and charity.

War and trade carried this culture slowly around the eastern coasts of the Mediterranean; and before 1000 B.C. Phoenician traders had scattered its seeds more widely in many regions. Five hundred years later, Persia saved the slow gains of the ages from barbarian ravagers, and united and organized all the civilized East under an effective system of government.

80. The Dark Side. — This Oriental culture, however, was marred by serious faults.

Its benefits were for relatively few. The immense wealth, for instance, was spent chiefly by the kings in gorgeous pomp and splendor.

The form of government generally was the absolute monarchy. The king was the sole source of law; participation of the people or even of a nobility in legislation and government was practically unknown. The people worshiped the monarch with slavish submission.

In Art much *was unnatural.* Sculpture mingled the monstrous and grotesque with the human; and architecture sought to rouse admiration by colossal size, rather than by elegance. Most literature was pompous and stilted, or defaced by extravagant fancies, — like the story of a king who lived many thousand years before his first gray hair appeared.

Learning was allied to absurd and evil superstition. Men's minds were blinded because they had wandered from the true notion of God and of man's relation towards Him. Progress was hampered by the unrestrained passions of the strong and unscrupulous. *Most religions (along with better features) fostered lust and cruelty.*

There was little variety in the different civilizations of the Orient. They differed in certain minor ways, but not as the later European nations did. *Thus they lacked a wholesome rivalry to stimulate them to continued progress.* Each civilization reached its best stage early, and then hardened into set customs.

81. The Question of Further Progress. — Whether the Oriental world would have made further progress, if left to itself, we cannot know surely. It seems not likely. China and India, we know, made similar beginnings, but became stationary, and have remained so for centuries since. In like fashion, the Oriental civilizations which we have been studying appear to have been growing stagnant. Twice as long a period had already elapsed since their beginning, as has sufficed for all our Western growth. Very probably, they would have crystallized, with all their faults, had not new actors appeared. To these new actors and their new stage we now turn.

Suggestions for Review

Let the class prepare review questions, each member five or ten, to ask of the others. Criticize the questions, showing which ones help to bring out important facts and contrasts and likenesses, and which are merely trivial or curious. The author of this volume does not think it worth while to hold students responsible for dates in Part I, unless, perhaps, for a few of the later ones. The table in § 158 below may be used for cross reference and reviews. It is well to make lists of important names or terms for rapid drill, demanding brief but clear explanation of each term, *i.e.*, *cuneiform, shekel, Hyksos, papyrus.* Read over the "theme sentences," in quotation, at the top of Chapters or Divisions (on pages 1, 11, 15, 80), and see whether the class feel, in part at least, their applications.

Sample Questions: (1) Why is Chaldea (whose civilization has been overthrown) better worth our study than China (where an ancient civilization still exists)? (2) In what did the Egyptians excel the Babylonians? (3) In what did the Babylonians excel the Egyptians? (4) In what did the Persians excel both? (5) Trace the growth of the map for civilized countries. (6) Name four contributions to civilization, not mentioned in § 79, but important enough to deserve a place there if space permitted.

Caution: Make sure that the terms "empire," "state," "tributary state," "civilization," have a definite meaning for the student. (See preceding text or footnotes.)

It does not seem to the author advisable to recommend young high school students to read widely upon the Oriental peoples in connection with the first year in history. The material in Davis' *Readings* is admirable for all classes. And a few select titles for the school library are given in the appendix, from which the teacher may make assignments if it seems best.

ITALY

Appollnia

ILLYRIA

MACEDONI

Methone

P. EONES

Longitude East

40

EPIRUS

Olympus M.

Thermaic G.

CORCYRA

MOLOSSIA

Tempe

Ossa M.

THESSALY

Pene

Larissa

Ambracia

ACTIUM

ACARNANIA

Stratus

Thermop.

AETOLIA

Œta M.

ITHACA

Parnassus M.

Chaer

CEPHALLENIA

Delphi

PHOCIS

Coronea

BŒ

38

Patræ

G. of Corinth

Thespiæ

ACHAEA

Sicyon

Meg

ZACYNTHUS

Corinth

Ist.

Olympia

ARCADIA

Argos

Myce

Alpheus F.

Mantinea

ARGOLIS &

Ep

Tegea

Argolicus

P

MESSENE

MESSENIA

E

L

LACONIA

O

Sparta

36

P

O

N

Tænarium Pr.

CYT

M

GREECE
AND
ADJOINING COASTS

SCALE OF MILES

0   25   50   75   100

EXPLANATION:

⸺ IONIANS

⸺ DORIANS

⸺ ÆOLIANS

⸺ ROUTE OF XERXES

18

20

22

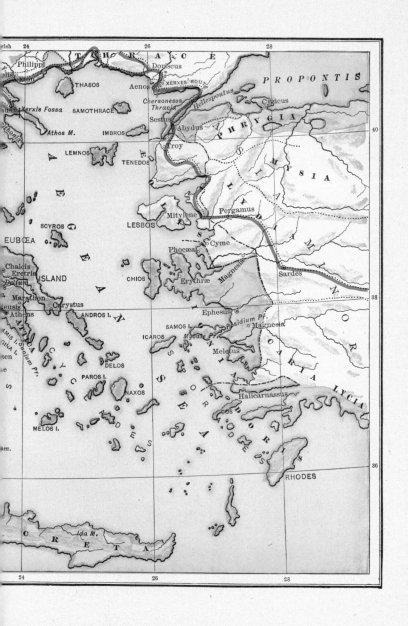

T   H   R   A   C   E

Philippi
lis
lon

THASOS

Xerxis Fossa   SAMOTHRACE

Athos M.   IMBROS

Doriscus

Aenos   XERXES ROUTE

Chersonesus,
Thracia

Sestus

PROPONTIS

Cyzicus

Hellespontus

PHRYGIA

40

LEMNOS

TENEDOS

Abydus

Troy

MYSIA

A   E   G   E   A   N

SCYROS

EUBŒA

Chalcis
Eretria
Delium

ISLAND

Marathon

Carystus

eusis

Athens

AMIS I.   Sunium Pr.
ÆGINA I.
zen

ANDROS I.

Mitylene

LESBOS

Pergamus

Cyme

Phocæa

CHIOS

Erythræ   Magnesia

Sardes

38

Ephesus

Posidium Pr.

Magnesia

SAMOS I.

ICAROS   Mycale Pr.

Meletus

C   Y   C   L   A   D   E   S

DELOS

PAROS I.

NAXOS

S   P   O   R   A   D   E   S

Halicarnassus

CARIA

LYCIA

MELOS I.

RHODES

36

am.

Ida M.

C   R   E   T   A

PART II

THE GREEKS

We now turn to another empire, that of the Greeks. It is not an exterior one but a dominion of the spirit. It extends over the whole world. It lasts as long as civilization with its arts and sciences will remain the pride of the human mind. — JOHN B. VON WEISS.

STUDY OF THE MAPS AFTER PAGES 98 AND 104

Note the three great divisions : *Northern Greece* (Epirus and Thessaly) ; *Central Greece* (a group of eleven districts, to the isthmus of Corinth) ; and the *Peloponnesus* (the southern peninsula). Name the districts from Phocis south, and the chief cities in each, as shown on the map. Which districts have no coast ? Locate Delphi, Thermopylae, Tempe, Parnassus, Olympus, Olympia, Salamis, Ithaca, eight islands, three cities on the Asiatic side. Draw the map with the amount of detail just indicated. **Examine the map frequently in preparing the next lesson.** (*The index tells on what map each geographical name used in the book can be found,* — *except in a few cases, like* Pacific Ocean.)

CHAPTER VII

INFLUENCE OF GEOGRAPHY

82. **Europe contrasted with Asia.** — Asia and Egypt had developed the earliest civilizations. But, for at least half of their four thousand years, another culture had been rising slowly along the coasts and islands of southern Europe. After its separation from the parent stock this European civilization saw a rather independent development. It was influenced in many ways by that of the Oriental nations, but it always kept a distinct character of its own. *The difference was due*, in part at least, *to differences in physical geography.* Four features of European geography were specially important: —

Europe is a peninsula. The sea is easy of access.[1]

Europe has a more temperate climate than the semitropical river valleys of Asia; and *food crops demand more cultivation.* These conditions called for greater exertion upon the part of man. Moreover, the natural products of Europe were more varied than those of Asia. This led to greater variety in human occupations. The beginnings of civilization were slower in Europe; but man was finally to count for more there than in Asia.

In contrast with the vast Asiatic plains and valleys, *Europe is broken into many small districts*, fit to become the homes of distinct peoples. Thus many separate civilizations grew up in touch with one another. Their natural boundaries kept one from absorbing the others. So they remained mutually helpful by their rivalry and intercourse.

Europe could not easily be conquered by the Asiatic empires. This consideration was highly important. Some districts of Asia, such as western Syria and parts of Asia Minor, had a physical character like that of Europe. Accordingly, in these places, civilizations had begun, with a character like that of later European peoples. But these states were reached easily by the forces of the earlier and mightier river-empires; and in the end the "Asiatic character" was always imposed upon them. Europe was saved, partly by its remoteness, but more by the Mediterranean.

83. The Mediterranean has been a mighty factor in European history. Indeed, through all ancient history, European civilization was merely "Mediterranean civilization." It never ventured far from the coasts of that sea. The Mediterranean was the great *highway* for friendly intercourse, and the great

---

[1] Through all "ancient history" (§ 4), "Europe" means southern and central Europe. Russian Europe, indeed, is really part of Asia in geography, and it has always been Asiatic rather than European in civilization.

barrier against Asiatic conquest. Thus, Persia subdued the
Asiatic Greeks, almost without a blow: the European Greeks
she failed to conquer even by supreme effort.

To understand this value of the sea as a barrier, we must keep in
mind the character of ships in early times. The sea was the easiest
road for merchants, traveling in single vessels and certain of friendly
welcome at almost any port. But oars were the main force that drove
the ship (sails were used only when the wind was very favorable); and
the small vessels of that day could not carry many more people than
were needed to man the benches of oarsmen. To transport a large
army, in this way, with needful supplies, — in condition, too, to meet
a hostile army at the landing place, — was almost impossible.

84. **Greece was typical of Europe** in geography and civilization.
The Greeks called themselves *Hellenes* (as they do still).
Hellas meant not European Greece alone, but *all the lands of
the Hellenes.* It included the Greek peninsula, the shores and
islands of the Aegean, Greek colonies on the Black Sea, to the
east, and in Sicily and southern Italy, to the west, with scattered patches elsewhere along the Mediterranean.

Still, the central peninsula remained the heart of Hellas.
Epirus and Thessaly had little to do with Greek history.
Omitting them, the area of Greece is less than a fourth of that
of New York. In this little district are found all the characteristic traits of European geography. It has been well called
the "*most European of European lands,*" *and it became the first
home of European culture.*

85. **Greek Geography and its Influence**. — Certain factors in
Greek geography deserve special mention even though we repeat part of what has been said of Europe as a whole.

a. The islands and the patches of Greek settlements on
distant coasts made *many distinct geographical divisions.* Even
the little Greek peninsula counted more than twenty such units,
each shut off from the others by its strip of sea and its mountain walls. Some of these divisions were about as large as an
American township, and the large ones (except Thessaly and
Epirus) were only seven or eight times that size.

The little states which grew up in these divisions differed widely from one another. Some were monarchies; some, oligarchies; some, democracies.[1] In some, the chief industry was trade; in some, it was agriculture. In some, the people were slow and conservative; in others, they were enterprising and progressive. Oriental civilizations, we have seen (§ 80), were marked by too great *uniformity;* the civilizations of European countries have been marked by a wholesome *diversity.* This character was found especially among the Greeks.

b. Mountain people, living apart, are usually rude and conservative; but *from such tendencies Greece was saved by the sea.* The sea made friendly intercourse possible on a large scale, and brought Athens as closely into touch with Miletus (in Asia) as with Sparta or Olympia. This value of the sea, too, held good for different parts of "European Greece" itself. The peninsula has less area than Portugal, but a longer coast line than all the Spanish peninsula. The very heart of the land is broken into islands and promontories, so that it is hard to find a spot thirty miles distant from the sea.

c. Certain products of some districts made commerce very desirable. The mountain slopes in some parts, as in Attica, grew grapes and olives better than grain. Wine and olive oil had much value in little space. Thus they were especially suited for commerce. Moreover, such mountain districts had a limited grain supply; and, if population was to increase, the people were driven to trade. Now, sailors and traders come in touch constantly with new manners and new ideas, and they are more likely to make progress than a purely agricultural people. Exchanging commodities, they are ready to exchange ideas also. The *seafaring* Greeks were "always seeking some new thing."

---

[1] A monarchy, in the first meaning of the word, is a state ruled by one man, a "monarch." An oligarchy is a state ruled by a "few," or by a small class. A democracy is a state where the whole people govern. In ancient history the words are used with these meanings. Sometimes "aristocracy" is used with much the same force as oligarchy. (In modern times the word "monarchy" is used sometimes of a government like England, which is monarchic only in form, but which really is a democracy.)

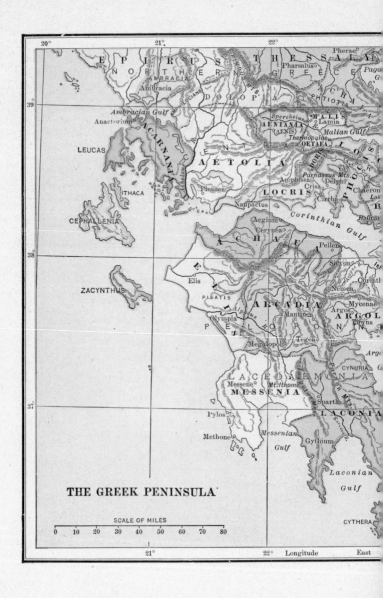

THE GREEK PENINSULA

SCALE OF MILES

0   10   20   30   40   50   60   70   80

SCIATHOS ICOS

PEPARETHOS

LESBOS

39°

Artemisium

SCYROS

PSYRA

CHIOS

Chalcis

Eretria

Delium

O Thebes

Tanagra

Oenophyta

Asopus R.

Phyle Aphidna

Decelia

Parnes Mt.

Marathon

Eleusis Acharnae

Pentelicus Mt.

MEGARIS Athens

Nisaea

SALAMIS Piraeus

Phalerum Hymettus Mt.

Saronic Gulf

Aegina

38°

ANDROS

TENOS

ICARIA

CEOS GYAROS

SYROS RHENEA

CYTHNOS DELOS

HYDREA

SERIPHOS PAROS DONUSSA

NAXOS

37°

SIPHNOS

MELOS SICINOS IOS

PHOLEGARDROS

THERA ANAPHE

Greenwich 24° 25° 26°

d. These early seekers *found valuable new things within easy reach.* Fortunately, this most European of all European lands lay nearest of all Europe to the old civilizations of Asia and Egypt. Moreover, it *faced this civilized East* rather than the barbarous West. On the other side, toward Italy, the coast of Greece is cliff or marsh, with only three or four good harbors. On the east, however, the whole line is broken by

SCENE IN THE VALE OF TEMPE. — From a photograph.   Cf. § 173.

deep bays, from whose mouths, chains of inviting islands lead on and on. In clear weather, the mariner may cross the Aegean without losing sight of land.

e. Very important, too, was *the appearance of the landscape.* A great Oriental state spread over vast plains and was bounded by terrible immensities of desolate deserts. But, except in Thessaly, Greece contained no plains of consequence. It was a land of intermingled sea and mountain, *with everything upon a moderate scale.* There were no mountains so astounding as to

awe the mind. There were no destructive earthquakes, or tremendous storms, or overwhelming floods. Oriental man had
bowed in superstitious dread before the mysteries of nature,
with little attempt to explain them. But in Greece, nature
was not terrible; and men began early to search into her
secrets. In like manner, Oriental *despotism* gave way to Greek
freedom. No doubt, too, the moderation and variety of the
physical world had a part in producing the many-sided genius
of the people and their lively but well-controlled imagination.
And the varied beauty of hill and dale and blue, sunlit sea, the
wonderfully clear, exhilarating air, and the soft splendor of
the radiant sky helped to give them intense joy in mere living.

86. Summary. — We have noted five features of Greek geography: the many separate districts; the sea roads; the in-
ducements to trade; the vicinity of the open side to Eastern
civilization; and the moderation, diversity, and beauty of
nature. Each of these five features became a force in history.
The Greeks produced many varieties of society, side by side,
to react upon one another. They learned quickly whatever the
older civilizations could teach them. They never submitted
long to arbitrary government, as the great Asiatic peoples did.
Above all other peoples, they developed *a love for harmony and
proportion*. Moderation became their ideal virtue.

EXERCISE. — Review the topic — Influence of Geography upon History
— up to this point. See Index, *Physical Geography.*

CHAPTER VIII

HOW WE KNOW ABOUT "PREHISTORIC" HELLAS

87. The Homeric Poems. — The Greeks were late in learning
to use writing, and so our knowledge of early Greek civilization
is imperfect. Until recently, what knowledge we had came
mainly from the two oldest works of Greek poetry, the *Iliad*
and the *Odyssey*. The later Greeks believed that these were
composed about 1100 B.C. by a blind minstrel[1] named Homer.
We still call them "the Homeric poems," though some scholars
believe that each collection was made up of ballads by many bards.
The poems were not put into manuscript until about 600 B.C.;
but they had been handed down orally from generation to generation for centuries. The *Iliad* describes part of the ten-year
siege of Troy (*Ilium*) in Asia. A Trojan prince had carried
away the beautiful Helen, wife of Menelaus, king of Sparta;
and, under the leadership of the great king Agamemnon,
brother of Menelaus, the chiefs had rallied from all parts of
Greece to recover her. Finally they captured and burned the
city. The *Odyssey* narrates the wanderings of Odysseus
(Ulysses), one of the Greek heroes, in the return from the war.

The Trojan war may be fact or fiction.[2] In either case, the
pictures of society in the poems must be true to life. In rude
ages a bard may invent stories, but not manners and customs.[3]

---

[1] In early times, the poet did not write his poems. He chanted them, to the
accompaniment of a harp or some such instrument, at festivals or at the meals
of chieftains. Such a poet is called a minstrel, or bard, or harper.

[2] A well-known Homeric scholar has just published an ingenious book to
prove that there was a real Trojan war, and that it was fought by the Greeks
to secure control of the Hellespont — and so of the Black Sea trade. Teachers
will find this latest contribution to the Homeric problem intensely interesting:
Walter Leaf, *Troy : A Study in Homeric Geography*, Macmillan.

[3] *To-day* a novelist inclines naturally to make the people in his story talk
and act like the people in real life around him. To be sure, now, he may try,

Thus these Homeric poems teach us much about what the Greeks of 1000 or 1100 B.C. thought, and how they lived.

88. Remains in the Soil. — Quite recently another source of information has been opened to us. Students of Greek history strangely neglected *the remains buried in the soil,* long after the study of such objects in the Orient had disclosed many wonders; but in 1870 A.D. Dr. Schliemann, a German scholar, turned to this kind of investigation. He hoped to prove the Homeric stories true. His excavations, and those of others since, have done a more important thing. They have added much to our knowledge of Homer's time, *but they have also opened up two thousand years of older culture, of which Homer and the later Greeks never dreamed.*

89. Henry Schliemann's own life was as romantic as any story in Homer. His father was the pastor in a small German village. The boy grew up with perfect faith in fairies and goblins and tales of magic treasure connected with the old history of the place. His father told him the Homeric stories, and once showed him a fanciful picture of the huge "Walls of Troy." The child was deeply interested. When he was told that no one now knew just where Troy had stood, and that the city had left no traces, he insisted that such walls *must* have left remains that could be uncovered by digging in the ground; and his father playfully agreed that sometime Henry should find them. Later, the boy learned that the great scholars of his day did not believe that such a city as Troy had ever existed. This aroused in him a fierce resentment; and to carry out his childhood dream of finding the great walls of Homer's city became the passion of his life. To do this he must have riches. He was very poor. Six years he worked as a grocer's boy; then, for many years more as clerk for various larger firms. All this time he studied zealously, learning many languages. This made it possible for his employers to send him to foreign countries, in connection with their business. In this way he found opportunities to amass wealth for himself, and, at the age of forty-eight, he was ready to begin his real work.

---

purposely, to represent a past age (historical novel), or he may try foolishly to represent some class of people about whom he knows little. But *in an early age*, like that of the Homeric poems, a poet cannot know any society except the simple one about him, and he knows all phases of that. If he tells a story at all, even of a former age, he makes his actors like men of his own time.

Three incidents in the explorations are treated in the following paragraphs.

90. Excavations at Troy. — Dr. Schliemann began his excavation at a little village in "Troy-land," three miles from the shore, where vague tradition placed the scene of the *Iliad*. The explorations continued more than twenty years and disclosed the remains of *nine* distinct towns, one above another.

The oldest, some fifty feet below the present surface, was a rude village, whose inhabitants knew only stone implements. The second showed powerful walls with a strong citadel which had been destroyed by fire. Its civilization was marked by bronze weapons and gold ornaments. Dr. Schliemann thought this city was Homer's Troy. But we know now that it passed away more than a thousand years before Homer's time, and no doubt the very memory of its civilization had perished before the real Troy was built. Above it, came the remains of three inferior settlements, and then — *the sixth layer from the bottom* — a much larger and finer city, which had perished in conflagration some twelve hundred years before Christ. Extensive explorations conducted after Schliemann's death made it clear that this sixth city corresponded strikingly to the descriptions contained in the *Iliad*. There is therefore no reason to doubt its identity with Homeric Troy.

Above this Homeric Troy came an old Greek city, a magnificent city of the time of Alexander the Great, a Roman city, and, finally, the squalid Turkish village of to-day.

91. Excavations at Mycenae. — Homer places the capital of Agamemnon, leader of all the Greeks, in Argolis at "Mycenae, rich in gold." Here, in 1876, Schliemann uncovered the remains of an ancient city, with peculiar, massive ("Cyclopean") walls. Within, were found a curious group of tombs, where lay in state the embalmed bodies of ancient kings, —

"in the splendor of their crowns and breastplates of embossed plate of gold; their swords studded with golden imagery; their faces covered strangely in golden masks. The very floor of one tomb was thick with gold dust — the heavy gilding from some perished kingly vestment. In another was a downfall of golden leaves and flowers. And amid this profusion of fine fragments were rings, bracelets, smaller crowns, *as for children*, dainty butterflies for ornaments, and [a wonderful] golden flower on a silver stalk."

One tomb, with three female bodies, contained 870 gold objects, besides multitudes of very small ornaments and countless gold beads. In another, five bodies were "literally smothered in jewels." And, with these ornaments, there were skillfully and curiously wrought weapons for the dead, with whetstones to keep them keen, and graceful vases of marble and alabaster, carved with delicate forms, to hold the funeral food

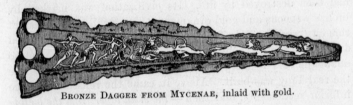

BRONZE DAGGER FROM MYCENAE, inlaid with gold.

and wine. Near the entrance lay bodies of slaves or captives who had been offered in sacrifice.

92. These discoveries confirmed much in "Homer." Like "Troy," so this ancient Mycenae had perished in fire long before Homer's day. But similar cities must have survived, in some parts of Hellas, to be visited by the wandering poet. From remains of many palaces, it may be seen now that the picture of Menelaus' palace in the *Odyssey* (VII, 84 ff.) was drawn from life, — the friezes of glittering blue glass, the walls flashing with bronze and gleaming with plated gold, the heroes and their guests feasting through the night, from gold vessels, in halls lighted by torches held on massive golden statues.

93. Excavations in Crete. — Schliemann's discoveries amazed and aroused the world. Scores of scholars have followed him, exploring the coasts of the Aegean at many points. The most wonderful discoveries of all have been made in Crete, — mainly since the year 1900. Old legends of the Greeks represented that island as one source of their civilization and as the home of powerful kings before Greek history began. These legends used to be regarded as fables; but we know now that they were based upon true tradition. At Knossos, a palace of

THE GATE OF THE LIONS AT MYCENAE.

The huge stone at the top of the gate, supporting the lions, is 15 feet long and 7 feet thick. Enemies could reach the gate only by passing between long stone walls — from behind which archers could shoot down upon them.

"*King Minos*" has been unearthed, spreading over more than four acres of ground, with splendid throne rooms, and with halls and corridors, living rooms, and store rooms. In these last, there were found multitudes of small clay tablets covered with writing, — apparently memoranda of the receipt of taxes. No one can yet read this ancient Cretan writing; but the sculptures and friezes on the walls, the paintings on vases, and the gold designs inlaid on sword blades teach us much about this forgotten civilization. Especially amazing are the admirable

MOUTH OF PALACE SEWER AT KNOSSOS, with terracotta drain pipes — showing method of joining pipes. From Baikie.

bath rooms of the palace, with a drainage system which has been described as "superior to anything of the kind in Europe until the nineteenth century." The pipes could be flushed properly, and a man-trap permitted proper inspection and repair. Back of the Queen's apartments stood a smaller room with a baby's bath. Like Troy and Mycenae, the remains show that Knossos was burned and ravaged — about 1500 B.C.

CHAPTER IX

THE FIRST CIVILIZATION OF HELLAS

94. Antiquity of "Cretan Culture." — For a long time the civilization of Greece was not known to have existed before

HEAD OF A BULL, from a Knossos relief.

800 or about 1000 B.C. at the most. That people more or less civilized were living in the Greek lands and islands when the pyramids rose in Egypt was vaguely believed by many and doubted or denied by others. Yet it remained a riddle to all how the Greeks could have suddenly appeared on the scene with a civilization which was not only a full-grown but also a very peculiar one, vastly different from that of the East.

The discoveries of Dr. Schliemann and his later successors, however, have brought to light the fact that the coasts of the Aegean Sea were alive with human activity for a long period

before the Trojan war.   There was some kind of civilization in
these regions nearly as early as in Egypt and Babylonia.   Our
sole source for this knowledge are relics.   So far it has not been
possible to decipher any of the inscriptions belonging to that
remote age.   Much has been learned from the condition of the
ruins, the cause of their destruction, and the evident attempts,
successful or unsuccessful, at rebuilding them.   The many
pictorial representations of human life also contributed a considerable share.

" VAPHIO CUPS": 3½ inches high; 8 ounces each.   Found at Vaphio, in the
Peloponnesus, in 1889 A.D., and dating back at least to 1800 or 2000 B.C.
Probably Cretan in origin.   Very delicate and yet vigorous goldsmith
work.   See the scroll on the page opposite.

For some time historians called this civilization *Mycenean*, a
name still applied occasionally to the last period of it.   It
was also styled *Minoan*, from Minos, the great Cretan lawgiver.
But it seems better simply to use the name of *Cretan civilization* for the whole period preceding the Homeric age.   In the
island of Crete it evidently reached its highest perfection.
This island, stretching as it does its extended body across the
mouth of the Aegean Sea, and yet not too far distant from the
coasts of Egypt and Syria, served as a stepping stone from
these countries to Greece and Europe.   In fact, many of its
first inhabitants seem to have come from Phoenicia and

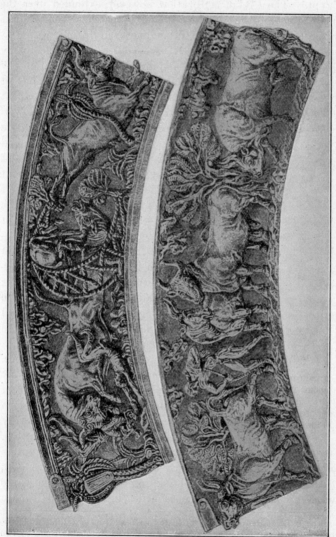

Scroll from the Vaphio Cups.—Stages in the netting and taming of wild bulls. The complete scroll shows them at the plow.

Egypt.[1] The Cretan civilization, however, extended over the entire coast of the Aegean Sea and in patches from Cyprus in the East as far west as Sardinia and even Spain.

95. Origin and Nature. — It is of course impossible to say how much of the achievements of pre-diluvian civilization the first comers brought with them to the coasts and islands of the Aegean Sea. There seems to have been a period, about 4000 or 3500 B.C., when their settlements, like the lowermost of the "towns" discovered by Schliemann on the site

of ancient Troy, consisted of plain round huts and their implements were made of stone. Yet they were by no means without refinement. The ornamentation of their hand-made pottery — they did not know the potter's wheel — shows skill and love of beauty. The better sort of knives and arrowheads was made from a peculiar dark and hard stone which is found in any considerable quantity in the island of Melos only; this seems to indicate that no little trade was going on along these coasts, which in all likelihood was not confined to stone. As we have seen, Schliemann's second city, a very early settlement, contains bronze relics.

VASE FROM KNOSSOS (about 2200 B.C.), with characteristic sea-life ornament. From Baikie.

When and whence this metal and the art of working it was acquired is a matter of conjecture. But the connection of Phoenicia with Crete and the Aegean Sea was very lively during those early times (see § 54). Finds in Egyptian ruins of a very ancient date and Egyptian relics unearthed in Crete show that there must have been at times at least a rather brisk intercourse between Crete and Egypt as well. As a consequence Egyptian and Eastern

[1] The bulk of the population of historic Greece was of a different stock. They belonged to the Japhetites or Aryans, and had probably come by two ways, Asia Minor and Europe.

arts and inventions and every kind of progress found their way to Crete and further to the Aegean territory and Europe.

But these achievements were not admitted or copied slavishly. They were rather adapted and improved upon than simply adopted. Cretan civilization on the island and in its whole sphere of influence took an entirely individual course. The nature of the habitations, the character of the people and their different ideals and ideas worked out a kind of culture which was not found elsewhere. We may call it the beginning of European civilization.

96. The Best Stages. — At all events, by 2500 B.C., Crete had advanced far in the bronze age of culture; and for the next thousand years her civilization (in material things, at least) was quite equal to that of Egypt. The old hand-made pottery gave way to admirable work on the potter's wheel; and the vase paintings, of birds and beasts and plant and sea life, are vastly more lifelike and graceful than any that Egyptian art can show. The walls of houses were decorated with a delicate " egg-shell " porcelain in artistic designs. Gold inlay work, for the decoration of weapons, had reached great perfection.

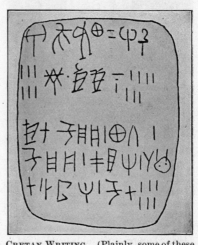

CRETAN WRITING. (Plainly, some of these characters are numerals. Others have a strong likeness to certain Greek letters, especially in the oldest Greek writing.)

A system of syllabic writing had been developed, seemingly more advanced than the Egyptian. Unhappily scholars have not yet found a key to it; but some believe that it may have been the common ancestor of the Phoenician and the Greek alphabets.[1] The palace at Knossos (§ 93) was built about 2200 B.C., and rebuilt and improved about 1800. Its monarch must have ruled all the island, and probably (as the Greek legends taught) over wide regions of the sea. The city had no walls to shut out an enemy : Crete relied upon her sea power to ward off invaders. We may think of the Cretan lawgiver, Minos, seated on his throne at Knossos, ruling over the surrounding seas, at about the time Abraham left Ur to found the Hebrew race, or a little before the lawgiver, Hammurabi, established the Old Babylonian Empire, or as a contemporary of some of the beneficent pharaohs of the Middle Kingdom in Egypt.

So-called THRONE OF MINOS in the palace at Knossos. Says Baikie (*Sea Kings of Crete*, 72) : " No more ancient throne exists in Europe, or probably in the world." Compare its associations with those of the throne of Charlemagne. (§ 799.)

The life at court is portrayed to us in the frescoes of the palace walls. Sometimes the dependants of the prince march into the royal castle in stately procession to offer their gifts and, perhaps, pay tribute to their master. Sometimes the court is filled with gayly dressed courtiers and ladies. The nobles wear their hair in three long curls. The women were not banished from society life as in later Greece, but moved freely in the company of men as in mediaeval and modern

[1] One old Roman writer (Diodorus Siculus) has preserved the interesting fact that the Cretans themselves in his day claimed to have been the inventors

times. These lords and ladies appear sitting, standing, ges-
ticulating in animated conversation.   Occasionally the court is
represented on a balcony or large veranda intently watching
some game or performance, perhaps a bull fight or the taming

COOKING UTENSILS, found in one tomb at Knossos.

and training of wild bulls.   The bull was a favorite subject of
Cretan art.   See the illustrations in these pages.[1]

The chief article of the men's *dress* was a linen cloth hanging from the waist or fashioned into short trousers, like the
dress of the men seen on the Egyptian monuments.   To this
the nobles sometimes, when not in war or hunting, added a

---

of the alphabet. He says: "Some pretend that the Syrians were the inventors of letters, and that the Phoenicians learned from them and brought the
art of writing to Greece. . . . But the Cretans say that the first invention
came from Crete, and that the Phoenicians only changed the form of the letters and made the knowledge of them more general among the peoples."
Modern Cretans had forgotten this claim for many centuries, but recent discoveries go far to prove it true.

[1] Compare also the later story of the Athenian hero Theseus and the
Cretan Minotaur (bull) in any collection of Greek legends, as in Hawthorne's
Tanglewood Tales.

short sleeveless mantle, fastened over one shoulder with a jewelled pin; their belt, drawn tight about the waist, always carried a dagger, inlaid with gold figures. The women's dress was very elaborate, with fine sewing and exquisite embroidery. It resembled much more the female dress of modern days than did that of the women of later Greece and Rome. The skirts were bell-shaped, like the fashion of some fifty years ago, and flounced with ruffles. Men and women alike wore gold bracelets, and the women added long coils of beaded necklaces.

Each home wove its own cloth, as we learn from the loom-weights in every house. Each home, too, had its stone mortars for grinding the daily supply of meal. Kitchen utensils were varied and numerous. They include perforated skimmers and strainers, and charcoal carriers, and many other devices strangely modern in shape. Most cooking was done over an open fire of sticks —though sometimes there

CRETAN VASE of later period, showing a tendency to use "conventionalized" ornament. Critics believe that such vases indicate a period of decay in Cretan art.

was a sort of recess in a hearth, over which a kettle stood. When the destroying foe came upon Knossos, one carpenter left his kit of tools hidden under a stone slab; and among these we find "saws, hammers, adze, chisels heavy and light, awls, nails, files, and axes." They are of bronze, of course, but in shape they are so like our own that it seems probable that this handicraft passed down its skill without a break from the earliest European civilization to the present. One huge cross-cut saw, like our lumberman's, was found in a mountain town, — used probably to cut the great trees there into columns for the palaces.

97. The dark side of this splendid civilization has to do with its government and the organization of society. Here, Oriental features prevailed. The monarch was absolute; and a few nobles were the only others who found life easy and pleasant. The masses were far more abject and helpless than in later Greek history. The direct cause of the destruction of Cretan culture was a series of barbarian invasions; but the remains show that the best stages of art had already passed away. Probably the invasions were so completely successful only because of internal decay, such as usually comes to despotic states after a period of magnificence. Some excavators think they find evidence that the invaders were assisted by an uprising of the oppressed masses. In any event, fortunately, many of the better features of this early Aegean civilization were adopted by the conquerors and preserved for time to come.

FOR FURTHER READING. — *Specially suggested:* Davis' *Readings*, Vol. I, No. 32, gives an interesting extract from an account of Cretan remains by one of the discoverers. Bury's *History of Greece*, 7–11, on *Cretan culture;* 11–33, on *remains near Mycenae* (half these pages are given to illustrations); 65–69, on the *Homeric poems*. The student may best omit or disregard Professor Bury's frequent discussions as to whether Cretans or Trojans were "Greeks." The important thing about each new wave of invasion is *not its race*, but its *kind of culture*, and where that culture came from.

Additional, for students who wish wider reading: Hawes, *Crete the Fore-runner of Greece;* or Baikie, *Sea Kings of Crete*. (Appendix.)

CHAPTER X

THE HOMERIC AGE

ORIGIN

98. The Achaeans. — Between 1500 and 1200 B.C. a great change took place in Greece. The civilization pictured by Homer differs greatly from the earlier one. *It was not a development from the earlier:* it was a separate culture, from a different source. The Mycenaeans and Cretans buried their dead, worshiped ancestors, used no iron, and lived frugally, mainly on fish and vegetable diet. Homer's Greeks burn their dead, adore a sun god, use iron swords, and feast all night mightily on whole roast oxen. So, too, in dress, manners, and personal appearance, as far as we can tell, the two are widely different. The early Greeks, as their pictures show, were short, dark, black-eyed, like the modern Greeks and like all the other aborigines of southern Europe. But Homer describes his Greeks, *or at least his chieftains*, as tall, fair, yellow-haired, and blue-eyed. In many ways, too, their civilization was ruder and more primitive than the one it replaced.

This second civilization of Hellas is called *Achaean*, — the name which "Homer" gives to the Greeks of his time. These Achaeans were part of a vigorous race dwelling in central Europe. They were semibarbarians in that home; *but in some way they had learned the use of iron.* About 1500 B.C., bands of these fair-haired, blue-eyed, ox-eating warriors, drawn by the splendor and riches of the south, broke into Hellas, as barbarians of the north so many times since have broken into southern Europe. These mighty-limbed strangers, armed with long iron swords, established themselves among the short,

120

dark, bronze-weaponed natives, dwelt in their cities, became their chiefs, married their women, and possessed the land.

99. Nature of their Invasion. — The occupation of the land by the invaders was a slow process, involving unrecorded misery, generation after generation, for the gentler, peace-loving natives. An Egyptian inscription of the period declares that "the islands were restless and disturbed," — and indeed the Achaean rovers reached even Egypt in their raids (§ 31). During most of the period, the newcomers merely filtered into Hellas, band by band, seizing a little island, or a valley, at a time. Occasionally, larger forces warred long and desperately about some stronghold. Knossos, without defensive walls, fell early before a fleet of sea-rovers. But in walled cities, like Troy and Mycenae, the old civilization lived on for three centuries. Much of the time, no doubt, there was peace and intercourse between the Achaeans and such cities; but finally the invaders mustered in force enough to master even these. Homer's ten-year Trojan War may be based upon one of these closing struggles.

The fair-haired Achaeans imposed their language upon the older natives (as conquerors commonly do); but, in course of time, their blood was absorbed into that of the more numerous conquered people — as has happened to all northern invaders into southern lands, before and since. The physical characteristics of Homer's Achaeans left no more trace in the later Greeks, than the tall, yellow-haired Goths who conquered Spain and Italy in the fifth century after Christ have left in those countries.

The Achaean and Cretan **cultures** *blended more equally than the two* **races** *did,* — though not till the splendor and most of the art of the older civilization had been destroyed. The change of language explains in part the loss of the art of writing, — which probably had been the possession of only a small class of scribes, in any case. But the common people, we may be sure, clung tenaciously to their old customs and habits of life, and especially to their religion. When next we see the Greek civilization clearly, the old worship of ancestors, of which the Homeric poems contain no mention, had reappeared and mingled with the newer worship of the Achaean gods.

Some features of the Achaean age are described below.

THE TRIBAL ORGANIZATION

100. The Clan. — In early times the smallest unit in Greek society was not a family like ours, but a clan (or gens). Each clan was a group of kindred, *an enlarged kind of family.* Some clans contained perhaps a score of members; others contained many score.

The nearest descendant of the forefather of the clan, counting from oldest son to oldest son, was the *clan elder,* or "king." *Kinship* and *worship* were the two ties which held a clan together. These two bonds were really one, *for the clan religion was a worship of clan ancestors.* If provided with pleasing meals at proper times and invoked with magic formulas (so the belief ran), the ghosts of the ancient clan elders would continue to aid their children. The food was actually meant for the ghost. Milk and wine were poured into a hollow in the ground, while the clan elder spoke sacred formulas inviting the dead to eat.[1]

This worship was secret. The clan tomb was the altar, and the clan elder was the only lawful priest. For a stranger even to see the worship was to defile it; for him to learn the sacred formulas of the clan worship was to secure power over the gods.[2] It followed that *marriage became a " religious " act.* The woman renounced her own gods, and was accepted by her husband's gods into their clan. Her father, of course, or some male rela-

---

[1] Travelers describe similar practices among primitive peoples to-day. A Papuan chief prays: " Compassionate Father! Here is food for you. Eat it, and be kind to us! "

[2] Primitive races think of words as in some strange way related to the things they stand for (as the spirit to the body). This is one reason for belief in " charms." Those who knew the right words could " charm " the gods to do their will. The Romans, in the days of their power, always kept the real name of their chief god a secret, lest some foe might compel or induce him to surrender the city.

tive, renounced for her, and gave her to the bridegroom by whose gods she was now protected. After that, she and her future children were in law and in religion no longer "related" to her father and his clan. Legal relationship, and inheritance of property, came through males only.

101. Later Family Worship. — In like manner in later times, as the families of the clan became distinct units, each came to have its separate family worship. The Hearth was the family altar. Near it were grouped usually images of the household gods who watched over the family. The father was the priest. Before each meal, he poured out on the Hearth the *libation*, or food-offering, to the family gods and asked their blessing. The family tomb was near the house, "so that the sons," says Euripides (a later Greek poet; § 221), "in entering and leaving their dwelling, *might always meet their fathers and invoke them*."

102. The Tribe. — Long before history began, clans united into larger units. In barbarous society the highest unit is the tribe, which is a group of clans living near together and *believing in a common ancestor*. In Greece the clan elder of the leading clan was the *king of the tribe and its priest*.

103. The Tribal City. — Originally a tribe dwelt in several clan villages in the valleys around some convenient hill. On the hilltop was the place of common worship. A ring wall, at a convenient part of the slope, easily turned this sacred place into a *citadel*. In hilly Greece many of these citadels grew up *near together;* and so, very early, groups of tribes combined further. Perhaps one of a group would conquer the others and compel them to tear down their separate citadels and to move their temples to its center. *This made a city.* The chief of the leading tribe then became the priest-king of the city.

Sometimes, of course, a tribe grew into the city stage without absorbing other tribes; but, in general, as clans federated into tribes, so *tribes federated into cities*, either peaceably or through war. The later Athenians had a tradition that in very early times the hero *Theseus* founded their city by bringing together four tribes living in Attica.

104. The City the Political Unit. — *If the cities could have combined into larger units, Greece might have become a " nation-state,"* like modern England or France. But the Greeks, in the time of their glory, never got beyond a city-state. To them the same word meant "city" and "state." A union of cities, by which any of them gave up its complete independence, was repugnant to Greek feeling. One city might hold other cities in subjection; but *it never admitted their people to any kind of citizenship.*[1] Nor did the subject cities dream of asking such a thing. What they wanted, and would never cease to strive for, was to recover their separate independence. *To each Greek, his city was his country.*

It followed, through nearly all Greek history, that the *political*[2] relations of one city with another five miles away were foreign relations, as much as its dealings with the king of Persia. *Wars, therefore, were constant and cruel. Greek life was concentrated in small centers. This made it vivid and intense; but the division of Greek resources between so many hostile centers made that life brief.*

GOVERNMENT OF THE EARLY CITY–STATE

105. The King. — The city had three political elements — king, council of chiefs, and popular assembly. In these we may see the germs of later monarchic, aristocratic, and democratic governments. (For these terms, see § 85, note.)

The king was *leader in war, judge in peace,* and *priest* at all times. His power was much limited by custom and by the two other political orders.

106. A council of chiefs aided the king, — and checked him. These chiefs were originally the clan elders and the members of the royal family. *Socially* they were the king's equals; and *in government* he could not do anything in defiance of their wish. If a ruler died without a grown-up son, the council could elect a king, although they chose usually from the royal family.

---

[1] Can the student see a connection between this fact and the "exclusive" character of clan and tribal and city-worship, as described above?

[2] "Political" means "relating to government." The word must be used frequently in history. In other relations, as in trade and religion and culture, the Greek cities did not think of one another as foreigners, to any such degree as in political matters.

107. The Assembly. — The common freemen came together for worship and for games; and sometimes the king called them together, to listen to plans that had been adopted by him and the chiefs. Then the freemen shouted approval or muttered disapproval. They could not start new movements. There were no regular meetings and few spokesmen, and the general reverence for the chiefs made it a daring deed for a common man to brave them. If the chiefs and king agreed, it was easy for them to get their way with the Assembly.

However, even in war, when the authority of the nobles was greatest, the Assembly had to be *persuaded: it could not be ordered*. Homer shows that sometimes a common man ventured to oppose the "kings."

Thus, in one Assembly before Trcy, the Greeks break away to seize their ships and return home. Odysseus hurries among them, and by persuasion and threats forces them back to the Assembly, until only Thersites bawls on, — " Thersites, uncontrolled of speech, whose mind was full of words *wherewith to strive against the chiefs*. Hateful was he to Achilles above all, and to Odysseus, *for them he was wont to revile*. But now *with shrill shout he poured forth his upbraidings even upon goodly Agamemnon*." Odysseus, it is true, rebukes him sternly and smites him into silence, while the crowd laughs. " Homer " sang to please the chieftains, his patrons, — and so he represents Thersites as a cripple, ugly and unpopular ; but there must have been such popular opposition to the chiefs, now and then, or the minstrel would not have mentioned such an incident at all. Says a modern scholar, — A chieftain who had been thwarted, perhaps, by some real Thersites during the day, " would over his evening cups enjoy the poet's travesty, and long for the good old times when [Odysseus] could put down impertinent criticism by the stroke of his knotty scepter." [1]

SOCIETY AND INDUSTRY

108. Society was simple. The Homeric poems attribute wealth and luxury to a few places (where probably some fragments of the Cretan civilization survived); but these are

---

[1] Davis' *Readings*, Vol. I, No. 33, reproduces the best Homeric account of an " Assembly " in war time. It contains also the Thersites story complete.

plainly exceptions to the general rule. When the son of Odysseus leaves his native Ithaca and visits Menelaus, he is astounded by the splendor of the palace, with its "gleam as of sun and moon," and whispers to his companion : —

"Mark the flashing of bronze through the echoing halls, and the flashing of gold and of amber and of silver and of ivory. Such like, methinks, is the court of Olympian Zeus. . . . Wonder comes over me as I look." [1]

But mighty Odysseus had built *his* palace with his own hands. It has been well called — from the poet's description — "a rude farmhouse, where swine wallow in the court." And the one petty island in which Odysseus was head-king held scores of yet poorer "kings." So, too, when Odysseus is shipwrecked on an important island, he finds the daughter of the chief king — the princess Nausicaa — doing a washing, with her band of maidens (treading out the dirt by trampling the clothes with their bare feet in the water of a running brook). Just before, the "queen" was pictured, busy in gathering together the palace linen for this event. *Such descriptions are the typical ones in the poems.*

109. Manners were harsh. In the Trojan War, the Greeks left the bodies of the slain enemy unburied, to be half devoured by packs of savage dogs that hung about the camp for such morsels. The common boast was to have given a foe's body to the dogs.[2] When the noble Trojan hero, Hector, falls, the Greek kings gather about the dead body, "*and no one came who did not add his wound.*" The chiefs fought in bronze and iron armor, usually in chariots. The common free men followed on foot, without armor or effective weapons, and seem to have counted for little in war. Ordinary prisoners became slaves as a matter of course. But when the chiefs were taken, they were

---

[1] Read the story in the *Odyssey*, or in Vol. I, No. 37, of Davis' *Readings*.

[2] The *Iliad* opens with the story of a pestilence, which almost drove the Greeks from Troy. The poet ascribes it to the anger of the Sun-god, Apollo, who shot his arrows upon the camp. Little wonder that the sun's rays, in a warm climate, should produce pestilence, under such conditions!

murdered in cold blood, unless they could tempt the victor to spare them for ransom. Female captives, even princesses, expected no better fate than slavery.

On the other hand, there are hints of natural and happy family life, of joyous festivals, and games and dances, and of wholesome, contented work.[1]

110. Occupations. — *The mass of the people were small farmers,* though their houses were grouped in villages.[2] Even the kings tilled their farms, in part at least, with their own hands. Odysseus can drive the oxen at the plow and "cut a clean furrow"; and when the long days begin he can mow all day with the crooked scythe, "pushing clear until late eventide." *Slaves were few,* except about the great chiefs. There they served as household servants and as farm hands; and they seem to have been treated kindly.[3] There had appeared, however, *a class of miserable landless freemen,* who hired themselves to farmers. When the ghost of Achilles (the invincible Greek chieftain) wishes to name to Odysseus the most unhappy lot among mortals, he selects that of the hired servant (§ 112).

Artisans and smiths were found among the retainers of the great chiefs. They were highly honored, but their skill was far inferior to that of the Cretan age. Some shields and inlaid weapons, always spoken of as the work of Hephaestus, the god of fire and of metal work, may have passed into the hands of the Achaeans from that earlier period.

A separate class of traders had not arisen. The chiefs, in the intervals of farm labor, turned to trading voyages now and then, and did not hesitate to increase their profits by *piracy.* It was no offense to ask a stranger whether he came as a pirate or for peaceful trade. (*Odyssey,* III, 60–70.)

---

[1] Davis' *Readings,* Vol. I, No. 35.

[2] For farm life, see an extract in Davis' *Readings,* Vol. I, No. 39.

[3] When Odysseus returned from his twenty years of war and wandering, he made himself known first to a faithful swineherd and one other servant — both slaves; and "They threw their arms round wise Odysseus and passionately kissed his face and neck. So likewise did Odysseus kiss their heads and hands."

111. Religious Ideas.—It has been said above that the Achaeans worshiped the forces of nature as gods. Their lively fancy *personified these in the forms and characters of men and women*—built in a somewhat more majestic mold than human men. The great gods lived on cloud-capped Mount Olympus, and passed their days in feasting and laughter and other pleasures. When the chief god, Zeus, slept, things sometimes went awry, for the other gods plotted against his plans. His wife Hera was exceedingly jealous—for which she had much reason—and the two had many a family wrangle. Some of the gods went down to aid their favorites in war, and might even be wounded by human weapons.

The twelve great Olympian deities were as follows (the Latin names are given in parentheses) :—

Zeus (Jupiter), the supreme god; god of the sky; "father of gods and men."

Poseidon (Neptune), god of the sea.

Apollo, the sun god; god of wisdom, poetry, prophecy, and medicine.

Ares (Mars), god of war.

Hephaestus (Vulcan), god of fire—the lame smith.

Hermes (Mercury), god of the wind; messenger ; god of cunning, of thieves, and of merchants.

Hera (Juno), sister and wife of Zeus; queen of the sky.

Athene (Minerva), goddess of wisdom; female counterpart of Apollo.

Artemis (Diana), goddess of the moon, of maidens, and of hunting.

Aphrodite (Venus), goddess of love and beauty.

Demeter (Ceres), the earth goddess—controlling fertility.

Hestia (Vesta), the deity of the home ; goddess of the hearth fire.

The Greeks thought also of all the world about them as peopled by a multitude of lesser local gods and demigods—spirits of spring and wood and river and hill—all of whom they personified in their way as youths or maidens. It was surely better to give the gods human forms, than the revolting bodies of beasts and reptiles (§ 24), though both are in sad contrast to the original idea of the one true God "Who made heaven and earth." In a multitude of legends the Greek poets gave to these gods a certain charm, which has made their stories a lasting possession of the world's culture,[1] — and which indeed kept this worship alive among the later Greeks long after the primitive ideas in that worship were really outgrown. Sometimes we find expressed noble religious sentiments. In the *Odyssey* the poet exclaims: "Verily, the blessed gods love not froward deeds, but they reverence justice and the righteous acts of men." All the gods, however, are represented as subject to human passion and guilty of low vices. Athene and, perhaps, Diana, are the only figures less repugnant to Christian ideals.

112. Ideas of a Future Life. — The Greeks believed in a place of terrible punishment (*Tartarus*) for a few great offenders *against the gods*, and in an *Elysium* of supreme pleasure for a very few others particularly favored by the gods. But for the mass of men the future life was to be "a washed-out copy of the brilliant life on earth" — its pleasures and pains both shadowy. Thus Odysseus tells how he met Achilles in the home of the dead : —

" And he knew me straightway, *when he had drunk the dark blood* [of a sacrifice to the dead] ; yea, and he wept aloud, and shed big tears as he stretched forth his hands in his longing to reach me. But it might not be, *for he had now no steadfast strength nor power at all in moving*, such as was aforetime in his supple limbs. . . . But lo, other spirits of the dead that be departed stood sorrowing, and each one asked of those that were dear to them." — *Odyssey*, xi, 390 ff.

For Further Reading. — *Specially suggested:* Davis' *Readings*, Vol. I, Nos. 33–38 (most of these already referred to in footnotes). *Additional:* Bury, pp. 69–79.

---

[1] The legends of heroes and demigods, like Hercules, Theseus, and Jason, are retailed for young people charmingly by Hawthorne, Gayley, Guerber, and Kingsley. The stories have no historical value that could be made clear in a book like this.

CHAPTER XI

FROM THE ACHAEANS TO THE PERSIAN WARS
(1000–500 B.C.)

A NEW AGE

113. The Dorian Conquest. — The Achaean conquests closed about 1200 B.C. For two centuries Hellas was troubled only by the usual petty wars between small states. But, about 1000 B.C., the revival of culture was checked again for a hundred years by new destructive invasions from the north.

The new barbarians called themselves *Dorians*. They seem to have been closely allied in language to the Achaeans; and they were probably merely a rear guard which had stopped for two hundred years somewhere in northern Hellas. They conquered because they had adopted a new and better military organization. The Achaeans fought still in Homeric fashion, — the chiefs in chariots, and their followers as an unwieldy, ill-armed mob. The Dorians introduced the use of heavy-armed infantry, with long spears, in regular array and close ranks.

By 900 B.C., the movements of the tribes had ceased. The conquering Dorians had settled down, *mainly in the Peloponnesus.* This district had been the center of the Mycenaean and Achaean glory, but it now lost its leadership in culture. When civilization took a new start in Hellas, soon after 900, it was from new centers — *in Attica and in Asia Minor.*

114. Phoenician Influence. — *The civilization which the Achaeans and Dorians had destroyed at Mycenae and Crete was restored to them in part by the Phoenicians.* After the overthrow of Cretan power, Phoenicia for many centuries was the leading sea-power of the Mediterranean (1500–600 B.C.). Especially

130

among the islands and coasts of the Aegean, did her traders
barter with the inhabitants (much as English traders did two
hundred years ago with American Indians), tempting them
with strange wares of small value, and counting it best gain of
all if they could lure curious maidens on board their black
ships for distant slave markets. In return, however, they made
many an unintentional payment. Language shows that the
Phoenicians gave to the Greeks the names (and so, no doubt,
the use) of linen, myrrh, cinnamon, frankincense, soap, lyres,
cosmetics, and writing tablets. The forgotten art of writing
they introduced again, — this time with a true alphabet. *But
the lively Hellenes were not slavish imitators.* Whatever the
strangers brought them, they improved and made their own.

115. The Gap in our Knowledge. — The Dorians had no
Homer, as the Achaeans had, nor did they leave magnificent monuments, as the Mycenaeans did. Accordingly, after
Homer, there is a *blank in our knowledge for nearly five centuries.* Great changes, however, took place during these
obscure centuries; and in a rough way we can see what they
were, *by comparing Homeric Greece with the historic Greece that
is revealed when the curtain rises again.*

This "rising of the curtain" took place about 650 B.C. By
that time the Greeks had begun to use the alphabet freely.
The next 150 years, however, merely continued movements
which were already well under way; and the whole period,
from the Dorian conquest to the year 500, can be treated as a
unit (§§ 116 ff.).

To that half thousand years belonged six great movements. (1) The
Hellenes awoke to a feeling that they were one people as compared with
other peoples. (2) They extended Hellenic culture widely by colonization. (3) The system of government everywhere underwent great
change. (4) Sparta became a great military power, whose leadership
in war the other Greek states were willing to recognize. (5) Athens
became a democracy. (6) A great intellectual development appeared,
manifested in architecture, painting, sculpture, poetry, and philosophy.

Each of the six movements will be described briefly.

I. UNITY OF FEELING

116. Greeks came to think of all Hellenes as one race, compared with other peoples — in spite of many subdivisions among themselves. The *Iliad* does not make it clear whether Homer looked upon the Trojans as Greeks or not. Apparently he cared little about the question. Five hundred years later such a question would have been a first consideration to every Greek. The Greeks had not become one nation: that is, they had not come under the same government. But they had come to believe in a kinship with each other, to take pride in their common civilization, and to set themselves apart from the rest of the world. The three chief forces which had created this oneness of feeling were *language, literature,* and the *Olympian religion,* with its games and oracles.

a. The Greeks understood each other's dialects, while the men of other speech about them they called "Barbarians," or babblers (*Bar'-bar-oi*). *This likeness of language made it possible for all Greeks to possess the same literature.* The poems of Homer were sung and recited in every village for centuries; and the universal pride in Homer, and in the glories of the later literature, had much to do in binding the Greeks into one people.

b. The poets invented a system of relationship. The first inhabitant of Hellas, they said, was a certain *Hellen,* who had three sons, Aeolus, Dorus, and Xuthus. Xuthus became the father of Achaeus and Ion. Aeolus, Dorus, Achaeus, and Ion were the ancestors of all Hellenes, — in the four great divisions, *Aeolians, Dorians, Achaeans,* and *Ionians. This system of fables made it easier for the Greeks to believe themselves connected by blood.*

c. Three special features of the Olympian religion helped to bind Greeks together, — the *Panhellenic Games,* the *Delphic Oracle* and the various *Amphictyonies* (§§ 117, 118, 119).

117. The Panhellenic Games. — To the great festivals of some of the gods, men flocked from all Hellas. This was especially

true of the Olympic games.. These were celebrated each fourth
year at Olympia, in Elis, in honor of Zeus. The contests consisted of foot races, chariot races, wrestling, and boxing. The
victors were felt to have won the highest honor open to any
Greek. They received merely an olive wreath at Olympia;
but at their homes they were honored with inscriptions and

RUINS OF THE ENTRANCE TO THE STADIUM (*athletic field*) AT OLYMPIA.

statues. All Greeks, and only they, could compete in Pan-
hellenic games. There was a strong feeling that all the wars
between Greek states should be suspended during the festival.

To these games came merchants, to secure the best market
for rare wares. Heralds proclaimed treaties there — as the best
way to make them known through all Hellas. Poets, orators,
and artists gathered there; and gradually the intellectual contests and exhibitions became the most important feature of
the meeting. The oration or poem or statue which was praised

at Olympia had received the approval of the most intelligent judges that could be brought together anywhere in the world.

These intellectual contests, however, did not become part of the sacred games. Nor was any prize given to the winner. — The four-year periods between the Olympic games were called *Olympiads*. All events were dated from what was believed to be the first recorded Olympiad, beginning in 776 B.C. An *admirable account of the Olympic Games* is given in Davis' *Readings*, Vol. I, No. 44. Less famous, though by no means without importance, were the Panhellenic games held at other places and at different intervals.

118. The Delphic Oracle. — Apollo, the sun god, was also the god of prophecy. One of his chief temples was at Delphi, far up the slopes of Mount Parnassus, amid wild and rugged scenery. From a fissure in the ground, within the temple, volcanic gases poured forth. A priestess would, when desired, inhale the gas until she passed into a trance (or seemed to do so); and, while in this state, she was supposed to see into the future, by the aid of the god. *The advice of this "oracle" was sought by men and by governments throughout all Hellas.* (See further in Davis' *Readings*, Vol. I, Nos. 41–43.)

119. Amphictyonies. — There was an ancient league of Greek tribes to protect the temple at Delphi. This was known as *the Amphictyonic League* (league of "dwellers-round-about"). Smaller amphictyonies, for the protection of other temples, were common in Greece. In early Greek history, they were the only hint of a movement toward a union of states. All these leagues, it is true, were strictly *religious* in purpose, and not at all like *political* unions. The Delphic Amphictyony, however, did in a way represent the whole Greek people. All important states sent delegates to its "Council," which held regular meetings; and every division of the Greek race felt that it had a share in the oracle and in its League.

120. Dorians and Ionians. — At the cost of some digression, this is the best place to note that through all later Greek history (after 600 B.C.) *the two leading races were the Dorians and the Ionians.* (See § 116 *b*, above.)

By 600 B.C. the Dorians had their chief strength in the Peloponnesus, while the Ionians held Attica and most of the islands of the Aegean. The Ionians seem to have been descendants of the original inhabitants of Greece, mixed with tribes of the Achaean invasion.

Athens was the leading city of the Ionians. The Athenians were sea-farers and traders; they preferred a democratic government; they were open to new ideas — "always seeking some new thing"; and they were interested in art and literature. Sparta was the leading city of the Dorians. The Spartans were a military settlement of conquerors, in a fertile valley, organized for defense and ruling over slave tillers of the soil. They were *warriors*, not traders; *aristocratic*, not democratic; *conservative*, not progressive; *practical*, not artistic.

Some writers used to explain the differences between Athens and Sparta on the ground of *race*, and teach that all Ionians were *naturally* demo-cratic and progressive, while all Dorians were *naturally* aristocratic and conservative. But it has been pointed out that Dorian colonies in Italy and Sicily (like Syracuse) resembled Athens more than they did Sparta. *Their physical surroundings were more like those of Athens, also.* To-day scholars look with suspicion upon all attempts to explain differences in civilization on the ground of inborn race tendencies. For Sparta and Athens, the explanation certainly is found mainly in the difference in physical surroundings.

II. EXPANSION BY COLONIZATION

121. First Period. — While Greek civilization was becoming more united in feeling, it was becoming more scattered in space. The old tribes which the Dorians drove out of the Peloponnesus jostled other tribes into motion all over Greece, and some of the fugitives carried the seeds of Greek culture more widely than before along the coasts of the Aegean.

This period of colonization lasted about a century, from 1000 to 900 B.C. Its most important fact was the Hellenizing of the western coast of Asia Minor. Some of this district had been Greek before; but now large reinforcements arrived from the main Greek peninsula, and all non-Hellenic tribes were subdued or driven out. Large bodies of Ionian refugees from the Peloponnesus had sought refuge in Ionian Attica. But Attica could not support them all; and soon they began to cross the sea to Asia Minor. There they established them-selves in twelve great cities, of which the most important were *Miletus* and *Ephesus*. The whole middle district of that coast took the name *Ionia*, and was united in an amphictyony.

122. Second Period. — A century later, there began a still wider colonizing movement, which went on for two hundred years (800–600 B.C.), doubling the area of Hellas and spreading it far outside the old Aegean home. The cause this time was not war. Greek cities were growing anxious to seize the Mediterranean commerce from the Phoenicians. *The new colonies were founded largely for trading stations.*

Thus Miletus sent colony after colony to *the north shore of the Black Sea*, to control the corn trade there. Sixty Greek towns fringed that sea and its straits. The one city of Chalcis, in Euboea, planted thirty-two colonies *on the Thracian coast*, to secure the gold and silver mines of that region. On the west, *Sicily* became almost wholly Greek, and *southern Italy* took the proud name of *Magna Graecia* (Great Greece). Indeed, settlements were sown from end to end of the Mediterranean. Among the more important of the colonies were *Syracuse* in Sicily, *Tarentum, Sybaris,* and *Croton* in Italy, *Corcyra* near the mouth of the Adriatic, *Massilia* (Marseilles) in Gaul, *Olynthus* in Thrace, *Cyrene* in Africa, *Byzantium* at the Black Sea's mouth, and *Naucratis* in Egypt (§ 32).[1]

123. Method of Founding Colonies. — Many motives besides the commercial assisted this movement. Sometimes a city found its population growing too fast for its grain supply. Often there was danger of class struggles, so that it seemed well to get rid of the more adventurous of the poorer citizens. Perhaps some daring youth of a noble family longed for a more active life than he found at home, and was glad to become the head of a new settlement on a distant frontier.

In any case the oracle at Delphi was first consulted. If the reply was favorable, announcements were made and volunteers

---

[1] Map study : on outline maps, or on the board, locate the districts and cities mentioned in §§ 121 and 122.

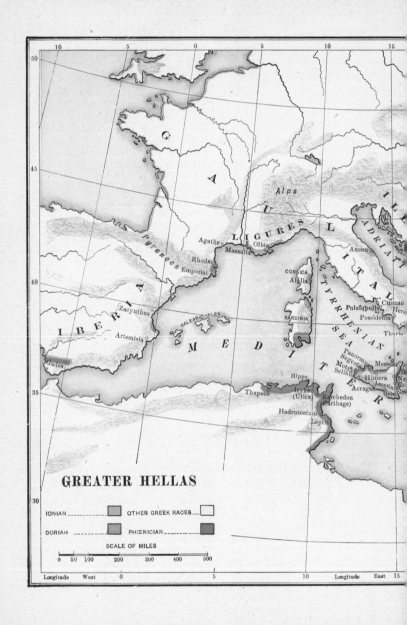

GREATER HELLAS

IONIAN ---------- OTHER GREEK RACES ----

DORIAN ---------- PHŒNICIAN ----------

SCALE OF MILES

0   50   100   200   300   400   500

Longitude   West   0   5   10   Longitude   East   15

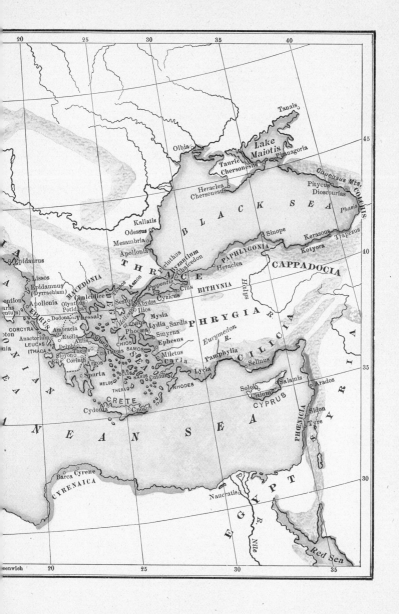

were gathered for the expedition. The mother city always gave the sacred fire for the new city hearth, and appointed the "founder." This "founder" established the new settlement with religious rites and distributed the inhabitants, who thronged in from all sides, into *artificial* tribes and clans.

RUINS OF THE ATHLETIC FIELD AT DELPHI. Second only to the Olympic Games, and similar to them, was the Festival at Delphi in honor of Apollo.

The colonists ceased to be citizens of their old home, and the new city enjoyed complete independence. The colony recognized a religious connection with its "metropolis" (mother city), and of course there were often strong bonds of friendship between the two; but there was no political union between them — until Athens invented a new form of colony which will be described later (§ 148).

III. CHANGES IN GOVERNMENT

124. The Kings overthrown by Oligarchies. — Between 1000 and 500 B.C. the "kings" disappeared from every Greek city except Sparta and Argos, and even in those cities they lost most of their old power. The change was the work of the nobles; and that class divided the royal power among themselves. Monarchies gave way to oligarchies.

A Homeric king, we have seen, had three kinds of duties: he was *war chief*, *judge*, and *priest*. The office of war chief could least safely be left to the accident of birth. Accordingly the nobles took away this part of the king's duties first, turning it over to officers whom they elected from among themselves. Then, as judicial work increased with the growth of city life, special judges were chosen to take over that part of the king's work. The priestly dignity was connected most closely with family descent (§§ 101, 102): therefore it was left longest a matter of inheritance.

This, then, was the general order of the changes by which *the rule of one man became the rule of " the few."* The process was gradual; the means and occasion varied. A contest between two rivals for the throne, or the dying out of a royal line, or a weak king or a minor, — any of these conditions made it easy for the nobles to encroach upon the royal power.

125.. Oligarchies overthrown by Tyrants. — Originally, the aristocratic element consisted of the council of clan elders (§ 106), but with time it had become modified in many ways. Sometimes the families of a few great chiefs had come to overshadow the rest. In other places, groups of conquering families ruled the descendants of the conquered. Sometimes, perhaps, wealth *helped* to draw the line between " the few" and "the many." At all events, *there was in all Greek cities a sharp line between two classes,* — one calling itself " the few," " the good," " the noble"; and another called by these " the many," " the bad," " the base."

" The few" had succeeded the kings. " The many" were oppressed and misgoverned, and they began to clamor for relief. They were too ignorant as yet to maintain themselves against the intelligent and better united " few"; but the way was prepared for them by the " tyrants" (§ 126).

Why does it matter who controls the government? The student should begin to think upon this matter. Government is not a matter of dignity mainly, but a very practical matter. It touches our daily life very closely. In one of our States, for many years past, a certain railroad has controlled the legislature. Therefore it has escaped taxation, for the most part, upon its immense wealth; and every poor man in the State has had to pay unduly high taxes in consequence, leaving less money for his children's shoes and books. The same railroad has been permitted to charge exorbitant rates on freight. Every farmer has received too little for his wheat; and every citizen has paid too much for flour. So for forty years, in our own day and country, big business interests have striven constantly to own congress and legislatures and judges and governors, so as to get or keep monopolies or tariff advantages or other special privileges, by which they have heaped up riches — which, in the long run, have been drawn from the homes of the working people. In early society, class distinctions are drawn more sharply, and class rule was even more tyrannical. "The few" are usually wiser than "the many"; but all history proves that class rule by "the good" is sure to be a selfish, bad rule.

126. "Tyrants" pave the Way for Democracies. — Before 500 B.C. every city in the Greek peninsula, except Sparta, had its tyrant, or had had one. In the outlying parts of Hellas, tyrants were common through later history also, but by the year 500 they had disappeared from the main peninsula; and so the *two centuries from 700 to 500 B.C. are sometimes called the "Age of Tyrants."*

In *Greek history a tyrant is not necessarily a bad or cruel ruler: he is simply a man who by force seizes supreme power.* But arbitrary rule was hateful to the Greeks, and the murder of a tyrant seemed to them a good act. Sometimes, too, the selfishness and cruelty of such rulers justified the detestation which still clings to the name. But at the worst the tyrants seem to have been a necessary evil, to break down the greater evil of the selfish oligarchies. Many tyrants were generous, far-sighted rulers, building public works, developing trade, patronizing art and literature; but their main value in history was this: *they paved the way for democracy.*

Sometimes a tyrant had been an ambitious noble ; sometimes a man of the people, by birth. In either case, he usually won his mastery by coming forward, in some crisis of civil strife, as the champion of "the many." When he had made himself tyrant of his city, he surrounded himself with paid soldiers ; but he sought also to keep the favor of the masses, who had helped him to the throne. The nobles he could not conciliate. These he burdened with taxes, oppressed, exiled, and murdered. The story goes that Periander, tyrant of Corinth, sent to the tyrant of Miletus to ask his advice in government. The Milesian took the messenger through a grain field, striking off the finest and tallest ears as they walked, and sent him back without other answer.

Thus when the tyrants themselves were overthrown, democracy had a chance. The nobles were weaker than before, and the people had gained confidence. In the Ionian cities, the next step was usually a democratic government. In Dorian parts of Greece, more commonly there followed an aristocracy. But this was always much broader, and less objectionable, than the older oligarchies. The tyrants had done their work effectively.[1]

This, then, was the *general order* of change : the kings give way to oligarchies ; the oligarchies are overthrown by tyrants ; and the tyrants, unintentionally, prepare the way for the rule of the people. We shall now trace the changes, with more detail, in the two leading cities of Hellas, — Sparta and Athens. *The first had less change than any other city. The second led the movement.*

IV. RISE OF SPARTA TO MILITARY HEADSHIP

127. Changes in Early Sparta. — The invading Dorians founded many petty states in the Peloponnesus. For a time one of the weakest of these was Sparta. Her territory covered only a

---

[1] EXERCISE. — Contrast the "tyrants" with the Homeric kings, — as to origin of power; as to limitation by custom and public opinion; as to security in their positions.

few square miles. It was shut off from the sea, and it was surrounded by powerful neighbors.

The later Spartans attributed their rise from these conditions to the reforms of a certain *Lycurgus.* Certainly, about the year 900, whether the reformer's name was Lycurgus or not, the Spartans adopted peculiar institutions which made them a marked people. The new laws and customs disciplined and hardened them; and they soon entered upon a brilliant career of conquest. Before 700, they had subdued all Laconia; before 650, Messenia also; while the other states of the Peloponnesus, except hostile Argos, had become their allies.

128. Government. — Sparta had *two kings.* An old legend explained this peculiar arrangement as due to the birth of twin princes. At all events in this city the royal power was weakened by division, and so the nobles were less tempted to abolish it.

There was also a *Senate* of thirty elders. In practice, this body was the most important part of the government. The kings held two of the seats, and the people elected the twenty-eight other senators.

No one under sixty years of age could be chosen. The candidates were led through the Assembly in turn, and as each passed, the people shouted. Judges, shut up in a room from which they could not see the candidates, listened to the shouts and gave the vacancy to the one whose appearance had called out the loudest welcome. Aristotle, a later Greek writer, calls this method " childish " ; but it has an interesting relation to our *viva-voce* voting, where a chairman decides, in the first instance, by noise.

A *popular Assembly* of all Spartans chose senators and other officers, and decided important matters laid before it — subject to a veto by the Senate. The Assembly had no right to introduce new measures, and the *common* Spartan could not even take part in the debate.

About 725 B.C. new magistrates, called *Ephors,* became the chief rulers. Five Ephors *were chosen each year by the Assembly,* and any Spartan might be elected. The Ephors called the Assembly, presided over it, and acted as judges in all important matters. One or two of them accompanied the king in war, with power to control his movements, and even to arrest him and put him to death. In practice, *the Ephors acted as the servants of the Senate*, which indeed really *controlled* the nominations and elections of these officers.

To the Greeks, all delegation of power, even to officers elected for short terms, seemed undemocratic. They would not have called our government by President, Congress, and Supreme Court a democracy at all. Our government is sometimes called a " *representative* democracy." To the Greeks, democracy always meant " *direct* democracy," — a government in which each freeman took somewhat the same part that a member of Congress does with us — a system such that each citizen voted, not occasionally, to elect representatives, but constantly, on all matters of importance, — which matters he might also discuss in the ruling Assembly of his city. Even one of our State governments with the " initiative " and " referendum " would have seemed to the Greek a very mild sort of " direct democracy." By his standard, Sparta was exceedingly aristocratic.

129. Classes in Laconia. — Moreover, *the Spartans as a whole were a ruling class in the midst of subjects eight or ten times their number.* They were simply a camp of some nine thousand conquerors (with their families) living under arms in their unwalled city. They were wholly given to camp life. They had taken to themselves the most fertile lands in Laconia, but they did no work. Each man's land was tilled by certain slaves, or *Helots*.

The Helots numbered four or five to one Spartan. They were slaves, not to individual Spartans, but to the government. Besides tilling the Spartan lands, they furnished light-armed troops in war; but they were a constant danger. A secret police of active Spartan youth busied itself in detecting plots among them, and sometimes carried out secret massacres of the more intelligent and ambitious slaves.

Indeed it was *lawful* for any Spartan to kill a Helot without trial; and sometimes crowds of Helots vanished mysteriously when their numbers threatened Spartan safety. On one occasion, in the great struggle with Athens in the fifth century (§§ 192 ff.), the Spartans gave the Helots heavy armor, but afterward they became terrified at the possible consequences. Thucydides (the Greek historian of that period) tells how they met the danger: —

"They proclaimed that a selection would be made of those Helots who claimed to have rendered the best service to the Spartans in the war, and promised them liberty. The announcement was intended to test them : it was thought that those among them who were foremost in asserting their freedom would be most high-spirited and most likely to rise against their masters. So [the Spartans] selected about two thousand, who were crowned with garlands, and went in procession round the temples. They [the Helots] were supposed to have received their liberty, *but not long afterwards the Spartans put them all out of the way, and no man knew how any of them came to their end.*"

The inhabitants of the hundred small subject towns of Laconia were free men, *but they were not part of the Spartan state.* They kept their own customs and shared in the government of their cities, under the supervision of Spartan rulers. They tilled lands of their own, and they carried on such trades and commerce as existed in Laconia.

These subject Laconians were three or four to one Spartan; and they furnished, in large measure, the heavy-armed soldiers of the Spartan army. The Ephors could put them to death without trial, but they seem, as a rule, to have been well treated and well content.

Thus the inhabitants of Laconia were of three classes : *a small ruling body of warriors, living in one central settlement ; a large class of cruelly treated, rural serfs, to till the soil for these aristocratic soldiers ; another large class of well-treated subjects, — town-dwellers, — who, however, had no share in the Spartan government.*

130. "**Spartan Discipline.**" — Sparta kept its mastery in Laconia by sleepless vigilance and by a rigid discipline. That discipline is sometimes praised as "the Spartan training." Its sole aim was to make soldiers. It succeeded in this ; but it was harsh and brutal.

The family, as well as the man, belonged absolutely to the state. The Ephors examined each child, at its birth, to decide whether it was fit to live. If it seemed weak or puny, it was exposed in the mountains to die. The father and mother could not save it. If it was strong and healthy, it was returned to its parents for a few years. But after a boy reached the age of seven, he never again slept under his mother's roof: he was taken from home, to be trained with other boys under public officers, until he was twenty.

The boys were taught reading and a little martial music, but they were given no other mental culture. The main purpose of their education was to harden and strengthen the body and to develop self-control and obedience. On certain festival days, boys were whipped at the altars to test their endurance; and Plutarch (a Greek writer of the second century A.D.) states that they often died under the lash rather than utter a cry. This custom was much like the savage "sun-dance" of some American Indian tribes. Indeed, several features of Spartan life that are ascribed by legend to Lycurgus seem rather to have been survivals of a barbarous period that the Spartans never wholly outgrew.

From twenty to thirty, the youth lived under arms in barracks. There he was one of a mess of fifteen. From his land he had to provide his part of the barley meal, cheese, and black broth, with meat on holidays, for the company's food. The mess drilled and fought side by side, so that in battle each man knew that his daily companions and friends stood about him. These many years of constant military drill made it easy for the Spartans to adopt more complex tactics than were possible for their neighbors. They were trained in small regiments and companies, so as to maneuver readily at the word of command. This made them superior in the field. They stood to the other Greeks as disciplined soldiery always stand to untrained militia.

At thirty the man was required to marry, in order to rear more soldiers; but he must still eat in barracks, and live there

most of the time. He had no real home. Said an Athenian,
" The Spartan's life is so unendurable that it is no wonder he
throws it away lightly in battle."

There was certain virtue, no doubt, in this training. The
Spartans had the quiet dignity of born rulers. In contrast with
the noisy Greeks all about them, their speech was brief and
pithy ("laconic" speech). They used only iron money. And
their plain living made them appear superior to the weak in-
dulgences of other men. After the introduction of Ephors,
their form of government did not change for five hundred
years; and this changeless character called forth admiration
from the other Greeks, who were accustomed to kaleidoscopic
revolutions. Spartan women, too, kept a freedom which unhappily was lost in other Greek cities. Girls were trained in
gymnastics, much as boys were; and the women were famous
for beauty and health, and for public spirit and patriotism.

131. The value of the Spartans to the world lay in the fact that *they
made a garrison for the rest of Greece*, and helped save something better
than themselves. In themselves, they were hard, ignorant, narrow.
They did nothing for art, literature, science, or philosophy. *If the Greeks
had all been Spartans, we could afford to omit the study of Greek history.*

For Further Reading. — All students should read the charming
account of Spartan customs contained in Plutarch's *Life of Lycurgus.*
Davis' *Readings* has several pages of extracts from the more valuable
part.

Exercise. — Name the three classes of people in Laconia. Which one
alone had full political rights ? What were the four parts of the government ? State the powers of each.

V. BEGINNING OF DEMOCRACY AT ATHENS

132. **Consolidation of Attica**. — *Athens was the only city in Attica* — a considerable territory. Like Sparta, Athens was the
result of more consolidation than was common with Greek cities.
In other districts as large as Attica or Laconia there were
always groups of independent cities. Boeotia, for instance,
contained twelve cities, jealous of one another; and Thebes,

the largest among them, could at best hope for only a limited leadership over her rivals.

In Attica, before history really began, the beginnings of several cities had been consolidated in one (§ 103). Indeed, consolidation had been carried even farther than with Sparta. Athens was the *home* of all the free inhabitants of Attica, not merely the *camp* of one ruling tribe.

133. Favorable Conditions. — Attica is one of the most easily defended districts of all Greece — against any force not absolutely overwhelming. It is a peninsula; and on the two land sides, where it borders Megaris and Boeotia, it is reached only through fairly difficult passes. These facts explain, in part, why Attica was the one spot of southern Greece not overrun by conquerors at the time of the Dorian migration. Naturally, it became a refuge for Ionian clans driven from the Peloponnesus. The richest and strongest of these were adopted into the tribes of Attica. Others became dependants. The frequent and peaceful introduction of new blood helped to make the people progressive and open to outside influence.

134. Decline of the Homeric Kingship. — Like other Greek cities, Athens lost her kings in the dim centuries before we have any real history. The nobles began to restrict the royal power about 1000 B.C. The king's title had been *king-archon*. Alongside the king-archon the nobles first set up, from among themselves, a *war-archon* (*polemarch*). Then they created a *chief-archon*, usually called *the Archon*, to act as judge and as chief executive of the government. After that, the king-archon was only the city-priest. In 752, the office was made elective, for ten-year terms. For some time longer the king-archon was always chosen from the old royal family; but finally the office was thrown open to any noble. At last, in 682 B.C., the archons were all made annual officers, and the number was increased to nine, because of the growing judicial work.

135. Rule by the Nobles. — The nobles were known as *Eupatrids* (well-born). They were the chiefs of the numerous clans in Attica. Their council was called *the Areopagus*, from the name of the hill where it met. The Areopagus chose the archons (from nobles, of course), and ruled Attica. The other tribesmen had even less influence than in Homeric times. *They no longer had a political Assembly.*

136. Economic [1] Oppression. — The nobles tyrannized over the common tribesmen in economic matters. *Most of the land had come to belong to the nobles.* They tilled it mainly by tenants, who paid *five sixths* of the produce for rent. A bad season or hostile ravages compelled these tenants to borrow seed or food, and to mortgage themselves for payment. If a debtor failed to pay promptly, he and his family could be dragged off in chains and sold into slavery.

Besides the great landlords and their tenants, there was a class of small farmers owning their own lands; but often these men also were obliged to borrow of the nobles. In consequence, many of them passed into the condition of tenants. Aristotle, the great philosopher (§ 316), says : —

" The poor with their wives and children were the very bondsmen of the rich, who named them Sixth-men, because it was for this wage they tilled the land. The entire land was in the hands of a few. If the poor failed to pay their rents they were liable to be haled into slavery. . . . They were discontented also with every other feature of their lot, for, to speak generally, *they had no share in anything.*" — *Constitution of Athens*, 2.

137. The first advance was to base political power in part upon wealth. The supremacy of the nobles had rested largely on their superiority in war. They composed the " knights," or heavy-armed cavalry of Attica. In comparison with this cavalry, the early foot soldiery was only a light-armed mob. But, before 650, the Athenians adopted the Dorian plan of a heavy-armed infantry (" hoplites "), with shield, helmet, and long spear. *The serried ranks of this infantry proved able to repel cavalry.* The importance of the nobles in war declined, and there followed some decrease in their political power.

---

[1] "Economic" means " with reference to property," or " with reference to the way of getting a living." The word must not be confused with " economical."

Each man furnished his own arms for war.   So, in order that each might know just what military service was required from him, all tribesmen were divided into **four classes**, *according to their yearly income from land*.[1]   The first and second classes (the richest ones) were obliged to serve as knights, or cavalry. Doubtless at first these were all nobles.   The third class were to arm themselves as hoplites.   The fourth class were called into the field less often, and only as light-armed troops.

This " census " was *designed only to regulate service in the army*, but it became a basis for the *distribution of political power.* All the heavy-armed soldiery — *the three higher classes* — came to have the right to vote on questions of peace and war, and in time they grew into a *new political Assembly.*   This Assembly elected archons and other officers. *Thus political rights ceased to be based wholly on birth, and became partly a matter of wealth.*

GREEK SOLDIER.

138. Civil Strife. — In general, however, the nobles seemed almost as safely intrenched under the new system by their wealth as they had been before by birth.   Their rule continued selfish and incompetent; and nothing had been done to cure the sufferings of the poor.   The people grew more and more bitter ; and, at length, ambitious adventurers began to try to overthrow the oligarchy and make themselves tyrants.   One young conspirator, *Cylon*, with his forces, actually seized the Acropolis, the citadel of Athens.   The nobles rallied, and Cylon was defeated; but the ruling oligarchy had received a fright, and they now made a great concession (§ 139).

---

[1] 500-measure men, 300-measure men, 200-measure men, and those whose income was less than 200 measures of wheat.   (The Greek " measure " was a little more than half a bushel.)

139. Draco: Written Laws. — Until 621 b.c., Athenian law had been a matter of *ancient custom*. It was not written down, and much of it was known only to the nobles. All judges, of course, were nobles; and they abused their power in order to favor their own class. Therefore the Athenians clamored for a written code. They did not ask yet for *new* laws, but only that the old laws might be definitely fixed and known to all.

The nobles had long resisted this demand. But in 621, after the attempt of Cylon, they consented that *Draco,* one of the archons, should draw up a written code. This was done; and the "laws of Draco" were engraved on wooden blocks and set up where all might see them. Draco did not make new laws: he merely put old customs into fixed written form. The result was to make men feel how harsh and unfit the old laws were, — "*written in blood rather than ink,*" as was said in a later age. The Athenians now demanded new laws.

140. Solon. — Just at this time Athens produced a rare man who was to render her great service. *Solon* was a descendant of the old kings. In his youth he had been a trader to other lands, even going as far as Egypt (§ 23). He was already famous as a poet, a general, and a philosopher; and he was to show himself also a statesman.

Solon's patriotism had been proven. At one time the internal quarrels had so weakened Athens that little Megara had captured Salamis. In control of this island, it was easy for Megara to seize ships trying to enter the Athenian ports. Efforts to recover this important place failed miserably; and, in despair, the Athenians had voted to put to death any one who should again propose the attempt. Solon shammed madness, — to claim a crazy man's privilege, — and, appearing suddenly in the Assembly, recited a warlike, patriotic poem which roused his countrymen to fresh efforts. Solon was made general; and he recovered Salamis and saved Athens from ruin.

Now, in peril of civil war, the city turned naturally to Solon. He was known to sympathize with the poor. In his poems he had blamed the greed of the nobles and had pleaded for reconciliation between the classes. All trusted him, and the poor loved him. He was elected *Archon, with special authority,* to make new laws and to remodel the government. This office he held for two years, *594 and 593 B.C.*

141. The "Shaking-off of Burdens." — The first year Solon swept away economic evils. *Three measures righted past wrongs :* —

a. The old tenants were given full ownership of the lands which they had formerly cultivated for the nobles.[1]

b. All debts were canceled so as to give a new start.

c. All Athenians in slavery in Attica were freed.

Two measures aimed to prevent a return of old evils : —

d. It was made illegal to reduce Athenians to slavery.

e. To own more than a certain quantity of land was forbidden.

In later times the whole people celebrated these acts of Solon each year by a "Festival of the Shaking-off of Burdens."

142. Political Reform. — These economic changes resulted in political change, since political power was already based upon landed property. Up to the time of Solon, the nobles had owned most of the land. But now much of it had been *given* to the poor, and henceforth it was easy for any rich man to *buy* land. Many merchants now rose into the first class, while many nobles sank into other classes. Soon, the Eupatrid name disappeared.

Moreover, in the second year of his Archonship, *Solon introduced direct political changes which went far toward making Athens a democracy.*

a. A Senate was created, to prepare measures for the Assembly to act upon. The members were chosen each year *by lot,*[2] so that neither wealth nor birth could control the election. This new part of the government became the *guiding* part.

b. The Assembly (§ 137) *was enlarged both as to size and*

---

[1] In one of his poems, Solon speaks of " freeing the enslaved land," by removing the stone pillars which had marked the nobles' ownership.

[2] The lot in elections was regarded as an appeal to the gods, and its use was accompanied by religious sacrifices and by prayer. The early Puritans in New England sometimes used the lot in a similar way.

power. The "fourth class" (light-armed soldiery) were admitted to vote in it — though they were not allowed to hold office of any kind. This enlarged Assembly of all Athenian tribesmen *discussed* the proposals of the Senate and *decided* upon them; *elected* the archons; and *could try them for misgovernment* at the end of their year of office.

c. *The Areopagus* was no longer a council of nobles only. *It was composed of ex-archons*. Thus, it was elected, indirectly, by the Assembly. It had lost most of its powers to the Senate and Assembly; but it remained a court to try murder cases, and to exercise a supervision over the morals of the citizens, with power to impose fines for extravagance, insolence, or gluttony.

143. Additional Measures. — Solon also replaced Draco's bloody laws with a milder code; introduced a coinage (§ 70); made it the duty of each father to teach his son a trade; limited the wealth that might be buried with the dead; and restricted women from appearing in public.

144. The sixth century B.C. was one of great progress in Athens. In *682 B.C.*, a few noble families still owned most of the soil, possessed all political power, and held the rest of the people in virtual slavery.

In *593 B.C.*, when Solon laid down his office, nearly all Athenian tribesmen were landowners. All were members of the political Assembly, which decided public questions.

Some elements of aristocracy were left. To hold office, a man had to possess enough wealth to belong to one of the three higher classes, and some offices were open only to the wealthiest class. But if this Athenian progress seems slow to us, we must remember that in nearly all the American states, for some time after the Revolutionary War, important offices and the right to vote were open only to men with property.

145. Anarchy Renewed. — The reforms of Solon did not end the fierce strife of factions. Bitter feuds followed between the *Plain* (wealthy landowners), the *Shore* (merchants), and the *Mountain* (shepherds and small farmers). Twice within ten years, disorder prevented the election of archons.

146. Pisistratus, 560–527. — From such anarchy the city was saved by *Pisistratus.* In 560 B.C.[1] this noble made himself tyrant, by help of the Mountain (the most democratic faction). Twice the aristocracy drove him into exile, once for ten years. But each time he recovered his power, almost without bloodshed, because of the favor of the poorer people.

His rule was mild and wise. He lived simply, like other citizens. He even appeared in a law court, to answer in a suit against him. And he always treated the aged Solon (his kinsman) with deep respect, despite the latter's bitter opposition. Indeed, *Pisistratus governed through the forms of Solon's constitution,*[2] and enforced Solon's laws, *taking care only to have his own friends elected to the chief offices.* He was more like the "boss" of a great political "machine" than like a "tyrant." During the last period of his rule, however, he did banish many nobles and guarded himself by mercenary soldiers.

Pisistratus encouraged commerce; enlarged and beautified Athens; built roads, and an aqueduct to bring a supply of water to the city from the hills; and drew to his court a brilliant circle of poets, painters, architects, and sculptors, from all Hellas. The first written edition of the Homeric poems is said to have been put together under his encouragement. During this same time, *Anacreon* (§ 155) wrote his graceful odes at Athens, and *Thespis* (§ 155) began Greek tragedy at the magnificent festivals there instituted to Dionysus (god of wine). The tyrant gave new splendor to the public worship, and set up rural festivals in various parts of Attica, to make country life more attractive. He divided the confiscated estates of banished nobles among landless freemen, and thus increased the number of peasant landholders. Attica was no longer torn by dissension.

"Not only was he in every respect humane and mild and ready to forgive those who offended, but in addition he advanced money to the poorer people to help them in their labors.

---

[1] Two years before Cyrus became king of Persia.

[2] *Constitution,* here and everywhere in early history, means not a written document, as with us, but the general usages of government in practice.

"For the same reason [to make rural life attractive] he instituted local justices, and often made expeditions in person into the country to inspect it, and to settle disputes between persons, that they might not come to the city and neglect their farms. It was in one of these progresses, as the story goes, that Pisistratus had his adventure with the man in the district of Hymettus, who was cultivating the spot afterwards known as the 'Tax-free Farm.' He saw a man digging at very stony ground with a stake, and sent and asked what he got out of such a plot of land. 'Aches and pains,' said the man, 'and out of these Pisistratus must get his tenth.' Pisistratus was so pleased with the man's frank speech and industry that he granted him exemption from taxes."—ARISTOTLE, *Constitution of Athens*, 17.

147. Expulsion of the Son of Pisistratus, 510 B.C. — In 527, Pisistratus was succeeded by his sons Hippias and Hipparchus. Hipparchus, the younger brother, lived an evil life, and in 514 he was murdered because of a private grudge.[1] The rule of Hippias had been kindly, but now he grew cruel and suspicious, and Athens became ready for revolt.

Clisthenes, one of a band of exiled nobles, saw his opportunity to regain his home. The temple of Apollo at Delphi had just been burned, and Clisthenes engaged to rebuild it. He did so with great magnificence, using the finest of marble where the contract had called only for common limestone. After this, whenever the Spartans consulted the oracle, no matter what the occasion, they were always ordered by the priestess to *"first set free the Athenians."* The Spartans had no quarrel with Hippias; but repeated commands from such a source could not be disregarded. In 510, a reluctant Spartan army, with the Athenian exiles, expelled the tyrant.

148. Vigor of Free Athens. — The Athenians were now in confusion again; but they were stronger than before the rule of Pisistratus, and better able to govern themselves. The oligarchy strove to regain its ancient control; but Clisthenes wisely threw his strength upon the side of the people, and drove out the oligarchs. The Thebans and Euboeans seized

---

[1] Davis' *Readings*, Vol. I, No. 53, gives the patriotic song of Athens that commemorated this event.

this time of confusion to invade Attica from two sides at once; but they were routed by a double engagement in one day. A Spartan army restored the oligarchs for a moment, but was itself soon besieged in the Acropolis and captured by the aroused democracy.

A century later an Athenian dramatist (Aristophanes, § 221) portrayed the Athenian exultation (and hinted some differences between Athenian and Spartan life) in the following lines: —

> . . . " For all his loud fire-eating,
> The old Spartan got a beating,
> And, in sorry plight retreating,
>   Left his spear and shield with me.
> Then, with only his poor shirt on,
> And who knows what years of dirt on,
> With a bristling bush of beard,
>   He slunk away and left us free."

The Athenians had enjoyed little fame in war, "but now," says Aristotle, "they showed that men will fight more bravely for themselves than for a master." Indeed, they were not content simply to defend themselves. Chalcis in Euboea was stormed, and its trade with Thrace (§ 122) fell to Athens.

Athens now began a new kind of colonization, sending four thousand citizens to possess the best land of Chalcis, and to serve as a garrison there. *These men retained full Athenian citizenship.* They were known as *cleruchs*, or out-settlers. In this way Athens found land for her surplus population, and fortified her influence abroad.

During these struggles, Clisthenes proposed further reforms in the government. The people adopted his proposals, *and so made Athens a true democracy.* (See §§ 149–152.)

149. There were four main evils for Clisthenes to remedy.

a. The constitution of Solon, though a great advance toward democracy, *had left the government still largely in the hands of the rich.* The poorest "class" (*which contained at least half of all the citizens*) could not hold office; and the Assembly had not learned how to use its new powers.

  b. The jealousy between the Plain, the Shore, and the Mountain (§ 145) still caused great confusion.

  c. All voting was by clans; and there was strong temptation for each clan merely to rally around its own chief.

  d. There was a bitter jealousy between the Athenian tribesmen (the citizens) and a large body of non-citizens. The presence of these calls for a further explanation.

  150. The Non-citizen Class. — Solon's reforms had concerned tribesmen only. But in the ninety years between Solon and Clisthenes, *the growing trade of Athens had drawn many aliens there.* These men were enterprising and sometimes wealthy; but though they lived in the city, *they had no share in it.* *No alien could vote or hold office, or sue in a law court* (except through the favor of some citizen), *or take part in a religious festival, or marry an Athenian, or even own land in Attica.* The city might find it worth while to protect his property, in order to attract other strangers; but he had no secure rights. *Nor could his son, or his son's son, or any later descendant acquire any rights merely by continuing to live in Athens.*

  A like condition was found in other Greek cities; but rarely were the aliens so large or so wealthy a class as in commercial Athens. Discontent might at any moment make them a danger. Clisthenes' plan was to take them into the state, and so make them strengthen it.

  151. Geographical Tribes. — *Clisthenes began his work by marking off Attica into a hundred divisions, called demes.* Each citizen was enrolled in one of these, and his son after him. *Membership in a clan* had always been the proof of citizenship Now that proof was to be found in this *deme-enrollment.*

  The hundred demes were distributed among ten "tribes," or wards; but the ten demes of each tribe were not located close together. *They were scattered as widely as possible,* so as to include different interests. Voting in the Assembly was no longer by the old blood tribes, but by these ten new "territorial" tribes. By this one device, Clisthenes remedied three of the four great evils of the time (*b, c, d,* in § 149).

(1) A clan could no longer act as a unit, since its members made parts, perhaps, of several "tribes." So the influence of the clan chiefs declined. (2) Men of the Shore and of the Mountain often found themselves united in the same tribe, and the old factions died out. (3) While Clisthenes was distributing citizens among the new geographical units, *he seized the chance to enroll the non-citizens also in the demes.* Thus, fresh, progressive influences were again adopted into Athenian life.

It must not be supposed, however, that aliens *continued* to gain admission in the future, as with us, by easy naturalization. The act of Clisthenes *applied only to those then in Athens, and to their descendants.* In a few years another alien class grew up, with all the old disadvantages.

152. **The Assembly** kept its old powers, and gained new ones. It began to deal with foreign affairs, taxation, and the details of campaigns. It no longer confined itself to proposals from the "Council of Five Hundred" (the new name for the Senate). Any citizen could move amendments or introduce new business. The Assembly now elected *ten "generals"* yearly, who took over most of the old authority of the archons.

These new arrangements corrected much of the first evil noted in § 149. *The "fourth class" of citizens was still not eligible to office.* Otherwise, Athens had become a democracy. To be sure, it took some time for the Assembly to realize its full power and to learn how to control its various agents; but its rise to supreme authority was now only a matter of natural growth.

Solon and Clisthenes were the two men who stood foremost in the great work of putting government into the hands of the people. The struggle in which they were champions is essentially the same contest that is going on to-day. The student will have little difficulty in selecting names, in America and in European countries, to put in the list which should be headed with the names of these two Athenians.

153. Ostracism. — One peculiar device of Clisthenes deserves mention. It was called *ostracism*, and it was designed to head off civil strife.   Once a year the Assembly was given a chance to vote by ballot (on pieces of pottery, "ostraka"), each one against any man whom he deemed dangerous to the state.   If six thousand citizens thought that *some one* ought to go into exile for the safety of the state, then that man had to go *against whom the largest number of the six thousand votes were cast.*   Such exile was felt to be perfectly honorable ; and when a man came back from it, he took at once his old place in the public regard.

EXERCISE : QUESTIONS ON THE GOVERNMENT. — *For the Eupatrid government.* — 1. What represented the monarchic element of Homer's time ?   2. What the aristocratic ?   3. What the democratic ?   4. Which element had made a decided gain in power ?   5. Which had lost most ?   6. Which of the three was least important ?   7. Which most important ?
  For the government after Solon. — 1. What was the basis of citizenship ?   2. What was the basis for distribution of power among the citizens ?   3. Was the introduction of the Senate a gain for the aristocratic or democratic element ?   4. What powers did the Assembly gain ?   5. Which two of these powers enabled the Assembly to control the administration ?
  Students should be able to answer similar questions on the government after Clisthenes' reforms.   It would be a good exercise for the class to make out questions themselves.

VI. INTELLECTUAL DEVELOPMENT

154. Architecture, painting, and sculpture had not reached full bloom in the sixth century, but they had begun to show a character distinct from Oriental art.   Their chief centers in this period were Miletus and Ephesus (in Ionia) and Athens. Architecture was more advanced than painting or sculpture. It found its best development, not in palaces, as in the old Cretan civilization, but in the temples of the gods.   In every Greek city, the temples were the most beautiful and the most prominent structures.

The plan of the Greek temple was very simple.   People did not gather within the building for service, as in our churches. They only brought offerings there.   The inclosed part of the building, therefore, was small and rather dark, — containing only one or two rooms, for the statues of the god and the altar and the safe-keeping of the offerings. It was merely the god's house, where people could visit him when they wished to ask favors.

In shape, the temple was rectangular. The roof projected beyond the inclosed part of the building, and was supported not by the walls, but by a row of columns running around the four sides. The gables (*pediments*) in front and rear were low, and were filled with statuary, as was also the *frieze*, between the cornice and the columns. Sometimes there was a second frieze upon the walls of the building inside the colonnade.

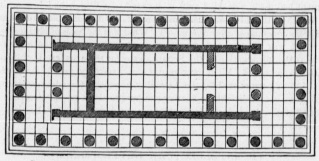

GROUND PLAN OF THE TEMPLE OF THESEUS AT ATHENS.

The building took much of its beauty from its colonnades; and *the chief differences in the styles of architecture were marked by the columns and their capitals.* According to differences in these features, a building is said to belong to the *Doric*, *Ionic*, or *Corinthian* "order."

In the Doric order the column has *no base* of its own, but rests directly upon the foundation from which the walls rise. The *shaft* is grooved lengthwise with some twenty flutings. The *capital* is severely simple, consisting of a circular band of stone, swelling up from the shaft, capped by a square block, without ornament. Upon the capitals rests a plain band of massive stones (*the architrave*), and above this is the frieze, which supports the roof. The frieze is divided at equal spaces by *tri-*

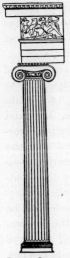

IONIC ORDER.

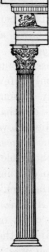

**CORINTHIAN
ORDER.**

glyphs, a series of three projecting flutings; and
the spaces between the triglyphs are filled with
sculpture.

The Doric style is the simplest of the three
orders. It is almost austere in its plainness, giving a sense of self-controlled
power and repose. Some-
times it is called a *masculine*
style, in contrast with the
more ornate and *feminine*
character of the Ionic order.

The Ionic order came into
general use later. In this
style, the column *has a base*
arranged in three expanding
circles. The shaft is *more
slender* than the Doric. The
swelling bell of the capital
is often *nobly carved, and it
is surmounted by two spiral
rolls.* The frieze has *no triglyphs :* the sculpture upon
it is one continuous band.

The Corinthian order is a later
development and does not belong
to the period we are now consid-
ering. It resembles the Ionian ;
but the capital is taller, lacks
the spirals, and is more highly
ornamented, with forms of leaves
or animals. For illustrations of
the Doric and Ionic orders, see also pages 162, 163, and
especially page 216. For the Corinthian, see page 486.

DORIC COLUMN. — From
the Temple of Theseus
at Athens.

1, the shaft ; 2, the capital ;
3, the frieze ; 4, cornice ;
5, part of roof, showing the
low slope.

155. Poetry. — In poetry there was more progress even than in architecture. The earliest Greek
poetry had been made up of *ballads,* celebrating

wars and heroes.   These ballads were stories in verse, sung by
wandering minstrels.   The greatest of such compositions rose
to *epic poetry*, of which the *Iliad* and *Odyssey* are the noblest
examples.   Their period is called the *Epic Age*.

In the seventh and sixth centuries, most poetry consisted of
odes and songs *in a great variety of meters*, — corresponding to

the more varied life
of the time. Love and
pleasure are the favor-
ite themes, and the
poems describe *feel-
ings* rather than out-
ward events. They
were intended to be
sung to the accom-
paniment of the lyre
(a sort of harp). They
are therefore called
lyrics ; and the sev-
enth and sixth cen-
turies are known as
the *Lyric Age*.

It is possible to
name here only a few
of the many famous
lyric poets of that

A DORIC CAPITAL. — From a photograph of a detail of the Parthenon. See § 219 for the date
and history.

age.   *Sappho*, of Lesbos, wrote exquisite and melodious love
songs, of which a few fragments survive.   Her lover *Alcaeus*
(another Lesbian poet) described her as "Pure Sappho, violet
tressed, softly smiling."   The ancients were wont to call her
"the poetess," just as they referred to Homer as "the poet."
Simonides wrote odes to arouse Hellenic patriotism ; *Anacreon*
has been spoken of in connection with the brilliant court of
Pisistratus.   *Tyrtaeus*, an Attic war-poet, wrote chiefly for the
Spartans, and became one of their generals.   *Corinna* was a
woman poet of Boeotia.   *Pindar*, the greatest of the lyric poets,

came from the same district. He delighted especially to celebrate the rushing chariots and glorious athletes of the Olympic games.

Two other great poets, representing another kind of poetry, belong to this same period. *Hesiod* of Boeotia lived about 800 B.C. He wove together into a long poem old stories of the creation and of the birth and relationship of the gods. This *Theogony* of Hesiod was the most important single work in early Greek literature, after the Homeric poems. Hesiod wrote also remarkable home-like poems on farm life (*Works and Days*).[1] The other writer was *Thespis,* who *began dramatic poetry* (plays) at Athens, under the patronage of Pisistratus.

156. Philosophy. — In the sixth century, too, Greek philosophy was born. Its home was in Ionia. There first the Greek mind set out to explain the origin of things. *Thales* of Miletus, "father of Greek philosophy," taught that all things came from Water, or moisture. His pupil *Anaximenes* called Air, not Water, the universal "first principle." *Pythagoras* (born at Samos, but teaching in Magna Graecia) sought the fundamental principle, not in any kind of matter, but in *Number,* or *Harmony. Xenophanes* of Ionia affirmed that the only *real* existence was that of God, one and changeless — "not in body like unto mortals, nor in mind." The changing world, he said, did not really exist: it was only a deception of men's senses. *Heracleitus* of Ephesus, on the other hand, held that "ceaseless change" was the very principle of things: the world, he taught, had evolved from a fiery ether, and was in constant flux.

Some of these explanations of the universe seem childish to us. They may represent honest attempts of men who had lost the primitive revelation. They do not in any way approach Christian philosophy. *This early philosophy, however, was closely related to early science.* Thales

---

[1] This was really a textbook on farming, — the first textbook in Europe. Hesiod wrote it in verse, because prose writing in his day was unknown. The earliest composition of any people is usually in meter.

was the first Greek to foretell eclipses. (He could predict the period, but not the precise day or hour.) Those who laughed at philosophers, liked to tell of him that, while gazing at the heavens, he fell into a well. He may have obtained his knowledge of astronomy from Egypt, which country we know he visited (§ 32). *Anaximander*, another philosopher of Miletus,

WEST FRONT OF THE PARTHENON TO-DAY. Doric style. See § 219.

made maps and globes. The Pythagoreans naturally paid special attention to mathematics and especially to geometry; and to Pythagoras is ascribed the famous demonstration about the square on the hypotenuse of a right triangle.

The Pythagoreans connected "philosophy" particularly with *conduct*. The harmony in the outer world, they held, must be matched by a harmony in the soul of man. Indeed, all these sages taught lofty moral truths. (See Davis' *Readings*, Vol. I, No. 98.) Greek philosophy lifted itself far above the moral level of Greek religion.

157. Summary of the Five Centuries. — During the five centuries from 1000 to 500 B.C., the Hellenes had come to think of themselves as one people (though not as one nation), and had developed a brilliant, jostling society. During more than half the period they had been busy sowing Hellenic cities broadcast along even the distant Mediterranean shores. They had found a capable military leadership in Sparta. They had everywhere rid themselves of the old monarchic rule, by a

WEST FRONT OF TEMPLE OF VICTORY AT ATHENS. — From the ruins to-day. Ionic style. See § 218.

long series of changes; and, in Athens in particular, they had gone far toward creating a true democracy. They had experienced an artistic and intellectual development *which made their civilization in many regards nobler and more promising than any the world had yet seen. Moreover, this civilization was to be part of our own.* The remains of Egyptian or Babylonian sculpture and architecture arouse our admiration and interest as curiosities; but they are foreign to us. With the remains of a Greek temple, or a fragment of a Greek poem, of the year 500, we feel at home. *It might have been built, or written, by our own people.*

158. The following table of dates shows the correspondence in time of leading events in the Oriental and the Greek world down to the period when the two worlds come into close relations. Down to about 800, dates are mostly estimates (§ 31). *This table is not given to be memorized*, but merely to be read and referred to.

HELLAS	THE EAST
B.C.	B.C.
	5000 Records of advanced Bronze cultures in valleys of Nile and Euphrates
3500 Rising Aegean " New Stone " culture	3400–2400 " Old Kingdom " in Egypt, centered at Memphis ; Menes ; Cheops ; pyramids
	2800 Sargon : empire from Euphrates to Mediterranean
2500 Bronze culture in Crete and other Aegean centers	
2500 or 2400 Destruction of Schliemann's " Troy " (the " Second City ")	2400–2000 " Middle Kingdom " in Egypt, centered at Thebes : Lake Moeris ; Red Sea canal ; commerce with Crete
	2234 Beginning of recorded astronomical observations at Babylon (§ 49)
2000 (?) " Minos of Crete "	2000 Abraham emigrates from Ur
	2000–1600 Egyptian Decline : Hyksos ; Hebrews enter Egypt
	1917 (?) Hammurabi : " First Babylonian " Empire ; voluminous cuneiform literature
1600 Phoenicians in the Aegean	1600–1330 " New Empire " in Egypt
1500–1200 Achaean conquests	
1500 Destruction of Knossos	
	1475 Egyptian brief conquest of the East : *first union of the Oriental world*
1300 Destruction of Mycenae	
1200 Destruction of Homer's " Troy " (the " Sixth City ")	1320 Hebrew exodus
1100 Homeric Poems	1100 Beginnings of Assyrian Empire — Tiglath-Pileser I

HELLAS (*continued*)	THE EAST (*continued*)
	1055–975 David and Solomon
1000 Dorian conquests	1000 (?) Zoroaster
900 Rise of Sparta	
900–800 Ionian colonization	850 (?) Carthage founded
800–650 Greek colonization of Mediterranean coasts	
776 First recorded Olympiad	745 True Assyrian Empire — Tiglath-Pileser II
700–500 " Age of Tyrants "	722 Sargon carries the Ten Tribes of Israel into captivity
	672 Assyria conquers Egypt : *second union of Oriental world*
	653–525 Last period of Egyptian independence — open to Greeks; visits by Solon and Thales ; circumnavigation of Africa
650–500 " Lyric Age "	650 (?) First coinage, in Lydia
	630 Scythian ravages
	625–538 Second Babylonian Empire : Babylonian captivity of the Jews
594–593 Solon's reforms	556 Croesus, king in Lydia
560–527 Pisistratus	558–529 Cyrus the Great founds Persian Empire — *third union of the Oriental World*
510 Expulsion of Tyrants from Athens	

500 Ionian Revolt (§§ 164, 165)

(Eastern and Western civilizations in conflict)

FOR FURTHER READING. — *Specially suggested :* (1) Davis' *Readings*, Vol. I, Nos. 40–56. These very nearly fit in with the order of treatment in this book, and several numbers have been referred to in footnotes.   It is desirable for students each day to consult the *Readings*, to see whether they can find there more light on the lesson in *this* book.

(2) Bury (*on colonization*), 86–106, 116–117 ; (*on Sparta*), 120–134 ; (*on "Lycurgus"*), 134–135 ; (*on certain tyrants*), 149–155 ; (*oracles and festivals*), 159–161 ; (*work of Solon*), 180–189.

EXERCISE. — Distinguish between *Sparta* and *Laconia*. How did the relation of *Thebes* to *Boeotia* differ from that of Sparta to Laconia? Which of these two relations was most like that of *Athens* to *Attica* ? Have you any buildings in your city in which Greek columns are used ? Of which order, in each case ?   (Take several leading buildings in a large town.)   Explain the following terms : constitution ; Helot ; Eupatrid ; tyrant ; Lycurgus ; Clisthenes ; Areopagus ; archon ; deme ; clan ; tribe ; a " tribe of Clisthenes."

(To *explain* a term, in such an exercise, is to make such statements concerning it as will at least prevent the term being confused with any other. Thus if the term is *Solon*, it will not do to say, " A Greek lawgiver," or " A lawgiver of the sixth century B.C." The answer *must* at least say, " An *Athenian* lawgiver of about 600 B.C." ; and it *ought* to say, " An Athenian lawgiver *and democratic reformer* of about 600 B.C." Either of the first two answers is worth *zero*.)

CHAPTER XII

THE PERSIAN WARS

We have now reached a point where the *details* of Greek history are better known, and where a more connected *story* is possible. This story begins with the *Persian Wars*.

THE TWO ANTAGONISTS

159. Persia. — In §§ 69–77, we saw how — within a time no longer than an average human life — Persia had stretched its rule over the territory of all former Oriental empires, besides adding vast regions before unknown. By 500 B.C. (the period to which we have just carried Greek history), Persia reached into the peninsula of Hindoostan in Asia, and, across Thrace, up to the Greek peninsula in Europe (map, after page 88). On this western frontier lay the scattered groups of Greek cities, bustling and energetic, but small and disunited. *The mighty world-empire now advanced confidently to add these little communities to its dominions.*

Persia, in many ways, was the noblest of the Asiatic empires; but its civilization was distinctly Oriental (with the general character that has been noted in §§ 80 ff.). The Greek cities, between 1000 and 500 B.C., had created a wholly different sort of culture, which we call European, or Western (§§ 82, 86). *East and West now joined battle.* The Persian attack upon Greece began a contest between two worlds, which has gone on, at times, ever since, — with the present "Eastern Question" and our Philippine question for latest chapters.

160. **Three sections of Hellas** were prominent in power and culture: *the European peninsula,* which we commonly call Greece; *Asiatic Hellas,* with its coast islands; and *Sicily and Magna Graecia* (§ 122). Elsewhere, the cities were too scattered, or too small, or too busy with their own defense against surrounding savages, to count for much in the approaching contest. Asiatic Hellas fell easily to Persia before the real struggle began. Then the two other sections were attacked simultaneously, Greece by Persia, Sicily by Carthage.

Carthage was a Phoenician colony on the north coast of Africa (see map after page 86). It had built up a considerable empire in the western Mediterranean; and, in Sicily, it had already, from time to time, come into conflict with Greek colonies. Sicily was an important point from which to control Mediterranean trade. Carthage now made a determined attempt to drive out her rivals there.

The Greeks believed that the Persian king urged Carthage to take this time for attack, so that Magna Graecia and Sicily might not be able to join the other Greeks in resisting the main attack from Persia. At all events, such was the result. The Greek cities in Sicily and Italy were ruled by tyrants. These rulers united under *Gelon* of Syracuse, and repelled the Carthaginian onset. *But the struggle kept the Western Greeks from helping their kinsmen against the Persians.*

161. Conditions in Greece itself at this critical moment were unpromising. The forces that could be mustered against the master of the world were small at best; but just now they were further divided and wasted in internal struggles. Athens was at war with Aegina and with Thebes; Sparta had renewed an ancient strife with Argos (§ 96), and had crippled her for a generation by slaying in one battle almost the whole body of adult Argives.[1] Phocis was engaged in war with Thessalians on one side and Boeotians on the other. Worse than all this, many cities were torn by cruel class strife at

---

[1] The old men and boys, however, were still able to defend Argos itself against Spartan attack. This touches an important fact in Greek warfare: *a walled city could hardly be taken by assault;* it could fall only through extreme carelessness, or by treachery, or starvation. *The last danger did not often exist.* The armies of the besiegers were made up of citizens, not of paid troops; and they could *not keep the field long themselves.* They were needed at home, and it was not easy for them to secure food for a long siege.

home, — oligarchs against democrats. *One favorable condition,* however, calls for attention (§ 162).

162. The Peloponnesian League. — In a sense, Sparta was the head of Greece. She lacked the enterprise and daring that were to make Athens the city of the coming century ; but her government was firm, her army was large and disciplined, and so far she had shown more genius than any other Greek state in organizing her neighbors into a military league. *Two fifths of the Peloponnesus she ruled directly* (Laconia and Messenia), and the rest (except Argolis and Achaea) formed a confederacy for war, with Sparta as the head.

THE PELOPONNESIAN LEAGUE
(500 B.C.)

It is true the union was very slight. On special occasions, at the call of Sparta, the states sent delegates to a conference to discuss peace or war; but there was no constitution, no common treasury, not even a *general* treaty to bind the states together. Indeed, one city of the league sometimes made war upon another. Each state was bound to Sparta by its *special* treaty ; and, if Sparta was attacked by an enemy, each city of the " league " was expected to maintain a certain number of troops for the confederate army. Loose as this Peloponnesian league was, it was the greatest war power in Hellas; *and it seemed the one rallying point for disunited Greece in the coming struggle* (§ 130, close). Except for the presence of this war power, few other Greeks would have dared to resist Persia at all.

OPENING OF THE STRUGGLE IN IONIA

163. Conquest of the Ionian Greeks. — For two centuries before 500 B.C., the Asiatic Hellenes excelled all other branches of the Greek race in culture. Unfortunately for them, the empire of Lydia arose near them. That great state was unwilling to be shut off from the Aegean by the Greek cities, and it set out to conquer them. For some time, the little Greek states kept their independence; but when the energetic Croesus (§ 70) became king of Lydia, he subdued all the cities on the coast of Asia Minor. Croesus, however, was a warm admirer of the Greeks, and his rule over them was gentle. They were expected to acknowledge him as their over-lord and to pay a small tribute in money; but they were left to manage their own affairs at home, and were favored in many ways.

When Cyrus the Persian attacked Croesus (§ 72), the Asiatic Greeks fought gallantly for Lydia. After the overthrow of Croesus, they tried to come to terms with Cyrus. Cyrus was angry because they had refused his invitations to join him in the war, and he would make them no promises. Fearing severe punishment, they made a brief struggle for independence. They applied, in vain, to Sparta for aid. Then Thales (§ 156) suggested a federation of all Ionia, with one government and one army; but the Greeks could not rise to so wise a plan (cf. § 104). So the Ionian cities fell, one by one, before the arms of Cyrus; and under Persian despotism their old leadership in civilization soon vanished.

164. The " Ionian Revolt," 500 B.C. — The Persian conquest took place about 540 B.C. Before that time the Ionians had begun to get rid of tyrants. But the Persians set up a tyrant again in each city, as the easiest means of control. (This shows something of what would have happened in Greece itself, if Persia had won in the approaching war.) Each tyrant knew that he could keep his power only by Persian support.

In the year 500, by a general rising, the Ionians deposed their tyrants once more, formed an alliance with one another,

and broke into revolt against Persia. Another appeal to
Sparta[1] for help proved fruitless; but Athens sent twenty
ships, and little Eretria sent five. " These ships," says Herodotus, " were the beginnings of woes, both to the Greeks and to
the barbarians."

At first the Ionians and their allies were successful. They
even took Sardis, the old capital of Lydia, far in the interior.
But treachery and mutual suspicion were rampant; Persian
gold was used skillfully; and one defeat broke up the loose
Ionian league. Then the cities were again subdued, one by
one, in the five years following.

FIRST TWO ATTACKS UPON THE EUROPEAN GREEKS
(492–490 B.C.)

**165. What was the relation of the Ionian Revolt to the Persian
invasion of Greece?** According to legend, the Persian king
attacked Greece to punish Athens for sending aid to the
Ionian rebels. Herodotus says that Darius (§ 76) was so
angered by the sack of Sardis that, during the rest of his
life, he had a herald cry out to him thrice each day at dinner,
— "O King, remember the Athenians!" This story has the
appearance of a later invention, to flatter Athenian vanity.
Probably Athens *was* pointed out for special vengeance, by her
aid to Ionia; *but the Persian invasion would have come, anyway,*
and it would have come some years sooner, had not the war in
Ionia kept the Persians busy.

The expanding frontier of the Persian empire had reached

---

[1] The story of the appeal to Sparta is told pleasantly by Herodotus (extract in Davis' *Readings*, Vol. I, No. 57). It should be made a topic for a
special report by some student to the class. (This seems a good place to call the
attention of teachers to one feature of the present textbook. The story just
referred to might easily be put into the text; but it would take up much space;
and though interesting, it has little historical value. At least, it is in no way
essential for understanding the rest of the history. More important still, —
any student who has Herodotus accessible can tell the story as well as this
book could do it. *This is the kind of outside reading that any student likes
to do, and a kind that any student is perfectly able to do.*)

Thessaly just before 500 B.C., and the same motives that had carried Persian arms through Thrace and Macedonia would have carried them on into Greece. Persia was still in full career of conquest. The Greek peninsula was small; but its cities were becoming wealthy, and Persia coveted them for their ships and their trade. *The real significance of the Ionian war was that it helped to delay the main Persian onset until the Greeks were better prepared. The Athenians had been wise, as well as generous, in aiding the Ionians.*

166. First Expedition against Greece, 492 B.C. Mount Athos.— Immediately after the end of the Ionian revolt Darius began vast preparations for the invasion of Greece. A mighty army was gathered at the Hellespont under *Mardonius*, son-in-law of the king; and a large fleet was collected. This was to sail along the coast, in constant touch with the army, and furnish it, day by day, with provisions and other supplies. In 492, these forces set out, advancing along the shores of the Aegean. But the army suffered from constant attacks by the savage Thracian tribes; and finally, as the fleet was rounding the rocky promontory of Mount Athos, a terrible storm dashed it to pieces. With it were wrecked all hopes of success. Mardonius had no choice but to retreat into Asia.

167. Second Expedition, 490 B.C. Marathon.— This failure filled Darius with wrath. Such a check in an expedition against the petty Greek states was wholly unexpected. Mardonius, though an able general, was disgraced, and preparations were begun for a new expedition.

Meantime, in 491, heralds were sent to all the Greek cities to demand "earth and water," in token of submission. The islands in the Aegean yielded at once. In continental Greece the demand was in general quietly refused; but, in Athens and Sparta, indignation ran so high that even the sacred character of ambassadors did not save the messengers. At Athens they were thrown into a pit, and at Sparta into a well, and told to "take thence what they wanted."

In the spring of 490, the Persians were ready for the second expedition. This time, taking warning from the disaster at Mount Athos, the troops were embarked on a mighty fleet, which proceeded directly across the Aegean. Stopping only to receive the submission of certain islands by the way, the fleet reached the island of Euboea without a check.

There Eretria (§ 164) was captured, through treachery. The city was destroyed, and most of the people were sent in chains to Persia. Then the Persians landed on the plain of *Marathon* in Attica, to punish Athens. Hippias, the exiled tyrant (§ 147), was with the invaders, hoping to get back his throne as a servant of Persia; and he had pointed out this admirable place for disembarking the Persian cavalry.

At first most of the Athenians wished to fight only behind their walls. Sooner or later, this must have resulted in ruin, especially as there were some traitors within the city hoping to admit Hippias. Happily *Miltiades*, one of the ten Generals (§ 152), persuaded the commanders to march out and attack the Persians at once.[1]

From the rising ground where the hills of Mount Pentelicus meet the plain, the ten thousand Athenian hoplites faced the Persian host for the first struggle between Greeks and Asiatics on European ground. Sparta had promised aid; and, at the first news of the Persian approach, a swift runner (Phidippides) had raced the hundred and fifty miles of rugged hill country to implore Sparta to hasten. He reached Sparta on the second day; but the Spartans waited a week, on the ground that an old law forbade them to set out on a military expedition before the full moon. The Athenians felt bitterly that Sparta was ready to look on, not unwillingly, while the "second city in Greece" was destroyed.

At all events, Athens was left to save herself (and our Western world) as best she could, with help from only one city. This was heroic little *Plataea*, in Boeotia, near by. Athens had sometimes protected the democratic government of that

---

[1] This story should be read in Herodotus, or, even better in some ways, in the extracts in Davis' *Readings*, with Dr. Davis' admirable introductions.

city from attack by the powerful oligarchs of Thebes. The Plataeans remembered this gratefully, and, on the eve of the battle, marched into the Athenian camp with their full force of a thousand hoplites. Then Athenians and Plataeans won a marvelous victory over perhaps ten times their number[1] of the most famous soldiery in the world. The result was due to the generalship of Miltiades, and to the superior equipment of the Greek hoplite.

Miltiades drew out his front as thin as he dared, to prevent the long Persian front from overlapping and "flanking" him.

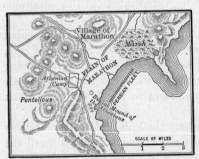

PLAN OF MARATHON. Cf. map, page 184.

To accomplish this, he weakened his center daringly, *so as to mass all the men he could spare from there in the wings.* He meant these wings to bear the brunt of battle, and ordered them to advance more rapidly than the thin center. Then he moved his forces down the slope toward the Persian lines.

While yet an arrow's flight distant, the advancing Greeks broke into a run, according to Miltiades' orders, so as to cover the rest of the ground before the Persian archers could get in their deadly work. Once at close quarters, the heavy weapons of the Greeks gave them overwhelming advantage. Their dense, heavy array, charging with long, outstretched spears, by its sheer weight broke the light-armed Persian lines, which were

---

[1] The figures, on the next page, for the slain, are probably trustworthy; but all numbers given for the Persian army, in this or other campaigns, are guesses. Ancient historians put the Persians at Marathon at from a quarter to half a million. Modern scholars are sure that no ancient fleet could possibly carry any considerable part of such a force, — and, indeed, it is clear that the ancient authorities had no basis for their figures. Modern guesses — they are nothing better — put the Persian force at Marathon all the way from 100,000 down to 20,000.

utterly unprepared for conflict on such terms. The Persians fought gallantly, as usual; but their darts and light scimetars made little impression upon the heavy bronze armor of the Greeks, while their linen tunics and wicker shields counted for little against the thrust of the Greek spear. For a time, it is true, the Greek center had to give ground; but the two

MARATHON TO-DAY. — From a photograph. The camera stood a little above the Athenian camp in the Plan on the opposite page. That camp was in the first open space in the foreground, where the poplar trees are scattered. The land beyond the strip of water is the narrow peninsula running out from the "Marsh" in the Plan.

wings, having routed the forces in front of them, wheeled upon the Persian center, crushing upon both flanks at the same moment, and drove it in disorder to the ships. One hundred ninety-two Athenians fell. The Persians left over sixty-four hundred dead upon the field.

The Athenians tried also to seize the fleet; but here they were repulsed. The Persians embarked and sailed safely away. They took a course that might lead to Athens. Moreover, the

Greek army had just seen sun-signals flashing to the enemy from some traitor's shield in the distant mountains; and Miltiades feared them to be an invitation to attack the city in the absence of the army. To check such plots, he sent the runner Phidippides to announce the victory to Athens. Already exhausted by the battle, Phidippides put forth supreme effort, raced the twenty-two miles of mountain road from Marathon, shouted exultantly to the eager, anxious crowds, — "Ours the victory," — and fell dead.[1]

Meanwhile Miltiades was hurrying the rest of his wearied army, without rest, over the same road. Fortunately the Persian fleet had to sail around a long promontory (map, page 180), and when it appeared off Athens, the next morning, Miltiades and his hoplites had arrived also. The Persians did not care to face again the men of Marathon; and the same day they set sail for Asia.[2]

168. Importance of Marathon. — Merely as a military event Marathon is an unimportant skirmish; but, in its results upon human welfare, it is among the few really "decisive" battles of the world. Whether Egyptian conquered Babylonian, or Babylonian conquered Egyptian, mattered little in the long run. Possibly, whether Spartan or Athenian prevailed over the other mattered not much more. But it did matter whether or not the huge, inert *East* should crush the new life out of the *West*. Marathon decided that the West should live on.

For the Athenians themselves, Marathon began a new era. Natural as the victory came to seem in later times, it took high courage on that day to stand before the hitherto unconquered Persians, even without such tremendous odds. "The Athenians," says Herodotus, "were the first of the Greeks to face

---

[1] The student will like to read, or to hear read, Browning's poem, *Pheidippides*, with the story of both runs by this Greek hero. Compare this story with Herodotus' account in Davis' *Readings*, Vol. I, No. 59. The famous run from the battlefield to the city is the basis of the modern "Marathon" race, in which champion athletes of all countries compete.

[2] The full story of this battle should be read as Herodotus tells it. It is given in Davis' *Readings*, Vol. I, Nos. 59, 60.

the Median garments, . . . whereas up to this time the very
name of Mede [Persian] had been a terror to the Hellenes."
Athens broke the spell for the rest of Greece, and grew herself to
heroic stature in an hour.   The sons of the men who conquered
on that field could find no odds too crushing, no prize too
dazzling, in the years to come.   It was now that the Athenian
character first showed itself as Thucydides described it a century
later : " The Athenians are the only people who succeed to
the full extent of their hope, *because they throw themselves without reserve into whatever they resolve to do."*

ATHENS — FROM MARATHON TO THERMOPYLAE

169. Internal Faction Crushed. — Soon after Marathon, Egypt
revolted against Persia.   *This gave the Greeks ten years more for
preparation;* but, except in Athens, little use was made of the
interval.   In that city the democratic forces grew stronger
and more united, while the oligarchs were weakened.

One incident in this change was the ruin of Miltiades, the
hero of Marathon.   Miltiades was originally an Athenian noble
who had made himself tyrant of Chersonesus (map after
page 94).   Not long before the Persian invasion, he had
brought upon himself the hatred of the Great King,[1] and had
fled back to Athens.   Here he became at once a prominent
supporter of the oligarchic party.   The democrats tried to
prosecute him for his previous " tyranny "; but the attempt
failed, and when the Persian invasion came, the Athenians
were fortunate in having his experience and ability to guide
them.   Soon after Marathon, however, Miltiades failed in an
expedition against Paros, into which he had persuaded the
Athenians ; and then the hostile democracy secured his
overthrow.   He was condemned to pay an immense fine, and
is said to have died soon afterward in prison.

*This blow was followed by the ostracism of some oligarchic
leader each season for several years,* until that party was utterly

---

[1] Report the story from Herodotus, if a translation is accessible.

broken. Thus Athens was saved from its most serious internal dissension.

170. Themistocles makes Athens a Naval Power. — The victorious democrats at once divided into new parties. The more moderate section was content with the constitution of Clisthenes and was disposed to follow old customs. Its leader was *Aristides*, a calm, conservative man, surnamed "the Just." The radical wing, favoring new methods and further change, was led by *Themistocles*. Themistocles was sometimes less scrupulous and upright than Aristides, but he was one of the most resourceful and far-sighted statesmen of all history.

Themistocles desired passionately one great departure from past custom in Athenian affairs. He wished to make Athens a naval power. *He saw clearly that the real struggle with Persia was yet to come, and that the result could be decided by victory on the sea.* Such victory was more probable for the Greeks than victory on land. Huge as the Persian empire was, it had no seacoast except Egypt, Phoenicia, and Ionia. It could not, therefore, so vastly outnumber the Greeks in ships as in men ; and if the Greeks could secure command of the sea, Persia would be unable to attack them at all.

But this proposed naval policy for Athens broke with all tradition, and could not win without a struggle. Seafarers though the Greeks were, up to this time they had not used ships much in war. Attica, in particular, had almost no navy. The party of Aristides wished to hold to the old policy of fighting on land, and they had the glorious victory of Marathon to strengthen their arguments. Feeling ran high. Finally, in 483, the leaders agreed to let a vote of ostracism decide between them. Fortunately, Aristides was ostracized (§ 153), and for some years the influence of Themistocles was the strongest power in Athens.

While the voting was going on (according to Herodotus) a stupid fellow, who did not know Aristides, asked him to write the name Aristides on the shell he was about to vote. Aristides did so, asking, however, what harm Aristides had ever done the man. "*No* harm," replied the voter; "in

deed, I do not know him; but I am tired of hearing him called 'the Just.' "
Read the other anecdotes about Aristides in Davis' *Readings*, Vol. I, No. 61.

Themistocles at once put his new policy into operation.
Rich veins of silver had recently been discovered in the mines
of Attica.   These mines *belonged to the city*, and a large revenue from them had accumulated in the public treasury.   It
had been proposed to divide the money among the citizens ;
but Themistocles persuaded his countrymen to reject this
tempting plan, and instead to build a great fleet.   Thanks to
this policy, in the next three years Athens became the greatest naval power in Hellas.   The decisive victory of Salamis
was to be the result (§ 179).

THE THIRD ATTACK, 480–479 B.C.

171. Persian Preparation. — Meantime, happily for the world,
the great Darius died, and the invasion of Greece fell to his
feebler son, *Xerxes*.   Marathon had proved that no Persian
fleet by itself could transport enough troops; so the plan of
Mardonius' expedition (§ 166) was tried again, *but upon a
larger scale, both as to army and fleet.*

To guard against another accident at Mt. Athos, a canal for
ships was cut through the isthmus at the back of that rocky
headland, — a great engineering work that took three years.
Meantime, supplies were collected at stations along the way ;
the Hellespont was bridged with chains of boats covered with
planks ;[1] and at last, in the spring of 480, Xerxes in person
led a mighty host of many nations into Europe.

Ancient reports put the Asiatics at from one and a half
million to two million soldiers, with followers and attendants
to raise the total to five millions.   Modern critics think
Xerxes may have had some half-million troops, with numerous
followers.   In any case, the numbers vastly exceeded those
which the Greeks could bring against them.   A fleet of twelve
hundred ships accompanied the army.

---

[1] Read Herodotus' story of Xerxes' wrath when the first bridge broke, and
how he ordered the Hellespont to be flogged (Davis' *Readings*, Vol. I, No. 64).

172. The Greek Preparation. — *The danger forced the Greeks into something like common action:* into a greater unity, indeed, than they had ever known.   Sparta and Athens joined in calling *a Hellenic congress* at Corinth, on the isthmus, in 481 B.C. The deputies that appeared bound their cities by oath to aid one another, and pledged their common efforts to punish any states that should join Persia.   Ancient feuds were pacified. Plans of campaign were discussed, and Sparta was formally recognized as leader.   In spite of Athens' recent heroism, the belief in Sparta's invincibility in war was too strong to permit any other choice.

Messengers were sent also to implore aid from outlying portions of Hellas, but with little result.   Crete excused herself on a superstitious scruple.   Corcyra promised a fleet, but took care it should not arrive; and the Greek tyrants in Sicily and Magna Graecia had their hands full at home with the Carthaginian invasion (§ 160).

The outlook was full of gloom.   Argos, out of hatred for Sparta, and Thebes, from jealousy of Athens, had refused to attend the congress, and were ready to join Xerxes.   Even the Delphic oracle, which was of course consulted in such a crisis, predicted ruin and warned the Athenians in particular to flee to the ends of the earth.

173. The Lines of Defense. — Against a land attack the Greeks had three lines of defense.   The first was at the Vale of Tempe near Mount Olympus, where only a narrow pass opened into Thessaly.   The second was at Thermopylae, where the mountains shut off northern from central[1] Greece, except for a road only a few feet in width.   The third was behind the Isthmus of Corinth.

174. Plan of Campaign. — At the congress at Corinth *the Peloponnesians had wished selfishly to abandon the first two lines.* They urged that all patriotic Greeks should retire at once within the Peloponnesus, the final citadel of Greece, and for-

---

[1] For these terms, see map study, page 99.

tify the isthmus by an impregnable wall. This plan was as foolish as it was selfish. Greek troops might have held the isthmus against the Persian land army; but the Peloponnesus was readily open to attack by sea, and the Persian fleet would have found it easier here than at either of the other lines of defense to land troops in the Greek rear, *without losing touch with its own army*. Such a surrender of two thirds of Greece, too, would have meant a tremendous reinforcement of the enemy by excellent Greek soldiery. Accordingly, *it was finally decided to resist the entrance of the Persians into Greece by meeting them at the Vale of Tempe*.

175. The Loss of Thessaly. — Sparta, however, had no gift for going to meet an attack, but must always await it on the enemy's terms. A hundred thousand men should have held the Vale of Tempe; but only a feeble garrison was sent there, and it retreated before the Persians appeared. Through Sparta's incapacity for leadership, Xerxes entered Greece without a blow. Then the Thessalian cities, deserted by their allies, joined the invaders with their powerful cavalry.

176. Thermopylae: Loss of Central Greece. — This loss of Thessaly made it evident, even to Spartan statesmen, that to abandon central Greece would strengthen Xerxes further; and it was decided in a half-hearted way to make a stand at Thermopylae. The pass was only some twenty feet wide between the cliff and the sea, and the only other path was one over the mountain, equally easy to defend. Moreover, the long island of Euboea approached the mainland just opposite the pass, so that the Greek fleet *in the narrow strait* could guard the land army against having troops landed in the rear.

The Greek fleet at this place numbered 270 ships. Of these the Athenians furnished half. The admiral was a Spartan, though his city sent only sixteen ships. The land defense had been left to the Peloponnesian league. This was the supremely important duty; but the force, which Sparta had sent to attend to it, was shamefully small. The Spartan king, *Leonidas*, held the pass with three hundred Spartans and a few thousand allies. *The main force of Spartans was again left at home, on the ground of a religious festival.*

The Persians reached Thermopylae without a check. Battle was joined at once on land and sea, and raged for three days. Four hundred Persian ships were wrecked in a storm, and the rest were checked by the Greek fleet in a sternly contested con-

THERMOPYLAE.

From a photograph: to show the steepness of the mountain side.

flict at *Artemisium*. On land, Xerxes flung column after column of chosen troops into the pass, to be beaten back each time in rout. But on the third night, *Ephialtes*, "the Judas of Greece," guided a force of Persians over the mountain path, which the Spartans had left only slightly guarded. Leonidas knew that he could no longer hold his position. He sent home his allies; but he and his three hundred Spartans remained to die in the pass which their country had given them to defend. They charged joyously upon the Persian spears, and fell fighting, to a man.[1]

Sparta had shown no capacity to command in this great crisis. Twice her shortsightedness had caused the loss of vital positions. But at Thermopylae her citizens had set Greece an example of calm heroism that has stirred the world ever since. In later times the burial place of the Three Hundred was marked by this inscription, "Stranger, go tell at Sparta that we lie here in obedience to her command."

177. Destruction of Athens. — Xerxes advanced on Athens and was joined by most of central Greece. The Theban oligarchs, in particular, welcomed him with genuine joy. The Peloponnesians would risk no further battle outside their own peninsula. They withdrew the army, and fell back upon their first plan of building a wall across the isthmus. *Athens was left open to Persian vengeance.*

The news threw that city into uproar and despair. The Delphic oracle was appealed to, but it prophesied utter destruction. Themistocles (perhaps by bribery) finally secured from the priestess an additional prophecy, that when all else was destroyed, "wooden walls" would still defend the Athenians. Many citizens then wished to retire within the wooden palisade of the Acropolis; but Themistocles, the guiding genius of the stormy day, persuaded them that the oracle meant the "wooden walls" of their ships.

The Greek fleet had withdrawn from Artemisium, after the Persians won the land pass; and the Spartan admiral was bent upon retiring at once to the position of the Peloponnesian army, at the isthmus. By vehement entreaties, Themistocles persuaded him to hold the whole fleet for a day or two at Athens, to help remove the women and children and old men to Salamis and other near-by islands. More than 200,000

---

[1] One Spartan, who had been left for dead by the Persians, afterward recovered and returned home. But his fellow-citizens treated him with pitying contempt ; and at the next great battle, he sought and found death, fighting in the front rank.

people had to be moved from their homes.   There was no time
to save property.   The Persians marched triumphantly through
Attica, burning villages and farmsteads, and laid Athens and
its temples in ashes.

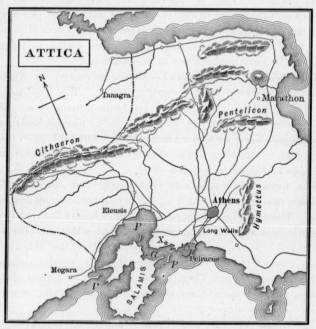

G, the Greek fleet at Salamis. PPP, the Persian fleet. X, the Throne
of Xerxes.   (The " Long Walls " were not built until later; § 200.)

178. Strategy of Themistocles. — But Themistocles, in delay-
ing the retreat of the fleet, planned for more than escape. *He
was determined that the decisive battle should be a sea battle, and
that it should be fought where the fleet then lay.* No other spot
so favorable could be found.   The narrow strait between the
Athenian shore and Salamis would embarrass the Persian numbers, and help to make up for the small numbers of the Greek
ships.   Themistocles saw, too, that if they withdrew to

Corinth, as the Peloponnesians insisted, all chance of united action would be lost. The fleet would break up. Some ships would sail home to defend their own island cities; and others, like those of Megara and Aegina, feeling that their cities were deserted, might join the Persians.

The fleet had grown now to 378 ships. The Athenians furnished 200 of these. With wise and generous patriotism, they had yielded the chief command to Sparta, but of course Themistocles carried weight in the council of captains. It was

THE BAY OF SALAMIS. — From a photograph.

he who, by persuasion, entreaties, and bribes, had kept the navy from abandoning the land forces at Thermopylae, before the sea fight off Artemisium. A similar but greater task now fell to him. Debate waxed fierce in the all-night council of the captains. Arguments were exhausted, and Themistocles had recourse to threats. The Corinthian admiral sneered that the allies need not regard a man who no longer represented a Greek city. The Athenian retorted that he represented two hundred ships, and could make a city, or take one, where he chose; and, by a threat to sail away to found a new Athens in Italy, he forced the allies to remain. Even then the decision would have been reconsidered, had not the wily Themistocles made use of a strange stratagem. With pretended friendship, he sent a secret message to Xerxes, notifying him of the weakness and dissensions of the Greeks, and *advising him to block up the straits to prevent their escape.*

Xerxes took this treacherous advice. Aristides, whose ostracism had been revoked in the hour of danger, and who now slipped through the hostile fleet in his single ship to join his countrymen, brought the news that they were surrounded. *There was now no choice but to fight.*

179. The Battle of Salamis. — The Persian fleet was twice the size of the Greek, and was itself largely made up of Asiatic Greeks, while the Phoenicians and Egyptians, who composed the remainder, were famous sailors. The conflict the next day lasted from dawn to night, but the Greek victory was complete.

> " A king sat on the rocky brow [1]
> Which looks o'er sea-born Salamis;
> And ships by thousands lay below,
> And men in nations, — all were his.
> He counted them at break of day,
> And when the sun set, where were they? "

Aeschylus, an Athenian poet who was present in the battle, gives a noble picture of it in his drama, *The Persians.* The speaker is a Persian, telling the story to the Persian queen-mother: —

> " Not in flight
> The Hellenes then their solemn paeans sang,
> But with brave spirits hastening on to battle.
> With martial sound the trumpet fired those ranks:
> And straight with sweep of oars that flew thro' foam,
> They smote the loud waves at the boatswain's call . . .
> And all at once we heard a mighty shout —
> '*O sons of Hellenes, forward, free your country;*
> *Free, too, your wives, your children, and the shrines*
> *Built to your fathers' Gods, and holy tombs*
> *Your ancestors now rest in.   The fight*
> *Is for our all.'* . . .

---

[1] A golden throne had been set up for Xerxes, that he might better view the battle. These lines are from Byron.

> . . . And the hulls of ships
> Floated capsized, nor could the sea be seen,
> Filled as it was with wrecks and carcasses ;
> And all the shores and rocks were full of corpses,
> And every ship was wildly rowed in flight,
> All that composed the Persian armament.
> And they [Greeks], as men spear tunnies, or a haul
> Of other fishes, with the shafts of oars,
> Or spars of wrecks, went smiting, cleaving down ;
> And bitter groans and wailings overspread
> The wide sea waves, till eye of swarthy night
> Bade it all cease . . . Be assured
> That never yet so great a multitude
> Died in a single day as died in this."

180. Two incidents in the celebration of the victory throw light upon Greek character.

The commanders of the various city contingents in the Greek fleet voted a prize of merit to the city that deserved best in the action. The Athenians had furnished more than half the whole fleet ; they were the first to engage, and they had especially distinguished themselves ; they had seen their city laid in ashes, and only their steady patriotism had made a victory possible. *Peloponnesian jealousy, however, passed them by for their rival, Aegina, which had joined the Spartan league.*

A vote was taken, also, to award prizes to the two most meritorious commanders. Each captain voted for himself for the first place, while *all voted for Themistocles for the second.*

181. The Temptation of Athens. — On the day of Salamis the Sicilian Greeks won a decisive victory over the Carthaginians at *Himera.* For a while, that battle closed the struggle in the West. In Greece the Persian chances were still good. Xerxes, it is true, fled at once to Asia with his shattered fleet; but he left his general, the experienced Mardonius, with three hundred thousand chosen troops. Mardonius withdrew from central Greece for the time, to winter in the plains of Thessaly; but he would be ready to renew the struggle in the spring.

The Athenians began courageously to rebuild their city. Mardonius looked upon them as the soul of the Greek resistance, and in the early spring, *he offered them an alliance,* with many favors and with the complete restoration of their city at

Persian expense. Sparta was terrified lest the Athenians should accept so tempting an offer, and sent in haste, with many promises, to beg them not to desert the cause of Hellas. There was no need of such anxiety. The Athenians had already sent back the Persian messenger: "Tell Mardonius that so long as the sun holds on his way in heaven, the Athenians will come to no terms with Xerxes." They then courteously declined the Spartan offer of aid in rebuilding their city, and *asked only that Sparta take the field early enough so that Athens need not be again abandoned without a battle.*

Sparta made the promise, but did not keep it. Mardonius approached rapidly. The Spartans found another sacred festival before which it would not do to leave their homes; and the Athenians, in bitter disappointment, a second time took refuge at Salamis. *With their city in his hands, Mardonius offered them again the same favorable terms of alliance.* Only one of the Athenian Council favored even submitting the matter to the people, — and he was instantly stoned by the enraged populace, while the women inflicted a like cruel fate upon his wife and children. Even such violence does not obscure the heroic self-sacrifice of the Athenians. Mardonius burned Athens a second time, laid waste the farms over Attica, cut down the olive groves (the slow growth of many years), and then retired to the level plains of Boeotia.

182. Battle of Plataea, 479 B.C. — Athenian envoys had been at Sparta for weeks begging for instant action, but they had been put off with meaningless delays. The fact was, *Sparta still clung to the stupid plan of defending only the isthmus,* — which was all that she had made real preparations for. Some of her keener allies, however, at last made the Ephors see the uselessness of the wall at Corinth if the Athenians should be forced to join Persia with their fleet, as in that case, the Persians could land an army anywhere they chose in the rear of the wall. So Sparta decided to act; and she gave a striking proof of her resources. One morning the Athenian envoys, who had given up hope, announced indig-

nantly to the Spartan government that they would at once
return home. To their amazement, they were told that during
the night 50,000 Peloponnesian troops had set out for central
Greece.

The Athenian forces and other reinforcements raised the total
of the Greek army to about 100,000, and the final contest with
Mardonius was fought near the little town of *Plataea*. Spartan
generalship blundered sadly, and many of the allies were not
brought into the fight; but the stubborn Spartan valor and the
Athenian skill and dash won a victory which became a massacre
It is said that of the 260,000 Persians engaged, only 3000
escaped to Asia. The Greeks lost 154 men.

183. The Meaning of the Greek Victory. — The victory of
Plataea closed the first great period of the Persian Wars. A
second period was to begin at once, but it had to do with freeing
the Asiatic Greeks. That is, *Europe took the offensive. No
hostile Persian ever again set foot in European Greece.*

A Persian victory would have meant the extinction of the
world's best hope. The Persian civilization was Oriental
(§§ 80, 81). Marathon and Salamis decided that the despotism of the East should not crush the rising freedom of
the West in its first home.

To the Greeks themselves their victory opened a new epoch.
They were victors over the greatest of world-empires. It was
a victory of intellect and spirit over matter. Unlimited confidence gave them still greater power. New energies stirred in
their veins and found expression in manifold forms. The
matchless bloom of Greek art and thought, in the next two
generations, had its roots in the soil of Marathon and Plataea.

Moreover, slow as the Greeks had been to see Sparta's poor
management, most of them could no longer shut their eyes
to it. Success had been due mainly to the heroic self-sacrifice and the splendid energy and wise patriotism of Athens.
And that city — truest representative of Greek *culture* — was
soon to take her proper place in the *political* leadership of
Greece.

EXERCISES. — 1. Summarize the causes of the Persian Wars. 2. Devise and memorize a series of *catch-words* for rapid statement, that shall suggest the outline of the story quickly. Thus : —

Persian conquest of Lydia and so of Asiatic Greeks ; revolt of Ionia, 500 B.C. ; Athenian aid ; reconquest of Ionia. *First expedition against European Greece*, 492 B.C., through Thrace : *Mount Athos. Second expedition*, across the Aegean, two years later : capture of Eretria ; landing at Marathon ; excuses of Sparta ; arrival of Plataeans ; *Miltiades and battle of Marathon, 490 B.C.*

(Let the student continue the series. *In this way, the whole story may be reviewed in two minutes*, with reference to every important event.)

FOR FURTHER READING. — *Specially suggested :* Davis' *Readings* gives the whole story of Xerxes' invasion as the Greeks themselves told it, in Vol. I, Nos. 62–73, — about 47 pages. Nowhere else can it be read so well ; and the high school student who does read that account can afford to omit modern authorities. If he reads further, it may well be in one of the volumes mentioned below, mainly to see how the modern authority has used or criticised the account by Herodotus.

Additional : Cox's *Greeks and Persians* is an admirable little book : chs. v–viii may be read for this story. Bury is rather critical ; but the student may profitably explore his pages for parts of the story (pp. 265–295). Many anecdotes are given in Plutarch's *Lives* (" Themistocles " and " Aristides ").

CHAPTER XIII

ATHENIAN LEADERSHIP, 478–431 B.C.

(FROM THE PERSIAN WAR TO THE PELOPONNESIAN WAR)

The history of Athens is for us the history of Greece. — HOLM.

GROWTH OF THE ATHENIAN EMPIRE

184. Athens Fortified. — Immediately after Plataea, the Athenians began once more to rebuild their temples and homes. Themistocles, however, persuaded them to leave even these in ashes and first surround the city with walls. Some Greek cities at once showed themselves basely eager to keep Athens helpless. Corinth, especially, urged Sparta to interfere; and, to her shame, Sparta did call upon the Athenians to give up the plan. Such walls, she said, might prove an advantage to the Persians if they should again occupy Athens. Attica, which had been ravaged so recently by the Persians, was in no condition to resist a Peloponnesian army. So, neglecting all private matters, the Athenians toiled with desperate haste — men, women, children, and slaves. The irregular nature of the walls told the story to later generations. No material was too precious. Inscribed tablets and fragments of sacred temples and even monuments from the burial grounds were seized for the work. To gain the necessary time, Themistocles had recourse to wiles. As Thucydides (§ 224) tells the story : —

" The Athenians, by the advice of Themistocles, replied that they would send an embassy to discuss the matter, and so got rid of the Spartan envoys. Themistocles then proposed that he should himself start at once for Sparta, and that they should give him colleagues who were not to go immediately, but were to wait until the wall had reached a height which could be defended. . . . On his arrival, he did not at once present himself officially to the magistrates, but delayed and made excuses,

191

and when any of them asked him why he did not appear before the Assembly, he said that he was waiting for his colleagues who had been detained. . . . The friendship of the magistrates for Themistocles induced them to believe him, but when everybody who came from Athens declared positively that the wall was building, and had already reached a considerable height, they knew not what to think. Aware of their suspicions, Themistocles asked them not to be misled by reports, but to send to Athens men of their own whom they could trust, to see for themselves.

" The Spartans agreed ; and Themistocles, at the same time, privately instructed the Athenians to detain the Spartan envoys as quietly as possible, and not let them go till he and his colleagues had got safely home. For by this time, those who were joined with him in the embassy had arrived, bringing the news that the wall was of sufficient height, and he was afraid that the Lacedaemonians,[1] when they heard the truth, might not allow him to return. So the Athenians detained the envoys, and Themistocles, coming before the Lacedaemonians, at length declared, in so many words, that Athens was now provided with walls and would protect her citizens : henceforward, if the Lacedaemonians wished at any time to negotiate, they must deal with the Athenians as with men who knew quite well what was best for their own and the common good."

185. The Piraeus. — Themistocles was not yet content. Athens lay some three miles from the shore. Until a few years before, her only port had been an open roadstead, — the Phalerum ; but during his archonship in 493, as part of his plan for naval greatness, Themistocles had given the city a magnificent harbor, by improving the bay of the *Piraeus*, at great expense. Now he persuaded the people to *fortify* this new port. Accordingly, the Piraeus, on the land side, was surrounded with a massive wall of solid masonry, clamped with iron, sixteen feet broad and thirty feet high, so that old men and boys might easily defend it against any enemy. *The Athenians now had two walled cities*, each four or five miles in circuit, and only four miles apart.

186. Commerce and Sea Power. — The alien merchants, who dwelt at the Athenian ports, had fled at the Persian invasion;

---

[1] Lacedaemonia is the name given to the whole Spartan territory. See map after page 98.

but this new security brought them back in throngs, to contribute to the power and wealth of Athens. Themistocles took
care, too, that Athens should not lose her supremacy on the sea.
Even while the walls of the Piraeus were building, he secured
a vote of the Assembly ordering that twenty new ships should
be added *each year* to the fleet.

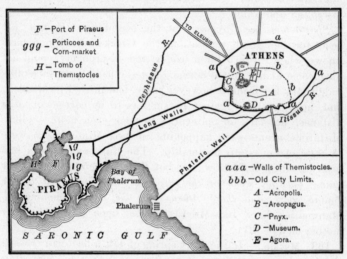

PLAN OF ATHENS AND ITS PORTS.[1]

187. Attempt at One League of All Hellas. — While the Greek army
was still encamped on the field of victory at Plataea, it was agreed to
hold there each year a Congress of all Greek cities. For a little time
back, danger had forced a make-shift union upon the Greeks. The plan
at Plataea was a wise attempt to make this union into a permanent confederacy of all Hellas. *The proposal came from the Athenians*, with
the generous understanding that Sparta should keep the headship. The
plan failed. Indeed, the jealous hostility of Sparta regarding the fortification of Athens showed that a true union would be difficult. *Instead of
one confederacy, Greece fell apart into two rival leagues.*

---

[1] The "Long Walls" were not built until several years after the events
mentioned in this section. See § 200.

188. Sparta and Athens. — Though Sparta had held command in the war, still the repulse of Persia had counted most for the glory of Athens. Athens had made greater sacrifices than any other state. She had shown herself free from petty vanity, and had acted with a broad patriotism. She had furnished the best ideas and ablest leaders; and, even in the field, Athenian enterprise and vigor had accomplished as much as Spartan discipline and valor.

Sparta had been necessary at the beginning. Had it not been for her great reputation, the Greeks would not have known where to turn for a leader, and so, probably, could not have come to any united action. But she had shown miserable judgment; her leaders, however brave, had proved incapable [1]; and, now that war against Persia was to be carried on at a distance, her lack of enterprise became even more evident. Meantime, events were happening in Asia Minor which were to *force* Athens into leadership. The European Greeks had been unwilling to follow any but Spartan generals on sea or land; *but the scene of the war was now transferred to the Ionian coast, and there Athens was the more popular city.* Many cities there, like Miletus, looked upon Athens as their mother city (§ 121).

189. Mycale. — In the early spring of 479, a fleet had crossed the Aegean to assist Samos in revolt against Persia. A Spartan commanded the expedition, but three fifths of the ships were Athenian. On the very day of Plataea (so the Greeks told the story), these forces won a *double* victory at *Mycale*, on the coast of Asia Minor. They defeated a great Persian army, and seized and burned the three hundred Persian ships. *No Persian fleet showed itself again in the Aegean for nearly a hundred years.* Persian garrisons remained in many of the islands, for a time; but Persia made no attempt to reinforce them.

---

[1] Two of her kings were soon to play traitorous parts to Sparta and Hellas. Special report: King Leotychides in Thessaly. See also Pausanias at Byzantium, § 190. *The boasted Spartan training did not fit her men for the duties of the wider life now open to them.*

190. The Ionian Greeks throw off Spartan Leadership. — The victory of Mycale was a signal for the cities of Ionia to revolt again against Persia. The Spartans, however, shrank from the task of defending Hellenes so far away, *and proposed instead to remove the Ionians to European Greece.* The Ionians refused to leave their homes, and the Athenians in the fleet declared that Sparta should not so destroy " Athenian colonies." *The Spartans seized the excuse to sail home,* leaving the Athenians to protect the Ionians as best they could. The Athenians gallantly undertook the task, and began at once to expel the Persian garrisons from the islands of the Aegean.

The next spring (478) Sparta thought better of the matter, and sent *Pausanias* to take command of the allied fleet. Pausanias had been the general of the Greeks at the battle of the Plataea; but that victory had turned his head. He treated the allies with contempt and neglect. At last they found his insolence unbearable, and asked the Athenians to take the leadership. Just then it was discovered that Pausanias had been negotiating treasonably with Persia, offering to betray Hellas. Sparta recalled him, to stand trial,[1] and sent another general to the fleet. The allies, however, refused to receive another Spartan commander. *Then Sparta and the Peloponnesian league withdrew wholly from the war.*

191. The Confederacy of Delos. — After getting rid of Sparta, the first step of the allies was to organize a confederacy. The chief part in this great work fell to *Aristides,* the commander of the Athenian ships in the allied fleet. Aristides proposed a plan of union, and appointed the number of ships and the amount of money that each of the allies should furnish each year. The courtesy and tact of the Athenian, and his known honesty, made all the states content with his proposals, and his arrangements were readily accepted.[2]

The union was called the *Confederacy of Delos,* because its

---

[1] Special report: the story of the punishment of Pausanias.

[2] EXERCISE. — 1. Could Themistocles have served Athens at this time as well as Aristides did ?   2. Report upon the later life of Themistocles.

seat of government and its treasury were to be at the island of Delos (the center of an ancient Ionian amphictyony). Here an annual congress of deputies from the different cities of the league was to meet. Each city had one vote.[1] Athens was the "president" of the league. Her generals commanded the fleet, and her delegates presided at the Congress. In return, Athens bore nearly half the total burdens, in furnishing ships and men, — far more than her proper share.

The purpose of the league was to free the Aegean completely from the Persians, and to keep them from ever coming back. The allies meant to make the union *perpetual*. Lumps of iron were thrown into the sea when the oath of union was taken, as a symbol that it should be binding until the iron should float. *The league was composed mainly of Ionian cities, interested in commerce.* It was a natural rival of Sparta's *Dorian inland league.*

192. The League did its work well. Its chief military hero was the Athenian *Cimon*, son of Miltiades.[2] Year after year, under his command, the allied fleet reduced one Persian garrison after another, until the whole region of the Aegean — all its coasts and islands — was free. Then, in 466, Cimon *carried the war beyond the Aegean* and won his most famous victory at the mouth of the *Eurymedon*, in Pamphylia (map following page 136), where in one day he destroyed a Persian land host and captured a fleet of 250 vessels.

193. Naturally, the League grew in size. It came to include nearly all the islands of the Aegean and the cities of the northern and eastern coasts. The cities on the straits and shores of the Black Sea, too, were added, and the rich trade of that region streamed through the Hellespont to the Piraeus. After the victory of the Eurymedon, many of the cities of the Carian and Lycian coasts joined the confederacy. Indeed, the cities of the league felt that all other Greeks of the Aegean

---

[1] Like our states in Congress under the old Articles of Confederation.

[2] There is an interesting account of Cimon (three pages) in Davis' *Readings*, Vol. I, No. 74, from Plutarch's *Life*.

and of neighboring waters were *under obligation to join*, since they all had part in the blessings of the union. Aristophanes speaks of a " thousand cities " in the league, but only two hundred and eighty are known by name.

194. Some members of the League soon began to shirk. As soon as the pressing danger and the first enthusiam were over, *many cities chose to pay more money, instead of furnishing ships and men.* They became indifferent, too, about the congress, and left the management of all matters to Athens. Athens, on the other hand, was ambitious, and eagerly accepted both burdens and responsibilities. The fleet became almost wholly Athenian. Then it was no longer necessary for Athens to consult the allies as to the management of the war, and the congress became of little consequence.

Another change was still more important. Here and there, cities began to refuse even the payment of money. This, of course, was secession. Such cities said that Persia was no longer dangerous, and that the need of the league was over. But the Athenian fleet, patrolling the Aegean, was all that kept the Persians from reappearing; and Athens, with good reason, held the allies by force to their promises.

The first attempt at secession came in 467, when the union was only ten years old. Naxos, one of the most powerful islands, refused to pay its contributions. Athens at once attacked Naxos, and, after a stern struggle, brought it to submission. *But the conquered state was not allowed to return into the union.* It lost its vote in the congress, and *became a mere subject of Athens.*

195. The "Athenian Empire." — From time to time, other members of the league attempted secession, and met a fate like that of Naxos. Athens took away their fleets, leveled their walls, made them pay a small tribute. Sometimes such a city had to turn over its citadel to an Athenian garrison. Usually a subject city was left to manage its internal government in its own way; but it could no longer have political alliances with other cities.

Just how many such rebellions there were we do not know; but before long the loyal cities found themselves treated much like those that had rebelled. *The confederacy of equal states became an empire, with Athens for its "tyrant city."* The meetings of the congress ceased altogether. The treasury was removed from Delos to Athens, and the funds and resources of the union were used for the glory of Athens.

Athens, however, did continue to perform faithfully the work for which the union had been created; and on the whole, despite the strong tendency to city independence, the subject cities seem to have been well content. Even hostile critics confessed that the bulk of the people looked gratefully to Athens for protection against the oligarchs. Athens was the true mother of Ionian democracy. As an Athenian orator said, *"Athens was the champion of the masses, denying the right of the many to be at the mercy of the few."* In nearly every city of the empire the ruling power became an Assembly like that at Athens.

By 450 B.C. Lesbos, Chios, and Samos were the only states of the league which had not become "subject states"; and even they had no voice in the government of the empire. Athens, however, had other independent allies that had never belonged to the Delian Confederacy — like Plataea, Corcyra, Naupactus, and Acarnania in Greece; Rhegium in Italy; and Segesta and other Ionian cities in Sicily.

FOR FURTHER READING. — *Specially suggested:* The only passage in Davis' *Readings* for this period is Vol. I, No. 74, on Cimon. Bury, 228–242, covers the period. *Instead of* Bury, the student may well read Chapter 1 in Cox's *Athenian Empire.* Plutarch's *Themistocles* and *Aristides* continue to be valuable for *additional* reading.

FIRST PERIOD OF STRIFE WITH SPARTA, 461–445 B.C.

196. Jealousy between Athens and Sparta. — Greece had divided into two great leagues, under the lead of Athens and Sparta. These two powers now quarreled, and their strife made the history of Hellas for many years. The first hostile step came from Sparta. In 465, Thasos, a member of the

Confederacy of Delos, revolted; and Athens was employed for two years in conquering her. During the struggle, Thasos asked Sparta for aid. Sparta and Athens were still nominally in alliance, under the league of Plataea (§ 186); but Sparta grasped at the opportunity and secretly began preparations to invade Attica.

197. Athenian Aid for Sparta. — This treacherous attack was prevented by a terrible earthquake which destroyed part of Sparta and threw the whole state into confusion. The Helots revolted, and Messenia (§ 127) made a desperate attempt to regain her independence. Instead of attacking Athens, Sparta, in dire need, called upon her for aid.

At Athens this request led to a sharp dispute. The democratic party, led by *Ephialtes*[1] and *Pericles*, was opposed to sending help; but *Cimon* (§ 192), leader of the aristocratic party, urged that the true policy was for Sparta and Athens to aid each other in keeping a joint leadership of Hellas. Athens, he said, ought not to let her yoke-fellow be destroyed and Greece be lamed. This generous advice prevailed; and Cimon led an Athenian army to Sparta's aid.

198. An Open Quarrel. — A little later, however, the Spartans began to suspect the Athenians, groundlessly, of the same bad faith of which they knew themselves guilty, and sent back the army with insult. Indignation then ran high at Athens; and the anti-Spartan party was greatly strengthened. Cimon was ostracized (461 B.C.), and the aristocratic faction was left leaderless and helpless for many years.

At almost the same time Ephialtes was murdered by aristocrat conspirators. Thus, leadership fell to Pericles. Under his influence *Athens formally renounced her alliance with Sparta.* Then the two great powers of Greece stood in open opposition, ready for war.

199. A Land Empire for Athens. — Thus far the Athenian empire had been mainly a *sea power*. Pericles planned to

---

[1] This, of course, was not the Ephialtes of Thermopylae.

extend it likewise over inland Greece, and so to supplant Sparta. He easily secured an alliance with Argos, Sparta's sleepless foe. He established Athenian influence also in Thessaly, by treaties with the great chiefs there, and thus secured the aid of the famous Thessalian cavalry. Then Megara, on

PERICLES.
A portrait bust, now in the Vatican at Rome.

the Isthmus of Corinth, sought Athenian alliance, in order to protect itself against Corinth, its powerful neighbor. This involved war with Corinth, but Pericles gladly welcomed Megara because of its ports on the Corinthian Gulf. He then built long walls running the whole width of the narrow isthmus from sea to sea, joining Megara and these ports. In control of these walls, Athens could prevent invasion by land from the Peloponnesus.

200. Activity of Athens. — A rush of startling events followed. Corinth and Aegina, bitterly angry because their old commerce had now been drawn to the Piraeus, declared war on Athens. Athens promptly captured Aegina, and struck Corinth blow after blow even in the Corinthian Gulf. At the same time, without lessening her usual fleet in the Aegean, she sent a mighty armament of 250 ships to carry on the war against Persia, by assisting Egypt in a revolt. Such a fleet called for from 2500 to 5000 soldiers and 50,000 sailors.[1]

---

[1] A Greek warship of this period was called a "three-banker" (*trireme*), because she was rowed by oarsmen arranged on *three benches*, one above

The sailors came largely from the poorer citizens, and even from the non-citizen class.

Pericles turned next to Boeotia, and set up friendly democracies in many of the cities there to lessen the control of oligarchic and hostile Thebes.   The quarrel with Sparta had

SIDE OF PART OF A TRIREME. — From a relief at Athens. In this trireme the highest " bank " of rowers rested their oars on the gunwale. Only the oars of the other two banks are visible.

become open war; and an Athenian fleet burned the Laconian dock-yards. A Spartan army crossed the Corinthian Gulf and

---

another. The wars which the Greeks waged in these three-bankers were hardly more fierce than those that modern scholars have waged — in ink — about them. Some have held that each group of three oarsmen held only one oar. This view is now abandoned — because of the evidence of the " reliefs " on Greek monuments. Plainly each group of three had three separate oars, of different lengths; but we do not know yet how they could have worked them successfully. The oars projected through port-holes, and the 174 oarsmen were protected from arrows by the wooden sides of the vessel. Sometimes — as in the illustration above — the upper bank of rowers had no protection. There were about 20 other sailors to each ship, for helmsman, lookouts, overseers of the oarsmen, and so on. And a warship never carried less than ten fully armed soldiers. The Athenians usually sent from 20 to 25 in each ship.

The ships were about 120 feet long, and less than 20 feet wide. The two masts were always lowered for battle. Two methods of attack were in use. If possible, a ship crushed in the side of an opponent by ramming with its sharp bronze prow. This would sink the enemy's ship at once. Almost as good a thing was to run close along her side (shipping one's own oars on that side just in time), shivering her long oars and hurling her rowers from the benches. This left a ship as helpless as a bird with a broken wing.

appeared in Boeotia, to check Athenian progress there. It won a partial victory at *Tanagra* (map after page 102), — the first real battle between the two states, — but immediately retreated into the Peloponnesus. The Athenians at once reappeared in the field, crushed the Thebans in a great battle at *Oenophyta*, and became masters of all Boeotia. At the same time *Phocis* and *Locris* allied themselves to Athens, so that she seemed in a fair way to extend her land empire over all central Greece, — to which she now held the two gates, Thermopylae and the passes of the isthmus. A little later *Achaea*, in the Peloponnesus itself, was added to the Athenian league.

The activity of Athens at this period is marvelous. It is impossible even to mention the many instances of her matchless energy and splendid daring for the few years after 460, while the empire was at its height. For one instance : just when Athens' hands were fullest in Egypt and in the siege of Aegina, Corinth tried a diversion by invading the territory of Megara. Athens did not recall a man. She armed the youths and the old men past age of service, and repelled the invaders. The Corinthians, stung by shame, made a second, more determined attempt, and were again repulsed with great slaughter. It was at this time, too, that the city completed her fortifications, by building the *Long Walls* from Athens to her ports (maps, pages 184 and 193). These walls were 30 feet high and 12 feet thick. They made Athens absolutely safe from a siege, so long as she kept her supremacy on the sea ; and they added to the city a large open space where the country people might take refuge in case of invasion.

201. Loss of the Land Empire. — How one city could carry on all these activities is almost beyond comprehension. But the resources of Athens were severely strained, and a sudden series of stunning blows well-nigh exhausted her. The expedition to Egypt had at first been brilliantly successful,[1] but unforeseen disaster followed, and the 250 ships and the whole

---

[1] Athenian success here would have shut Persia off completely from the Mediterranean, and so from all possible contact with Europe.

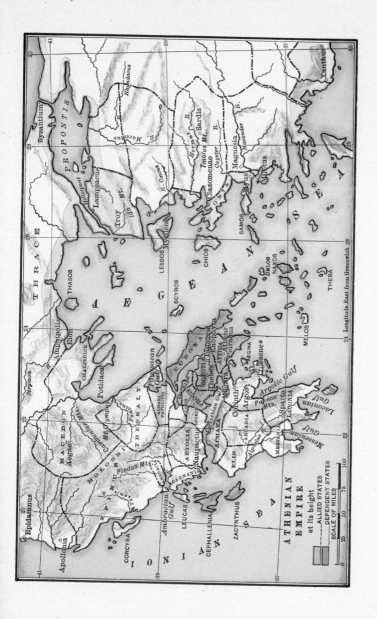

army in Egypt were lost.[1] This stroke would have annihilated any other Greek state, and it was followed by others. Megara, which had itself invited an Athenian garrison, now treacherously massacred it and joined the Peloponnesian league. A Spartan army then entered Attica through Megara; and, at the same moment, Euboea burst into revolt. All Boeotia, too, except Plataea, fell away. The oligarchs won the upper hand in its various cities, and joined themselves to Sparta.

202. The Thirty Years' Truce. — The activity and skill of Pericles saved Attica and Euboea; but the inland possessions and alliances were for the most part lost, and in 445 B.C. a *Thirty Years' Truce* was concluded with Sparta. A little before this, the long war with Persia had closed.

For fifteen years Athens had almost unbroken peace. Then the truce between Sparta and Athens was broken, and the great Peloponnesian War began (§§ 241 ff.). That struggle ruined the power of Athens and the promise of Greece. Therefore, before entering upon its story, we will stop here for a survey of Greek civilization at this period of its highest glory, in Athens, its chief center.

For Further Reading. — *Specially suggested:* Davis' *Readings,* Vol. I, Nos. 73–75 (4 pages); Bury, 352–363. *Additional:* Cox's *Athenian Empire,* and the opening chapters of Grant's *Greece in the Age of Pericles.*

THE EMPIRE AND THE IMPERIAL CITY IN PEACE

203. Three Forms of Greatness. — Athens had *great material power* and a *high political development* and *wonderful intellectual greatness. The last is what she especially stands for in history.* But the first two topics have already been partly discussed, and may be best disposed of here before the most important one is taken up.

A. Military Strength

The Athens of the fifth century was a great state in a higher sense than most of the kingdoms of the Middle Ages. . . . *For the space of a*

---

[1] Special report.

*half century her power was quite on a par with that of Persia, . . . and
the Athenian Empire is the true precursor of those of Macedonia and
Rome.* — HOLM, II, 259.

204. Material Power. — The last real chance for a united
Hellas passed away when Athens lost control of central Greece.
But at the moment the loss of land empire did not seem to
lessen Athens' strength. She had saved her sea empire, and
consolidated it more firmly than ever. *And, for a generation more, the Greeks of that empire were the leaders of the world
in power, as in culture.* They had proved themselves more than
a match for Persia. The mere magic of the Athenian name
sufficed to keep Carthage from renewing her attack upon the
Sicilian Greeks. The Athenian colonies in Thrace easily held
in check the rising Macedonian kingdom. Rome, which three
centuries later was to absorb Hellas into her world-empire, was
still a barbarous village on the Tiber bank. In the middle of
the fifth century B.C. *the center of power in the world was imperial Athens.*

205. Population. — The cities of the empire counted some
three millions of people. The number seems small to us ; but
it must be kept in mind that *the population of the world was
much smaller then than now,* and that the Athenian empire was
made up of cultured, wealthy, progressive communities.

To be sure, slaves made a large fraction of this population.
Attica itself contained about one tenth of the inhabitants of the
whole empire, perhaps 300,000 people (about as many as live
in Minneapolis). Of these, one fourth were slaves, and a
sixth were aliens. This left some 175,000 citizens, of whom
perhaps 35,000 were men fit for soldiers. Outside Attica,
there were 75,000 more citizens, — the *cleruchs* (§ 148), whom
Pericles had sent to garrison outlying parts of the empire.

206. Colonies. — The cleruchs, unlike other Greek colonists,
kept all the rights of citizenship. They had their own local
Assemblies, to manage the affairs of each colony. But they kept
also their enrollment in the Attic demes and could vote upon
the affairs of Athens and of the empire — *though not unless*

they came to Athens in person. They were mostly from the poorer classes, and were induced to go out to the new settlements by the gift of lands sufficient to raise them at least to the class of hoplites (§ 137). Rome copied this plan a century later. Otherwise, *the world was not to see again so liberal a form of colonization until the United States of America began to organize " Territories."*

207. Revenue. — The empire was rich, and the revenues of the government were large, for those days. Athens drew a yearly income of about four hundred talents ($400,000 in our values) from her Thracian mines and from the port dues and the taxes on alien merchants. The tribute from the subject cities amounted to $600,000. This tribute was fairly assessed, and it bore lightly upon the prosperous Greek communities. *The Asiatic Greeks paid only one sixth as much as they had formerly paid Persia;* and the tax was much less than it would have cost the cities merely to defend themselves against pirates, had Athenian protection been removed.

Indeed, the whole amount drawn from the subject cities would not keep one hundred ships manned and equipped for a year, to say nothing of building them. When we remember the standing navy in the Aegean and the great armaments that Athens sent repeatedly against Persia, it is plain that she continued to bear her full share of the imperial burden. She kept her empire because she did not rob her dependencies — as most empires had done, and were to do for two thousand years longer.

B. Government

208. Steps in Development. — Seventy years had passed between the reforms of Clisthenes and the truce with Sparta. The main steps of progress in government were five.

The office of *General* had grown greatly in importance.

The *Assembly* had extended its authority to all matters of government, in practice as well as in theory.

Jury courts (§ 211, below) had gained importance.

The poorest citizens (§ 152) had been made eligible to office.

The state had begun to pay its citizens for public services.

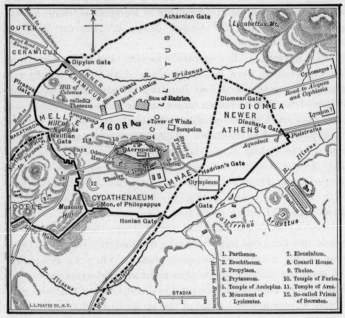

MAP OF ATHENS, with some structures of the Roman period.—The term "Stoa," which appears so often in this map, means "porch" or portico. These porticoes were inclosed by columns, and their fronts along the Agora formed a succession of colonnades. Only a few of the famous buildings can be shown in a map like this. The "Agora" was the great public square, or open market place, surrounded by shops and porticoes. It was the busiest spot in Athens, the center of the commercial and social life of the city, where men met their friends for business or for pleasure.

The constitution was not made over new at any one moment within this period, as it had been earlier, at the time of Solon and of Clisthenes. Indeed, the change was more in the *spirit of the people* than in the written law. The first three steps mentioned (the increased power of the Generals and of the Assembly and jury courts) came altogether from a gradual change *in practice.* The other two steps had been brought about by piecemeal *legislation.* The guiding spirit in most of this development was *Pericles.*

209. "**Generals**" and "**Leaders of the People.**" — When Themistocles put through important measures, like the improvement of the Piraeus (§ 185), he held the office of Archon; but when Cimon or Pericles guided the policy of Athens, they held the office of General. *The Generals had become the administrators of the government.* It was usually they who *proposed* to the Assembly the levy of troops, the building of ships, the raising of money, the making of peace or war. Then, when the Assembly decided to do any of these things, the Generals *saw to the execution of them. They were subject absolutely to the control of the Assembly, but they had great opportunities to influence it :* they could call special meetings at will, and they had the right to speak whenever they wished.

But any man had full right to try to persuade the Assembly, whether he held office or not ; and the more prominent speakers and leaders were known as "leaders of the people" (demagogues). Even though he held no office, a "leader of the people," trusted by the popular party, exercised a greater authority than any General could *without* that trust. To make things work smoothly, therefore, it was desirable that the Board of Generals should contain the "leader of the people" for the time being. Pericles was recognized "demagogue" for many years, and was usually elected each year president of the Board of Generals.

210. The Assembly [1] met on the Pnyx,[2] a sloping hill whose side formed a kind of natural theater. There were forty regular meetings each year, and many special meetings. Thus a patriotic citizen was called upon to give at least one day a week to the state in this matter of political meetings alone.

---

[1] On the Assembly, there is an admirable treatment in Grant's *Age of Pericles*, 141–149.   [2] See plan of Athens, page 206.

The Assembly had become thoroughly democratic and had made great gains in power since Clisthenes' time. All public officials had become its obedient servants. The Council of Five Hundred (§ 152) existed not to guide it, but to do its bidding. The Generals were its creatures, and *might be deposed by it any day.* No act of government was too small or too great for it to deal with. *The Assembly of Athens was to the greatest empire of the world in that day all, and more than all, that a New England town meeting ever was to its little town.* It was as if the citizens of Boston or Chicago were to meet day by day to govern the United States, and, at the same time, to attend to all their own local affairs.

211. "Juries" of citizens were introduced by Solon, and their importance became fully developed under Pericles. Six thousand citizens were chosen by lot each year for this duty, from those who offered themselves for the service — mostly the older men past the age for active work. One thousand of these were held in reserve. The others were divided into *ten jury courts* of five hundred men each.

The Assembly turned over the trial of officials to the juries. With a view to this duty, each juror took an oath " above all things to favor neither tyranny nor oligarchy, nor in any way to prejudice [injure] the sovereignty of the people." The juries also settled all disputes between separate cities of the empire; they were courts of appeal for important cases between citizens in a subject city; and they were the ordinary law courts for Athenians. An Athenian jury was " both judge and jury ": it decided each case by a majority vote, *and there was no appeal from its verdict.*

Thus these large bodies had not even the check that our small juries have in trained judges to guide them. No doubt they gave many wrong verdicts. Passion and pity and bribery all interfered, at times, with even-handed justice ; *but, on the whole, the system worked astonishingly well.* In particular, any citizen of a subject city was sure to get redress from these courts, if he had been wronged by an Athenian officer. And rich criminals found it quite as hard to bribe a majority of 500 jurors as such offenders find it among us to " influence " some judge to shield them with legal technicalities.

212. State Pay. — Since these courts had so great weight, and since they tried political offenders, it was essential that they should not fall wholly into the hands of the rich. To prevent this, Pericles introduced a small payment for jury duty. The amount, three obols a day (about nine cents), would furnish a day's food for one person in Athens, but it would not support a family.

Afterward, Pericles extended public payment to other political services. Aristotle (a Greek writer a century or so later) says that some 20,000 men — over half the whole body of citizens — were constantly in the pay of the state. Half of this number were soldiers, in garrisons or in the field. But, besides the 6000 jurymen, there were the 500 Councilmen, 700 city officials,[1] 700 more officials representing Athens throughout the empire, and many inferior state servants; *so that always from a third to a fourth of the citizens were in the civil service.*[2]

Pericles has been accused sometimes of " corrupting " the Athenians by the introduction of payment. But there is no proof that the Athenians were corrupted; and, further, such a system was inevitable when the democracy of a little city became the master of an empire. It was quite as natural and proper as is the payment of congressmen and judges with us.

213. Athenian Political Ability. — Many of the offices in Athens could be held only once by the same man, *so that each Athenian citizen could count upon serving his city at some time in almost every office.* Politics was his occupation; office-holding, his regular business.

Such a system could not have worked without a high *average* of intelligence in the people. It *did* work well. With all its faults, the rule of Athens in Greece was vastly superior to the rude despotism that followed under

---

[1] Overseers of weights and measures, harbor inspectors, and so on.

[2] *Civil* service is a term used in contrast to *military* service. Our postmasters are among the civil servants of the United States, as a city engineer or a fireman is in the city civil service.

Sparta, or the anarchy under Thebes (§§ 253, 267). It gave to a large part of the Hellenic world a peace and security never enjoyed before, or after, until the rise of Roman power. Athens itself, moreover, was governed better and more gently than oligarchic cities like Corinth.

"The Athenian democracy made a greater number of citizens fit to use power than could be made fit by any other system. . . . The Assembly was an assembly of citizens — of average citizens without sifting or selection; but it was an assembly of citizens *among whom the political average stood higher than it ever did in any other state.* . . . The Athenian, by constantly hearing questions of foreign policy and domestic administration argued by the greatest orators the world ever saw, received a political training which nothing else in the history of mankind has been found to equal." [1]

214. The Final Verdict upon the Empire. — It is easy to see that the Athenian system was imperfect, tried by our standard of government; but it is more to the point to see that it was an advance over anything ever before attempted.

It is to be regretted that Athens did not continue to admit aliens to citizenship, as in Clisthenes' day. It is to be regretted that she did not extend to the men of her subject cities that sort of citizenship which she did leave to her cleruchs. But the important thing is, that she had moved farther than had any other state up to this time. The admission of aliens by Clisthenes and the cleruch citizenship (§ 206) were notable advances. *The broadest policy of an age ought not to be condemned as narrow.*

215. Parties: A Summary. — A few words will review party history up to the leadership of Pericles. All factions in Athens had united patriotically against Persia, and afterward in fortifying the city; but the brief era of good feeling was followed by a renewal of party strife. The Aristocrats rallied around Cimon, while the two wings of the democrats were led at first, as before the invasion, by Aristides and Themistocles.

---

[1] Freeman's *Federal Government.* Read a spicy paragraph in Wheeler's *Alexander the Great,* 116, 117.

Themistocles was ostracized, and his friend Ephialtes became the leader of the extreme democrats. When Ephialtes was assassinated (§ 196), Pericles stepped into his place.

216. Pericles. — The aristocratic party had been ruined by its pro-Spartan policy (§§ 197, 198). The two divisions of the democrats reunited, and for a quarter of a century Pericles was in practice as absolute as a dictator. Thucydides calls Athens during this period " a democracy in name, ruled in reality by its ablest citizen."

Pericles belonged to the ancient nobility of Athens, but to families that had always taken the side of the people. His mother was the niece of Clisthenes the reformer, and his father had impeached Miltiades (§ 169), so that the enmity between Cimon and Pericles was hereditary. The supremacy of Pericles rested in no way upon the flattering arts of later popular leaders. His proud reserve verged on haughtiness, and he was rarely seen in public. He scorned to show emotion. His stately gravity and unruffled calm were styled Olympian by his admirers — who added that, like Zeus, he could on occasion overbear opposition by the majestic thunder of his oratory.

The great authority of Pericles came from no public office. He was elected General, it is true, fifteen times, and in the board of ten generals, he had far more weight than any other had; but this was because of his *unofficial* position as " leader of the people " (§ 209). General or not, he was *master* only so long as he could carry the Assembly with him ; and he was compelled to defend each of his measures against all who chose to attack it. The long and steady confidence given him honors the people of Athens no less than it honors Pericles himself. His noblest praise is that which he claimed for himself upon his deathbed, — that, with all his authority, and despite the bitterness of party strife, " no Athenian has had to put on mourning because of me."

Pericles stated his own policy clearly. As to the empire, he sought to make Athens at once the *ruler* and the *teacher* of

Hellas, — the political and intellectual center. Within the city itself, he wished *the people to rule*, not merely in theory, but in fact, as the best means of training them for high responsibilities.

C. INTELLECTUAL AND ARTISTIC ATHENS

217. The True Significance of Athens. — After all, in politics and war, Hellas has had superiors. Her true service to mankind and her imperishable glory lie in her literature, her philosophy, and her art. *It was in the Athens of Pericles that these forms of Greek life developed most fully*, and this fact makes the real meaning of that city in history.

218. Architecture and Sculpture. — Part of the policy of Pericles was to adorn Athens from the surplus revenues of the empire. The injustice of this is plain; but the result was to make the city the most beautiful in the world, so that, ever since, her mere ruins have enthralled the admiration of men. Greek art was just reaching its perfection; and everywhere in Athens, under the charge of the greatest artists of this greatest artistic age, arose temples, colonnades, porticoes, — inimitable to this day.

" No description can give anything but a very inadequate idea of the splendor, the strength, the beauty, which met the eye of the Athenian, whether he walked round the fortifications, or through the broad streets of the Piraeus, or along the Long Walls, or in the shades of the Academy, or amidst the tombs of the Ceramicus ; whether he chaffered in the market place, or attended assemblies in the Pnyx, or loitered in one of the numerous porticoes, or watched the exercises in the Gymnasia, or listened to music in the Odeum or plays in the theaters, or joined the throng of worshipers ascending to the great gateway of the Acropolis. And this magnificence was not the result of centuries of toil; *it was the work of fifty years.* . . . Athens became a vast workshop, in which artisans of every kind found employment, all, in their various degrees, contributing to the execution of the plans of the master minds, Phidias, Ictinus, Callicrates, Mnesicles, and others." — ABBOTT, *Pericles*, 303–308.

The center of this architectural splendor was the ancient citadel of the Acropolis. That massive rock now became the

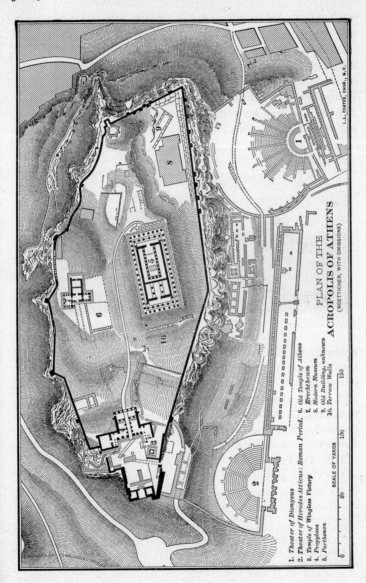

L.L. POATES, ENGR., N.Y.

PLAN OF THE
ACROPOLIS OF ATHENS
(BOETTICHER, WITH OMISSIONS)

1. Theater of Dionysus
2. Theater of Herodes Atticus: Roman Period.
3. Temple of Wingless Victory
4. Propylaea
5. Parthenon

6. Old Temple of Athens
7. Erechtheum
8. Modern Museum
9. Old Building, unknown
10. Terrace Walls

SCALE OF YARDS

0   50   100   150

"holy hill." No longer needed as a fortification, it was crowned with white marble, and devoted to religion and art. It was inaccessible except on the west. Here was built a stately stairway of sixty marble steps, leading to a series of noble colonnades and porticoes (*the Propylaea*) of surpassing beauty. From these the visitor emerged upon the leveled top of the Acropolis, to find himself surrounded by temples and statues, any one of which alone might make the fame of the proudest

THE ACROPOLIS TO-DAY.

modern city. Just in front of the entrance stood the colossal bronze statue of *Athene the Champion*, whose broad spear point, glittering in the sun, was the first sign of the city to the mariner far out at sea. On the right of the entrance, and a little to the rear, was the temple of the *Wingless Victory*[1]; and near the center of the open space rose the larger structures of the *Erechtheum*[2] and the *Parthenon*.

219. The Parthenon ("maiden's chamber") was the temple of the virgin goddess Athene. It remains absolutely peerless in its loveliness among the buildings of the world. It was in the Doric style,[3] and of no great size, — only some 100 feet by

[1] See the illustration on page 163.

[2] A temple to Erechtheus, an ancestral god of Attica. See page 216.

[3] See § 154 for explanation of this and other terms used in this description. See also pages 160, 162, 216, 225, for illustrations of the Parthenon.

250, while the marble pillars supporting its low pediment rose only 34 feet from their base of three receding steps. The effect was due, not to the sublimity and grandeur of vast masses, but to the perfection of proportion, to exquisite beauty of line, and to the delicacy and profusion of ornament. On this structure, indeed, was lavished without stint the highest art of the

PROPYLAEA OF THE ACROPOLIS TO-DAY.

art capital of all time. The fifty life-size and colossal statues in the pediments, and the four thousand square feet of smaller reliefs in the frieze were all finished with perfect skill, even in the unseen parts. The frieze represents an Athenian procession, carrying offerings to the patron goddess Athene at the greatest religious festival of Athens. Nearly 500 different figures were carved upon this frieze.[1] As with all Greek tem-

[1] These reliefs are now for the most part in the British Museum and are often referred to as the *Elgin Marbles*, from the fact that Lord Elgin secured them, shortly after 1800, for the English government. The student can judge of the original position of part of the sculpture on the building from the illustration of the Parthenon on page 225. The frieze within the colonnade

ples, the bands of stone above the columns were painted in brilliant reds and blues; and the faces of the sculptures were tinted in lifelike hues.

In Christian times the Parthenon became a church of the B. V. Mary. The Turks changed it into a mosque. During a siege they kept large stores of powder in it. In 1687 an enemy's cannon ball exploded the magazine, blowing the temple into ruins, much as we see them to-day.

ERECHTHEUM (foreground) AND PARTHENON. This view gives the contrast between the delicacy of the Ionic style and the simple dignity of the Doric. Cf. § 154.

220. Phidias. — The ornamentation of the Parthenon, within and without, was cared for by *Phidias* and his pupils. Phidias still ranks as the greatest of sculptors.[1] Much of the work on the Acropolis he merely planned, but the great statues of

---

(§ 154) cannot be shown in this picture. It was a band of relief, about four feet in width, running entirely around the temple.

[1] Phidias has been rivaled, if at all, only by his pupil, *Praxiteles*. The *Hermes* of Praxiteles is one of the few great works of antiquity that survive to us. See page 258.

Athene were his special work. The bronze statue has already
been mentioned. Besides this, there was, *within the temple*,
an even more glorious statue in gold and ivory, smaller than
the other, but still five or six times larger than life.[1] Professor Mahaffy has said of all this Parthenon sculpture: —

> " The beauty and perfection of all the invisible parts are such that the
> cost of labor and money must have been enormous. There is no *show*

FIGURES FROM THE PARTHENON FRIEZE.

> whatever for much of this extraordinary finish, which can only be seen
> by going on the roof or by opening a wall. Yet the religiousness of the
> unseen work [2] has secured that what *is* seen shall be perfect with no
> ordinary perfection."

---

[1] These two works divide the honor of Phidias' great fame with his *Zeus*
at Olympia, which, in the opinion of the ancients, surpassed all other sculpture
in grandeur. Phidias said that he planned the latter work, thinking of
Homer's *Zeus*, at the nod of whose ambrosial locks Olympus trembled.

[2] Compare Longfellow's lines, —

> " In the older days of art,
> Builders wrought, with utmost care,
> Each obscure and unseen part, —
> For the gods see everywhere."

221. The Drama. — In the age of Pericles, the chief form of poetry became the *tragic drama* — the highest development of

SOPHOCLES — a portrait-statue, now in the Lateran Museum at Rome.

Greek literature. As the tenth century was the epic age, and the seventh and sixth the lyric (§ 155), so the fifth century begins the dramatic period.

The drama *began* in the songs and dances of a chorus in honor of Dionysus, god of wine, at the spring festival of flowers and at the autumn vintage festival. The *leader* of the chorus came at length to recite stories, between the songs. Thespis (§ 146) at Athens, in the age of Pisistratus, had developed this leader into an *actor*, — *apart from the chorus and carrying on dialogue with it.* Now *Aeschylus* added another actor, and his younger rival, *Sophocles*, a third.[1] Aeschylus, Sophocles, and their successor, *Euripides*, are the three greatest Greek dramatists. Together they pro-

---

[1] The Greek tragedy never permitted more than three actors upon the stage at one time. The Greek drama cannot be compared easily with the

duced some two hundred plays, of which thirty-one survive. Their plays were all *tragedies*.

Comedy also grew out of the worship of the wine god, — not from the great religious festivals, however, but from the rude village merrymakings. Even upon the stage, comedy kept traces of this rude origin in occasional coarseness; and it was

THEATER OF DIONYSUS — present condition.

sometimes misused, to abuse men like Pericles and Socrates. Still, its great master, *Aristophanes*, for his wit and genius, must always remain one of the bright names in literature.

222. The Theater. — Every Greek city had its "theaters." A theater was a semicircular arrangement of rising seats, often cut into a hillside, with a small stage at the open side of the circle for the actors. There was no inclosed building, except sometimes a few rooms for the actors, and there was

modern. Sophocles and Shakespeare differ somewhat as the Parthenon differs from a vast cathedral. In a Greek play the scene never changed, and all the action had to be such as could have taken place in one day. That is, the "unities" of time and place were strictly preserved, while the small number of actors made it easy to maintain also a "unity of action."

none of the gorgeous stage scenery which has become a chief feature of our theaters. Neither did the Greek theater run every night. Performances took place at only two periods in the year — at the spring and autumn festivals to Dionysus — for about a week each season; and the performance of course had to be in the daytime.

The great *Theater of Dionysus,* in Athens, was on the southeast slope of the Acropolis — the rising seats, cut in a semicircle into the rocky bluff, looking forth, beyond the stage, to the hills of southern Attica and over the blue waters of the Aegean. It could seat almost the whole free male population.[1]

Pericles secured from the public treasury the admission fee to the Theater for each citizen who chose to ask for it. This use of "theater money" was altogether different from the payment of officers and jurors. It must be kept in mind that the Greek stage was the modern pulpit and press in one. The practice of free admission was designed to advance religious and intellectual training, rather than to give amusement. *It was a kind of public education for grown-up people.*

223. Oratory was highly developed. Among no other people has public speaking been so important and so effective. Its special home was Athens. For almost two hundred years, from Themistocles to Demosthenes (§ 272), great statesmen swayed the Athenian state by the power of sonorous and thrilling eloquence; and the emotional citizens, day after day, packed the Pnyx to hang breathless for hours upon the persuasive lips of their leaders. The art of public speech was studied zealously by all who hoped to take part in public affairs.

Unhappily, Pericles did not preserve his orations. The one quoted below (§ 229) seems to have been recast by Thucydides in his own style. But fortunately we *do* still have many of the orations of Demosthenes, of the next century; and from them we can understand how the union of fiery passion, and

---

[1] The stone seats were not carved out of the hill until somewhat later. During the age of Pericles, the men of Athens sat on the ground, or on stools which they brought with them, all over the hillside.

convincing logic, and polished beauty of language, made oratory rank with the drama and with art as the great means of public education for Athenians.

224. History. — *Prose* literature now appears, with history as its leading form. The three great historians of the period are

Herodotus, Thucydides, and *Xenophon.* For charm in story-telling they have never been excelled. Herodotus was a native of Halicarnassus (a city of Asia Minor). He traveled widely, lived long at Athens as the friend of Pericles, and finally in Italy composed his great *History of the Persian Wars,* with an introduction covering the world's history up to that event. Thucydides, an Athenian general, wrote the history of the Peloponnesian War (§§ 241 ff.) in which he took part. Xenophon belongs rather to the next century. He also was an

THUCYDIDES.

A portrait bust; now in the Capitoline Museum at Rome.

Athenian. He completed the story of the Peloponnesian War, and gave us, with other works, the *Anabasis,* an account of the expedition of the Ten Thousand Greeks through the Persian empire in 401 B.C. (§ 257).

225. Philosophy.[1] — The age of Pericles saw also a rapid development in philosophy, — and this movement, too, had Athens for its most important home. *Anaxagoras* of Ionia,

---

[1] This section can best be read in class, and talked over. It may well be preceded by a reading of § 156 upon the *earlier* Greek philosophy.

the friend of Pericles, taught that the ruling principle in the universe was Mind: "In the beginning all things were chaos; then came Intelligence, and set all in order.'" He also tried to explain comets and other strange natural phenomena, which had been looked upon as miraculous.

But, like *Democritus* and *Empedocles* of the same period, Anaxagoras turned in the main from the old question of a fundamental principle to a new problem. The philosophers of the sixth century had tried to answer the question, — How did the universe come to be? The philosophers of the age of Pericles asked mainly, — How does man *know* about the universe? That is, *they tried to explain the working of the human mind.* These early attempts at explanation were not very satisfactory, and so next came the *Sophists,* with a skeptical philosophy. Man, the Sophists held, cannot reach truth itself, but must be content to know only *appearances.* They taught rhetoric, and were the first of the philosophers to accept pay.[1]

Socrates, the founder of a new philosophy, is sometimes confounded with the Sophists. Like them, he abandoned the attempt to understand the material universe, and ridiculed gently the attempted explanations of his friend, Anaxagoras. He took for his motto, "*Know thyself,*" and considered philosophy to consist in *right thinking upon human conduct.* True wisdom, he taught, is *to know* what is good *and to do* what is right; and he tried to make his followers see the difference between justice and injustice, temperance and intemperance, virtue and vice.

Thus Socrates completes the circle of ancient philosophy. The whole development may be summed up briefly, as follows : —

1. Thales and his followers (§ 156) tried to find out how the world came to be — out of what "first principle" it arose (water, fire, etc.).

---

[1] Thus these philosophers were accused of advertising for gain, to teach youth "how to make the worse appear the better reason," and the name "sophist" received an evil significance. Many of the Sophists, however, were brilliant thinkers, who did much to clear away old mental rubbish. The most famous were *Gorgias,* the rhetorician, a Sicilian Greek at Athens, and his pupil, *Isocrates.*

2. Anaxagoras and his contemporaries tried to find out how man's mind could understand the outside world. (His teaching that *mind* was the real principle of the universe formed a natural step from 1 to 2.)

3. The Sophists declared all search for such explanations a failure — beyond the power of the human mind.

4. Socrates sought to know, not about the outside world at all, but about himself and his duties.

226. The Man Socrates. — Socrates was a poor man, an artisan who carved little images of the gods for a living; and he constantly vexed his wife, Xanthippe, by neglecting his trade, to talk in the market place. He wore no sandals, and dressed meanly. His large bald head and ugly face, with its thick lips and flat nose, made him good sport for the comic poets. His practice was to entrap unwary antagonists into public conversation by asking innocent-looking questions, and then, by the inconsistencies of their answers, to show how shallow their opinions were. This proceeding afforded huge merriment to the crowd of youths who followed the bare-footed philosopher, and it made him bitter enemies among his victims. But his method of argument (which we still call "the Socratic method") was a permanent addition to our intellectual weapons; and his beauty of soul, his devotion to knowledge, and his largeness of spirit make him the greatest name in Greek history. When seventy years old (399 B.C.) he was accused of impiety and of corrupting the youth. He refused to defend himself in any ordinary way, and was therefore declared guilty. His accusers then proposed a death penalty. It was the privilege of the condemned man to propose any other penalty, and let the jury choose between the two. Instead of proposing a considerable fine, as his friends wished, Socrates said first that he really ought to propose that he be maintained in honor at the public expense, but, in deference to his friends' entreaties, he finally proposed a small fine. The angered jury, by a close vote, pronounced the death penalty.

227. Socrates on Obedience to Law and on Immortality. — Socrates refused also to escape before the day for his execution.

Friends had made arrangements for his escape, but he answered their earnest entreaties by a playful discourse, of which the substance was, — " Death is no evil ; but for Socrates to 'play truant,' and injure the laws of his country, would be an evil." After memorable conversations upon immortality, he drank the fatal hemlock with a gentle jest upon his lips.[1]   His execution is the greatest blot upon the intelligence of the Athenian democracy.

It happened that the trial had taken place just before the annual sailing of a sacred ship to Delos to a festival of Apollo. According to Athenian law, no execution could take place until the return of this vessel. Thus for thirty days, Socrates remained in jail, conversing daily in his usual manner with groups of friends who visited him. Two of his disciples (Plato and Xenophon) have given us accounts of these talks. On the last day, the theme was immortality. Some of the friends fear that death may be an endless sleep, or that the soul, on leaving the body, may " issue forth like smoke . . . and vanish into nothingness."   But Socrates comforts and consoles them, — convincing them, by a long day's argument, that the soul is immortal, and picturing the lofty delight he anticipates in applying his Socratic questionings to the heroes and sages of olden times, when he meets them soon in the abode of the blest.   Then, just as the fatal hour arrives, one of the company (Crito) asks, " In what way would you have us bury you ? " Socrates rejoins : —

" ' In any way you like : only you must first get hold of me, and take care that I do not walk away from you.'   Then he turned to us, and added, with a smile : ' I cannot make Crito believe that *I* am the same Socrates who has been talking with you. He fancies that I am another Socrates whom he will soon see a dead body — and he asks, How shall he bury me? I have spoken many words to show that *I* shall leave you and go to the joys of the blessed ; but these words, with which I comforted you, have had, I see, no effect upon Crito. And so I want you to be

---

[1] Special report: the trial and death of Socrates. See Plato's *Apology*, Xenophon's *Memorabilia*, and other accounts.

surety for me now, as Crito was surety [bail] for me at my trial, — but
with another sort of promise. For he promised the judges that I would
remain ; but you must be my surety to him that I shall *not* remain. Then
he will not be grieved when he sees merely my *body* burned or buried. I
would not have him sorrow at my lot, or say, Thus we follow Socrates to
the grave ; for false words such as these infect the soul. Be of good
cheer, then, my dear Crito, and say that you are burying my body only —
and do with that what is usual, or as you think best.' " [1]

228. Summary. — **The amazing extent and intensity of Athenian
culture** overpower the imagination. With few exceptions, the

THE ACROPOLIS, as " restored " by Lambert.

famous men mentioned in §§ 220–225 were Athenian citizens.
In the fifth century B.C. *that one city gave birth to more great
men of the first rank*, it has been said, *than the whole world has
ever produced in any other equal period of time.*

Artists, philosophers, and writers swarmed to Athens, also,
from less-favored parts of Hellas; for, despite the condemnation
of Socrates, no other city in the world afforded such freedom
of thought, and nowhere else was ability, in art or literature,

---

[1] Anecdotes of Socrates are given in Davis' *Readings*, Vol. I, Nos. 89–92.

so appreciated. The names that have been mentioned give but a faint impression of the splendid throngs of brilliant poets, artists, philosophers, and orators, who jostled each other in the streets of Athens. This, after all, is the best justification of the Athenian democracy. Abbott (*History of Greece*, II, 415), one of its sternest modern critics, is forced to exclaim, " Never before or since has life developed so richly as it developed in the beautiful city which lay at the feet of the virgin goddess." [1]

229. The Tribute of Pericles to Athens. — The finest glorification of the Athenian spirit is contained in the great funeral oration delivered by Pericles over the Athenian dead, at the close of the second year of the Peloponnesian War. Thucydides gives the speech and represents no doubt the ideas, if not the words, of the orator : —

" And we have not forgotten to provide for our weary spirits many relaxations from toil. We have our regular games and sacrifices throughout the year ; at home the style of our life is refined, and the delight which we daily feel in all these things helps to banish melancholy. Because of the greatness of our city, the fruits of the whole earth flow in upon us ; so that we enjoy the goods of other countries as freely as of our own. . . .

" And in the matter of education, whereas our adversaries from early youth are always undergoing laborious exercises which are to make them brave, we live at ease, and yet are equally ready to face the perils which they face. . . . If then we prefer to meet danger with a light heart but without laborious training, and with a courage which is gained by habit and not enforced by law, are we not greatly the gainers ?

" *We are lovers of the beautiful, yet simple in our tastes ; and we cultivate the mind without loss of manliness.* Wealth we employ, not for talk and ostentation, but when there is a real use for it. To avow poverty with us is no disgrace ; the true disgrace is in doing nothing to avoid it. An Athenian citizen does not neglect the state because he takes care of his own household ; and even those of us who are engaged in business have a very fair idea of politics. We alone regard a man who takes no interest in public affairs, not as a harmless, but as a useless character. . . .

---

[1] The patron deity of Athens was Pallas Athene, the virgin goddess, whose temple, the Parthenon, crowned the Acropolis.

"In the hour of trial Athens alone is superior to the report of her. No enemy who comes against her is indignant at the reverses which he sustains at the hands of such a city; no subject complains that his masters are unworthy of him. And we shall assuredly not be without witnesses. There are mighty monuments of our power which will make us the wonder of this and of succeeding ages. . . . For we have compelled every land and every sea to open a path for our valor, and have everywhere planted eternal memorials of our friendship and of our enmity. . . .

"To sum up: I say that *Athens is the school of Hellas*, and that the individual Athenian in his own person seems to have the power of adapting himself to the most varied forms of action with the utmost versatility and grace. . . .

"*I would have you day by day fix your eyes upon the greatness of Athens, until you become filled with the love of her;* and when you are impressed by the spectacle of her glory, reflect that this empire has been acquired by men who knew their duty and had the courage to do it, and who in the hour of conflict had the fear of dishonor always present to them. . . .*"

230. Three limitations in Greek culture must be noted.

a. It rested necessarily on slavery, and consequently could not honor labor, as modern culture at least tries to do. The main business of the citizen was government and war. Trades and commerce were left largely to the free non-citizen class, and unskilled hand labor was performed mainly by slaves. As a rule, it is true, this slavery was not harsh. In Athens, ordinarily, the slaves were hardly to be distinguished from the poorer citizens. They were frequently Greeks, of the same speech and culture as their masters. In some ways, this made their lot all the harder to bear; and there was always the *possibility* of cruelty. In the mines, even in Attica, the slaves were killed off brutally by merciless hardships.

b. Greek culture was for males only. It is not probable that the wife of Phidias or of Thucydides could read. The women of the working classes, especially in the country, necessarily mixed somewhat with men in their work. But among the well-to-do, women had lost the freedom of the simple and rude

society of Homer's time, without gaining much in return. Except at Sparta, where physical training was thought needful

WOMEN AT THEIR TOILET. — From a vase painting.

for them, they passed a secluded life even at home, in separate women's apartments. They had no public interests, ap-

WOMEN AT THEIR TOILET. — The rest of the vase painting shown above.

peared rarely on the streets, and never met their husbands' friends. At best, they were only higher domestic servants. The chivalry of the mediæval knight toward woman and the love and respect of the Christian man in general for his wife were equally unthinkable by the best Greek society.

This rule is merely emphasized by its one exception. No account of the Athens of Pericles would be complete without the mention of Aspasia. She was a native of Miletus and came to Athens as a perfect stranger. But she succeeded in winning the love of Pericles. He married her, though being a foreigner she could not figure as his wife before the Athenian Law. Her dazzling beauty and wit made his house the focus of a large circle of prominent men. Anaxagoras, Socrates, Phidias, Herodotus, the charming group of brilliant friends of Pericles, delighted in her conversation. Pericles consulted her on the

GREEK WOMEN AT THEIR MUSIC
From a vase painting.

most important public matters. But she is almost the only woman who need be named in Greek history.

c. The most intellectual Greeks of that age had not thought of finding out the truths of nature by *experiment*. The ancients had chiefly such knowledge of the world about them as they had *chanced upon*, or such as they could attain by *observation of nature as she showed herself to them*. To ask questions, and make nature answer them by systematic experiment, is a method of reaching knowledge which in its widest development belongs to later times. But, before the Greeks, men had reached about all the mastery over nature that was possible without that method.

This limitation had a remarkable consequence, namely the simplicity, nay almost complete absence, of those material comforts which rest upon the many inventions and discoveries of later centuries. There were no railroads nor telegraphs — not to speak of wireless communication — no electric or gas lights, no refrigerator cars or even ice boxes. Even the best houses were without plumbing or drains of any sort; beds without sheets or springs; rooms without fire; traveling without bridges; clothes without buttons or even a hook and eye. The Greek had to tell time without a watch, and to cross the seas without a compass.

This fact, however, is rather instructive than bewildering. There is a higher civilization, more essential than merely material achievements. A band of robbers is not civilized, if it uses a train of automobiles or establishes telephonic connection between its various headquarters. The Greeks excelled in intellectual civilization, which has a much nobler claim, because of its nearer relation to man's spiritual nature. For hours the entire population of Greek cities could listen to and enjoy such high class drama as those of the Hellenic masters. In our days only the educated are able to appreciate these plays. The average Athenian no doubt excelled the average man of our times in brain power, and the Greek mind performed wonders in literature and art and philosophy. It is through features like these that Greek life has had such a lasting influence upon all later ages.

The lack of control over nature had another serious drawback. Without our modern scientific knowledge and modern machinery it had never been possible for man to produce wealth fast enough so that *many* could take sufficient leisure for refined and graceful living. Even with us this ability is not accompanied by a proper distribution of our wealth, too much of which remains in the hands of a proportionately small number. In the Greek system it seems to have been still less possible to give to many an ample share. There was too little to go round. The material civilization of the relatively few rested necessarily on slavery.

231. The Moral Side of Greek civilization falls considerably short of the intellectual. The two religions, of the clan and of the Olympian gods, both kept their hold upon the people even in the age of Pericles. But neither had much to do with moral conduct. The good sense and clear thinking of the Greeks had preserved their religion, whatever they understood by this term, from many of the repulsive features found in Oriental beliefs. But their moral ideas are to be sought rather in their philosophy, literature, and history than in their mythological stories. In fact they could learn little morality from the example given to them by the Olympians (§ 111).

The Greeks accepted a rather unlimited search for pleasures as natural and proper. Self-sacrifice had little place in their moral code. They lacked altogether the Jewish and Christian sense of sin. Even the Babylonians were far ahead of them in this matter (§ 53). Their chief motive for right conduct, as far as it went, was a certain admiration, based on natural grounds, of moderation and temperance. Individual characters at once lofty and lovable were not numerous. Trickery and deceit mark most of the greatest names, and not even physical or moral bravery can be called a national characteristic. The wily Themistocles, rather than Socrates or Pericles, is the typical Greek. As in literature and arts so in moral corruption were the Greeks the teachers of Rome. In beautiful Hellas grew up that degradation which in due time was to spread along the shores of the Mediterranean. It was to reach maturity when adopted by the future masters of the world.

At the same time some Greek teachers inculcate morality. They found in themselves the courage to listen to the voice of their conscience and to assert what they saw was right. They may have caught the dim rays of original revelation, or obtained inspiration from the sacred books of the Jews. Yet none of these men in any way reached the Jewish and Christian ideals.

232. Illustrative Extracts. — The following passages illustrate the moral ideas of the best of the Greeks. They are taken from Athenian writers of the age of Pericles, and represent the mountain peaks of Greek thought, by no means its average level.

a. From Aeschylus.

" The lips of Zeus know not to speak a lying speech."

" Justice shines in smoke-grimed houses and holds in regard the life that is righteous ; she leaves with averted eyes the gold-bespangled palace which is unclean, and goes to the abode that is holy."

b. Antigone, the heroine of a play by *Sophocles*, has knowingly incurred penalty of death by disobeying an unrighteous command of a wicked king. She justifies her deed proudly, —

> " Nor did I deem thy edicts strong enough
> That thou, a mortal man, should'st overpass
> *The unwritten laws of God that know no change.*"

c. From Socrates to his Judges after his condemnation to death (Plato's *Apology*). — " Wherefore, O judges, be of good cheer about death, and know this of a truth — that no evil can happen to a good man, either in life or after death. He and his are not neglected by the gods. . . . The hour of departure has arrived, and we go our ways — I to die, you to live. Which is better, God only knows."

d. From Plato (the greatest disciple of Socrates, § 315). — " My counsel is that we hold fast ever to the heavenly way and follow justice and virtue. . . . Thus we shall live dear to one another and to the gods, both while remaining here, and when, *like conquerors in the games*, we go to receive our reward."

e. A Prayer of Socrates (from Plato's *Phaedrus*). — " Beloved Pan, and all ye other gods who haunt this place, give me beauty in the inward soul ; and may the outward and inward man be at one. May I reckon the wise to be the wealthy, and may I have such a quantity of gold as none but the temperate can carry."

(The quotations from Socrates' talks after his condemnation, given in § 227 above, give more material of this kind. Fuller passages will be found in Davis' *Readings*, Vol. I, Nos. 89–92.)

FOR FURTHER READING. — *Specially suggested :* Davis' *Readings*, Vol. 1, Nos. 76–80 (11 pages, mostly from Plutarch and Thucydides) ; and Nos. 88–97 (24 pages) ; Bury, 363–378.

Additional : Valuable and very readable treatments will be found in any of the three excellent volumes mentioned for the two preceding topics, — Cox's *Athenian Empire.* Plutarch's *Pericles* ought to be inviting, from the extracts in Davis' *Readings*.

Exercise. — Count up and classify the *kinds* of sources of our knowledge about the ancient world, — so far as this book has alluded to sources of information.   *Note here the suggestions for "fact-drills," on page 299, and begin to prepare the lists.*

CHAPTER XIV

LIFE IN THE AGE OF PERICLES

233. **Houses,** even those of the rich, were very simple. The poor could not afford more; and the rich man thought his house of little account. It was merely a place to keep his women folk and young children and some other valuable property, and to sleep in. His real life was passed outside.

A "well-to-do" house was built with a wooden frame, covered with sun-dried clay. Such buildings have not left many remains; and most of what we know about them comes from brief references in Greek literature. On the opposite page is given the ground plan of one of the few private houses of the fifth century which has been unearthed in a state to be traced out. This house was at Delos; and it was something of a mansion, for the times.

Houses were built flush with the street, and on a level with it, — without even sidewalk or steps between. The door, too, usually opened out — so that passers-by were liable to bumps, unless they kept well to the middle of the narrow street. In this Delos mansion, the street door opened into a small vestibule (*A*), about six feet by ten. This led to a square "hall" (*D, D, D, D*), which was the central feature of every Greek house of importance. In the center of the hall there was always a "court," *open to the sky,* and surrounded by a row of columns. The columns were to uphold their side of the hall ceiling, — since the hall had no wall next the court, but was divided from it only by the columns. In the Delos house, the columns were ten feet high (probably higher than was usual), and the court was paved with a beautiful mosaic. Commonly, however, all floors in private houses, until some three centuries later, were made of concrete.

234

Under part of the hall were two cellars or cisterns; and from the hall there opened six more rooms. The largest (*H*) was the dining room and kitchen, with a small recess for the chimney in one corner. The other rooms were store rooms, or sleeping rooms for male slaves and unmarried sons. Any occasional overflow of guests could be taken care of by couches in the hall. This whole floor was for males only.

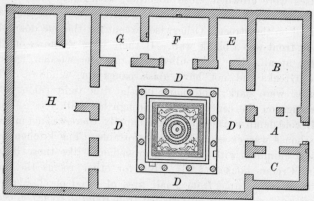

PLAN OF A FIFTH-CENTURY DELOS HOUSE.
After Gardiner and Jevons.

Some houses (of the very rich) had only one story. In that case there was at the rear a second half for the women, connected with the men's half by a door in the partition wall. This rear half of the house, in such cases, had its own central hall and open court, and an arrangement of rooms similar to that in the front half. But more commonly, as in the Delos house, there was an upper story for the women, reached by a steep stairway in the lower hall, and projecting, perhaps, part way over the street. Near the street door, on the outside, there was a niche in the wall for the usual statue of Hermes; and a small niche in room *F* was used probably as a shrine for some other deity.

The doorways of the interior were usually hung with curtains; but store rooms had doors with bronze locks. Bronze keys are sometimes found in the ruins, and they are pictured in use in vase paintings. The door between the men's and women's apartments was kept locked: only the master of the house, his wife, and perhaps a trusted slave, had keys to it. The Delos house had only one outside door; but often there was a rear door into a small, walled garden. City houses were crowded close together, with small chance for windows on the sides. Sometimes narrow slits in the wall opened on the street. Otherwise, except for the one door, the street front was a blank wall. If there were windows on the street at all, they were filled with a close wooden lattice. The Greeks did not have glass panes for windows. The houses were dark; and most of the dim light came from openings on the central court, through the hall.

In cold damp weather (of which, happily, there was not much), the house was exceedingly uncomfortable. The kitchen had a real chimney, with cooking arrangements like those in ancient Cretan houses (§ 96). But for other rooms the only artificial heat came from small fires of wood or charcoal in braziers, — such as are still carried from room to room, on occasion, in Greece or Italy or Spain. The choking fumes which filled the room were not much more desirable than the cold which they did little to drive away. Sometimes a large open fire in the court gave warmth to the hall. At night, earthenware lamps, on shelves or brackets, furnished light. *There were no bathrooms, and no sanitary conveniences.*

Poor people lived in houses of one or two rooms. A middle class had houses nearly as large as the one described above; but they rented the upper story to lodgers. Professional lodging houses had begun to appear, with several stories of small rooms, for unmarried poor men and for slaves who could not find room in the master's house.

234. The residence streets were narrow and irregular, — hardly more than crooked, dark alleys. They had no pavement, and they were littered with all the filth and refuse from the houses. Slops, from upper windows, sometimes doused unwary passers-by. Splendid as were the *public* portions of Athens, the residence quarters were much like a squalid Oriental city of to-day. In the time of Pericles, wealthy men were just beginning to build more comfortably on the hills near the city; but war kept this practice from becoming common till a much later time.

GREEK GIRLS AT PLAY. — From a vase painting.

235. The Family. — In the Oriental lands which we have studied, a man was at liberty to have as many wives in his household as he chose to support. Poor men usually were content with one; but, among the rich, polygamy was the rule. A Greek had only one wife. Imperfect as Greek family life was, the state laws recognized " monogamous " marriages only.

The Homeric poems give many pictures of lovely family life; and the Homeric women meet male guests and strangers with a natural dignity and ease. In historic Greece, as we have noted (§ 230), this freedom for women had been lost — except, in some degree, at Sparta. Marriage was arranged by parents. The young people as a rule had never seen each other. Girls were married very young — at fifteen or earlier

— and had no training of any valuable sort. Among the
wealthy classes, they spent the rest of their days indoors —
except on some rare festival occasions. The model wife
learned to oversee the household; but in many homes this was
left to trained slaves, and the wife dawdled away the day list-
lessly at her toilet or in vacant idleness. The vase pictures
show her commonly with a mirror. Unwholesome living led
to excessive use of red and white paint, and other cosmetics,
to imitate the complexion of early youth.

Law and public opinion allowed the father to " expose " a
new-born child to die. This horrible practice of legalized
murder was common among the poor. Boys, however, were
valued more than girls. They would offer sacrifices, in time,
at the father's tomb, *and they could fight for the city.* Divorce
was lawful, and the husband easily found a sufficient plea for
it. With the Greeks, too, matrimony had fallen far from its
original perfection.

Till the age of seven, boys and girls lived together in the
women's apartments. Then the boy began his school life
(§ 240). The girl continued her childhood until marriage.
Much of her time was spent at music and in games. One very
common game was like our " Jackstones," except that it was
played with little bones. Not till the evening before her marriage did the girl put away her doll, — offering it then solemnly
on the shrine of the goddess Artemis. These laws and customs
obtained more or less in all Greece. The views and usages of
Sparta, however, differed from them in many regards (§ 130).

236. Greek dress is well known, as to its general effect, from
pictures and sculpture. Women of the better classes wore
flowing garments, fastened at the shoulders with clasp-pins,
and gathered in graceful loose folds at the waist. Outside the
house, the woman wore also a kind of long mantle, which was
often drawn up over the head.

The chief article of men's dress was a shirt of linen or
wool, which fell about to the knees. For active movements,
this was often clasped with a girdle about the waist. Over

this was draped a long mantle, falling in folds to the feet.
This is well shown in the statue of Sophocles, on page 218.
Sometimes, this mantle was carried on the arm. The soles
of the feet were commonly protected by sandals; but there
was also a great variety of other foot gear. Socrates' habit
of going barefooted was the rule at Sparta for men under
middle age; and some Spartan kings made it their practice
all their lives.

Even these statements do not make emphatic enough the very simple
nature of men's dress. The inner garment was merely a piece of cloth
in two oblong parts (sometimes partly sewn together), fastened by pins,
so as to hold it on. The outer garment was one oblong piece of cloth,
larger and not fastened at all.

A VASE PAINTING, showing the Trojan prince enticing away Helen. The
painting is of the fifth century, and shows fashions in dress for that time.

237. Occupations. — Good "society" looked down upon all
forms of money-making by personal exertion. A physician
who took pay for his services they despised almost as much
as they did a carpenter or shoemaker. This attitude is natural
to a slaveholding society. Careless thinkers sometimes admire
it. But it contains less promise for mankind than does even
our modern worship of the dollar, bad as that sometimes is.
The Greek wanted money enough to supply all the comforts

that he knew about; but he wanted it to come without *his* earning it. He was very glad to have slaves earn it for him.

Most of the hand labor was busied in tilling the soil. The farmer manured his land skillfully; but otherwise he made no advance over the Egyptian farmer — who had not been compelled to enrich his land. Some districts, like Corinth and Attica, could not furnish food enough for their populations from their own soil. Athens imported grain from other parts

GREEK WOMEN, in various activities. — From a vase painting.

of Hellas and from Thrace and Egypt. This grain was paid for, in the long run, by the export of manufactures. In the age of Pericles, *large factories* had appeared. (See Davis' *Readings*, Vol. I, No. 76, for a list of twenty-five handicrafts connected with the beautifying of the Acropolis.) In these factories, the place taken now by machinery was taken then, in large part, by slaves. The owner of a factory did not commonly own all the slaves employed in it. Any master of a slave skilled in that particular trade might "rent" him out to the factory by the month or year.

In Attica, then, the villages outside Athens were mainly occupied by farmers and farm laborers. Commerce (as well as much manufacturing) was centered in the Piraeus, and was managed directly, for the most part, by the non-citizen class.

In Athens, the poorer classes worked at their trades or in their shops from sunrise to sunset — with a holiday about one day in three. Their pay was small, because of the competition of slave labor; but they needed little pay to give them most of the comforts of the rich — except constant leisure. And we must understand that the Greek artisan — sometimes even the slave — *took a noble pride in his work.* The stone masons who chiseled out the fluted columns of the Parthenon felt themselves fellow workmen with Phidias who carved the pediments. In general, the Greek workman seems to have

worked deliberately and to have found a delight in his work which was so common among the artisans of the Middle Ages in Europe, but which has been largely driven out of modern life by our greater subdivision of labor and by our greater pressure for haste.

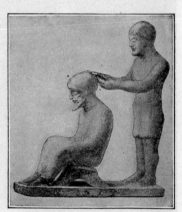

A BARBER IN TERRA-COTTA.
From Blümner.

An Athenian citizen of the wealthy class usually owned lands outside the city, worked by slaves and managed by some trusted steward. Probably he also had capital invested in trading vessels, though he was not likely to have any part in managing them. Some revenue he drew from money at interest with the bankers; and he drew large sums, too, from the "rent" of slaves to the factories.

238. A Day of the Leisure Class. — Like the poorer citizens, the rich man rose with the sun. A slave poured water over his face and hands, or perhaps over his naked body, from a basin. (Poor men like Socrates bathed at the public fountains.) He then broke his fast on a cup of wine and a dry crust of bread. Afterward, perhaps he rode into the country, to visit one of his farms there, or for a day's hunting.

If, instead, he remained within the city, he left his house

at once, stopping, probably, at a barber's, to have his beard
and finger nails attended to, as well as to gather the latest
news from the barber's talk. In any case, the later half of
the morning, if not the first part, would find him strolling
through the shaded arcades about the market place, among
throngs of his fellows, greeting acquaintances and stopping for
conversation with friends — with whom, sometimes, he sat on

ATHENE.

the benches that
were interspersed
among the colon-
nades. At such
times, he was al-
ways followed by
one or two hand-
some slave boys,
to run errands.
At midday, he re-
turned home for
a light lunch. In
the afternoon, he
sometimes slept.
Or, if a student,
he took to his rolls
of papyrus. Or,
if a statesman,

perhaps he prepared his speech for the next meeting of the
Assembly. Sometimes, he visited the public gaming houses or
the clubs. During the afternoon,— usually toward evening,
— he bathed at a public bathing house, hot, cold, or vapor
bath, as his taste decided ; and here again he held conversation
with friends, while resting, or while the slave attendants rubbed
him with oil and ointment. The bath was usually preceded by
an hour or more of exercise in a gymnasium.

Toward sunset, he once more visited his home, unless he was
to dine out. If the evening meal was to be, for a rare occasion,
at home and without guests, he ate with his family,— his wife

sitting at the foot of the couch where he *reclined ;* and soon afterward he went to bed. More commonly, he entertained guests — whom he had invited to dinner as he met them at the market place in the morning — or he was himself a guest elsewhere.

The evening meal deserves a section to itself (§ 239). First let us note that such days as we have just described were not allowed to become monotonous at Athens. For several years of his life, the citizen was certain to be busied most of the time in the service of the state (§ 212). At other times, the meetings of the Assembly and the religious festivals and the theater took at least one day out of every three.

239. The evening banquet played a large part in Greek life. As guests arrived, they took their places in pairs, on couches, which were arranged around the room, each man reclining on his left arm. Slaves removed the sandals or shoes, washing the dust from the feet, and passed bowls of water for the hands. They then brought in low three-legged tables, one before each couch, on which they afterward placed course after course of food.

The Greeks of this period were not luxurious about eating. The meals were rather simple. Food was cut into small pieces in the kitchen. No forks or knives were used at table. Men ate with a spoon, or, more commonly, with the fingers; and at the close, slaves once more passed bowls for washing the hands. When the eating was over, the real business of the evening began — with the wine. This was mixed with water; and drunkenness was not common; but the drinking lasted late, with serious or playful talk, and singing and story-telling, and with forfeits for those who did not perform well any part assigned them by the "master of the feast" (one of their number chosen by the others when the wine appeared). Often the host had musicians come in, with jugglers and dancing girls. Respectable women never appeared on these occasions. Only on marriage festivals, or some special family celebration, did the women of a family meet male guests at all.

240. Education. — Education at Athens, as in nearly all Greece, was in marked contrast with Spartan education (§ 130). *It aimed to train harmoniously the intellect, the sense of beauty, the moral nature, and the body.* At the age of seven the boy

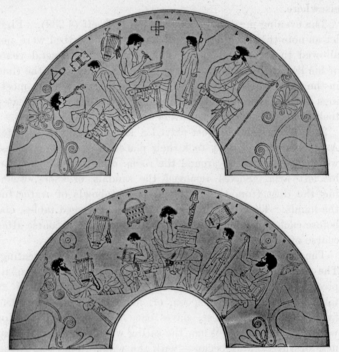

SCHOOL SCENES. — A BOWL PAINTING.

Instruments of instruction, mostly musical, hang on the walls. In the first half, one instructor is correcting the exercise of a boy who stands before him. Another is showing how to use the flute. The seated figures, with staffs, are "pedagogues."

entered school, but he was constantly under the eye not only of the teacher, but of a trusted servant of his own family, called a pedagogue.[1] The chief subjects for study were Homer

---

[1] The word meant "boy-leader." Its use for a "teacher" is later.

and music. Homer, it has well been said, was to the Greek at once Bible, Shakespeare, and Robinson Crusoe. The boy learned to write on papyrus with ink. But papyrus was costly, and the elementary exercises were carried on with a sharp instrument on tablets coated with wax. No great proficiency was expected from the average rich youth in writing — since he would have slaves do most of it for him in after life. The schoolmaster indulged in cruel floggings on slight occasion (Davis' *Readings*, Vol. I, No. 94).

When the youth left school, he entered upon a wider training, in the political debates of the Assembly, in the lecture halls of the Sophists, in the many festivals and religious processions, in the plays of the great dramatists at the theaters, and in the constant enjoyment of the noblest and purest works of art.

Physical training began with the child and continued through old age. No Greek youth would pass a day without devoting some hours to developing his body and to overcoming any physical defect or awkwardness that he might have. All classes of citizens, except those bound by necessity to the workshop, met for exercise. The result was a perfection of physical power and beauty never attained so universally by any other people.

IMAGINATIVE EXERCISES. — This period affords excellent material for exercises based upon the training of the historic imagination. Let the student absorb all the information he can find upon some historical topic, until he is filled with its spirit, and then reproduce it *from the inside*, with the dramatic spirit — as though he lived in that time — not in the descriptive method of another age. The following topics are suggested (the list can be indefinitely extended, and such exercises may be arranged for any period) : —

1. A captive Persian's letter to a friend after Plataea.

2. A dialogue between Socrates and Xanthippe.

3. An address by a Messenian to his fellows in their revolt against Sparta.

4. Extracts from a diary of Pericles.

5. A day at the Olympic games (choose some particular date).

CHAPTER XV

THE PELOPONNESIAN WAR

(431–404 B.C.)

241. Causes. — Athens and Sparta were at the opposite poles of Greek civilization. Athens stood for progress. Sparta was the champion of old ways. A like contrast ran through the two leagues of which these cities were the heads. The cities of the Athenian empire were Ionian in blood, democratic in politics, commercial in interests. Most of the cities of the Peloponnesian league were Dorian in blood and aristocratic in politics, and their citizens were landowners. This difference between the Athenian and Spartan states gave rise to mutual distrust. It was easy for any misunderstanding to ripen into war.

Still, if *none* of the cities of the Peloponnesian league had had any interests on the sea, the two powers might each have gone its own way without crossing the other's path. But Corinth and Megara (members of Sparta's league) were trading cities, like Athens; and, after the growth of the Athenian empire, they felt the basis of their prosperity slipping from under them. They had lost the trade of the Aegean, and Athens had gained it. And now Athens was reaching out also for the commerce of the western coasts of Greece. Next to Sparta, Corinth was the most powerful city in the Peloponnesian league ; and she finally persuaded Sparta to take up arms against Athens, before the Thirty Years' Truce (§ 202) had run quite half its length.

242. The immediate occasion for the struggle was found in some aid which Athens gave Corcyra against an attack by Corinth in 432 B.C.

Corcyra was the third naval power in Greece. Corinth was second only to Athens.   Corinth and Corcyra had come to blows, and Corcyra asked to be taken into the Athenian league. Athens finally promised *defensive* aid, and sent ten ships with instructions to take no part in offensive operations. A great armament of 150 Corinthian vessels appeared off the southern coast of Corcyra. Corcyra could muster only 110 ships. In the battle that followed, the Corinthians were at first completely victorious. They sank or captured many ships, and seemed about to destroy the whole Corcyran fleet. Then the little Athenian squadron came to the rescue, and by their superior skill quickly restored the fortune of the day.

But in the negotiations that followed, between Athens and the Peloponnesian league, this matter of Corcyra fell out of sight, and the quarrel was joined on broader issues.[1]   Sparta finally sent a haughty ultimatum, posing, herself, as the champion of a free Hellas against tyrant Athens, which had enslaved the Aegean cities. " Let Athens set those cities free, and she might still have peace with Sparta." A timid party, of Athenian aristocrats, wished peace even on these terms. But the Assembly adopted a dignified resolution moved by Pericles : —

" Let us send the ambassadors away," said he, " with this answer : That we will grant independence to the cities . . . as soon as the Spartans allow their subject states [Messenia and the subject towns of Laconia] to be governed as they choose, and not by the will and interest of Sparta. Also, *that we are willing to offer arbitration*, according to the treaty [the treaty of the Thirty Years' Truce]. And that we do not want to begin the war, but shall know how to defend ourselves if we are attacked."

As Pericles frankly warned the Assembly, this reply meant conflict. And so in 431 began the " Peloponnesian War."

243. Resources and Plans. — The Peloponnesian league could muster a hundred thousand hoplites, against whom in that day no army in the world could stand; but it could not keep many men in the field longer than a few weeks.   Sparta could

---

[1] Special report: the narrative of the deliberations at Sparta regarding war or peace (note especially Thucydides' account of the Corinthian speech regarding Sparta and Athens in Davis' *Readings*, Vol. I, No. 77).

not capture Athens, therefore, and must depend upon ravaging Attic territory and inducing Athenian allies to revolt.

Athens had only some twenty-six thousand hoplites at her command, and half of these were needed for distant garrison duty. But she had a navy even more unmatched on the sea than the Peloponnesian army was on land. Her walls were impregnable. The islands of Euboea and Salamis, and the open spaces within the Long Walls, she thought, could receive her country people with their flocks and herds. The corn trade of south Russia was securely in her hands. The grain ships could enter the Piraeus as usual, however the Spartans might hold the open country of Attica. Athens could easily afford to support her population for a time from her annual revenues, to say nothing of the immense surplus of 6000 talents ($6,000,000) in the treasury.

When war began, the Spartans marched each year into Attica with overwhelming force, and remained there for some weeks, laying waste the crops, burning the villages, and cutting down the olive groves, up to the very walls of Athens. At first, with frenzied rage, the Athenians clamored to march out against the invader; but Pericles strained his great authority to prevent such a disaster, and finally he convinced the people that they must bear this insult and injury with patience. Meantime, an Athenian fleet was always sent to ravage the coasts and harbors of Peloponnesus and to conquer various exposed allies of Sparta. Each party could inflict considerable damage, *but neither could get at the other to strike a vital blow.* The war promised to be a matter of endurance.

Here Athens seemed to have an advantage, since she had the stronger motive for holding out. She was fighting to preserve her empire, and could not give up without ruin. Sparta could cease fighting without loss to herself; and Pericles hoped to tire her out.

244. The Plague in Athens. — The plan of Pericles might have been successful, had the Spartans not been encouraged by a tragic disaster which fell upon Athens and which no one in that day could have foreseen. A terrible plague had been ravaging western Asia, and in the second year of the war it reached the Aegean. In most parts of Hellas it did no great harm; but in Athens it was peculiarly deadly. The people of all Attica, crowded into the one city, were living under unusual and unwholesome conditions; and the pestilence returned each summer for several years. It slew more than a fourth of the population, and paralyzed industry and all ordinary activities. Worse still, it shattered, for years, the proud and joyous self-trust which had come to the Athenian people after Marathon.

Thucydides, an eye witness, has described the ravages of the plague and explained their cause. "When the country people of Attica arrived in Athens," he says, "a few had homes of their own, or found friends to take them in. But far the greater number had to find a place to live on some vacant spot or in the temples of the gods and chapels of the heroes. . . . Many also camped down in the towers of the walls or wherever else they could; for the city proved too small to hold them." Thucydides could see the unhappy results of these conditions, *after* the plague had fallen on the city; and he adds, with grim irony, that "while these country folk were dividing the spaces between the Long Walls and settling there," the government (Generals and Council) were "paying great attention to mustering a fleet for ravaging the Peloponnesian coasts."

Then, in dealing with the horrible story of the plague, Thucydides shows how these conditions prepared for it. "*The new arrivals from the country* were the greatest sufferers, — lodged during this hot season in stifling huts, where death raged without check. The bodies of dying men lay one upon another, and half-dead creatures reeled about the streets, poisoning all the fountains and wells with their bodies, in their longing for water. The sacred places in which they had camped were full of corpses [a terrible sacrilege, to Greeks]; for *men, not knowing what was to become of them, became wholly careless of everything.*"

245. Twenty-seven Years of War. — Still, the Athenians did recover their buoyant hope; and the war dragged along with varying success for twenty-seven years, with one short and ill-kept truce, — a whole generation growing up from the cradle to manhood in incessant war. A story of the long struggle in detail would take a volume. *The contest was not of such lasting importance as the preceding struggle between the Greek and Persian civilizations;* and only a few incidents require mention.

246. Athenian Naval Supremacy. — On the sea the superiority of Athens consisted not merely in the size of her navy, *but even more in its skill.* The other Greeks still fought, as at the time of Salamis, by dashing their ships against each other, beak against beak, and then, if neither was sunk, by grappling the vessels together, and fighting as if on land. The Athenians, however, had now learned to maneuver their ships, rowing swiftly about the enemy with many feints, and seizing the opportunity to sink a ship by a sudden blow at an exposed point. Their improved tactics revolutionized naval warfare; and for years small fleets of Athenian ships proved equal to three times their number of the enemy.[1] Gradually, however, the Peloponnesians learned something of the Athenian tactics, and this difference became less marked.

247. New Leaders. — The deadliest blow of the plague was the striking down of Pericles, who died of the disease, in the third year of the war. Never had the Athenians so needed his controlling will and calm judgment. He was followed by a new class of leaders, — men of the people, like *Cleon* the tanner, and *Hyperbolus* the lampmaker, — men of strong will and much force, but rude, untrained, unscrupulous, and ready to surrender their own convictions, if necessary, to win the favor of the crowd. Such men were to lead Athens into many blunders and crimes. Over against them stood only a group of incapable aristocrats, led by *Nicias,* a good but stupid man, and *Alcibiades,* a brilliant, unprincipled adventurer.

---

[1] Special report to illustrate these points: the story of Phormio's victories in the Corinthian Gulf in 431.

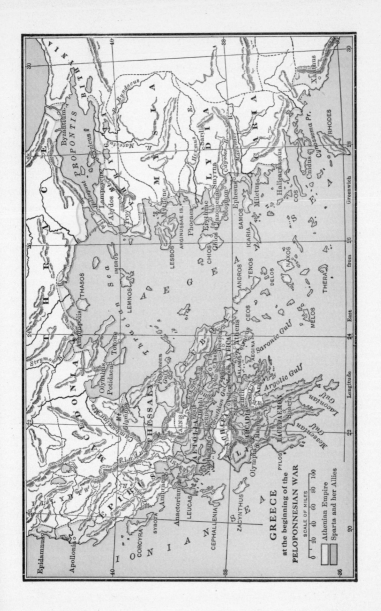

GREECE

at the beginning of the

PELOPONNESIAN WAR

SCALE OF MILES

0   20   40   60   80   100

Athenian Empire

Sparta and her Allies

Athens was peculiarly unfortunate in her statesmen at this period. She produced no Themistocles, or Aristides, or Cimon, or Pericles; and Phormio and Demosthenes, her great admirals, were usually absent from the city. Sparta, on the other hand, produced two greater generals than ever before in her history: *Brasidas*, whose brilliant campaigns overthrew Athenian supremacy on the coast of Thrace; and *Lysander*, who was finally to bring the war to a close.

248. Athenian Disaster in Sicily. — The turning-point in the war was an unwise and misconducted Athenian expedition against Syracuse.[1] Two hundred perfectly equipped ships and over forty thousand men — among them eleven thousand of the flower of the Athenian hoplites — were pitifully sacrificed by the superstition and miserable generalship of their leader, Nicias (413 B.C.).

Even after this crushing disaster Athens refused peace that should take away her empire. Every nerve was strained, and the last resources and reserve funds exhausted, to build and man new fleets. The war lasted nine years more, and part of the time Athens seemed as supreme in the Aegean as ever. Two things are notable in the closing chapters of the struggle, — the attempt to overthrow democracy in Athens, and Sparta's betrayal of the Asiatic Greeks to Persia (§§ 249, 250).

249. The Rule of the Four Hundred. — For a century, the oligarchic party had hardly raised its head in Athens; but in 411, it attempted once more to seize the government. Wealthy men of moderate opinions were wearied by the heavy taxation of the war. The democracy had blundered sadly and had shown itself unfit to deal with foreign relations, where secrecy and dispatch were essential; and its new leaders were particularly offensive to the old Athenian families.

Under these conditions, the officers of the fleet conspired with secret oligarchic societies at home. Leading democrats were assassinated; and the Assembly was terrorized into sur-

---

[1] Syracuse, a Dorian city and a warm friend to Sparta, had been encroaching upon Ionian allies of Athens in Sicily.

rendering its powers to a council of *Four Hundred* of the oligarchs. But this body proved generally incompetent, except in murder and plunder, and it permitted needless disasters in the war. After a few months, the Athenian fleet at Samos deposed its oligarchic officers; and the democracy at home expelled the Four Hundred and restored the old government.

Route of the Long Walls, looking southwest to the harbor, some three and one half miles distant. From a recent photograph.

250. Sparta betrays the Asiatic Greeks. — In 412, immediately after the destruction of the Athenian army and fleet in Sicily, Persian satraps appeared again upon the Aegean coast. *Sparta at once bought the aid of their gold by promising to betray the freedom of the Asiatic Greeks,* — to whom the Athenian name had been a shield for seventy years. Persian funds now built fleet after fleet for Sparta, and slowly Athens was exhausted, despite some brilliant victories.

251. Fall of Athens. — In 405, the last Athenian fleet was surprised and captured at *Aegospotami* (Goat Rivers). Apparently the officers had been plotting again for an oligarchic revolution; and the sailors had been discouraged and demoralized, even if they were not actually betrayed by their commanders.

Lysander, the Spartan commander, in cold blood put to death the four thousand Athenian citizens among the captives.[1]

This slaughter marks the end. Athens still held out despairing but stubborn, until starved into submission by a terrible siege. In 404, the proud city surrendered to the mercy of its foes. Corinth and Thebes wished to raze it from the earth; but Sparta had no mind to do away with so useful a check upon those cities. She compelled Athens to renounce all claims to empire, to give up all alliances, to surrender all her ships but twelve, and to promise to "follow Sparta" in peace and war. The Long Walls and the defenses of the Piraeus were demolished, to the music of Peloponnesian flutes; and Hellas was declared free !

Events were at once to show this promise a cruel mockery. *The one power that could have grown into a free and united Greece had been ruined, and it remained to see to what foreign master Greece should fall.*

For Further Reading. — *Specially suggested:* Davis' *Readings*, Vol. I, Nos. 81–86 (16 pages), gives the most striking episodes of the war, as they were told by the Athenian historians of the day, Thucydides and Xenophon. Plutarch's *Lives* ("Alcibiades," "Nicias," and "Lysander") is the next most valuable authority.

The following modern authorities continue to be useful (and may be consulted for special reports upon the period, if any are assigned) : Bury, chs. x, xi ; the closing parts of Grant's *Age of Pericles* and of Abbott's *Pericles;* and Cox's *Athenian Empire.* Bury gives 120 pages to the struggle, — too long an account for reading, but useful for special topics.

---

[1] Special reports: (1) Cleon's leadership. (2) The trial of the Athenian generals after the victory of Arginusae. (3) The massacre of the Mytilenean oligarchs (story of the decree and the reprieve). (4) Massacre of the Melians by Athens, 415 B.C. (5) Note the merciless nature of the struggle, as shown by other massacres of prisoners: *i.e.*, Thebans by Plataeans, 431 B.C.; Plataeans by Thebans, 427 B.C.; thousands of Athenians in the mines of Syracuse; the four thousand Athenians after Aegospotami. (6) The career of Alcibiades. (7) The Thracian campaigns. (8) The Sicilian expedition. (9) The Siege of Plataea.

Material for such reports will be easily found in the books named at the end of this chapter.

CHAPTER XVI

FROM THE FALL OF ATHENS TO THE FALL OF HELLAS

(404–338 B.C.)

252. Decline of Hellas. — The Athenian empire had lasted seventy glorious years. Nearly an equal time was yet to elapse before Hellas fell under Macedonian sway; but it need not detain us long. Persia had already begun again to enslave the Greeks of Asia; Carthage again did the like in Sicily; and in the European peninsula the period was one of shame or of profitless wars. It falls into three parts: thirty-three years of Spartan supremacy; nine years of Theban supremacy; and some twenty years of anarchy.

SPARTAN SUPREMACY, 404–371 B.C.

253. " Decarchies." — After Aegospotami, Sparta was mistress of Greece more completely than Athens had ever been, but for only half as long; and most of that time was given to wars to maintain her authority. She had promised to set Hellas free; but the cities of the old Athenian empire found that they had exchanged a mild, wise rule for a coarse and stupid despotism.[1] *Their old tribute was doubled; their self-government was taken away ; bloodshed and confusion ran riot in their streets.*

Everywhere Sparta overthrew the old democracies, and set up oligarchic governments. Usually the management of a city was given to a board of ten men, called a *decarchy* ("rule of ten"). These oligarchies, of course, were dependent upon Sparta.[2] To defend them against any democratic rising, there

---

[1] Cox, *Athenian Empire*, 229–231, gives an admirable contrast between the Athenian and the Spartan systems.

[2] Note the likeness between this Spartan method and the Persian practice of setting up tyrannies, dependent upon Persia, in the Ionian cities (§ 164).

was placed in many cities a Spartan garrison, with a Spartan military governor called a *harmost*. The garrisons plundered at will; the harmosts grew rich from extortion and bribes; the decarchies were slavishly subservient to their masters, while they wreaked upon their fellow-citizens a long pent-up aristocratic vengeance, in confiscation, outrage, expulsion, assassination, and massacre.

254. Spartan Decay. — In Sparta itself luxury and corruption replaced the old simplicity. As a result, the number of citizens was rapidly growing smaller. Property was gathered into the hands of a few, while many Spartans grew too poor to support themselves at the public mess (§ 130). These poorer men ceased to be looked upon as citizens. They were not permitted to vote in the Assembly, and were known as "Inferiors." The 10,000 citizens, of the Persian War period, shrank to 2000.

The discontent of the "Inferiors" added to the standing danger from the Helots. A plot was formed between these classes to change the government; and only an accident prevented an armed revolution.[1] Thus, even at home, the Spartan rule during this period rested on a volcano.

255. The "Thirty Tyrants" at Athens. — For a time even Athens remained a victim to Spartan tyranny, like any petty Ionian city. After the surrender, in 404, Lysander appointed a committee of thirty from the oligarchic clubs of Athens "to reëstablish the constitution of the fathers." Meantime, they were to hold absolute power. This committee was expected to undo the reforms of Pericles and Clisthenes and even of Solon, and to restore the ancient oligarchy. As a matter of fact they did worse than that: they published no constitution at all, but instead they filled all offices with their own followers and plotted to make their rule permanent.

These men were known as "the Thirty Tyrants." They called in a Spartan harmost and garrison, to whom they gave the fortress of the Acropolis. They disarmed the citizens, ex-

---

[1] Special report : the conspiracy of Cinadon at Sparta.

cept some three thousand of their own adherents. Then they began a bloody and greedy rule. Rich democrats and alien merchants were put to death or driven into exile, in order that their property might be confiscated.[1] The victims of this proscription were counted by hundreds, perhaps by thousands. Larger numbers fled, and, despite the orders of Sparta, they were sheltered by Thebes. That city had felt aggrieved that her services in the Peloponnesian War received no reward from Sparta, and now she would have been glad to see Athens more powerful again.

256. Athens again Free. — This reign of terror at Athens lasted over a year. Then, in 403, one of the democratic exiles, *Thrasybulus*, with a band of companions from Thebes, seized the Piraeus. The aliens of the harbor rose to his support. The Spartan garrison and the forces of the Thirty were defeated. A quarrel between Lysander and the Spartan king prevented serious Spartan interference, and the old Athenian democracy recovered the government.

The aliens and sailors of the Piraeus had fought valiantly with the democrats against the Thirty. Thrasybulus now urged that they be made full citizens. That just measure would have made up partly for Athens' terrible losses in the Peloponnesian War. Unfortunately, it was not adopted; but in other respects, the restored democracy showed itself generous as well as moderate. A few of the most guilty of the Thirty were punished, but for all others a general amnesty was declared.

The good faith and moderation of the democracy contrasted so favorably with the cut-throat rule of the two recent experiments at oligarchy, that Athens was undisturbed in future by revolution. Other parts of Greece, however, were less fortunate, *and democracy never again became so generally established in Hellenic cities as it had been in the age of Pericles.*

257. "March of the Ten Thousand." — Meantime, important events were taking place in the East. In 401, the weakness of

---

[1] Davis' *Readings*, Vol. I, No. 100, gives a famous instance.

the Persian empire was strikingly shown. *Cyrus the Younger*, brother of the king Artaxerxes, endeavored to seize the Persian throne. While a satrap in Asia Minor, Cyrus had furnished Sparta the money to keep her fleet together before the battle of Goat Rivers; and now, through Sparta's favor, he was able to enlist ten thousand Greeks in his army.

Cyrus penetrated to the heart of the Persian empire; but in the battle of *Cunaxa,* near Babylon, he was killed, and his Asiatic troops routed. The Ten Thousand Greeks, however, proved unconquerable by the Persian host of half a million. By treachery the leaders were entrapped and murdered; but under the inspiration of *Xenophon* [1] the Athenian, the Ten Thousand chose new generals and made a remarkable retreat to the Greek districts on the Black Sea.

258. Renewal of the Persian Wars. — Until this time the Greeks had waged their contests with Persia only along the *coasts* of Asia. After the Ten Thousand had marched, almost at will, through so many hostile nations, the Greeks began to dream of conquering the Asiatic *continent.* Seventy years later, Alexander the Great was to make this dream a fact. First, however, the attempt was made by *Agesilaus,* king of Sparta.

Sparta had brought down upon herself the wrath of Persia, anyway, by favoring Cyrus; and Agesilaus burned with a noble ambition to free the Asiatic Greeks, who, a little before (§ 250), had been abandoned to Persia by his country. Thus war began between Sparta and Persia. In 396, Agesilaus invaded Asia Minor with a large army, but was checked, in full career of conquest, by events at home (§ 259).

259. A Greek League against Sparta, 395 B.C. — No sooner was Sparta engaged with Persia than enemies rose up in Greece itself. Thebes, Corinth, Athens, and Argos formed an alliance against her, and the empire she had gained at Goat Rivers was shattered by *Conon.* Conon was the ablest of the Athenian generals in the latter period of the Peloponnesian War. At

---

[1] Cf. § 224 and § 41. Xenophon's *Anabasis* is our authority for these events.

Goat Rivers he was the only one who had kept his squadron in order; and after all was lost, he had escaped to Rhodes and entered Persian service. Now, in 394, in command of a Persian fleet (mainly made up of Phoenician ships) he completely destroyed the Spartan naval power at the battle of *Cnidus.*

THE HERMES OF PRAXITELES.

The arms and legs of the statue are sadly mutilated, but the head is one of the most famous remains of Greek art. Cf. § 220, note.

Spartan authority in the Aegean vanished. Conon sailed from island to island, expelling the Spartan garrisons, and restoring democracies; and in the next year he anchored in the Piraeus and rebuilt the Long Walls. Athens again became one of the great powers; and Sparta fell back into her old position as mere head of the inland Peloponnesian league.

260. Peace of Antalcidas, 387 B.C. — After a few more years of indecisive war, Sparta sought peace with Persia. In 387, the two powers invited all the Greek states to send deputies to Sardis, *where the Persian king dictated the terms.* The document read: —

" King Artaxerxes deems it just that the *cities in Asia, with the islands of Clazomenae and Cyprus,* should belong to himself. The rest of the Hellenic cities, both great and small, he will leave independent, save Lemnos,

Imbros, and Scyros, which three are to belong to Athens as of yore. Should any of the parties not accept this peace, I, Artaxerxes, together with those who share my views [the Spartans], will war against the offenders by land and sea." — XENOPHON, *Hellenica*, v, 1.

Sparta held that these terms dissolved all the other leagues (like the Boeotian, of which Thebes was the head), but that they did not affect her own control over her subject towns in Laconia, nor weaken the Peloponnesian confederacy.

Thus Persia and Sparta again conspired to betray Hellas. Persia helped Sparta to keep the European Greek states divided and weak, as they were before the Persian War; and Sparta helped Persia to recover her old authority over the Asiatic Greeks. By this iniquity the tottering Spartan supremacy was bolstered up a few years longer.

Of course the shame of betraying the Asiatic Greeks must be shared by the enemies of Sparta, who had used Persian aid against her ; *but the policy had been first introduced by Sparta in seeking Persian assistance in 412 against Athens* (§ 250) ; *and so far no other Greek state had offered to surrender Hellenic cities to barbarians as the price of such aid.*

261. Spartan Aggressions. — Sparta had saved her power by infamy. She used it, with the same brutal cunning as in the past, to keep down the beginnings of greatness elsewhere in Greece.

Thus, Arcadia had shown signs of growing strength; but Sparta now broke up the leading city, Mantinea, and dispersed the inhabitants in villages. In Chalcidice, the city of Olynthus had organized its neighbors into a promising league. A Spartan army compelled this league to break up. While on the way to Chalcidice, part of this army, *by treachery, in time of peace, seized the citadel of Thebes.* And, when the Athenian naval power began to revive, a like treacherous, though unsuccessful, attempt was made upon the Piraeus.

262. Thebes a Democracy. — These high-handed outrages were to react upon the offender. First there came a revolution at Thebes. The Spartan garrison there had set up an oligarchic Theban government which had driven crowds of citizens into

exile. Athens received them, just as Thebes had sheltered
Athenian fugitives in the time of the Thirty Tyrants; and
from Athens *Pelopidas*, a leader of the exiles, struck the return
blow.[1] In 379, Thebes was surprised and seized by the exiles,
and the government passed into the hands of the democrats.
Then Thebes and Athens joined in a new war upon Sparta.

263. Leuctra; the Overthrow of Sparta. — The war dragged
along for some years; and in 371 B.C., the contending parties,

wearied with fruitless
strife, concluded peace.
But when the treaty was
being signed, *Epaminon-
das*, the Theban repre-
sentative, *demanded the
right to sign for all Boeotia*, as Sparta had signed
for all Laconia. Athens
would not support Thebes
in this position. So
Thebes was excluded
from the peace; and
Sparta turned to crush her. A powerful army at once invaded
Boeotia, — and met with an overwhelming defeat *by a smaller
Theban force at Leuctra.*

This amazing result was due to the military genius of Epaminondas. Hitherto the Greeks had fought in long lines, from
eight to twelve men deep. Epaminondas adopted a new
arrangement that marks a step in warfare. He massed his
best troops in a solid column, *fifty men deep*, on the left, opposite the Spartan wing in the Peloponnesian army. His other
troops were spread out as thin as possible. The solid phalanx

---

[1] The story is full of adventure. Pelopidas and a number of other daring
young men among the exiles returned secretly to Thebes, and, through the aid
of friends there, were admitted (disguised as dancing girls) to a banquet
where the Theban oligarchs were already deep in wine. They killed the
drunken traitors with their daggers. Then, running through the streets, they
called the people to expel the Spartans from the citadel.

was set in motion first; then the thinner center and right wing advanced more slowly, so as to engage the attention of the enemy opposite, but not to come into action until the battle should have been won by the massed column.

In short, Epaminondas massed his force against *one part* of the enemy. The weight of the Theban charge crushed through the Spartan line, and trampled it under. Four hundred of the seven hundred Spartans, with their king and with a thousand other Peloponnesian hoplites, went down in ten minutes.

The mere loss of men was fatal enough, now that Spartan citizenship was so reduced (the number of full citizens after this battle did not exceed fifteen hundred); but the effect upon the military prestige of Sparta was even more deadly. At one stroke Sparta sank into a second-rate power. None the less, Spartan character never showed to better advantage. Sparta was always greater in defeat than in victory, and she met her fate with heroic composure. The news of the overthrow did not interfere with a festival that was going on, and only the relatives of the *survivors* of the battle appeared in mourning.

THEBAN SUPREMACY

264. Epaminondas. — For nine years after Leuctra, Thebes was the head of Greece. This position she owed to her great leader, *Epaminondas*, whose life marks one of the fair heights to which human nature can ascend. Epaminondas was great as general, statesman, and philosopher; but he was greatest as a man, lofty and lovable in nature. In his earlier days he had been looked upon as a dreamer; and when the oligarchs of Thebes drove out Pelopidas and other active patriots (§ 262), they only sneered while Epaminondas continued calmly to talk of liberty to the young. Later, it was recognized that, more than any other man, he had prepared the way for the overthrow of tyranny; and after the expulsion of the oligarchs he became the organizer of the democracy.

265. Sparta surrounded by Hostile Cities. — Epaminondas sought to do for Thebes what Pericles had done for Athens.

While he lived, success seemed possible. Unhappily, the few years remaining of his life he was compelled to give mainly to war. Laconia was repeatedly invaded. During these campaigns Epaminondas freed Messenia,[1] on one side of Sparta, and organized Arcadia, on the other side, into a federal union, — so as to "surround Sparta with a perpetual blockade." The great Theban aided the Messenians to found a new capital, *Messene;* and in Arcadia he restored *Mantinea,* which Sparta had destroyed (§ 261). In this district he also founded *Megalopolis,* or "the Great City," by combining forty scattered villages.

266. **Athens (jealous of Thebes) saved Sparta** from complete destruction, but drew Theban vengeance upon herself. Epaminondas built fleets, swept the Athenian navy from the seas, and made Euboea a Theban possession. Thessaly and Macedonia, too, were brought under Theban influence; and the young *Philip,* prince of Macedon, spent some years in Thebes as a hostage.

267. **Mantinea.** — The leadership of Thebes, however, rested solely on the supreme genius of her one great statesman, and it vanished at his death. In 362, for the fourth time, Epaminondas marched against Sparta, and at *Mantinea* won another great victory. The Spartans had been unable to learn; and went down again before the same tactics that had crushed them nine years earlier at Leuctra. Mantinea was the greatest land battle ever fought between Hellenes, and nearly all the states of Greece took part on one side or the other. But the victory bore no fruit; for Epaminondas himself fell on the field, and his city sank at once to a slow and narrow policy.

No state was left in Greece to assume leadership. A turbulent anarchy, in place of the stern Spartan rule, seemed the only fruit of the brief glory of the great Theban.

268. **Failure of the City-state.** — The failure of the Greek cities to unite in larger states made it certain that sooner or later they must fall

---

[1] Messenia had been a mere district of Laconia for nearly two centuries and a half. Its loss took from Sparta more than a third of her whole territory.

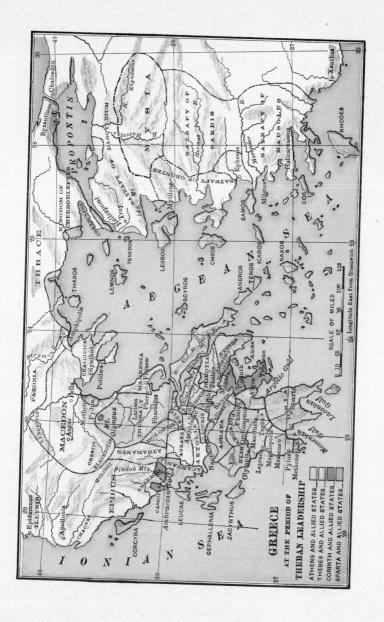

GREECE

AT THE PERIOD OF
THEBAN LEADERSHIP

ATHENS AND ALLIED STATES.
THEBES AND ALLIED STATES.
CORINTH AND ALLIED STATES.
SPARTA AND ALLIED STATES.

SCALE OF MILES
0 10 25   50   75   100   125

Longitude East from Greenwich

to some outside power.   Sparta and Thebes (with Persian aid) had
been able to prevent Athenian leadership; Thebes and Athens had
overthrown Sparta; Sparta and Athens had been able to check Thebes.
Twenty years of anarchy followed; and then Greece fell to a foreign
master.   On the north there had been growing up a *nation-state;* and
the city-state could not stand before that stronger organization.

    FOR FURTHER READING. — *Specially suggested:* Davis' *Readings*,
Vol. I, Nos. 100 ("Thirty Tyrants"), 101 (Epaminondas), and 102
(Leuctra).   Plutarch's *Lives* ("Agesilaus" and "Pelopidas").
    Additional: Bury, 514–628.

THE MACEDONIAN CONQUEST

269. Macedon. — The Macedonians were part of the "outer
rim of the Greek race."   They were still barbaric, and
perhaps were mixed somewhat with non-Hellenic elements.
Shortly before this time, they were only a loose union of
tribes; but *Philip II* (§ 270) had now consolidated them into
a real nation.   The change was so recent that Alexander the
Great, a little later, could say to his army: —

    " My father, Philip, found you a roving, destitute people, without fixed
homes and without resources, most of you clad in the skins of animals,
pasturing a few sheep among the mountains, and, to defend these, waging
a luckless warfare with the Illyrians, the Triballans, and the Thracians
on your borders.   He gave you the soldier's cloak to replace the skins,
and led you down from the mountains into the plain, making you a
worthy match in war against the barbarians on your frontier, so that you
no longer trusted to your strongholds, so much as to your own valor,
for safety.   He made you to dwell in cities and provided you with
wholesome laws and institutions.   Over those same barbarians, who
before had plundered you and carried off as booty both yourselves and
your substance, he made you masters and lords." [1]

270. Philip II of Macedon is one of most remarkable men in
history.[2]   He was ambitious, crafty, sagacious, persistent, unscrupulous, an unfailing judge of character, and a marvelous
organizer.   He set himself to make his people true Greeks by

---

[1] See the rest of this passage in Davis' *Readings*, Vol. I, No. 107.
[2] Wheeler's characterization, *Alexander the Great*, 5–7, is admirable.

making them the leaders of Greece. He was determined to secure that headship for which Athens, Sparta, and Thebes had striven in vain.

271. Philip's Methods. — At Philip's accession Macedon was still a poor country without a good harbor. The first need was an outlet on the sea. Philip found one by conquering the Chalcidic peninsula. Then his energy developed the gold mines of the district until they furnished him a yearly revenue of a thousand talents — as large as that of Athens at her greatest power.

PHILIP II.
From a gold medallion by Alexander.

Next Philip turned to Greece itself. Here he used an adroit mingling of cunning, bribery, and force. In all Greek states, among the pretended patriot statesmen, there were secret servants in his pay. He set city against city; and the constant tendency to quarrels among the Greeks played into his hands.

272. Demosthenes. — The only man who saw clearly the designs of Philip, and constantly opposed them, was *Demosthenes* the Athenian. Demosthenes was the greatest orator of Greece. To check Macedonia became the one aim of his life; and the last glow of Greek independence flames up in his passionate appeals to Athens that she defend Hellas against Macedon as she had once done against Persia.

"Suppose that you have one of the gods as surety that Philip will leave *you* untouched, in the name of all the gods, it is a shame for you in ignorant stupidity to sacrifice the rest of Hellas!"

The noble orations (the *Philippics*) by which Demosthenes sought to move the Athenian assembly to action against Philip

are still unrivaled in literature,[1] but they had no permanent
practical effect.

273. The Macedonian Army. — The most important work of
Philip was his army. This was as superior to the four-months

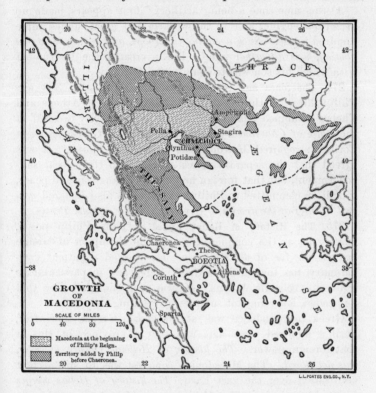

citizen armies of Hellas as Philip's steady and secret diplomacy
was superior to the changing councils of a popular assembly.
The king's wealth enabled him to keep a disciplined force
ready for action. He had become familiar with the Theban
phalanx during his stay at Thebes as a boy (§ 266). Now he

---

[1] Cf. § 223. Special report : Demosthenes.

enlarged and improved it, so that the ranks presented five rows of bristling spears projecting beyond the front soldier. The flanks were protected by light-armed troops, and the Macedonian nobles furnished the finest of cavalry.

At the same time a field "artillery" first appears, made up of curious engines able to throw darts and great stones three hundred yards. *Such a mixture of troops, and on a permanent footing, was altogether novel.* Philip created the instrument with which his son was to conquer the world.

274. Chaeronea and the Congress of Corinth. — In 338 B.C. Philip threw off the mask and invaded Greece. Athens and Thebes combined against him, — to be hopelessly crushed at the *battle of Chaeronea.* Then a congress of Greek states at Corinth *recognized Macedonia as the head of Greece.* It was agreed that the separate states should keep their local self-government, but that foreign matters, including war and peace, should be committed to Philip. Philip was also declared *general in chief of the armies of Greece for a war against Persia.*

275. The History of Hellas Ended. — Thus Philip posed, wisely, not as the conqueror, but as the champion of Greece against the foe of all Hellenes. He showed a patient magnanimity, too, toward fickle Greek states, and in particular he strove to reconcile Athens. He was wise enough to see that he needed, not reluctant subjects, but willing followers.

Greek independence was at an end. Greece thereafter, until a hundred years ago, was only a province of this or that foreign power. *The history of Hellenic culture, however, was not closed.* The Macedonian conquest was to spread that civilization over the vast East. *The history of Hellas merges in the history of a wider Hellenistic world.*

FOR FURTHER READING. — *Specially suggested:* Davis' *Readings,* Vol. I, Nos. 103–107. Bury, ch. xvi ; *or* (better if accessible) Wheeler's *Alexander the Great,* 14–18 and 64–80.

EXERCISE. — Review the period from Aegospotami to Chaeronea by "catch-words" (see Exercise on page 190).

PART III

THE GRAECO-ORIENTAL WORLD

With Alexander the stage of Greek influence spreads across the world, and Greece becomes only a small item in the heritage of the Greeks.

— MAHAFFY.

The seed-ground of European civilization is neither Greece nor the Orient, but a world joined of the two. — BENJAMIN IDE WHEELER.

◆

CHAPTER XVII

THE MINGLING OF EAST AND WEST

276. Alexander the Great. — Philip of Macedon was assassinated in 336, two years after Chaeronea. He was just ready to begin the invasion of Asia; and his work was taken up by his son *Alexander*.

Father and son were both among the greatest men in history, but they were very unlike. In many ways Alexander resembled his mother, Olympias, a semi-barbaric princess from Epirus, — a woman of intense passions and generous enthusiasms. Says Benjamin Ide Wheeler : —

" While it was from his father that Alexander inherited his sagacious insight into men and things, and his brilliant capacity for timely and determined action, it was to his mother that he undoubtedly owed that passionate warmth of nature which betrayed itself not only in the furious outbursts of temper occasionally characteristic of him, but quite as much in a romantic fervor of attachment and love for friends, a delicate tenderness of sympathy for the weak, and a princely largeness and generosity of soul toward all, that made him so deeply beloved of men and so enthusiastically followed." — *Alexander the Great*, 5.

As a boy, Alexander had been fearless, self-willed, and restless, with fervent affections.[1] These traits marked his whole career. He was devoted to Homer, and he knew the *Iliad* by heart. Homer's Achilles he claimed for an ancestor and took for his ideal. His later education was directed by *Aristotle* (§ 315), and from this great teacher he learned to admire Greek art and science and to come closely into sympathy with the best Greek culture.

277. Restoration of Order. — At his father's death Alexander was a stripling of twenty years. He was to prove a rare mili-

ALEXANDER.   ALEXANDER IN A LION-HUNT.
Two sides of a gold medallion of Tarsus.

tary genius. He never lost a battle and never refused an engagement; and, on occasion, he could be shrewd and adroit in diplomacy; but at this time he was known only as a rash boy. No one thought that he could hold together the empire that had been built up by the force and cunning of the great Philip. Revolt broke out everywhere; but the young king showed himself at once both statesman and general. With marvelous rapidity he struck crushing blows on this side and on that. A hurried expedition restored order in Greece; the savage tribes of the north were quieted by a rapid march beyond the Danube;

---

[1] Special report: anecdotes from Plutarch regarding Alexander's boyhood.

then, turning on rebellious Illyria, Alexander forced the mountain passes and overran the country.

Meanwhile it was reported in the south that Alexander was killed or defeated among the barbarians. Insurrection again blazed forth; but with forced marches he suddenly appeared a second time in Greece, falling with swift and terrible vengeance upon Thebes, the center of the revolt. The city was taken by storm and leveled to the ground, except the house of Pindar (§ 155), while the thirty thousand survivors of the population were sold as slaves. The other states were terrified into abject submission, and were treated generously. Then, with his authority firmly reestablished, Alexander turned, as the champion of Hellas, to attack Persia.

ALEXANDER.
The "Copenhagen" head. Probably by a pupil of the sculptor Skopas.

278. The Persian Campaigns. — In the spring of 334 B.C. Alexander crossed the Hellespont with thirty-five thousand disciplined troops. The army was quite enough to scatter any Oriental force, and as large as any general could then handle in long and rapid marches in a hostile country; but its size contrasts strangely with that of the huge horde Xerxes had led against Greece a century and a half before.

The route of march and the immense distances traversed can be best traced by the map. The conquest of the main empire occupied five years, and the story falls into three distinct chapters, each marked by a world-famous battle.

a. Asia Minor: Battle of the Granicus. — The Persian satraps of Asia Minor met the invaders at the Granicus, a small stream in ancient Troyland. With the personal rashness that was the one blot upon his military skill, Alexander himself led the Macedonian charge through the river and up the steep bank into the midst of the Persian cavalry, where he barely escaped death. The Persian nobles fought, as always, with gallant self-devotion, but in the end they were utterly routed. Then a body of Greek mercenaries in Persian pay was surrounded and cut down to a man. No quarter was to be given Hellenes fighting as traitors to the cause of Hellas.

The victory cost Alexander only 120 men, and it made him master of all Asia Minor. During the next few months he set up democracies in the Greek cities, and organized the government of the various provinces.

b. The Mediterranean Coast: Battle of Issus. — To strike at the heart of the empire at once would have been to leave behind him a large Persian fleet, to encourage revolt in Greece. Alexander wisely determined to secure the entire coast, and so protect his rear, before marching into the interior. Accordingly he turned south, just after crossing the mountains that separate Asia Minor from Syria, to reduce Phoenicia and Egypt. Meantime the Persians had gathered a great army; but at *Issus* Alexander easily overthrew their host of six hundred thousand men led by King Darius in person. Darius allowed himself to be caught in a narrow defile between the mountains and the sea. The cramped space made the vast numbers of the Persians an embarrassment to themselves. They soon became a huddled mob of fugitives, and the Macedonians wearied themselves with slaughter.

Alexander now assumed the title, King of Persia. The siege of Tyre (§ 57) detained him a year; but Egypt welcomed him as a deliverer, and by the close of 332, *all the sea power of the Eastern Mediterranean was his.*[1] While in Egypt he showed his

---

[1] Carthage dominated the western waters of the Mediterranean — beyond Italy; but she had nothing to do with naval rivalries farther east.

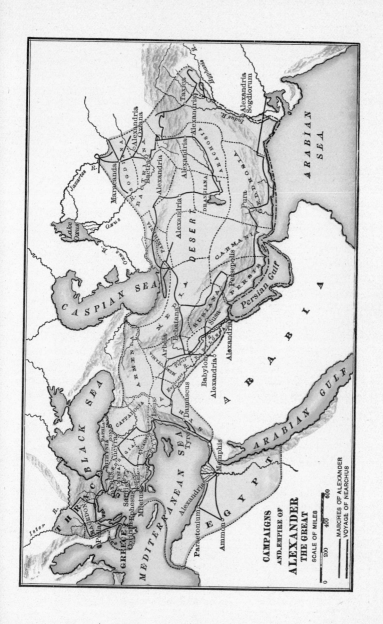

CAMPAIGNS
AND EMPIRE OF
ALEXANDER
THE GREAT

SCALE OF MILES

0   200   400   600

MARCHES OF ALEXANDER
VOYAGE OF NEARCHUS

ARABIAN
SEA

ARABIAN GULF

MEDITERRANEAN SEA

BLACK SEA

CASPIAN SEA

Persian Gulf

ARABIA

DESERT

EGYPT

THRACE

GREECE

MACEDON

Alexandria
Sogdiorum

Taxila

Hydaspes
Hyphasis

Indus R.

Alexandria
Oxiana

Maracanda

SOGDIANA

BACTRIANA

Bactra

ARIA

Alexandria

Alexandria

ARACHOSIA

GEDROSIA

Pura

CARMANIA

Persepolis

PERSIA

Alexandria

SUSIANA

Susa

Ecbatana

MEDIA

Arbela

ARMENIA

CAPPADOCIA

Babylon
Alexandria

Euphrates

Tigris

Damascus

Tyre

Issus

BITHYNIA

Sinope

Ister R.

Lake Oxus

Oxus R.

Jaxartes R.

Jaxartes R.

DRANGIANA

GANDAHARIA

PARTHIA

HYRCANIA

MESOPOTAMIA

ASSYRIA

Alexandria

Memphis

Parætonium

Ammonium

Sardis
Ephesus
Miletus

Byzantium
Cyzicus

Halicarnassus

constructive genius by founding *Alexandria,* a city destined for many centuries to be a commercial and intellectual center for the world.

c. The Tigris-Euphrates District: Battle of Arbela. — Darius now proposed that he and Alexander should divide the empire between them. Rejecting this offer contemptuously, Alexander took up his march for the interior. While following the ancient route from Egypt to Assyria (§ 6) he visited Jerusalem, was received with great honor by the high priest and granted the Jews considerable privileges. He met Darius near *Arbela,* not far from ancient Nineveh. Alexander purposely allowed him choice of time and place, and by a third decisive victory *proved* the hopelessness of resistance. Darius never gathered another army. The capitals of the empire — Babylon, Susa, Ecbatana, Persepolis — surrendered, with enormous treasure in gold and silver, and *the Persian Empire had fallen (331 B.C.).*

The Granicus, Issus, and Arbela rank with Marathon, Salamis, and Plataea, as "decisive" battles. The earlier set of three great battles gave Western civilization a chance to develop. This second set of three battles resulted in a new type of civilization, springing from a union of East and West. No battle between these two periods had anywhere near so great a significance.

279. **Campaigns in the Far East.** — The next six years went, however, to much more desperate warfare in the eastern mountain regions, and in the Punjab.[1] Alexander carried his arms as far east from Babylon as Babylon was from Macedonia. He traversed great deserts; subdued the warlike and princely chiefs of Bactria and Sogdiana up to the steppes of the wild Tartar tribes beyond the Oxus; twice forced the passes of the Hindukush (a feat almost unparalleled); conquered the valiant mountaineers of what is now Afghanistan; and led his army into the fertile and populous plains of northern India. He crossed the Indus, won realms *beyond* the ancient Persian province of the Punjab, and planned still

---

[1] A district of northern India.

more distant empires; but on the banks of the Hyphasis River his faithful Macedonians refused to be led farther, to waste away in inhuman perils; and the chagrined conqueror was compelled to return to Babylon. This city he made his capital, and here he died of a fever two years later (323 B.C.) in the midst of preparations to extend his conquests both east and west.[1] These last years, however, were given mainly to organizing the empire (§ 280).

280. Merging of East and West. — Alexander began his conquest to avenge the West upon the East. But he came to see excellent and noble qualities in Oriental life, and he rose rapidly to a broader view. He aimed no longer to hold a world in subjection by the force of a small conquering tribe, but rather *to mold Persian and Greek into one people on terms of equality.* He wished to marry the East and the West, — "to bring them together into a composite civilization, to which each should contribute its better elements."

Persian youth were trained by thousands in Macedonian fashion to replace the veterans of Alexander's army; Persian nobles were welcomed at court and given high offices; and the government of Asia was intrusted largely to Asiatics, on a system similar to that of Darius the Great (§ 76). Alexander himself adopted Persian manners and customs, and he bribed and coaxed his officers and soldiers to do the like. All this was part of a deliberate design to encourage the fusion of the two peoples. The Macedonians protested jealously, and even rebelled, but were quickly reduced to obedience.

" The dream of his youth melted away, but a new vision in larger perspective arose with ever strengthening outlines in its place. The champion of the West against the East faded in mist, and the form of a world monarch, standing above the various worlds of men and belonging to none, but molding them all into one, emerged in its stead." — WHEELER, *Alexander the Great,* 376.

---

[1] Topic: anecdotes of Alexander's later years; the change in his character. Wheeler's *Alexander* gives an ardent defense.

281. Hellenism the Active Element. — At the same time Alexander saw that to fulfill this mission he must throw open the East to Greek ideas. The races might mingle their blood; the Greek might learn much from the Orient, and in the end be absorbed by it; *but the thought and art of little Hellas, with its active energy, must leaven the vast passive mass of the East.*

One great measure, for this end, was the founding of chains of cities, to bind the conquests together and to become the homes of Hellenic influence. Alexander himself built seventy of these towns (usually called from his name, like the Alexandria in Egypt). Their walls sprang up under the pick and spade of the soldiery along the lines of march. One great city, we are told, walls and houses, was completed in twenty

ALEXANDER AS APOLLO.
Now in the Capitoline Museum.

days. Sometimes these places were mere garrison towns on distant frontiers, but oftener they became mighty emporiums at the intersection of great lines of trade. There was an Alexandria on the Jaxartes, on the Indus, on the Euphrates, as well as on the Nile. The sites were chosen wisely, and many of these cities remain great capitals to this day, like Herat and Kandahar.[1]

282. Greek Colonies in the Orient. — This building of Greek cities was continued by Alexander's successors. Once more, and on a vaster scale than ever before, the Greek genius for

---

[1] Iskandar, or Kandahar, is an Oriental form of the Greek name Alexander.

colonization found vent. *Each new city had a Greek nucleus.* Usually this consisted only of worn-out veterans, left behind as a garrison; but enterprising youth, emigrating from old Hellas, continued to reinforce the Greek element. The native village people roundabout were gathered in to make the bulk of the inhabitants; and these also soon took on Greek character. From scattered, ignorant rustics, they became artisans and merchants, devotedly attached to Greek rule and zealous disciples of Greek culture.

The cities were all built on a large and comfortable model. They were well paved. They had ample provision for lighting by night, and a good water supply. They had police arrangements, and good thoroughfares. Even in that despotic East, they received extensive privileges and enjoyed a large amount of self-government: they met in their own assemblies, managed their own courts, and collected their own taxes. For centuries they made the backbone of Hellenism throughout the world. Greek was the ordinary speech of their streets; Greek architecture built their temples, and Greek sculpture adorned them; they celebrated Greek games and festivals; and, no longer in little Hellas alone, but over the whole East, in Greek theaters, vast audiences were educated by the plays of Euripides. The culture developed by a small people became the heritage of a vast world.

The unity of this widespread civilization cannot be insisted upon too strongly. Political unity was soon lost; but the oneness of culture endured for centuries, and kept its character even after Roman conquest. Over all that vast area there was for all cultivated men a common language, a common literature, a common mode of thought. *The mingling of East and West produced a new civilization, — a Graeco-Oriental world.*

In our own day, Western civilization is again transforming the Orient, leaving the railroad, the telegraph, free schools, and republican government in its line of march, — a march that reaches even farther than Alexander ever did. Between Alexander's day and ours, no like phenomena has been seen on any scale so vast. But this time the West does not give so large a part of its blood to the East; nor does the East *react* upon the West, as it did after Alexander (§ 283).

283. Reaction upon Hellas. — Hellas itself lost importance. It was drained of its intellect and enterprise, because adventurous young Greeks wandered to the East, to win fortune and distinction. And the victorious Hellenic civilization was modified by its victory, even in its old home. Sympathies were broadened. The barrier between Greek and barbarian faded away. Greek ideals were affected by Oriental ideals.

In particular, we note two forms of reaction upon Greek life, — the economic and the scientific (§§ 284, 285).

284. Economic Results. — Wealth was enormously augmented. The vast treasure of gold and silver which Oriental monarchs had hoarded in secret vaults was thrown again into circulation, and large sums were brought back to Europe by returning adventurers. These adventurers brought back also an increased desire for Oriental luxuries. Thus, trade was stimulated; a higher standard of living arose; manifold new comforts and enjoyments adorned and enriched life.

Somewhat later, perhaps as a result of this increase of wealth, there came other less fortunate changes. *Extremes of wealth and poverty appeared side by side,* as in our modern society : the great cities had their hungry, sullen, dangerous mobs; and socialistic agitation began on a large scale. These last phenomena, however, concerned only the closing days of the Hellenic world, just before its absorption by Rome.

285. Scientific Results. — A new era of scientific progress began. Alexander himself had the zeal of an explorer, and one of the most important scientific expeditions ever sent out by any government is due to him while he was in India. When he first touched the Indus, he thought it the upper course of the Nile; but he built a great fleet of two thousand vessels, sailed down the river to the Indian Ocean, and then sent his friend Nearchus to explore that sea and to trace the coast to the mouth of the Euphrates. After a voyage of many months, Nearchus reached Babylon. He had mapped the coast line, made frequent landings, and collected a mass of observations and a multitude of strange plants and animals.

Like collections were made by Alexander at other times, to be sent to his old instructor Aristotle, who embodied the results of his study upon them in a *Natural History* of fifty volumes. The Greek intellect, attracted by the marvels in the new world opened before it, turned to scientific observation and arrangement of facts. This impulse was intensified by the discovery of a long series of astronomical observations at Babylon (§ 49) and of the historical records and traditions of the Orientals, reaching back to an antiquity of which the Greeks had not dreamed. The active Greek mind, seizing upon this confused wealth of material, began to put in order a great system of knowledge about man and nature.

286. Summary. —Thus the mingling of East and West gave a product different from either of the old factors. Alexander's victories are not merely events in military history. They make an epoch in the onward march of humanity. They enlarged the map of the world once more, and they made these vaster spaces the home of a higher culture. *They grafted the new West upon the old East, — a graft from which sprang the civilization of imperial Rome.*

Alexander died at thirty-two, and his empire at once fell into fragments, Had he lived to seventy, it is hard to say what he might not have done to provide for lasting political union, and perhaps even to bring India and China into the current of our civilization.

For Further Reading. — *Specially suggested:* Davis' *Readings*, Vol. I, Nos. 108–118 (24 pages, mostly from Arrian, a second century writer and the earliest authority who has left us an account of Alexander). Bury, 736–836.

CHAPTER XVIII

THE GRAECO-ORIENTAL WORLD

THE POLITICAL STORY

287. Wars of the Succession. — Alexander left no heir old enough to succeed him. On his deathbed, asked to whom he would leave his throne, he replied grimly, "To the strongest." As he foresaw, at his death his leading generals instantly began to strive with each other for his realm; and for nearly half a century the political history of the civilized world was a horrible welter of war and assassination. These struggles are called the *Wars of the Succession* (323–280 B.C.).

288. The Third Century B.C. — Finally, about 280 B.C., something like a fixed order emerged; then followed a period of sixty years, known as the *Glory of Hellenism.* The Hellenistic [1] world reached from the Adriatic to the Indus, and consisted of: (1) three great kingdoms, *Syria, Egypt,* and *Macedonia;* (2) a broken chain of smaller monarchies scattered from *Media* to *Epirus* [2] (some of them, like *Pontus* and *Armenia*, under dynasties descended from Persian princes); and (3) single free cities like *Byzantium.* Some of these free cities united into leagues, which sometimes became great military powers — like one famous confederation under the leadership of *Rhodes.*

289. Resemblance to Modern Europe. — *Politically in many ways all the vast district bore a striking resemblance to modern Europe.* There was a like division into great and small states, ruled by dynasties related by intermarriages; there was a common civilization, and a recognition of common interests as

---

[1] *Hellenic* refers to the old Hellas; *Hellenistic*, to the wider world, of mixed Hellenic and Oriental character, after Alexander.

[2] There is a full enumeration in Mahaffy's *Alexander's Empire*, 90–92.

against outside barbarism or as opposed to any non-Hellenic power, like Rome; and there were jealousies and conflicts similar to those in Europe in recent centuries. There were shifting alliances, and many wars to preserve "the balance of power" or to secure trade advantages. There was a likeness to modern society, too, as we shall see more fully later, in the refinement of the age, in its excellences and its vices, the great learning, the increase in skill and in criticism. (Of course the age was vastly inferior to that of modern Europe.) It follows that the history of the third century is a history of many separate countries (§§ 292 ff.). But there was one event of general interest.

290. The Invasion by the Gauls. — Here we have to speak for the first time of *the Gauls or Celts.* (See § 8.) This nation had emigrated, as indeed had the other nations of Europe, from Asia. After inhabiting for some time parts of present Germany, they finally fixed their abodes somewhere northwest of the Alps. They soon occupied all present France, Britain, and Ireland, and a great part of Spain. To the south of Europe they were far more known for their prowess and thirst for conquest and plunder than for the other qualities to which they owe their place in history, namely, their remarkable talent for technical and literary skill and a still greater aptitude for religious enthusiasm. For the time being they were in a period of unrest. Large multitudes of them migrated to northern Italy and settled there. One of their bands penetrated into the very heart of the peninsula, defeated a Roman army and plundered and burned the city of Rome itself (§ 375). Other hordes traveled further west and settled in various places along the Danube, without, however, making them the goal of their wanderings. In fact, in their unsubdued aggressiveness they became for some time a standing menace to the civilized nations on the shores of the Aegean Sea.

One of these Gallic invasions, in B.C. 278, was the first really formidable attack upon the Eastern world since the Scythians

had been chastised by the early Persian kings (§ 75). Fortunately it did not take place before the ruinous wars of the
succession were over. The Gauls poured into exhausted Macedonia and advanced into Greece as far as Delphi. They made
a raid on the famous temple of Apollo to carry off its immense
treasures. But somehow they were routed in disorder. Apollo,
it was said, had driven them away with his thunderbolts. After
horrible ravages they carried havoc into Asia. For a long
period every great sovereign of the Hellenic world turned his
arms upon them, until they were finally settled as peaceful
colonists in a region of Asia Minor, which took the name
Galatia from these new inhabitants.[1] — The Hellenistic patriotism roused by this attack played a part in the splendid outburst of art and literature which followed.

291. Decline of the Hellenistic World. — About 220, the widespread Hellenistic world began a rapid decline. In that
year the thrones of Syria, Egypt, and Macedonia fell to youthful heirs; and all three of these new monarchs showed a
degeneracy which is common in Oriental ruling families after
a few generations of greatness. Just before this year, as we
shall see (§ 310), the last promise of independence in Greece
itself had flickered out. Just after it, there began an attack
from Rome, which was finally to absorb this Hellenistic East
into a still larger world.

Before turning to the growth of Rome, however, we will note (1) the
history, in brief, of the leading Hellenic states from Alexander to the
Roman sway; (2) with more detail, an interesting attempt at federal
government in Greece itself; and (3) the character of Hellenistic culture
in this period.

SOME SINGLE EASTERN STATES IN OUTLINE

292. Syria was the largest of the great monarchies. It comprised most of Alexander's empire in Asia, except the small

---

[1] These new inhabitants preserved their national individuality for several
centuries. St. Paul addressed one of his letters to "the Galatians."

states in Asia Minor. In the Wars of the Succession, it fell
to *Seleucus*, one of the Macedonian generals; and his descendants (Seleucidae) ruled it to the Roman conquest. They

PYLON OF PTOLEMY III AT KARNAK. The reliefs represent that conqueror
in religious thanksgiving, sacrificing, praying, offering trophies to the gods.
At the top is the "conventionalized" winged sundisk. Cf. page 36. Note
the general likeness to the older Egyptian architecture.

excelled all other successors of Alexander in building cities
and extending Greek culture over distant regions. Seleucus
alone founded seventy-five cities.

About 250 B.C. Indian princes reconquered the Punjab, and the Parthians arose on the northeast, to cut off the Bactrian provinces from the rest of the Greek world. Thus Syria shrank to the area of the ancient Assyrian Empire, — the Euphrates-Tigris basin and old Syria proper, — but it was still, in common opinion, the greatest world-power, until its might was shattered by Rome in 190 B.C. at *Magnesia.*

293. Egypt included Cyprus, and possessed a vague control over many coast towns of Syria and Asia Minor. Immediately upon Alexander's death, one of his generals, *Ptolemy,* chose Egypt for his province. His descendants, all known as Ptolemies, ruled the land until Cleopatra yielded to Augustus Caesar (30 B.C.), though it had become a Roman protectorate [1] somewhat before that time.

The early Ptolemies were wise, energetic sovereigns. . They aimed to make Egypt the commercial emporium of the world, and to make their capital, Alexandria, the world's intellectual center. Ptolemy I established a great naval power, improved harbors, and *built the first lighthouse.* Ptolemy II (better known as *Ptolemy Philadelphus*) restored the old canal from the Red Sea to the Nile (§§ 28, 32), constructed roads, and fostered learning more than any great ruler before him (§ 319). Ptolemy III, in war with Syria, carried his arms to Bactria, and on his return mapped the coast of Arabia. Unlike earlier conquerors, he made no attempt to add territory to his realm by his victories, but only to secure trade advantages and a satisfactory peace. The later Ptolemies were weaklings or infamous monsters, guilty of every folly and crime; but even they continued to encourage learning.

294. Macedonia ceased to be of great interest after the death of Alexander, except from a military point of view. Its position made it the first part of the Greek world to come into hostile contact with Rome. King Philip V joined Carthage in a war against Rome, a little before the year 200 B.C.

---

[1] That is, Rome had come to control all the relations of Egypt with foreign countries, although its government continued in name to be independent.

A series of struggles resulted; and Macedonia, with parts of Greece, became Roman in 146 B.C.

295. Rhodes and Pergamum. — Among the many small states, two deserve special mention. *Rhodes* headed a confederacy of cities in the Aegean, and in the third century she became the leading commercial state of the Mediterranean. Her policy was one of peace and freedom of trade. *Pergamum* was a small Greek kingdom in Asia Minor, which the genius of its rulers (the Attalids) made prominent in politics and art. When the struggles with Rome began, Pergamum allied itself with that power, and long remained a favored state.

THE ACHAEAN LEAGUE IN GREECE

296. The Political Situation. — During the ruinous Wars of the Succession, Greece had been a favorite battleground for the great powers, Egypt, Syria, and Macedonia. Many cities were laid waste, and at the close of the contests, the country was left a vassal of Macedonia. To make her hold firmer, Macedonia set up tyrants in many cities. From this humiliation, Greece was lifted for a time by a new power, the *Achaean League*, which made a last effort for the freedom of Hellas.

297. Earlier Confederations. — In early times, in the more backward parts of Greece, there had been many rude federations of tribes, as among the Phocians and Locrians; but in city-Greece no such union had long survived.

The failure of the *Confederacy of Delos* has been told. During the supremacy of Sparta (about 400 B.C.) another still more interesting federal union appeared for a brief time on the northern coast of the Aegean. *Olynthus*, a leading Greek city in the Chalcidic district, built up a confederacy of forty states, to check the Thracian and Macedonian barbarians, who had begun to stir themselves after the fall of the Athenian power. This league is called the *Olynthian Confederacy*. Its cities kept their local independence ; but they were merged, upon equal terms, into a large state more perfect than any preceding federal union. *The citizens of any one city could intermarry with those of any other, and they could dwell and acquire landed property anywhere within the league; while no one city had superior privileges over the others*, as Athens had had in the

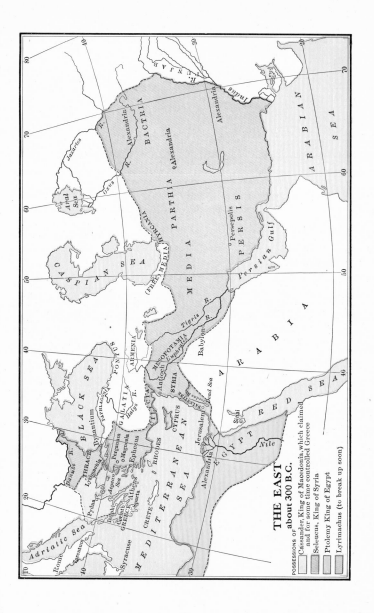

THE EAST
about 300 B.C.

POSSESSIONS of Cassander, King of Macedonia, which claimed and for some time controlled Greece

Seleucus, King of Syria

Ptolemy King of Egypt

Lyrimachus (to break up soon)

Delian League. After only a short life, as we have seen, this promising union was crushed ruthlessly by jealous Sparta (§ 261).

298. Aetolian League. — Now, after 280 B.C., two of the ancient tribal federations which had survived in obscure corners of Greece — Achaea and Aetolia — began to play leading parts in history.

Of these two, the *Aetolian League* was the less important. Originally it seems to have been a loose union of mountain districts for defense. But the Wars of the Succession made the Aetolians famous as bold soldiers of fortune, and the wealth brought home by the thousands of such adventurers led to a more aggressive policy on the part of the league. The people remained, however, rude mountaineers, " brave, boastful, rapacious, and utterly reckless of the rights of others." They played a part in saving southern Greece from the invading Gauls (§ 290), but their confederacy became more and more an organization for lawless plunder.

299. Achaean League : Origin. — In Achaea there was a nobler history. A league of small towns grew into a formidable power, freed most of Greece, brought much of it into a federal union, with all members on equal terms, and for a glorious half century maintained Greek freedom successfully.

The story offers curious contrasts to the period of Athenian leadership two hundred years earlier. Greece could no longer hope to become one of the great military powers ; we miss the intellectual brilliancy, too, of the fifth century ; but the period affords even more instructive political lessons — especially to Americans, interested, as we are, in federal institutions. The most important political matter in Greek history in the third century B.C. is this experiment in federal government.

The people of Achaea were unwarlike, and not very enterprising or intellectual. In all Greek history they produced no great writer or great artist. They did not even furnish great statesmen, — for all the heroes of the league were to come from outside Achaea itself. Still, the Achaean League is one of the most remarkable federations in history before the adoption of the present Constitution of the United States.

We know that there was some kind of a confederation in Achaea as early as the Persian War. Under the Macedonian rule, the league was destroyed and tyrants were set up in several of the ten Achaean cities. But, about 280 B.C., four small towns revived the ancient confederacy. This union swiftly drove out the tyrants from the neighboring towns, and absorbed all Achaea. One generous incident belongs to this part of the story: *Iseas*, tyrant of Cerynea, voluntarily gave up his power and brought his city into the league.

So far Macedonia had not interfered. The Gallic invasion just at this time spread ruin over all the north of Hellas, and probably prevented hostile action by the Macedonian king. Thus the federation became securely established.

300. Government. — During this period the constitution was formed. The chief authority of the league was placed in a *Federal Assembly*. This was not a *representative* body, but a mass meeting: it was made up of all citizens of the league who chose to attend. To prevent the city where the meeting was held from outweighing the others, each city was given only one vote. That is, ten or twelve men — or even one man — from a distant town cast the vote of that city, and counted just as much as several hundred from a city nearer the place of meeting. The Assembly was held twice a year, for only three days at a time, and in some small city, so that a great capital should not overshadow the rest of the league. It chose yearly a *Council of Ten*, a *Senate*, and a *General* (or president), with various subordinate officers. The same General could not be chosen two years in succession.

This government raised federal taxes and armies, and represented the federation in all foreign relations. Each city remained a distinct state, with full control over all its internal matters — but no city of itself could make peace or war, enter into alliances, or send ambassadors to another state. That is, the Achaean League was a true federation, and not a mere alliance; and its cities corresponded closely to the American States under our old Articles of Confederation.

301. Faults in the Government. — In theory, the constitution was extremely democratic : in practice, it proved otherwise. Men attended the Assembly at their own expense. Any Achaean *might* come, but *only the wealthy could afford to do so,* as a regular thing. Moreover, since the meetings of the Assembly were few and brief, great authority had to be left to the General and Council. Any Achaean was eligible to these offices; but *poor men could hardly afford to take them, because they had no salaries. The Greek system of a primary assembly was suited only to single cities. A primary assembly made the city of Athens a perfect democracy : the same institution made the Achaean League intensely aristocratic.*

The constitution was an advance over all other Greek federations, but it had two other faults. (1) It made little use of representation, which no doubt would have seemed to the Achaeans undemocratic (§ 128), but which in practice would have enabled a larger part of the citizens to have a voice in the government; and (2) all cities, great or small, had the same vote.

This last did not matter much at first, for the little Achaean towns did not differ greatly in size; but it became a plain injustice when the union came later to contain some of the most powerful cities in Greece. However, this feature was almost universal in early confederacies,[1] and it was the principle of the American Union until 1789.

302. First Expansion beyond Achaea. — The power of the General was so great that the history of the league is the biography of a few great men. The most remarkable of these

---

[1] The one exception was the Lycian Confederacy in Asia Minor. The Lycians were not Greeks, apparently; but they had taken on some Greek culture, and their federal union was an advance even upon the Achaean. It was absorbed by Rome, however, in 54 A.D., before it played an important part in history. In its Assembly, the vote was taken by cities, *but the cities were divided into three classes : the largest had three votes each, the next class two each, and the smallest only one.* In the Philadelphia Convention, in 1787, several American statesmen wished to adopt this Lycian plan for our States in the Federal Congress.

leaders was *Aratus* of Sicyon. Sicyon was a city just outside Achaea, to the east. It had been ruled by a vile and bloody tyrant, who drove many leading citizens into exile. Among these exiles was the family of Aratus. When a youth of twenty years (251 B.C.) Aratus planned, by a night attack, to overthrow the tyrant and free his native city. The daring venture was brilliantly successful; but it aroused the hatred of Macedon, and, to preserve the freedom so nobly won, Aratus brought Sicyon into the Achaean federation.

303. Aratus.[1] — Five years later, Aratus was elected General of the league, and thereafter, he held that office each alternate year (as often as the constitution permitted) until his death, thirty-two years later.

Aratus hated tyrants, and longed for a free and united Greece. He extended the league far beyond the borders of Achaea, and made it a champion of Hellenic freedom. He aimed at a noble end, but did not refuse base means. He was incorruptible himself, and he lavished his vast wealth on the union; but he was bitterly jealous of other leaders. With plenty of daring in a dashing project, as he many times proved, he lacked nerve to command in battle, and he never won a real victory in the field. Still, despite his many defeats, his persuasive power and his merits kept him the confidence of the union to the end of a long public life.

304. Growth of the League; Lydiadas. — In his second generalship, Aratus freed Corinth from her Macedonian tyrant by a desperate night attack upon the garrison of the citadel. That powerful city then entered the union. So did Megara, which itself drove out its Macedonian garrison. The league now commanded the isthmus, and was safe from attack by Macedonia. Then several cities in Arcadia joined, and, in 234, Megalopolis (§ 265) was added, — at that time one of the leading cities in Greece.

---

[1] Aratus is the first statesman known to us from his own memoirs. That work itself no longer exists, but Plutarch drew upon it for his *Life*, as did Polybius for his *History*.

Some years earlier the government of Megalopolis had become a tyranny: *Lydiadas,* a gallant and enthusiastic youth, seized despotic power, meaning to use it for good ends.[1] The growth of the Achaean League opened a nobler way: *Lydiadas resigned his tyranny,* and as a private citizen brought the Great City into the union. This act made him a popular hero, and Aratus became his bitter foe. The new leader was the more lovable figure, — generous and ardent, a soldier as well as a statesman. Several times he became General of the league, but even in office he was often thwarted by the disgraceful trickery of the older man.

THE ACHAEAN AND AETOLIAN LEAGUES,
ABOUT 225 B.C.

305. The Freeing of Athens and Argos. — For many years Aratus had aimed to free Athens and Argos — sometimes by heroic endeavors, sometimes by assassination and poison. In 229, he succeeded. He *bought* the withdrawal of Macedonian troops from the Piraeus, and Athens became an ally, though not a member, of the league.[2] The tyrant of Argos was persuaded or frightened into following the example

---

[1] This was true of several tyrants in this age, and it was due no doubt in part to the new respect for monarchy since Alexander's time, and in part to new theories of government taught by the philosophers.

[2] The old historic cities, Athens and Sparta, could not be brought to look favorably upon such a union.

of Iseas and Lydiadas, — as had happened meanwhile in many smaller cities, — and Argos joined the confederacy.

The league now was the commanding power in Hellas. It included all Peloponnesus except Sparta and Elis. Moreover, all Greece south of Thermopylae had become free, — largely through the influence of the Achaean league, — and most of the states not inside the union had at least entered into friendly alliance with it. But now came a fatal conflict with Sparta.

306. Need of Social Reforms in Sparta. — The struggle was connected with a great reform within that ancient city. The forms of the "Lycurgan" constitution had survived through many centuries, but now Sparta had only seven hundred full citizens (cf. §§ 254, 263). This condition brought about a violent agitation for reform. And about the year 243, *Agis*, one of the Spartan kings, set himself to do again what Lycurgus· had done in legend.

307. Agis was a youthful hero, full of noble daring and pure enthusiasm. He gave his own property to the state and per-suaded his relatives and friends to do the like. He planned to abolish all debts, and to divide the land among forty-five hundred Spartan "Inferiors" (§ 254) and fifteen thousand other Laconians, so as to refound the state upon a broad and democratic basis. Agis could easily have won by violence; but he refused such methods, and sought his ends by con-stitutional means only. The conservative party rose in fierce opposition. By order of the Ephors, the young king was seized, with his noble mother and grandmother, and murdered in prison, — " the purest and noblest spirit that ever perished through deeming others as pure and noble as himself."

308. Cleomenes. — But the ideals of the martyr lived on. His wife was forced to marry *Cleomenes*, son of the other king; and, *from her, this prince adopted the hopes of Agis.* Cleomenes became king in 236. He had less of high sensitiveness and of stainless honor than Agis, but he is a grand and colossal figure. He bided his time; and then, when the Ephors were planning to use force against him, he struck first.

Aratus had led the Achaean League into war[1] with Sparta in order to unite all the Peloponnesus; but the military genius of Cleomenes made even enfeebled Sparta a match for the great league. He won two great victories. Then, the league being helpless for the moment, he used his popularity to secure reform in Sparta. The oligarchs were plotting against him, but he was enthusiastically supported by the disfranchised multitudes. Leaving his Spartan troops at a distance, he hurried to the city by forced marches with some chosen followers. There he seized and slew the Ephors, and proclaimed a new constitution, which contained the reforms of Agis.

309. Sparta Victorious over the League. — Cleomenes designed to make this new Sparta the head of the Peloponnesus. He and Aratus each desired a free, united Greece, but under different leadership. Moreover, Sparta now stood forth the advocate of a kind of socialism, and so was particularly hateful to the aristocratic government of the league.

The struggle between the two powers was renewed with fresh bitterness. Cleomenes won more victories, and then, with the league at his feet, he offered generous terms. He demanded that Sparta be admitted to the union as virtual leader. This would have created the greatest power ever seen in Greece, and, for the time, it would have made a free Hellas sure. The Achaeans were generally in favor of accepting the proposal; but Aratus — jealous of Cleomenes and fearful of social reform — broke off the negotiations by underhanded methods.

310. Aratus calls in Macedon. — Then Aratus bought the aid of Macedon against Sparta, *by betraying Corinth,* a free member of the league and the city connected with his own most glorious exploit. As a result, *the federation became a protectorate of Macedonia,* holding no relations with foreign states except through that power. The war now became a struggle

---

[1] In a battle in this war Aratus held back the Achaean phalanx, while Lydiadas, heading a gallant charge, was overpowered by numbers.

for Greek freedom, waged by Sparta under her hero king against the overwhelming power of Macedon assisted by the confederacy as a vassal state. Aratus had undone his own great work.

The date (222 B.C.) coincides with the general decline of the Hellenic world (§ 291). For a while, Sparta showed surprising vigor, and Cleomenes was marvelously successful. The league indeed dwindled to a handful of petty cities. But in the end Macedonia prevailed. Cleomenes fled to Egypt, to die in exile; and Sparta opened her gates for the first time to a conquering army. The league was restored to its old extent, but its glory was gone. It still served a useful purpose in keeping peace and order over a large part of Peloponnesus, but it was no longer the champion of a free Hellas.

311. Final Decline. — Soon after, war followed between Achaea and Aetolia. This contest became a struggle between Macedonia and her vassals on the one side, and Aetolia aided by Rome on the other; for as Achaea had called in Macedonia against Sparta, so now Aetolia called in Rome against Achaea and Macedonia, — and Greek history closed.

Some gleams of glory shine out at the last in the career of *Philopoemen* of Megalopolis, the greatest general the Achaean League ever produced, and one of the noblest characters in history; but the doom of Achaea was already sealed. "Philopoemen," says Freeman, "was one of the heroes who struggle against fate, and who are allowed to do no more than to stave off a destruction which it is beyond their power to avert." These words are a fitting epitaph for the great league itself.

HELLENISTIC SOCIETY

312. General Culture. — From 280 to 150 B.C. was the period of chief splendor for the new, widespread Hellenism. It was a great and fruitful age. Society was refined; the position of woman improved; private fortunes abounded, and private houses possessed works of art which, in earlier times, would have been found only in palaces or temples. For the reverse side, there was corruption in high places, and hungry and threatening mobs at the base of society.

Among the countless cities, all homes of culture, five great intellectual centers appeared — Athens, Alexandria, Rhodes, Pergamos, Antioch. The glory of Alexandria extended over the whole period, which is sometimes known as the Alexandrian age; the others held a special preëminence, one at one time, one at another. Athens, however, always excelled in philosophy, and Rhodes in oratory.[1]

313. Literature. — The many-sided age produced new forms in art and literature: especially, (1) *the prose romance*, a story of love and adventure, the forerunner of the modern novel; (2) *the pastoral poetry* of *Theocritus*, which was to influence Virgil and Tennyson; and (3) *personal memoirs*. The old Attic comedy, too, became the "New Comedy" of *Menander* and his followers, devoted to satirizing gently the life and manners of the time.

In general, no doubt, the tendency in literature was toward critical scholarship rather than toward great and fresh creation. Floods of books appeared, more notable for style than matter. Treatises on literary criticism abounded; the science of grammar was developed; and poets prided themselves upon writing all kinds of verse equally well. Intellectually, in its faults, as in its virtues, the time strikingly resembles our own.

314. Painting and Sculpture. — Painting gained prominence. *Zeuxis, Parrhasius,* and *Apelles* are the most famous Greek names connected with this art, which was now carried to great perfection. According to popular stories, Zeuxis painted a cluster of grapes so that birds pecked at them, while Apelles painted a horse so that real horses neighed at the sight.

Despite the attention given to painting, Greek sculpture produced some of its greatest work in this period. Multitudes of splendid statues were created — so abundantly, indeed, that even the names of the artists are not preserved.

315. Greek Philosophy after Socrates. — **Plato.** We may dis-

---

[1] Caesar and Cicero studied oratory at Rhodes.

tinguish three periods, corresponding to the three chief divisions of remaining Greek history.[1]

For the Period of Spartan and Theban Leadership. — The most famous disciple of Socrates is known to the world under the name *Plato*, the "broad-browed." This name and that of his pupil Aristotle are among the greatest in the history of thought. Plato elaborated a vast and consistent system of Philosophy. He strikingly displays before us the infinite greatness, goodness, and wisdom of God — One God — His sovereignty over the world, the spirituality and immortality of the soul and the reward of virtue and punishment of vice. He also preserved some traditions of man's original innocence, his fall from grace, and the existence of superior intelligences between God and man. But many of his teachings rest on no solid reasonings and the gross errors mixed with them show the limitation of most highly gifted human minds.

Truth and error are most strangely mixed in his theory of Ideas. Nothing is in existence except by partaking of an idea. A man is kind, for instance, only because he has in him a share of the idea of kindness. The idea itself is eternal and indestructible. The ideas in our minds were not acquired; we possessed them before we came into our present existence. In spite of such and similar deficiencies his philosophy, taken as a whole, exhibits a noble, powerful, and poetic mind, grappling with the important problems of life and of the world around us with considerably more success than any of his predecessors.

316. Aristotle. — *The Macedonian Period. Aristotle,* for twenty years Plato's disciple, by far outshines his master. He gave to the world the most comprehensive system of universal knowledge, whose basic principles will ever be recognized by the thinkers of the world. In his investigations he proceeds directly from life and experience. There has hardly ever been a man in whom the keenest power of observation

---

[1] It is impossible to do justice to Greek philosophy in general and much less to the present period in a book like this. Histories of philosophy, as Turner's or Coppens', must be consulted if full information is desired.

was combined with so much intellectual penetration, bold gen-
eralizing, and careful deduction. The ideas in our minds are
acquired through the operation of the senses, which convey to
the intellect the material upon which the latter begins its
activity and rises to spiritual (immaterial) concepts. Ideas
are eternal only as far as the knowledge of things was from
all eternity in the infinite mind of God.

Aristotle's system, though not free from serious shortcomings, is so perfect that its chief outlines and very much of its
details became the fundamental doctrines of the great Christian philosophers of the Middle Ages. St. Thomas and the
other scholastics refer to him simply as " The Philosopher."

Reverend William Turner thus ends his estimate of Aristo-
telian Philosophy : —

" Aristotle's philosophy is the synthesis and culmination of the specula-
tions of pre-Socratic and Socratic schools. His doctrine of causes is an
epitome of all that Greek philosophy had up to his time accomplished.
But it is especially with Plato, his master, that Aristotle is to be compared,
and it is by his additions to Platonic teaching that he is to be judged.
Plato built out of the ruins of pre-Socratic speculation a complete meta-
physical structure according to a definite plan, — a structure beautiful in
its outlines, perfect in its symmetry, but insecure and unstable, like one
of those golden palaces of fairyland, which we fear to approach and
examine lest it vanish into airy nothingness. Aristotle, on the contrary,
drew his plan with a firmer hand ; he laid the foundation of his philosophy deep on the rock bottom of experience, and although all the
joints in the fabric are not equally secure, the care and consistency with
which the design is executed are apparent to every observer. It was left
for Scholastic philosophy to add the pinnacle to the structure, which
Aristotle had carried as far towards completion as human thought could
build unaided." (*Hist. of Philos.*, p. 157.)

317. Minor Philosophic Systems. — *After Alexander.* Two
schools are best described by stating that they tried to answer
the question : How can man become happy ? *The Stoics,* so
called from the Stoa[1] where their founder *Zeno* used to teach,

---

[1] For explanation of this term see description of map on page 206. Zeno
taught in the hall called " the Painted " from its famous wall paintings.
Besides the fact that it was situated north of the *Agora* little is known about

replied : By practicing virtue, *i.e.* by complete submission to the laws of man's nature and of the world around us. All passions and emotions must be subdued and annihilated. Everything happens with an unchangeable necessity ; bear patiently and without feeling what cannot be avoided. *Epicurus* and the *Epicureans* taught : Calculate so that you may derive from your life the greatest possible amount of pleasure and the smallest amount of pain. The caution, feeble enough in itself, that this requires frugality, simple habits, friendship, and abstinence from excess, was widely disregarded by the practical followers of this theory. It must be borne in mind, however, that both these answers are only the necessary conclusions from their cardinal concepts of the world and the divinity, which were completely wrong. Stoics as well as Epicureans believed in a kind of general brotherhood of men.

At this time the *Skeptics* (Considerers) made their appearance, who maintained everything must be doubted ; one should not worry about anything that occurs, because it might after all not even be real. The *Eclectics* did not attempt to introduce anything like a real new philosophy. They looked only for some common basis on which to found a system of practical conduct. For this purpose they " selected " whatever they thought correct in any system. Hence their name.

One more school should be mentionod here, though it belongs chiefly to an earlier period, namely the *Cynics*. They are somewhat similar in doctrine to the Stoics ; in fact, Zeno the Stoic was one of them for some time. They were one-sided followers of Socrates. According to them the essence of virtue is self-control, by which they understood the complete absence of all material and accidental needs. They ostentatiously threw away all the comforts of life and sneered at the relations of family life and the love and laws of country and religion. With the immorality of the

---

its location. Similarly Plato's school is often styled the *Academics*, from the Academy, a building somewhere in the outskirts of the city, where he used to assemble his hearers. Aristotle would walk about with his disciples in the shady avenues of the Lyceum (see map), while conversing with them; hence the name of *Peripatetics* was given to them, from a Greek verb meaning to walk up and down.

time, which they pretended to combat, they also rejected its morality and culture. All was nothing to them, because they said they needed nothing and nobody. One of them, Diogenes, lived for many years in a tub.[1] The word Cynic means doglike. It is easy to see the connection between the name and their conduct.

318. New Character of Philosophy. — Philosophy, after Socrates, took on a more moral and practical character. Educated people desired to have some rules and principles according to which to guide themselves in their actions. Philosophers became the teachers of conduct. As far as they reflected the truths proclaimed by nature in every man's heart or the glimpses of supernatural revelation which had survived or been obtained through some contact with the Hebrews, they did a great service to mankind and contributed their share towards the reception of Christianity. In the complete absence of any real religious teaching they performed in an imperfect way the office of our clergy. But after all, they benefited only the man of leisure. The people in the street, the toilers and slaves, were not as much as thought of when the philosopher discoursed gravely on happiness or the moral rights and duties of man.

319. Libraries and "Museums" ("Universities"). — The closing age of Hellenistic history saw the forerunner of the modern university. The beginning was made at Athens. Plato (§ 315), by his will, left his gardens and other property to his followers, organized in a club. Athenian law did not recognize the right of any *group* of people to hold property, unless it were a religious body. Therefore this club claimed to be organized for the worship of the *Muses*, who were the patrons of literature and learning; and the name *museum* was given to the institution. *This was the first endowed academy, and the first union of teachers and learners into a corporation.*[2]

---

[1] Special report: the stories of Diogenes.
[2] A corporation is a body of men recognized by the law as a "person" so far as property rights go.

The idea has never since died out of the world. The model and name were used a little later by the Ptolemies at Alexandria in their *Museum*. This was a richly endowed institution, with large numbers of students. It had a great library of over half a million volumes (manuscripts), with scribes to make careful copies of them and to make their meaning more clear, when necessary, by explanatory notes. It had also observatories and botanical and zoölogical gardens, with collections of rare plants and animals from distant parts of the world. The librarians, and the other scholars who were gathered about the institution, devoted their lives to a search for knowledge and to teaching; and so they corresponded to the faculty of a modern university.

"The external appearance [of the Museum] was that of a group of buildings which served a common purpose — temple of the Muses, library, porticoes, dwellings, and a hall for meals, which were taken together. The inmates were a *community* of scholars and poets, on whom the king bestowed the honor and privilege of being allowed to work at his expense with all imaginable assistance ready to hand. . . . The managing board was composed of priests, but the most influential post was that of librarian." — HOLM, *History of Greece*, IV, 307.

One enterprise, of incalculable benefit to the later world, shows the zeal of the Ptolemies in collecting and translating texts. Alexandria had many Jews in its population, but they were coming to use the Greek language. Philadelphus, for their benefit, had the Hebrew Scriptures translated into Greek. This is the famous *Septuagint* translation, so called from the tradition that it was the work of *seventy* scholars.

320. Science made greater strides than ever before in an equal length of time. Medicine, surgery, botany, and mechanics became real sciences for the first time. *Archimedes* of Syracuse discovered the principle of the lever, and of specific gravity, and constructed burning mirrors and new hurling engines which made effective siege artillery.[1] *Euclid*, a Greek at Alexandria, building upon the old Egyptian knowledge, produced the geometry which is still taught in our schools with

---

[1] See Davis' *Readings*, Vol. II, No. 27.

little addition. *Eratosthenes* (born 276 B.C.), the librarian at Alexandria, wrote a systematic work on geography, invented delicate astronomical instruments, and devised the present way of measuring the circumference of the earth — with results nearly correct. A little later, *Aristarchus* taught that the earth moved round the sun; and *Hipparchus* calculated eclipses, catalogued the stars, wrote books on astronomy, and

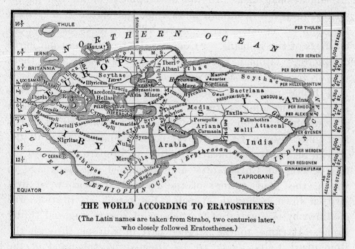

THE WORLD ACCORDING TO ERATOSTHENES

(The Latin names are taken from Strabo, two centuries later, who closely followed Eratosthenes.)

founded the science of trigonometry. Aristotle had already given all the proofs of the sphericity of the earth that are common in our text-books now (except that of actual circumnavigation) and *had asserted that men could probably reach Asia by sailing west from Europe*. The scientific spirit gave rise, too, to actual voyages of exploration into many regions; and daring discoverers brought back from northern regions what seemed wild tales of icebergs gleaming in the cold aurora of the polar skies.

The lighthouse built by the first Ptolemy on the island of *Pharos*, in the harbor of Alexandria, shows that the new civilization had begun to make practical use of science to advance human welfare. The tower rose 325 feet into the air, and from the summit a group of polished reflecting mirrors threw its light at night far out to sea.

321. The Greek contributions to our civilization can hardly be named in detail as those of the Oriental nations. Egypt and Babylonia gave us some very important outer features. Greece as it were infused a new spirit. Hers was essentially an educational task. In the development of all the purely secular branches of human knowledge and endeavor no nation has had an equally large share. The Greeks became the teachers of the Romans. " Conquered Greece caught her fierce conqueror." Roman poetry and oratory and whatever there was of Roman philosophy shaped itself after Greek models. And Rome passed on the treasure she had received to the peoples of the later centuries. Thus Greece through Rome is still teaching in our schools. The chief principles of Christian philosophy were taken over bodily from the sages of the Ægean Sea. Greek education helped to prepare the world for the coming of Christianity and furnished the language in which the glad tidings of the New Testament were first written down in human speech. Yet Greek civilization was modified by the matter-of-fact genius of conquering and ruling Rome. It came to the largest part of Europe through the Romanized Celts, again to be affected by the mind of the Teutons. There is above all the paramount influence of the religion of Jesus Christ with its Heaven-born truths and ideals. None of these factors may be omitted when judging of the influence of Greece upon our present civilization.

REFERENCES FOR FURTHER STUDY. — *Specially suggested :* Davis' *Readings*, Vol. I, Nos. 119–125 (19 pages, mostly from Polybius, Arrian, and Plutarch, the three Greek historians of that age).

Additional : Plutarch's *Lives* ("Aratus," "Agis," "Cleomenes," "Philopoemen "), Mahaffy's *Alexander's Empire*.

EXERCISE. — Review the various confederacies, — Peloponnesian, Delian, Olynthian, Achaean, noting likenesses and contrasts. Review the period from Chaeronea to the death of Alexander by "catch words."

REVIEW EXERCISES ON PARTS II AND III

A. Fact Drills on Greek History

1. The class should form a *Table of Dates* gradually as the critical points are reached, and should then *drill* upon it until it says itself as the alphabet does. The following dates are enough for this drill in Greek history. The table should be filled out as is done for the first two dates.

776 B.C.	First recorded Olympiad	338 B.C.
490 "	Marathon	222 "
405 "		146 "
371 "		

2. *Name in order fifteen battles*, between 776 and 146 B.C., stating for each the parties, leaders, result, and importance. (*Such tables also should be made by degrees as the events are reached.*)

3. *Explain concisely the following terms or names:* Olympiads, Ephors, Mycenaean Culture, Olympian Religion, Amphictyonies, Sappho. (*Let the class extend the list several fold.*)

B. Topical Reviews

This is a good point at which to review certain " culture topics," — *i.e.*, agriculture, industrial arts, life of rich and poor, philosophy, literature, art, religion, science, — tracing each separately from the dawn of history.

Make a table showing the chief divisions of Greek history, with subdivisions.

JULIUS CAESAR. — The British Museum bust.

PART II
ROME AND THE WEST

PART IV

ROME

The center of our studies, the goal of our thoughts, the point to which all paths lead and the point from which all paths start again, is to be found in Rome and her abiding power. — FREEMAN.

———◆———

CHAPTER XIX

THE PLACE OF ROME IN HISTORY

322. Preceding History. — Our civilization began seven thousand years ago in the fertile valleys of Egypt and western Asia. Slowly war and trade spread it around the eastern coasts of the Mediterranean. *But the contributions of this Oriental civilization to the future were mainly* material. About 600 B.C. the Greeks, in their Aegean home and in their many settlements scattered along all the Mediterranean coasts, became the leaders in civilization. They made marvelous advance in art, literature, philosophy, and in some sciences. *Their chief contributions were* intellectual. After about three hundred years, under Alexander the Great, they suddenly conquered the East and formed a Graeco-Oriental world.

323. The historical "center of gravity" now shifted once more to the West. The Italian peninsula, west of Greece, had long had intercourse with Hellas and the Orient. Greek cities dotted its southern shores; and its continuation — the island of Sicily — had been for centuries a battleground between Greek and Carthaginian. Italian cities, too, traded widely in the eastern Mediterranean. Italy was not a new land to history; but, until 200 B.C., it was merely an outlying fragment of the world

303

of history. *Then it suddenly became the center of historical interest.*

During the three centuries between the Persian War and the Achaean League, one of the Italian cities had been growing into a power which was soon to become the master of the world, and to make new advances in civilization. This power was *Rome.*

324. Rome stands for government and law, as distinctly as Greece stands for art and intellectual culture. The masterwork of Rome was to make empire and to rule it. The Romans themselves recognized this. Their poet Virgil wrote : —

" Others, I grant, indeed, shall with more delicacy mold the breathing brass ; from marble draw the features to the life ; plead causes better ; describe with a rod the courses of the heavens, and explain the rising stars. *To rule the nations with imperial sway be* **thy** *care, O Roman.* These shall be thy arts : to impose terms of peace, to spare the humbled, and to crush the proud."

Rome began as a village of rude shepherds and peasants by the bank of the Tiber. Her history is the story of the growth of a village into a city-state, the growth of that city-state into a united Italy, and the further growth of that Italy into a world-state. Rome did first for the villages of its surrounding hills what Athens did for the villages of Attica. It went on to do for all Italy what Athens had tried in vain to do for all Greece. Then it did lastingly for *all* the Mediterranean world what Alexander did — for a moment — for the eastern half. Shortly before the birth of Christ it had organized the fringes of the three continents bordering the Mediterranean into one Graeco-Roman society.

The Greeks, aside from their own contributions to civilization, had *collected* the arts and sciences of all the nations of antiquity. Rome *preserved* this common treasure of mankind, and herself *added* laws and institutions which have influenced all later time. The Roman Empire, says the historian Freeman, is the central *" lake in which all the streams of ancient history lose themselves, and which all the streams of modern history flow out of."*

325. The Roman and the Greek. — It was not Rome's genius in war, great as that was, which enabled her to make the world Roman. *It was her political wisdom and her organizing power.* The Romans were stern and harsh, but they were also just, obedient, reverent of law. They were a disciplined people, and they loved order. The work of the Greeks and that of the Romans are happily related. *Each is strong where the other is weak.* The Greeks gave us philosophy and art; the Romans, political institutions and systems of law.

" The Greeks had more genius; the Romans more stability. . . . They [the Romans] had less delicacy of perception, . . . but they had more sobriety of character and more endurance. . . . Versatility belonged to the Greek, virility to the Roman." — FISHER, *Outlines of Universal History*, 125.

" If it be true, as is sometimes said, that there is no literature which rivals the Greek except the English, it is perhaps even more true that the Anglo-Saxon is the only race which can be placed beside the Roman in creative power in law and politics." — GEORGE BURTON ADAMS.

CHAPTER XX

THE LAND AND THE PEOPLES

326. Meaning of the Name " Italy." — *Modern* Italy, bounded by the Alps and the sea, is made up of two distinct halves, — the level valley of the Po extending from east to west, and the slender mountainous peninsula reaching from it south into the Mediterranean. But until about 27 B.C., the first of these two, the Po valley, was always considered part of Gaul. It was called *Cisalpine Gaul*, or *Gaul this side the Alps*. During all early Roman history the name *Italy* belonged not to this valley, but *only to the true peninsula with the Apennine range for its backbone*. This district is about as large as Alabama.

Like Greece, Italy was specially fitted by nature for the work it was to do. In particular, there were three ways in which its geography affected its history. Each of these calls for a paragraph (§§ 327–329).

327. Unity. — Italy was more fit than Greece for *internal union*, which is the only safe basis for *external* empire. *The geographical divisions are larger, and less distinct, than the divisions in Greece*, and so the inhabitants were more easily united under one government. The fertile plains were better suited to agriculture and grazing than were the lands of Greece, while the coast lacked the many harbors and the island-studded sea that invited the earliest Hellenes to commerce. Civilization came somewhat later; but the foundations of empire were more securely laid.

328. Direction of the First Expansion. — Geography determined also the direction of Italy's first conquests. The Apennines are nearer the eastern coast than the western, and so, on the eastern side, the short rocky spurs and swift torrents lose

306

themselves quickly in the Adriatic.   The western slope is
nearly twice as broad; here are rivers and fertile plains, and,
as a result, most of the few harbors and the important states.

   Thus Italy and Greece stood back to back (§ 85 *d*).   Greece
faced the old Oriental civilizations.   *Italy faced west* toward
Spain, and, through Sicily, toward Africa.   When she was
ready for outside work, she gave herself to conquering and
civilizing these western lands, inhabited by fresh, vigorous
peoples.   Only after this had been accomplished did she
come into hostile contact with the Graeco-Oriental world — except for the small Greek states in southern Italy.

   329. The Central Mediterranean Land. — European culture began in the peninsula which was at once "the most European
of European lands " and also the European land nearest to the
older civilizations of the East (§§ 84, 85).   Just as naturally,
*the state which was to unite and rule all the coasts of the Mediter-
ranean had its home in the central peninsula* which divides that
inland sea.   When her struggle for empire began, her central
position enabled Italy to cut off the Carthaginian power in
Africa and Spain from its allies in the East and to conquer her
enemies one by one.

   EXERCISE. — Map study : note that *Liguria, Gallia Cisalpina*, and
Venetia are outside the true Italy (§ 326) ; fix the position of *Etruria,
Latium, Campania, Samnium*, and the *Sabines ;* observe that the *Arnus*
(Arno), in Etruria, the *Tiber*, between Etruria and Latium, and the
Liris, between Latium and Campania, are the most important rivers.
Their basins were early homes of culture in Italy.

   330. A Mingling of Races. — For some centuries in the period we are to study, Italy was the mistress of the world.   Before that time, as since, she had been overrun by invaders.   In
prehistoric times, the fame of her fertility and beauty had
tempted swarm after swarm of barbarians across the Alps and
the Adriatic ; and already at the opening of history the land
held a curious mixture of races.

   331. Chief Divisions. — The center of the peninsula was the
home of the *Italians*, who were finally to give their language

and law to the whole land. They fell into two branches. The western Italians were lowlanders, and were called *Latins.* Their home was in Latium. The eastern and larger section of Italians were highlanders, and were again subdivided into Sabines, Samnites, Volscians, and so on.

The more important of the other races were the *Greeks* in the south and the *Gauls*[1] and *Etruscans* in the north. The

REMAINS OF AN ETRUSCAN WALL AND ARCH AT SUTRI.

Greeks (of Magna Graecia) have been referred to in earlier pages. The Gauls held the Po valley. They were merely a portion of the Gauls from beyond the Alps, and remained semi-barbarians until a late period.

The Etruscans were a mysterious people — " the standing riddle of history." At an early time they had held the Po and all the western coast from the Alps to the Greek cities of the south. But before exact history begins, the Campanians, de-

[1] See § 290.

ITALY

REFERENCE MAP

SCALE OF MILES

0   25   50   100

scendants of the Samnites, and the Latins had driven them from all lands south of the Tiber, while the Gauls had expelled them from the Po valley. Thus they had become restricted to the central district, Etruria, just across the Tiber from the Latins.

The Etruscans remained, however, the most civilized people in Italy until the Greek settlements began. They were mighty and skillful builders, as their many interesting ruins show. They had a system of writing, and have left multitudes of

ETRUSCAN TOMBS AT ORVIETO.

inscriptions, in a language to which scholars can find no key. They became celebrated early for their work in bronze and iron, and they were the first people in Italy to engage in commerce. But before they sent out trading ships themselves, they welcomed those of the Phoenicians, and perhaps those of the Cretans. Their early tombs contain many articles of Egyptian and Phoenician and early Greek workmanship, brought them by these early traders, who doubtless taught them many arts. *The Etruscans, in turn, were Rome's first teachers*, before

that task fell to the Greeks of south Italy.   Etruscan builders
reared the walls of early Rome, drained her marshes, and fringed
the Tiber-side with great quays.   The Roman's dress (the toga),
his house, his favorite amusements (the cruel sports of the am-

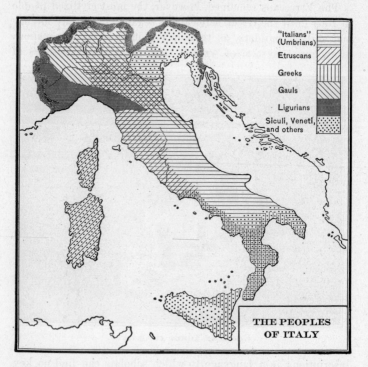

THE PEOPLES
OF ITALY

phitheater), and much of his religion (especially the divination
and soothsaying) were Etruscan in origin ; while from the same
source he learned his unrivaled power to build for all time.[1]

---

[1] The Church has still to fight against some survivals of the ancient paganism and divination among the Tuscan peasantry. — The ancient method of
discovering the will of the gods by examining the entrails of animals (offered
in sacrifice) was very similar — even in little details — to the custom of the
old Babylonians. It seems almost certain that this and other Etruscan
"charms" must have come, in some way, from Babylonia.

332. " Fragments of Forgotten Peoples." — Besides these four great races — Italians, Greeks, Etruscans, and Gauls — whom Rome was finally to fuse into one strong and noble nation, there were also fragments of earlier peoples in ancient Italy. In the southern mountains were the Iapygians; in the marshes of the northeast, the Veneti; and, in the extreme northwest, between the Alps and the sea, the wild *Ligurians.* These last were rude hill-men, who had fought savagely for their crags and caves with Etruscans and Gauls, and were long to harass the Roman legions with guerilla warfare. Later, they furnished Rome an admirable light infantry.

333. Geographical Advantages of Rome. — At first Rome was simply one of many Italian towns. Her rise to greatness rested, in part, at least, upon four geographical conditions.

a. Rome is the central city of the peninsula, and so had advantages for consolidating Italy like those enjoyed by Italy afterward for unifying the Mediterranean coasts. It was not by accident that Mediterranean dominion fell to the *central city* of the *central peninsula.*

ROME AND VICINITY

b. The Tiber was the one navigable river of Italy. In old times ships sailed up the river to Rome, while barges brought down to her wharves the wheat and wine of the uplands. The site had the advantages of a port, but was far enough from the coast to be safe from sudden raids by pirates. There is no doubt that Rome's greatness in Latium was largely due to her *commercial site.*[1]

c. Early Rome was a " mark state" of the Latins; that is, it bordered upon hostile peoples. Just across the Tiber lay the Etruscans, and in the eastern mountains dwelt the Sabines, — rude highlanders, fond of raiding their richer neighbors of the plains. *The Romans were the champions of the Latins against*

---

[1] Mommsen, I, 59–62, has a striking account of the Tiber traffic.

both these foes. Thus they came to excel the other Latins in war. Their position was favorable, also, to some mingling of tribes; and Roman traditions assert that such a mingling did take place (§ 335).

d. *Rome was "the city of the* **seven** *hills."* Italian towns, like the Greek (§ 103), had their origin each in some acropolis, or hill fortress; and even in Latium there were many settlements, like Alba Longa or Praeneste, that frowned from more formidable heights than those held by Rome. *But nowhere else was there in the midst of a fertile plain a* **group of hills.** The importance of this will be shown soon (§ 338).

For Further Reading. — Davis' *Readings*, Vol. II, No. 1, gives a description of Italy and its peoples by an old Roman writer. An excellent brief modern account is to be found in Howe and Leigh, 1–19.

CHAPTER XXI

LEGENDARY HISTORY

The two pages of this chapter are more suitable for reading in class than for ordinary recitation.

334. **Old Writers and Sources.** — The Romans had no Homer[1] for their early civilization; and they did not begin to write the history of their city until about 200 B.C., — more than two centuries after Herodotus and Thucydides wrote the history of Greece. Even then the first histories were meager skeletons. To make even such a story for the earlier centuries of Roman life, the first Roman historians found only two kinds of material — scant official records and unreliable family chronicles.

The records comprised only lists of magistrates, with brief notices of striking events and of peculiar phenomena, like an eclipse. Even these barren records had been destroyed up to the year 390 B.C. (when the Gauls sacked the city), and had been restored, imperfectly, from memory.

The great clans fed their pride by family histories, and especially by historical funeral orations (§ 397) ; but these were all based upon oral tradition, which was readily distorted by inventions and wild exaggerations, to suit family glory.

From such sources, early in the second century B.C., *Fabius Pictor* (§ 624) wrote the first connected history of Rome. He and his successors (mostly Greek slaves or adventurers) trimmed and patched their narratives ingeniously to get rid of gross

---

[1] Some modern scholars, however, believe that there must have been a copious ballad literature among the people, from which early historians could draw. Macaulay's *Lays of Ancient Rome* was an attempt to reproduce such ballads as Macaulay thought must once have existed. A criticism of this idea may be found in Ihne's *Early Rome*, 18, 19.

inconsistencies, filled the many gaps by borrowing freely from incidents in Greek history, and so produced an attractive story. These early works are now lost; but, two hundred years later, they furnished material for *Livy* and *Dionysius*, whose accounts of the legendary age were accepted as real history [1] until after 1800 A.D.

335. Legends of Regal Rome. — According to the legendary story, Rome was ruled from 753 to 510 B.C. by seven successive kings. The founder, *Romulus*, was the son of Mars (God of War) and of a Latin princess. As a babe he had been exposed to die, but was preserved and suckled by a wolf. He grew up among rude shepherds; with their aid he built a city on the Palatine Mount above the old wolf's den; here he gathered about him outlaws from all quarters, and these men seized the daughters of a Sabine tribe for wives. This led to war, and finally to the union of the Romans and the Sabines, who then settled upon one of the neighboring hills. Romulus organized the people into tribes, curias, and clans; appointed a Senate; conquered widely; and was finally taken up to heaven by the gods in a thunderstorm, or, as some thought, was killed by jealous aristocrats. *Numa*, the next king, elected after a year's interregnum, established religious rites, and gave laws and arts of peace, which were taught him by the nymph Egeria in a sacred grove by night. *Tullus Hostilius*, a warlike conqueror, is a shadowy Romulus, and *Ancus Marcius* is a faint copy of Numa. The fifth king was *Tarquin the First*, an Etruscan adventurer, who was succeeded by *Servius Tullius*, son of a slave girl. Servius reorganized the government, and was followed by a second Tarquin, *Tarquin the Proud*, whose oppression led to his expulsion and to the establishment of a Republic. The last three seem to have been "tyrants" in the Greek sense (§ 126). They favored the common people (the *plebs*) against the aristocratic *patricians*, extended the sway of Rome, and constructed great and useful works.

336. Modern Scholars and these Legends. — To scholars of the time of the American Revolution, Romulus and Tarquin were as real as Queen Elizabeth or Christopher Columbus. Early in the nineteenth century, however, scholars began to inquire into inconsistencies in the Roman narrative. Such investigation soon forced the world to give up the old history.

---

[1] Livy himself spoke modestly of the unreliability of much of his material for the early period; but later writers repeated his story without his cautions.

No one now regards the stories of the kings as history. Indeed, no one pretends to know more than a general outline of Roman history before 390 B.C.; and for a century after that date the details are very uncertain. Since 1900 A.D., however, excavations have taught us much. The opinions of modern scholars regarding this early period will be stated briefly in the next chapter.

CHAPTER XXII

CONCLUSIONS ABOUT ROME UNDER THE KINGS

THE GROWTH OF THE CITY

337. **Early Latium** contained thirty Latin tribes, each settled around some hill-fort. At first, Rome was by no means the most important of these centers. In the early days the leading settlement was Alba Longa (the Long White City), which was the head of a rude Latin union, — like a Greek amphictyony (§ 119), but somewhat more political in character.

338. **The Union of the Seven Hills at Rome.** — The oldest part of Rome seems to have been a settlement on the crest of the *Palatine*, a square hill and the central one of the group of low hills on the south side of the Tiber. Some village had held a place there from the Stone Age of the Latins, — at least 1200 years before Christ, — and it is still possible to trace solidly built walls of this "square town" belonging to a prehistoric date.[1] This citadel served as a military outpost of the Latins, to hold the Tiber frontier against the Etruscans on the north bank.

Early settlements were made also on at least two other of the seven hills, — the Quirinal and the Caelian. Roman tradition says that one of these towns was founded by an invading tribe of Sabines, and the other by a conquering Etruscan tribe. No doubt, there was a long period of war between the three hill-forts, with occasional truces, during which the townsmen met for trade on the common ground of the marshes between the hills. Finally, the three settlements were united into one state, with the tribes on an equal footing, one with another.

---

[1] The historic Romans believed that their city was founded in 753 B.C., and they dated all events from that year. Excavations show that they might have claimed much greater antiquity.

Then the low ground between these hills became the place for political assemblies (*Comitium*), and for the common market place (*Forum*); and the steep Capitoline, a little to one side,

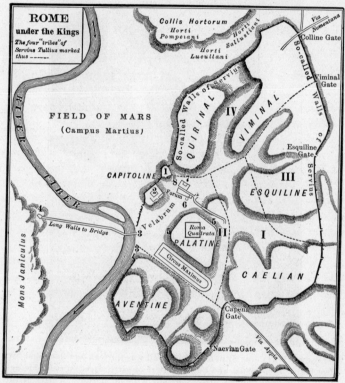

**ROME
under the Kings**
The four "tribes" of Servius Tullius marked thus - - - -

FIELD OF MARS
(Campus Martius)

Collis Hortorum
Horti Pompeiani
Horti Sallustiani
Horti Lucullani

Via Nomentana
Colline Gate
So-called Walls of Servius
Viminal Gate
So-called Walls of Servius

QUIRINAL
IV
VIMINAL

CAPITOLINE
Esquiline Gate
III
ESQUILINE

RIVER TIBER

Forum
6
8
1
2

Mons Janiculus
4
Long Walls to Bridge
3
Velabrum
5
Roma Quadrata
II
PALATINE
5
I

CAELIAN

3
Circus Maximus

AVENTINE

Capena Gate
Via Appia
Naevian Gate

1. Citadel (Arx).
2. Temple of Jupiter (Capitolinus).
3. "Quays of the Tarquins."
4. Citadel at Janiculum.
5. "Wall of Romulus."
6. Temple of Vesta.
7. Senate House (Curia).
8. Comitium.

became the common citadel. The later kings (the "tyrants" perhaps) drained the marshes and inclosed all the seven hills within one wall, taking in also much open space for further city growth. Until a few years ago, the remains of a great drain (*Cloaca Maxima*) and of a massive wall were thought to belong to these early works; but they are now supposed to be of later date, replacing the ruder structures of the kings. The

SO-CALLED WALL OF SERVIUS. This wall was thirteen feet thick and fifty feet high. It consisted of a huge rampart of earth, faced on each side by a wall of immense stones fitted together without mortar. A part of this colossal structure has recently been uncovered on the Aventine.

present remains, however, belong to a very early period, and are pictured in these pages.

The gain from this union was not merely in physical power. That was the least of it. Early societies are fettered rigidly by custom, so that the beginnings of change are inconceivably slow. In Rome, the union of distinct societies broke this bondage at a period far earlier than common. Necessity compelled the three tribes to adopt broader views of their relations toward one another. They became accustomed to variety of customs, and they found how to live together peaceably even when their ways differed. Compromise took the place of inflexible custom. *Thus began the process of association that was later to unite Italy*, and Rome was started upon the development of her marvelous system of law.

CLOACA MAXIMA. As it appeared before a recent restoration.

339. Growth beyond the Walls. — The territory of the city must still have been for a while only a narrow strip along the river, limited on every side by the stream or by the lands of other towns. But before the year 500 B.C., war with the neighboring Sabines, Etruscans, and Latins had produced great expansion. *Rome had come to hold a third of Latium and to control the whole south bank of the Tiber from the sea to the highlands* (about eighteen miles either way from the city). At the Tiber mouth, *Ostia*, the first Roman colony, had been founded for a port; and, on the *north* side of the river, Rome had seized *Mount Janiculum* and fortified it against the Etruscans. Several of the conquered Latin towns had been razed and their inhabitants brought to Rome. Even Alba Longa had been destroyed, and Rome had succeeded to the *headship of the Latin confederacy.*

EARLY ROMAN SOCIETY

340. Homes. — The first Romans, when not fighting, were farming or shepherding their flocks. Their life was plain and simple. Their houses were like those of the primitive people all about the Mediterranean (§ 95), — small huts, often only one room, with no chimney or window. The open door and an opening in the peaked roof let out the smoke from the hearth fire, and let in light. Daylight entered through the open door, and a slight cavity directly below the roof-opening received the rain.

341. Religion centered about the home and the daily tasks. For each house the door had its protecting god *Janus*, two-faced, looking in and out; and each hearth fire had the goddess *Vesta.* When the city grew powerful, it had a city *Janus*, and a city *Vesta.* In the ancient round temple of Vesta, the holy fire of the city was kept always bright by the priestesses (*Vestal Virgins*), who had to keep pure in thought and act, that they might not pollute its purity. For the fire to go out, or be defiled in any way, would mean disaster or ruin for the city.

Next to the house gods came the gods of the farm: Tellus (*Earth*), the deity in the soil; Saturn, the god of sowing; Ceres, the goddess who made the grain grow; Venus, another goddess of fruitfulness; and Terminus, a god who dwelt in each boundary pillar, to preserve the bounds of the farm — and, later, to guard the boundaries of the state.

The early Romans had also an ancestor worship at each family tomb, and each Latin tribe had its ancestral or at least its patron deity. The war-god, Mars, father of the fabled Romulus, was the special god of Rome. At the head of all the tribal gods of Latium stood Jupiter (Father Jove); and when Rome became the central Latin power, Jupiter became the center of the Roman religion.

The later Romans borrowed some of the Greek stories about the gods,[1] to establish a sort of relationship among their deities; but they lacked imagination and poetic feeling, and

AN EARLY ROMAN COIN (AS). The head is a representation of Janus; the reverse side shows the prow of a ship.

they could not create a rich and beautiful mythology, as the Greeks had done.

The Roman gods were less like men than the Greek gods were. They remained vague and misty. In consequence Roman religion seems to us a "dreary round of ceremonies," with little of adoration, no poetry, and no love. As a matter of prudence, the will of the gods was sought out by a study of omens. Worship consisted of a strict observance of ceremonies. Divine favor could be lost by failure to use precise gestures in a service, or by the omission or addition of a single word. On the other hand, the intricacies of the worship had somewhat the value of a conjurer's charm. If the ceremony was carried through in the proper manner,[2] it almost compelled the aid of the gods.

---

[1] For the correspondence of Greek and Roman gods, see § 111.
[2] Hull, *Archaic Religions*, p. 65, "Magic *vs.* Religion."

342. Pontiffs and Augurs. — Under these conditions there grew up in Rome (as in other Italian towns) two important " colleges " of city priests,[1] — *pontiffs* and *augurs*.

a. The pontiffs had general oversight of the state religion; and they were also the guardians of human seïence. Their care of the exact dates of religious festivals made them the keepers of the calendar and of the rude records of the city (§ 334). They had oversight also of weights and measures; and they themselves described their knowledge as " the science of all things human and divine."

b. The gods at Rome manifested their will not by oracles but by omens, or *auspices*. These auspices were sought especially in the conduct of birds, and in the color and size of the entrails of animals (§ 331, note). The interpretation of such signs became a kind of science, in the possession of a college of augurs.

343. Political Value. — The Roman religion became a mighty political instrument. No public act (vote, election, or battle) could be begun without divine approval. If the gods were properly consulted concerning a proposed measure and had manifested their approval, then, the Romans felt, they were under obligation to see it carried through.[2]

The thrifty Roman mind drove hard bargains, too, with the gods. The soothsayers called for fresh animals until the entrails gave the signs desired by the ruling magistrate, and then the gods were just as much bound as if they had shown favor at the first trial. The sky was watched until the desired birds did appear, and, in the later periods, tame birds were kept to give the required indications.

The priests and augurs, too, were the servants of the state, not its masters. They did not make a distinct hereditary class, but were themselves warriors and statesmen; and, as priests, they acted only at the command of the civil magistrate. The

---

[1] A " college " is simply a " collection " of persons. The members of each college held office for life, and themselves filled vacancies in their number.

[2] Munro's *Source Book*, 16, illustrates this point.

augurs sought no omen, and made no announcement, except when directed to do so.[1]

344. Patricians and Plebeians. — The descendants of the original three tribes (§ 338) formed "the Roman people," in a strict sense. The tribesmen were *patricians* (men "with fathers"). For a long time, they were the only citizens — along with the clans and families whom they "adopted" from time to time. They alone could vote or hold office or sue in the courts.

But, like the Greek cities, Italian cities contained many non-citizens. In Rome this class was especially large, partly because the city had brought within its walls many clans from conquered cities, and partly because adventurers and refugees thronged naturally to a prosperous commercial center. These non-citizens were *plebeians* (or the plebs). Some of them were rich; but none of them had any part in the religion, or law, or politics of the city. They could not intermarry with citizens. Policy and custom required the city to protect their lives and property ; but they had no absolute security against an unscrupulous patrician. *Their struggle to win rights and privileges makes the early political history of Rome.*

345. Patrician society was organized in *families, clans* (gentes), and *curias*.

a. The *family* counted far more than in Greece. The Roman father had a peculiar power over his sons and grandsons as long as he lived, even when they were grown men and perhaps in the ruling offices of the city. When his son took a wife, she, too, leaving her own family, came under his control. His own daughters passed by marriage from his hand under that of some other house-father. Roman law recognized no relationship through females. The father ruled his household, *and the households of his male descendants*, as priest, judge, and king. He could sell, or slay, his wife, unmarried daughter, grown-up son, or son's wife ; and all that was theirs was his. No appeal lay from him to any higher judge. In

---

[1] Munro's *Source Book*, 12, has a good illustration of the power of augurs.

practice, however, the father was influenced somewhat by near relatives and by public opinion and religious feeling. A man was declared accursed if he sold a married son into slavery, though no law could punish him. It is a curious fact that, despite the legal slavery of women, the Roman matrons had a dignity and public influence unknown in Greece.

b. The Roman *gentes* correspond to the Greek clans. In patrician Rome there were 300 of these units.

c. The 300 clans were grouped in 30 *curias*.[1] In early historical times, the curias were the most important division of the people, both for worship and for government. Each curia possessed its own religious festivals, its own priest, its temple and sacred hearth. In the political Assembly of the people the curia was the unit for voting.

346. The patrician government had three parts, — king, Senate, and Assembly (as in Homeric Greece). The king stood to the state as the father to the family, and was somewhat more important than the early Greek kings were.

The Senate seems to have been originally a council of the 300 chiefs of the clans. In historic Rome it long kept the number 300, but the kings won the power to fill vacancies. The Senate could *advise* the king, and it could *veto* any change in old custom.

When a king died before his successor had been appointed, there was an *interregnum* ("interval between kings"). The Senators ruled by turns, for five days each, as *inter-reges* ("kings for an interval"). The first inter-rex was chosen by lot. Each one then named his successor, and any one after the first could nominate a permanent king. No election could take place except upon such nomination. Each inter-rex for his brief rule kept the kingly power in full.

The Assembly was a meeting of the patricians in curias. It met only at the call of the king. Its approval was necessary for offensive war and for any change in old customs,[2] and for

---

[1] These precise figures suggest that there had been some artificial rearrangement of these natural units — such as that ascribed to Romulus.

[2] Early societies have very little law-making. This process of definitely changing an old custom, on rare occasions, corresponds to modern legislation.

the adoption of new clans; and, after an interregnum, it elected a king on the nomination of some inter-rex. The early Assembly did not debate: it only listened to the king's words.

TWO PREHISTORIC REVOLUTIONS

347. Plebeians gain Some Rights. — The first great change in the Roman government was the partial admission of the plebeians. Legend asserts that this was the work of Servius. Certainly the change was connected with a reform of the Roman army.

Originally, the army was made up of "the Roman people" — the patricians and their immediate dependents. But as the plebeians grew in numbers, the king needed their service in war. Toward the close of the period of the kings, Rome was a city of eighty thousand or one hundred thousand people. According to the legend, Servius called upon eighteen hundred of the wealthiest citizens to serve as cavalry (*equites* or *knights*), and then, for infantry service, divided all other landowners, *plebeian* and *patrician*, into five classes, according to their wealth.

Eight thousand had property enough so that they could be required to provide themselves with complete armor. They made the front ranks of the phalanx. Behind them stood the second and third classes, less completely equipped, but still ranking as "heavy-armed." The poorer fourth and fifth classes served as light-armed troops. Each of the five classes was subdivided into *centuries*, or companies of 100 men each. In all there were 193 centuries, — a fighting force of nearly 20,000 men.

In early society the *obligation to fight* and the *right to vote* go together (cf. § 137). Questions of peace and war and the election of military officers were naturally referred to the war host. Thus, gradually the army of centuries became in peace an Assembly of Centuries, which took to itself all the political powers of the old Assembly of Curias.

348. Aristocratic Character Maintained. — The army gradually changed its form, but the political Assembly of Centuries crystallized in the original shape. In this way, the patricians maintained most of their power. As the population increased, the poorer classes grew in numbers faster than the rich; *but they did not gain political weight* because the *number* of centuries was not changed. *The centuries of the lower classes came to contain many more than a hundred men each, while those of the knights and first class contained far less; but each century, full or skeleton, still counted one vote.*

Thus the *knights* and the *first class* (98 of the 193 centuries), even after they had come to be a small minority of the people, *could outvote all the rest.* They still voted first, too, just as when they stood in the front ranks for battle; and so oftentimes they settled a question without any vote at all by the other classes. And since the knights and the first class must have remained largely patrician, it is clear that in disputes between the patricians and plebeians the aristocratic party could rule.

None the less it was a great gain that the position of a man was fixed, not by birth and religion, but by his wealth. The arrangement of the centuries still prevented complete political equality; *but the first great barrier against the rise of democracy was broken down.*

349. "**Tyrants.**" — A second great change took place about the year 500. This was the disappearance of kingship.[1] Probably many more than seven kings ruled at Rome. The last three (as the legends suggest) were probably "tyrants," supported by the plebeians against the patricians. Thus the overthrow of kingship seems to have been an aristocratic victory.

350. Expulsion of the "Tyrants." — The later Romans believed that the last Tarquin oppressed the people and that the cruel deeds of his son finally roused the people to fury, so that they drove the family from Rome, abolished the kingship, and, in place of a king for life, chose two consuls for a year. This revolution is ascribed to the year 510, — the same year in which the Pisistratids were finally driven from Athens. But

---

[1] Compare these early revolutions with those at Athens (§§ 134–137).

while the Greek story is strictly historical, the Roman is mere legend. In after centuries the Romans hated the name king, and the feeling was created largely by the stories of Tarquin's cruelty. Probably, however, these stories were the inventions of the aristocrats long after the "expulsion."[1] Certainly "king" did not at once become a detested name. At Rome, as at Athens (§ 134), there remained a king-priest (*rex sacrorum*), whose wife also kept the title of queen (*regina*). The legends themselves represent another Tarquin (Lucius Tarquinius Collatinus) as one of the first two consuls; nor is there any evidence that at first the consuls ruled only for one year. All that we really know is, that, in prehistoric Rome, *the aristocratic patricians in some way reduced and finally abolished kingship.*

" The struggle was doubtless longer and sharper, and the new constitution more gradually shaped, than tradition would have us believe. Possibly, too, this revolution at Rome was but part of a wide-spreading wave of change in Latium and central Italy, similar to that which in Greece swept away the old heroic monarchies." — PELHAM, *Outlines of Roman History*, 41.

351. The Consuls have been called "*joint kings for one year.*" The kingship had become elective, and it was divided between two men. The term of office, too, was finally limited to one year. But for that year the new consuls were "kings," nearly in full. They called and dissolved Assemblies at will. They alone could propose measures or nominate magistrates. They filled vacancies in the Senate. They ruled the city in peace, and commanded the army in war.

352. Practical Checks. — In practice, however, three important checks appeared upon the power of the consuls. (1) Either consul might find any of his acts absolutely forbidden by his

---

[1] Students should tell some of these stories as they are given in Livy: for instance, Lake Regillus, Brutus and his sons, Horatius at the Bridge, and the Porsenna anecdotes. The second and third of these are reproduced in Davis' *Readings*, Vol. II, Nos. 7 and 8. This is a good place for the student, who has not before done so, to become acquainted with Macaulay's *Lays of Ancient Rome.*

colleague. (2) When they laid down their office, they became responsible to the centuries and the courts for their past acts. (3) Their short term made them dependent upon the advice of the permanent Senate, — against whose will it became almost impossible for them to act.

A fourth limitation was less important. The kings had held power of life and death, without appeal; but one of the early consuls, *Valerius Publicola*, secured a law that if a consul condemned a citizen to death, he must permit an appeal to the Assembly — except in war, when he kept the old power in full.

353. The Senate's Gain. — Moreover, the relation of the Senate to a one-year consul was very different from its old subordinate relation to a life-king. The king had been jealous of its powers; the consul's highest ambition was to get into its ranks. Its *advice* became more and more a command, until, in fact, it became the main part of the government.

354. The Dictatorship. — In time of peril, the division of power between two consuls, with the possibility of a deadlock, might easily be fatal to the city. The remedy was found in temporary revivals of the old kingship under a new name. Either consul, at the request of the Senate, might appoint a *dictator*. This officer was absolute master of Rome, save that his term of office could not exceed *six months*. He was the two consuls in one, with half their length of office. He had power of life and death in the city as in the army ; and he could not be questioned for his acts even when he had laid down his powers. *He could not, however, nominate a successor.*

For Further Reading. — Davis' *Readings*, Vol. II, Nos. 2–6, illustrate various phases of Roman religion ; Pelham's *Outlines*, 15–17, treats of the proofs of separate settlements on the seven hills.

Additional readings of value on the matter of this chapter may be found in Ihne's *Early Rome*, chs. v–ix. Students are advised to read one of these. The best treatment of the consulship is Ihne's *Early Rome*, chs. x–xii.

CHAPTER XXIII

CLASS STRUGGLES IN THE REPUBLIC, 510-367 B.C.

355. The Expulsion of the Kings followed by Class Conflicts. — The first century and a half of the Republic was a stern conflict between patricians and plebeians. Torn and distracted by the internal struggle, Rome made little gain externally, and indeed for a time she lost territory.

The peculiar mark of the long internal struggle was the absence of extreme violence. The vehement class conflicts in Greek cities were marked by bloody revolutions and counter-revolutions; the contest in Rome was carried on " with a calmness, deliberation, and steadiness that corresponded to the firm, persevering, sober, practical Roman character." When the victory of the plebs was once won, the result was correspondingly permanent.

THE POSITION OF THE CLASSES AFTER 510 B.C.

356. A Patrician Oligarchy. — *The overthrow of the kings was in no sense a democratic movement. It left Rome an oligarchy.* The last kings had leaned upon the lower orders. The plebeians found themselves the losers in politics, in law, and in property rights, by the change.

a. They could hold no office ; they could control only a minority of votes in the Assembly; and they had no way even to get a measure considered. At best, they could vote only upon laws proposed by patrician magistrates, and they could help elect only patrician officers, who had been nominated by other patricians. The patrician Senate, too, had a final veto upon any vote of the centuries; and, in the last resort, the patrician consuls could always fall back upon the patrician augurs to prevent a possible plebeian victory.[1]

---

[1] The augurs could prevent a vote by declaring the auspices unfavorable.

b. In law suits there was a like loss to the plebeians. The kings had found it to their interest to see justice done the plebs, but now law became again a patrician possession. It was unwritten, and to the plebs almost unknown. It was easy, therefore, in any dispute for a patrician to take shameful advantage.

c. The laws regarding debt were cruelly severe,[1] and here the patricians found their opportunity for oppression. The plebeians were liable to fall into debt for two reasons, — which require separate treatment (§§ 357, 358).

357. The patricians now robbed the plebeians of their share in the public land. When Rome conquered a hostile city, she took away a half or a third of its territory. The kings had sometimes settled colonies of landless plebeians upon such land, but the greater portion of the new territory became a common pasture ground. It belonged to the state, and a small tax was paid for the right to graze cattle upon it.

Strictly, even under the kings, only the patricians had the right to use this grazing land, but the kings had extended the privilege to the plebs also. The patricians now resumed their sole right, and thus reduced to painful straits the poorer plebeians who had eked out a scanty income from their small farms by such aid.[2] At the same time, the sending out of colonies of landless plebeians was stopped, partly because little land was won now for a long time, and partly because the patricians insisted upon keeping for themselves any that was secured.[3]

358. The conditions of warfare, also, bore more heavily upon the small farmer than upon the great landlord. The farmer was called away frequently to battle; he had no servants to till his fields in his absence; and his possessions were more exposed

---

[1] See the extracts in Munro's *Source Book*, 54, 55.

[2] To make matters worse, the patrician officers ceased to collect the grazing tax. Thus the public land was enjoyed by the patricians as private property, without purchase or tax, while, as a result, the tax on plebeian farms had to be increased, to supply the falling off to the treasury.

[3] An excellent brief treatment of the public land is given in Tighe, 82–88, and in Mommsen, I, 343–346.

to hostile forays than were the strongly fortified holdings of his greater neighbor. Thus he might return to find his crops ruined by delay or his homestead in ashes, and he could no longer apply to the king — the patron of the plebs — for assistance.

359. Results. — Thus, more and more, the plebeians were forced to borrow tax money from patrician money lenders or to get advances of seed corn and cattle from a neighboring patrician landlord. The debtor's land and his person were both mortgaged for payment. On failure to pay, the plebeian debtor became the property of the creditor. He was compelled thereafter to till his land (no longer his) for the creditor's benefit; or, if he refused to accept this result, he was cast into a dungeon, loaded with chains, and torn with stripes.

360. Dissatisfaction of the Rich Plebeians. — To be sure, there were many plebeians who were rich in goods and lands, but they, too, were bitterly dissatisfied. This was true especially of the descendants of the ruling families of the conquered Latin towns whose populations had been removed to Rome. These men were aggrieved because they were not allowed to hold office or to intermarry with the old Roman families. Thus they became the natural leaders and organizers of the mass of poorer plebeians.

THE STRUGGLE

361. Objects. — The struggle of the plebeians to right these wrongs filled a century and a half (510–367 B.C.). At first the masses clamored for relief from the cruel laws regarding debt, and for a share in the public lands. The leaders cared more for equality with the patricians in the law courts and for social equality and political office. Gradually the whole body of the plebeians, also, began to demand these things *because they found that whatever economic rights they won were of no value, so long as the laws were carried out only by patrician officials.*

362. Methods. — Livy (§ 334) gives a graphic story of the first great clash between the classes (497 B.C.). Probably the story

is essentially correct. (It is given in full in Davis' *Readings,*
II, No. 9.) It may be summed up briefly as follows: —

The plebs, driven to despair by the cruelty of patrician creditors, refused
to serve in a war against the Volscians, until the consul won them over
by freeing all debtors from prison. But when the army returned victorious, the other consul refused to recognize his colleague's acts ; he arrested

BRIDGE OVER THE ANIO TO-DAY, on the road from Rome to the " Sacred
Mount."

the debtors again, and enforced the law with merciless cruelty. On a
renewal of the war, the betrayed plebs again declined to fight ; but finally
Manius Valerius (of the great Valerian house "that loves the people
well ") was made dictator, and him they trusted. Victory again followed ;
but Valerius was unable to get the consent of the Senate to his proposed
changes in the law. So the plebeian army, still in battle array outside the
gates, marched away to a hill across the Anio, some three miles from
Rome, where, they declared, they were going to build a Rome of their own.
The " strike " brought the patricians to some real concessions (§ 363), and
the plebs returned from the " Sacred Mount."

This story resembles that of later conflicts. Once more, at
least, during foreign war, the plebeian army " struck," and on

other occasions it prepared to do so. Between these great crises, there was much bitter strife, with a few bloody conflicts in the city streets. Sometimes the plebs succeeded in driving a patrician consul into exile, after his term of office ; and at least one plebeian leader, *Genucius,* fell a victim to patrician daggers. The patricians were especially bitter toward any of their own order who were great-souled enough and brave enough to dare take the side of the people.

The first such hero was *Spurius Cassius.* He had served Rome gloriously in war and in statesmanship (§ 373). Finally, as consul, he proposed a reform in the selfish patrician management of the public lands. The patricians raised the cry that he was trying to win popular favor so as to make himself tyrant. The foolish plebeians allowed themselves to be frightened by the charge : they deserted their champion, and he was put to death. Under like conditions, two other heroes, *Spurius Maelius* and *Marcus Manlius,* the man who had saved Rome from the Gauls (§ 375), fell before like charges. Sometimes the later aristocratic historians blackened the memory of such "traitors" even further. There was *Appius Claudius,* who joined the plebeians, in 451 B.C., in an effort to secure fixed *written* laws (§ 364]. He was put to death by the patricians, and his overthrow was afterward represented as the work of a popular rising. Claudius, said the patrician story, seized the free maid *Virginia* as his slave girl; her father, Virginius, a popular officer, to save her from such shame, slew her with his own hand, and then called upon the army to avenge his wrongs ; his comrades marched upon the tyrants and overthrew them.

The story of Virginia has become so famous that the student ought to know it. We cannot tell whether or not there is any truth in it. Possibly Claudius did put the cause of the people in danger by selfish tyranny, and gave the patricians a handle against him ; but in any case we may be sure this was not the real cause of his overthrow ; and the popular rising, we know, was directed, not against him, but at his patrician murderers who were trying to cheat the people out of their previous gains. (See Ihne, *Early Rome,* 175.)

The other most instructive feature of the contest is the way in which the aristocratic class by trick and superior skill, over and over again, took back with one hand what they had been forced to surrender with the other; so that the masses had to win their cause many times, to really secure the fruits of victory.

The steps by which the plebs rose to equality with the patricians are treated in the following sections (363–372).

363. Tribunes. — The first secession gave the plebs the right to choose *tribunes,* with power to protect oppressed plebeians against cruel laws. It was agreed that the tribunes should have the right to stop any magistrate in any act by merely calling out *veto* ("I forbid") — just as one consul could "veto" another. This veto could be exercised only within the city (not in war), and *by the tribunes in person.* Hence a tribune's door was left always unlocked, so that a plebeian in trouble might have instant admission. At first two tribunes were elected each year. Later the number was increased to ten. The person of a tribune was declared sacred; and a curse was invoked upon any man who should interfere with their acts — which, however, did not save the tribune Genucius from assassination (§ 362).

At the close of a patrician consul's term of office, too, the tribune could impeach him, and bring him up for trial before the Assembly, for offenses against the people. The power of veto, too, was extended until a tribune could forbid even the putting of a question to vote in the Assembly; and from a seat just outside the Senate door he could stop any proceeding in that body by crying out a loud *veto.* Thus the tribunes could bring the whole patrician government to a standstill.

"Absolute prohibition was in the most stern and abrupt fashion opposed to absolute command ; and the quarrel was settled (?) by recognizing and regulating the discord."— MOMMSEN, I, 354, 355.

364. Written Laws. — About 460 B.C. the plebeians began to demand written laws. (Compare with the Athenian demands, before Draco.) The patricians opposed the demand furiously;

but after a ten-year contest a board of ten men (*Decemvirs*) was elected to put the laws into writing. Their laws were engraved on twelve stone tables, in short, crisp sentences, and set up where all might read them.

These " Laws of the Twelve Tables " were the basis of all later Roman law. Like the first written laws at Athens, they were very severe, and were for the most part simply old customs reduced to writing. The new thing about them was that they were now known to all, and that they applied to plebeian and patrician alike.[1]

365. The Assembly of Tribes. — At some early date (legend says in the days of Servius), the city and its territory outside the walls had been divided into twenty-one "wards," or "tribes," for the military levy. Like the "tribes" of Clisthenes at Athens, these tribes were *territorial,* and had nothing to do with the three patrician blood tribes. In some way the meeting of the inhabitants of these local units grew into a regular " Assembly." The plebeians, who had no complete organization in clans and curias, made use of this new Assembly of Tribes for purposes of government. It was here they chose their tribunes, and adopted their plans, and passed decrees (*plebiscita*) binding upon all of their order. The tribunes called this Assembly together and presided over it, as the consuls did with the Assembly of Centuries. Probably a patrician had a right to attend the meeting of the " tribe" in which he lived ; but at this stage he would not care to do so.

The plebeians, finding themselves helpless in the Assembly of Centuries, began to insist upon bringing oppressive patrician consuls for trial before this Assembly of Tribes. Then, a little later, they demanded that the *plebiscites* of their Assembly should be law, binding upon the whole state, just as the decrees of the Assembly of Centuries were. This point they finally carried, though the Senate kept a veto upon the decrees of both Assemblies.

---

[1] See extracts in Munro's *Source Book*, 54–55.

Thus a half century of conflict had failed indeed to admit the plebeians into the patrician state ; but it had instead set up a double state, — a plebeian state over against the old patrician state ; Assembly of Tribes and its tribunes over against the Assembly of Centuries and its consuls. There was no real arbiter between the two states, and no check upon civil war except the Roman moderation and preference for constitutional methods. *The next work was to fuse these two governments into one.*

366. Social Fusion. — The plebeians used their new powers to win further victories. Soon after its recognition, the Assembly of Tribes decreed that plebeians should have the right to marry with patricians. Then the Senate was forced to approve this plebiscite by the threat of another secession.

From this time, the two orders began to mix in social matters, and this prepared the way for political fusion. Those patricians who had plebeian relatives were not likely to oppose bitterly the demands of that class for political honors. Still the final contest was a long one. About the same time (445 B.C.) the plebeians began a seventy-eight-year struggle for admission to the office of the consul (§§ 367 ff.).

367. Consular Tribunes. — In 445 the tribes voted that the people should be allowed to choose a plebeian for one of the consuls. The Senate refused to allow the " religious " office of consul to be " polluted," but they offered a compromise. Accordingly it was decided to have no consuls in some years, but instead to elect *military tribunes with consular power, and this office was to be open to both patricians and plebeians.*

368. Censors. — At the same time, with their old stronghold threatened, the patricians prepared an inner fortress for defense of their privileges. A new office, the *censorship*, was created, to take over the religious part of the consul's duty and his most important powers. To this office, *only patricians* could be elected. Every fifth year two censors were chosen, with power to revise the lists of the citizens and of the Senate. By their mere order they could deprive any man of citizenship, or degrade a senator. They also exercised a general moral oversight over the state.[1]

---

[1] Ihne's *Early Rome*, 184–189, has an admirable treatment of the censors. Either censor could veto action by the other. Their tremendous power was used commonly with moderation, and not for partisan ends.

369. Patrician Maneuvers. — It had been left to the Senate to decide each year whether consuls or consular tribunes should be elected. The Senate used this authority to secure the election of consuls (who, of course, had to be patricians) twenty times out of the next thirty-five years. And even when consular tribunes were chosen, the patrician influence in the Assembly of Centuries kept that office for their own order every time for almost half a century.

370. The Licinian Laws, 367 B.C. — In 400, 399, and 396, however, the plebeians won in the election of the consular tribunes, and thereafter they never lost ground. An invasion by the Gauls in 390 (§ 375) almost ruined Rome and thrust aside party conflict for a time; but in 377 the final campaign began. Under the wise leadership of the tribune *Licinius Stolo,* the whole body of plebeians united firmly on a group of measures. These were proposed to the Assembly by Licinius, and are known as the *Licinian Rogations.*

The three most important demands were: —

(1) that the office of consul should be restored, and that *at least one consul* each year should be a *plebeian;*

(2) that no citizen *should hold more than 500 jugera of the* **public** *lands* (an acre is nearly two jugera);

(3) that payment of debts might be postponed for three years, and that the interest already paid should be deducted from the amount of the debt.

The first measure was what the leaders, like Licinius, cared most for The second and third secured the support of the masses. These measures, also, were wise and helpful. The one regarding debts had been made necessary by the distress that followed the invasion by the Gauls. The land acts were not acts of confiscation, from any point of view. Like the early attempt of Spurius Cassius (§ 362), they were a righteous effort to recover the people's property from wealthy patrician squatters.

371. Final Victory of the Plebs. — The proposal of these reforms was followed by ten years of bitter wrangling. Each year the plebeians reëlected Licinius and passed the decrees anew in the Assembly of the Tribes. Each time the Senate vetoed the measures. Then the tribunes, by their veto power, prevented the election of magistrates during the year, and so left the state without any regular government.[1] At last the patricians tried to buy off the masses, by offering to yield on the matters of debts and lands if they would drop the demand regarding the consulship. But Licinius succeeded in holding his party together for the full program of reform; and, in 367, the Senate gave way and the plebeian decrees became law.

372. Political Fusion completed, 367-300 B.C. — The long struggle was practically over, and the body of the patricians soon accepted the result with good grace. Just at first, to be sure, they tried again to save something from the wreck by creating a third, and patrician, consul — called *the praetor* — for supreme judicial control in the city.[2] But all such devices were in vain. Plebeian consuls could nominate plebeians for other offices. A plebeian secured the office of dictator in 356; another became censor in 351, and one was chosen praetor in 337. In 300 even the sacred colleges of pontiffs and augurs were thrown open to them.

Appointments to the Senate were commonly made from those who had held office, and so *that body, also, gradually became plebeian.* By the year 300, the old distinction between patricians and plebeians had practically died out.

For Further Reading. — *Specially recommended:* Davis' *Readings*, II, Nos. 9 and 10 (which have been noticed in footnotes and text above); Ihne's *Early Rome*, 135-151, 165-190; *or* How and Leigh, 52-58, 65-77, 91-94.

Additional: Pelham's *Outlines*, 54-69, gives in compact form a somewhat different view of these class struggles.

---

[1] During the peril of a foreign attack, however, they withdrew from this extreme ground and permitted consuls to be chosen. Read Livy's account of the long contest in Davis' *Readings*, II, No. 10.

[2] The consul had had three functions, religious, civil, and military. As the plebs gained ground, the patricians first reserved the religious duties to the patrician censor, and now the chief civil powers to the patrician praetor, intending to share with the plebs only the military office.

CHAPTER XXIV

THE UNIFICATION OF ITALY, 367-266 B.C.

PROGRESS BEFORE 367 B.C.

373. Gains under the Kings, and the Reaction to 449 B.C. —
The story of Rome's early wars is full of patriotic legends,[1]
but the general trend of her growth is fairly clear. Under
the kings she had conquered widely; but, after 510, the Latin
towns became independent again and much territory was seized
by the Etruscans. For the next sixty years Rome fought for
life. Etruscan, Volscian, and Sabine armies often appeared
under her very walls, and many times the peril was made more
deadly by the fierce conflict of classes within the city.

In 493, it is true, the Latin league was united to Rome, by
treaty,[2] as an equal ally, and so a bulwark was provided
against the Volscians (map, page 305). But the chief danger
lay in the Etruscans, and from this enemy Rome was saved,
mainly, by outside events. Just at this time the Gauls of the
north broke the power of Etruria on land, and the tyrants of
Syracuse (§ 160) shattered her superiority on the sea.

374. The Period 449-367: Slow Gains — After the decemvirs
(§ 364), when the bitterest internal dissensions were past, Rome
began to make steady gains. By slow degrees she became
again the mistress of the Latin league; and, in 396, after
fourteen long wars, she finally destroyed *Veii*, a dangerous
rival, only a few hours' walk distant, in Etruria. Here she
began the merciless policy which she was to show toward

---

[1] The story of Cincinnatus (§ 409) is given in Davis' *Readings*, II, No. 11.
Special report : a Roman triumph (see especially Munro's *Source Book*, 38-40).

[2] This important treaty was the work of Spurius Cassius (§ 362).

many rival capitals in time to come, by exterminating the population and laying waste the site of the city.

375. The Gauls.[1] — Six years later the city was again for a time in danger of utter destruction. In 390, a horde of Gauls, who had overrun Etruria, defeated the Roman army in the battle of the *Allia*, twelve miles from the walls, and cut it off from the city. Fortunately, the barbarians squandered three days in pillage, and so gave time to save Rome. The sacred

THE CITY SEAL OF SYRACUSE.   A COIN OF SYRACUSE ABOUT
(A coin of 480 B.C.)   400 B.C.

fire was hastily removed; the helpless inhabitants fled; and a small garrison, under the soldier *Marcus Manlius* (§ 362), garrisoned the Capitoline citadel.

The Gauls sacked the rest of the city and held it seven months. But their host was ravaged by the deadly malaria of the Roman plain (which has more than once been Rome's best protection); they had little skill or patience for a regular siege; and finally they withdrew on the payment of a ransom.

THE REAL ADVANCE, 367–266 B.C.

376. United Rome and her Rapid Growth. — Rome recovered rapidly from the Gallic conquest; and the slow growth of

---

[1] See §§ 290 and 331. — Special reports: the geese of the capitol; Brennus, the Gallic chief, and his sword at the scales; the later fiction of the Roman victory. See Davis' *Readings*, II, Nos. 12, 13.

territory up to this time contrasts strikingly with the swift advance that was to come in the next hundred years. The difference was due mainly to the difference in internal conditions. *The long strife of classes closed in 367 B.C.* (§ *371*). *The process of amalgamation that had originally merged the three separate hill towns into the patrician state had at length fused this patrician state and the newer plebeian state into one Roman people. Now this united Rome turned to the work of uniting Italy. This task filled a century.*

377. The Champion of Italian Civilization. — Other states in Italy had suffered by the Gauls as much as Rome, or more. Rome at once stood forth as the champion of Italian civilization against the barbarians. After her own immediate peril was past, she followed up the invaders of Italy in strenuous campaigns, until they withdrew to the Po valley. In like manner, she was soon to be recognized as the champion of the civilized lowland Italians against the more savage Italian tribes of the Apennine valleys (§ 331). It was in such ways that Rome at first earned her right to empire.

378. The Lowlands of Central Italy. — The Latin towns had seized the opportunity of the Gallic invasion to throw off Roman leadership; but another short war made Rome again the mistress of Latium. The southern half of Etruria, too, was soon seized; and on both north and south the new acquisitions were garrisoned by Roman colonies.

Next Campania was added. The cities of that fertile plain were being ravaged by the rude "Hill" Samnites, and so they appealed to Rome for aid. Rome repulsed the mountain tribes; and, in return, the cities of the Campanian plain became her tributaries.

379. The Last Latin Revolt. — Now that the Samnites seemed no longer dangerous, the Latins once more broke into revolt. This was the great *Latin War of 338 B.C.* In the end, the rising was crushed and the Latin league dissolved. Its public land became Roman. Some of its cities were brought into the Roman state, — their inhabitants being listed as citizens in the

Roman "tribes." The less fortunate cities were bound to Rome as subjects, *each by its separate treaty,* and they were allowed no intercourse with one another (except through Rome) either in politics or in trade.

380. Last Struggle for Central Italy : Samnite Wars. — The leadership of central Italy now lay between Rome, the great city-state of the lowlands, and the warlike Samnite tribes, which were spread widely over the southern Apennines. The decisive struggle between the two began in 326, and lasted, with brief truces, to 290 B.C. Both combatants were warlike, and they were not unequally matched. The Samnites trusted partly for defense to their mountain fastnesses; and Rome found safety in the chains of fortress colonies she had been building (§ 384).

Early in the war (321 B.C) the Samnites won an overwhelming victory. The whole Roman army was entrapped at the *Caudine Forks* in a narrow pass between two precipices. The Samnite leader, *Pontius,* made a treaty with the consuls by which the Romans were to withdraw all their posts from Samnium and to stop the war. He then let the captives go, after sending them "under the yoke." [1] The fruits of the victory, however, were lost, because the Romans refused to abide by the treaty.

According to the Roman story, the Senate declared that only the Roman Assembly, not the consuls alone, had power to make such a treaty. In place of their rescued army, they delivered to the Samnites the two consuls, naked and in chains, saying, through the herald : "These men have wronged you by promising, without authority, to make a treaty with you. Therefore we hand them over to you." Then one of the consuls (who is said to have suggested the whole plan) pushed against the Roman herald, and said, "I am now a Samnite, and, by striking the Roman herald, I have given the Romans the right to make war upon the Samnites." The Romans pretended that these forms released them from all obligation, and resumed the war.

---

[1] This humiliation consisted in obliging the captives to come forth one by one, clad only in shirts, and pass, with bowed head, between two upright spears upon which rested a third.

Then the Samnites built up a great alliance, which soon came to contain nearly all the states of Italy, together with the Cisalpine Gauls. But, using to the full the advantage of her central position (§ 333), Rome beat these foes, one by one, before they could unite their forces; and at the close of the long conflict (290 B.C.) she had become mistress of all the true peninsula, except the Greek cities of the south.

381. War with Pyrrhus. — Ten years later began the last great war for territory in Italy. The Greek cities at this moment were harassed by neighboring mountaineers, and they called in Roman aid, as Campania had done sixty years before. Thus Roman lordship became established throughout the south, except in Tar-

A COIN OF PYRRHUS.

entum. That great city wished to keep her independence, and sought help from *Pyrrhus*, the chivalrous king of Epirus.

Pyrrhus was one of the most remarkable of the Greek military adventurers who arose after the death of Alexander. He came to Italy with a great armament and with vast designs.

COIN OF PYRRHUS, struck in Sicily.

He hoped to unite the Greek cities of Magna Graecia and Sicily, and then to subdue Carthage, the ancient enemy of Hellenes in the West. That is, he planned to play in western Hellas and in Africa the part already played by Alexander in eastern Hellas and in Asia.

Pyrrhus knew little of Rome; but at the call of Tarentum he found himself engaged as a Greek champion with this new power. He won some victories, chiefly through his elephants, which the Romans had never before encountered. Then most of southern Italy deserted Rome to join him ; but, anxious to carry out his wider plans, he offered a favorable peace. Under the leadership of an aged and blind senator, *Appius Claudius*,[1] defeated Rome answered haughtily that she would treat with no invader *while he stood upon Italian soil*. Pyrrhus chafed at the delay, and finally hurried off to Sicily, leaving his victory incomplete. The steady Roman advance called him back, and a great Roman victory at *Beneventum* (275 B.C.) ruined his dream of empire and gave Rome that sovereignty of Italy which she had just claimed so resolutely. In 266, she rounded off her work by the conquest of that part of Cisalpine Gaul which lay south of the Po.

FOR FURTHER READING. — *Specially recommended :* Davis' *Readings*, II, Nos. 13–15 ; and Pelham's *Outlines*, 68–97 (the best compact treatment of the conquest of Italy).

Additional: There is an excellent brief summary of Rome's *method* in Smith's *Rome and Carthage*, 27.

EXERCISE. — (1) Review the growth of Rome, 510–266 B.C., by catchwords (see p. 186), with the important dates. (2) Make a list of terms for rapid explanation (see p. 162), from chapters xix–xxiv, especially from chapter xxiii.

---

[1] See the story from Livy in Davis' *Readings*, II, No. 15. For Appius Claudius, see also §§ 395, 399 a, and 402.

CHAPTER XXV

UNITED ITALY UNDER ROMAN RULE

382. **Rome and Subject Italy.** — Italy now contained some 5,000,000 people. More than a fourth of these (some 1,400,000) were *Roman citizens.* The rest were *subjects,* outside the Roman state. These figures do not include slaves; but there were not yet many slaves in Italy.

THE ROMAN STATE

383. **Classes of Citizens.** — It had come to pass that the majority of Roman citizens did not live at Rome. Large parts of Latium and Etruria and Campania had become "suburbs" of Rome (although in the midst even of these districts there were many subject communities); and other towns of Roman citizens were found in distant parts of Italy. Indeed, partly because of *difference in place of residenc*e, the citizens fall into three classes: (1) the inhabitants of *Rome itself,* (2) members of *Roman colonies,* and (3) members of *Roman municipia* (§§ 384, 385).

384. **Colonies.** — From an early date (§ 339) Rome had planted colonies of her citizens about the central city as military posts. The colonists and their descendants kept *all the rights of citizens.* Each colony had control over its *local* affairs in an Assembly of its own; but in order to vote upon matters that concerned the state the colonists had to come to Rome at the meeting of the Assembly there. This, of course, was usually impossible. *Representative government had not been worked out; and hence it was not possible for all the people of a large state to have an equal opportunity to attend meetings of the Assembly and to take part in political affairs.*

385. **Municipia.** — While Rome ruled parts of her conquests as subject communities, there were also many conquered towns which she *incorporated into the state in full equality.* This had

345

become the case with most of the Latin cities, with the Sabine towns, and with some other communities.

A town so annexed to the Roman state was called a *municipium*. Like a Roman colony, the inhabitants of a municipium managed their own local affairs, and, by coming to Rome, they could vote in the Assembly of the Tribes upon all Roman and imperial questions. They had also all the other rights of citizens. The municipia and the colonies differed chiefly in the matter of origin.

Besides the colonies and municipia, there were also many small hamlets of Roman citizens settled upon the public lands in distant parts of Italy. The dwellers in such hamlets kept their citizenship in Rome itself or in some colony or municipium, according to their origin.

The *municipia* represent a political advance,—a new contribution to empire-making. Athens had had cleruchies corresponding to the Roman colonies (§§ 148, 206), but she had never learned to give citizenship to conquered states. Therefore Rome, by 266 B. C., had a "citizen" body five times as large as Athens ever had. Later, Rome extended the principle of municipia to distant parts of Italy, and finally even more widely.

386. Organization in "Tribes." — To suit this expansion of the state, the twenty-one Roman "tribes" (§ 365) were increased gradually to thirty-five, — four in the city, the rest in adjoining districts. At first these were real divisions of territory, and a man changed his "tribe" if he changed his residence. At the point we have reached, however, this was no longer true. A man, once enrolled in a given tribe, remained a member, no matter where he lived, and his son after him; and as new communities were given citizenship, they were enrolled in the old thirty-five tribes, — sometimes whole new municipia, far apart, in the same tribe. Each tribe kept its one vote in the Assembly.

387. Privileges and Burdens of Citizens. — Rome and her citizens owned directly one third the land of Italy. All Roman citizens, too, had certain valued rights, as follows : —

a. Private Rights: (1) the right to acquire property, with the protection of the Roman law, in any of Rome's possessions;

and (2) the right of intermarriage in any Roman or subject community.

b. Public rights: (1) the right to vote in the Assembly of the Tribes; (2) the right to hold any offices; and (3) the right to appeal to the Assembly if condemned to death or to bodily punishment.

In return for these privileges, the citizens furnished half the army of Italy and paid all the *direct* taxes.

THE SUBJECTS

388. Three Classes of Subjects. — Rome was not yet ready to give up the idea of a city-state; and so, beyond a certain limit, all new acquisitions of territory were necessarily reduced to some form of subjection. Outside the Roman state was subject-Italy, in three main classes, *Latin Colonies, Prefectures,* and *"Allies."*

389. The Latin Colonies. — Highest in privilege among the subjects stood the Latins. This name did not apply now to the old Latin towns (nearly all of which had become municipia), but to a new kind of colonies sent out by Rome after 338, far beyond Latium.

These colonists were not granted citizenship, as were the *Roman colonies,* but only the *Latin right,* based on the rights enjoyed by the towns of the Latin Confederacy under the ancient alliance with Rome (§ 373). That is, their citizens had the *private rights* of Romans; and they might acquire full *public rights* also, and become Roman citizens in all respects, *by removing to Rome and enrolling in one of the tribes.* At first this removal was permitted to any member of a Latin colony who left a son in his own city to represent him; *but in the later colonies the privilege was restricted to those who had held some magistracy in the colony. In local affairs,* like the Roman colonies and the municipia, *the Latin colonies had full self-government.*

The poorer landless citizens of Rome could well afford the slight sacrifice of citizenship that came from joining a Latin colony, in return for the gain they secured as the aristocracy of a new settlement. There were thirty-five Latin colonies in

Italy before the Carthaginian invasion (§ 439). They numbered originally from three hundred to six thousand male colonists each, and they grew by drawing in settlers from the Italian populations about them. They are notable in three respects : —

a. They were a chief instrument in *Romanizing Italy* in language and institutions. Inscriptions show that they copied the Roman city constitution, even to such names as consuls and tribunes.

b. From a military point of view, like the Roman colonies, they were *garrisons,* protecting the distant parts of the peninsula against revolt or invasion. An enemy could rarely assail their walls successfully ; and he was rash indeed to pass on, leaving them to fall upon his rear.

c. Politically, they added a new element of *elasticity* to the rigid system of citizenship common in ancient states. They formed a link *between full citizens* and *permanent subjects.*

390. The class of prefectures was the least enviable, but it was very small. It consisted of three or four conquered towns, too deep offenders to warrant them in asking either the " Latin right " or " alliance." Apparently, they were all old municipia, which had been degraded in punishment for rebellion. They bore all the burdens of Roman citizenship, and some of them had part of the *private rights ; but they had no self-government.* Alone of all cities in Italy, they had their local government administered for them by *prefects* sent out from Rome.

391. The Italian " Allies." — Most numerous of all the inhabitants of Italy stood the mass of subject Greeks, Italians, and Etruscans, under the general name of *Italian Allies.* These cities ranked in privilege next to the Latin colonies ; but among themselves they differed greatly in condition. Each one was bound to Rome by its separate treaty, and these treaties varied widely. None of the " Allies," however, had either the private or public rights of Romans, and they were *isolated jealously one from another ;* but in general they bore few burdens and enjoyed local self-government and Roman protection.

392. The following table shows the gradations of Italian communities, and the way in which one class merged into another.

1. Rome
2. Roman
    Colonies } full rights, but able to exercise political power only
    and   } by coming to Rome to the Assembly.
    Municipia }

3. Latin Colonies: private rights of Roman citizens, and possibility of acquiring full citizenship.

4 "Allies": local self-government and Roman protection; lightly burdened, but no Roman rights.

5. Prefectures: no self-government.

ROME AND HER SUBJECTS: SUMMARY

393. Advantages and Restrictions of the Subjects. — No one of the "subject cities" (Latin colony, municipium, or prefecture) had any one of the three great rights of making war, concluding treaties, or coining money. With the exception of the small class of prefectures, they did retain nearly complete self-government in other matters. Each kept its own Assembly, Senate, and magistrates; and, in general, each retained its own law and custom. They paid no tribute, except to provide their *small* share of troops for war.

Thus where Rome refused to confer citizenship, she did, with rare insight and magnanimity, lessen burdens and leave local freedom. At the same time she bestowed order, tranquillity, and prosperity. The calamities of great wars strike our imagination; but they cause infinitely less suffering than the everlasting petty wars of neighbors, with pillage and slaughter diffused everywhere. Roman supremacy put a stop to these endless and wasting feuds. Moreover, so far as Italy was concerned, the field of conflict, even in Rome's great wars, was thenceforth to be mostly beyond her borders.

394. Rome's Policy. — The citizens enrolled in the thirty-five Roman tribes were the rulers of Italy. None others possessed any of the imperial power. They, or their officers, decided upon war and peace, made treaties, issued the only coinage permitted, and fixed the number of soldiers which the subject cities must furnish for war.

It should be noted that there are two phases of the Roman genius for rule, — one admirable and the other mean but effective.

a. Incorporation and Tolerance.   Rome grew strong first by a wise and generous *incorporation* of her conquests.   With this

THE APPIAN WAY TO-DAY, WITH RUINS OF THE AQUEDUCT OF CLAUDIUS IN THE BACKGROUND. The Aqueduct was carried for long distances on arches. It was built nearly four centuries later than the Appian Way. See pp. 468, 490.

strength, she won wider physical victories. And over her subjects she won also spiritual dominion by her intelligence, justice, and firmness, and especially by a marvelous *toleration* for local customs and rights.

b. Jealousy and Isolation.   At the same time, Rome strictly *isolated* the subject communities from one another. She dissolved all tribal confederacies; she took skillful advantage of the grades of inferiority that she had created among her dependents *to foment jealousies* and to play off one class of communities against another. Likewise, within each city, she set class against class, on the whole favoring an aristocratic organization. In politics as in war, the policy of her statesmen was "*Divide and conquer.*"

Thus Rome combined the imperial system of Athens (with improvements) with phases of that of Sparta. The general result was admirable. The rule of Rome in Italy was not an absolutism, as it was to be later over more distant conquests. The whole Italian stock had become consolidated under a leading city. In form, and to a great degree in fact, Italy was a confederacy; but it was a confederacy *with all the connecting lines radiating from Rome — a confederacy under a Queen-city.* The allies had no connection with each other except through the head city. Even the physical ties — the famous roads that marked her dominion and strengthened it — "all led to Rome."

395. The Roman roads were a real part of the Roman system of government. They were bonds of union. Rome began her system of magnificent roads in 312 B.C. by building the *Via Appia* to the new possessions in Campania. This was the work of the censor Appius Claudius (§ 402). Afterward all Italy, and then the growing empire outside Italy, was traversed by a network of such roads. Nothing was permitted to obstruct their course. Mountains were tunneled; rivers were bridged; marshes were spanned for miles by viaducts of masonry.

The construction was slow and costly. First the workmen removed all loose soil down to some firm strata, preferably the native rock. Then was laid a layer of large stones, then one of smaller, and at least one more of smaller ones still, — all bound together — some two feet in thickness — by an excellent cement. The top was then carefully leveled and smoothly paved with huge slabs of rock fitted to one another with the greatest nicety. These roads made the best means of communication the world was to see until the time of railroads. They were so carefully constructed, too, that their remains, in good condition to-day, still "mark the lands where Rome has ruled." They were designed for military purposes; but they helped other intercourse and held Italy together socially.   (Cf. § 77, for Persian roads.)

For Further Reading in these Divisions (The Roman State and the Subjects) : *Specially recommended*, Pelham's *Outlines*, 97–107.

CHAPTER XXVI

GOVERNMENT OF THE ROMAN REPUBLIC

396. The officers of chief dignity, from least to greatest were : —

Aediles (two), with oversight over police and public works ;

Praetors (two), with the chief judicial power ;

Consuls (two), commanders in war and leaders in foreign policy ;

Censors (two), § 368 ;

Dictator (one), in critical times only (§ 354).

These five were called *curule offices,* because the holders, dividing among them the old royal power, kept the right to use the curule chair — the ivory "throne"[1] of the old kings. There were also the two *inferior aediles,* the eight *quaestors* (in charge of the treasury and with some judicial power), and the ten *tribunes.* This last office, though less in dignity than the curule offices, was perhaps most important of all. The tribune's old duties were gone; but he had become a political leader, and he kept his tremendous power of veto.

Except the censor these officers held authority for only one year (the dictator for only a half-year), but they exercised great power. The magistrate still called and adjourned Assemblies as he liked ; he alone could put proposals before them ; and he controlled debate and amendment.

397. A new aristocracy had appeared, *composed of the descendants of curule officers.* Each such official, by law, transmitted to his descendants the right to keep upon the walls of their living rooms the wax masks of ancestors, and to carry them in

---

[1] This symbol of dignity was very simple,— much in the character of an ivory camp-stool.

a public procession at the funeral of a member of the family.
A chief part of such a funeral was an oration commemorating

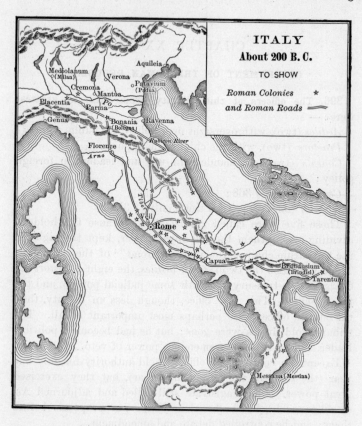

the virtues and deeds of the ancestors, whose images were present.[1] Families with this privilege were called *nobles* (nobiles).

Before the year 300 B.C., the nobles began to be jealous of
the admission of "new men" to their ranks; and their united
influence soon controlled nearly all curule elections in favor of

---

[1] See Davis' *Readings*, II, No. 19, on Roman state funerals.

some member of their own order. To make this easier, they secured a law fixing the order in which these offices could be attained. No one could be elected aedile until he had held the quaestorship, nor praetor till he had been aedile, nor consul till he had been praetor. Then the nobles had to watch the elections only of the first rank of officers. By controlling these, they could control admission to their order.[1] *Thus all the nobles became practically an hereditary oligarchy of a few hundred families.* And since senators had to be appointed from those who had held curule offices, each "noble" family was sure to have a senator among its near relatives, if not in its own home. "Nobles" became equivalent to *the Senatorial order*.

398. The Assemblies. — The Assemblies by curias, by centuries, and by tribes *continued to exist side by side;* but the center of gravity had shifted again, — as once before from the curias to the centuries, so now from the centuries to the tribes. The political function of the Curiate Assembly had become purely formal in very early times (§ 346). The Centuriate Assembly continued to elect consuls, censors, and praetors; but its law-making power and the choice of all other officers had passed to the Assembly of Tribes. Of course, as this change took place, the rich citizens took their place in this Assembly;[2] but in deciding the vote of a tribe, each member, rich or poor, counted like any other member.

399. Changes in the Assemblies. — During the century between the Licinian Laws and the war with Pyrrhus, three or four legal reforms were adopted, to make the political Assemblies more powerful and more democratic.

a. In 312, a reforming censor, Appius Claudius, enrolled the landless citizens in the tribes. Up to this time, only land-

---

[1] Davis' *Readings*, II, No. 14 (section on the *Aedileship of Flavius*), illustrates the hostility of the aristocrats to the " new men," and gives also the story of democratic reforms. See, too, Dr. Davis' introduction to No. 14. For a compact modern treatment, see Pelham's *Outlines*, 170–172.

[2] A descendant of an old patrician family now belonged to all three Assemblies ; a plebeian belonged to the Assembly of Centuries and to the Assembly of Tribes.

holders had had a voice there.   Appius carried this extension of
the franchise unconstitutionally, in defiance of the veto of his
colleague.   The aristocratic party did not venture to undo the
act, but they did modify it : a few years later another censor
put all the landless class into the four city tribes alone, so that
the city poor might not outvote the rural landowners.[1]

b. About the same time a change took place in the Centuriate Assembly, by which each of the *five classes* (§ 348) secured
an equal voice, and wealth lost most of its supremacy.

c. In 287, after some dissension and a threatened secession,
*the Hortensian Law took from the Senate its veto upon the plebi-
scites of the tribes.* Somewhat earlier the Senate had lost all
veto over the elections in the centuries.

These changes made Rome a democracy, in law; but
in practice they were more than counterbalanced by the way
in which the nobles controlled the Senate and the curule
offices.

400. The Senate. — Indirectly, the Senate had been made
elective.   The censors were required to fill vacancies in that
body first from those who had held curule offices, and ordinarily
this left them little choice.   The senatorial veto upon the Assemblies, too, had been taken away.   So far as written law was
concerned, the Senate was only an advisory body.

None the less it was really the guiding force in the government.
It contained the wisdom and experience of Rome.   The pressure of constant and dangerous wars, and the growing com-
plexity of foreign relations even in peace, made it inevitable
that this far-seeing, compact, experienced body should assume
authority which in theory belonged to the clumsy, inexperienced
Assembly.   "*Rome,*" says Ihne, "*became a complete aristocracy
with democratic forms;* or, as Mommsen puts it, "While the
burgesses [citizens] acquired the semblance, the Senate acquired the substance, of power."

Each magistrate expected, after his brief term of office,

---

[1] Davis' *Readings*, II, No. 14, gives Livy's aristocratic account of this contest.

to become permanently a member of the Senate. Therefore he guarded its dignity and dreaded its anger. Thus, as the magistrate controlled the Assemblies, so the Senate controlled the magistrate. No consul would think of bringing a law before the people without the previous approval of the Senate (so that indirectly that body, rather than the Assembly, had become the real legislature.) As a last resort, it could usually count upon one or more of the ten tribunes, and could block any action it disliked by his veto. No officer would draw money from the treasury without the Senate's consent. It declared and managed wars. It received ambassadors and made alliances. And certainly, for over a hundred years, by its sagacity and energy, this "assembly of kings"[1] justified its usurpation, earning Mommsen's epithet, — "the foremost political corporation of all time."

401. **Democratic Theory and Aristocratic Practice.** — In theory the Democracy was supreme through its popular Assemblies. In practice the Aristocrats controlled the government through their monopoly of the curule offices and of the all-directing Senate.

This condition began before the Pyrrhic War, or about 300 B.C., and it lasted nearly three hundred years. During the first part of this time (until about 200 B.C.) the rule of the nobles, though marked sometimes by a narrow class spirit, was patriotic, vigorous, and beneficent.[2] *After the year* 200, *it became both weak and selfish. Then power slipped from the incapable Aristocracy into the hands of military chiefs, — the forerunners of the Empire* (§§ 520 ff.).

402. **Excursus: a Democratic Aristocrat.** — The greatest name in this period of Roman history is that of Appius Claudius, the censor of the years 312–307. The Claudian gens were of the proudest patrician rank, but, like the Valerii (§ 362), they too "loved the people well." It was an earlier Appius Claudius who carried through the reforms of the Decemvirs (§ 362). This later Appius, also, was reviled by Livy,

---

[1] This was the description of the Senate which an ambassador from Pyrrhus (§ 382) carried back to his master. [2] See Davis' *Readings*, II, No. 18.

who wrote for the aristocrats; but, even in the story of his foes, he stands out as a great, progressive statesman. As censor, he built the first Roman aqueduct, to bring pure water to Rome from the mountains twelve miles away, and he constructed the Appian Way (§ 395), the first of the famous Roman roads. In order to carry through these important public works, he kept his office during the whole five years, until the next appointment,[1] greatly to the wrath of the aristocracy.

More important still were the social and political reforms of Appius. He filled the vacancies in the Senate with plebeians (the old distinction had not then died out), and even with the sons of freedmen; and he gave the landless citizens of Rome political power by enrolling them in the " tribes " (§ 399). No doubt, he aided the valuable law-reforms of the aedile Flavius (§ 399, note), who, Livy tells us, owed his election to the strength Appius had given to the democratic faction.

At some time after the expiration of his censorship Appius became blind. His aristocratic foes called this a punishment from the gods, in return for his attacks upon the " constitution of the fathers." But the blind old man, years after his censorship, could still dominate the policy of Rome upon occasion. It was he who checked the Senate when it was about to make peace with Pyrrhus after the early Roman defeats, first enunciating clearly the Roman claim to supremacy in all Italy. Appius also was a lover of learning. He made a collection of legal decisions; and his written speeches and wise maxims were much quoted in later Rome.

For Further Reading on the Republican constitution: *Specially recommended:* Davis' *Readings*, II, No. 17 (the account of Polybius, a scholarly Greek historian who wrote about 150 B.C.) ; and Pelham's *Outlines*, 159–167 (Senate), 167–172 (curule officers).

---

[1] Censors were appointed each five years. Customarily, they performed their duties, and laid down their office, by the close of the first eighteen months. But there was no way to compel one to shorten his term in this way.

CHAPTER XXVII

THE ARMY

403. **The Flexible Legion**. — The instrument with which the Roman state conquered the world can best be surveyed at this point, although the changes noted in § 406 took place somewhat later.

The Roman army under the kings was similar to the old Dorian organization. In Italy, as in Greece, the "knights" of very early times had given way, before history fairly begins, to a dense hoplite array, usually eight deep. In Greece the next step was to deepen and close the ranks still further into the massive Theban and Macedonian phalanx. In Italy, instead, they were broken up into three successive lines, and each line was divided further into small companies. The companies were usually six men deep with twenty in each rank; and between each two companies there was a space equal to the front of a company. Thus, if one line fell back, the companies of the line behind could advance through the intervals. Within a company, too, each soldier had about twice the space permitted in the phalanx. The front rank of companies contained the raw recruits. Experienced soldiers made up the second line of companies. The third line contained only veterans, and was usually held in reserve, to deliver a decisive blow at a critical moment in the battle.[1]

IRON HEAD OF A JAVELIN.

(Such a head was about three feet long, and was fitted into a wooden shaft of about the same length. Each soldier of the two front rows of companies carried two javelins.)

---

[1] The legion usually had ten "companies" in each of its three lines. Can the student draw a diagram of a legion in battle array, from the description above?

The arms of legion and phalanx differed also. The phalanx depended upon long spears. While it remained unbroken and could present its front, it was invulnerable; but if disordered by uneven ground, or if taken in flank, it was doomed. The legion used the hurling javelin to disorder the enemy's ranks before immediate contact (as moderns have used musketry), and the famous Roman short sword for close combat (as moderns, till recently, have used the bayonet). Flexibility, individuality, and constancy took the place of the collective lance thrust of the unwieldy phalanx.[1] For defensive armor, a legionary wore (1) a bronze *helmet;* (2) a *corselet*, of interwoven leather straps, about the body, holding a plate of iron; (3) a short leather skirt, strengthened with metal plates, hanging lower than the corselet; (4) metal greaves on the legs; and (5), on the left arm, an oblong shield with a convex surface, to make the weapons of the enemy glance off.

The legion numbered about five thousand, and was made up of Roman citizens. Each legion was accompanied by about five thousand men from the Allies. These *auxiliaries* served on the wings of the legion as light-armed troops, and they furnished also whatever cavalry the army had. The strength of the Roman army, however, lay in the infantry and especially in the legions.

404. The Roman camp was characteristic of a people whose colonies were garrisons. Where the army encamped — even if for only a single night — there grew up in an hour a fortified city, with earth walls and regular streets.[2] This system allowed the Romans often " to conquer by sitting still," declining or giving battle at their own option; while, too, when they

---

[1] The reserve line of the legion carried spears instead of javelins. The two great fighting instruments, legion and phalanx, were not to come into final conflict until after 200 B.C. Meantime they remained supreme in the East and West respectively.

[2] The importance of these camps, as the sites and foundation plans of cities over Europe, is shown by the frequency of the Roman word *castra* (camp) in English place-names, as in *Chester, Rochester, Winchester, Dorchester, Manchester*, etc.

did fight, they did so "under the walls of their city," with a fortified and guarded refuge in their rear.

405. Discipline.[1] — The terrible discipline of early times remained. Without trial, the general could scourge or behead

THE ROMAN CAMP.

any man serving in his camp. Still more fearful was the practice of *decimating* a faulty corps (putting to death every tenth man).

406. Changes with Extension of Service: a Professional Army; Proconsuls. — Rome now began a long series of great wars,

---

[1] An interesting extract from Polybius is given in Munro's *Source Book*, 28, 29.

waged, for the most part, outside Italy. Great changes resulted in the army. Service with the legions long remained the highest duty of the citizen, and each man between the ages of seventeen and forty-six was liable to active duty. But, alongside this citizen army, there was to grow up a *professional army*. New citizen legions were raised each year for the summer campaigns, as before, though more and more, even in these legions, the officers were veterans and were becoming a professional class; but the legions sent to Sicily, Spain, or Africa were kept under arms sometimes for many years.[1]

Such facts led to another change, *with important political consequences*. To call home a consul each year from an unfinished campaign in these distant wars became intolerably wasteful. The remedy was found in prolonging the commander's term, under the title of *proconsul*. This office was destined to become the strongest force in the Republic and a chief step toward the coming Empire.

---

[1] In particular, the long struggle in Spain during the War with Hannibal and after it (§§ 447, 456) operated in this way. Twenty thousand soldiers were required for that province each year for half a century. There soon grew up a practice of settling such veterans, upon the expiration of their service, in military colonies in the provinces where they had served — the lands thus given them being regarded as a kind of service pension. In this way communities of Roman citizens were to be spread over the provinces, *to Italianize the world*, as a like system of colonization had already Romanized Italy.

CHAPTER XXVIII

ROMAN SOCIETY, 367–200 B.C.

407. The Noblest Period. — From 367 to about 200 B.C. is the period of greatest Roman vigor. The old class distinctions (between patrician and plebeian) had died out. A new aristocracy of office was growing up, but it was still in its best age, its "age of service." There was soon to come a new class struggle between rich and poor — but this had not yet begun.

It was the Roman people of these two splendid centuries who made Rome the mistress first of Italy and then of the world. That conquest was not completed in this period; but it was really decided by the events of these years. The final steps were carried out by an inferior Rome; for the conquests — *beyond Italy* — were no sooner started than they began to work woeful changes in the conquering people. We stop, therefore, at this point to survey Roman society — as we have just done with the Roman government — at its noblest stage.

408. Industries. — The Roman citizens, in the main, were still yeomen farmers, who worked hard and lived plainly. Each such farmer tilled his few acres with his own hands and the help of his own sons. Each eighth day, he came to the city with a load of produce for the "market." The early practice of raising cattle had given way largely to the cultivation of wheat, barley, garden vegetables, and fruit; but horses, cattle, sheep, and hogs still counted in the farm produce. Many modern garden vegetables were not yet known, and the Roman variety was certainly no larger than the Egyptian of a much earlier time (§ 17); but we read frequently of beans, onions, turnips, cabbages, and of such fruits as figs, olives, apples, plums, and pears.

363

In the city itself (as no doubt in all Italian towns), the craftsmen were organized in "unions" (*gilds*). These gilds were not for the purpose of raising wages, as with us, nor mainly for improving the character of the work, as in later centuries in Europe. They were associations for friendly intercourse, and, to some extent, for mutual helpfulness among the members in times of misfortune. They illustrate the extraordinary Roman capacity for organization and group action, — in marked contrast to the individuality of Greek life. Legend tells us that King Numa organized the gilds of carpenters, shoemakers, dyers, laundrymen, potters, coppersmiths, and flute players. Certainly these gilds were very ancient at Rome. Weavers and bakers were to appear a little later; but during this period these industries were carried on in each household. The oldest gild known to us — that of the flute players, who furnished music for the sacred festivals — is the only one, so far as we know, which ever entered upon a strike for greater privileges. (See Davis' *Readings*, II, No. 14.)

Commerce (*trade to other lands*) paid huge profits to the successful merchants (those who did not too often lose vessels by shipwreck or pirates). The few rich Romans still disdained the business for themselves, but they had begun to use their capital in it through their slaves or former slaves (freedmen).

409. Wealth. — There were few citizens of great wealth or in extreme poverty. The rapid gains of territory, after 367, made it possible to relieve the city poor by grants of land or by sending them out in colonies. Still, the attitude of the Roman landed citizen toward the merchant, the small shopkeeper, and the artisan was not unlike that of the Athenian gentleman (§ 237). But the Roman "gentleman" of this age was not yet a mere owner of farms, like the Athenian of Pericles' time: he was himself the farmer.

The legend of the patrician *Cincinnatus*[1] of the fifth century (called from the plow on his three-acre farm to become dicta-

---

[1] § 350, note.

tor and save Rome from the Aequians, and returning to the
plow again, all in sixteen days) is more than matched by the
sober history of *Manius Curio*, the conqueror of the Samnites
and of Pyrrhus.

This great Roman was a Sabine peasant and a proud aristocrat.   Plutarch tells us that, though he had "triumphed" [1]
thrice, he continued to live in a cottage on a little three-acre
plot which he tilled with his own hands.   Here the Samnite
ambassadors found him dressing turnips in the chimney corner,
when they came to offer him a large present of gold.   Curio
refused the gift : " A man," said he, " who can be content with
this supper hath no need of gold; and I count it glory, not to
possess wealth, but to rule those who do."

410. Money. — The oldest Roman word for money (*pecunia*)
came from the word for herd (*pecus*).   This points to a time
when payments were made chiefly in cattle, as with many semi-
barbaric tribes in modern times.   But before definite Roman
history begins, a copper coinage had been introduced.   Even
before the *coinage,* the Romans had " estimated " in copper (*aes*),
counting by the pound weight.   Silver was not used either for
money or for household purposes until after the union of Italy ;
and even at a later date a senator was struck from the list by a
reforming censor, because he owned ten pounds of silver plate.

411. Home and Manner of Life. — The family and religion as yet
showed little change from the early state described in §§ 340,
341.   The house had added rooms on sides and rear, and openings for windows ; but it was still exceedingly simple, like the
life within.   A plain table, wooden couches, and a few stools,
and simple cooking utensils comprised the furniture.   Artificial
warmth and light were secured by " braziers " and lamps, like
those of the Greeks (§ 233).   The Roman took his chief meal
at midday (not in the evening, as the Greeks did).   In early
times, the main food was a " porridge " of ground meal boiled
in water.   Pork, especially in the form of sausage, was the

---

[1] Special report : a Roman "triumph."   See Munro's *Source Book*, 38-40.

favorite meat. Bread, from ground wheat or barley, was baked in flat, round cakes. Water or milk was the common drink, but wine mixed with water was coming into general use, after the fashion of the Greeks. The Romans who conquered Pyrrhus and Hannibal were a frugal, temperate people.

412. Dress was as simple as the food. The Roman kept the primitive loin cloth of linen. Over this he drew a short-sleeved woolen shirt (*tunic*) falling to the knees. This made the common dress of the house, workshop, and field. In public the Roman wore an outer garment — a white woolen blanket, thrown about him in graceful folds. This was the famous Roman *toga*. For defense against rain or cold, sometimes a cloak also was worn. Women wore a long and a short tunic, and for the street, a blanket-wrap. Foot-gear was like that of the Greeks. Stockings and hats were alike unknown. Women were fond of jewelry, — rings, bracelets, pins, and chains; and each man wore a seal-ring. Members of the senatorial families wore also broad gold rings.

413. Education was elementary. Until seven, the children were in the mother's care. After that age, boys went to a private school, taught by some Greek slave or freedman. As in Greece, the pupil was attended by a "pedagogue." He learned merely to read, write, and, in a limited degree, to compute with Roman numerals. The only textbook was the Twelve Tables, which were learned by heart. Physical training was found in athletic games in the Campus Martius (p. 311), where the young Romans contended in running, wrestling, and in the use of the spear, sword, and javelin. The Roman took his exercise, not in regular gymnasium training, like the Greeks or the modern German, but more like the English and Americans. For amusements, there were chariot races and the theater; but the racers and actors were slaves or freedmen, not Romans. The Roman and the Greek views of the stage and of athletic contests were at opposite poles.

414. Science and Learning. — Literature, under Greek influence, was just beginning at the close of the period. So, too, with

art. Roads, bridges, and aqueducts were built in the last half
of the period on a magnificent scale; and the use of the round
arch was so developed that we often speak of that architectural
feature as "the Roman arch."

415. Roman morals and ideals are revealed in much of the
preceding story. The finest thing in Roman character was
the spirit of self-immolation for Rome, — the willingness to

A BOXING MATCH.

sink personal or party advantage for the public weal. Next to
this, and allied to it, is the capacity for organization, for working *together* for a common end. *Roman history is not the
history of a few brilliant leaders: it is the story of a people.*

Undue praise has been given sometimes to the stern excellence
of early Rome. It is cheap moralizing to point out the barbaric
virtues of a rude society in comparison with the luxury of
refined times, and omit more important considerations. The
real picture is by no means without shadows. The Roman was
abstemious, haughty, obedient to law, self-controlled. His
ideal was a man of iron will and stern discipline, devoted to
Rome, contemptuous of luxury, of suffering, and even of human
sympathy if it conflicted with his duty to the state. His model

was still the first consul, Brutus, who in legend sent his guilty sons to the block unmoved;[1] and the great Latin war (338 B.C.) furnished a historical consul, *Manlius*, who, as Livy tells us, gloomily executed his gallant son for a glorious act of insubordination.[2]

With such men for her heroes, it is not strange that Rome made some peculiar boasts. For instance, the noble Samnite, Pontius, the victor of Caudine Forks, had magnanimously spared the Roman army (§ 380); but when he became prisoner in turn, Rome saw only cause for pride in basely dragging him through the city in a triumph, and then starving him to death in a dungeon. The Romans were coarse, cruel, and rapacious, as well as lofty-minded, brave, and obedient.

416. The Beginning of Greek Influence. — In manners and in morals Rome was a fair type of the Italians proper. The Etruscans and Greeks were softer and more luxurious, with more abject poverty among the masses.

After the war with Pyrrhus, the connection with Magna Graecia introduced Greek culture into Roman society, and wealth and luxury began slowly to appear. At first the Romans as a whole did not show to advantage under the change. Too often it seemed only to veneer their native coarseness and brutality. At the same time, with the better minds, it did soften and refine character into a more lovable type than Italy had so far seen: and, from this time, Greek art and thought more and more worked upon Roman society.

This change certainly is not to be mourned. It was not this that ruined Rome. It was the manifold results of world-empire, soon to follow. The old Roman training had made citizens fit to grapple with the problems of uniting Italy into one nation, and of ruling and protecting that home land. But Roman training and character broke down utterly before the vastly more complex problems and temptations of foreign conquests.

---

[1] § 350, close.   [2] Special report.

CHAPTER XXIX

THE WINNING OF THE WEST, 264-146 B.C.

THE RIVALS — ITALY AND CARTHAGE

417. Italy in 264 B.C. was one of five great Mediterranean states. When she completed the union of Italy (§ 381), Alexander the Great had been dead nearly fifty years. The long Wars of the Succession had closed, and the dominion of the eastern Mediterranean world was divided between the three great Greek kingdoms, Syria, Egypt, and Macedonia, with their numerous satellites (§§ 289, 292 ff.). In the western Mediterranean Carthage held undisputed sway. Now, between the three powers of the East and the single mistress of the West stood forth a new state, Roman Italy, destined to absorb them all.

The struggle for supremacy between these five Mediterranean powers filled the next hundred and twenty years. The first half of the period went to Roman conquests in the West at the expense of Carthage.

418. Carthage the Natural Rival of Rome in the West. — Carthage and Rome had been allied, just before, against Pyrrhus, their common enemy. But that gallant adventurer had seen that they were natural rivals; and, as he abandoned the West, he exclaimed longingly, "How fair a battlefield we are leaving for the Romans and Carthaginians!" In less than ten years the hundred-year conflict began.

Carthage was an ancient Phoenician colony, on the finest harbor in North Africa. Her government, in form, was a republic, somewhat like Rome, but in reality it was a narrow oligarchy controlled by a few wealthy families. She was now at the height of her power. Polybius (§ 462) called her the richest city ·in the world. To her old naval supremacy she had added a vast

369

land empire, including North Africa,[1] Sardinia, Corsica, half
of Sicily, and the coasts of Spain. The western Mediterranean
she regarded as a Punic[2] lake: foreign sailors caught tres-
passing there were cast into the sea. But the Greeks of South
Italy had traded in those waters for five hundred years; and
Rome, now mistress and protector of those cities, was bound

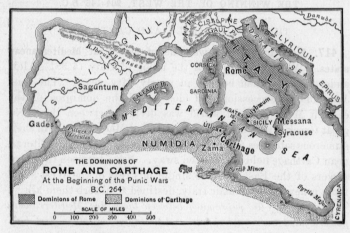

THE DOMINIONS OF
ROME AND CARTHAGE
At the Beginning of the Punic Wars
B.C. 264

Dominions of Rome   Dominions of Carthage

SCALE OF MILES
0   100   200   300   400   500

soon to defend their trading rights against this "closed door"
of Carthaginian policy.

419. Carthaginian Character. — Her Roman foes represented
Carthage as wanting in honesty; and with biting irony they
invented the term, "Punic faith," as a synonym for treachery.
Carthage herself is "a dumb actor on the stage of history."
She once had poetry, oratory, and philosophy, but none of it
escaped Roman hate, to tell us how Carthaginians thought and
felt. Rome wrote the history; but, even from the Roman
story, the charge of faithlessness and greed is most apparent
against Rome.

---

[1] In Africa alone Carthage ruled three hundred cities, and her territory
merged into the desert where tributary nomads roamed.

[2] "Punic" is another form for "Phoenician," and is used as a shorter ad-
jective for "Carthaginian."

However, the civilization of Carthage was of an Oriental type (§ 80). Her religion was the cruel and licentious worship of the Phoenician Baal and Astarte. Her armies were a motley mass of mercenaries. And though, like the mother Phoenician states, she scattered wide the seeds of a material culture, like them, also, she showed no power of assimilating inferior nations. The conquests of Rome were to be Romanized; *but six centuries of Punic rule had left the Berber tribes of Africa* (§ 10) *wholly outside Carthaginian society.*

420. The contrast between the political systems of the two rivals is equally striking. Even her nearest and best subjects Carthage kept in virtual slavery. Says Mommsen (*History of Rome*, II, 155) : —

" Carthage dispatched her overseers everywhere, and loaded even the old Phoenician cities with a heavy tribute, while her subject tribes were practically treated as state slaves. In this way there was not in the compass of the Carthagino-African state a single community, with the exception of Utica, that would not have been politically and materially benefited by the fall of Carthage ; in the Romano-Italic, there was not one that had not much more to lose than to gain in rebelling against a government which was careful to avoid injuring material interests, and which never, at least by extreme measures, challenged political opposition."

421. The Issue at Stake. — Thus, whatever our sympathy for Carthage and her hero leaders, we must see that the victory of Rome was necessary for the welfare of the human race. *The struggle was the conflict of Greece and Persia repeated by more stalwart actors on a western stage.*

The conflict consists of a series of three wars. The second is the decisive struggle, to which, it is often said, the first and third stand merely as prologue and epilogue.

THE FIRST PUNIC WAR (THE WAR FOR SICILY)

422. The *occasion* for the First Punic War was found in Sicily. When Rome conquered South Italy, she came necessarily into relations with the Greeks in that island. Sicily is really a con-

tinuation of the Italian peninsula. It reaches to within ninety
miles of the African coast. A sunken ridge on the bed of the
sea shows that it once joined the two continents, and it still
forms a stepping-stone between them. For this middle land,
European and African struggled for centuries. For two hundred years now it had been divided, Syracuse holding the
eastern half, Carthage the western.

While Rome was still busy with the Pyrrhic war, an event
happened which renewed the conflict for Sicily and was finally
to draw Rome in as a chief actor. A band of Campanian mer-

COIN OF HIERO II OF SYRACUSE.

cenaries, on their way home from service under the tyrant of
Syracuse, seized the city of Messana, murdering all the men
and taking possession of their wives and goods. The robbers
called themselves *Mamertines* ("Sons of Mars"), and for several
years, from their walled stronghold, they ravaged and plundered the northeast corner of Sicily. Now, in 265, they were
hard pressed by Hiero II, the ruler of Syracuse, and one faction called in Carthage while another party appealed to Rome
for protection.

Both Syracuse and Carthage were allies of Rome, and it was
not easy for that state to find excuse for defending the robbers.
The desire to check Carthage and to extend Roman power, however, outweighed all caution as well as all moral considerations. And, indeed, there was real danger in Carthage establishing herself in Messana, close to the Italian coast. Even so,

the Senate could come to no decision; but the people, to whom it referred the question, voted promptly to send troops to Sicily; *and, in 264, Roman legions for the first time crossed the seas.* The war with Carthage that followed is known as the *First Punic War.*

423. Strength of the Parties. — Carthage was mistress of an empire huge but scattered and heterogeneous. Rome was the head of a small but compact nationality. Each state contained, or ruled over, about 5,000,000 people. The strength of Carthage lay in her wealth and in her navy. Her weak points were: the jealousy felt by the ruling families at home toward their own successful generals; the difficulty of dealing with her mercenaries; the danger of revolt among her Libyan subjects; *and the fact that an invading army, after one victory, would find no resistance outside her walls, since her jealousy had leveled the defenses of her tributary towns in Africa.*

Rome was strong in the patriotism and vigor of her people, in the discipline of her legions, *and in the fidelity of her allies.* Her weakness lay in the total lack of a navy, and in the want of a better military system than the one of annually changing officers and short-term soldiers. (The changes in the army referred to in § 406 above had not yet taken place. They were to result from this war.)

424. Importance of Sea Power. — The war lasted twenty-three years, and is ranked by Polybius (a Greek historian of the next century) above all previous wars for severity. Few conflicts illustrate better the value of naval superiority. At first the Carthaginians were undisputed masters of the sea. They therefore reinforced their troops in Sicily at pleasure, and ravaged the coasts of Italy to the utter ruin of seaboard prosperity. Indeed, for a time they made good their warning to the Roman Senate before the war began, — that against their will no Roman could wash his hands in the sea.

425. Rome becomes a Sea Power. — But the Romans, with sagacity and boldness, built their first war fleet and soon met the ancient Queen of the Seas on her own element. Winning command there temporarily,[1] in 256, they invaded Africa itself. The consul *Regulus* won brilliant successes there, and even laid siege to Carthage. But, as winter came on, the short-term Roman armies were mostly recalled, according to custom, and the weak remnant was soon killed or captured.

426. Legend of Regulus. — Five years later, the weary Carthaginians sent the captive Regulus home with offers of peace and exchange of prisoners, binding him by oath to return to Carthage if Rome rejected the terms. Later Roman legend tells proudly how Regulus, arrived at Rome, advised the Senate not to make peace or ransom captives who had disgraced themselves by surrender, and how then, despite all entreaties, he steadfastly left Rome, holding his eyes on the ground to avoid sight of wife and child, to return to Carthage and to a cruel death by torture. (See Davis' *Readings*, II, No. 20.) The story at least illustrates Roman ideals of patriotic self-devotion and of faithfulness to the plighted word.

427. The Carthaginian hero of the war is strictly historical. In 247, the general *Hamilcar* appeared in Sicily. He established himself with a small force on the summit of a rugged mountain, and from this citadel with a mere handful of troops, he held large Roman armies in check for six years, by his remarkable skill in war. His troops grew their own food and forage on the barren mountain slopes; and from time to time Hamilcar swooped down, eagle-like, to strike telling blows, — earning from friend and foe the surname *Barca* (the Lightning).

---

[1] Special report ; the new naval tactics of the Romans (Mommsen, II, 173–176). Despite real genius in the device by which Rome, to a great degree, changed a naval into a land battle, her immediate victory at sea over the veteran navy of Carthage is explicable chiefly on the supposition that the " Roman " navy was furnished by the " allies " in Magna Graecia. The story of Polybius, that Rome built her fleet in two months on the model of a stranded Carthaginian vessel, and meantime trained her sailors to row sitting on the sand (see Munro, 79–80), must be in the main a quaint invention. See How and Leigh, 152. Mommsen (II, 43–46) outlines the history of the Roman navy for sixty years before the war, and (II, 172–176) gives a possible meaning to the old account by Polybius.

428. Rome's Patriotism and Enterprise. — Rome's first attempts upon the sea had been surprisingly successful, but soon terrible reverses befell her there. In quick succession she lost four great fleets with large armies on board, mainly through lack of seamanship in her commanders. One sixth of her citizens had perished ; the treasury was empty; and, in despair, the Senate was about to abandon the effort to secure the sea. In this crisis Rome was saved by the public spirit of private citizens. *Lavish loans built and fitted out two hundred vessels,* and this fleet won an overwhelming victory, which closed the war.

These loans were made by " companies " of merchants and capitalists which had recently begun to appear in Rome. The loans were not secured. The Republic merely promised to repay them when it might be able. If Rome had lost once more, they never would have been repaid. The whole proceeding is very like the way in which, in our Civil War, after Bull Run, our Northern banking syndicates loaned vast sums to the government, without security, to save the Union.

429. Peace : Sicily becomes Roman. — Carthage had lost command of the sea and could no longer reinforce her armies in Sicily. Moreover, she was weary of the war and of the losses it brought to her commerce; and, in 241, she sued for peace. To obtain it, she withdrew from Sicily and paid a heavy war indemnity. Hiero, who after the first years of the war had become a faithful ally of Rome, remained master of Syracuse. *The rest of Sicily passed under the rule of Rome.*

FROM THE FIRST TO THE SECOND PUNIC WAR, 241–218 B.C.

430. Use of the Interval. — Sagacious Romans looked forward to another struggle with Carthage. That conflict, however, did not come for *twenty-three years.* Meantime, *Rome pushed wider the borders of Italy* (§§ 431–433), *and organized her new conquests upon the "provincial" plan* (§ 435).

431. Sardinia and Corsica. — When the mercenaries of Carthage were withdrawn from Sicily to Africa, they were left unpaid and they soon broke into revolt. The Libyan tribes joined the rising, and a ferocious struggle followed between

Carthage and the rebels. The war is known as the War of the Mercenaries, and sometimes as the Truceless War. At last Hamilcar Barca stamped out the revolt in Africa. But meantime the movement had spread to Sardinia and Corsica; and, in 238, the rebels offered these islands to Rome. The temptation was too much for Roman honor. The offer was shamelessly accepted, and a protest from distracted Carthage was met by a stern threat of war. The islands became Roman possessions. The Tyrrhenian Sea had become a Roman lake.

432. The Adriatic a Roman Sea. — This period marks also the first Roman enterprise *to the east* of Italy. Illyria had risen into a considerable state, in friendly relations with Macedonia. The Illyrian coasts were the homes of countless pirates, who swarmed forth in great fleets to harry the commerce of the adjoining waters. Finally these pirates even captured Corcyra. Other Greek towns complained loudly to Rome. Rome sent a haughty embassy to demand order from the Illyrian queen. The embassy was assaulted murderously, and Rome declared war. In a brief campaign (229 B.C.) she swept the pirates from the Adriatic and forced Illyria to sue for peace. The Adriatic had become a Roman waterway. At this time, *Rome kept no territory on the eastern coast;* but the Greek cities had learned to look to her for protection, and accordingly Macedonia began to regard her with a jealous eye.

433. Cisalpine Gaul. — A few years later came a great addition of territory on the north. Rome had begun to plant colonies on the border of Cisalpine Gaul. Naturally the Gauls were alarmed and angered, and, in 225, for the last time they threatened Italy. They penetrated to within three days' march of Rome; but Italian patriotism rallied around the endangered capital, and the barbarians were crushed.

Then Rome resolutely took the offensive, and, by 222, Cisalpine Gaul had become a Roman possession, garrisoned by numerous colonies and traversed by a great military road. *At last Rome had pushed her northern boundary from the low Apennines to the great crescent wall of the Alps.*

434. Summary of Roman Expansion to 222 B.C. — The steps of Roman expansion from 367 to 222 may be summarized in a few words. The period 367–266 consolidated Apennine Italy.   In the next fifty years this narrow " Italy " had been rounded out to its true borders by three great steps : (1) The First Punic War, filling half the period, added Sicily. (2) The other great islands bounding Italian waters on the west were seized soon after, treacherously, from Carthage in the hour of her death struggle with her revolted troops. (3) Then, having provoked the Gauls to war, Rome became mistress of the valley of the Po.   Meantime Roman authority had been successfully asserted, also, in the sea bordering Italy on the east.

435. Organization of the Conquests outside of Italy. — On the whole, Rome had been generous and wise in her treatment of united Italy ; *but all her conquests since the war with Pyrrhus* (Cisalpine Gaul as truly as the islands) *were looked upon as outside of Italy* (§ 255).   The distance of the new possessions from Rome, the fact that the islands could not be reached by "roads," and the character of Cisalpine Gaul seemed to make impossible for these districts the kind of government given to the "allies" and municipia in Italy proper.   Unfortunately, Rome was unable to invent a new form of government, and so she fell back upon the idea of prefectures (§ 390).   The new acquisitions became strictly subject possessions of Rome, and they were ruled much as the prefectures were in Italy.

Sicily (241 B.C.) was managed temporarily by a Roman praetor; but in 227, when some semblance of order had been introduced into Sardinia and Corsica, the Senate adopted a permanent plan of government for all these islands.   Two additional praetors, it was decided, should be elected each year, — one to rule Sicily, the other for the two other islands.   The two governments received the name of *provinces*.

*This was the beginning of **the provincial system*** that was to spread finally far beyond these " suburbs of Italy."   Soon afterward Cisalpine Gaul was organized in a like manner, though it was not given the title of a province until much later.   The system will be described in §§ 498–503.

THE SECOND PUNIC WAR (SOMETIMES STYLED "THE WAR FOR SPAIN"), 218–202 B.C.

436. Occasion. — Carthage was not ready to give up control of the Western Mediterranean without another struggle. Rome's policy of "blunder and plunder" in seizing Sardinia gave her excuse enough to renew the contest if she could find leaders and resources. These were both furnished by the *Barca* family.

From Rome's high-handed treachery in Sardinia, Hamilcar Barca imbibed a deathless hatred for that state; and immediately after putting down the War of the Mercenaries he began to prepare for another conflict. To offset the loss of the great Mediterranean islands, he sought to extend Carthaginian dominion over Spain. The mines of that country, he saw, would furnish the needful wealth, and its hardy tribes, when disciplined, would make an infantry which might meet even the legions of Rome.

437. Hannibal. — When Hamilcar was about to cross to Spain, in 236, he swore his son *Hannibal* at the altar to eternal hostility to Rome. Hannibal was then a boy of nine years. He followed Hamilcar to the wars, and, as a youth, became a dashing cavalry officer and the idol of the soldiery. He used his camp leisure to store his mind with all the culture of Greece. At twenty-six he succeeded to the command in Spain. In rare degree he possessed the ability to secure the devotion of fickle, mercenary troops. He was a statesman of a high order, and possibly the greatest captain in history. The Second Punic War takes its keenest interest from his dazzling career. Even the Romans called that struggle the "War with Hannibal."

No friendly pen has left us a record of Hannibal. Roman historians sought to stain his fame with envious slander. But, through it all, his character shines out chivalrous, noble, heroic. Says Colonel Dodge,[1] "There is not in history a figure more noble in purity, more radiant in patriotism, more heroic in genius, more pathetic in its misfortunes."

---

[1] Author of various military biographies.

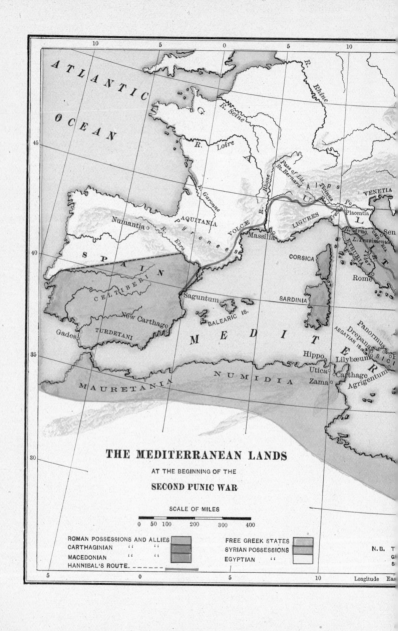

THE MEDITERRANEAN LANDS

AT THE BEGINNING OF THE

SECOND PUNIC WAR

SCALE OF MILES

0 50 100   200   300   400

ROMAN POSSESSIONS AND ALLIES
CARTHAGINIAN   "   "
MACEDONIAN   "   "
HANNIBAL'S ROUTE ---------

FREE GREEK STATES
SYRIAN POSSESSIONS
EGYPTIAN   "

Longitude Eas

BLACK SEA

Olbia

Bosporus

Chersonesus

PAPHLAGONIA

THRACE

Byzantium

Heraclea

GALATIA

or

Danube

Epidamnus

MACEDONIA

Cydna

Cynoscephalæ

Pergamus

Magnesia

Ephesus

KINGDOM OF THE SELEUCIDÆ

Tarsus

Antioch

Cannæ

tum

ac

CORCYRA

Epirus

THESSALY

ÆTOLIA

Elis

Corinth

Athens

Mænander

CARIA

CILICIA

SYRIA

sana

egium

Megalopolis

Sparta

LYCIA

acuse

CRETE

RHODES

CYPRUS

Salamis

NEAN SEA

Cyrene

Barca

CYRENAICA

Alexandria

E   G   Y   P   T

Nile

RED SEA

438. Hannibal at Saguntum; Rome declares War, 218 B.C. — Hannibal continued the work of his great father in Spain. He made the southern half of that rich land a Carthaginian province and organized it thoroughly. Then he rapidly carried the Carthaginian frontier to the Ebro, collected a magnificent army of over a hundred thousand men, and besieged Saguntum, an ancient Greek colony near the east coast. Fearing Carthaginian advance, Saguntum had sought Roman alliance; and now, when Carthage refused to recall Hannibal, Rome, in alarm and anger, declared war (218 B.C.).

439. Hannibal's Invasion of Italy. — The Second Punic War (218–202 B.C.) was somewhat shorter than the First, but it was an even more strenuous struggle. Rome had intended to take the offensive. Indeed, she dispatched one consul in a leisurely way to Spain, and started the other for Africa by way of Sicily. But Hannibal's audacious rapidity threw into confusion all his enemy's plans. In five months he had crossed the Pyrenees and the Rhone, fighting his way through the Gallic tribes; forced the unknown passes of the Alps, under conditions that made it a feat paralleled only by Alexander's passage of the Hindukush; and, leaving the bones of three fourths of his army between the Ebro and Po, startled Italy by appearing in Cisalpine Gaul, with twenty-six thousand "heroic shadows."

440. His First Victories. — With these "emaciated scarecrows" the same fall Hannibal swiftly destroyed two hastily gathered Roman armies — at the *Ticinus* and at the *Trebia*. Then the recently pacified Gallic tribes rallied turbulently to swell his ranks. The following spring he crossed the Apennines, ambushed a Roman army of forty thousand men, blinded with morning fog, near *Lake Trasimene*, and annihilated it, and then carried fire and sword through Italy.

441. Quintus Fabius Maximus was now named dictator, to save Rome. That wary old general adopted the wise policy of delay ("Fabian policy") to wear out Hannibal and gain breathing time for Rome. He would not give battle, but he followed close at the Carthaginian's heels, from place to place. Even Hannibal could not catch Fabius unawares; and he did not dare to attack the intrenched Roman camps. But Hannibal had to win victories to draw the Italian "Allies" from Rome, or he would have to flee from Italy. He ravaged savagely, as he marched, to provoke the Roman commander to battle, but in vain; and his position grew critical. So far, not a city in Italy had opened its gates to him as a shelter.

442. Cannae. — But in Rome many of the common people murmured impatiently, nicknaming Fabius *Cunctator* (the Laggard). Popular leaders, too, began to grumble that the Senate protracted the war in order to gain glory for the aristocratic generals; and the following summer the new consuls were given ninety thousand men — by far the largest army Rome had ever put in the field, and several times Hannibal's army — with orders to crush the daring invader. The result was the battle of *Cannae* — "a carnival of cold steel, a butchery, not a battle." Hannibal lost six thousand men. Rome lost sixty thousand dead and twenty thousand prisoners. A consul, a fourth of the senators, nearly all the officers, and over a fifth of the fighting population of the city perished. Hannibal sent home a bushel of gold rings from the hands of fallen Roman nobles.[1]

443. Fidelity of the Latins and Italians to Rome. — The victory, however, yielded little fruit. Hannibal's only real chance within Italy had been that brilliant victories might break up the Italian confederacy and bring over to his side the subjects of Rome. Accordingly, he freed his Italian prisoners without ransom, proclaiming that he warred only on Rome and that he came to liberate Italy.

The mountain tribes of the south, eager for plunder, did join him, as did one great Italian city, *Capua*. Syracuse, too, renounced its Roman alliance and joined its ancient enemy Carthage. And three years later, a cruel Roman blunder drove

---

[1] There is an excellent account of the battle in How and Leigh, 194–198.

some of the Greek towns of south Italy into Hannibal's arms. But the other cities — colonies, Latins, or Allies — closed their gates against him as resolutely as Rome herself, — and so gave marvelous testimony to the excellence of Roman rule and to the national spirit it had fostered.

444. Rome's Grandeur in Disaster. — Rome's own greatness showed grandly in the hour of terror after Cannae, when any other people would have given up the conflict in despair. A plot among some faint-hearted nobles to abandon Italy was stifled in the camp; and the surviving consul, Varro, courageously set himself to reorganize the wreckage of his army.

Varro had been elected, in a bitter partisan struggle, as the champion of the democratic party, against the unanimous opposition of the aristocracy. With undoubted merits in personal character, he had proved utterly lacking in military talent. Indeed, he had forced his wiser colleague to give battle, and his poor generalship was largely responsible for the disaster. He now returned to Rome, expecting to face stern judges. At Carthage, a general, so placed, would have been nailed to a cross or thrown under the feet of enraged elephants. Even in Athens, as Dr. Davis says, he would probably have had to drink the fatal cup of hemlock. At Rome, faction and criticism were silenced, and the aristocratic Senate showed its nobility by publicly giving thanks to the democratic and luckless general " because he had not despaired of the Republic."

Even Cannae was not the end of disaster. Before the close of the year another army under a new consul was cut to pieces, and by losses elsewhere the Senate had fallen to less than half its numbers;[1] but with stern temper and splendid tenacity Rome refused even to receive Hannibal's envoys or to consider his moderate proposals for peace. According to one story, Rome refused in this crisis to ransom prisoners. Much as she needed her soldiers back, she preferred, so the story goes, to teach her citizens that they ought at such a time to die for the Republic, rather than surrender.

A third of the adult males of Italy had fallen in battle within

---

[1] The next year 177 new members were added, to bring the number up to the normal 300.

three years, or were in camp, so that all industry was demoralized. Still, taxes were doubled, and the rich gave cheerfully, even beyond these crushing demands. The days of mourning for the dead were shortened by a decree of the government. Rome refused to recall a man from Sicily or Spain. Instead *she sent out new armies to those places*, and by enrolling slaves, old men, boys, and the criminals from the prisons (arming them with the sacred trophies in the temples), she managed to put two hundred and fifty thousand troops into the field.

Rome learned, too, from disaster. The legions and generals sent to Spain, Sicily, and other distant lands were no longer recalled at the end of the year. They were enlisted "for the war." Here lay the beginnings of important constitutional changes (§ 406).

445. Lack of Concerted Action by Rome's Foes. — Hannibal was now in no peril in Italy. He could maintain himself there indefinitely, with his allies in the south of the peninsula. But he made no more headway. His possible chances for success lay in arousing a general Mediterranean war against Rome, or in receiving himself strong reinforcements from Carthage. Philip V of Macedonia did ally himself with Hannibal, but he acted timidly and too late. Carthage showed a strange apathy when victory was within her grasp. She made no real attempt even to regain her ancient command of the sea, and so could not send troops to Hannibal, or defend her ally, Syracuse, from Roman vengeance.

446. The War in Sicily. — Meantime Rome guarded her coasts with efficient fleets and transported her armies at will. Especially did she strain every nerve for success abroad, where Hannibal's superb genius could not act against her. Syracuse had been besieged promptly by land and sea, and (212) after a three years' siege, it was taken by storm. This siege is memorable for the scientific inventions of Archimedes (§ 320), used in the defense.[1] The philosopher himself was killed during the

---

[1] See Davis' *Readings*, II, No. 27, for the fullest account by an ancient authority.

sack of the city, and one more commercial rival of Rome was wiped from the map. Its works of art (the accumulations of centuries) were destroyed or carried to Rome, and it never recovered its old eminence in culture, commerce, or power.

447. The War in Spain. — Hannibal's one remaining chance lay in reinforcements by land, from his brother, Hasdrubal, whom he had left in command in Spain. But, step by step, the Roman Scipio brothers, with overwhelming forces, pushed back the Carthaginian frontier in that peninsula, and for many years ruined all Hannibal's hopes. At last, in 211, Hasdrubal won a great victory, and the two Scipios perished; but Rome promptly hurried in fresh forces under the young *Publius Cornelius Scipio,* who, in masterly fashion, for three years more, continued the work of his father and uncle.

448. Changed Character of the War in Italy. — In Italy itself, the policy of Fabius was again adopted, varied by the telling blows of the vigorous soldier, Marcellus, who was called the " Sword " of Rome, as Fabius was called her " Shield." Hannibal's hopes had been blasted in the moment of victory. Rome fell back upon an iron constancy and steadfast caution. Her Italian subjects showed a steady fidelity even more ominous to the invader. Carthage proved neglectful, and her allies lukewarm.

Against such conditions all the great African's genius in war and in diplomacy wore itself out in vain. For thirteen years after Cannae he maintained himself in Italy without reinforcement in men or money, — always winning a battle when he could engage the enemy in the field, — and directing operations as best he might in Spain, Sicily, Macedonia, and Africa. But it was a war waged by one supreme genius against the most powerful and resolute nation in the world. Says Dr. Davis, *" The greatest military genius* who ever lived attacked *the most military people* which ever existed — and the genius was defeated after a sixteen years' war."

449. " Hannibal at the Gates." — One more dramatic scene marked Hannibal's career in Italy. The Romans had besieged

Capua. In a daring attempt to relieve his ally, Hannibal marched to the very walls of Rome, ravaging the fields about the city. The Romans, however, were not to be enticed into a rash engagement, nor could the army around Capua be drawn from its prey. The only result of Hannibal's desperate stroke was the fruitless fright he gave Rome, — such that for generations Roman mothers stilled their children by the terror-bearing phrase, "Hannibal at the Gates!" Roman stories relate, however, that citizens were found, even in that hour of fear, to show a defiant confidence by buying eagerly at a public sale the land where the invader lay encamped. And even Hannibal must have felt misgivings when his scouts reported that from another gate a Roman army had just marched away contemptuously, with colors flying, to reinforce the Roman troops in Spain.

450. Capua. — Hannibal finally drew off, and Capua fell, — to meet a fate more harsh even than that of Syracuse. That "second city of Italy" ceased to exist as a city. Its leading men were massacred; most of the rest of the population were sold as slaves; and colonies of Roman veterans were planted on its lands. The few remaining inhabitants were governed by a prefect from Rome.

Syracuse and Capua had been faithless allies. They had been also rivals in trade; and their cruel fate was due quite as much to Roman greed as to Roman vengeance. Cf. § 374.

451. Hannibal's Forces Worn Out. — And so the struggle entered upon its last, long, wasting stage. It became a record of sieges and marches and countermarches. Hannibal's genius shone as marvelous as ever, earning him from modern military critics the title, "Father of Strategy"; but there are no more of the dazzling results that mark the first campaigns. Hannibal's African and Spanish veterans died off, and had to be replaced as best they might by local recruits in Italy; and gradually the Romans learned the art of war from their great enemy.

"With the battle of Cannae the breathless interest in the war ceases; its surging mass, broken on the walls of the Roman fortresses, . . . foams away in ruin and devastation through south Italy, — ever victorious, ever receding. Rome, assailed on all sides by open foe and forsworn friend, driven to her last man and last coin, ' ever great and greater grows ' in the strength of her strong will and loyal people, widening the circle round her with rapid blows in Sicily, Sardinia, Spain, and Macedon, while she slowly loosens the grip fastened on her throat at home, till in the end . . . the final fight on African sands at the same moment closes the struggle for life and seats her mistress of the world." — How and Leigh, 199.

452. The Second Carthaginian Invasion. — Meantime, in Spain, Hannibal's brother, Hasdrubal, had been contending against the crushing force of the Scipios, with the skill and devotion of his family. Finally, in 208, by able maneuvers, he eluded the Roman generals, and started with a veteran army to reinforce Hannibal. Rome's peril was never greater than when this second son of Barca crossed the Alps successfully with fifty-six thousand men and fifteen elephants. Just before, several of the most important " Latin colonies " had given notice that they could not much longer sustain the ravages of the war. If the two Carthaginian armies joined, Hannibal would be able to march at will through Italy, and Rome's faithful allies would no longer close their gates against him.

453. The Metaurus. — The Republic put forth its supreme effort. One hundred and fifty thousand men were thrown between the two Carthaginian armies, which together numbered some eighty thousand. By a fortunate chance the Romans captured a messenger from Hasdrubal and so learned his plans, while Hannibal was still ignorant of his approach. This gave a decisive advantage. The opportunity was well used. The consul, *Claudius Nero*, with audacity learned of Hannibal himself, left part of his force to deceive that leader, and, hurrying northward with the speed of life and death, joined the other consul and fell upon Hasdrubal with crushing numbers at the *Metaurus.* The ghastly head of his long-expected brother, flung with brutal contempt into his camp,[1] was the first notice to Hannibal of the ruin of his family and his cause.

---

[1] This deed was in strange contrast to the chivalrous treatment that Hannibal gave to the bodies of Marcellus and of the Roman generals at Cannae and elsewhere.

454. The War in Africa. — Still Hannibal remained invincible in the mountains of southern Italy. But Rome now carried the war into Africa. After Hasdrubal left Spain, Scipio rapidly subdued the whole peninsula, and, in 204, he persuaded the Senate to send him with a great army against Carthage itself. Two years later, to meet this peril, Carthage recalled Hannibal. That great leader obeyed sadly, "leaving the country of his enemy," says Livy, "with more regret than many an exile has left his own."

This event marks the end of all hope of Carthaginian success. The same year (202 B.C.) the struggle closed with Hannibal's first and only defeat, at the battle of *Zama*.[1] Carthage lay at the mercy of the victor, and sued for peace. She gave up Spain and the islands of the western Mediterranean; surrendered her war elephants and all her ships of war save ten; paid a huge war indemnity, which was intended to keep her poor for many years; and became a dependent ally of Rome, promising to wage no war without Roman consent. Scipio received the proud surname *Africanus*.[2] The Greek cities of the south and the mountain tribes that had joined Hannibal lost lands and privileges. And Cisalpine Gaul was thoroughly Romanized by many a cruel campaign.

455. Rome Mistress of the West. — Rome had been fighting for existence, but she had won world-dominion. *In the West no rival remained.* Her subsequent warfare there was to be only

---

[1] Zama was a village a little to the south of Carthage. Read the story of the battle in Davis' *Readings*, II, No. 28. Special report: the career of Hannibal after the war.

[2] Commonly a Roman had three names. The gentile name was the *nomen*, the most important of the three; it came in the middle. The third (the *cognomen*) marked the family. The first (*praenomen*) was the individual name (like our baptismal name). Then a Roman often received also a surname for some achievement or characteristic. Thus *Publius Cornelius Scipio Africanus* was the individual Publius of the Scipio family of the great Cornelian gens, surnamed Africanus for his conquest of Africa. The first name was often abbreviated in writing. The most common of these abbreviations were: C. for Caius (Gaius); Cn. for Gnaeus; L. for Lucius; M. for Marcus; P. for Publius; Q. for Quintus; T. for Titus.

with unorganized barbarians. In the East the result was to show more slowly; but there, too, Roman victory was now only a *matter of time*. No civilized power was again to threaten Rome by invading Italy, and the mighty kingdoms of Alexander's realms were to be absorbed, one by one, into her empire.

This imperial destiny was more than Rome had planned. Italy she had designed to rule. The West had fallen to her as the heir of Carthage. In the East she hesitated honestly, until events thrust dominion upon her there also (ch. xxxi).

This hesitancy in the East was due, in part at least, to respect for Greek civilization, to which Rome was beginning to owe more and more. It is quite true, though, that, even this early, the commercial interests at Rome, excited by greed for fresh booty, used much secret influence to foment new wars and extend Roman dominion. This commercial greed was later to become a main cause of Roman expansion (cf. § 483).

CHAPTER XXX

THE WEST FROM 201 TO 146 B.C.

SPAIN

456. Spain's Heroic War for Independence. — Rome's rule in Spain was still largely a rule only in name. To make it real, there was much work yet to do. A land route to that country had to be secured; and the mountain tribes in the peninsula and in its bordering islands had to be thoroughly subdued. This involved tedious wars, not always waged with credit to Roman honor.

In Spain two new provinces were created, for which two governors were elected annually by the Roman Senate. Some of these governors proved rapacious; others were incompetent; and the proud and warlike tribes of Spain were driven into a long war for independence.

The struggle was marked by the heroic leadership of the Spanish patriot, *Viriathus,* and by contemptible Roman baseness. A Roman general massacred a tribe which had submitted. Another general procured the assassination of Viriathus by hired murderers. Rome itself rejected treaties after they had saved Roman armies. Spanish towns, which had been captured after gallant resistance, were wiped from the face of the earth, so that other towns chose wholesale suicide rather than surrender to Roman cruelty.

457. Final Romanization. — Still, despite these miserable means, Roman conquest in the end was to be a blessing to Spain. The struggle in the most inaccessible districts went on until 133, but long before that year the greater part of the land had been Romanized. Traders and speculators flocked to the seaports. For more than half a century twenty thousand soldiers were left under arms in the province. These legionaries, quartered in Spain for many years at a time, married Spanish wives, and when relieved from military service, they gladly received lands in Spain, as a sort of pension, and settled down in military colonies, to spread Roman language and customs among the neighboring natives.[1] No sooner were the restless interior tribes fully subdued than there appeared the promise — to be well kept later — that Spain would become "more Roman than Rome itself."

458. South Gaul. — Meantime (about 188) Rome had secured a land road, through southern Gaul, from Italy to Spain. This was obtained in the main by friendly alliance with the ancient Greek city Massilia; but there was also some warfare with the native tribes, which laid the foundations for a new Roman province in South Gaul in the near future.

THE THIRD PUNIC WAR (The War for Africa)

459. Rome seeks Perfidious Pretext against Carthage. — Even before Spain was pacified, hatred and greed had led Rome to seize the remaining realms of Carthage. That state was now powerless for harm. But Roman fear was cruel; commercial envy was rapacious and reckless; and (after some fifty years) a long series of persecutions forced a needless conflict upon the unhappy Carthaginians. The Third Punic War was marked by black perfidy on the part of Rome and by the final desperate heroism of Carthage.

First, that city was called upon to surrender Hannibal to Roman vengeance.[2] Then it was vexed by constant annoyances in Africa on the part of Massinissa, Prince of Numidia. Massinissa had been Rome's ally in the latter part of the Second

---

[1] It was in this way that communities of Roman citizens were to be spread over other provinces, as they were acquired, one by one, *to Italianize the world*, as a like system of colonization had formerly Romanized Italy.

[2] Hannibal escaped to the East. But Roman petty hatred followed him from country to country, until, to avoid falling into Roman hands, he took his own life, "proving in a lifelong struggle with fate, that success is in no way necessary to greatness."

Punic War, and had been rewarded by new dominions carved out of Carthaginian territory. Now, *encouraged by Rome*, he encroached more and more, seizing piece after piece of the district that had been left to the vanquished city.

Repeatedly Carthage appealed to Rome, but her just complaints brought no redress. The Roman commissioners that were sent to act as arbiters — with secret orders beforehand to favor Massinissa — carried back to Rome only a greater fear of the reviving wealth of Carthage, and told the astonished Roman Senate of a city with crowded streets, with treasury and arsenals full, and with its harbors thronged with shipping. From this time (157 B.C.) the narrow-minded but zealous *Cato* closed every speech in the Senate, no matter what the subject, with the phrase "*Delenda est Carthago*" (Carthage must be blotted out). More quietly but more effectively, the Roman merchant class strove to the same end, to prevent Carthage from recovering its ancient trade in the Mediterranean.

460. Carthage is treacherously Disarmed. — Carthage was cautious, and gave no handle to Roman hate, until at last, when Massinissa had pushed his seizures almost up to her gates, she took up arms against his invasion. By her treaty with Rome she had promised to engage in no war without Roman permission; and Rome at once snatched at the excuse to declare war.

In vain, terrified Carthage punished her leaders and offered abject submission. The Roman Senate would only promise that the city should be left independent if it complied with the further demands of Rome, to be announced on African soil. The Roman fleet and army proceeded to Carthage, and an act of masterful treachery was played out by successive steps.

First, at the demand of the Roman general, Carthage sent as hostages to the Roman camp three hundred boys from the noblest families, amid the tears and outcries of the mothers. Then, on further command, the city dismantled its walls and stripped its arsenals, sending, in long lines of wagons, to the Roman army 3000 catapults and 200,000 stand of arms, with vast military supplies. Next the shipping was all surrendered. Finally, now that the city was supposed to be utterly defenseless, came the announcement that it must be destroyed and the people removed to some spot ten miles inland from the sea, on which from dim antiquity they had founded their wealth and power.

461. Heroic Resistance. — Despair blazed into passionate wrath, and the Carthaginians fitly chose death rather than ruin and exile. Carelessly enough, the Roman army remained at a distance for some days. Meanwhile the dismantled and disarmed town became one great workshop for war. Women gave their hair to make cords for catapults; the temples were ransacked for arms, and torn down for timber and metal; and to the angry dismay of Rome, Carthage stood a four years' siege, holding out heroically against famine, pestilence, and war.

At last the legions forced their way over the walls. For seven days more the fighting continued from house to house, until at last a miserable remnant surrendered. The commander at the last moment made his peace with the Roman general; but his disdainful wife, taunting him from the burning temple roof as he knelt at Scipio's feet, slew their two boys and cast herself with them into the ruins.

462. Carthage is "blotted out": the Province of Africa. — For many days the city was given up to pillage. Then, *by express orders from Rome*, it was burned to the ground, and its site was plowed up, sown to salt, and cursed (146 B.C.).

To carry out this crime fell to the lot of one of the purest and noblest characters Rome ever produced, — *Publius Scipio Aemilianus,* the nephew and adopted grandson of Scipio Africanus, known himself as *Africanus the Younger.* As he watched the smoldering ruins (they burned for seventeen days) with his friend Polybius the historian, Scipio spoke his fear that some day Rome might suffer a like fate, and he was heard to repeat Homer's lines : —

> " Yet come it will, the day decreed by fate,
>   The day when thou, Imperial Troy, must bend,
>   And see thy warriors fall, thy glories end."

What was left of the ancient territory of Carthage became the *Province of Africa*, with the capital at Utica. Two centuries later, under the Roman Empire, North Africa became a chief seat of Roman civilization.

FOR FURTHER READING. — *Specially recommended :* Davis' *Readings*, II, Nos. 20–29 (extracts from Livy and Polybius); Pelham, 122–133, or, much better for this subject, How and Leigh, chs. 19–22. *Additional material* of value and interest will be found in Smith's *Rome and Carthage* (Epoch series) ; W. W. How's *Hannibal ;* and especially in Plutarch's *Lives* ("Fabius" and "Marcellus").

REVIEW EXERCISE. — Catchword review of Roman expansion in the West from 264 to 146.

CHAPTER XXXI

THE WINNING OF THE EAST, 201–146 B.C.

The expansion of Rome in the fifty years after the Second Punic War went on continuously both west and east. The two stories, however, had little connection; and they are given in this book in separate chapters. We have dealt with the West for that half century in Chapter XXX. Now we turn to the East.

AN ATTEMPT AT PROTECTORATES

463. Earlier Beginnings : the First Macedonian War. — Ever since the repulse of Pyrrhus, Rome had been drifting into contact with the Greek kingdoms of the East. With Egypt she had a friendly alliance and close commercial intercourse. Between the First and the Second Punic War, too, she had chastised the formidable pirates of the Illyrian coasts, and so, as the guardian of order, had come into friendly relations with some of the cities in Greece (§ 432).

Further than this, Rome showed no desire to go. But, in 214, Philip V of Macedonia joined himself to Hannibal against Rome (§ 432). The war with Macedonia which followed is known as the *First Macedonian War*. Rome entered upon it only to prevent a Macedonian invasion of Italy, and she waged it by means of her Aetolian allies.[1] It closed in 205, before the end of the Second Punic War, without any especial change in eastern affairs; *but it made later struggles natural.*

464. Second Macedonian War. — In 205, Philip V of Macedon and Antiochus of Syria tried to seize Egypt, left just then to a boy king. Egypt was an ally of Rome. Moreover, it was

---

[1] Aetolia had sought Roman protection against Macedonia and had been recognized as an " ally " (§ 310).

already becoming the granary of the Mediterranean, and Rome could not wisely see it pass into hostile hands. Philip also attacked Athens, another of Rome's allies. So, as soon as Rome's hands were freed by the peace with Carthage, the Senate persuaded the wearied Assembly to enter upon the *Second Macedonian War* (201–196 B.C.).

At first Philip won some success; but in 198 the Senate intrusted the war to *Flamininus*, who was to be the first Roman conqueror in the East. Flamininus was one of the group of young Romans around Scipio Aemilianus imbued with Hellenic culture and chivalrous ideals. His appointment proved particularly grateful to the Greek allies of Rome, and his excellent generalship quickly put Philip on the defensive. The decisive battle was fought at *Cynoscephalae* (Dog's heads), a group of low hills in Thessaly; and the result was due, not to generalship, but to the fighting qualities of the soldiery. The two armies were of nearly equal size. They met in mist and rain, and the engagement was brought on by a chance encounter of scouting parties. *The flexible legion proved its superiority over the unwieldy phalanx* (§ 403). The Roman loss was 700; the Macedonian, 13,000.

Philip was left at the mercy of the victor, but the chivalrous Flamininus gave generous terms. Macedonia, it is true, sank into a second-rate power, and became a dependent ally of Rome. But Rome herself *took no territory.* Macedonia's possessions in Greece were taken from her, and Flamininus proclaimed that the Greeks were "free." The many Greek states, along with Rhodes and Pergamum and the other small states of Asia, became Rome's grateful allies. In name they were equals of Rome; in fact, they were *Roman protectorates.* That is, Rome controlled all the *foreign relations* of each of them, — at least, whenever she cared to do so.

465. The War with Antiochus of Syria. — Meanwhile Antiochus had sheltered Hannibal and had been plundering Egypt's possessions in Asia. Now he turned to seize Thrace, Greece, Pergamum, and Rhodes. Rome sincerely dreaded a conflict with the "Great King," the Lord of Asia, but she had no choice. The struggle proved easy and brief. In the second campaign, in 190, Roman legions for the first time invaded Asia, and at *Magnesia*,[1] in Lydia, they shattered the power of Syria. That kingdom was reduced in territory and power, somewhat as Macedonia had been, *but Rome still kept no territory* for herself. Her allies were rewarded with gifts of territory; and the Hellenic cities and small states of Asia were declared free, and really became friendly dependents of Rome.

466. The System of Protectorates.[2] — *Thus, in eleven years (200–190 B.C.) after the close of the Second Punic War, Rome had set up a virtual protectorate over all the realms of Alexander's successors.*

To Rome herself, this expansion of power was to prove a curse; but to her dependent realms it was a blessing. The Greek states were embroiled ceaselessly in petty quarrels among themselves, and they were endangered constantly by the greed of their greater neighbors. From all sides came appeals to Rome to prevent injustice. The disturbing powers were Macedonia, Syria, and the Aetolian and Achaean Leagues. The forces which stood for peace were Egypt, Rhodes, Pergamum, and the small states of European Greece. It was these pacific states which especially claimed protection from Rome.

The weakness of the eastern states drew the great western power on and on, and her own methods became less and less scrupulous. Cruelty and cynical disregard for obligations more and more stamped her conduct. But, after all, as How and Leigh well say, "compared with the Ptolemies, Seleucids, and Antigonids,[3] her hands were clean and her rule bearable. In that intolerable eastern hubbub, men's eyes turned still with envy and wonder to the stable and well-ordered Republic of the West."

---

[1] The Roman commander was Lucius Scipio, who took the name *Asiaticus*; but credit was really due to his brother Publius, who accompanied him.

[2] Cf. § 293.   [3] A ruling family in Macedonia.

467. Rome and Judea. — After the death of Alexander the Great, the Jews first belonged to the kingdom of Egypt. But in 203 B.C. Antiochus the Great definitely annexed them to Syria. His second successor conceived the plan of Hellenizing all his dominions. But the Jews refused to give up their religion. When he met with resistance a most cruel religious persecution began. The Holy Scriptures were burned. We all know of the heroic "Maccabean mother" who saw her seven sons tortured to death before her own eyes. Finally, the priest Matathias headed an insurrection, which effected a complete liberation of the country. This result was, next to divine assistance, due chiefly to the valor of Matathias' son, Judas, called Makkab (the hammer). Seeing, however, how difficult his position was, Judas applied to Rome for help. Similar appeals were made by Judas' successors, the "Maccabees." It was, naturally speaking, greatly due to Rome's desire to see Syria crippled, that the Jews were able to maintain their freedom from about 145 to 63 B.C. In the latter year Rome saw fit to deprive them of their independence. The foreigner Herod, with his family, replaced the Maccabees, but parts of the country were at times under direct Roman administration.

It should be remarked here that by this time the Jews had spread widely over foreign countries. In all the larger cities they inhabited separate quarters. They had obtained nearly everywhere from the authorities the privileges which enabled them to lead a life in accordance with their peculiar laws. About the time of King Herod these "Jews of the Dispersion" were probably more numerous than those living in Palestine itself. (See Acts. ii.)

ADDITIONAL READING TO § 467. — The selections from the Books of the Maccabees in Coppens and the corresponding chapters in Eckers are fascinating for young people. See also "The Jews of the Dispersion" in Fouard, *St. Peter*, pp. 38–58, Longfellow's little drama, *Judas Maccabæus*, and Morisson, *The Jews under Roman Rule*, pp. 3 to 118.

THE PROTECTORATES ARE ANNEXED AS PROVINCES

468. A Gradual Change. — Conditions in the East were un-stable. Rome could not stop with protectorates. They had neither the blessings of real liberty nor the good order of true provinces. And so gradually Rome was led to a process of *annexation of territory* in the civilized East, as before in the barbarous West. By 146 B.C. this change was well under· way. In the next hundred years — before the day of the Caesars — the original *influence over "allies"* had everywhere been trans-formed into *dominion over subject provinces*.

469. A deplorable change in Roman character took place early in this period. Appetite for power grew with its exercise. Jealousy appeared toward the prosperity of even the truest ally. *A class of ambitious nobles* craved new wars of conquest *for the sake of glory and power;* and the growing class of *merchants and money lenders* (who now indirectly dominated the govern-ment) hungered raveningly for conquests in order to secure more special privileges in the form of trade monopolies and the management of finances in new provinces. Thus, to extend her sway in the East, where at first she had hesitated so mod-estly, Rome finally sank to violence and perfidy as high-handed and as base as had marked her treatment of Carthage in the West, at the beginning of the same period.

We can note here only three or four chief steps in the long process of Eastern annexation.

470. Macedonia. — Rome's gentle treatment of the Greek states after the Second Macedonian War (§ 464) was due largely to a true admiration for Greek civilization and Greek history. But this feeling was soon lost in contempt for Greek fickleness and weakness and inability for concerted action — and in greed for Greek riches. On their side, the Greek cities at first had welcomed Rome joyfully as a guardian of Hellenic liberty. But high-handed Roman officials, with their assumption of mas-tery, and their frequent contemptuous disregard of treaties, soon made these cities look back regretfully to the rule of

Macedonia, which at least had had understanding and sympathy for Greek character.

Perseus of Macedonia (son of Philip V) took advantage of this revulsion of feeling to form alliances with the Greek states in the hope of recovering a true national independence. This brought on a *Third Macedonian War*, and the Roman victory of *Pydna* (168 B.C.) closed the life of the ancient kingdom of Macedonia.[1] That state was broken up into four petty "republics," which were declared free, but which were provinces of Rome in all but name and good order. They paid tribute, were disarmed, and were forbidden intercourse with one another; but they did not at first receive a Roman governor. Some years later a pretended son of Perseus tried to restore the monarchy; and this attempt led to the full establishment of the Roman "Province of Macedonia," with a Roman magistrate at its head (146 B.C.).

471. Rearrangements in Greece. — Pydna had been followed also by important rearrangements in *Greece*, and the factions there, which had sympathized with Perseus in his hopeless struggle, had been cruelly punished. In the succeeding years the Roman Senate was called upon to listen to ceaseless weari-

---

[1] Plutarch (*Life of Aemilius Paulus*) describes the gorgeous "triumph" of the Roman general on his return. For three days a festal procession paraded the city, to the temple of Jupiter on the Capitoline. Throngs of white-robed citizens watched the procession from scaffolds, which had been erected for the purpose in all convenient places. On the first day, two hundred and fifty wagons carried by the statues and paintings which had been plundered from Macedonian cities. On the next day passed many wagons, carrying Macedonian standards and armor, followed by three thousand men loaded with the silver money and silver plate which had been secured in the booty. On the third day came a procession of men carrying gold spoil, followed by the conqueror in a splendid chariot, behind which walked the conquered king with his three young children.

Rome so filled her coffers with treasure by this plunder that the Republic never thereafter taxed her citizens. And besides this public plunder, the Roman general had paid his soldiers by permitting them to sack seventy helpless rich cities in Epirus. The unspeakable suffering and misery, — the ruined lives and broken families, — in every such city is simply beyond the power of the imagination to picture.

some complaints from one Greek city or party against another.
The Roman policy was sometimes vacillating, sometimes contemptuous.   Finally the Achaeans were goaded into open rebellion.   The Achaean League fell easily before Roman arms, in
146 B.C.   Corinth had been the chief offender.   By order of

RUINS AT CORINTH, as they appeared in 1905. The Roman destruction was
so complete that the site of Corinth has yielded less to the modern ex-
cavator than almost any other famous ancient center. The building in
the foreground was a temple of Apollo — the only Doric temple known
whose columns are monoliths. In the background is the ancient citadel,
Acrocorinth.

the Senate that city was burned and its site cursed, and its
people murdered or sold as slaves.

Greece was not yet made a province, but it was treated as
Macedon had been just after Pydna, and was virtually ruled
by the Roman governor of Macedon.   Thus the one year 146
B.C. saw the last territory of Carthage made a Roman province
and the first province formed in the old empire of Alexander,
together with the destruction of the ancient cities of Carthage
and Corinth.   A century later Greece became the *Province of
Achaea.*

The destruction of Corinth was a greater crime than that of Carthage, Syracuse, Capua, or the other capitals that Roman envy laid low. Corinth was a great emporium of Greece, *and its ruin was due mainly to the jealousy of the commercial class in Rome.* Its art treasures, so far as preserved, became the plunder of the Roman state ; but much was lost. Polybius saw common soldiers playing at dice, amid the still smoking ruins, on the paintings of the greatest masters.

472. The Province of Asia. — A few years after Macedonia became a province, the king of Pergamum willed to Rome his realms, which became the *Province of Asia* (133 B.C.).

After the battle of Magnesia (§ 470), Pergamum had been enlarged so that it included most of western Asia Minor. This region was now known as " Asia." It is in this sense that the word " Asia " is used in the Acts of the Apostles ; as, for instance, when Paul says, that, after going through Phrygia, he was forbidden "to pass into Asia," and again later, that " all they who dwelt in Asia " heard the word.

473. Rhodes and Roman Greed. — Further progress in the East in this period consisted in jealously reducing friendly allies, like Rhodes, to the condition of subjects, and in openly setting up protectorates over Egypt and Syria. It is in this series of events that Rome's lust for power and greed for money begin to show most hatefully. She had no more generosity for a faithful ally than she had magnanimity toward a fallen foe ; and her treatment of Rhodes gains little by contrast with her perfidious dealings with Carthage. Rhodes, of course, never had been or could be a danger to Rome's power. Indeed she had been a most faithful and trusting friend. But the Roman merchants looked avariciously upon her wide-spread commerce; and a sham excuse was seized upon greedily to rob that helpless friend of her territory and trade.

SUMMARY

474. Rome the Sole Great Power. — In 264 B.C. Rome had been *one of five* Great Powers (§ 357). By the peace of 201 after Zama, Carthage disappeared from that list. In the next fifty years Cynoscephalae, Magnesia, Pydna, and arrogant

Roman diplomacy removed three of the others.   In 146, Rome
was the *sole* Great Power.   She had annexed as provinces all
the dominions of Carthage and of Macedonia.   Egypt and
Syria had become protectorates and were soon to be made provinces.   All the smaller states had been brought within the
Roman " sphere of influence."   Rome held the heritage of Alexander as well as that of Carthage.   There remained no state

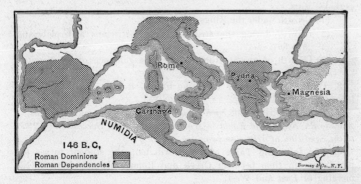

able to dream of equality with her.   *The civilized world had*
become a Graeco-Roman World, under Roman sway.

   475. The Latin West and the Greek East. — At the same time,
while Rome was really mistress in both East and West, her relations
with the two sections were widely different.   In the West, Rome appeared on the stage as the successor of Carthage ; and to the majority
of her Western subjects, despite terrible cruelties in war, she brought
better order and higher civilization than they had known.   Thus *the*
Western world became Latin.
   In the East, Rome appeared first as the liberator of the Greeks.   The
provincial system and the good Roman order were introduced slowly ;
and to the last, the East remained Greek, not Latin, in language, customs, and
thought.   The Adriatic continued to divide the Latin and Greek civilizations
when the two shared the world under the sway of Rome.

   For Further Reading. — *Specially recommended :* An admirable
brief treatment of the expansion in the East is given in Pelham, 140–157.
The student will do well to read either this or the longer treatment, with

more story, in How and Leigh, chs. 25–27. *Additional :* Plutarch's *Lives*
(" Aemilius Paulus," " Flamininus ") as usual, and Mahaffy's *Alexander's
Empire*, chs. 27–31. There is a noble summary of the whole period of
Roman expansion in Freeman's *Chief Periods*, 45–59, but the book is not
very likely to be found in a high school library.

REVIEW EXERCISES. — 1. Catchword review of Rome's progress in the
East.

2. Connected review of the general topic of Rome's growth by large
periods ; thus, —

    (1) Growth under the Kings.

    (2) Growth during the strife between patricians and plebeians,
        510–367.

    (3) Growth of united Rome (under the guidance of the Senate),
        367–146.

3. Catchword review of the same topic — Roman expansion — from
legendary times to 146 B.C.

4. *Catchword review of each of the three great eastern kingdoms, —
Macedonia, Syria, and Egypt, — from the Wars of the Succession (§ 287)
to the condition of a Roman province.*

5. The following Table of Dates will help the student to see the
parallelism in time between Greek and Roman history, down to the
merging of East and West.

GREECE		ROME	
B.C.		B.C.	
510 . .	Expulsion of the Pisis-tratidae	510 . .	Legendary Expulsion of the Tarquins
509 . .	Constitution of Clis-thenes		
500–494 .	The Ionic revolt	494 . .	First secession of the plebs : Tribunes
492–479 .	Attack by Persia and Carthage		
490 . .	Marathon	486 . .	Agrarian proposal of Spurius Cassius
480 . .	Thermopylae, Salamis, Himera		
477 . .	Confederacy of Delos		
468 . .	Eurymedon		
		462 . .	Proposal for written laws
461–429 .	Leadership of Pericles		
458 . .	Long Walls at Athens		

GREECE	ROME
B.C.	B.C.
454 . . Athenian disaster in Egypt	451–449 . The Decemvirs; the Twelve Tables; second secession of the plebs
445 . . Thirty Years' Truce	445 . . Intermarriage between the orders legalized
	444 . . Consular tribunes
	443 . . Censors
438 . . The Parthenon completed	
431–404 . Peloponnesian War	
415–413 . The Sicilian expedition	
411 . . The " Four Hundred " at Athens	409 . . Plebeians attain the quaestorship
405 . . Aegospotami	
404–371 . Supremacy of Sparta	
401 . . March of the Ten Thousand Greeks	400 . . Plebeians attain the consular tribuneship
399 . . Execution of Socrates	
396 . . Agesilaus invades Asia	
394 . . Cnidus	
393 . . Athens' Long Walls rebuilt	390 . . Gauls sack Rome
387 . . Peace of Antalcidas	
383–379 . Sparta crushes the Chalcidic Confederacy	
371 . Leuctra	367 . . The Licinian Laws
371–362 . Theban leadership	
362 . . Battle of Mantinea	
	356 . . Plebeians attain the dictatorship
359–336 . Philip king of Macedon	
351 . . First Philippic of Demosthenes	351 . . Plebeians attain the censorship
348 . . Death of Plato	
	343–341 . First Samnite War
338 . . Chaeronea	340–338 . The Latin War
	337 . . The plebeians attain the praetorship
336–323 . Rule of Alexander the Great	
334 . . The Granicus	
333 . . Issus	

GREECE	ROME
B.C.	B.C.
332 . . Siege of Tyre; Alexandria founded	332 . . The Tribes increased to twenty-nine
331 . . Arbela	
325 . . Expedition of Nearchus	326–304 . Second Samnite War
323–276 . Wars of the Succession	321 . . Caudine Forks
	312 . . Appius Claudius, censor
	300 . . Plebeians become augurs and pontiffs
285–247 . Ptolemy Philadelphus	298–290 . Third Samnite War
280 . . The Achaean League	**280–275 . War with Pyrrhus**
278 . . The Gallic invasion	266 . . Conquest of the Gauls to the Rubicon
245 . . Aratus, general of the Achaean League	264–241 . First Punic War: Sicily becomes Roman
241 . . Agis at Sparta	241–238 . The Mercenary War
235 . . Struggle between Achaean League and Sparta; Cleomenes' reforms	225–222 . Cisalpine Gaul becomes Roman
220 . . Marked decline in the Graeco-Oriental kingdoms	**218–201 . Second Punic War;** Spain a Roman province
	216 . . Cannae

215–205 . First Macedonian War

                   207 . . Battle of the Metaurus

                   202 . . Zama

201–196 . Second Macedonian War

197 . . Cynoscephalae ; Macedonia a dependent ally

192–188 . War with Syria

189 . . Magnesia ; Syria a dependent ally

171–167 . Third Macedonian War

168 . . Pydna

149–146 . Third Punic War

146 . . Destruction of Carthage and Corinth; Macedonia and Africa become Roman provinces ; Greece dependent

133 . . The Province of Asia

CHAPTER XXXII

NEW STRIFE OF CLASSES, 146–49 B.C.

PRELIMINARY SURVEY

476. The history of the Roman Republic falls into three great divisions : —

a. The internal conflict between plebeians and patricians (a century and a half, 510–367). This period closed with the fusion of the old classes into a united people.

b. The expansion of this united Rome (a little more than two centuries): over Italy, 367–266 ; over the Mediterranean coasts, 264–146.

c. A new internal strife (less than a century, 146–49).

The first two periods we have already surveyed. The third is the subject of the present chapter and the two following ones.

477. New Period of Class Conflicts. — The senatorial oligarchy (§ 400) carried Rome triumphantly through her great wars, but it failed to devise a plan of government fit for the conquests outside Italy. It knew how to conquer, but not how to rule. Gross misgovernment followed abroad. This corrupted the citizens and lowered the moral tone at home, until the Republic was no longer fit to rule even Italy or herself. *There resulted a threefold conflict : in Rome, between rich and poor ;* [1] *in Italy, between Rome and the "Allies" ; in the empire at large, between Italy and the provinces.*

478. New External Danger. — Moreover, Rome had left no other state able to keep the seas free from pirates or to guard the frontiers of the civilized world against barbarians. It was therefore her plain duty to police the Mediterranean lands

---

[1] This class struggle, unlike that between patricians and plebeians, bears closely upon that of our day.

herself. But erelong this simple duty was neglected; the seas swarmed again with pirate fleets, and new barbarian thunderclouds, unwatched, gathered on all the frontiers.

479. The Plan of Treatment. — Each of these evils will be surveyed in detail (§§ 480–505). Then we shall notice how the senatorial oligarchy grew more and more irresponsible and incompetent. It was not able itself to grapple with the new problems which expansion had brought, and it jealously crushed out each individual statesman who tried to heal the diseases of the state in constitutional ways (§§ 507–530). Thus, when the situation became unbearable, power fell to a series of military chiefs — Marius, Sulla, Pompey, Caesar. The despotic usurpations of these leaders led to a new system of government which we call the Empire.

THE EVILS IN ROME

480. Industrial and Moral Decline due to the Great Wars. — Rome had begun to decline in morals and in industries before the end of the Second Punic War. *Even a glorious war tends to demoralize society.* It corrupts morals and creates extremes of wealth and poverty. Extreme poverty lowers the moral tone further. So does quick-won and unlawful wealth. Then the moral decay of the citizens at both extremes shows in the state as political disease. The Second Punic War teaches this lesson to the full.

In that war Italy lost a million lives — the flower of the citizen body, including thousands of her most high-spirited and great-souled youth, who, in peace, would have served the state nobly through a long life. The race was made permanently poorer by that terrible hemorrhage. The adult Roman citizens fell off from 298,000 to 214,000. Over much of the peninsula the homesteads had been hopelessly devastated; while years of camp life, with plunder for pay, had corrupted the simple tastes of the old yeomen. In the ruin of the small farmer, Hannibal had dealt his enemy a deadlier blow than he ever knew.

Trade, too, had stagnated; and so illegitimate profits were eagerly sought. The merchants who had risked their wealth so enthusiastically to supply their country in her dire need after Cannae (§ 444) began to indemnify themselves, as soon as that peril was over, by fraudulent war contracts. We are told even that sometimes they over-insured ships, supposed to be loaded with supplies for the army in Spain or Africa, and then scuttled them, to get the insurance money from the state.

Thus the farmers had been impoverished. In the cities there gathered a starving rabble. And between these masses and the old senatorial oligarchy there sprang up a new aristocracy of wealth. Its members were known as *equites* (knights).[1] Its riches were based on rapacious plunder of conquered countries, on fraudulent contracts with the government at home, on reckless speculation, and on unjust appropriation of the public lands (for the restriction of the Licinian law (§ 370) had become a dead letter, and the wealthy classes again used the state lands as private property).

481. This new " capitalistic " system demands further notice. Rome became the money center of the world. Its capitalists, organized in partnerships and in stock companies, had their central offices in Rome, along the *Via Sacra* (the first " Wall Street "), and branch offices in the most important provincial centers, like Alexandria, Ephesus, and Antioch. Through numerous agents, scattered over the Roman world, they managed the " public works " (the construction of aqueducts, theaters, sewers, etc.) for distant provincial cities — at huge profits — or they loaned the cities the money for such necessary improvements — at from 12 to 50 per cent interest. A specially profitable business of such companies was " farming the taxes" of rich provinces (§ 500).

482. Trade Monopolies. — Some of these companies were organized to engross the trade or the production of certain commodities, so as unduly to raise the price. About 200 B.C. we read of an " oil trust " in Rome (*olive* oil, of course, which was an important element in Italian and Greek living). Plainly

---

[1] This order must not be confused with the early *military* knights (§ 348).

these illegal "combinations in restraint of trade" (such as the United States has been trying to control since 1890) were common in Rome after the Second Punic War. In 191 B.C., a Roman drama refers incidentally to a "corner in grain" which was then distressing the people. Two years later, this trade monopoly had become so serious that the government had to step in, for the public safety. The aediles prosecuted the "malefactors of great wealth" under an ancient law of the Twelve Tables, and heavy fines were imposed upon them. Plainly the government could not let speculators so directly rob the Roman populace of bread, without danger of revolution; but ordinarily the capitalistic syndicates went their extortionate ways unhindered.

483. The Money Power and the Government. — The senatorial families were forbidden by law (in 218) to engage in foreign trade or to take government contracts. Therefore the "money kings" who desired a certain policy by the government could not themselves enter the Senate to secure it (as they sometimes have done in America). But none the less, *indirectly*, the moneyed interests did control the government.

This condition *began* in the Punic Wars; and, as in part has been shown, it began with the patriotic action of the men of wealth. Year by year, during that long and desperate struggle, the Senate needed immense sums of money, such as the Roman treasury had never before known. There was no time to build up a new state system of finance. The Senate asked aid from the companies of capitalists. These companies equipped Roman fleets and armies, and furnished the "sinews of war" by which Hannibal was held in check. But, in return, the state came to depend upon the moneyed powers even after the danger was past. Then grew up a very real, though wholly informal, alliance between the "interests" and the government.

The capitalists kept in close touch with the governing class in various ways. They loaned money to aspiring young nobles, to help them attain their political ends; and in return they expected and received favors when these nobles became influential leaders at Rome or the governors of provinces abroad. A provincial governor could easily induce a rich city to give fat contracts to his favorite Roman syndicate; or he could enable the syndicate to squeeze from a debtor city the last penny of extortionate interest which its government had carelessly or foolishly or wrongfully promised.

The syndicates were of no political party. Like "big business" in our own time, they sought to control or own every leader and party which might be sometime able to serve them. Moreover, small shares of the stock companies were widely distributed, so that the whole middle class of citizens was interested in every prospect of enlarged dividends. Such citizens could be counted upon to support any project of the moneyed interests with their votes in the Assembly, and with their shoutings in the street mobs. Indeed there were many striking resemblances between the relation of Roman "big business" to the Roman state and the relation between the great corporations and the government in our own day and country.[1]

484. The Rise of Luxury. — With the equites and the nobles, the old Roman simplicity gave way to sumptuous luxury. There was a growing display in dress and at the table, in rich draperies and couches and other house furnishings, in the houses themselves, in the celebration of marriages, and at funerals. As the Roman Juvenal wrote later: "Luxury has fallen upon us—more terrible than the sword; the conquered East has avenged herself by the gift of her vices." The economic phenomena, good and bad, that had occurred in the Greek world (§§ 283–286) after the conquests of Alexander, were now repeated on a larger scale in Italy — with a difference: *the coarser Roman resorted too often to tawdry display and to gluttony or other brutal excesses from which the temperate Greek turned with disgust.*

---

[1] In this treatment of Roman capitalism after 200 B.C., the author has drawn freely from two recent books of great value, — Dr. William Stearns Davis' *Influence of Wealth in Imperial Rome*, and Dr. Frank Frost Abbott's *Common People of Ancient Rome*.

From this time, the Romans indulged in extremes of luxury which had not been dreamed of by the Athenians of Pericles' day. They had far more elegant houses, bigger troops of slaves, and much more ostentation of all sorts.

Exaggerated copies of the Greek public baths (§ 238) appeared in Rome. These became great public clubhouses, where the more voluptuous and idle citizens spent many hours

RUINS OF THE HOUSE OF M. OLCONIUS AT POMPEII.[1]

a day. Besides the various rooms for baths, — hot, tepid, or cold, — there were in a bathing house swimming pools, libraries, and, often, museums. There were also many colonnades with benches and couches; and the extensive gardens contained delightful shady walks, along whose borders stood, now and then, noble statues, the booty of some Hellenic city.

485. Excursus: Homes. — Rome's narrow streets seemed narrower than ever, now that buildings rose several stories

---

[1] Cf. § 583 for the preservation of Pompeian remains.

high, to house the growing city population. They were dirty,
too, and, as in Greek cities (§ 233), they ran between blank
walls, so far as the lower stories of the houses were concerned.

The private houses of wealthy men had come to imitate the
Greek type. We have already noticed (§ 411) that the original
"house" had become a central hall (*atrium*) with rooms on
the sides and rear. This *atrium* now became a *front* hall, where
the master of the house received his guests. It was shut off
from the street by a vestibule and porter's room. Its central
opening to the sky still admitted light and air, and it now held
a marble basin to catch the rain. Often an ornamental foun-
tain was now introduced, to play constantly into this basin,
surrounded by statues. In the rear was a second court, more
fully open to the sky, with flower beds and blooming shrubbery.
About this court (*peristyle*), which was bordered by rows of
columns, stood many rooms for the women and for various
domestic occupations. Each house had its kitchens and several
dining rooms, large and small, where stood tables, each surrounded on three sides by luxurious couches, in place of the
old-fashioned hard benches. The Romans had now adopted
the Greek practice of reclining at meals. Each fashionable
house, too, had its bathrooms, one or more, and its library.
The pavement of the courts, and many floors, were ornamented with artistic mosaic. The walls were hung with
costly, brilliantly colored tapestries, and ceilings were richly
gilded. Sideboards held beautiful vases and gold and silver
plate, and in various recesses stood glorious statues. Each such
house now had its second story.

Besides his town house, each rich Roman had one or more
country houses (*villas*), with all the comforts of the city —
baths, libraries, museums, — and also with extensive park-like
grounds, containing fishponds, vineyards, and orchards. To
care for the complex needs of this new luxurious life, every
man of wealth kept troops of slaves in his household.

486. Gladiatorial Games. — Alongside this private luxury,
there grew *the practice of entertaining the populace with shows.*

These were often connected with religious festivals, and were of many kinds. It was the special duty of the aediles to care for public entertainment, but gradually many candidates for popular favor began to give shows of this kind.

Among these new shows were the horrible *gladiatorial games.* These came, not from the Greek East, but from neighbors in Italy. They were an old Etruscan custom (§ 331, close), and were introduced into Rome about the beginning of the Punic Wars. A gladiatorial contest was a combat in which two men fought each other to the death for the amusement of the spectators. The practice was connected with ancient human sacrifices for the dead, and at Rome the first contests of this kind took place only at the funerals of nobles. By degrees, however, they became the most popular of the public amusements and were varied in character. A long series of combats would be given at a single exhibition, and many couples, armed in different ways, would engage at the same time. Sometimes wild beasts, also, fought one another, and sometimes beasts fought with men.

At first the gladiators were captives in war, and fought in their native fashion, for the instruction as well as the entertainment of the spectators. Later, slaves and condemned criminals were used. Finally this fighting became a profession, for which men prepared by careful training in gladiatorial schools.

487. Greek Culture. — Alongside these evil features there was some compensation in a new inflow of Greek culture. Men like Flamininus and the Scipios absorbed much of the best spirit of Greek thought; and there was a general admiration for Greek art and literature. For a long time to come, however, this did not make Rome herself productive in art or literature. Greek became the fashionable language; Greek marbles and pictures were carried off from Greek cities to adorn Roman palaces. But Rome, in this period, produced few great sculptors or painters, and such books as appeared were mainly the work of Greek adventurers (§ 624).

488. Continued Decline of the Yeomanry. — The rift between rich and poor went on widening after the great wars were over. Rome soon had its hungry masses of unemployed laborers in the city and its land question in the country.

Those of the yeomanry who had survived the ruin of war (§ 480) were fast squeezed off the land by economic conditions

REMAINS OF A COURT OF A PRIVATE RESIDENCE AT POMPEII.
(*House of the Vettii.*)

resulting from Rome's conquests. The nobles, who could not invest their riches in trade, secured vast landed estates in the provinces out of confiscated lands sold by the state or by cheap purchase from the ruined natives. From such large farms in Sicily and in the African "grain provinces" they supplied Italian cities with grain cheaper than the Italian farmer could raise it on his less fertile soil. The large landlord in Italy turned to cattle grazing or sheep raising or to wine and oil culture. The small farmer had no such escape; for these forms of industry called for large tracts and slave labor. For grazing, or often simply for pleasure resorts, the new capitalists and the nobility wanted even vaster domains. So they bought out the near-by small farmers.

489. Force and Fraud by the Rich. — The decreased profits in grain raising made many small farmers (already ruined) willing to sell — though they could look forward to no certain future, and must expect a total change in their life. And when the small farmer would not sell, the rich and grasping landlord sometimes had recourse to force or fraud, to get the coveted patch of land. This was especially true in the more secluded regions, where, despite all discouragements, the yeomen clung stubbornly to their ancestral fields. In pathetic words the Latin poet Horace (§ 626) describes the violence and trickery used by the great man toward such helpless victims.[1] The yeoman's cattle were likely to die mysteriously, or his growing crops were trampled into the ground over night; or constant petty annoyances wore down his spirit, until he would sell at the rich man's price. Redress at law, as in our own times, was usually too costly and too uncertain for a poor man in conflict with a rich one.

490. Summary. — The wars in the East continued to supply cheap slaves for the landlords; and the dispossessed yeoman could find no employment in the country. Thus we have a series of forces all tending to the same end : —

a. the cheap grain from the provinces ;

b. the introduction of a new industry better suited to large holdings and to slave labor ;

c. the growth of large fortunes eager for landed investment ;

d. the growth of a cheap slave supply.

In some parts of Italy, of course, especially in the north, many yeomen held their places. But over great districts, only large ranches could be seen, each with a few half-savage slave herdsmen and their flocks, where formerly there had nestled

---

[1] See Davis' *Readings*, II, No. 38, for this process of the disappearance of the yeomen, and note the reference there also to violence by the rich.

numerous cottages on small, well-tilled farms, each supporting its independent family of Italian citizens. *As a class*, the small farmers, formerly the backbone of Italian society in peace and war alike, drifted from the soil.

491. Emigration. — What became of this dispossessed yeomanry, from whom formerly had come conquerors, statesmen, and dictators? Many had foresight and energy enough to make their way at once to Gaul or Spain, while their small capital lasted. In these semi-barbarous western provinces, for a century, a steady stream of sturdy peasant emigrants from Italy spread the old wholesome Roman civilization and confirmed the Roman rule, while at the same time they built up comfortable homes or even large fortunes for themselves. But to Italy their strength was lost.

492. A City Mob. — But a whole class of people could not be expected to leave their native land. For multitudes, lack of money, or sickness in the family, or other misfortune would make this impossible. Love of the homeland and mere custom would hold larger numbers. Thus the great bulk of the ex-farmers merely drifted to the cities of Italy, and especially to the capital.

If Italy had been a manufacturing country, they might finally have found a new kind of work in these city homes. But the Roman conquests in the East prevented this. In the Eastern provinces manufacturing of all sorts was much more developed than in Italy; and now Roman merchants found it cheaper to import Oriental goods than to build up a system of factories at home. Rome had become the center of *exchange* for the Roman world, but not a producer of wealth. It ceased to develop home resources and fed upon the provinces. Some increase in simple manufactures there was, of course; but such work was already in the hands mainly of skilled Oriental slaves or freedmen, of which an ever growing supply was brought to Rome.

Thus the ex-farmers found no more employment in the city than in the country. However willing or eager to work, there was no place for them in the industrial system. They soon spent the small sums they had received for their lands, and then they and their sons sank into a degraded city rabble which became the ally and finally the master of cunning politicians, who amused it with festivals and gladiatorial shows, and who were finally to support it, at state expense, with free grain. The lines of an English poet, almost two thousand years later, regarding similar phenomena in his own country, apply to this Italy : —

> " Ill fares the land, to hastening ills a prey,
> Where wealth accumulates, and men decay ! " [1]

493. Political Results : Decay of the Constitution. — The economic changes, we have seen, had replaced the rugged citizen farmer with an incapable, effeminate nobility and a mongrel, hungry mob, reinforced by freed slaves. *With this moral decline came political decay.* The constitution in theory remained that of the conquerors of Pyrrhus and of Hannibal, but in reality it had become a plaything, tossed back and forth between factions in the degenerate state. Old ideas of loyalty, obedience, regard for law, self-restraint, grew rare. Young nobles flattered and caressed the populace for votes.[2] Bribery grew rampant. Statesmen came to disregard all checks of the constitution in order to carry a point.

494. Decay of the Assembly. — Indeed, had Rome kept all its old virtue, the old constitution would no longer have served good ends. It was outgrown. By the close of the Punic Wars Rome was a mighty city of perhaps a million people, and the mistress of an empire that reached from the Atlantic to the Euphrates. But she still tried to govern herself and her

---

[1] The student may find this interesting and important change in Italian life easier to understand by comparing it with the like change in England just before the time of Shakspere. Look this up in any good English history.

[2] Few were those who could defy the hissings of the mob as did the younger Africanus : " Silence, ye step-children of Italy.' Think ye I fear those whom I myself brought in chains to Rome ! "

dominions by the simple machinery which had grown up before 367, when she was a little village in Latium. To rule the larger Rome of 266 B.C., mistress of Italy only, had tasked this form of government and had shown some weaknesses. For its present task it was wholly unfitted.

Nowhere did this show more clearly than in the Assembly. Rome was too large to decide public questions by mass meeting; and it did not know how to invent our modern democratic machinery of balloting in small precincts, with such devices as the referendum and the recall. But there were other reasons, also, apart from mere size, why the Assembly failed. The new city mob controlled the four city tribes. The other seventeen of the older rural "tribes" (§ 365) were originally made up of small yeomanry near Rome. That class had mainly disappeared; and Roman nobles or bankers, who had bought up its lands, now made most of the voters in these tribes. To some extent, the like was true of the fourteen other rural tribes which had been added later (§ 386) and which were scattered up and down Italy. In these, it is true, the great majority of voters were still the small farmers — if only they could all be got together at the Assembly in Rome. But this was almost impossible. Ordinarily the wealthy class of Italian landowners could control the votes of these tribes also. Thus the old stronghold of democracy in the government had been seized, for most purposes, by the aristocracy.

495. Decline of the Senate. — Meantime the senatorial oligarchy closed up its ranks still further. By custom, the lowest curule office, the aedileship, was so burdened with costly spectacles for the populace that only men of great wealth, or the most reckless gamesters, could start upon a political career. This was even worse than the undemocratic Greek practice (outside Athens) of paying no salaries to officials. Secure in their own fortunes, the nobles let things go at will, grasping for themselves the profits of empire, but shirking its responsibilities. Among the cowardly and dissolute aristocrats there were noble exceptions; but Mommsen, who so generously applauded the Senate of 200 B.C. (§ 400), says of its successor eighty years later : —

"It sat on the vacated throne with an evil conscience and divided hopes, indignant at the institutions of the state which it ruled, and yet incapable of even systematically assailing them, vacillating in all its conduct except where its own material advantage prompted a decision, a picture of faithlessness toward its own as well as the opposite party, of inward inconsistency, of the most pitiful impotence, of the meanest selfishness, — an unsurpassed ideal of misrule."

EVILS IN ITALY

496. The distinction between citizens and subjects (§§ 388 ff.) **was drawn more sharply.** Admission to Roman citizenship from

AN EXCAVATED STREET IN POMPEII.

without almost ceased. New Latin colonies were no longer founded, because the wealthy classes wanted to engross all vacant land in Italy. Laws restricted the old freedom of

Latin migration to Rome, and confounded the Latins with the other " Allies."

497. Roman Insolence toward " Subject Italians."—This sharpening of the line between " Romans " and " subjects " tended to create envy on one side and haughtiness on the other. Rome began openly to treat the " Allies " as subjects. They were given a smaller share of the plunder in war than formerly, and they were ordered to double their proportion of soldiers for the army. Roman citizens, on the other hand, had their old burdens lightened. Taxation upon them ceased wholly after the Second Punic War, when the Carthaginian " war indemnity " glutted the treasury.

Worse than such distinctions was the occasional insolence or brutality of a Roman official. In one town the city consul was stripped and scourged because the peevish wife of a Roman magistrate felt aggrieved that the public baths were not vacated quickly enough for her use. In another, a young Roman idler, looking on languidly from his litter, caused a free herdsman to be whipped to death for a light jest at his expense.[1] Such tyranny was the harder to bear because, more than Rome, the Italian towns had kept their old customs and old virtues. It was a poor return, in any case, for the Italian loyalty that had saved Rome from Hannibal.

EVILS IN THE PROVINCES[2]

498. The Provincial System and its Deterioration. — By 133, there were eight provinces, — Sicily, Sardinia and Corsica, Hither Spain, Farther Spain, Africa, Illyria (which had been conquered after the third Macedonian War), Macedonia, and Asia. Cisalpine Gaul, Southern Gaul, and Greece were

---

[1] These incidents were stated by Caius Gracchus (§ 514) in the year 123, in his fiery pleas for reform.

[2] Pelham, 174–186, 327–329; Arnold, *Roman Provincial Administration*, 40–88. On the governor's tyranny, Cicero's *Oration against Verres*, or the chapter on " A Roman Magistrate " in Church's *Roman Life in the Days of Cicero*.

Roman possessions and were soon to be provinces. The growth of provincial government had been a matter of patchwork and makeshifts. There had been no comprehensive view of Roman interests and no earnest desire to govern for the good of the provincials. Both these things had to wait for the Caesars. At first, to be sure, the Roman administration was more honest, capable, and just than the Carthaginian or the Greek. But irresponsible power bred recklessness and corruption. Deterioration soon set in; and, before the year 100, it was doubtful whether the West had gained by the fall of Carthage. It took the Empire with its better aims and methods to dispel the doubt.

499. Marks of a Province. — At the worst, existing institutions were everywhere respected, with true Roman tolerance. As in Italy, however, the different cities were jealously isolated from one another. As in Italy, too, there were various grades of cities. To most of them was left their self-control for purely local concerns, and some were, in name, independent "allies," with special exemption from taxes. But in general, the distinctive marks of a province, as opposed to Italian communities, were (1) *payment of tribute* in money or grain,[1] (2) *disarmament*, and (3) *the absolute rule of a Roman governor*.

500. Tax Farming. — Rome adopted for her provinces the method of taxation which she found in force in many of them. She did not herself at this time build up a system of tax collectors. She "farmed out" the right to collect taxes from each province. That is, she sold the right, usually at public sale, to the highest bidder. Of course, the Senate first fixed the proportion of produce or amount of money which each part of the province was to pay. Then the contractor, or "farmer," paid down a lump sum, and had for himself all that he could squeeze from the province, above that sum and the expenses of his agent.

---

[1] The "Allies" in Italy furnished men, but did not pay tribute. The position of the provincial cities was less honorable in Roman eyes, and it was more liable to abuse (§ 500).

The evil was that this arrangement constantly tempted the contractor to extort too much from the helpless provincials, — which was especially easy when the tax was collected "in kind." If an agent seized twice the allowed "tenth," it would be practically impossible afterward to prove the fact; even if there had been a fair judge to hear the case. But the only judge was the Roman governor of the province, who often was hand-in-glove with the contracting Roman capitalist, from whom, perhaps, he received a share of the plunder. The whole corrupt and tyrannical system was essentially the same as that by which Turkey has ground down her Christian provinces in southwestern Europe for five hundred years.

501. The Governor. — The actual working of the whole provincial system rested with the governor, and everything tended to make him a tyrant. He was appointed by the Senate from those who had just held consulships or praetorships, and he had the title of pro-consul or pro-praetor. His power over his district, even in peace, was as great as the consul exercised at the head of an army. He had no colleague. There was no appeal from his decrees. There was no tribune to veto his act. He had soldiery to enforce his commands. His whole official staff went out from Rome with him, and were strictly subordinate to him.

The persons of the provincials were at his mercy. In Cisalpine Gaul a governor caused a noble Gaul, a fugitive in his camp, to be beheaded, merely to gratify with the sight a worthless favorite who lamented that he had missed the gladiatorial games at Rome.[1] There was even less check upon the governor's financial oppression. All offices were unpaid; the way to them was through vast expense; and the plundering of a province came to be looked upon as the natural means of repaying one's self for previous outlay and for a temporary exile from Rome. Provincial towns were ordered by Roman law to supply the governor's table (including all his staff, of course).

---

[1] See Davis' *Readings*, II, No. 37.

Under color of this, the governor often seized priceless art treasures (costly vases and statuary), as table ornaments, bringing them back with him to Rome. In short, the senatorial nobility passed around the provinces among themselves as so much spoil.

502. The Trial of Corrupt Governors. — A governor might be brought to trial, it is true; but only *after* his term had expired; and only *at Rome.* Poor provincials, of course, had to endure any abuse without even seeking redress; and in any case it was rarely possible to secure conviction even of the grossest offenders. The only court for such trials was made up of senators. Thus many of the judges were themselves interested in similar plunderings, either in person, or through a son or brother or cousin; and with the best of them, class spirit stood in the way of convicting a noble.

When other means failed to secure acquittal, the culprit could fall back on bribery. When a certain Verres was given the province of Sicily for three years, Cicero tells us, he cynically declared it quite enough: "In the first year he could secure plunder for himself; in the second for his friends; in the third for his judges."

503. The Provinces the "Estates of the Roman People." — It was not the senatorial class alone, however, who enriched themselves from the provinces. All Rome, and indeed all Italy, drew profit from them.

The state now secured its immense revenues from taxation of the provincials, and from its domains and mines in the provinces. *The equites,* organized in companies ("publicans") or as private speculators, swarmed in by thousands, to conduct all public works with corrupt contracts, to "farm" the taxes, to loan money at infamous interest, and to rob the unhappy provincials mercilessly in many other ways. *The populace* looked to the provinces for cheap grain and for wild-beast shows and other spectacles.

"Italy was to rule and feast: the provinces were to obey and pay." And withal it was nobody's business in particular tó see that these "farms of the Roman people" were not rapidly and wastefully exhausted.

SLAVERY

We have now surveyed the three great evils mentioned in § 477. The fourth peril (the danger of barbarian inroads) can be best dealt with in the narrative to follow (§§ 523, 547, etc.). *But Rome's most dangerous barbarians were in her midst;* and a few words must be given now to the evils of *Roman slavery.*

504. Extent and Brutal Nature.[1] — In the last period of the Republic, slavery was unparalleled in its immensity and degradation. Mommsen is probably right in saying that in comparison with its abyss of suffering all Negro slavery is but as a drop. Captives in war were commonly sold by the state or given away to wealthy nobles. To keep up the supply of slaves, man hunts were regularly organized on the frontiers, and some of the provinces themselves were desolated by kidnappers. At the market in Delos ten thousand slaves were sold in a single day.

The student must not think of slaves in ancient times as usually of a different color and race from the masters. The fact that they were commonly of like blood, and often of higher culture, gave to ancient slavery a peculiar character, when compared with more modern slavery. The slaves came in part from the cultured East, but they came also from the wildest and most ferocious barbarians, — Gauls, Goths, Moors. The more favored ones became schoolmasters, secretaries, stewards. The most unfortunate were savage herdsmen and the hordes of branded and shackled laborers, who were clothed in rags and who slept in underground dungeons.

The maxim of even the model Roman, Cato (§ 506), was to work slaves like so many cattle, selling off the old and infirm. "The slave," said he, "should be always either working or

---

[1] Beesly, *The Gracchi,* 10–14; Davis' *Readings,* II, Nos. 32–34.

sleeping." With the worst class of masters the brutal Roman nature vented itself in inhuman cruelties. The result was expressed in the saying — "So many slaves, so many enemies." The truth of this maxim was to find too much proof.

505. Slave Wars. — In the year 135 came the first of a long series of slave revolts. Seventy thousand insurgent slaves were masters of Sicily for four years. They defeated army after army that Rome sent against them, and desolated the island with indescribable horrors before the revolt was stamped out. Thirty years later, when Rome was trembling before a Teutonic invasion (§ 523), occurred a Second Sicilian Slave War — more formidable even than the first, lasting five years. Other slave risings took place at the same time.

Another thirty years, and there came a terrible slave revolt in Italy itself, headed by the gallant *Spartacus*. Spartacus was a Thracian captive who had been forced to become a gladiator. Escaping from the gladiatorial school at Capua, with a few companions, he fled to the mountains. There he was joined by other fugitive slaves and outlaws until he was at the head of an army of seventy thousand men. He kept the field three years, and for a time threatened Rome itself.

CHAPTER XXXIII

THE GRACCHI

(*Attempts at Peaceful Reform*)

TIBERIUS GRACCHUS, 133 B.C.

506. **Attempts at Reform before the Gracchi.** — The evils that
have been described had not come upon Rome without being
noted by thoughtful men. The chief needs of the state may
be summed up under two heads. First, the government needed
to be taken from the incapable senatorial class and given to
some organization that would more truly represent all classes
of citizens. Second, the poor in the cities needed to be restored to the land as farmers. No attempt had been made
to accomplish either of these things, but there had been one
notable effort at another kind of reform.

This was the work of *Marcus Porcius Cato*. Cato was a
Roman of the old school, — austere, upright, energetic, patriotic,
but coarse and narrow. From a simple Sabine farmer, he had
risen to the highest honors of the state. He had been just old
enough to join the army at the beginning of the Second Punic
War, in which he fought valiantly for sixteen years from Trasimene to Zama; and, half a century later, as we saw (§ 459), he
had a chief part in bringing on the Third Punic War. Thus
his long public life covered the period of chief Roman decline.

Cato longed ardently to restore "the good old days" of
Roman simplicity. As censor (195 B.C.) he tried in a way
to bring back those days. He repressed luxury sternly, and
struck from the Senate some of the proudest names because
of private vices. But he had no far-reaching views. He tried,
not to direct the stream of change into wholesome channels,
but to dam it. He spent his force foolishly in fighting the

new Hellenic culture and the rising standard of comfort. He did not touch the real evils, or suggest any remedy for their causes. Indeed, instead of himself remaining a yeoman farmer, like the Manius (§ 409) whom he took for his model, he became the owner of great plantations worked by slave labor.[1]

For a time there seemed one other chance. After 146 B.C. Scipio Africanus the Younger was the foremost man in Rome. He was liberal, virtuous, cultivated. Many looked hopefully to him for reform. But though more of a statesman than Cato, he lacked Cato's courage. He shrank from a struggle with his order; and when he laid down his censorship, he betrayed his despair by praying the gods, not in the usual words, to *enlarge* the glory of Rome, but to *preserve* the state.

Some slight reforms there were. For instance, the ballot was introduced into the Assembly, so that the rich might have less chance for bribery. But such measures did not reach the root of the disease of the state. The older statesmen were too narrow or too timid; and the great attempt fell to two youths, the Gracchi brothers, throbbing with noble enthusiasm and with the fire of genius.

507. Tiberius Gracchus[2] was still under thirty at his death. He was one of the brilliant circle of young Romans about Scipio. His father had been a magnificent aristocrat. His mother, *Cornelia*, a daughter of the older Africanus, is as famous for her fine culture and noble nature as for being the "Mother of the Gracchi." Tiberius himself was early distinguished in war and marked by his uprightness and energy. *This was the first man to strike at the root of the economic, moral, and political decay of Italy, by trying to rebuild the yeoman class.*

508. The Agrarian[3] **Proposals of Tiberius.** — Tiberius obtained the tribuneship for the year 133, and at once brought forward

---

[1] The student should read Plutarch's " Cato " in the *Lives*. See, too, Davis' *Readings*, II, Nos. 33, 36, 37.

[2] Read Beesly's *The Gracchi*, 23–37.

[3] " Agrarian " refers to land, especially agricultural land ; from Latin *ager*.

an agrarian law. It was simply the land clause of the obsolete Licinian law in a gentler but more effective form. The proposal was threefold.

a. Each holder of state land was to surrender all that he held in excess of the legal limit (cf. § 370), *receiving in return absolute title to the three hundred acres left him.*[1]

b. The land reclaimed was to be given in small holdings (some eighteen acres each) to poor applicants, so as to re-create a yeomanry. And to make the reform lasting, these holders and their descendants were to possess their land *without right to sell.* In return, they were to pay a small rent to the state.

c. To provide for changes, and to keep the law from being neglected, there was to be a *permanent board* of three commissioners to superintend the reclaiming and distributing of land.

509. The Struggle. — Gracchus urged his law with fiery eloquence : —

" The wild beasts of Italy have their dens, but the brave men who spill their blood for her are without homes or settled habitations. Their generals do but mock them when they exhort their men to fight for their sepulchers and the gods of their hearths ; for among such numbers there is perhaps not one who has an ancestral altar. The private soldiers fight and die to advance the luxury of the great, and they are called masters of the world without having a sod to call their own."

The Senate of course opposed the proposal, and the wealthy men, who had so long enjoyed what did not belong to them, cried out that the measure was confiscation and robbery. Tiberius brought the question directly before the tribes, as he had the right to do ; and the town tribes, and all the small farmers left in the rural tribes, rallied enthusiastically to his support. The Senate fell back upon a favorite device. It put up one of the other tribunes, Octavius, to forbid a vote. After many pleadings, Tiberius resorted to a revolutionary measure. In spite of his colleague's veto, he put to the Assembly the question

---

[1] This was generous treatment, and neither confiscation nor demagogism. It was further provided that an old holder might keep about 160 acres more for each of his sons.

whether he or Octavius should be deposed; and when the vote was given unanimously against Octavius, Tiberius had him dragged from his seat.[1] Then the great law was passed.

510. Further Conflict. — At this time the last king of Pergamum, by will, left his treasure to the Roman people.[2] Gracchus proposed to divide the money among the new peasantry to stock their farms. He also proposed to extend Roman citizenship to all Italy. The Senate fell back upon an ancient cry: it accused him of trying to make himself king (§ 362), and threatened to try him at the end of his term. To complete his work, and to save himself, Gracchus asked for reëlection. The first two tribes voted for him, and then the Senate, having failed in other methods, declared his candidacy illegal.[3] The election was adjourned to the next day. The end was not difficult to foresee.

511. Tiberius murdered. — Tiberius put on mourning and asked the people only to protect his infant son. It was harvest time, and the farmers were absent from the Assembly, which was left largely to the worthless city rabble. On the following day the election was again forbidden. A riot broke out, and the more violent of the senators and their friends, charging the undecided mob, put it to flight and murdered Gracchus — a patriot-martyr worthy of the company of the Cassius, Manlius, and Maelius of earlier days. Some three hundred of his adherents also were killed and thrown into the Tiber. Rome, in all her centuries of stern, sober, patient, constitutional strife, had never witnessed such a day before.[4]

512. The work of Gracchus lived. Partisanship ran so high that the whole aristocratic party approved the outrage, rather than abandon their champions to the vengeance of the people. Accordingly the Senate declared the murder an act of patriotism, and followed up the reformer's partisans with mock trials

---

[1] On the morality of this act, cf. Beesly's *The Gracchi*, 32, 33.

[2] Along with his realms; see § 472.

[3] Read Beesly, 35.

[4] Davis, *Readings*, II, No. 39, gives Plutarch's account.

and persecutions (fastening one of them, says Plutarch, in a chest with vipers).

It did not dare, however, to interfere with the great law that had been carried. A consul for the year 132 inscribed on a monument, that he was the first who had installed farmers in place of shepherds on the public domains. The land commission (composed of the friends of Tiberius) did its work zealously, and in 125 B.C. the citizen list of Rome had increased by eighty thousand farmers.

This " back to the land " movement was a vast and healthful reform.[1] If it could have been kept up vigorously, it might have turned the dangerous rabble into sturdy husbandmen, and so removed Rome's chief danger. But of course to reclaim so much land from old holders led to many bitter disputes as to titles; and, after a few years, the Senate took advantage of this fact to abolish the commission.

CAIUS GRACCHUS (123-121 B.C.)

513. Character and Aims. — Immediately after this aristocratic reaction, and just nine years after his brother's death, *Caius Gracchus* took up the work.   He had been a youth when Tiberius was assassinated.   Now he was Rome's greatest orator, —a dauntless, resolute, clear-sighted man, long brooding on personal revenge and on patriotic reform.   Tiberius, he declared, appeared to him in a dream to call him to his task: " Why do you hesitate?   You cannot escape your doom and mine — to live for the people and to die for them! "   A recently discovered letter from Cornelia indicates, too, that his mother urged him on.

Tiberius had striven only for economic reform.   Caius saw the necessity of buttressing that work by political reform. Apparently he meant to overthrow the Senate and to set up a new constitution something like that of Athens under Pericles.

---

[1] Beesly, 39.

514. Political Measures, to win Allies. — The city mob Gracchus secured by a *corn law* providing for the sale of grain to the poor in the capital at half the regular market price, the other half to be made up from the public treasury. Perhaps he regarded this as a necessary poor-law, and as compensation for the public lands that still remained in the hands of the wealthy. It did not pauperize the poor, since such distributions by private patrons (especially by office-seekers) were already customary on a vast scale. It simply took this charity into the hands of the state. If Gracchus' other measures could have been carried through, the need for such temporary charity would have been removed. But, however well meant, this measure certainly introduced a vicious system of *legislative bribery* where in the end the well-meaning patriot was sure to be outbidden by the reckless demagogue. For the moment, however, it won the Assembly.

The equites also Caius won, by taking the law courts from the Senate to place in their hands.

515. Economic Reform. — With these political alliances to back him, Caius took up his brother's work. The land commission was reëstablished, and its work was extended *to the founding of Roman colonies in distant parts of Italy.* Still more important, — Caius *introduced the plan of Roman colonization outside Italy.* He sent six thousand colonists from Rome and other Italian towns to the waste site of Carthage; and he planned other such foundations. *The colonists were to keep full Roman citizenship.*

If this statesmanlike measure had been allowed to work, it would not only have provided for the landless poor of Italy : it would also have Romanized the provinces rapidly, and would have broken down the unhappy distinctions between them and Italy.

516. Personal Rule. — Then Caius turned to attack senatorial government. To a great degree *he drew all authority into his own hands.* By various laws he took away power from the Senate, and himself ruled in its place. He had tried to pro-

vide against his brother's fate by a law expressly legalizing re-
election to the tribuneship, and he served two terms, virtually
as dictator.

"With unrivaled activity," says Mommsen, "he concentrated the
most varied and complicated functions in his own person. He himself
watched over the distribution of grain, selected jurymen, founded colonies in person, notwithstanding that his magistracy legally chained him
to the city, regulated highways and concluded business contracts, led the
discussions of the Senate, settled the consular elections; in short, he
accustomed the people to the fact that one man was foremost in all
things, and threw the lax and lame administration of the Senate into the
shade by the vigor and dexterity of his personal rule."

517. Attempt to extend Citizenship to Italians. — Caius also
pressed earnestly for political reform *outside the city.*   He

TEMPLE OF APOLLO AT POMPEII.

proposed, wisely and nobly, to confer full citizenship upon the
Latins, and Latin rights upon all Italy. But the tribes, jealous
of any extension of their privileges to others, were quite ready

to desert him on these matters. The "knights" and the merchants, too, had grown hostile, from jealousy of the proposal to rebuild commercial rivals like Corinth and Carthage.

The Senate seized its chance. It set on another tribune, *Drusus,* to outbid Caius by promises never meant to be kept. Drusus proposed to found twelve large colonies at once in Italy and to do away with the small rent paid by the new peasantry. There was no land for these colonies, but the mob thoughtlessly followed the treacherous demagogue and abandoned its true leader. When Gracchus stood for a third election he was defeated.

518. Murder of Caius. — Now that he was no longer protected by the sanctity of the tribuneship (§ 363), the nobles, headed by the consul (a ferocious personal enemy), were bent upon his ruin. The chance was soon found. The Senate tried to repeal the law for the colony at Carthage. This attempt caused many of the old supporters of Caius to come into the Assembly from the country. Remembering the fate of Tiberius, some of them came in arms. The nobles cried out that this meant a conspiracy to overthrow the government. The consul called the organized senatorial party to arms, offered for the head of Gracchus its weight in gold (*the first instance of head money in Roman civil strife*), and charged the unorganized and unprepared crowd. A bloody battle followed in the streets. Gracchus, taking no part in the conflict himself, was slain. Three thousand of his adherents were afterward strangled in prison.

519. Overthrow of the Work of the Two Brothers. — The victorious Senate struck hard. It resumed its sovereign rule. The proposed colonies were abandoned, and the great land reform itself was undone. *The peasants were permitted to sell their land, and the commission was abolished.* The old economic decay began again, and soon the work of the Gracchi was but a memory.

Even that memory the Senate tried to erase. Men were forbidden to speak of the brothers, and Cornelia was not allowed to wear mourning for her sons. One lesson, however, had been taught: the Senate had drawn the sword; and when a Marius or a Caesar should attempt again to take up the work of the Gracchi, he would appear as a military master, to sweep away the wretched oligarchy with the sword or to receive its cringing submission (chs. xxxiv ff.).

"The net result of the work [of Caius] was to demonstrate the hopelessness of any genuine democracy. . . . The two Gracchi, . . . in their hope to regenerate Italy, were drawn on to attempt a political revolution, whose nature they did not realize. . . . They were not revolutionists, but they were the fathers of revolution. They aimed at no tyranny, but they were the precursors of the principate [Empire]." — How and Leigh.

For Further Reading. — Ancient writer: Plutarch's *Lives* ("Tiberius Gracchus" and "Caius Gracchus"); Modern writers: Beesly, *The Gracchi*, or How and Leigh, 331–359.

CHAPTER XXXIV

MILITARY RULE: MARIUS AND SULLA (106-78 B.C.)

520. The Biographical Character of Roman History in the Last Century of the Republic. — In earlier times Rome had been greater than any of her citizens. *But after 146, the history of the Republic is summed up in a series of biographies,* and soon the only question is, which man will finally seize the sovereignty. This phase of the Roman Republic really begins with the younger Africanus and closes with Julius Caesar; but it is with Marius and Sulla (halfway between) that the new character first shows without disguise, because these men were the first to carry political measures by the use of the army.

521. The War with Jugurtha. — For some twenty years after the murder of the Gracchi, the Senate's misrule was undisturbed. But a prolonged fourteen-year border war in Africa again revealed its corruption and incapacity in glaring light, and brought military masters to the front.

Jugurtha, grandnephew of Massinissa (§ 459), — brave, crafty, cruel, — had made himself king of Numidia by the assassination of a series of princes dependent upon Rome. He bribed Roman investigating commissioners; bought a consul who had been sent to attack him; and, being summoned to Rome after massacring thousands of Italians and Romans in Africa, he bought his acquittal from the Senate itself (Davis' *Readings*, II, No. 40). But an indignant tribune brought the matter directly before the tribes, and so stirred their indignation that war at last was prosecuted in earnest.

522. New Leaders. — Its progress revealed the utter corruption of the army, but it finally called out two great captains. One was the rude soldier *Marius*, son of a Volscian day laborer,

434

who had risen from the ranks, and who by the votes of the people, against the wish of the Senate, was made consul to carry on the war. The other was his aristocratic lieutenant, *Sulla.*

By skill and good fortune, and by a daring exploit of Sulla's, Marius was able to bring the war to a close during his year of office. Jugurtha was captured. Marius celebrated a splendid triumph at Rome (January 1, 104 B.C.), in which the captive king was dragged through the streets in chains at the wheel of his conqueror's chariot, and then cast into an underground dungeon to starve.

523. The Cimbri and Teutones. — Meantime a storm had broken upon the northern frontier. The *Cimbri* and *Teutones*, two German peoples, migrating slowly with families, flocks, and goods, in search of new homes in the fertile south, had reached the passes of the Alps in the year 113. These barbarians were huge, flaxen-haired, with fierce blue eyes, and they terrified the smaller Italians by their size, their terrific shouts, and their savage customs.

· A Roman consul who tried to entrap the strangers treacherously was defeated and slain; but, leaving Italy on one side for the time, the Germans crowded into Gaul. There they harried the native tribes at will, and, after defeating four more Roman armies (the last with slaughter that recalled the day of Cannae), they finally threatened Italy itself. At the same time the Second Slave War had broken out in Sicily (§ 505).

524. Marius the " Savior of Rome." — Rome had found a general none too soon. Marius was just finishing his work in Africa. In his absence he was reëlected consul — despite the law which required a candidate to appear in person and which forbade an immediate reëlection in any case. The Germans gave him precious time, by turning for two years more into Spain. It was this unaccountable blunder that saved panic-stricken Italy. Marius used the interval in drilling troops and reorganizing the army. Then, in the summer of 102, at *Aquae Sextiae* (Aix), in southern Gaul, he annihilated the two hundred thou-

sand warriors of the Teutones, with all their women and
children, in a huge massacre (Davis' *Readings*, II, No. 41)   The
next summer he destroyed in like manner the vast horde of
the Cimbri, who had penetrated to the Po.   The first German
nation to attack Rome had been given graves in her soil, and
Italy was saved for five hundred years.

525. Civil Disorder. — In defiance of the constitution, Marius
had been reëlected consul each year while the peril lasted.
Thus he had held the consulship five successive years.   This
began to look like a military monarchy.   Perhaps it would have
been well if Marius *had* made himself king.   Or, better still,
had he been enough of a statesman, he might have used his
great power to secure the reforms needed by the Republic.   He
did not try to do either thing.

He was given another consulship; but he was as incapable in
politics as he was great in war.   The feeling between democrats
and aristocrats ran high, and finally broke into street war (De-
cember, 100 b.c.).   Marius looked on while his radical friends

THEATER AT POMPEII.

were massacred. Then he found himself in disgrace with both parties; and in chagrin he retired for some years into obscurity. Meantime another war brought to the front the other great general of the time, the champion of the aristocrats (§ 526).

526. The Social War. — There had grown up in the Senate a small liberal party bent upon reform. Their leader was the tribune *Drusus,* son of the Drusus who had opposed the Gracchi. In the year 91, Drusus took up the Gracchi's work and proposed to extend citizenship to the Italians. He was assassinated; and the nobles carried a law threatening with death any one who should renew the proposal. Then the Italians rose in arms and set up a republic of their own.

Once more Rome fought for life, surrounded by a ring of foes. The *Social War* (war with the Socii, or "Allies") was as dangerous a contest as the imperial city ever waged (91–88 B.C.). Two things saved her. First: she wisely divided her foes by granting citizenship to all who would at once lay down their arms. Second: Sulla showed a magnificent generalship, outshining Marius as the savior of Rome. Marius served with credit; but he was disliked by the Senate and was suspected by all of favoring the demands of the Italians.

527. All Italy enters the Roman State. — The "Allies" were crushed, *but their cause was victorious.* When the war was over, Rome gradually incorporated into the Roman state all Italy south of the Po, *raising the number of citizens* from 400,000 to 900,000. The cities all became municipia, and their burgesses secured the full Roman citizenship. This was the most notable reform in the last century of the Republic.

528. A New Reformer: Sulpicius. — The Italian "Allies" who joined Rome in the war had all been placed in eight tribes. Thus, at most, they could influence only eight out of thirty-five votes, though they made half the citizen body. Now that many more Italians were to be enrolled, the popular party proposed to remedy this injustice and to distribute all the new additions among the thirty-five tribes. This attempt was the occasion for the brooding civil war to break forth.

The tribune *Sulpicius,* a friend of Drusus, carried a law providing for the distribution of the new citizens. In trying to prevent it, Sulla provoked a riot, from which he himself barely escaped with his life through the aid of his rival Marius. Just before this, the Senate had appointed Sulla to manage a war against *Mithridates* the Great, king of Pontus. Now, fearing a military revolution, Sulpicius induced the tribes to give this command to Marius instead.

529. Civil War. — Sulla fled to his army at Capua ; and, though all but one of his officers left him, he marched upon Rome. *For the first time a Roman magistrate used a regular army to reduce the capital (88 B.C.).* After a brief but furious resistance, the unorganized democrats under Marius were scattered, and Sulla became the military master of the city. He repealed the Sulpician laws, executed a few democratic leaders, set a price upon the head of Marius, tried to buttress the Senate by hasty laws, and then departed for the East, where Roman dominion was rapidly crumbling. With grim irony, the head of Sulpicius was set upon the rostrum in the Forum, whence his lips had so often swayed the Assembly.

530. Massacre. — On the departure of Sulla the democratic párty rallied to undo his legislation. The aristocrats surrounded the Assembly with armed forces, and ruthlessly cut down ten thousand men, until the streets ran with blood. But the democratic leader *Cinna* escaped. He was welcomed by the Italians and the country tribes, and returned to besiege the city. Marius, too, came back from adventurous exile,[1] — a grim, vengeful, repulsive old man, with some thousands of freed slaves for his bodyguard. Rome was captured ; the gates were closed ; and for four days and nights the senatorial party were hunted down and butchered by the desperadoes of Marius, despite the indignant pleadings of other democratic leaders, like the generous *Sertorius.*

531. Marius and Cinna proclaimed themselves consuls, *with-*

---

[1] Special report : stories of Marius' hairbreadth escapes while in exile.

out even the form of an election. They then outlawed Sulla, repealed his legislation, and restored the Sulpician law regarding the Italians. In the midst of his orgy of triumph Marius died. Then Sertorius with regular troops stamped out the band of slave assassins; but Cinna remained political master of Rome for four years.

532. Sulla's War with Mithridates. — For thirty years the indolent Senate had looked on carelessly while danger gathered head in the East. Finally the storm had burst. The powerful states of Pontus, Armenia, and Parthia had grown into independent kingdoms, each of them, for long time past, encroaching upon Rome's protectorates. Now, Mithridates VI, king of Pontus, suddenly seized the Roman province of "Asia" (Asia Minor). The people hailed him as a deliverer, and joined him enthusiastically to secure freedom from the hated extortion of Roman tax-collectors and money-lenders. Eighty thousand Italians, scattered through the province, — men, women, and children, — were massacred, almost in a day, by the city mobs. Then Mithridates turned to Macedonia and Greece. Here, too, the people joined him against Rome. Athens welcomed him as a savior from Roman tyranny; and twenty thousand more Italians were massacred in Greece and in the Aegean islands. Rome's dominion in the Eastern world had crumbled at a touch.

A COIN OF MITHRIDATES VI.

This was the peril that had called Sulla from Rome. Outlawed by the democrats at home, without supplies, with only a small army, he restored Roman authority in the East in a series of brilliant campaigns. Then he returned to glut his vengeance and to restore the nobles to power (83 B.C.).

533. The New Civil War. — Italy was almost a unit for the democrats, but Sulla's veterans made him victor after a desolating two years' struggle. Toward the close of the war, the Samnites rose, for the last time, under another Pontius, and marched straight upon Rome, "to burn the den of the wolves that have so long harried Italy." The city was barely saved by Sulla's forced march and desperate night-victory at the *Colline Gate*.

534. Rule of Sulla. — Sulla was now undisputed master of Rome. At his suggestion, the Senate declared him *permanent dictator*[1] (81 B.C.).

SULLA.

His first work was to crush the democratic party by systematic massacre. Lists of names were posted publicly day by day, and any desperado was invited to slay the proscribed men at two thousand dollars a head. Sulla's friends were given free permission to include private enemies in the lists. Debtors murdered their creditors. The wealth of the proscribed men was confiscated, and many a man's only offense was that he owned property which was desired by some follower of Sulla. "Unhappy wretch that I am," cried one gentleman who had stepped up unsuspectingly to look at the list and who found his own name there ; "my villa pursues me ! "

---

[1] The old constitutional office of dictator had become obsolete ; the new permanent dictatorship of Sulla, and later of Caesar, is merely a name for a new kingship.

When entreated at last by the servile Senate to let it be known when he would be through with slaughter, Sulla characteristically replied that he did not recall any more enemies just then, but that those whom he had forgotten would have to be included in some future proscription. Forty-seven hundred Romans of wealth and position perished. Even worse massacres followed over Italy. At Praeneste alone, twelve thousand men were put to death in one day. Sulla thought he had stamped out the embers of the Marian party. Only Sertorius, the noblest Roman of the age, held Spain for the democrats; and the youth Julius Caesar, a nephew of Marius' wife and the husband of Cinna's daughter, was in hiding in the mountains.[1]

535. Restoration of Senatorial Rule. — Sulla next set about reëstablishing oligarchic rule. He enlarged the Senate to six hundred and by law made all officers dependent upon it. The tribuneship (whence had come all the popular movements) was restricted: no tribune could bring any proposal before the tribes, or even address them, without the Senate's permission. By various other changes the part of the people in the government was weakened.

536. "Sulla the Fortunate." — After a three years' absolutism, Sulla abdicated, — to go back to his debaucheries, and to die in peace shortly after as a private citizen. He is a monstrous enigma in history — dauntless, crafty, treacherous, dissolute, licentious, refined, absolutely unfeeling and selfish, and with a mocking cynicism that spiced his conversation and conduct. He called himself the favorite of the Goddess of Chance, and was fond of the title "Sulla the Fortunate." No other civilized man has ever so organized murder. Few have had so clear a grasp of ends and made such unscrupulous use of means.

---

[1] Sulla had had Caesar (a boy of seventeen) in his power and had meant to put him to death. Finally, at the entreaties of friends, he spared him, exclaiming, however, "There is many a Marius hidden in that young fop."

Apparently Sulla believed sincerely in senatorial government; but he had striven against his age, and his work hardly outlived his mortal body.

FOR FURTHER READING. — Ancient writers : Plutarch, *Lives* ("Marius" and "Sulla"). Davis' *Readings*, II, No. 42, contains Plutarch's story of Sulla's massacres. Munro's *Source Book* has good extracts from ancient historians on the Civil War and the Jugurthine War.

Modern writers: Beesly, *The Gracchi, Marius and Sulla;* How and Leigh, 360–449.

CHAPTER XXXV

POMPEY AND CAESAR, 78–49 B.C.

537. **General View.** — The history of the next thirty years — to the rule of Caesar — has two phases. (1) In Italy, it is a question as to what leader shall become master. (2) Abroad, it is marked by Pompey's conquests and his organization of Roman dominion in the East to the Euphrates, and by Caesar's like work in the West to the Rhine and the North Sea. The rivalry for supreme power at Rome narrowed down to these two men, and happily victory fell to Caesar, incomparably the abler and nobler of the two. (Reread § 520.)

538. **Pompey and Crassus** were two of Sulla's officers, who, by the death of their chief, were left in special prominence. Both, of course, belonged to the oligarchic party. Crassus was not only a soldier, but also a scheming man of business. He had built up the greatest fortune in Rome, by the purchase of confiscated property during the Sullan proscriptions. " Pompey the Great," with more honesty and good nature, was a man of mediocre ability, vain, sluggish, cautious to timidity, without broad views. Still, for twenty years, until the rise of Caesar, he was far the greatest power in Rome.

539. **Sertorius in Spain.** — During the rule of Sulla, Spain had been the one remaining refuge of the democrats. While that party had been in power (83 B.C.), one of their leaders, Sertorius (§ 530), had been sent to Spain as governor. He proved a great general and a broad-minded statesman. His rule was gentle and just, and the Spaniards were devoted to him. In the brief time allowed him, he did much to advance the prosperity of the province and to introduce there the best elements of Roman civilization.[1] Aided by the natives, he

---

[1] Special report: anecdotes of Sertorius. Read Plutarch's *Life*.

had easily maintained himself against the officers Sulla sent to drive him out.

540. Pompey's First Chance at a Crown. — Sulla had made it plain that the path to the throne lay through a position as proconsul in a rich province for a term of years, with a war that would call for a large army. Pompey had not yet held any of the offices leading to a proconsular appointment;[1] but, upon Sulla's death, he compelled the Senate to send him to Spain against Sertorius, *with an indefinite term* and absolute powers (77 B.C.). After some years of warfare, Sertorius was basely assassinated, and then Pompey quickly reduced Spain to obedience. In the year 71, he returned triumphantly to Italy. Meantime had come the rising of Spartacus (§ 505). This revolt had just been crushed by Crassus; but Pompey arrived in time to cut to pieces a few thousand of the fugitives, and to claim a large share of the credit.

Thus there were two generals in Italy, each at the head of a victorious army. The Senate feared both, and foolishly refused them the honor of a triumph. This led the generals to join their forces and ally themselves for a moment with the democratic leaders. Their armies encamped at the gates of the city, and the two generals obtained the desired triumphs and their election to the consulship. Then, to pay the democrats, they undid the chief work of their old master, Sulla, by restoring the tribunes and censors with their ancient powers.

The crown was now within the reach of Pompey. He longed for it, but did not dare stretch out his hand to grasp it; and the politicians skillfully played off the two military chiefs against each other until they agreed to disband their armies simultaneously. The crisis was past. Pompey, who had expected still to be the first man in Rome, found himself of very little account among the senatorial talkers, and, for some years, he sulked in retirement.

541. The Cilician Pirates. — In 67, military danger called Pompey again to the front. The navy of Rome had fallen to

---

[1] It was customary to give such places only to ex-consuls or ex-praetors.

utter decay, and swarms of pirates terrorized the seas. They even set up a formidable state, with its headquarters on the rocky coasts of Cilicia, and negotiated with kings as equals. They paralyzed trade along the great Mediterranean highway. They even dared to ravage the coasts of Italy, and carry off the inhabitants for slaves. Finally they threatened Rome itself with starvation by cutting off the grain fleets.

To put down these plunderers, Pompey was given supreme command *for three years in the Mediterranean and in all its coasts for fifty miles inland.* He received also unlimited authority over all the resources of the realm. Assembling vast fleets, he swept the seas in a three months' campaign.

542. Pompey in the East. — Then Pompey's command was extended *indefinitely* in order that he might carry on war against Mithridates of Pontus, who for several years had again been threatening Roman power in Asia Minor. Pompey was absent on this mission five years — a really glorious period in his career, and one that proved the resources and energies of the commonwealth unexhausted, if only a respectable leader were found to direct them. He waged successful wars, crushed dangerous rebellions, conquered Pontus and Armenia, annexed wide provinces, and extended the Roman bounds to the Euphrates. He restored order, founded cities, and deposed and set up kings in the dependent states. When he returned to Italy, in 62, he was the leading figure in the world.

In his triumph, 324 princes walked captive behind his chariot, and triumphal banners proclaimed that he had conquered twenty-one kings and twelve millions of people, and doubled the revenues of the state. Again the crown was within his grasp. Again he let it slip, expecting it to be thrust upon him.[1]

543. Cato and Cicero. — During Pompey's absence, new actors had risen to prominence. Three deserve special mention, be-

---

[1] Davis' *Readings*, II, No. 45, gives the account by Appian (§ 627) of Pompey's conquests and of his " triumph."

cause they represent three distinct forces. *Cato the Younger,*
great-grandson of Cato the Censor, was a brave, honest, bigoted

CICERO.

aristocrat, bent upon preserving the oligarchic Republic. *Cicero,* the greatest orator of Rome, was a
refined scholar and a representative of the wealthy
middle class. He desired
reform, and at first he inclined toward the demo-
cratic party; but, alarmed
by their violence and rude-
ness, he finally joined the
conservatives, in the idle
hope of restoring the early
republican constitution.[1]

Neither of these two
men deserves the name of
statesman. "Both," says

a modern historian of Rome, "were blinded to real facts —
Cato by his ignorance, Cicero by his learning." The third man
was to tower immeasurably above these and all other Romans
(§ 544).

544. Caius Julius Caesar was the chief democratic leader, and
perhaps the greatest genius of all history. He was of an old
patrician family that claimed divine descent through Aeneas[2]
and his son Iulus (Julius). His youth had been dissolute, but
bold; and he had refused with quiet dignity to put away his
wife (the daughter of Cinna) at Sulla's order, though Pompey
had not hesitated to obey a like command. In Pompey's
absence he had served as quaestor and praetor, and he strove

---

[1] Cicero has been bitterly accused of cowardly and shifty politics. Warde-
Fowler's *Caesar* is sympathetic in its treatment. There is an excellent statement in Pelham, 247–252.

[2] A fabled prince of Troy in the Trojan War, the hero of Virgil's *Aeneid.*

ardently to reorganize the democratic party. In public speeches he ventured to praise Marius and Cinna as champions of the people; and in the year 64, by a daring stroke, he again set up at the Capitol the trophies of Marius, which had been torn down in the rule of Sulla.

545. Conspiracy of Catiline. — Caesar had tried also to counterbalance Pompey's power by securing a province in Egypt; but his hopes had been dashed by a strange incident. One of the democratic agitators was the profligate *Catiline*. This man organized a reckless conspiracy of bankrupt and ruined adventurers, like himself. He planned to murder the consuls and the senators, confiscate the property of the rich, and make himself tyrant. This conspiracy was detected and crushed by Cicero, the consul (63 B.C.). The movement was not one of the democratic party proper. It belonged to the disreputable extremists who always attach themselves to a liberal party; but the collapse reacted upon the whole popular party, and Caesar's plans were necessarily laid aside. The same year, his career seemed closed by Pompey's return, and he was glad to withdraw from Italy for a while to the governorship of Spain, which at that time had no army and was not an important province.

546. The "First Triumvirate." — The jealous and stupid Senate again drove Pompey into the arms of the democrats. It refused to give his soldiers the lands he had promised them for pay, and delayed even to ratify his wise political arrangements in the East.

Pompey had disbanded his army, and, for two years, he fretted in vain. Caesar seized the chance and formed a coalition between Pompey, Crassus, and himself. This alliance is sometimes called the "First Triumvirate."[1] Caesar furnished the brains and obtained the fruits. He became consul (59 B.C.) and set about securing Pompey's measures. The Senate refused even to consider them. Caesar laid them directly before the Assembly. A tribune, of the Senate's party, interposed his veto. Caesar looked on calmly while a mob of

---

[1] For a caution regarding this term, see § 565, note.

Pompey's veterans drove the tribune from the Assembly. To delay proceedings, Caesar's colleague in the consulship then announced that he would consult the omens. According to religious law, all action should have ceased until the result was known. Caesar serenely disregarded this antiquated check, and carried the measures by the votes of the Tribes. Next he demolished the remains of Sulla's constitution. He had stepped into the first place in Rome.

547. Conquest of Gaul. — At the close of his consulate Caesar secured the governorship of the Gallic provinces, that is, of Cisalpine Gaul or Northern Italy, and that southeastern part of Transalpine Gaul which was under the Roman power, the present Provence. This enabled him to begin one of the most important tasks of his life, the conquest of the whole of Gaul. (See § 290.)

The country would indeed make a splendid acquisition. The land was very fertile, the Celtic inhabitants a vigorous race. Though they lacked Roman training, their personal bravery was an object of general admiration. They practiced agriculture, but were much more famous for cattle breeding. Their habitations generally formed villages or towns, which were often well fortified. They used the Greek alphabet. They were proficient in the working of metals and extracting them from the soil. They knew music and poetry, and carried on a brisk commerce. Their priesthood, the Druids, was under a common high priest. A kind of general council was held yearly near the city of Chartres, "the Center of the Celtic Earth." Their religion, however, contained many hideous traits, for instance, human sacrifices.[1]

Political jealousy among the various tribes and fierce strifes within them, oppression of the people by the chiefs, and the still migratory habits of some tribes greatly aided Caesar's

---

[1] See Caesar's *Gallic War*, Book VI, Ch. 11 ff. Special reports: The Druids; Caesar in Britain; the bridge across the Rhine; the revolt of Vercingetorix.

efforts. He forced the Helvetians who threatened an inroad into the small Roman province to return to their Alpine homes, and drove back across the Rhine a German host under Ariovistus, after they had already settled in Gaul. Then, in a series of masterly campaigns of eight years, he made Gaul Roman. In the seventh year he had to quell a most formidable and well-organized uprising, in which for the first and last time the whole country was united under an able leader, the brilliant and chivalrous Vercingetorix.

548. Result of the Conquest of Gaul. — To the Romans it gave the rich lands from the Pyrenees to the Rhine; it extended the Mediterranean empire to the shores of the Atlantic and the North Sea; it opened up an immense field for Roman business and a new source to replenish the Roman army with excellent recruits.

The danger of a Teutonic inroad like that of the Cimbri and Teutons was averted. "Let the Alps now sink," exclaimed Cicero; "the gods raised them to shelter Italy from the barbarians, but they are no longer needed." Rome obtained leisure to develop its civilization and organization and to prepare the way for the coming of Christianity.

Practically all the Celts of the continent were now brought under Roman influence. Theirs was not a political vocation. But they were to assimilate the elements of Graeco-Roman civilization and to be a chief factor in transmitting it to the nations of the future. (See § 620.) Except for the work of Caesar, "our civilization would have stood in hardly more intimate relation to the Romano-Greek than to the Assyrian culture."[1]

549. Caesar and Pompey. — The close of the first five years of Caesar's rule in Gaul saw him easily superior to his colleagues, and able to seize power at Rome if he chose. But it was never his way to leave the work in hand unfinished. He renewed the "triumvirate" in 55 B.C., securing the Gauls for five years more for himself, giving Spain to Pompey, and Asia to Crassus.

---

[1] Mommsen, V, 100–102, has an admirable statement.

Crassus soon perished in battle with the Parthians,[1] a huge, barbaric empire, then reaching from the Euphrates to the Indus. Then it became plain that the question whether Caesar or Pompey was to rule at Rome could not long be postponed. The Senate was growing frantic with fear of Caesar and his victorious legions. Pompey, jealous of his more brilliant rival, drew nearer to the Senate again, and was adopted by that terrified body as its champion. He was made *sole consul* with supreme command in Italy, and at the same time, his *indefinite proconsular powers abroad* were continued to him.

Caesar' office as proconsul was about to expire. He had finished his work in Gaul in the nick of time, and was free to take up even greater designs. He still shrank from civil war. He hoped to secure the consulship for the next year; and he seems to have hoped, in that case, to carry out reforms at Rome without violence. Accordingly he made offer after offer of conciliation and compromise. All offers were rebuffed by Pompey and the Senate. To stand for consul, under the law, Caesar must disband his army and come to Rome in person. There would be an interval of some months when he would be a private citizen. The aristocrats boasted openly that in this helpless interval they would destroy him. Caesar finally offered to lay down his command and disband his troops, if Pompey were ordered to do the same. This, too, was refused. Then, by a series of acts marked by trickery and bad faith, the aristocrats tried to take away Caesar's army before the settled time. Finally they carried a decree that he must disband his troops before a certain day or be declared a public enemy. Two tribunes vetoed the decree, but were mobbed, and fled to Caesar's camp. Civil war was at hand.

FOR FURTHER READING. — Davis' *Readings*, II, Nos. 46–49, gives an excellent view of Roman political and social conditions during the First Triumvirate.

---

[1] Special report: Crassus' campaign.

PART V

THE ROMAN EMPIRE (THE GRAECO-ROMAN WORLD)

Rome was the whole world, and all the world was Rome.
— SPENSER, *Ruins of Rome.*

Even now a sovereign who should thus hold all the lands round the Mediterranean Sea, and whose borders should be the Rhine, the Danube, and the Euphrates, would be incomparably the strongest ruler in the world. . . . As has been often pointed out, when Rome ruled she was not only the greatest, but practically the only Power of which the statesman and the philosopher took any cognizance.
— HODGKIN, in *Contemporary Review*, January, 1898, p. 53.

Republican Rome had little to do either by precept or example with modern life; imperial Rome, everything. — STILLÉ, *Studies*, 17.

———◆———

CHAPTER XXXVI

FOUNDING THE EMPIRE: JULIUS AND AUGUSTUS (49 B.C.–14 A.D.)

THE FIVE YEARS OF JULIUS CAESAR (49–44 B.C.)

550. Monarchy Inevitable. — From the time of the Gracchi, Rome had been moving toward monarchy. *Owing to the corruption of the populace in the capital*, the tremendous power of the tribune had grown occasionally into a virtual dictatorship (as with Caius Gracchus and Sulpicius). *Owing to the growing military danger on the frontiers*, the mighty authority of a one-year proconsul of a single province was sometimes extended, by special decrees, over vaster areas for indefinite time (as with Marius, Sulla, Pompey, Caesar). *To make a monarch needed but to unite these two powers, at home and abroad, in one person.*

551. Caesar the Hope of the Subject Nations. — These two conditions (the corruption of the Roman citizens and the danger of barbarian invasion) made monarchy *inevitable*. A third condition made it *right*. This was *the need for better government in the provinces,* — **far the greater part of the Roman world.**

Here is the merit of Caesar. There might have arisen a purely selfish despot. It is Caesar's honor that he, more than any other statesman of the time, felt this third need. He rose to power as the champion of the suffering subject-populations. He had come to see that in any case the only government for that age was one-man rule. But his special aim was to mold the distracted Roman world into a mighty empire *under equal laws.* From the champion of the city mob against an aristocratic ring, he had become the champion of wide nationalities against the same narrow clique *and* the mob of a single city.

Already, as proconsul, on his own authority, *he had admitted the Cisalpine Gauls to all the privileges of citizenship.* In the midst of arduous campaigns, he had kept up correspondence with leading provincials in all parts of the empire. Other Roman conquerors had spent part of their plunder of the provinces in adorning Rome with public buildings. Caesar had expended vast sums *in adorning and improving provincial cities,* not only in his own districts of Gaul and Spain, but also in Asia and Greece. All previous Roman armies had been made up of Italians. Caesar's army was drawn from Cisalpine Gaul, and indeed partly from Gaul beyond the Alps. The subject peoples were learning to look to him as their best hope against senatorial rapacity ; and the great body of them wished for monarchy as the only escape from anarchy and oligarchic misrule.

552. Despotism a Medicine for Roman Decay. — To call Caesar right in his day, is not to call monarchy right in all times and places. No institution can be judged apart from the surrounding conditions. A " Caesar " in Rome in 200 B.C. would have been a criminal ; the real Caesar in 50 B.C. was a benefactor.

To say that monarchic government was the happiest solution *possible* for Rome is not to call it an unmixed good. No very happy outcome was possible to the Roman world, which was destitute of representative institutions and based on slavery. *But a despotism can get along on less virtue and intelligence than a free government can.* The evils that were finally to overthrow the Empire five centuries later *had all appeared in force in the last century of the Republic.* Ruin seemed imminent. The change to the imperial system restored prosperity and staved off the final collapse for a time as long as separates us from Luther or Columbus.

The interval was precious. Under Roman protection, priceless work was yet to be done for humanity. *But finally the medicine of despotism exhausted its good effect;* and the collapse, threatened in the first century B.C., came in the fifth century A.D.

553. Caesar crosses the Rubicon : Campaign in Italy. — Plainly Caesar had not made preparation for civil war. He had only one legion with him in Cisalpine Gaul. The other ten (an irresistible force) were far distant. But the Senate had at last made him choose between civil war and ruin both to himself and to all his noble hopes for the Roman world. Promptly he chose war, and, in January, 49 B.C., he led his one legion into Italy.

A Roman proconsul was strictly forbidden by law to bring an army into Italy; and the story goes that as Caesar crossed the Rubicon — the little stream between his province and Italy — he exclaimed, "The die is cast!" He never again looked back. With audacious rapidity he moved directly upon the much larger forces that ponderous Pompey was mustering slowly; and in sixty days, almost without bloodshed, he was master of the peninsula.

554. Spain and Greece. — Pompey still controlled most of the empire; but Caesar held the capital and the advantage of Italy's central position. Turning to Spain, in three months he dispersed the armies of Pompey's lieutenants there. Then following Pompey himself to Greece, in a critical campaign in 48 B.C. he became master of the world. The decisive battle was fought at *Pharsalus* in Thessaly. Caesar's little army had been living for weeks on roots and bark of trees, and it numbered less than half Pompey's well-provided troops. Pompey had his choice of positions, and he had never been beaten in the field. It looked for a time as though Caesar had rashly invited ruin. From such peril he snatched overwhelming victory.

The result is explained largely by the character of the opposing commanders. Pompey, despite his career of unbroken success, was "formed for a corporal and forced to be a general"; while Caesar, though caring not at all for military glory, was one of the greatest captains of all time. Almost as much the armies differed in real fighting power. Warde-Fowler's summary is masterly (*Caesar*, 299):—

POMPEY — the Copenhagen bust.

"The one host was composed in great part of a motley crowd from Greece and the East, representing that spurious Hellenic civilization that for a century had sapped the vigor of Roman life; the other was chiefly drawn from the Gallic populations of Italy and the West, fresh, vigorous, intelligent, and united in devotion and loyalty to a leader whom not even defeat could dishearten. With Pompeius was the spirit of the past; and his failure did but answer to the failure of a decaying world. With Caesar was the spirit of the future; and his victory marks the moment when humanity could once more start hopefully upon a new line of progress."

555. Remaining Campaigns. — Other wars hindered the great work of reorganization. Egypt and Asia Minor each required

a campaign. In Egypt, under the influence of the wily
queen, *Cleopatra*, Caesar seems to have wasted a few months.
He partly atoned for this delay by his swift prosecution of the

JULIUS CAESAR — the Naples bust.

war in Asia against the son of Mithridates. This campaign
Caesar reported pithily to the Senate, "I came, I saw, I conquered."

Meantime, Cato and the senatorial party had raised troops in Africa and called in the aid of the Numidian king. Caesar crushed them at *Thapsus*. Somewhat later, Pompey's sons and the last remnants of their party were overthrown in Spain at *Munda*.

Cato, stern Republican that he was, committed suicide at Utica, after this defeat, unwilling to survive the commonwealth. His death was admired by the ancient world, and cast an undeserved halo about the expiring Republican cause. More than anything else, it has led many later writers to treat Caesar as the ambitious destroyer of his country's liberty. The story may be read in Plutarch's *Life of Cato*.

556. Policy of Reconciliation. — The first efforts of the new ruler went to reconcile Italy to his government. All respectable

THE FORUM AT POMPEII.

classes there had trembled when he crossed the Rubicon, expecting new Marian massacres or at least a new war upon property. But Caesar maintained strict order, guarded property carefully, and punished no political opponent who laid down arms.

Only one of his soldiers had refused to follow him when he decided upon civil war. Caesar sent all this officer's property after him to Pompey's camp. He continued the same policy, too, toward the nobles who left Italy to join Pompey. On the field of victory, he checked the vengeance of his soldiers, calling upon them to remember that the enemy were their fellow-citizens; *and, after Pharsalus, he employed in the public service any Roman of ability, without regard to the side he had fought on.*

In Gaul, Caesar's warfare had been largely of the cruel kind so common in Roman annals; but his clemency in the civil war was without example. It brought its proper fruit: almost at once all classes, except a few extremists, became heartily reconciled to his government.

557. The Form of the New Monarchy. — For the most part, the old Republican *forms* continued. The Senate deliberated, and consuls and praetors were elected, as before. *But Caesar drew the most important powers into his own hands.* He received the *tribunician power*[1] *for life,* and likewise the authority of a *life censor.* He was already head of the state religion as *Pontifex Maximus.* Now he accepted also a *dictatorship for life* and the title of *Imperator* for himself *and his descendants.*

"Imperator" (from which comes our "Emperor") had meant simply "general," or "supreme commander." It suggested the absolute power of the master of the legions in the field. This power (the closest survival of the ancient *imperium* of the kings) was now conferred upon a civil officer in the city itself. Caesar's power really resulted from *a union* (§ 550) *of the tribunician power in the city* with *the proconsular power over all the provinces.* The title Imperator sums up this union, and indicates supreme authority throughout the empire.

Probably Caesar would have liked the title of king, since the recognized authority that went with it would have helped to maintain order. But when he found that term still hate-

---

[1] Caesar was from an old patrician family, and so could not hold the office of tribune (§§ 308, 324). Therefore he devised this new grant of "tribunician power," to answer the purpose.

ful to the populace, he seems to have planned this *hereditary Imperatorship* for the title of the new monarchy.

558. Constructive Reform. — Caesar's reforms embraced Rome, Italy, and the provinces. A bankrupt law released all debtors from further claims, if they surrendered their property to their creditors,[1] — and so the demoralized society was given a fresh start. A commission, like that of the Gracchi, was put at work to reclaim and allot public lands. Landlords were required to employ at least one free laborer for every two slaves. Italian colonization in the provinces was pressed vigorously. In his early consulship (59 B.C.), Caesar had refounded Capua; now he did the like for Carthage and Corinth, and these noble capitals which had been criminally destroyed by the narrow jealousy of the Roman oligarchy, rose again to wealth and power. Eighty thousand landless citizens of Rome were provided for beyond seas; and by these and other means the helpless poor in the capital, dependent upon free grain, were reduced from 320,000 to 150,000. Beyond doubt, with longer life, Caesar would have lessened the evil further.

Soon after the time of the Gracchi, it became necessary to extend the practice of *selling cheap grain* to *distributing free grain*, at state expense, to the populace of the capital. This became one of the chief duties of the government. To have omitted it would have meant starvation and a horrible insurrection. For centuries to come, the degraded populace was ready to support any political adventurer who seemed willing and able to satisfy lavishly its cry for "bread and games." To have attacked the growing evil so boldly is one of Caesar's chief titles to honor. His successors abandoned the task.

Rigid economy was introduced into all branches of the government. Taxation was equalized and reduced. A comprehensive census was taken for all Italy, and measures were under way to extend it over the empire, as was done later by Augustus. Caesar also began the codification of the irregular mass of Roman law, created a great *public* library, built a new

---

[1] This principle has been adopted in modern legislation.

Forum, began vast public works in all parts of the empire, and reformed the coinage and the calendar.

The Roman calendar had been inferior to the Egyptian and had got three months out of the way, so that the spring equinox came in June. To correct the error, Caesar made the year 46 ("the last year of confusion") consist of four hundred and forty-five days, and for the future, instituted the system of leap years, as we have it, except for a slight correction by Pope Gregory in the sixteenth century. The reform was based upon the Egyptian system (§ 23).

THE ROMAN FORUM TO-DAY — looking south.

559. The system of provincial government was made over. The old governors had been irresponsible tyrants, with every temptation to plunder. Under Caesar they became *trained servants* of a stern master *who looked to the welfare of the whole empire.* Their authority, too, was lessened, and they were surrounded by a system of checks in the presence of other officials who were dependent directly upon the Imperator. Soon the governors came to be paid fixed salaries, and were not allowed even to accept presents from the provincials.

560. Wider Plans. — Even more important was Caesar's plan *to put the provinces upon an equality with Italy.* " As provinces they were to disappear, to prepare for the renovated Romano-Greek nation a new and more spacious home, of whose several parts no one .existed merely for the others, but all for each and each for all." [1] *All Cisalpine Gaul was incorporated in*

THE ROMAN FORUM TO-DAY — looking north.

Italy, and Roman citizenship was enormously multiplied *by the addition of whole communities in Farther Gaul, in Spain, and elsewhere.* Leading Gauls, too, were *admitted to the Senate,* whose membership was raised to 900. It was a strange thing, no doubt, to see the tall, fair-haired barbarians, speaking with uncouth and almost unintelligible accent, intermingled on the benches of the Senatehouse with the proud Italian aristo-crats, even though the new members had laid aside the breeches, at which Rome jeered, for the white, purple-bordered togas of Senators. But Caesar hoped to make the Senate into a

[1] Mommsen, V, 415–417, also 427, 428.

Grand Council which would really represent the needs and feelings of the whole empire.

561. The Unforeseen Interruption. — In a few months Caesar had won the favor of the Roman populace, the sympathy of the respectable classes in Italy, and the enthusiastic reverence of the provinces. He was still in the prime of a strong and active manhood, and had every reason to hope for time to complete his work.

No public enemy could be raised against him within the empire. One danger there was: lurking assassins beset his path. But with characteristic dignity he quietly refused a bodyguard, declaring it better to die at any time than to live always in fear of death. And so, in the midst of preparation for expeditions against the Parthians and Germans to secure the frontiers, the daggers of men whom he had spared struck him down.

A group of irreconcilable nobles plotted to take his life, — led by the envious *Cassius* and the weak enthusiast *Brutus*, whom Caesar had heaped with favors. They accomplished their crime in the Senatehouse, on the

MARCUS BRUTUS. — A bust now in the Capitoline Museum.

Ides of March (March 15), 44 B.C. Crowding around him, and fawning upon him as if to ask a favor, the assassins suddenly drew their daggers. According to an old story not credited by all, Caesar at first stood on his defense and wounded Cassius; but when he saw the loved and trusted Brutus in the snarling pack, he cried out sadly, " Thou, too, Brutus!" and drawing his toga about him with calm dignity, he resisted no longer, but sank at the foot of Pompey's statue, bleeding from three and twenty stabs.

562. Caesar's Character. — Caesar has been called the one original genius in Roman history. His gracious courtesy and unrivaled charm won all hearts, so that it is said his enemies dreaded personal interviews, lest they be drawn to his side. Toward his friends he never wearied in forbearance and love. In the civil war young Curio, a dashing but reckless lieutenant, lost two legions and undid much good work — to Caesar's great peril. Curio refused to survive his blunder, and found death on the field; and Caesar, with no word of reproach, refers to the disaster only to excuse it kindly by reference to Curio's youth and to " his faith in his good fortune from his former success."

No man ever excelled Caesar in quick perception of means, fertility of resource, dash in execution, or tireless activity. His opponent Cicero said of him: " He had genius, understanding, memory, taste, reflection, industry, exactness." Numerous anecdotes are told of the many activities he could carry on at one time, and of his dictating six or more letters to as many scribes at once. Says a modern critic, " He was great as a captain, statesman, lawgiver, jurist, orator, poet, historian, grammarian, mathematician, architect."

No doubt, " Caesar was ambitious." He was not a philanthropic enthusiast merely, but a broad-minded, intellectual genius, with a strong man's delight in ruling well. He saw clearly what was to do, and knew perfectly his own supreme ability to do it. Caesar and Alexander are the two great captains whose conquests have done most for civilization. Both were snatched away from their work by untimely death. But Caesar, master in war as he was, always preferred statesmanship, and was free from Alexander's boyish liking for mere fighting.

The seven campaigns in the five years after Caesar crossed

the Rubicon left less than eighteen months for reorganization. Even this short time was *in broken intervals,* between wars, while, too, the whole routine of ordinary government had to be taken care of.   The new work remained incomplete; and it is not always possible to tell just what Caesar planned to do.   But that which was actually accomplished dazzles the imagination. Caesar's genius, too, marked out the lines, along which, on the whole, his successors, less grandly, had to move.

The murder was as imbecile as it was wicked.   It struck the wise monarch, but not the monarchy, and left Caesar's work to be completed by smaller men after a new period of anarchy. There is no better way to leave " the foremost man of all this world," than to use the words of Mommsen :   " Thus he worked and created as never any mortal before or after him ; and as a worker and creator he still, after two thousand years, lives in the memory of the nations — the first and the unique Imperator Caesar ! " [1]

For Further Reading. — *Specially suggested :* Davis' *Readings,* II, Nos. 50–54 (7 pages) ; and, on Caesar's constructive work, Warde-Fowler's *Caesar,* 326–359, or How and Leigh, 539–551.

Additional : Plutarch's *Lives* (" Caesar," " Pompeius," " Cicero ") ; Warde-Fowler's *Caesar.*

FROM JULIUS TO OCTAVIUS, 44–31 B.C.

563. Flight of the Assassins. — Caesar's assassination led to fourteen years more of dreary civil war, before the Empire was finally established on a firm foundation.   The murderers had hoped to be greeted as liberators.   For the moment they were the masters of the city ; but, to their dismay, all classes (even the senatorial order) shrank from them.   In a few days they found themselves in extreme peril.   At Caesar's funeral his lieutenant and friend, Marcus Antonius (" Mark Antony ") was permitted to deliver the usual oration over the dead body.   His artful and fiery words roused the populace to fury against the

---

[1] Mommsen's fine summary, V, 441–442, and, for Caesar's character, the famous passage, pp. 305–314, should be read, if in the school library.

assassins.[1] The mob rose; all Italy was hostile; and the conspirators fled to the Eastern provinces, where Caesar had given
governorships to some of them, and where the fame of Pompey
was still a strength to the aristocrats.

564. In the West, control fell to two men, *Antonius* and
Octavius Caesar. Antonius, the orator of Caesar's funeral, was

a dissolute, resolute, daring soldier. Octavius was
a grand-nephew and
adopted son of Julius
Caesar. He was an un-
known sickly youth of
eighteen, and at first he
owed his importance
wholly to his connection
with the great dictator.
Each party despised, or
thought to use, "the
boy"; but he soon proved
himself the shrewdest and
strongest statesman of the
empire.

At first these two lead-
ers were rivals, each posing as the heir and suc-

OCTAVIUS CAESAR (AUGUSTUS) AS A BOY.
A bust now in the Vatican.

cessor of Caesar. By the shrewd policy of Octavius, however,
they united their forces, and, to secure the West thoroughly,
they took into partnership Lepidus, governor of Gaul and Spain.

565. Second Triumvirate. — The three men got themselves
appointed *triumvirs*[2] by the Senate (43 B.C.). They were

---

[1] Davis' *Readings*, II, No. 53, gives Appian's account of this speech. The
student may compare it with Shakspere's version in his drama, *Julius Caesar*.

[2] The term *triumvirate* is official in this use, while the so-called *first* triumvirate (§ 540) was an unofficial league, or ring, of public men. The triumvirate of 43 B.C. was a triple dictatorship; just as the ancient decemvirate
(§ 364) was a dictatorship of *ten* men.

given unlimited power for five years to reorganize the state; and this dictatorship they afterward extended at will.

The union was cemented with blood. To their shame, the triumvirs abandoned the merciful policy of Caesar. Their first deed was to get rid of their personal foes in Italy by a horrible proscription. Each marked off on the fatal list those whose deaths he demanded, and each surrendered an uncle, a brother, or a trusting friend to the others' hate. It was at this time that Cicero perished, abandoned by his friend Octavius to the hatred of Antonius. More than three thousand victims — all men of high position — were slain, and opposition in Italy was crushed.

566. Philippi. — Meantime Brutus and Cassius had been rallying the old Pompeiian forces in the East. Their army contained troops from Parthia, Armenia, Media, Pontus, and Thrace. Octavius and Antonius marched against them. Again the East and West met in conflict, and again the West won — at *Philippi* in Macedonia (42 B.C.). The "Republicans" never appeared again in arms.

567. Actium. — Then Octavius and Antonius set aside Lepidus and divided the Roman world between themselves. Soon each was plotting for the other's share. The East had fallen to Antonius. In Egypt he became infatuated with Cleopatra until he lost care even for his military fame and sank into sensual indolence, with only fitful gleams of his old energy.

Octavius was preparing to take advantage of this condition, when a pretext was made ready to his hand. Antonius bestowed rich provinces upon Cleopatra, and, it was rumored, he planned to supplant Rome by Alexandria as chief capital. The West turned to Octavius as its champion. In 31, the rivals met in the naval battle of *Actium* off the coast of Greece. This was the third of the decisive battles in the establishment of the Empire: Philippi had decided between monarchy and republic; Actium decided who was to be the monarch. Like both Pharsalus and Philippi, it also was a victory for the West.

OCTAVIUS AUGUSTUS, 31 B.C.–14 A.D.

568. The Empire under Republican Forms. — Actium made Octavius sole master of the Roman world. He proceeded to the East to restore order and to annex Egypt as a province. On his return to Rome in 29 B.C., the gates of the Temple of Janus were closed, in token of the reign of peace.[1] He declared a general amnesty, and thereafter welcomed to favor and public office the followers of his old enemies; and, by prudent and generous measures, he soon brought back prosperity to long-distracted Italy. In 27, he laid down his office of triumvir (which had become a sole dictatorship), and declared *the Republic restored.* The act really showed that he was absolute master and that *the Empire was safely established.*

To be sure, Octavius himself wrote (*Monumentum,*[2] xxxiv): "After that time I excelled all others *in dignity*, but *of power* I held no more than those who were my colleagues in any magistracy." And indeed Republican *forms* were respected scrupulously. The Senate deliberated; the Assembly met to elect consuls and the other officers of the old constitution. But, even in form, the Senate at once gave back to Octavius his most important authority in various ways,[3] and, in reality, supreme power lay in his hands as Imperator,[4] — master of the legions. This office Octavius kept, and the Senate now added to it the new title *Augustus*, which had before been used only of the gods. It is by this name that he is thenceforth known in history.

---

[1] These gates were always open when the Romans were engaged in any war. In all Roman history, they had been closed only twice before, — and one of these times was in the legendary reign of King Numa.

[2] See References, page 464. The student must be on his guard in reading such "sources": Augustus' account is true to the letter, not to the spirit.

[3] There is an excellent statement in Pelham, 407–409.

[4] Octavius, however, was so intrenched in popular favor that he did not need open support from the army. The legions were stationed mostly on the frontiers, far from Italy. Octavius did create a body of city troops, nine thousand in number, the *praetorian guards*, to preserve order at Rome; but, during his rule, even these guards were encamped outside the city.

Augustus, however, carefully refused the forms and pomp of monarchy, and exercised his real control of the government

AUGUSTUS. — Now in the Vatican.

through disguised channels, instead of ruling openly as Julius had done. He lived more simply than many a noble, and walked the streets like any citizen, charming all by his frank courtesy. He preferred to all his other titles the name of honor, *Princeps* (" Prince "), which was popularly conferred upon him and which signified " the first citizen " of the Republic.

Character of Augustus. — In his early career Augustus had proven himself able, adroit, unscrupulous, cold-blooded. He had shrunk from no cruelty, and had been moved by no passion. But absolute power, which drives small men to frenzy, warmed this cold, unlovely schemer into something akin to greatness. He became an impartial and faithful ruler, and took up the work of the great Julius, though with a more cautious spirit. The remaining forty years of his life he gave to unremitting toil in strengthening the Empire and in improving the condition of the people throughout the Roman world.

BRIDGE BUILT BY AUGUSTUS AT RIMINI, — a town on the Adriatic ten miles south of the Rubicon. The structure is still in perfect condition.

569. The Augustan Age. — Augustus had not the ambition of an insatiable conqueror. He was no Alexander the Great. The Roman world was wide enough for him. Yet he extended the boundaries of the empire, chiefly in the north, to secure safer

frontiers (§ 605). But his chief work lay in internal organization. He organized the administration of the capital. A
police department, a fire department, and a department for the
distribution of grain, each under its proper head, were created,
and the work of founding colonies outside Italy was renewed
on a large scale. In like manner, the needs of Italy and the
provinces received careful attention. Throughout the empire,
peace reigned. Order was everywhere established. Industry
revived and throve. Marshes were drained. Roads were built.
A postal system was organized. A great census of the whole
empire was carried out. The number of citizens was increased
by about one fifth, and many important public works were
carried through.

Above all, out of the long century of anarchy, Augustus reared
a new structure of imperial government (§§ 592–599), building so firmly that even his death did not shake his work. For
three centuries (until the time of Diocletian, § 662) his successors for the most part followed his general policy. He was
also a generous and ardent patron of literature and art,[1] and the
many famous writers of his reign (§ 626) gave splendor to his
memory. In the history of Latin literature, the *Augustan Age*
is synonymous with "golden age." The chief cities of the
empire were adorned with noble buildings, — temples, theaters,
porticoes, baths. Augustus tells us in a famous inscription
that in one year he himself began the rebuilding of eighty-two
temples, and of Rome he said, "I have found it brick and
left it marble."

The details of much of his work will appear more fully in
chapter xxxviii.

570. The Worship of the Dead Augustus. — At the death of
Augustus, the Senate decreed him divine honors. Temples
were erected in his honor, and he was worshiped as a god.

---

[1] In this patronage Augustus was imitated by many great nobles and especially by his minister *Maecenas*, whose fame in this respect outshines even
that of his master. Maecenas was the particular friend and patron of Virgil
and Horace.

This kind of idolatry was not at all new to the Romans.
It was connected with the idea of ancestor worship in
each family, and with the general worship of ancient heroes,
and was a way of recognizing the emperor as "the father of all
his people." The practice was adopted for the successors of
Augustus, and this worship of dead emperors soon became the
most general and widespread religious rite in the Roman
world. It proved to be a great obstacle to Christianity.

FOR FURTHER READING. — On the work of Augustus : — *specially suggested :* Davis' *Readings*, II, No. 56 (a six-page series of extracts from Augustus' inscription known as the *Monumentum Ancyranum*), and No. 59; Pelham's *Outlines*, 398–406.

Additional : Pelham's account of the Triumvirate (*Outlines*, 357–397).

REVIEW EXERCISES

1. Catchword review, 49–27 B.C.
2. Review the growth of Roman citizenship from early times (see index).
3. Review the theme sentences at the heads of chapters in Roman history up to this point, and note how they apply.
4. Fact drills.
   a. List of important battles in Roman history, to this point, with results of each.
   b. List of Rome's wars after 390 B.C.
   c. Dates. Continued drill on the list given on p. 295. Fill out the following table, and group other dates around these: —

510 (?) B.C.	"Expulsion " of the kings.	
390 "	Sack of Rome by the Gauls.	
367 "	___. ___ ___	
266 "	___ ___ ___	
218 "	(Cf. 222 B.C. in Greek History.)	
146 "	___ ___ ___	
133 "	___ ___ ___	
49 "	___ ___ ___	
31 "	___ ___ ___	

JESUS CHRIST AND HIS WORK

Jesus Christ, the Redeemer of the world, was born during the reign of Augustus and closed His life work under Tiberius. It seems more practical to treat of both His coming and His work in this place.

571. The Birth and Death of Jesus Christ. — The downfall of the national kingdom under the Maccabees had been hastened

CHURCH OF THE NATIVITY AT BETHLEHEM — on the site of the stable where Christ was born.

by the domestic strifes between the Pharisees and Sadducees, the religious leaders of the people. At times neither party shrank from violence and fraud to obtain its ends. The mass of the nation, however, though finally led into destruction by these blind guides, meant to be faithful to the law of Moses. The regulations concerning abstinence were observed generally, and the whole male population made the prescribed yearly pilgrimages to the temple of Jerusalem to worship the One

true God "Who made heaven and earth." They also perse-
vered in waiting for "Him who was to come," the "Anointed
of the Lord," the "Son of David," though their very idea of
the promised Redeemer had become much obscured and on the
whole more carnal than the words of Holy Scripture would
allow. The belief that a world power would take its rise
from among the Jews had even spread over wide countries in
Asia.

Finally, "the fullness of time" arrived, the moment when
the Almighty was to make good His promise solemnly given
to Adam and repeated to the patriarchs and prophets of Israel.
In Jerusalem an old man by the name of Simeon must have
attracted attention even during the religious and political conflicts which kept his country astir. It was rumored that he
would not see death until he had seen the "Anointed of the
Lord."

"In the forty-second year of Octavian Augustus, when the whole
world was at peace, JESUS CHRIST, eternal God and Son of the eternal
Father, desirous to sanctify the world by His most merciful coming, was
born in Bethlehem of Juda, having become man, of Mary the Virgin." —
(*Entry of the birth of Our Savior in the Roman martyrology.*)

The world at large took no notice of this most memorable
event. Even the nation whose whole existence had no other
purpose but to prepare for His coming, and which had been
crying to Heaven for it, now that He was there acted as if He
were of no concern for its national life; yet several happenings which took place during His infancy and childhood could
have convinced them of the extraordinary nature of this child.
Later during His public teaching He proved Himself by words
and miracles to be indeed the Messiah foretold by the prophets,
the Son of God. But then, Pharisees and Sadducees combined
against Him and He was crucified under the Roman governor
Pontius Pilate, having been delivered up by His own people.
After His death and resurrection, the organization founded by
Him, His Church, began to spread over the whole world.

The death of Jesus Christ on the cross was the redemption of the world. In view of this divine death the original relation of God to the human race was restored in all essential parts, and new favors of infinite magnitude were bestowed upon all those who would believe in Him. The promise of this event consoled the first parents when, after their fall, they were exiled from paradise. This event was foretold to the patriarchs and prophets, and foreshadowed for more than a thousand years in the sacrificial rites of the divine service held in the grandest temple of the world. This sacrifice of the God-Man on the cross is the central fact of human history.

572. The Doctrine of Christ was partly as old as the human heart, but partly it represented new gifts of knowledge from the fountainhead of divine truth. The Law of Nature, expressed in the Ten Commandments, again became the moral code of the world. Christ thereby restored the true relation of man to the one God " Who made heaven and earth." The emphasis now laid on the sacredness of human life and human personality wrought a complete revolution in the position of the poor, the slave, the child, and the woman. The family not only became again what the Creator of mankind wanted it to be when He instituted it in the beginning, but essentially more. Matrimony being made a sacrament, the family, too, was raised to the sphere of the supernatural. The seven sacraments, a system so sublime that only a divine intellect could devise it, affect and sanctify the entire human life with their silent influence. But the crowning point of Christ's teaching is the law of charity, " the bond of perfection." Charity sees in every man a brother redeemed by the blood of Christ and makes the practice of kindness a duty and even the characteristic feature of the new religion.

This religion, at the same time, satisfies the general craving of man for something like God's presence, and the desire to approach His infinite majesty with worthy sacrifices of adoration and petition. In the Holy Eucharist we possess " the tabernacle of God among mer " and are enabled to glorify Him by the sacrifice of the Mass, the ever repeated sacrifice of the

Cross: "In every place there is sacrifice and there is offered to my name a clean oblation." (Mal. i, 10, 11.)

Christianity solves the problem of suffering. Adversities and tribulations are only the means to obtain a more blissful future; even death loses its terror by the certainty of eternal life and a glorious resurrection.

Finally, all the abstract as well as all the practical truths are brought nearer to our human feelings and sympathies by the reality of the life among us, in a servant's garb, of the God-Man, Jesus of Nazareth, Who became like ourselves in all things, sin excepted.

573. The Christian Organization. — It is an essential tenet of Christ's doctrine that those who wish to receive the benefits resulting from His teachings must belong to a visible society, in which there is a well-defined difference between the governing and the governed. This society He called His Church. Christ's Apostles were commissioned to "preach to all nations, baptize them, and teach them to observe all things whatsoever I have commanded you." The nations of the world, therefore, were obliged to admit their preaching, to allow themselves to be baptized, and to submit to the further directions of the Apostles concerning the service of God. It is evident that this arrangement was to last until the end of the world, as long as men will be born with the consequences of the sin of Adam. Whatever offices Christ instituted for the purpose of the salvation of mankind were to exist as long as the world stands, and whatever assistance He promised will ever be granted to the incumbents of the offices he established.

Paramount among these offices is the position which was first entrusted to *St. Peter.* He was to be the rock upon which the Church is built. All the strength and stability of the Church was to come through him, just as an edifice cannot be stronger than the foundation upon which it rests. Not St. Peter's learning or strength of character was to keep him from error; no, but a special providence of God would govern all his official acts. "I have prayed for thee, that thy faith fail not," said Christ to him, and the effect of this divine prayer enabled him to strengthen his brethren. "Upon this Rock I shall build my Church, and the powers of hell shall not prevail against her." (Matt. xvi, 18.) St. Peter accordingly holds the place of eminence in the records of the young Church. He it is who, contrary to the views of the converts from Judaism, admits the first pagan, the Roman centurion Cornelius, to all the rights and privileges of Christians. (Acts x, 11.)

When St. John, the last of the Apostles, died in the year 100 A.D., there was in every greater community one *bishop* with full jurisdiction and responsibility, but assisted by priests and deacons and sometimes by other bishops. The subdivision into regular parishes took place rather slowly and only in the course of many centuries. Distant country districts, however, were taken care of in a somewhat parish-like fashion. (*Catholic Encyclopedia*, art. "Bishop," p. 582.) A measure of later times was also the erection of *Archbishoprics*, or ecclesiastical provinces, and of the *Patriarchal office* between the archbishops and the head of the Church.

In the beginning, the terms "bishop" (Latin, *Episcopus*) and "priest" (Latin, *Presbyter* or *Sacerdos*) designated promiscuously either of the two offices; but it was always exactly known which men were bishops in the present sense of the word, and which were "priests of the second rank." In view of the harmony and unselfishness prevalent in the first times, the faithful were allowed a certain influence in the management of the communities. Even in the selection of priests and bishops their voice was heard. But it was always the Apostles or the governing bishops, on whom the decision finally depended and who laid their hands on those thus presented.

FOR FURTHER READING. — Any chapter of the New Testament. Very appropriate in this connection is "The Foundation of the Church," Lecture III of Finlay, *The Church of Christ.*

CHAPTER XXXVII

THE EMPIRE OF THE FIRST TWO CENTURIES, 31 B.C.–180 A.D. AUGUSTUS TO AURELIUS

(The Story of the Emperors)

574. Treatment of this Period. — With the Age of Augustus the history of the Empire ceases to be centered in the city of Rome. Nor is it centered even in the emperors. Much depends, of course, upon the ruler ; but the great movements go on in a good deal the same way, no matter who sits upon the throne. Our study will not concern itself with court scandal. For the next three centuries our interest lies not so much in a *narrative* of any kind as in a *topical* survey of the institutions of the Empire, upon which, in large measure, modern society rests.

Such a topical study is given in the *next* chapter. But, since it is convenient to refer to the reigns as dates, *this* chapter gives a brief summary of the emperors. *This chapter is for reading and reference, not for careful study* at this stage. In *review*, *after* studying the topical treatment, important names and dates in this chapter may be memorized.

THE JULIAN CAESARS

575. Augustus, 31 B.C.–14 A.D. — The work of Augustus has been discussed, but a brief summary is added here. Augustus fixed the imperial constitution, *establishing despotism under Republican forms.* He *fixed the boundaries* of the empire (meeting with a check from the Germans in the defeat of the *Teutoburg Forest,*

A GOLD COIN OF AUGUSTUS.

§ 605). He restored *order*, promoted *prosperity*, carried out a *census* of the empire, extended *Roman citizenship*, constructed many vast *public works*. His age was the "golden age" of Latin literature. He "found Rome brick and left it marble." During his reign, *Christ was born.* To the end Augustus kept perfectly his chosen part of an uncrowned "first citizen." No doubt it was with gentle irony at this pretense, that he said to the friends about his death-bed — like an actor in the epilogue to a Roman drama — "If you think I have played well my part on the stage of life, applaud."

576. Tiberius, 14–37 A.D. — Augustus was succeeded by his stepson *Tiberius,* whom he had adopted as his heir. Tiberius was stern, morose, suspicious; but he was also an able, conscientious ruler. The nobles of the capital conspired against him, and were punished cruelly. The populace of Rome, too, hated him because he restricted the distribution of grain and refused to amuse them with gladiatorial sports. To keep the capital in order, Tiberius brought the praetorians (§ 569, note) into the city. He also made the law of treason (*majestas*) apply to *words* against the emperor, as well as to *acts* of violence; and he encouraged a system of paid spies. Such wretches sometimes *invented* plots, when there were none, so as to share in the confiscation of the property of the man they accused. So the people of Rome with some reason looked upon Tiberius as a gloomy tyrant. *But in the provinces he was proverbial for fairness, kindness, and good government.* "A good shepherd shears his sheep; he does not flay them," was one of his sayings. On one occasion, after a great earthquake in Asia Minor, he rebuilt twelve cities which had been destroyed there. In this reign occurred *the crucifixion of Christ.*

The great authority for this period is the Roman historian *Tacitus.* But Tacitus is affected by the prejudice of the Roman nobles, and he paints Tiberius in colors much too dark. (Munro's *Source Book,* 140–150, gives extracts.) The worst cruelties of Tiberius' reign were due, too, to his misplaced trust in *Sejanus,* his minister and commander of the praetorians. For a time this infamous miscreant virtually ruled the capital, while Tiberius, in disgust, withdrew to his beautiful retreat on the island of *Capri*, near the Bay of Naples, to manage the affairs of the empire at large. Finally Sejanus plotted against the life of Tiberius, and was himself put to death.

577. Caligula, 37–41. — In the absence of nearer heirs, Tiberius adopted his grandnephew *Caligula*. This prince had been a promising youth, but, crazed by power, or by a serious illness, he became a capricious madman, with gleams of ferocious humor. "Would that the Romans had all one

RUINS OF THE CLAUDIAN AQUEDUCT.
Near Rome; from a photograph. See also the same in the view of the *Appian Way*, on page 344.

neck!" he exclaimed, wishing that he might behead them all at one stroke. His deeds were a series of crimes and extravagant follies. The gladiatorial shows and the wild-beast fights of the amphitheater fascinated him strangely. It is said that sometimes, to add to the spectacle, he ordered spectators to be thrown to the animals, and he entered the arena himself as a gladiator, to win the applause of the people whom he hated. After four years, he was slain by officers of his guard. Thus ended one of the strangest figures who have ever possessed supreme power.

578. Claudius, 41–54. — Caligula had named no successor. For a moment the Senate hoped to restore the old Republic ; but the praetorians (devoted to the great Julian line) set up as emperor *Claudius*, the uncle of Caligula. Claudius had been a timid, gentle, awkward, well-meaning scholar and an author of several tiresome books. He ruled, in a large measure, through two of his freedmen, who committed many crimes and heaped up huge fortunes for themselves, but who were capable administrators. Claudius himself gave his time faithfully to the hard work of governing, with fairly good results. His reign is famous for a *great extension of citizenship* to provincials and for *legislation to protect slaves* against cruel masters.[1] *The Roman conquest of southern Britain* took place in this reign (§ 606).[2]

579. Nero (54–68), Claudius' stepson, became emperor as a likeable boy of sixteen. He had been trained by the philosopher *Seneca* (§ 627), and for two thirds of his reign he was ruled by this great thinker and by other wise ministers. The young emperor cared little for affairs of government, but was fond of art, and ridiculously vain of his skill in music and poetry. After some years his fears, together with a total lack of principle, led him to crime and tyranny. He poisoned his half-brother, and had his ambitious mother murdered. Wealthy nobles were put to death

BRONZE COIN OF NERO — to commemorate the closing of the doors of the Temple of Janus (cf. § 568).

in numbers, and their property confiscated, Seneca himself be-

---

[1] Munro, *Source Book*, 187.　　　　[2] Special report.

ing among the victims. Like Caligula, Nero entered the lists as a gladiator, and he sought popular applause also for his music and dancing.

During this reign, *half of Rome was laid in ashes* by the "Great Fire."[1] For six days and nights the flames raged

AGRIPPINA — mother of Nero.

unchecked, surging in billows over the slopes and through the valleys of the Seven Hills. By some, Nero was believed to have ordered the destruction, in order that he might rebuild in more magnificent fashion. On better authority he was reported to have enjoyed the spectacle from the roof of his palace, with music and dancing, singing meanwhile a poem he had composed on the "Burning of Troy."

The Christians also were accused of starting the fire, out of their supposed "hatred for the human race." (See below § 657.) Some color may have been given to the accusation by the fact that the Christians believed in a final destruction of the world. Making this a pretext Nero, to turn attention from himself, began the *first persecution of the Christians*, one of the most cruel in all history. Victims, tarred with pitch, were burned as torches in the imperial gardens, to light the indecent revelry of the court at night; and others, clothed in the skins of animals, were torn by dogs for the amusement of the mob. The persecution, however, was *confined to the capital*.

---

[1] Davis' *Readings*, II, No. 65.

Nero sank deeper and deeper in vice and crime. Except for the disgrace, his capricious tyranny did not reach far beyond the city of Rome; but finally the legions in the provinces revolted. The tyrant was deserted by all, and the Senate condemned him to death. To avoid capture he stabbed himself, exclaiming, "What a pity for such an artist to die!"

THE FLAVIAN CAESARS

580. The year 69 was one of wild confusion. The legions in Spain had proclaimed their general *Galba* emperor. Galba was soon thrust from the throne by *Otho*, supported by the praetorians. Otho, in turn, was overthrown by *Vitellius*, at the head of the army of the Rhine. Then the legions in Syria proclaimed their general, *Flavius Vespasianus* (*Vespasian*). From his name *Flavius*, he and his two sons are known as the *Flavian emperors*.

581. Vespasian (70–79) was the grandson of a Sabine laborer. He was a rude soldier,— stumpy in build, blunt in manner,

THE COLISEUM (*Flavian Amphitheater*) TO-DAY (§ 622).

homely in tastes, but honest, industrious, experienced, and broad-minded. He had distinguished himself in Britain and in Asia, and he knew the needs of the empire. He quickly made himself master, and brought to an end the disorder into which Nero's misrule had plunged the state. His reign was economical and thrifty, and was notable as an era of great public works and magnificent buildings (§ 622). He loved simple manners and homely virtues, and hated shams. So, at the end, as he felt the hand of death upon him, he said, with grim irony, "I think I am becoming a god," — in allusion to the fact that dead emperors were worshiped as divinities.

582. The siege and destruction of Jerusalem was the most striking event in Vespasian's reign. The kingdom of the Jews, which the heroic Maccabees established (§ 467), had been made a tributary state by Pompey, during his Eastern wars,

DETAIL FROM THE TRIUMPHAL ARCH OF TITUS — showing the seven-branched candlestick taken from the Temple at Jerusalem.

in the year 63 B.C. From 41 A.D. to 44, it was under Herod II (Agrippa), who was much loved by the people.

After his death, Judea was again placed under Roman governors and trouble began at once. It was not so much the severity of the Roman rule as the fact that they were now directly under the dominion of a foreigner, which drove the Jews into rebellion. The idea of a worldly Messias as an irresistible hero who would free the people of God, was fostered by the ever-increasing party of the Zealots, until it rose to a national frenzy. The avarice, cruelty, and incapacity of the governors did the rest. The peaceably inclined either joined the Zealots or fled the country, in which anarchy soon became general. Finally, in 66 A.D., the Roman officers could no longer maintain themselves, and the death struggle of the Jewish nation began.

Nero sent his general Vespasian with three legions to put down this revolt. Vespasian was about to lay siege to Jerusalem, when the struggle for the Empire called him to Italy. In the year 70 A.D., his oldest son, *Titus*, besieged and destroyed the city. The Jews made a desperate resistance, and when the walls were finally stormed, many of them slew their women and children and died in the flames. The miserable remnant for the most part were doomed to slavery. Simon Bar Giora, one of the principal Zealot leaders, was cruelly executed in Rome during the magnificent triumph of the conquerors. (See Morisson, *Jews under Rome*, pp. 153–180.)

583. Titus (79–81) had been associated in the government with his father. His kindness and indulgence toward all classes made him the most popular of all the emperors. Once at supper, not able to remember that he had made any one happy during the day, he exclaimed, " I have lost a day ! "

The most famous event of his two years' reign was the *destruction of Pompeii and Herculaneum*. (See map following p. 498.) The volcano Vesuvius was believed extinct, and its slopes were covered with villas and vineyards. With little warning it belched forth in terrible eruption, burying two cities and many villages. In the eighteenth century, by the chance digging of a well, the site of Pompeii, the largest of the two cities, was rediscovered. In recent years it has been excavated; and to-day a visitor can walk through the streets of an ancient city, viewing perfectly perserved houses, shops, temples, baths, theaters, ornaments, and utensils of the men of eighteen hundred years ago, just as they chanced to stand when the volcanic ashes and lava flood came upon them.[1]

584. Domitian (81–96), younger brother of Titus, was a strong, stern ruler. His general *Agricola* completed *the conquest of*

COIN OF DOMITIAN — struck to commemorate the completion of the Coliseum.

Britain to the highlands of Caledonia (Scotland). The southern part of the island was now to enjoy a long peace. Roman roads were built; camps grew into rich cities; merchants thronged to them; the country was dotted with beautiful villas. Britain became a Roman province with Roman civilization. To protect the southern districts against the inroads of the unconquered highlanders, Agricola built a line of fortresses from the Forth to the Clyde.

At home, *Domitian reduced the power of the Senate*, disregarding the threadbare pretense of a joint rule by Senate and Princeps. He took the office of *Censor for life*, and so could legally make and unmake senators at will. This power was retained by his successors, even when it was not used; and Domitian's reign therefore marks an important change toward the outward *form* of monarchy.

These facts led the Roman nobles to conspire against him. He put down their plots with cruelty, earning from their sympathizers the name of tyrant. Finally he was assassinated by members of his household. In this reign took place the *second persecution of the Christians.*

---

[1] Several illustrations of ancient life, as revealed by excavations at Pompeii, have been given in preceding pages.

THE ANTONINE CAESARS

585. Nerva (96–98). — The Senate chose the next ruler from
its own number; and that emperor with his four successors governed in harmony with it. . These princes are known as the *five
good emperors*. The first of the five was *Nerva*, an aged senator *of Spanish descent*, who died after a kindly rule of sixteen
months.

586. Trajan (98–117 A.D.) was the adopted son of Nerva.
He was a *Spaniard by birth* and a great general. Once more
the boundaries of the empire were advanced, though with
doubtful wisdom (§ 606). Trajan conquered *Dacia*, a vast district north of the Danube, and then attacked the Parthians in
Asia. That power was humbled, and new provinces were added
*beyond the Euphrates. These victories mark the greatest extent
of the Roman empire*.

Trajan's reign was the most famous in Roman history for the
*construction of roads and other useful public works throughout the
provinces*. Despite his wars, his rule was humane as well as
just. By loans from the treasury, he encouraged the cities of
Italy *to care for and educate many thousands of poor children*,[1]
and slaves were protected by strict laws against cruelty. A
slight persecution of Christians took place under this emperor.

587. Hadrian, a Spanish kinsman of Trajan, succeeded him
(117–138 A.D.). He was a wise and prudent man, and his rule
was one of *general reorganization*. He reformed the army and
strengthened its discipline, and at the same time he looked to
the fortification of the exposed frontiers. His most famous
work of this kind was the wall (Hadrian's Wall) in Britain,
from the Solway to the Tyne, to replace the less satisfactory
wall of Agricola, farther to the north. Wisely and courageously, he abandoned most of Trajan's conquests in Asia (disregarding the sneers and murmurs of nobles and populace), and
withdrew the frontier there to the old line of the Euphrates.

---

[1] Capes' *Antonines*, 19–21, gives the details.

Hadrian spent most of his twenty years' rule in inspecting the provinces. Now he is in Britain, now in Dacia; again in Gaul, or in Africa. Syria and Egypt were both visited. He spent several months in Asia Minor, and in Macedonia; and twice he visited Athens, his favorite city, which he adorned with splendid buildings. Indeed, everywhere memorials of his stay sprang up in useful public works, — aqueducts, baths, schools,

RUINS OF THE TEMPLE OF ZEUS BUILT BY HADRIAN AT ATHENS. — Note the Corinthian architecture (§ 154).

basilicas (§ 623), highways, temples. Hadrian organized the civil service of the empire, — the whole body of officers who carried on the administration. Every emperor, necessarily, had been surrounded by assistants and advisers; and sometimes these had been vicious adventurers or greedy freedmen. The nobles had felt it beneath their dignity to take regular office as secretary to a "Princeps." But Hadrian brought nobles and "knights" (§ 480) into such public service, and built up a body of trained public servants, who thereafter continued from reign to reign, with definite customs and ideals of government. In particular, Hadrian brought together the heads of important administrative divisions into a true *Privy Council*, to advise and inform the Emperor. A painful illness seems to have changed his mild character towards the end of his life. He passed a large number of unjust death sentences, even against senators. His adopted son and future successor, however, succeeded in many cases to prevent executions.

THE TOMB OF HADRIAN.

588. Antoninus Pius, 138–161 A.D., who had been adopted by Hadrian, was his successor. His reign was singularly *peaceful*, and might well have given rise to the saying, "Happy the people whose annals are meager." Antoninus himself was a pure and gentle spirit. His kindness and liberality, which he showed chiefly during an earthquake in Asia and a famine in Rome, won him general love and esteem and the title "Father of Mankind." He recognized merit everywhere, undertook great works for the embellishment of the capital, supported educational efforts, and devoted himself untiringly to the promotion of public welfare. Barbarous nations elected him arbiter of their disputes. Yet he proved himself a good commander in some expeditions in Africa and Britain. The chief feature of his rule was legislation *to prevent cruelty to slaves and to lessen suffering.*

MARCUS AURELIUS.

His adopted son wrote of him : "He was ever prudent and temperate. . . . There was in his life nothing harsh, nothing excessive, nothing overdone." (Davis' *Readings*, II, No. 69, gives two pages of this noble tribute.)

589. Marcus Aurelius Antoninus (161–180). — He was a *philosopher and student.* He belonged to the Stoic school (§ 317), but in him that stern philosophy, without losing its lofty tone, was softened by a gracious gentleness. His *Thoughts* (§ 628) is one of the noblest books written by a pagan.

The tastes of Marcus Aurelius made him wish to continue in his father's footsteps, but he had fallen upon harsher times. The barbarians renewed their attacks upon the Danube, the Rhine, and the Euphrates. The Emperor and his lieutenants beat them back, but at the cost of almost incessant war.

During one of these expeditions, in 174, an event took place which is famous as the ".miracle of the thunderstorm." The Romans were suffering great distress from lack of water, so much so that a defeat by the barbarians seemed certain. There was, however, in the army a detachment from a legion called FULMINEA, the "thundering legion," which was stationed somewhere in Armenia and consisted largely, if not entirely, of Christians. Upon the prayers of these Christians a thunderstorm arose and such a torrent of rain poured down, that it did not only refresh the Romans but also inflicted considerable damage on the enemy and facilitated the victory.[1]

A great Asiatic plague, too, swept over the empire. Not only did it cause terrible loss of life : it also demoralized society. The populace thought the disease a visitation from

COMMODUS — From a coin of
192 A.D.

---

[1] See *Catholic Encyclopædia*, under "Thundering Legion."

offended gods, and, in many parts of the empire, they were frantically excited against the Christians who refused to worship the gods of Rome. Thus the reign of Aurelius was marked by a cruel persecution.

590. Commodus, 180–192 A.D. — The "five good emperors" end with Marcus Aurelius. His son, Commodus, was an infamous wretch who repeated the crimes and follies of the worst of his predecessors. He was finally murdered by his officers.

591. Summary 31 B.C.–192 A.D.[1] — The first long period of 224 years was an age of settled government and regular succession, except for two or three slight disturbances and for the disorders of the one terrible year 69, at the close of Nero's reign. That brief anarchy subdivides the period into nearly equal parts. The five Julian emperors (*Romans* and related to the great Julius) covered just a century. After the three Flavians (*Italians*) came the six Antonines,[2] who also covered nearly a hundred years. They were *provincials*. The majority of the fourteen rulers were good men. Nearly all were good rulers. The few tyrants had short reigns, and their cruelties did not much affect the empire outside the capital city.

---

[1] We now count our years from the birth of Christ. The first Christians could not do this. Circumstances forced them to follow the methods which were in general use and which varied greatly. In the first half of the sixth century Dionysius Exiguus, abbot of a Roman monastery, "most learned in both languages," began the dating of events according to our present "*Christian Era.*" It is now admitted that he fixed the birth of the Savior about four years too late, an error which does not interfere with the practical application of the system. It took several centuries more before the Christian Era had dislodged all the others. (See *Catholic Encyclopedia*, under "Dionysius Exiguus.")

[2] This name (from Antoninus Pius) is sometimes applied to this entire group, from Nerva to Commodus.

CHAPTER XXXVIII

THE EMPIRE OF THE FIRST TWO CENTURIES

(*A Topical Treatment*[1])

THE IMPERIAL GOVERNMENT

Seldom has the government of so large a part of the world been carried on for so long a time with such good order. — MOMMSEN.

592. The "Principate." — We have noted how Augustus cloaked the new Monarchy in old Republican forms. In all his *words* and outward *forms*, he conciliated Republican feelings far more than Julius Caesar had done. *The Senate* exercised much real power. It was no longer a close oligarchy. It had become a chosen body of distinguished men, selected by the emperors from all parts of the realm; and it gave powerful expression to the feelings and needs of the empire. On the whole, this continued to be true for *three* centuries. Most of the better emperors treated the Senate with respect, and welcomed its help in carrying on the government.

Some writers call the government from Augustus to Diocletian by the name *Dyarchy*, to signify a "*joint rule*" of emperor and Senate. In reality, however, a strong emperor was an absolute monarch whenever he cared to assert his authority. Indeed, constitutionally, he could change the membership of the Senate at will (§ 584). Another term for the *disguised* despotism of these centuries is the *Principate*, from the title Princeps (§ 569).

---

[1] The plan of this chapter involves some repetition of chapter xxxvii. It is convenient, also, to carry some of the topics on through the following third century A.D., though that century is not treated as a whole until chapter xxxix.

593. Power of the Emperors.[1] — Even under Augustus, the duties of the consuls and other officers of the early Republican constitution were confined more and more to the city of Rome. For the government of the Empire, there grew up an imperial machinery, *centralized in one man.*

This machinery was partly old in origin, and partly new. Following the example of Julius Caesar (§ 557), each emperor *concentrated in his own person* a number of the most important offices of the later Republic, — *powers which had originally been intended to check one another.* Each emperor held the *tribunician power* and the *proconsular power* throughout all the provinces for life, and so was *leader of the city and master of the legions.* Usually he became *Pontifex Maximus,* the head of the state religion. With the power of *censor,* he could *appoint and degrade senators,* and so *could* at any time make himself absolute master of the Senate, or, as *Princeps,* he could lead the debates in the Senate, and virtually control its decrees, which had become the chief means of lawmaking. He appointed the governors of the provinces[2] and the generals of the legions, the city prefect, the head of the city police, and the prefect of the praetorians; and, at will, he called together his chief officers and friends to advise and assist in carrying on the government. Each successor of Augustus was hailed *Imperator Caesar Augustus.* (The imperial title *Caesar* survives in Kaiser, and perhaps in Tsar.)

594. The establishment of the Empire was a gradual process. It is dated sometimes from the year 27 B.C., when Octavius received the title of Augustus; sometimes from 31 B.C., when he became sole dictator; sometimes from 49 B.C., when Caesar crossed the Rubicon to become master of Rome.

But the process was not complete, even with Augustus. The

---

[1] There is an admirable discussion, unhappily long, in Pelham, 398–449, and a shorter one in Capes' *Early Empire,* 11–18.

[2] The Senate appointed the governors for some of the older provinces; but even for these the candidate favored by the Princeps was practically sure of appointment.

practical master was not yet the acknowledged monarch.   Another step was taken when, on Augustus' death, all the world
quietly recognized that he must have a successor.   To be sure,
in granting titles and authority to Tiberius, the Senate made
no reference to the *term* of his office; and Tiberius pretended
that he would lay it down as soon as the state no longer
needed him.   No one took these words seriously, however;
and soon it became the practice for the Senate to confer all the
imperial powers upon each new "imperator" *for life*.   The
appointment of the emperor by the praetorians, and then by
the legions, was another step toward making plain the character of the new military despotism.   Domitian's assumption
of a life-censorship (§ 584), and Hadrian's creation of a standing Privy Council, were other steps.   The most significant step
of all was yet to come — with Diocletian (§§ 662 ff.).

595. The uncertainty about the succession was the weakest
point in the imperial constitution.   Unlike Caesar, Augustus
did not venture to make any of the imperial titles hereditary.

INTERIOR OF COLISEUM TO-DAY.

In theory, just as the early Republican magistrates nominated their successors, so each emperor nominated the ablest man in his dominions to the Senate for his successor. But this principle was confused from the first by family claims, and later by the whims of the legions. The monarchy was neither elective nor hereditary, but in time it came to combine the evils of both systems. The best results were secured when an emperor, during his lifetime, associated a younger man in some of the imperial offices, and had him formally appointed by the Senate as the successor. Even then, the praetorian guards in Rome had to be conciliated by presents from each new ruler; and, after these two centuries, the throne became, for a hundred years, the sport of military adventurers (§§ 639–646).

MUNICIPAL GOVERNMENT

596. At Rome, the Assembly ceased to be a lawmaking body at the beginning of the Empire. During the forty years of Augustus, it continued to go through the *form* of electing consuls and other officers, and Augustus canvassed in person for its votes for himself and for his nominees. But Tiberius transferred all such elections to the Senate, and the Roman Assembly faded away. Even the *local* government of the capital (like that of Alexandria and some of the other *largest* cities) was placed wholly in the hands of officers *appointed* by the emperor or by the Senate.

597. Municipal institutions, for local self-government, did survive, however, in the thousands of smaller cities throughout the empire. Long after the Roman Assembly had passed away, popular assemblies in the cities of Gaul and of Dacia continued to elect each year their consuls (a sort of twin mayors), aediles, to oversee the police and the public works, and quaestors, to care for the city finances. Election placards, painted on the walls of the houses in Pompeii (§ 583) show that the contests for office were very real and quite modern in method.

Some 1500 political posters were painted on the walls of Pompeii's streets. Probably these all concerned one recent election; for when their purpose was served, the space would be whitewashed over, and used for new notices. These notices are painted in red letters from two to ten inches high, on a white background. Each man, apparently, could use his own wall to recommend his favorite candidates ; but hired and zealous "bill-posters" blazoned their placards even upon private buildings and upon funeral monuments. A baker is nominated for quaestor (city treasurer) on the ground that he sells " good bread " ; and nearby a leading aristocrat is supported as one of whom it is known that " he will guard the treasury." Trade gilds make some of these nominations, and even women take part in them, — though of course not in the voting. One " wide-open " candidate for " police commissioner " is attacked by an ironical wag in several posters — as in one that reads, "All the late-drinkers ask your support for Valia for the Aedileship.[1] "

In each town of this sort, the ex-magistrates made up a town council (senate), which voted local taxes, expended them for town purposes, and looked after town matters in general. The council's ordinances were submitted, in some towns, to an Assembly of citizens for ratification.

598. Tendency to centralize Local Government. — In the early Empire the spirit of local self-government was intense. Gradually, however, the interference of provincial governors sapped this hopeful political independence. The many varieties and irregularities of the local institutions in the different cities of a province caused vexatious delays, no doubt, to the central goverment. Strong rulers were sometimes disposed to sweep away the local institutions, in order to make the administration more uniform and to secure quicker results.

Finally, it came about that minute details were referred to the governor, and sometimes by him to the emperor, for decision. Oftentimes, the better intentioned the ruler, the stronger this evil tendency. Pliny (§ 628) was a worthy servant of a noble emperor; but we find Pliny writing to ask Trajan whether he shall allow the citizens of a town in his province of Bithynia to *repair* their public baths, as they desire, or

---

[1] Davis' *Readings*, II, No. 99, gives several of these Pompeiian posters, with other Pompeiian inscriptions. There is an interesting discussion of local city government under the Empire in Capes' *Early Empire*, 193–198.

whether he shall require them to *build new ones*,[1] and whether he shall not interfere to compel a wiser use of public moneys lying idle in another town, and to simplify varieties of local politics in other cities.[1]

Trajan, wiser than his minister, gently rebukes Pliny's over-zeal in this last matter and will have no wanton meddling with established rights and customs. But later rulers were not so far-sighted, and local life did decline before the spirit of centralization. Still, the *forms* of this municipal life never died out. The Empire passed them on through the Middle Ages [2] to our modern world.

599. The Provinces. — Above the towns there was no local *self*-government. The administration [3] of the provinces was regulated along the lines Julius Caesar had marked out, and the better emperors gave earnest study to provincial needs. But the imperial government, however paternal and kindly, was despotic and absolute. *Provincial Assemblies*, it is true, were called together sometimes, especially in Gaul, but only to give the emperor information or advice. These Assemblies were made up of delegates from the various towns in a province. At first sight, they have the look of representative legislatures, but they never acquired any real political power, except that they could petition the emperor against a tyrannical or incapable governor, — a petition always sure of careful consideration.

IMPERIAL DEFENSE

600. The Army. — The standing army counted thirty legions. The auxiliaries and naval forces raised the total of troops, at the highest, to some four hundred thousand. They were stationed almost wholly on the three exposed frontiers, — the Rhine, the Danube, and the Euphrates. The inner provinces,

---

[1] Read the excellent extracts from this correspondence in Davis' *Readings*, II, No. 75.   [2] See § 711, note.

[3] "Administration," in this common use, refers to the *machinery* by which the will of the government is carried out.

as a rule, needed only a handful of soldiers for police purposes. Twelve hundred sufficed to garrison all Gaul.

It is a curious fact that the many modern states which now fill the old Roman territory, with no outside barbarians to dread, keep always under arms twelve times the forces of the Roman emperors. One chief cause of the Empire, it will be remembered, had been the need for better protection of the frontiers. This need the Empire met nobly and economically.

601. Sources. — Roman citizens had long ceased to regard military service as a first duty. The army had become a standing body of disciplined mercenaries, with intense pride, however, in their fighting power, in their privileges, and in the Roman name. Even in the Early Empire, the recruits were drawn from the provinces rather than from Italy; and more and more the armies were renewed *from the frontiers where they stood.* In the third century *barbarian mercenaries*

A GERMAN BODYGUARD. — A detail from the Column of Marcus Aurelius.

were admitted on a large scale, and in the following period they came to make the chief strength of the legions. From the hungry foes surging against its borders, the Empire drew the guardians of its peace.

602. Industrial and Disciplinary Uses. — The Roman legions were not withdrawn wholly from productive labor. In peace, they were employed upon public works. "They raised the

marvelous Roman roads through hundreds of miles of swamp
and forest; they spanned great rivers with magnificent bridges;
they built dikes to bar out the sea, and aqueducts and baths to
increase the well-being of frontier cities." The steady discipline
of the legions afforded also a moral and physical training, for
which there were fewer substitutes then than now.

The legions proved, too, a noble school for commanders.
Merit was carefully promoted, and military incompetence disappeared. Great generals followed one another in endless series,
and several of the greatest emperors were soldiers who had
risen from the ranks.

603. A Social Value.— At the expiration of their twenty
years with the eagles,[1] the veterans became full Roman citizens
(no matter whence they had been recruited). They were commonly settled in colonies, with grants of land. Here they
became valuable members of the community, and, in particular,
they helped to mix the many races of the Roman world into one.
Spanish troops were stationed in Switzerland; Swiss, in Britain; Panonians, in Africa; Illyrians, in Armenia. They settled and married in these new homes. Augustus said that he
had spent over ten million dollars in purchasing lands for military colonies in the provinces; and this process continued,
generation after generation.

604. The Frontiers as Augustus found them.— Julius Caesar
left the empire bounded by natural barriers on three sides and
on part of the fourth: the North Sea and the Rhine to the
northwest, the Atlantic on the west, the African and Arabian
deserts on the south, Arabia and the upper Euphrates on the
east, and the Black Sea to the northeast.

The Euphrates limit was not altogether satisfactory. It surrendered to Oriental states half the empire of Alexander, and
let the great Parthian kingdom border dangerously upon the
Roman world. Julius seems to have intended a sweeping
change on this side; but none of his successors, until Trajan,

---

[1] The Roman military standards — with the form of eagles — are commonly
referred to in this way.

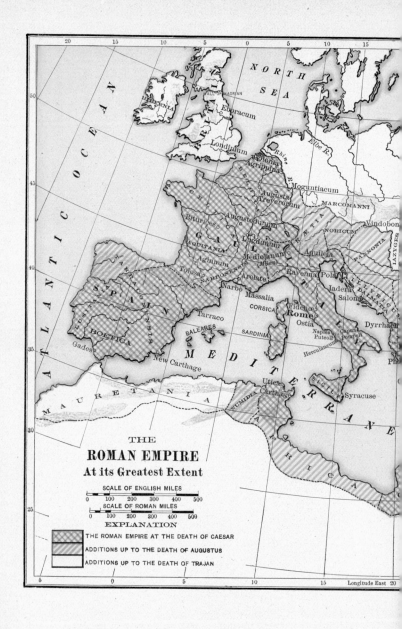

THE
ROMAN EMPIRE
At its Greatest Extent

SCALE OF ENGLISH MILES
0 100 200 300 400 500

SCALE OF ROMAN MILES
0 100 200 300 400 500

EXPLANATION

THE ROMAN EMPIRE AT THE DEATH OF CAESAR

ADDITIONS UP TO THE DEATH OF AUGUSTUS

ADDITIONS UP TO THE DEATH OF TRAJAN

NORTH SEA

ATLANTIC OCEAN

MEDITERRANEAN

HIBERNIA

Eboracum

Londinium

Colonia Agrippina

Moguntiacum

MARCOMANNI

Augusta Treverorum

Bituriges

GAUL

AQUITANIA

Augustodunum

Lugdunum

Mediolanum (Milan)

RAETIA

NORICUM

Vindobon

PANNONIA

IAZYGES

Aginnum

Tolosa

NARBONENSIS

Arelate

Narbo

Massalia

Aquileia

Ravenna

Pola

ILLYRICUM

DALMATIA

Iadera

Salona

SPAIN

TARRACONENSIS

Tarraco

BALEARES

CORSICA

SARDINIA

Fidenae

Rome

Ostia

Naples

Puteoli

Capua

Pompeii

ITALY

Dyrrhac

BOETICA

Gades

New Carthage

Utica

Carthage

NUMIDIA

AFRICA

Herculaneum

SICILY

Syracuse

Pha

MAURETANIA

Longitude East 20

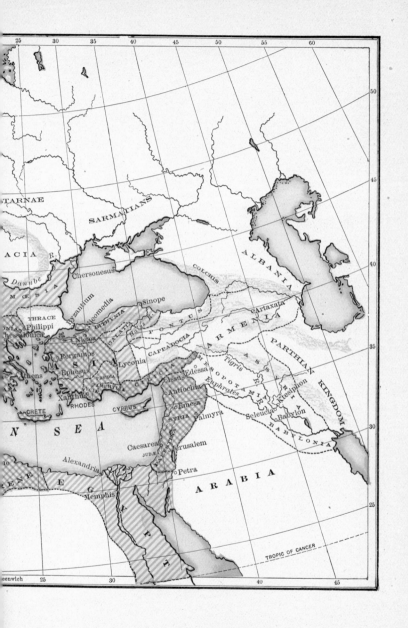

seriously thought of one.   The only other unsafe line was on the north, in Europe, between the Rhine and the Black Sea.

605. The Frontiers as Augustus corrected them. — Augustus aimed to make this northern line secure.   He easily annexed the lands south of the lower Danube (modern Bulgaria); and, after many years of stubborn warfare, he added the remaining territory between the Danube and the Alps.   The four great provinces, formed out of the conquered regions, were rapidly colonized and Romanized; and the line of the Danube was firmly secured.

In Germany, Augustus wished to move the frontier from the Rhine to the Elbe.   The line of the Danube and Elbe is much shorter than that of the Danube and Rhine, though it guards more territory (see map).   Moreover, it could have been more easily defended, because the critical opening between the upper courses of these rivers is filled by the natural wall of the mountains of modern Bohemia and Moravia.   But here the long success of Augustus was broken by his one failure. The territory between the Rhine and the Elbe was subdued, it is true, and it was held for some years.   But in the year 9 A.D. the Germans rose again under the hero Hermann. Varus, the Roman commander, was entrapped in the *Teutoburg Forest*, and in a three-days' battle his three legions were utterly annihilated (Davis' *Readings*, II, No. 62).

The Roman dominion was at once swept back to the Rhine. This was the first retreat Rome ever made from territory she had once occupied.   Roman writers recognized the serious nature of the reverse.   Said one of them: " From this disaster it came to pass that that empire which had not stayed its march at the shore of ocean did halt at the banks of the Rhine."

The aged Augustus was broken by the blow, and for days moaned repeatedly, "O Varus, Varus ! give me back my legions ! "   At his death, five years later, he bequeathed to his successors the advice to be content with the boundaries as they stood.   This policy was adopted, perhaps too readily.

Tiberius did send expeditions to chastise the Germans, and Roman armies again marched victoriously to the Elbe. The standards of the lost legions were recovered; but no attempt was made to restore the lost Roman province, and the Rhine became the accepted boundary.

Still, the general result was both efficient and grand. About the civilized world was drawn a broad belt of stormy waves and desolate sands, and at its weaker gaps — on the Rhine, the Danube, the Euphrates — stood the mighty, sleepless legions to watch and ward.

606. The Extreme Limits. — Claudius renewed Caesar's attempt to conquer *Britain* (§ 578). If the work had been car-

PART OF THE AQUEDUCT OF CLAUDIUS (cf. page 468), now used as a gate in a wall. Note parts of the arches in the wall.

ried to completion, it might have been well; but, after long, costly wars, the Roman power reached only to the edge of the highlands in Scotland. Thus a new frontier was added to the long line that had to be guarded by the sword, and little strength was gained to the empire. Trajan, with more provocation than that which had lured Claudius into Britain, added *Dacia* north of the lower Danube, and *Armenia, Mesopotamia,* and *Assyria,* in Asia (§ 586).

The two latter provinces were at once abandoned by Trajan's successor (§ 587). Dacia, however, even more than Britain, became Roman in speech, culture, and largely in blood ; and though it was abandoned after only a hundred years, in the weak period toward the close of the third century (§ 646), still the modern Roumanians claim to be Roman in race as well as in name. Britain was the next province to be given up, when the frontier began to crumble in earnest in the next great period of decay (§ 720). It had been Roman for three hundred and fifty years.

607. Frontier Walls. — Since the attempt had failed to secure the mountain barrier of Bohemia for part of the northern frontier, Domitian wisely constructed a line of forts and castles, with occasional long stretches of earth walls between, to protect the open frontier of 336 miles between the upper Danube and the middle Rhine. Better known, however, is the similar work built shortly after in Britain, called Hadrian's Wall (§ 587). Its purpose was to help shut out the wild Picts of the north. It extended from the Tyne to the Solway, and considerable remains of it still exist. Under Antoninus, a like structure was made farther north, just at the foot of the highlands, from the Clyde to the Forth, along the line of Agricola's earlier rampart.

Hadrian's Wall was seventy miles long, extending almost from sea to sea. It consisted of three distinct parts, (1) a stone wall and ditch, on the north ; (2) a double earthen rampart and ditch, about one hundred and twenty yards to the south ; and (3) between wall and rampart a series of fourteen fortified camps connected by a road. The northern wall was eight feet broad and twenty feet high, with turreted gates at mile intervals, and with numerous large towers for guard-stations.

LIFE IN THE EMPIRE

608. Good Government even by Bad Emperors. — The first two centuries were one long period of good government for the

Roman world. If the Caesars at Rome were weak or wicked, their follies or crimes were felt only by the nobles of the capital. The system of government had become so fixed that the world moved on along much the same lines whether a philanthropic Aurelius or a mad Caligula sat upon the throne.

It was not without good reason that the provincials raised their altars to more than one prince for whom the citizens [of Rome], also not without good reason, sharpened their daggers." — FREEMAN, *Chief Periods*, 69.

" It was in no mean spirit of flattery that the provincials raised statues and altars to the Emperors, to some even of the vilest who have ever ruled. . . . The people knew next to nothing of their vices and follies, and thought of them chiefly as the symbol of the ruling Providence which, throughout the civilized world, had silenced war and faction and secured the blessings of prosperity and peace, before unknown." — CAPES, *Early Empire*, 202.

609. Peace and Prosperity. — The year 69 (§ 580) was the only serious break in the quiet of the first two centuries. In Britain there was a revolt, under the queen *Boadicea*,[1] in 58 A.D. ; but, like the rising of the Germans under Hermann (§ 605), this was really a *frontier* war. A rebellion of some Gallic tribes, under their gallant chieftain *Civilis*,[1] was connected with the disorders of the year 69. The rebellion of the Jews (§ 582) came at almost the same time, and, to the empire at large, even this was only a trivial disturbance. " The distant clash of arms upon the Euphrates or the Danube scarcely disturbed the tranquillity of the Mediterranean lands."

As far as peace in itself is a blessing, the vast empire certainly was happy. Unfortunately, under the existing conditions the evils of Roman society had the best opportunity to increase unchecked (§§ 629 ff.). The slaves and the poor enjoyed little of the general prosperity. The dissolution of morals grew more and more. Without any obstacle the most shocking pagan rites found their way into ever wider circles (§ 657, *e*). Besides, the long peace contributed no doubt a very great share towards making the population less warlike. The legions were recruited chiefly from the frontier provinces and from the very barbarians against whom

---

[1] Special report.

they fought (§ 601). Thus for several reasons the time of this glorious "Roman peace" prepared the later downfall of the empire.

If it is true that the same countries never again saw so long a time of undisturbed tranquillity, they certainly never again saw a period of so general immorality, highly cultured barbarism, and enervation. Yet such reflexions should not diminish our admiration for what we may call the material splendor of these two hundred years and for the Roman genius and that universal-minded statesmanship which brought it about.

The providential importance of this remarkable period unquestionably lay in the opportunity it offered for the propagation of Christianity. The priest or bishop could travel unmolested. The Christian business man, soldier, or slave carried with him the Glad Tiding to the ends of the Roman domain and beyond. (See §§ 654, 652.)

610. Wealth and City Growth. — Everywhere rude stockaded villages changed into stately marts of trade, huts into palaces,

AQUEDUCT NEAR NÎMES, FRANCE, built by Antoninus Pius to supply the city with water from distant mountain springs; *present condition* of the long gray structure, where it crosses a deep valley. The water channels were carried across streams and valleys on arches like these, and through hills by tunnels. Some of these Roman aqueducts remained in use till very recent days.

footpaths into paved Roman roads. Roman irrigation made part of the African desert the garden of the world, where, from drifting sands, desolate ruins mock the traveler of to-day.[1] The regular symbol of Africa in art was a stately virgin with arms filled with sheaves of golden grain. In Gaul, Caesar found no real towns; but in the third century that province had 116 flourishing cities, with baths, temples, amphitheaters, works of art, roads, aqueducts, and schools of eloquence and rhetoric. One of the two Spanish provinces had 174 towns, each with a charter from some emperor defining its rights of self-government. Such grants were common, especially in the Western half of the empire.

Particular attention was paid in cities to the water supply. That of Rome was better than that of London or Paris to-day. The illustration on the preceding page explains the construction of Roman aqueducts. The cities had more and better public baths than the modern capitals of Europe or the cities of America. In Rome the *public* baths would accommodate more than 60,000 people at one moment.

The early Christians, though loyally patriotic, had no natural reason to be overfriendly toward the Pagan Empire, which persecuted them. But Tertullian, one of the greatest of the Christian authors wrote, about 200 A.D. : —

"Each day the world becomes more beautiful, more wealthy, more splendid. No corner remains inaccessible. Every spot is the scene of trade. Recent deserts now bloom with verdure. Forests give way to tilled acres; wild beasts retreat before domestic animals. Everywhere are houses, people, cities. Everywhere there is life."

611. Forms of Industry. — The empire pulsed with busy, throbbing life. In the main, it was a city life; but most cities rested *directly* on agriculture. There were a few great centers of trade, — Rome, with perhaps two million people, Alexandria and Antioch with half a million each, and Corinth, Carthage, Ephesus, and Lyons (Lugdunum) with some 250,000 each. These commercial cities were also centers of manufactures.

---

[1] Under French rule North Africa, in the last half of the nineteenth century, began to recover some of its former prosperity.

A letter, ascribed to Hadrian, declares that in Alexandria "No one is idle; some work glass, some make paper (papyrus), some weave linen. Money is the only god." The looms of Sidon and other old Phoenician cities ceaselessly turned forth their precious purple cloths. Miletus, Rhodes, and the other old Greek cities of the Asiatic coast, were famous for their woolen

A CITY GATE AT POMPEII.

manufactures. Syrian factories poured silks, precious tapestries, and morocco leather into the western trade. The silversmiths of Ephesus were numerous enough to stir up a formidable riot, on occasion.[1] In Rome the bakers' gild listed 254 different shops, and there were 2300 places where olive oil was for sale.[2]

In these larger towns there was always a rabble; and in

---

[1] *Acts of the Apostles*, xix, 23–41. That passage gives also a valuable picture of city political life under the empire.

[2] Olive oil had many uses in the ancient world, and was a necessity in every household.

Rome, Alexandria, and Antioch, the government regularly supported the unemployed by distributions of free grain. But after all, these large cities, taken all together, were only a small part of the Roman world, — holding perhaps a twentieth or twenty-fifth of the total population. Most of the other seventy-five or eighty million people lived in small towns, of 20,000 and less. We should learn to think of the empire as mapped into *municipia*, and understand that *each of these was a farming district, with the town for its core.*

The devouring of small farms by large landlords, which had ruined much of Italy in the second century B.C., began to show ominously in the provinces by the second century A.D.; but on the whole, for this period, especially in the western half of the empire, the farmers were a plain, sturdy peasantry, owning their own lands, or, generation after generation, tilling the same farms as tenants.[1] Market gardening was a profitable employment near the cities, and Varro (§ 625) tells of two old soldiers who, with half an acre of land, made $500 a year from their bees, — an amount equivalent to an income of several thousand dollars to-day.

As often in the Old World, this farming peasantry lived, not each family on its own farmstead as with us, but either in the city or in small hamlets grouped about it. (Cf. § 15.) Each town had its numerous gilds of artisans, weavers, fullers, and shopkeepers. Slaves performed most of the unskilled hand-labor in the towns. Thus a baker or a mason would usually have two or three or a dozen slaves to work under his direction. For the "gentleman class" (nobles) there were the occupations of law, the army, literature, and the farming of large estates. A middle class furnished merchants (as distinguished from shopkeepers), engineers, architects, bankers, teachers, and many of the men of letters. In medicine there was considerable subdivision of labor. We read of dentists, and of eye-and-ear specialists. Many so-called physicians

---

[1] For this last condition, even in Italy (in the North), see Davis' *Readings*, II, No. 88.

were cheap quacks, and many were slaves; but the more skilled members of this profession came from the middle class. One physician speaks of his income as 600,000 sesterces a year (about $24,000 in our money, or nearly $150,000 a year in purchasing power to-day); and many of them left large fortunes. Medicine, commerce, and banking, however, were not for the noble class.

612. Communication and Travel. — The roads were safe. Piracy ceased from the seas, and trade flourished as it was not to flourish again until the days of Columbus. The ports were crowded with shipping, and the Mediterranean was spread with happy sails. One Roman writer exclaims that there are as many men upon the waves as upon land.[1] An immense traffic flowed ceaselessly between Europe and Central Asia along three great arteries: one in the north by the Black Sea and by caravan (along the line of the present Russian trans-Caspian railway); one on the south by Suez and the Red Sea; one by caravan across Arabia, where, amid the sands, arose white-walled Palmyra, Queen of the Desert.

From frontier to frontier, communication was safe and rapid. The grand military and post roads ran in trunk-lines — a thousand miles at a stretch — from every frontier toward the central heart of the empire, with a dense network of ramifications in every province. Guidebooks described routes and distances. Inns abounded. The imperial couriers that hurried along the great highways passed a hundred and fifty milestones a day; *and private travel, from the Thames to the Euphrates, was swifter, safer, and more comfortable than the journeys in many modern lands until the days of railroads.*

Naturally, travel was very popular. The gravestones of ancient Syrian merchants are found to-day scattered from Roumania to France, and the monuments of Gallic traders in

---

[1] The ancient merchant vessel was not unlike the sailing ships engaged in Mediterranean coasting trade to-day. Multitudes of them could carry two or three hundred passengers, besides their freight, and we hear of an occasional "three-decker" which could carry a thousand or fifteen hundred people.

Asia witness to this ancient intercourse. One Phrygian merchant who died at home asserts on his gravestone that he had sailed "around Greece to Italy *seventy-two times!*" And men traveled for pleasure as well as for business. There was a keen desire in each great quarter of the empire to see the other regions which Rome had molded into one world. It seems to have been at least as common a thing for the gentleman of Gaul or Britain to visit the wonders of Rome and of the Nile as for the modern American to spend a summer in England and France. One great annoyance to modern travel, indeed, was absent. One language, or at most, two, answered all needs from London to Babylon. Whole families took pleasure trips in a body ; and, quite in modern fashion, they sometimes defaced precious monuments of the past with their scrawls. One of the most famous statues of Egypt bears a scratched inscription that it has been visited by a Roman "Gemellus" with "his dear wife, Rufilla" and their children. And a lonely Roman lady scrawled upon one of the pyramids her tearful lamentation that she was compelled to see these wonders "without you, dearest of brothers."

Much of this travel was in wheeled and cushioned carriages, which rolled smoothly along the perfectly faced stones of the Roman roads. But many people chose instead luxurious litters, each swung along by its eight even-paced Cappadocian slaves.[1] The motion was so easy, we are told by ancient authors, that reading and even writing were pleasant employments in them — as in a modern "Pullman."

Strangely enough, though the imperial postal service for official business was well organized throughout the empire, there was no public postal service for *private* correspondence. This was one reason why merchants had to travel so inces-

---

[1] This whole treatment is largely based on an invaluable study by William Stearns Davis, — *The Influence of Wealth in Imperial Rome.* That book is not designed for young high school students; but the lucid and interesting style makes it usable even by them, and a teacher will find many valuable readings in it.

santly in person — instead of doing business through corre-
spondents and agents in other provinces. There were many
private post companies, however, to carry people and letters
from city to city, and the wealthy sometimes sent letters
to distant lands by trusted slaves.

613. " **Foreign** " **Commerce.** — It was to be expected, with so
much travel in the Roman world, that the products of one
part of the empire would be known and used in every other
part. We are hardly surprised to find that women of the Swiss
mountains wore jewelry made in Asia Minor, or to learn that
Italian wines were drunk in Britain and in Cilicia. *But there
was also a vast commerce with regions beyond the boundaries
of the empire.* Roman writers are provokingly brief and vague
in their many allusions to this trade, and the barbarians, of
course, have left no records of it. We know that Caesar found
that the trader had preceded his legions to the most distant parts
of Gaul in his day ; and, just as English and Dutch traders
journeyed three hundred years ago far into the savage interiors
of America for better and better bargains in furs, so did
the indomitable Roman trader continue to press on into regions where the legions never camped. We know they visited
Ireland ; and both by sea and by overland routes from the
Danube, they found their way to the Baltic shores. Thence
they brought back amber, furs, and flaxen German hair with
which the dark Roman ladies liked to deck their heads. Such
goods the trader paid for in toys and trinkets and in wine and
sometimes in Roman arms and tools — as our colonial traders
got their furs from the Indians with beads and whisky and guns
and powder and knives. Roman iron arms have been found on
the Jutland coast,— probably left there in such commerce.

On the south, East Africa and Central Africa rewarded
the venturesome trader with ivory, spices, apes, rare marbles,
wild beasts, and negro slaves.

On the east, the trader reached civilized lands. Unhappily
it is just this trade that has the least history. A Latin poet
of Hadrian's time speaks of the " many merchants " who

reaped "immense riches" by venturesome voyages over the Indian Ocean "to the mouth of the Ganges." India, Ceylon, and Malasia sent to Europe indigo, spices, pearls, sapphires, and other precious stones. The East did not care for Western products in exchange, but had to be paid in coin; and in Trajan's time, Pliny the Elder (§ 627) estimated that India drew $2,000,000 a year in gold and silver away from the Roman world. From shadowy regions beyond India came the silk yarn which kept the Syrian looms busy. Chinese annals of the year 166 A.D. tell of an "embassy" from the Emperor Marcus Aurelius; and 200 years later they speak again of the port of Canton receiving from Roman traders glass and metal wares, amber, jewels, and drugs.

614. Banking and Panics. — Banking had long been an important business. The *early* Romans and Greeks often buried their money in the earth for safe keeping, but that practice had long ceased except with such ignorant or slothful rustics as are rebuked in Christ's parable. Instead, all over the Roman world, men placed money with the bankers, to receive it again with interest. The bankers, of course, had earned the interest (and their own profits) by lending the money out meanwhile at higher rates than they paid. As with our own day, so in the Roman empire, a large part of the business was done on borrowed capital furnished by bankers.

And as trade grew, it added another feature to the banking business. Innumerable merchants in every part of the empire would come, day by day, to owe one another large sums. To carry the coin from one frontier to another for each such debt would be costly — and indeed impossible for business of such volume as had grown up. So banks, as with us, had come to sell "bills of exchange," or drafts. A merchant in Alexandria who owed money to a citizen of Cologne could pay the amount into a home bank (plus some "premium" for the bank's service) and receive an order for the amount on a bank in Cologne. This slip of paper would then be sent to the creditor in Cologne, who could present it at his bank and get his money.

The Cologne bank, sooner or later, would have occasion to sell a draft upon the Alexandria bank, in like fashion. At some convenient time, the two banks would have to settle their balance in coin; but the amount to be carried from one to the other would be very small, compared with the total amount of business.

With such a wide-spread system of "credits," the Roman world, like our own, had its money flurries and "panics." A crop failure in Africa, or the loss of a richly laden merchant fleet by a hurricane in the Red sea, or a period of rash speculation in Gaul, was felt at once in the money market in every part of the empire. The failure of a great banking house in Antioch might drag down others in Rome and Alexandria. Thus in the year of Christ's crucifixion there happened the first great money panic in history, — an event which made much more noise in the Roman world than the vague rumor of a slight disturbance in Judea.

The Emperor Tiberius checked the disaster by promptly placing $4,000,000 in coin from the imperial treasury in certain central banks, to be loaned to hard-pressed debtors, and by ordering that debtors who could give ample security in real estate should have a three-years' extension of time. But it is clear that if the Roman world had many of the advantages which the modern world finds in a credit system, it had also the modern troubles.[1]

615. Taxation and Roads. — Taxation by the central government was heavy, no doubt, but during these two centuries it was less in amount than most of the provinces had had to pay to their earlier native rulers. Every farmer and landlord paid a tax on land. In the towns, every citizen and every trader paid a poll tax. Tariffs were sometimes collected at the frontiers of a province on goods entering or departing. Roman citizens paid a tax of five per cent on inheritances. Furthermore, Africa and Egypt paid a peculiar tax in grain. The Egyptian grain tax, some 144,000,000 bushels each year, was carried to Rome to feed the hungry masses, — largely in free distributions. Although the imperial tax was heavy, it was usually collected with the greatest possible consideration. In

---

[1] See Davis' *Readings*, II, No. 76. Dr. Davis has a striking picture of this panic in the opening chapter of his *Influence of Wealth in Imperial Rome*.

a bad season, in a given province, the amount was lessened promptly by imperial order. If an Egyptian village, in a dry year, received too little water from the Nile for its usual crop, the tribute in grain was remitted or lightened.

What did the government do for the people in return for the taxes it took from them? Many things which a government does to-day, it did not do then. It did not build hospitals or asylums, or maintain complete systems of education, or care systematically for the public health. It had no efficient laws for the preservation of morality or public decency. It was utterly powerless in protecting the working classes. But two things in particular it did do. It kept the "good Roman peace" of which so much has been said above, *and it built and kept in repair the Roman roads,* — the bonds of union and means of intercourse in the Roman world. This meant a huge expense. We happen to be informed that in Hadrian's rule a mile of road in southern Italy cost $4000. On the frontiers and in mountain districts, the cost must have been many times that amount. The one island of Sicily had a thousand miles of such roads. In France, 13,200 miles of road can still be traced. Every province shared in this great work, which was looked after by a special department of the government. Besides the imperial roads, each province was expected and sometimes required to build many radiating branches at its own expense.

616. The World becomes Roman. — Julius Caesar had begun the rapid expansion of Roman citizenship beyond Italy. Through his legislation the number of adult males with the franchise rose from some nine hundred thousand to over four million. Augustus was more cautious, but before his death the total reached nearly five million.[1] This represented a population of some twenty-five million people, in an empire of something more than three times that number, including slaves. Claudius made the next great advance, after a curious

---

[1] Augustus is our authority for both these sets of figures. See extract in Davis' *Readings,* II, No. 56.

debate in the Senate,[1] raising the total of adult male citizens, fit for military service, to about seven millions. Hadrian completed the enfranchisement of Gaul and Spain. The final step was taken a little later by Caracalla (§ 642), who made all free inhabitants of the empire full citizens in 212 A.D. This completed the process of political absorption that began when the Romans and Sabines of the Palatine and Quirinal made their first compact (§ 338).

By the time of Caracalla the franchise was no longer exercised, for the Roman Assembly had ceased except as a mob gathering. Moreover, most of the provincials had already come to possess many of the advantages of citizens. Caracalla probably acted from a desire to increase the revenues, — since citizens were subject to some taxes not paid by noncitizens. Still the gift of complete citizenship, with its eligibility to office and its rights before the law, was no slight gain. The apostle Paul before Festus, lays stress upon his privileges as a Roman citizen (Acts xvi, 37).

617. Unity of Feeling. — By its generous policy, by its prosperity and good government, by its uniform law, and its means of close communication, the empire won spiritual dominion over the hearts and minds of men. Rome molded the manifold races of her realms into one, — not by conscious effort or by violent legislation, but through their own affectionate choice. This Romanization of the provincials was very different from the violent measures used by Russia or Germany to-day to nationalize their mixed populations, and more like the unconscious absorption of many stocks in the United States. *Gaul, Briton, Dacian, African, Greek, called themselves Romans.* They were so, in life, thought, and feeling. The East kept its Greek tongue and a pride in its earlier civilization (§ 475); but it, too, turned from the glories of Miltiades and Leonidas for what seemed the higher honor of the Roman name. *And East and West alike used the Roman law and Roman political institutions.*

---

[1] Cf. § 587. Read the speech of the Emperor (Davis' *Readings*, II, No. 63), and note also the freedom and character of interruptions by the Senators.

The union of the Roman world was not, like that of previous empires, one of external force.[1] It was in the inner life of the people. The provincials had no reason to feel a difference between themselves and the inhabitants of Italy. From the provinces now came the men of letters who made Roman literature glorious, and the grammarians who defined the Roman language (§§ 626 ff.). They furnished nearly all the emperors.

PALACE OF THE ROMAN EMPERORS AT TRIER.

In their cities arose schools of rhetoric that taught the use of Latin even to youth born by the Tiber.

The poet Claudian, an Egyptian Greek of the *fourth* century, expressed this noble unity in patriotic lines : —

> " Rome, Rome alone has found the spell to charm
> The tribes that bowed beneath her conquering arm;

---

[1] Note that the physical conquests of Rome were chiefly made under the Republic. *The Empire was a defensive civilized state; and its wars, with rare exceptions, were not for conquest.*

> Has given one name to the whole human race,
> And clasped and sheltered them in fond embrace, —
> Mother, not mistress; called her foe her son ;
> And by soft ties made distant countries one.
> This to her peaceful scepter all men owe, —
> That through the nations, wheresoe'er we go
> Strangers, we find a fatherland.　Our home
> We change at will; we count it sport to roam
> Through distant Thule, or with sails unfurled
> Seek the most drear recesses of the world.
> Though we may tread Rhone's or Orontes'[1] shore,
> Yet are we all one nation evermore."

And at the very close of the dark fourth century, when to us the glory of Rome seems to have departed (§ 687), a Christian writer dwells glowingly upon this same unity : " We live, no

THE BLACK GATE (*Porta Nigra*) AT TRIER.
This is called the noblest Roman ruin in Germany.

---

[1] A Syrian river.

matter where we are in the world, *as fellow-citizens*, . . . inclosed within the circuit of one city and grown up at the same domestic hearth . . . an equal law has made all men equal." (See the rest of this tribute in Davis' *Readings*, II, No. 115.)

618. Diffusion of Social Life. — Life did not remain centered at Rome as in the first century B.C. To condense a passage from Freeman's *Impressions of Rome* : —

" Her walls were no longer on the Tiber, but on the Danube, the Rhine, and the German Ocean. Instead of an outpost at Janiculum, her fortresses were at York and Trier. Many of the emperors after the first century were more at home in these and other distant cities than in the ancient capital, — which they visited perhaps only two or three times in a reign, for some solemn pageant.[1] *In these once provincial towns the pulse of Roman life beat more strongly than in Old Rome itself.*"

619. The Universities. — The three great centers of learning were Rome, Alexandria, and Athens. In these cities there were *universities*, as we should call them now, with vast libraries and numerous professorships. The early Ptolemies in Egypt had begun such foundations at Alexandria (§ 319). Augustus followed their example at Athens, from his private fortune. Vespasian was the first to pay salaries from the public treasury ; and Marcus Aurelius began the practice of permanent *state endowments*. That is, the government gave large sums of money or valuable property, the *income* of which was to be used for the support of the institution receiving the gift, — as with our national land grants to State universities.

The professors had the rank of Senators, with good salaries, and with assured pensions after twenty years of service. At Rome there were ten chairs of Latin Grammar (language and literary criticism); ten of Greek; three of Rhetoric, which included law and politics;[2] and three of Philosophy, which included logic. These represent the three chief studies (the

---

[1] This statement holds good for most of the better emperors. As a rule it was the weak or wicked ones who spent their reigns in the capital.

[2] Because these were subjects to which rhetoric was especially applied and on account of which it was studied.

trivium) — language, rhetoric, and philosophy. There was also a group of mathematical studies, — music, arithmetic, geometry, astronomy (the *quadrivium*). In some universities special studies flourished. Thus, law was a specialty at Rome, and medicine at Alexandria.

620. Schools. — Below the universities, in all large provincial towns, there were "*grammar schools*." These were endowed by the emperors, from Vespasian's time, and corresponded in some measure to advanced high schools, or small colleges.

Those in Gaul and Spain were especially famous; in particular, the ones at Massilia, Autun, Narbonne, Lyons, Bordeaux, Toulouse.[1] The reputation of the instructors in the best schools drew students from all the empire. The walls of the class rooms were painted with maps, dates, and lists of facts. The masters were appointed by local magistrates, with life tenure and good pay. Like the professors in the universities, they were exempt from taxation and had many privileges.

In the small towns were many *schools of a lower grade*. But all this education was for the upper and middle classes, and for occasional bright boys from the lower classes who found some wealthy patron. Little was done toward dispelling the dense ignorance of the masses. Rich men and women, however, sometimes bequeathed money to schools in their home cities for the education of poor children.[2]

621. Architecture was the chief Roman art. With the Early Empire it takes on its distinctive character. To the Greek columns it adds the noble Roman arch, with its modification, the dome. As compared with Greek architecture, it has more massive grandeur and is more ornate. The Romans commonly used the rich Corinthian column instead of the simpler Doric or Ionic (§ 154).

---

[1] The Celts of Gaul took to the study of the Latin and Greek classics with enthusiasm. Among them the professional teacher was much more highly respected than in any other part of the empire. It foreshadowed their future mission. (See § 721, and Mommsen, *Roman Provinces*, Book VIII, Chap. III.)

[2] Davis' *Readings*, II, Nos. 79 and 80.

THE PANTHEON TO-DAY.

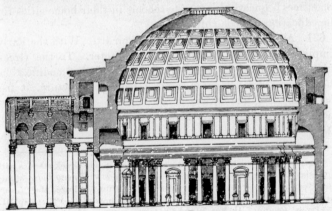

A SECTION OF THE PANTHEON.

622. Famous Buildings.— The most famous building of the Augustan Age is the *Pantheon*, — palace of all the gods of the Empire. It was built in the Campus Martius by the minister Agrippa.[1] It is a circular

The Coliseum, seen through the Arch of Titus. Cf. pp. 471, 478.

---

[1] Some recent archaeologists say that Hadrian built the Pantheon in its present form, retaining the inscription in honor of Agrippa from an earlier

structure, 132 feet in diameter and of the same height, surmounted by a majestic dome that originally flashed with tiles of bronze. The interior is broadly flooded with light from an aperture in the dome 26 feet in diameter. The inside walls were formed of splendid columns of yellow marble, with gleaming white capitals supporting noble arches, upon which again rested more pillars and another row of arches — up to the base of the dome. Under the arches, in pillared recesses, stood the statues of the gods of all religions ; for this grand temple was symbolic of the grander toleration and unity of the Roman world. Time has dealt gently with it, and almost alone of the buildings of its day it has lasted to ours.[1] It is now a church.

The *Coliseum* was begun by Vespasian and finished by Domitian. It is a vast stone *amphi*theater (*two* theaters, face to face) for wild beast shows and games. It covers six acres, and the walls rise 150 feet. It seated 45,000 spectators. For centuries, in the Middle Ages, its ruins were used as a quarry for the palaces of Roman nobles, but its huge size has prevented its complete destruction.

A favorite application of the arch was the *triumphal arch*, adorned with sculptures and covered with inscriptions, spanning a street, as if it were a city gate. Among the more famous structures of this kind in Rome were the arches of Titus, Trajan, Antoninus, and, later, of Constantine (see pages 509, 514, 515, etc.).

The Romans erected also splendid *mon-*

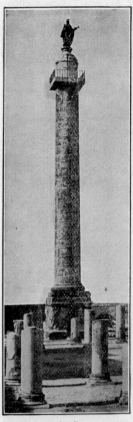

TRAJAN'S COLUMN.

building. Agrippa was an early friend of Augustus and a faithful assistant through his whole life. He was an able soldier and an ardent builder. In his patronage of art and architecture he filled a place like that of Maecenas in literature (§ 571, note). Agrippa's generalship won the battle of Actium. He became the son-in-law of Augustus, and, except for his death shortly before that of the Emperor, he would probably have succeeded to his power.

[1] Read the picture in Byron's *Childe Harold*, canto iv.

umental columns. The finest surviving example is *Trajan's Column*, one hundred feet high, circled with spiral bands of sculpture containing twenty-

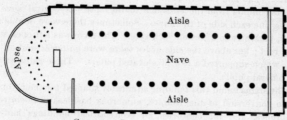

GENERAL PLAN OF A BASILICA.

five hundred human figures. It commemorated and illustrated Trajan's Dacian expedition.

623. Roman Basilicas and the Later Christian Architecture. — One other kind of building must have special mention. A little before

INTERIOR OF TRAJAN'S BASILICA, — a "restoration" by Canina.

the Empire, the Romans adopted the Greek basilica[1] and soon made it a favorite form of building for the law courts.

---

[1] So called from the hall at Athens where the *basileus archon* (king archon) heard cases at law involving religious questions. Cf. § 134.

The general plan was that of a great oblong hall, its length some two times its breadth, with a semicircular raised *apse* at the end, where sat the judges. The hall itself was divided by two long rows of pillars into three parts running from the entrance to the apse — a central *nave* and two *aisles*, one each side of the nave. Sometimes there were double rows of pillars, making two aisles on each side. The nave was left open up to the lofty roof; but above the side aisles there were *galleries* shut off by a parapet, which supported a row of elevated pillars. These galleries were for the general public.

The Christians found this building admirably adapted for their worship. After the conversion of the Empire, numerous basilicas were converted into churches, and for centuries all ecclesiastical buildings had this general plan. With slight changes, it grew into the plan of the medieval cathedral.

LITERATURE

Until just before the Empire, literature plays a small part in Roman life; and it has not been needful to mention it until now. To grasp the literary conditions under the Empire, however, it is desirable to review briefly the earlier period also. The following outline is designed only for reading and reference, not for careful study. If the teacher likes, it can be discussed in class, with open books.

624. Before the Age of Cicero. — Rome had no literature until the middle of the third century B.C. Then the influence of her conquest of Magna Graecia began to be felt. *Livius Andronicus*, a Greek slave from Tarentum, introduced the drama at Rome; but his plays, and those of his successor *Naevius*, were mainly translations from older Greek writers.

Ennius, also from Magna Graecia, comes in the period just after the Second Punic War. He translated Greek dramas, but his chief work was an epic on the legendary history of Rome.

Comedy was represented by two greater names, *Plautus* (of Italian origin) and *Terence* (a slave from Carthage). Both modeled their plays upon those of the Greek Menander (§ 313). Plautus (254–184 B.C.) is rollicking but gross. Terence (a generation later) is more refined.

To the period between the Second and Third Punic wars belong also *Cato's Origines* (an early history of Rome), an earlier history by *Fabius Pictor*, and the great history by the Greek *Polybius*, all of which have been referred to before in this volume.

625. The part of the first century B.C. preceding Augustus is sometimes known as the *Age of Cicero* from the name that made its chief glory. *Cicero* remains the foremost orator of Rome and the chief master of Latin prose.

Two great poets belong to the period : *Lucretius* the Epicurean, a Roman knight, who reaches a sublimity never attained by other Latin poets ; and *Catullus* from Cisalpine Gaul, whose lyrics are unsurpassed for delicacy, and who attacked Caesar with bitter invective, to meet gentle forgiveness.

History is represented by the concise, graphic, lucid narrative of *Caesar*, the picturesque stories of *Sallust* (who is our chief authority for the conspiracy of Catiline and the Jugurthine War), and by the inferior work of *Nepos* and *Varro*.

626. In the Augustan Age the stream broadens, and only the more important writers can be mentioned.

Horace (son of an Apulian freedman) wrote the most graceful of *Odes* and most playful of *Satires*, while his *Epistles* combine agreeably a serene common sense with beauty of expression.

Virgil (from Cisalpine Gaul) is probably the chief Roman poet. He is best known to school boys by his epic, the *Aeneid*, but critics rank higher his *Georgics* (exquisite poems of country life). In the Middle Ages Virgil was regarded as the greatest of poets, and Dante was proud to acknowledge him for a master.

Ovid (Roman knight) has for his chief work the *Metamorphoses*, a mythological poem.

Livy (of Cisalpine Gaul) and *Dionysius* (an Asiatic Greek) wrote their great *histories* of Rome in this reign. *Diodorus* (a Sicilian Greek) wrote the first general history of the world. Greek *science* is continued by *Strabo* of Asia Minor (living at Alexandria), who produced a systematic geography and speculated on the possibility of more continents.

627. In the first century, later than Augustus, were written the books of the *New Testament*. Their true author is God Himself. Together with the books of the Old Testament likewise inspired by God they stand preëminent among all other writings in dignity and influence. (See page xv.)

Prominent among the secular authors are the following: the poets *Lucan* and *Martial* (famous for his satirical wit), both Spaniards ; the Jewish historian *Josephus* (writing in Greek) ; the scientist *Pliny the Elder* (of Cisalpine Gaul), who perished in the eruption of Vesuvius in his scientific zeal to observe the phenomena ; the rhetorician *Quintilian* (a Spaniard) ; the philosophers *Epictetus* and *Seneca* (both Stoics), Seneca was a Roman noble, Epictetus a slave. Both taught a lofty philosophy, but the slave was the nobler both in teaching and in life.

628. In the second century contemporary society is charmingly illustrated in the *Letters* of *Pliny the Younger* (from Cisalpine Gaul),

ARCH OF TITUS.

and is gracefully satirized in the *Dialogues* of *Lucian* (a Syrian Greek).

In history we have : —

Appian (an Alexandrian Greek), who wrote (*in Greek*) a history of the different parts of the empire ;

Arrian (an Asiatic Greek), who wrote (*in Greek*) biographies of Alexander and his successors, and treatises on geography ;

Plutarch (a Boeotian), the author of the famous *Lives* (" the text-book of heroism ") and of a great treatise on *Morals* (*in Greek*) ;

Suetonius, the biographer of the first twelve Caesars ;

Tacitus (a Roman noble), author of the *Germania* (a description of the Germans), and of a great history of the Empire from Tiberius to Nerva. Unhappily only fragments survive, under the names of the *Annals* and the *Histories*.

Poetry is represented chiefly by the *Satires* of *Juvenal* (an Italian).

Science is represented by : —

Galen (an Asiatic Greek), who wrote treatises on medicine (*in Greek*), and who was revered for many centuries as the greatest medical authority ;

Ptolemy, an Egyptian astronomer and geographer, whose work (*in Greek*) was the chief authority for centuries. He taught that the earth was round, and that the heavens revolved about it for their center;

TRAJAN'S ARCH, AT BENEVENTUM.

Pausanias (an Asiatic Greek), a traveler and writer (*in Greek*).
Marcus Aurelius, the emperor (§ 589) (*in Latin*).

EXERCISE. — Note the significance in the use of Greek or Latin by the authors named above (cf. § 475). Observe the increase in prose literature.

MORALS

629. Unequal Distribution of Wealth. — Unfortunately the picture of the Roman World has many more dark colors than bright ones. The great wealth accumulated within the boundaries of the empire was in the hands of comparatively few. This was eminently the case in Rome and Italy. A few thousand families held the greater part of the landed property, while the rest of the citizens mostly lived in abject poverty. In Rome hundreds of thousands were the daily recipients of food which the state doled out gratis. Many of them indeed earned money besides, but the very institution encouraged idleness and was largely responsible for the crowds of unoccupied men and women, who hung around the streets, ready for any mischief, and who demanded state support as their right.

630. The Circus. — They demanded more ; they clamored for "bread and games." The games were the *circus* and the *theater*, admission to which was free to every one. Some of what the circus offered might be called innocent amusement. But by far the greater part of its performances were unspeakable horrors. There were the gladiatorial shows, in which, for the enjoyment of the spectators, men armed or unarmed were exposed to wild animals. Men were pitted against other men in mortal combat (§ 486). Those who voluntarily or involuntarily made this their business were called *gladiators*. To admire their bravery, to witness their sufferings, agony, and death, when torn by the beasts, or wounded, mutilated, and killed by their antagonists, was the choice delight not only of the people of the street but also of the most highly educated of the Romans, including delicate ladies, even the Vestal Virgins. For the latter, as for the imperial family and the senators, special places of honor were reserved.

Under Trajan one set of games continued 123 days. In a single day's games, when the Coliseum was first opened by Titus, 5000 animals were slain. The jaded spectators demanded ever new novelties, and the exhibitors sought out fantastic forms of combat. Thousands of men fought at once in hostile armies. Sea fights were imitated on artificial lakes. Distant regions were scoured for new varieties of beasts to slay and be slain. Women entered the arena as gladiators, and dwarfs engaged one another in deadly combat. The wealthy aristocrats laid wagers upon the skill of their favorite gladiators, as with us at a prize ring.

631. Theaters. — Another temple of depravity was the theater, where vice and cruelty appeared without disguise. The excesses which form part of the action of the play were actually committed on the stage. If the rôle of an actor required that he be scourged or executed, the scourging or execution was carried out in full reality before the spectators.

The fact that such "recreations" were enjoyed, nay passionately clamored for by the citizens and granted as a matter of course by the authorities, indicates of itself an extremely low standard of moral feeling. It was one of the ever present causes of a general and most shocking immorality.

632. Looseness of the Marriage Tie. — Matrimony was no longer sacred; divorces, always legal under Roman Law, now became of dreadful frequency. Many preferred criminal celibacy to honorable marriage. According to Roman custom fathers claimed it as their right to repudiate a new-born child and thus devote it to death by neglect. This became a widespread practice. Destruction of the blossoming life was in general vogue. The Roman writer Tacitus was surprised to find that child murder was considered a great crime among the Germans. Laws which imposed a special tax on bachelors and gave privileges to every father of three children did not have the desired effect.[1]

633. Slavery. — One of the greatest evils was slavery. The slaves of both sexes, old and young, were completely at the mercy of their masters and mistresses. They worked on

---

[1] On woman's degradation and elevation see F. N. Allies, *Formation of Christendom*, Vol. I, Lecture 5.

the farms or in the shops and offices or attended to the various duties of the household. In the palaces of the rich some of them were pampered, others enjoyed a kind of moderate comfort, but all depended constantly on their master's whims. A harsh and heartless treatment was the general rule.[1] Great, even excessive, cruelty, was of very frequent occurrence, particularly on the farms, and roused no comment. If sick or old, the slaves were not taken care of but were allowed to die of

THE WAY OF TOMBS AT POMPEII.

The higher stones, at the side of the street, are "burial stones," each with its inscription. The inscriptions quoted on page 529 come mainly from these stones.

starvation or exposure. Children of slaves were doomed to slavery, — that is, if their masters were willing to let them grow up at all. It was considered cheaper to buy slaves at the market than to raise slave children.

---

[1] On Slavery read Wiseman, *Fabiola*, Part I, Ch. 4.

634. Effects of Slavery. — That slavery was one of the most fruitful sources of all kinds of vices for the slave owner as well as for the unfortunate slave, needs no further explanation. The slave crowded out the free laborers in the country and this was one of the reasons for the disappearance of the small landholders who could no longer compete with the large estates worked by gangs of slaves. Among the slaves kept in the houses and establishments in the cities, there were artisans, clerks, managers, and female workers of all kinds. These constrained laborers took the bread from the poorer citizens who might have made their living by such occupations.

Most of these evils may be summed up under another head : *contempt for human life*, which finds further illustration in the frightfully increasing number of suicides.

635. Kindness. — There were, however, some few brighter colors in the dark picture. The Letters of Pliny reveal, in the court circle of his time, a society highminded and to some degree virtuous. A monument preserves the touching inscription, of a husband to his wife : "Only once did she cause me sorrow, and that was by her death." The tombstone of a physician declares that "to all the needy who came to him he gave his services free of charge." There was, in fact, in many places a show of charity. We hear of homes for poor children and orphan girls. Wealthy men loaned money below the rate of interest. After an accident near Rome the rich opened their houses and gave their wealth to relieve the sufferers. Nor is there any reason to presume that in every case this was done for the sake of self-glorification. Compassion is a natural trait in men, and to a character not wholly depraved beneficence affords a noble pleasure. Stoic philosophy (§ 317) with its doctrine of the equality of all men probably has something to do with this pagan charity. See note to § 637.

636. Liberality. — Every city, large or small, received gifts of money from its well-to-do citizens, not only to erect temples, libraries, and town halls, or to furnish gladiatorial shows and other amusements, but for the repair of pavements and the construction of sewers as well. But his liberality had one undesirable effect. The people came to do less and less for themselves, and fell more and more completely under the control of the great riches. They came to choose only wealthy

A DETAIL FROM TRAJAN'S COLUMN (page 520): Trajan sacrificing a bull at the bridge over the Danube, just completed by his soldiers. This bridge was a remarkable structure, — probably the most wonderful bridge in the world until the era of iron and steel bridge-work in the nineteenth century.

men for public office, because of the expectation of public benefaction from them. Even louder grew the cry for "bread and games."

637. Mitigation of Harsh Laws. — There were laws passed to mitigate the procedure in the courts, without however benefiting the Christians. Other laws were calculated to do away with some of the worst features of slavery. Occasionally the same crowd which feasted their eyes on the bloodshed of the circus would jeer at masters who were known to be unusually cruel to slaves. But all this did not materially change the lot of that oppressed class.[1]

638. Woman's Position. — According to the laws of the Roman republic, the wife, though generally treated with respect by her husband, was nevertheless legally his slave. The customs of imperial Rome practically freed her from this degradation. Women now engaged in various trades. They became women's physicians. They also did a great deal of writing, though none of their productions have survived until our age. But owing to the freedom which they did not know how to use, and subject to the depraving influences of circus, theater, and slavery, they were largely estranged from their natural position as queens of the household. Roman maidens, if they still deserved that name, no longer considered domestic happiness as the goal of their ambition. Thus woman contributed an ample share to the downfall of the empire, which was due in large measure to the degradation of matrimony.

FOR FURTHER READING. — Munchgesang, *In Quest of Truth*, gives information in the form of a narrative about a great variety of Roman conditions, production of books, meals, relation of children to parents, tenement houses, etc. Fouard, *Life of St. Peter*, pp. 272–315. Also the introductory chapter of Cardinal Rampolla's *Life of St. Melania*, on Roman morals, is instructive from this point of view. Cardinal Wiseman's *Fabiola*, a novel on the Church of the Catacombs, may be usefully studied concerning Roman morality and manners. Here belong *Readings*, 74–108, in Vol. II of Davis, some of which have already been quoted.

EXERCISE. — To the table of dates add A.D. 9, 14, 69, 180.

---

[1] The following quotation may be of interest concerning this point: " Perhaps it is a mere coincidence, but the fact is certain that the best epoch of the Roman law was precisely the reigns of the Severi and the Antonines (who were favorable to Christianity). The ideas of justice and equity professed by the eminent Roman lawyers of the third century had been held by Christians for over a century and a half. It is therefore highly probable that Christianity had something to do with the betterment of the Roman law of this time, especially as we notice a great setback during the reign of Julian the Apostate." Conway, *Studies in Church History*, p. 60. See also § 652.

CHAPTER XXXIX

THE DECLINE IN THE THIRD CENTURY

THE STORY OF THE EMPERORS

639. The "Barrack Emperors," 193–284 A.D. — The misrule of Commodus had again left the throne the sport of the soldiery. There followed ninety years of twenty-seven "barrack emperors," set up by the praetorians or the legions, and engaged in frequent civil war. All but four of the twenty-seven emperors were slain in some revolt ; and, of these four, two fell in battle against barbarian invaders.

640. The Throne for Sale. — After the murder of Commodus, the praetorians set up as Emperor a worthy Senator, Pertinax ; but in less than three months they mutinied and slew him. Then they *auctioned* off the imperial purple to the highest bidder, knocking it down to Julianus, a rich noble, who had offered $1000 apiece to each of the 12,000 guards. (See Davis' *Readings*, II, No. 71.)

The three great armies (on the Rhine, the Danube, and the Euphrates) answered this disgraceful news by rebellion. Each army "proclaimed" its favorite general. Septimius Severus, the commander on the Danube, was the nearest of the rivals to the capital. By swift action he secured the prize.

641. Septimius Severus (193–211) was a native of North Africa. He was a clear-headed, determined, industrious man, merciless and cruel toward his foes, but sternly conscientious about the duties of his great office. He restored order and unity to the empire, and repulsed the barbarians. Most of his reign was spent in the East, where the Parthians were growing more and more dangerous ; but he died in Britain — at the opposite frontier — where he had just been strengthening Hadrian's wall and repelling the Scots.   He greatly admired the Antonine emperors, and took the name Antoninus, in addition to his own. Another persecution of the Christians took place in his reign. For the watchword on the night of his death, he gave "Let us work" ("*Laboremus*").

642. Ten years of anarchy followed.   Severus' son, *Caracalla*, was a vicious weakling, whose six-year reign (211–217) is notable for the extension of citizenship to all free men in the empire (§ 616).   Caracalla was murdered by his guards, as were his two unimportant successors (Macrinus, 217–218, and Elagabalus, 218–222).

643. Alexander Severus (222–235) was a native of Syria.   Like his predecessors, he was set up, and finally murdered, by the soldiery.   He was a well-meaning, gentle youth (the nearest heir of the house of Septimius Severus); but he lacked the stern strength needful for his place.   His court was simple and pure.   "Do not to another what thou wouldst not have done to thyself" was the motto inscribed upon the entrance to the royal palace.   Septimius had had for his chief minister *Papinian,* a great jurist.   Alexander Severus, in like manner, was assisted by *Ulpian* (§ 637), the leading jurist of his day, and the chief adviser of the Emperor; but Ulpian was finally murdered by the soldiery at the helpless Emperor's feet.   The reign was troubled also on the frontiers by new enemies, — by a new Persian kingdom which had now overthrown the Parthians in the East, and, on the Rhine, by fresh German peoples. But, in spite of these troubles to court and to frontier, for the bulk of the empire the thirteen years of Severus were an oasis of peace and plenty in the dreary third century.

644. For the next thirty-three years (235–268) phantom emperors follow one another in bewildering confusion which it is profitless to trace.[1] Many reigns are counted by days, not by years.   Only one able ruler appeared (Decius, 249–251) ; and, after two years, he fell in a disastrous

---

[1] Maximus, 235–238. Gordianus I and II, Pupienus, Balbinus, 238. Gordianus III, 238–244. Philippus, 244–249. Decius, 249–251. Gallus, Æmilianus, Valerian, Gallienus, 251–268.

battle against the Goths near the Danube. This brief reign was marked by a stern persecution of the Christians. The most worthy of the successors of Decius in this troubled period was *Valerian ;* and he was defeated and captured by Sapor, the Persian king, and died in bitter and humiliating captivity. In the sixties, so many rival claimants for the throne appeared that the period is known as the Age of the " Thirty Tyrants."

645. Claudius II. — The Empire seemed in ruins. It was sunk in anarchy and split into fragments by the jealousies of rival legions; and while these false defenders turned their swords upon one another, the barbarians swarmed over every frontier and penetrated toward the heart of the Empire.

Happily strong hands grasped the scepter. The army itself wearied of disorder. In 268 it set a great general, Claudius, upon the throne. Claudius found his chief task with the Goths. That German people had worked their will in the Balkan provinces for almost twenty years — since the time of Decius. They were now defeated after a long campaign. Then Claudius died quietly in his bed, — the first emperor of whom that was true since Septimius Severus.

646. Aurelian. — To the world the death of Claudius mattered little, because his successor was an even greater ruler. *Aurelian* (270–275) was an Illyrian peasant, who had risen from the ranks to high military commands. The achievements of his reign of less than five years rival those of the first Caesar. He reorganized the army and *restored the Empire.* The barbarians were driven back beyond the Rhine and the Danube.[1] Gaul, which for some years had become virtually a separate kingdom, was recovered. Zenobia, the great Queen who had set up a rival Arabian empire at Palmyra, was brought captive to Rome (Davis' *Readings,* II, No. 73). Prosperity began to return; but death snatched away the Emperor, just when he was ready to take up the work of civil reform.

Once in this reign, the Alemanni, a German people, penetrated to the Po, and threw all Italy into a panic. When they had been repulsed, Aurelian built walls about Rome. Since

---

[1] Dacia was abandoned to them for their home.

Hannibal's day, that proud capital had feared no invader and
had spread out far beyond her earlier ramparts.   The new

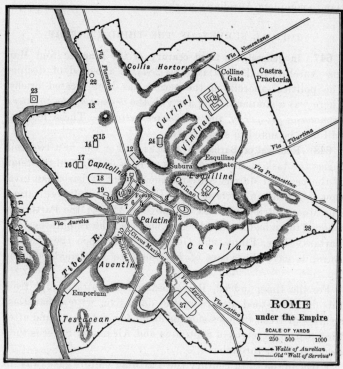

ROME
under the Empire

SCALE OF YARDS

0   250   500   1000

▬▬▬ *Walls of Aurelian*
───── *Old "Wall of Servius"*

1. Coliseum.	10. Temple of Jupiter Capitolinus.	19. Theater of Marcellus.
2. Arch of Constantine.		20. Forum Holitorium.
3. Arch of Titus.	11. Arch.	21. Forum Boarium.
4. Via Sacra.	12. Column of Trajan.	22. Mausoleum of Augustus.
5. Via Nova.	13. Column of Antoninus.	23. Mausoleum of Hadrian.
6. Vicus Tuscus.	14. Baths of Agrippa.	24. Baths of Constantine.
7. Vicus Jugarius.	15. Pantheon.	25. Baths of Diocletian.
8. Arch of Septimius Severus.	16. Theater of Pompey.	26. Baths of Titus.
	17. Portico of Pompey.	27. Baths of Caracalla.
9. Clivus Capitolinus.	18. Circus Flaminius.	28. Amphitheatrum Castrense.

walls of Aurelian, needful and grand as the work was, were
a somber symbol of a new age.

Six reigns[1] fill the next nine years, — three of them the reigns of able and well-meaning men; and then came Diocletian to complete Aurelian's work.

TOPICAL SURVEY OF THE THIRD CENTURY

647. In general, the third century of the Empire, from Marcus Aurelius to Diocletian (180–284), is a period of decline. The political anarchy of the period has been treated briefly. There was a similar falling away in the *defense of the frontiers,* in *material prosperity,* and in *literary activity.* These features will now be noted in some detail.

648. Renewal of Barbarian Attacks. — For the first two centuries the task of the legions was an easy one, but in the reign of the peaceful Marcus Aurelius the torrent of barbarian invasion began again to beat upon the ramparts of civilization. The Moorish tribes were on the move in Africa; the Parthians, whom Trajan had humbled, again menaced the Euphrates; and Tartars, Slavs, Finns, and Germans burst upon the Danube. Aurelius gave the years of his reign to campaigns on the frontier.

For the time, indeed, Rome beat off the attack; but from this date she stood always on the defensive, with exhaustless swarms of fresh enemies surging about her defenses; and after the prosperous reigns of Septimius and Alexander Severus they began to burst through.

Early in the third century the Parthian empire gave way to a new Persian kingdom under the Sassanidae kings. This Persian power for a time seemed the great danger to the Roman world. In 250 and 260 its armies poured across the Euphrates. The Emperor Valerian was taken prisoner (§ 644), and Antioch was captured. New German tribes, too, — the mightier foe, as events were to prove, — appeared on the European frontier. The *Alemanni* crossed the Rhine and maintained themselves in Gaul for two years (236–238). In the disorders of

---

[1] Tacitus, Florianus, Probus, Carus, Carinus, Numerianus; 275–282.

the fifties, bands of *Franks* swept over Gaul and Spain. The *Goths* seized the province of Dacia (§ 646), and raided the Balkan provinces. In the sixties, *Gothic* fleets, of five hundred sail, issuing from the Black Sea, ravaged the Mediterranean coasts, sacking Athens, Corinth, Argos, and Sparta (Davis' *Readings*, II, No. 72).

Claudius II and Aurelian, however, restored the old frontiers, except for Dacia, and chastised the barbarians on all sides. The worst of the evil was confined to the middle third of the century; but a fatal blow had been struck at the military fame of Rome.

649. Decline of Population and of Material Prosperity. — By the irony of fate, the reign of the best of emperors marks also another great calamity. In the year 166, a new Asiatic plague swept from the Euphrates to the Atlantic, carrying off, we are told, half the population of the empire.

From Aurelius to Aurelian, at brief intervals, the pestilence returned, desolating wide regions and demoralizing industry. Even vigorous young societies take a long time to recover from a single blow of this kind.[1] To the Roman Empire, the repeated disaster was the more deadly because *population had already become stationary*, if it were not indeed already on the decline. The causes have been hinted at in the chapter on Morals (§ 629 ff.), though there seem also to have been other influences at work. At any rate, the gaps left in the population by that disastrous pestilence remained unfilled.

The fatal disease of the *later empire* was want of men and a constant decrease of the population. Beside the causes already mentioned, the civil wars between the many rival emperors of this period involved a vast loss of life. Moreover, the barbarians, no longer kept back by strong rulers, sometimes swept off all the inhabitants of whole provinces into captivity. Marcus Aurelius once compelled the Quadi, a Teu-

---

[1] In the fourteenth century, Europe suffered from a pestilence known as the " Black Death "; it took England a hundred years to recover from the terrible ravages of that plague.

tonic people, to surrender 50,000 such Roman captives, a fact which shows how many thousands must have died in bitter slavery. Slavery within the empire was another powerful cause of this decline of population. As noticed before (§§ 633, 634), slaves practically had no offspring. Slaves, moreover, made the position of free laborers more and more precarious. If, therefore, the corruption of the lower classes was, perhaps, not so complete as that of the upper, economic conditions made the raising of children impossible for them.

Thus the result of the low standing of morality appeared more and more and grew from year to year more irremediable. The final victory of the new religion came too late to work an essential improvement.

Hand in hand with the decline of population went a decrease in material prosperity. Nor are any great names heard of in poetry or prose writing, in history or science. The only advance in secular matters is in Roman law. This is the age of Ulpian and other great jurists (§ 643). But even this progress closes with the reign of Alexander Severus.

The attacks upon Christianity by means of books, philosophical and otherwise, evoked a series of able Christian apologies. (See §§ 659, 682.) But the prominent Christian writers of the time, as Tertullian, Origenes, Clement of Alexandria, St. Cyprian, not only warded off attacks but performed admirable work for the study of the Bible and other branches of theological knowledge.[1] They prepared the way for the period of busy and brilliant Christian literature which was to follow a century later.

[1] Christian literature is one of the many subjects which can merely be hinted at in a general history. Church histories only can give it the space it deserves.

CHAPTER XL

RISE OF CHRISTIANITY

650. Propagation of Christianity among the Jews. — Fifty days after the resurrection of Jesus from the dead (§§ 571 ff.) the Holy Ghost descended upon the Apostles in the shape of fiery tongues, which appeared on the head of every one of them. At the same time the sound of a mighty wind was heard. It was the feast of Pentecost which had brought to Jerusalem "devout Jews from every nation under heaven." Attracted by the unwonted spectacle they assembled, and St. Peter, the first pope, preached the first missionary sermon. Three thousand souls entered the new-born Church on that day.

At first the Apostles confined their efforts to Jerusalem and the Holy Land, where numerous communities of fervent Christians soon grew up. Accounts of the new religion, which claimed to be the fulfillment of the Scriptures, reached the Jews of other cities and countries. Many of the pilgrims who year after year came to Jerusalem were converted, others at least heard of the doctrines of Christ. As a matter of fact, the starting point of Christianity in other cities was generally the quarter of the "Jews of the Dispersion" (§ 467). Unfortunately the Jews as a class found the kingship of this Messia too unworldly. They rejected His religion, just as their high priests had rejected Himself officially in Jerusalem.

651. Propagation among the Pagans. — A persecution under king Herod Agrippa (§§ 467, 583) scattered the flourishing congregation in Jerusalem far beyond the boundaries of Palestine. This resulted in the establishment of Christianity in many pagan cities, notably in Antioch, the intellectual and commercial center of the Orient. St. Peter himself was the first bishop of that city. Here the name of "Christians" was coined to denote the followers of Jesus. Soon the conversion of pagans, beginning with the baptism of Cornelius by St. Peter, assumed greater proportions. The Council of Jerusalem declared these converts free from the ceremonial laws of Moses. St. Paul, miraculously converted by an apparition of Jesus Himself, traveled through all the large cities of Asia Minor and Greece. He visited Rome and probably went even to Spain. More than any other Apostle did he make his special task the conversion of the "Gentiles," as the Jews called those not of their race, though he never preached to them before he had addressed himself to the Jews of the place. After laboring for some years in Antioch, St. Peter transferred his residence to the capital of the world, the city on the Tiber. Here Christianity was gaining converts from all classes of people, including the higher ranks of society.

The arrival of the humble fisherman made Rome what she was destined to be : the residence of the Vicars of Christ on earth. It was the greatest event in her history. St. Peter finally died a martyr's death by crucifixion during the persecution of Nero. St. Paul was beheaded on the same day. "These are the men, O Rome, through whom the splendor of the Gospel began to shine in thee, so that from a teacher of error thou becamest the disciple of truth. These are thy Fathers, who established thee in a much higher, much happier way than those who laid the foundation of thy walls. These are they that lifted thee up to thy present glory, that, being the head of the world by the Chair of Peter, thou rulest a wider domain than thy worldly empire ever embraced." (St. Leo I.)

652. Results. — Meanwhile the religion for which they died continued its peaceful march of victory throughout the Roman world and beyond its borders. It is estimated that by the middle of the second century, *i.e.* a little more than a hundred years after the death of Christ, there were about a million Christians. Within another hundred and fifty years this number had at least trebled, and may have amounted to ten millions. On the whole, the East became more rapidly and more thoroughly Christian than the West.

The truths of Christianity even simmered through into the pagan world. Since its coming we meet with thoughts of charity and kindness which were unknown before. We see rulers act according to principles diametrically opposite to the old and cold heartlessness and cruelty of the Roman character. This is visible in the government of the Antonines.[1] The new ideas were in the air; minds not wholly corrupt assimilated them without trying, in every case, to account for their presence.

653. Advantages of the True Religion. — Christianity had its most powerful ally in the natural desire of every human soul for truth and happiness. The teachings of the true religion, in themselves so extremely reasonable, and at the same time proposed in so simple a garb as to be equally intelligible to the learned and the unlearned, naturally made a strong appeal to these general cravings. There was, moreover, the virtuous life of the faithful, especially their charity, which, as the Christian writer Tertullian testifies, compelled great admiration from the pagans. There were the miracles, wrought by God on various occasions, chiefly during the sufferings of martyrs. There was, besides many other things, the missionary zeal of the converts, including women and slaves and, last not least, soldiers. Many Christian communities along the Rhine and Danube and other parts of the frontier were founded by soldiers whom duty called to these places.

654. How the World had been Prepared for the Spread of Christianity. 1. The Roman World. — "It was part of the Divine plan," says Pope Leo the Great, "that the several kingdoms and realms should be united under one empire, thus making all nations easily accessible to the preaching of the Gospel." At the time of David, Christianity could hardly have spread farther than the boundaries of his small dominion. Exclusiveness was one of the state maxims of the former age. Now all the frontiers around the Mediterranean had disappeared. The

---

[1] See § 637, note.

Syrian or Greek was no longer a stranger on the banks of the Rhine or in far-off Britain. As citizens or as members of an allied nation, the messengers of Christ could travel to any part of the vast world-empire of Rome. (See § 612 ff.)

The excellent roads, built chiefly for the use of the army, served equally for the merchant and the Apostle of Jesus Christ. The innumerable ships which plied the waters of the Mediterranean offered similar facilities for sea travel. Latin was the official language of the government, and was fast becoming the sole vernacular of the West. Greek had taken possession of the countries of the eastern Mediterranean and was also spoken in many cities of the West. In Rome it was nearly as common as Latin. It was the language of the educated the world over. These two languages, then, sufficed to carry a traveler from one end of the empire to the other and put him into intellectual communication with almost every inhabitant. At the time of David more than a score of languages would hardly have been enough.

655. 2. Roman Laws. — Rome practiced a remarkable tolerance of religious views. All gods of the universe were welcome in the capital, and remained unmolested in the length and breadth of the empire as long as they did not come into too glaring a conflict with Roman views of morality and did not endanger what was thought to be the interest of the state. Every freak of religion found an asylum in Rome. "Rome," says Leo the Great, "thought herself the wiser, the more religious folly she harbored within her walls." This enabled the Christians for a long time to live up to the tenets of their religion; the more so, as in the beginning they were identified with the Jews and participated in their privileges. (§ 650.)

Unions and societies, as a rule, were severely suppressed by the Roman government, lest they use their influence against the common welfare. But there was one great exception. The people were allowed to form funeral confraternities to secure for one another a decent burial. Any property devoted

to the purpose of such societies, and, above all, the graves themselves, were inviolable according to Roman views and laws.
Hence the Christians, organized into funeral societies, could
own common property and hold their meetings without being
molested by the authorities.

656. 3. Philosophy. — Greek philosophy had penetrated into
the circles of the educated of all cities. Though with no intention of addressing itself to the common people, and stopping
far short of a satisfactory solution of the problems of life, it
had to some extent prepared minds for greater seriousness of
thought and had spread ideas which facilitated assimilation of
the Christian truths. This was true of the Stoics in particular.
(See § 317.) They taught the necessity of virtue in general
and inculcated endurance in sufferings and hardships, death
included. They also believed in a common brotherhood of
men. Such and similar teachings might form the starting
point for conversions.

After the beginning of the Christian era, the conviction grew
among serious-minded men, that the ridiculous medley of their
gods and goddesses, all of whom were subject to the cravings
and vices of ordinary mortals, could not possibly benefit a
decaying race. (See Davis' *Readings*, No. 100.) The Neo-
Platonists and Neo-Pythagoreans now taught new systems of
religion. (See § 659.) The bannerbearers were in fierce opposition to the Church, which they thought to displace by giving
the impression that the ancient religion was just as good. But
to thinking minds the whole movement brought home very
forcibly the complete bankruptcy of the old superstitions and,
in the long run, could only assist in making converts to Christianity among the educated.

PERSECUTIONS OF THE CHRISTIANS

657. 1. Causes. — *The real reason* of the three hundred
years' persecution of the Church was the opposition of the
world and " the prince of this world " to God and His Son

Jesus Christ. "If they have persecuted Me they will also persecute you." (John xv, 20.)

But there were certain circumstances and conditions which, while by no means furnishing any true ground of antagonism, served as pretexts of legal procedure or resulted in rousing popular enmity against innocent men.

(a) It was highly perplexing to the Roman mind that a man of so despised a nation as the Jews and condemned by a Roman governor, should claim adoration; that poor unlettered fishermen should be bold enough to preach a religion which demanded the giving up of the most popular enjoyments, the circus and the theater, and to teach a life of general self-restraint, and even self-abasement.

(b) While the Romans were tolerant of foreign religions, they demanded at the same time that the Roman gods at least be not repudiated. The Christians, however, rejected all deities save their God "Who made heaven and earth." Hence the Romans called them atheists, that is, deniers of the gods. This opposition became very acute when worship of the deceased emperors gradually developed into a state religion which was strongly enforced. (See § 570.)

(c) To many a patriotic Roman the very idea of abandoning the ancient gods, so closely connected with all the periods of greatness in their history, seemed absurd.

(d) The fact that the Christians submitted to so many restrictions in matters of amusement and general conduct of life was made a pretext for the charge of hatred of the human race, a vague accusation, which, by its very indefiniteness, was apt to appeal to the thoughtless rabble.

(e) The Christians were declared guilty of the most horrible crimes: they would eat, it was said, the flesh of infants, adore goats' heads, etc. The secrecy with which their religious rites, especially the Holy Sacrifice and Communion, were surrounded to keep them from profanation may have given some pretext for these groundless rumors. It was also a well-known fact that many Oriental religions which began to spread in the

West, enjoined frightful orgies and repulsive debauchery.   To these calumnies must be added the custom mentioned by Tertullian of laying the blame for every calamity which befell the empire on the Christians. "When the Tiber rises above its banks, when the Nile does not overflow, if the earth quakes, if famine and pestilence come: up goes the cry, 'The Christians to the lions.'" [1]

It will be seen presently, that the persecution was always directed against the RELIGION itself.   Everything depended on the question of whether or not the accused person was a Christian.

658. 2. The Court Trials of the Christians. — Of course, all this did not justify any action of the Roman government against the Christians.   Though they refused to obey certain laws which were evidently contrary to the law of the One True God, they everywhere proved themselves loyal citizens and faithful subjects.   A thorough investigation would have brought out their complete innocence.   But the trials given them generally consisted simply in an attempt to make them deny their faith.   The judge applied all the means of persuasion, intimidation and tortures of the most terrible and hideous kind.   If they remained steadfast, he pronounced the penalty, which commonly consisted in some disgraceful and painful kind of death, or in banishment or lifelong work in the mines.   If they yielded, they were set free, though they were supposed to have been committing, perhaps for years, all the fearful transgressions which vulgar belief attributed to their religion.

659. 3. History of the Persecutions. — Nero was the first to inaugurate a persecution of the Christians, as we have seen in § 579.   The greatest victims of his cruelty were the Apostles Sts. Peter and Paul.   St. Peter died on the cross, St. Paul, a Roman citizen, by the sword.   See picture near

---

[1] This refers to the very common practice of exposing the Christians to the wild beasts for the amusement of "the Roman people." Countless martyrs thus suffered in the Coliseum. See § 662 and illustrations on pp. 481, 493, 519. Davis' *Readings*, Vol. II, No. 110.

§ 781.   From this time on it was the principle of the Roman government " that there must be no Christians."   This enabled the governors of the various provinces to proceed severely against them, even if the central authority was lenient or took no notice of them.   For nearly three hundred years there was seldom any time when, in some part of the wide empire, Christians were not suffering for their faith.   The TEN PERSECUTIONS, commonly named after the emperors who ordered or permitted them, are only so many highwater marks of the storm tide which never completely subsided.   We must admit, however, that these persecutors of the Church were not always bad rulers.   In a few instances they must even be credited with some amount of natural virtue.   Frequently, the populace demanded the death of the innocent disciples of Christ, and sympathizing or weak-kneed Pilates on the judgment seat or on the throne " gave sentence that their petition be granted." (Luc. xxiii, 24.)

The emperor Trajan, otherwise famous for his kindness, ordered a governor, Pliny, not to hunt out the Christians; but if accused and refusing to sacrifice to the gods, they were to be punished severely.[1]   Tertullian rightly remarks : " If we are such criminals as to deserve death, why are we not sought out for punishment ?   And if we are so harmless as to be allowed to live undisturbed according to our religion, why are we proceeded against if brought to trial ? "   Probably the emperor himself did not believe the Christians to be dangerous. But, in that case, it was a Pilate-like weakness to permit and even order them to be classed with robbers, traitors, and murderers.

In the third century the Church enjoyed comparative peace for about forty years.   But under *Decius* (250–253) a fiercer storm than ever broke upon it.   At no time had the government proceeded so systematically ; at no time were its efforts

---

[1] See Pliny's letter and the emperor's answer on pp. 219–222 in Davis' *Readings*, Vol. II.

directed with such consistency towards the destruction of the shepherds of the flock; never had the tortures been so exquisitely cruel, nor the governors and other judges so generally zealous in the execution of their master's mandate. During the first onslaught many fell away or bribed the officials for certificates, which stated that they had sacrificed to the gods.[1] But very great also was the number of those who followed in the footsteps of the former heroes and heroines. "The first systematic attempt of the Roman state to destroy Christianity by brute force proved a signal failure." When, some years after Decius' death, the persecution was renewed under the Emperor Gallus, it was met with an invincible fortitude all over the empire.

Yet the most methodical and therefore most terrible effort to eradicate the religion of the cross was still to come. It was the persecution under *Diocletian*. For more than fifteen years he rather favored the Christians. But towards the end of his reign his advisers, foremost the Caesar Galerius, succeeded in convincing him that Christianity formed a serious menace to the empire. With his usual energy he took up the struggle. He first ordered all the church edifices and other places of worship, as well as the sacred vessels and books, to be destroyed. The refusal to deliver up the latter caused many condemnations. A second decree concerned the bishops and clerics. The dungeons became so filled with them that there was no room left for real criminals. The persecutor did not so much seek their death as their defection from the faith. The rack and other horrible kinds of torture were freely used to induce them to sacrifice to the idols.

One edict was against the imperial domestics. "The Christians among them were slain in masses, some with the sword, some by fire." A last edict threatened the whole body of the Christians. In some places the executions amounted to a hundred a day, not to count those that were thrown to the

---

[1] See Davis, Vol. II, p. 111, which gives the text of such a certificate.

wild beasts in the amphitheaters. Numerous persons in the highest positions of the civil and military service were among the victims. One governor had an entire city whose population was Christian, surrounded by soldiers and set on fire, so that all men, women, and children perished in the flames.

After Diocletian's abdication the persecution was for many years continued by the several rulers of the East, but it was doomed to failure. (See §§ 672 and 675.) With it ended the period of bloody conflicts through which the Church had to pass. The prince of darkness who had been enthroned in his idols for thousands of years in the temples of antiquity fled before the coming of the Prince of Light and Peace.

During the period of persecution the Church was assailed with intellectual weapons also. There were literary attacks, both satirical and "scientific," upon the Christian religion, its founder, its promoters, and its members. The philosopher Celsus, in the second century, was the author of the most clever and most bitter assault in the form of a book. Other attacks employed a more indirect method. The Neo-Pythagoreans attempted to raise Pythagoras (see § 156) and the magician Apollonius to a level with Jesus Christ by representing them as great religious reformers, as models of human virtue and as miracle workers. The Neo-Platonists (see § 315) tried to purge paganism of its grossest superstitions. They explained the stories of the gods and goddesses as allegories, established a rough kind of monotheism and adopted a number of Christian teachings. The fight with them was taken up and carried through triumphantly by able Christian apologists, as the Syrian philosopher Justin, Clement and Origen of Alexandria, the Africans Tertullian and Cyprian. Unwittingly, all these pagan efforts helped to bring about a final victory of Christianity, because their very existence showed the hopelessness and insufficiency of the old religion. (See § 656.)

660. 4. The Catacombs. — During times of persecution the Christians in Rome held divine services in the catacombs. The catacombs are underground galleries, excavated in the soft rock in the neighborhood of the city of Rome, running in every direction, often on several levels or "stories," and widening here and there into rooms and more spacious halls. The uppermost of them are about thirty or forty feet below the surface. Their purpose was to serve as regular burial places for the Christians. On both sides of the galleries niches were hollowed out. After the bodies had been deposited in these, the niches were closed by stone slabs which usually received inscriptions. There were more notable graves for prominent persons and martyrs. If placed in a straight line, these galleries would stretch through the whole length of Italy;

CRYPT OF ST. CECILIA IN THE CATACOMBS OF ST. CALLIXTUS.
From the Cath. Encyclopedia.

After Constantine the Great had given liberty to the Christians, they still continued burying in the catacombs. It was not until the sacking of Rome by the Goths in 410 (§ 714) that this custom ceased. For two or three centuries more they remained the object of the greatest veneration. But about 1100 A.D. the memory of their very existence had disappeared. A partial rediscovery in 1578 led to some closer investigation. In the nineteenth century, however, John Baptist De Rossi, the real "Columbus of the Catacombs," founder of the science of Christian archæology, devoted all his energy and talent to the exploration of this forgotten world. With the encouragement of the popes he and his disciples accomplished a great deal in unearthing the hidden treasures of the Christian cities of the dead.

The treasures consist chiefly in a large number of inscriptions on the slabs which cover the niches, the walls of the galleries, recesses, and chapels. They were dictated by a living faith in the reality of the future life and the resurrection, and reveal a childlike belief in prayers for the dead and in the prayers of these for the living. A touching love between the faithful in general and the members of families in particular is expressed everywhere. A phrase occurring constantly is "In Pace," (rests) in peace. In many places the walls are embellished by mural pictures, especially representations of biblical scenes. A very frequent one is Christ as the Good Shepherd. Thus the catacombs are a very powerful corroboration of the unity of faith in all its essential dogmas.

Conclusion. — Christianity had to conquer the world in the face of overwhelming obstacles. All the physical force the mightiest of empires could muster was arrayed against the Church. As the world persecuted Christ, it also persecuted His followers. If we add to this the religious, moral, and social conditions prevailing in the Roman empire, and the fact that the new religion could have no attraction for man's natural inclinations, we gladly agree with those who see in its victory a miracle which alone would suffice to prove its divine origin.

For Further Reading. — Thos. W. Allies, *The Formation of Christendom*, vol. II, Lectures X, XI, XII. Arthur S. Barnes, *The Early Church in the Light of the Catacombs*, especially Part I. Also most of the books mentioned after § 638. Read the touching interview of the young martyr Perpetua with her father in Davis, Vol. II., No. 110, and the other selections on the persecutions, Nos. 109–112.

CHAPTER XLI

THE FOURTH CENTURY: DIOCLETIAN TO THEODOSIUS

(*The Story of the Emperors*[1])

DIOCLETIAN AND IMPERIAL REORGANIZATION

661. The Needs of the Empire. — The third century, we have seen, was a period of grave ·disorder. The throne was the sport of unruly legions and the prize of military adventurers. The usefulness of the Empire, however, was not over. Claudius II and Aurelian repulsed the perils from without, which the anarchy in government had encouraged; and then came *Diocletian* and *Constantine* to end the internal disorder itself (§§ 662 ff.).

That disorder had arisen in the main from two causes.

a. The machinery of government was too primitive. The emperor had too much to do. He could not ward off Persians on the Euphrates and Germans on the Rhine, and also supervise closely the government of the forty provinces. Moreover, some single provinces were so important that their governors, especially if also victorious generals, were almost the equals of the emperor in power. For the third century there had averaged a rebellion of a governor for nearly every year.

b. The succession to the throne was uncertain (§ 595). Sometimes the emperor named his successor; sometimes the Senate elected its own choice. Sometimes the new ruler was the creature of the praetorians, sometimes the favorite of a

---

[1] The fourth century, like the first two, is treated in two chapters — one for narrative and one for a topical study. For convenience, however, the character of the reorganized government is discussed in the first chapter, in connection with the reign of its creator *Diocletian*, and the victory of Christianity in connection with the reign of its champion *Constantine*.

frontier army. At times, the legions had ceased to wait for the throne to become vacant, and made vacancies at will. The result had been the century of "barrack emperors."

662. Diocletian (284–305 A.D.), a stern Illyrian soldier and the grandson of a slave, was himself one of these barrack emperors. He was the last and greatest of them, and he made them impossible thereafter. Seizing the scepter with a strong hand, he established victorious peace on all the frontiers, and

RUINS OF THE BATHS OF DIOCLETIAN.

Parts of the ruins are used to form the walls of modern buildings.

ruled firmly for twenty-one years. Toward the close of his reign he was induced to carry on the *most terrible and thorough of all the persecutions of the Christians.* His greatest work was his reorganization of the system of government.

663. "Partnership Emperors." — Diocletian introduced a system of "partnership emperors." He chose as a colleague *Maximian*, a rough soldier but an able man and a faithful friend. Each of the two took the same titles and dignity :

each was Imperator Caesar Augustus. The two *Augusti*
divided the empire, Diocletian taking the East, Maximian the
West. Each then divided his half into two parts, keeping one
under his own direct control, and intrusting the other to a
chosen heir with the title of *Caesar*. The Augusti (emperors)
kept their own capitals in the central and more settled provinces of the empire, — Diocletian at Nicomedia in Asia Minor,
and Maximian at Milan in North Italy. To the Caesars were
assigned the more turbulent and exposed provinces of the
extreme East and the extreme West, with the duty of guard-
ing the frontiers againt Persians and Germans.

Thus the empire was marked off into *four great sections*,
called *prefectures*, and each prefecture was put under the immediate supervision of one of the four rulers. This made
closer oversight possible. In great measure, also, it did away
with the danger of military adventurers seizing the throne.
Thereafter there were certain men especially pointed out in
advance for the succession. This was not so definitely fixed,
it is true, as to prevent all disputes. More than one war was
yet to be waged for the crown; but the number of possible
claimants was limited, and the evil was lessened.

664. Not a Division of the Empire. — This arrangement, however, was *not a partition of the empire*. It was only a division
of the burden of administration. The power of each emperor
in theory extended over the whole empire. An edict in any part
was published under their joint names. It was intended that
the rulers should act in harmony, and for much of the following
century they did so. *There were not two empires, or four. There
was only one.* In fact, though equal in dignity, the two emperors were usually not equal in power. Thus, throughout
his reign, Diocletian's strong will ruled his colleague.

665. New Machinery. — This division of duties between
four chief rulers was only the beginning of the reform. Below
the Augustus or the Caesar, in each prefecture, appeared *a series
of officials in regular grades*, as in an army, — each officer
under the immediate direction of the one just above him.

Before the time of Diocletian the forty provincial governors had stood directly below the emperor, who had to supervise them all himself. The bulky correspondence between Trajan and Pliny (§§ 598, 657) illustrates the minute oversight which industrious emperors attempted. But with average rulers, and with the greatest in times of special disturbance, such a system was likely to break down. Diocletian introduced better machinery. The *provinces* were subdivided so as to make about a hundred and twenty. These were grouped into thirteen *dioceses* each under a *vicar*. The dioceses were grouped into the four *prefectures*, each under its *prefect*, who was subject to a Caesar or Augustus in person. A prefect had under him three or five vicars; a vicar had under him several provincial governors. Each officer sifted all business that came to him from his subordinates, sending on to his superior only the more important matters.

666. Table of Prefectures and Dioceses. — The following table shows the grouping of these various units of government : —

	Prefectures	Dioceses		
THE EAST	East	East	15 provinces	
		Egypt	6 "	
		Asia	11 "	
		Pontus	11 "	
		Thrace	6 "	
	Illyricum	Macedonia and Greece	6 "	Countless municipalities
		Dacia	5 "	
THE WEST	Italy	Italy	17 "	
		Africa	6 "	
		Illyria	7 "	
	Gaul	Spain	7 "	
		The Gauls	17 "	
		Britain	5 "	

667. Further Precaution against Rebellion. — The provincial governors were now of too little importance to rebel success-

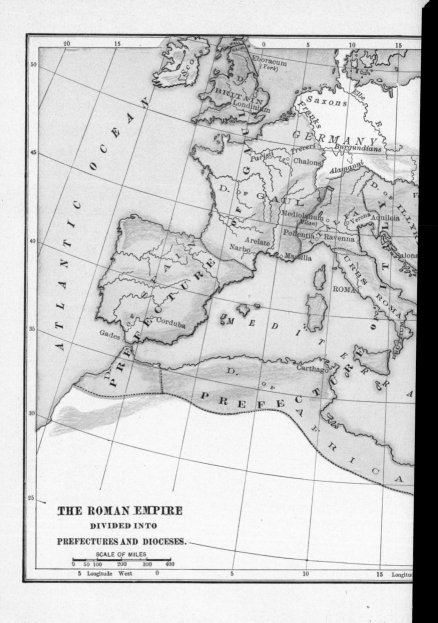

THE ROMAN EMPIRE

DIVIDED INTO

PREFECTURES AND DIOCESES.

SCALE OF MILES

0   50 100   200   300   400

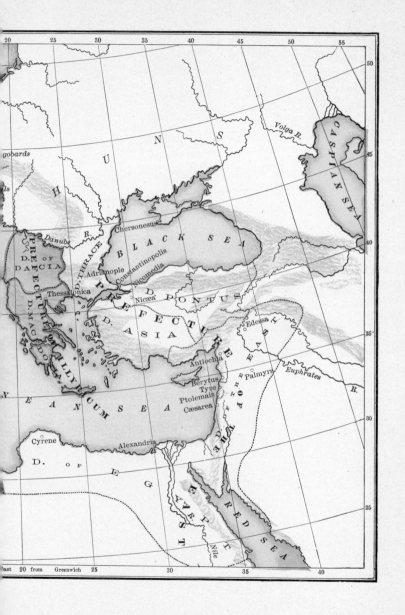

HUNS

gobards

ds

H E R   R.

Longobards

Danube

D. OF
DACIA

PREFECTURE

Thessalonica

D. MACEDON

PREFECTURE

Volga R.

CASPIAN SEA

Chersonesus

BLACK   SEA

D. THRACE

Adrianople
Constantinopolis
Nicomedia

Nicæa

D. PONTUS

PREFECTURE

D. ASIA

Edessa

Antioch

Berytus
Tyre
Ptolemais
Cæsarea

Palmyra

Euphrates   R.

N E A N   U M   S E A

Cyrene

Alexandria

D. OF
EGYPT

E   G   Y   P   T

RED SEA

Nile

st 20 from Greenwich 25   30   35   40

fully against the emperor, but another measure guarded still
further against such disorder. *The governors and vicars became
merely civil officials.* All *military* command was intrusted to
other officers, who were responsible directly to the emperor.
Thus the civil and military powers watched and checked each other.
(Cf. § 76 for this device in the ancient Persian empire.)

At the same time zealous precaution was taken against military adventurers. The powerful legions were broken up into
small regiments. These had less corps spirit than the larger
units had possessed and were less likely to rise against the central authority.

668. Highly Organized Administration. — Most of these reforms
were meant to distribute duties in a more workable way,
and to fix responsibility precisely. One more change aimed
at the same end. In the Early Empire the friends or servants
of the emperor were often given great power in the administration, but in an irregular and varying manner. Hadrian (§ 587)
had made these irregular assistants into regular officers and
advisers. Under Diocletian, each such officer became the head
of an extensive department of government, organized in many
ranks; and, along with this change at court, went also the mul-
tiplication of subordinate officials throughout the provinces.
(See Davis' *Readings*, II, No. 117.)

669. Despotic Forms. — To secure for the emperor's person
greater reverence, Diocletian adopted *the forms of monarchy.*
The Republican cloak of Augustus was cast aside, and the
Principate (§ 592) gave way to an open despotism. At last, absolutism was avowed, and adorned with its characteristic trap-
pings. The emperor assumed a diadem of gems and robes of
silk and gold. He dazzled the multitude by the oriental magnificence of his court, and fenced himself round, even from his
highest officers, with minute ceremonial and armies of function-
aries. When subjects were allowed to approach him at all, they
were obliged, in place of the old Republican greeting, to pros-
trate themselves slavishly at his feet.

Now the Senate of Rome — the last of the old Republican

influences — ceased to have part in the management of the empire. Thenceforth it was merely a city council, as the consuls and aediles had long before become mere city officials.

670. **Lawmaking,** up to this time, had belonged in form to the Senate. (But see § 593.) It now became openly one of the emperor's functions. The ruler made law either by publishing an *edict* to the world, or by addressing a *rescript* (set of directions) to provincial governors. The only other source of new laws thenceforward lay in the *interpretation* of old law, in doubtful cases, by the great judges (jurists) whom the emperor appointed.

The old Republican consuls had sometimes issued edicts, in crises, and the early emperors had often used that power freely. But *in theory*, until Diocletian's time, the consent of the Senate had been essential.

Judicial interpretation had long been important as a source of virtual lawmaking. The maxims of Ulpian (§ 657) had all the force of law.

671. **Summary : a Centralized Despotism.** — Like the reforms which had preserved the declining society of Caesar's day (§ 552), the changes introduced by Diocletian were in the direction of absolutism. The medicine had to be strengthened : soon its virtue would be exhausted. Only the poison would remain.

The government became a centralized despotism, a vast, highly complex machine. For a time its new strength warded off foreign foes, and it even stimulated society into fresh life. But the cost of the various courts and of the immense body of officials pressed upon the masses with crushing weight, and the omnipotence of the central government oppressed the minds of men. Patriotism died ; enterprise disappeared.[1]

---

[1] It is desirable for students to discuss in class more fully some of these forms of government of which the text treats. Absolutism refers to the *source of supreme power : i.e.,* in a system of absolutism, supreme power is in the hands of one person. "Centralization" refers to the *kind of administration.* A centralized administration is one carried on by a body of officials of many grades, all *appointed from above. Absolutism and centralization do not* **necessarily** *go together.* A government may come from the people, and yet rule through a centralized administration, as in France to-day. It may be absolute, and yet allow much freedom to local agencies, as in Turkey, or

To this despotic organization we owe thanks, however, for putting off the catastrophe in western Europe for two centuries more. In this time, *Christianity* won its battle over paganism, and *Roman law* took on a system (§ 737) that enabled it to live on under the barbarian conquest.

CONSTANTINE AND THE VICTORY OF CHRISTIANITY

672. From Diocletian to Constantine, 305–312. — In 303, after long hesitation, Diocletian began the most terrible of all the

HALL OF THE BATHS OF DIOCLETIAN — now the Church of St. Mary of the Angels.

persecutions of the Christian church. Two years later, in the midst of this contest, he laid down his power, to retire to pri-

---

in Russia in past centuries. But absolutism is likely to develop centralized agencies, as Russia has been doing rapidly of late.

Under a great genius, like Napoleon the First, a centralized government may for a time produce rapid benefits. But the system always decays, unless care is taken to *educate the people politically* and allow a large measure of local self-government.

vate life,[1] persuading his colleague Maximian to do the same. The two Caesars became emperors, — *Galerius* in the East and *Constantius* in the West. Each appointed a Caesar as an assistant and successor. But Constantius died in a few months, before the position of the new Caesars was firmly established, and this misfortune plunged the empire into new strife. For eight years, civil war raged between six claimants for the throne.

During these convulsions, the persecution of the Christians was still raging in the dominion of *Galerius.* But in A.D. 311, while sick with a loathsome disease, of which he soon died, he published a grudging *Edict of Toleration.* It declared that under the demoralizing conditions the emperor judged it wise "to permit them to resume their own worship, provided they did nothing contrary to good order." It was a remarkable act. For the first time the principle "that there may be Christians" was officially pronounced, the contrary of what had been in force since Nero. (§ 659.) Yet the decree did not restore confiscated property, nor grant the right to hold property, nor did it promise to the Christians equal rights with the pagans. The final clause, "provided they do nothing contrary to good order," admitted of any unfavorable interpretation. The announcement of special instructions for the judges was an ill omen. As a matter of fact the edict did not prevent other emperors from taking up the persecution again.

673. Constantine the Great was the son of that Constantius Chlorus who had been "Caesar" in Britain under Diocletian and who became joint emperor with Galerius, when the older emperors abdicated. Constantius had distinctly favored the Christians in his provinces. Almost immediately after his accession to the imperial throne, while still in Britain, he died; and his devoted army at once clothed his son with the purple robes,

---

[1] When pressed to assume the government again during the disorders that followed, Diocletian wrote from his rural retreat. "Could you come here and see the vegetables that I raise in my garden with my own hands, you would no more talk to me of empire." Cf. § 631.

hailing him Imperator. For some years Constantine was content to rule and reorganize his provinces in Britain and Gaul, preparing, at the proper moment, to interfere in the matter of civil strife in Italy, where one claimant was destroying another. In 312, he marched upon Maxentius, the worthless ruler who then held Rome.

One day, shortly after noontime, while pondering on the heavy odds that were against him, he and the soldiers who

THE MILVIAN BRIDGE TO-DAY.
Only the foundations belong to the ancient structure.

happened to be with him beheld a fiery cross in the skies with the inscription, " In this thou wilt conquer."[1] During the following night he had a vision of Christ, who told him to approach the enemy under the standard of the cross. This he did. The new standard, called " Labarum," preceded his host in the battle at the Milvian Bridge. Maxentius suffered a

---

[1] Davis' *Readings*, II, No. 113, gives the whole of the original account. The insinuation that Constantine deliberately took a false oath is unfounded.

crushing defeat and was drowned in the Tiber. Constantine publicly ascribed the victory to the God of the Christians.

In the following year, 313, Constantine together with Licinius, his ally, issued the famous Edict of Milan, by which full liberty was granted to the Christians. This event marks the beginning of a new era for Christianity, for the Roman empire, and for the world at large.

The battle at the Milvian Bridge made Constantine the sole ruler in the West. Licinius soon was the sole ruler in the East. During the years of peace that followed, however, Licinius displayed more and more hostility against the Christians and repudiated the Edict of Milan. Other differences increased the tension between him and Constantine. A new war broke out which assumed the character of a religious contest. In Licinius' camp Egyptian soothsayers and pagan priests predicted a victory of the Roman gods. In that of Constantine bishops prayed for victory. Licinius openly challenged the God of the Christians.

"These are our country's gods, and these we honor with a worship derived from our remote ancestors. But he who leads the army opposed to us has proven false to the religion of his fathers and has adopted atheistic sentiments, honoring, in his infatuation, some strange and unheard-of deity, with whose despicable standard he now disgraces the army, and confiding in whose aid he has taken up arms . . . not so much against us as against the gods he has forsaken. However, the present occasion shall decide . . . between our gods and those our adversaries profess to honor. For either it will declare the victory to be ours, and so most justly evince that our gods are the true helpers and saviors ; or else if the god of Constantine, who comes we know not whence, shall prove superior to our deities . . . let no one henceforth doubt what god he ought to worship."

The victory of Constantine at Chalcedon, 324, was widely accepted as a verdict in favor of Christianity. It at the same time made Constantine sole emperor of the entire Roman domain.

674. Constantinople. — Constantine definitely removed the capital from Rome. He established it at Byzantium, which he rebuilt on a magnificent scale. It now became "Constantinople," Constantine's city. There were several wise reasons for the removal. (1) The turbulent Roman populace still clung to the *name* of the old republic; a new and Eastern city without any of the old republican traditions would afford a more peaceful home for the Oriental monarchy now established. (2) Lying between the Danube and the Euphrates, Constantinople was a more convenient center than Rome from which to look to the protection of the frontiers, especially as the Persians were still thought the chief danger of the empire. (3) Constantinople was admirably situated to become a great center of commerce. Thus she could support a large population by her own industries far better than Rome which had little means of producing wealth. (4) It is often said that Constantine wished a capital which he could make Christian more easily and more thoroughly than old Rome. As a matter of fact, Constantinople became an entirely Christian city.

After this transfer of the capital and the imperial court Rome more and more changed into the city of the popes. In the course of time the successor of St. Peter became the most prominent man in Rome and all Italy. The papacy was thus enabled to develop its great resources more freely and independently. This effect, so highly providential, was probably never thought of by Constantine.

675. The Recognition of Christianity was the greatest part of Constantine's life work. The Edict of Milan was only its solemn introduction. Either at once or in the course of the next few years he ordered all confiscated property to be restored to the Christians and their Churches, gave the Church the power to hold property for religious purposes and bestowed great privileges on the clergy.[1] The bishops were better enabled to protect their flocks, especially the poor. Objectionable features began to be removed from the law books. By dropping the sacrifices to the gods, which officials had been obliged to perform, he made it possible for the Christians to

---

[1] The privileges of teachers (§ 620) were the model for the privileges now extended to the clergy.

hold public offices. On the other hand, paganism was not prohibited, but it was deprived of its character as the sole religion of the Roman state. There were now two religions, equally acknowledged by public authority. The emperor, however, let it be noticed that he preferred to have Christians around him.

676. Constantine's Views. — Constantine sincerely believed Christianity to be the only true religion, though it evidently

THE ARCH OF CONSTANTINE.

took a long time before his mind had assimilated all its truths. What strikes us most, at first sight, is the fact that he postponed his baptism until his death and spent all his life as a catechumen (one that is being prepared for baptism). Incredible as it sounds, this was not at all uncommon in his time. Wiser than he was his mother, St. Helena, who became at once a fervent Christian and made it her special task to have splendid churches erected on the holy places in Jerusalem, Bethlehem, and elsewhere. It is a beautiful trait in Constantine's character that he always showed a true filial devotion to her and bestowed upon her the greatest honors.

Considerations of statesmanship, however, were not absent when he took the momentous step which threw the history of the world into new channels. Numerically, indeed, the Christians were powerless, being at the most about one tenth of the population. Their organization, too, was neither intended nor fitted for military or political purposes. But what the state needed above all was morality restored and decaying society renewed, and this, his keen mind showed him, could be expected only from a religion whose members were prepared to die rather than violate their duty. He had the strength to follow his convictions and to face the antagonism of the pagan world. *In Constantine the imperial dignity obtained the position which Divine Providence had destined for it, namely, to be the protector of the Church of Jesus Christ.* This was entirely Constantine's view. Unfortunately, instead of confining himself to affairs within the province of the state, he often meddled with matters rather closely connected with doctrine. But taken all in all, the work of his long reign has been a great blessing to the world. Though he is no Saint, the Church gratefully remembers him in her martyrology as " the most pious emperor Constantine."

The victory of Christianity just at this time and the subsequent general conversion of the empire's population made possible the conversion and civilization of the barbarians who were to conquer the Empire politically.

FROM CONSTANTINE TO THEODOSIUS (337-395)

677. The Sons of Constantine (337-361). — Constantine divided the empire at his death between his three sons, Constantine II, Constans, and Constantius. Wars between Constantine and Constans and the rise and defeat of a usurper finally made Constantius sole emperor. More than any other emperor did Constantius meddle in ecclesiastical questions. He sided with the Arians (see § 682) and subjected the defenders of the

Catholic faith to a regular persecution. He proved an inefficient ruler, and the empire was invaded repeatedly by Persians and Teutons.

678. Julian the Apostate (361–363). — Finally the German Alemanni (§ 648) again broke into Gaul and threatened to become masters of that province. This peril summoned *Julian*, a cousin of Constantius, from his studies at Athens. The youthful philosopher was given command of the imperial armies in Gaul. He defeated the invaders in a great battle at *Strassburg*, and drove them again beyond the Rhine. The enthusiastic army, against his will, saluted him emperor, and soon afterward, on the death of Constantius, he succeeded to the throne.

Julian would have preferred to live the quiet life of a student. He spent his energy in conflict with two forces, both of which were to prove victorious, — the barbarians and the Church. This reign saw *the last official attempt to restore paganism*. Julian had been baptized and brought up in the Christian faith. He now openly apostatized, and began the fight against Christianity by a method entirely his own. Beside writing satires against the "Galileans," as he styled the Christians, he excluded them from the court, the higher offices, the bench and the bar, and *from the right of teaching or studying in the higher schools*. His aim was to make them appear a contemptible class; they might become "hewers of wood and drawers of water," but nothing more. Outside of this his edicts prescribed no persecution, but he allowed the governors to torture and murder Christians with impunity. Julian the Apostate fell in a war against the Persians, wounded by an arrow. It is said that he exclaimed, "Galilean, thou hast conquered." Whether this be true or not, it expressed the situation.

679. The Last Attempt at "Partnership Emperors." — On Julian's death, one of his officers, *Jovian*, was chosen emperor in the camp, and when he died, a few months later, the officers elected the vigorous *Valentinian* to succeed him. This ruler restored the system of "partnership emperors." He kept the

West under his own control and assigned the East to his brother *Valens*.

Valentinian (364–375) was an uncultured soldier, but proved an able ruler. The Alemanni, who had again broken across the Rhine, were repulsed, and other German tribes were chastised. He was succeeded in the West by his son *Gratian* (375–383). In the East, Valens was showing himself weak as well as cruel. *The Goths, a German people, were allowed (376 A.D.) to cross the Danube, to find homes as subjects within the empire* (§ 712). Enraged by the deceit of imperial officials, these barbarians soon rose in rebellion, and defeated and slew Valens in the battle of *Adrianople* (378 A.D.).

In the West, Gratian had in name associated his half-brother, *Valentinian II*, in the government; but Valentinian was a mere child, and now, in the great danger of the empire, Gratian gave the throne of the invaded East to *Theodosius*, an experienced general.

680. Theodosius (379–395) pacified the Goths and restored order. On the death of Gratian, he succeeded to the real authority in the West also. *This was the last real union of the whole empire under one ruler.* On his death the empire was divided between his two sons, Arcadius and Honorius. After 395 there was "The Empire in the East" and "The Empire in the West," *one* in theory.

Theodosius gave the deathblow to paganism by prohibiting it under pain of capital punishment. Paganism survived, however, for some time, chiefly in out-of-the-way places.[1] Theodosius was sincerely devoted to his Church. When the inhabitants of Thessalonica had killed some of his Gothic soldiers, he ordered a great massacre in that city, and some seven thousand citizens were killed without trial. Thereupon St. Ambrose, the bishop of Milan, his friend, informed him that he must submit to an ecclesiastical penance. This the emperor did "with religious humility" so genuine that the people interceded for him. "Stripping himself of every emblem of royalty, he publicly in church bewailed his sins."

---

[1] Hence the name *pagans*, from a Latin word meaning rustics. From a like fact the Christian Germans at a later time came to describe the remaining adherents of the old worship as *heathens* (heath-dwellers).

CHAPTER XLII

THE EMPIRE OF THE FOURTH CENTURY

(A Topical Study)

CHRISTIANITY

681. No longer hampered by repression and acknowledged and supported by civil authority the Church now began her public career of reformation. Her greatest mission was to restore the recognition and adoration of the One true God, " Who made heaven and earth," and to undo by the power of the Divine Savior the effects of Adam's sin in the souls of men. This is the foundation of all her other grand achievements. The sections of this book describing the morals of pagan Rome (§§ 629–634), outline the gigantic task she was to accomplish. The powerful and rich now heard that they had not only privileges but also strict duties towards the poor and dependent. The divine example of Jesus of Nazareth showed the dignity of manual labor. Man was again taught the sacredness of his own life and that of his fellow-men. The gladiatorial shows came to an end. The child's existence was safeguarded. Matrimony arose to the dignity of a sacrament and the married persons were instructed in their sacred duties towards children and each other. Charity was preached and practiced on a magnificent scale. Its precepts entered even into the cold regulations of the Roman law. Slavery was indeed not abolished with one blow. But the Church inculcated brotherly love, insisted on the equality of all men before God, and encouraged the voluntary liberation of slaves. The revised laws provided for their essential rights. All this, together possibly with other influences which if left alone would have been powerless, brought about a gradual disappearance of slavery without throwing the country into violent internal commotion.

True, the fact that the religion of the Cross now enjoyed honor and even preference caused a certain amount of worldliness to become noticeable among its followers. This indeed retarded the progress of its activity. But the final result is only the more remarkable.

682. Older Heresies. — While Christianity was harassed by the persecutions from without, its internal peace was threatened by dissensions within the fold. Some heresies were directed against the very essence of Christianity. Gnosticism and Manichaeism reintroduced with new and glaring errors the old system of the Persians (§ 78), in which there was no room for the doctrine of Redemption by Christ.

683. Arianism. — The Council of Nicaea. — After Constantine the Great had given liberty to the Church, new heresies raised their heads. The first and perhaps the most dangerous was *Arianism*. The priest Arius denied the divinity of Christ, leaving Him only the honor of being the noblest and greatest of all creatures, through whom all other things were made. Arius with his followers disturbed chiefly the oriental Churches. They propagated their error not only by scientific treatises, but also by all kinds of street-minstrelsy. To end the confusion caused by so fundamental an error, the first Ecumenical (general) Council was summoned to meet at *Nicaea* in Asia Minor in 325. With the consent of the pope, the emperor invited the bishops and defrayed the expenses of their journey and the maintenance of the assembly. Three hundred and eighteen bishops were present. Three legates of the pope presided, and though two of them were only priests, all signed the documents before the bishops. No one was more prominent than St. Athanasius, a deacon, who accompanied the bishop of Alexandria. With only two dissenting voices the august assembly drew up a brief summary of the Catholic doctrine, stating that Christ is the only Son of God, born of the Father from all eternity, true God of the true God, begotten not made, consubstantial with the Father. With some additions by later Councils this "Nicene Creed" still forms part of the Mass on Sundays and Feastdays. Arius and his adherents were banished by the emperor. (Dolan, *The Papacy and the First Councils.*)

Reaction of Arianism. — But the evil was not so easily eradicated. Constantine was prevailed upon to cancel the decree of banishment, and he and his successors became more and more entangled in the controversy. The Arians used all kinds of intrigue and violence. By the assistance of some heterodox emperors they at times seemed to be on the point of victory. Catholic bishops were deposed and exiled, and with their adherents subjected to brutal treatment. Blood flowed in many cities. After some sixty years, however, Arianism had disappeared within the Roman world.

Unfortunately, Arian bishops had spread their heresy among most of the German tribes who lived upon the borders. When these afterwards forced their way into the empire, they brought Arianism with them. Those Arian tribes who were not converted to Catholicity have vanished from history. Those only survived who professed the Nicene Creed.

684. Imperial Legislation. — Constantine had commenced the Christianization of the Roman law, and on the whole the succeeding emperors continued in his spirit. The new laws punished with death the killing of infants and slaves, and secured efficient protection for orphans. They abolished crucifixion as a mode of execution. They prohibited the gladiatorial combats, and although it took some time before these outrages really ceased, criminals were no longer condemned to fight in the arena.[1] The sanctity of matrimony was much better safeguarded. The legal formalities for the emancipation of slaves were considerably simplified, and the emancipated slave became at once a Roman citizen. Families of slaves were not to be separated when sold.

Laws were passed also against heretics and idolaters. Theodosius II declared it was the "first duty of the imperial majesty to protect the true religion, whose worship was in-

---

[1] See O'Reilly, *The Martyrs of the Coliseum*, (Novel), chapter 22, The Last Martyr.

timately connected with the prosperity of human undertakings." Certain heresies were punished with death. Great Christian authors opposed this secular legislation, though they finally granted that some repressive measures against heretics might be productive of good results. (See Catholic Encyclopedia, Vol. VIII, page 27.) The suppression of paganism began with the prohibition of the many unnatural excesses and superstitious abuses by which it was attended. Finally Theodosius I prohibited it under pain of death (§ 680). We do not know with what degree of severity all these laws were enforced. As to paganism some of its customs remained in vogue, even in the cities, as late as the end of the sixth century.

It is greatly to be deplored that the imperial lawgivers were less successful in other lines. Little was done for the benefit of the lower strata of society except slavery. Social and economic legislation continued in the direction it had taken under former emperors. It was meant for the welfare of the commonwealth. But since Diocletian the rulers considered themselves and the splendor of their court as the most necessary element in the government. (See §§ 661, 671.) This error was somewhat pardonable after the experience made with the rotten republican institutions. But the centralized form of administration tended to suppress individual ambition and enterprise. Society gradually crystallized in classes. For these and similar reasons the radical measures which should have been introduced grew more difficult every year. This will appear more clearly on the last pages of this chapter.

685. The Papacy. — The innate power of the papacy showed itself more and more. During the centuries of persecution the bishop of Rome had been appealed to in matters of both faith and discipline. The heretics coveted his favor, and thereby unwittingly bore witness to his character as head of the Church. But the occasions of using his supreme power were not numerous. It was different when the Christians moved with perfect safety throughout the whole empire. No doubt the fact that the successor of St. Peter was bishop of the imperial city enhanced his power; but no pope ever based his claim to supremacy on the fact that Rome was the Capital. Centuries later, ambitious patriarchs of Constantinople aspired

to the same position; the only ground they could allege for
their arrogant claim was that "New Rome," Constantinople,
was the head of the empire. The well-tried methods of
Roman administration, however, may have suggested more

THE LATERAN BASILICA, "ST. JOHN-IN-THE-LATERAN," ROME. — This site,
on which then stood the extensive palace of the "Laterani," was donated
to the popes by Constantine the Great. The present church structure,
however, is not the one erected under him. The palace served for more
than a thousand years as the regular residence of the Sovereign Pontiff.
The Lateran Palace of to-day, which is much smaller, now harbors the
Pontifical Museum of Christian Antiquities. The present Italian government declared this venerable ecclesiastical possession state property, but
leaves it provisionally under papal "administration."

than one detail in the disciplinary government of the universal
Church.

Donations to the Popes. — The popes were greatly assisted
in the fulfillment of their various duties by the liberality
of rich Romans. Constantine set the example by donating
large properties to the Apostolic See, and other ecclesiastical

institutions. Foremost among his donations to the pope was the Lateran palace. Eventually the pope became the richest landowner in Italy, a fact which enabled him to be, in the stormy period of the barbarian invasions, the benefactor of the poor and distressed in the whole world. Various emperors, moreover, bestowed on the popes regular governmental powers, such as the administration of the existing poorlaws and of other regulations concerning charity and justice. Thus the pope, though still a subject, enjoyed a position in Rome which was not very unlike that of a prince, the more so because, after the foundation of Constantinople, no emperor ever made the ancient capital his permanent residence.

686. Far-reaching missionary enterprises, which must be laid to the credit of the popes,[1] added new splendor to the See of Peter. The first to be mentioned under this head is the conversion of Ireland by its Apostle, St. Patrick. Although feeling himself called by God, he thought it his duty to obtain the authorization of the pope. Sent expressly by Celestine I, he went to Ireland in A.D. 432, and the result of his sixty years of labor was a fervently Catholic nation, and convents filled with devoted men and women. He impressed on his disciples that all difficult religious questions were to be settled by " the See Apostolic, that is, the Chair of the Apostle Peter, which has authority in the city of Rome." Scotland was gained for the faith by the zeal of his followers. Irish monks and monasteries carried on a most efficient missionary and reformatory activity in Central Europe. They also played a very important part in the conversion of Anglo-Saxon England.

Two other great missionaries, Sts. Augustine and Boniface, will be mentioned later on (§§ 747, 776).

---

[1] The name pope (" papa ") was originally only a term of affectionate, respect (" father ") applied to any bishop. It did not become the *official* name of the bishops of Rome until 1085. Special reports: Leo the Great and Gregory the Great.

SOCIETY IN THE FOURTH CENTURY

687. Exhaustion. — The three quarters of a century after the reunion of the empire under Constantine was marked by a fair degree of outward prosperity. But the secret forces that were sapping the strength of society continued to work, and early in the coming century (the fifth) the Empire was to crumble under barbarian attacks. *These inroads were no more formidable than those which had so often been rebuffed.* Apparently they were weaker (§ 752). The barbarians, then, are not to be considered as the chief cause of the " Fall." The causes were internal. The Roman Empire was overthrown from without by an ordinary attack, *because it had grown weak within.*

This weakness was not due, in any marked degree at least, to decline in the army. The army kept its superb organization, and to the last was so strong in its discipline and its pride that it was ready to face any odds unflinchingly. But more and more it became impossible to find men to fill the legions, or money to pay them. *Dearth of men (§ 649) and of money was the cause of the fall of the state. The Empire had become a shell.*[1]

688. Lack of money, rather than too much wealth, was one of the great evils. The empire did not have sufficient sources of supply of precious metals for the demands of business ; and what money there was was steadily drained away to India and the distant Orient (§ 613). This movement, which had been noticeable in the first century, had carried away hundreds of millions of dollars of coined money by the fourth century. The emperors were forced to mix silver and gold with cheaper metals in their coins. This reduced the purchasing power of money and demoralized business. Finally the lack

---

[1] The older writers explained the decay exclusively on moral grounds. Recent scholars recognize that the immediate causes of decline, though chiefly moral, were political and economic as well.

of coin forced even imperial officers to draw part of their salaries in produce, — robes, horses, wheat. Trade, in many districts, reverted to primitive barter. To pay taxes became more and more difficult. These evils continued to afflict Europe until the discovery of Mexico and Peru.

689. The classes of society in the fourth and fifth centuries differed widely from those of the first three centuries. At the top was the emperor to direct the machinery of government. At the bottom were the peasantry and artisans to produce food and wealth wherewith to pay taxes. Between these extremes were two aristocracies, — an imperial aristocracy for the empire at large, and a local aristocracy for every city.

690. The senatorial nobility, the higher aristocracy, now included many nobles who never sat in the Senate either at Rome or at the new capital Constantinople. It had swallowed up the old senatorial class of Rome, and most of the knights. *It was " a nobility of office."* That is, as with the modern Russian nobility, a family lost its rank unless from time to time it furnished officials to the government.

A noble of this class possessed great honor and some important privileges. He was a citizen of the whole empire, not of one municipality alone, and he did not have to pay *local* taxes. He bore, however, heavy imperial burdens. He might be called upon at any moment for ruinous expenses at the capital, in fulfilling some imperial command, or he might be required to assume some costly office at his own expense on a distant frontier. But only a few individuals were actually ruined by such duties. The lot of the great majority was a favored one. The great landed proprietors belonged to this class. The law allowed them to escape their proper share of the burdens of society ; and from those burdens which they were supposed to bear, they escaped in large measure by bribing the imperial officers.

691. The Curials. — Below the imperial nobility was the local nobility. Each city had its senate, or curia. The curials were not drafted into the armies, as the lower classes might be, nor were they subject to bodily punishment. They managed the finances of their city, and to some degree they still controlled its other local affairs. Those curials who rose to the high magistracies, however, had to bear large expense in providing shows and festivals for their fellow-townsmen, and all curials had costly duties in supplying the poor with corn.

More crushing still to this local nobility were the imperial burdens. The chief imperial tax was the land tax. The needs of the empire caused the amount to be increased steadily, while the ability of the people to pay steadily decreased. The curials were made the collectors of this tax in their city, *and were held personally responsible for any deficit.*

This duty was so undesirable that the number of curials tended to fall away. To secure the revenue, the emperors tried to prevent this decrease. *The curials were made a hereditary class, and were bound to their office.* They were forbidden to become clergy, soldiers, or lawyers; they were not allowed to move from city to city, or even to travel without special permission.

A place in the senate of his city had once been the highest ambition of a wealthy middle-class citizen; but in the fourth century it had become almost an act of heroism to assume the duty. A story is told that in a Spanish municipality a public-spirited man voluntarily offered himself for a vacancy in the curia, and that his fellow-citizens erected a statue in his honor. As the position grew more and more unendurable, desperate attempts were made to escape at any sacrifice. Of course the desirable escape was into the imperial nobility, but this was possible only to a few. Others, despite the law, sought refuge in the artisan gilds, in the church, or even in serfdom, in a servile marriage, or in flight to the barbarians.[1]

692. The middle class between the curials and the laborers, was rapidly disappearing. When a trader, small landowner, or professional man acquired a certain amount of land, he was compelled by law to become a curial; but the general drift was for such men to sink rather than rise.

---

[1] See Robinson's *Readings*, I, 29.

693. **The artisans** were grouped in gilds, or colleges, each with its own organization. *Each member was now bound to his gild, as the curial to his office.* The condition of artisans had become desperate. An edict of Diocletian's regarding prices and wages shows that a workman received not more than one tenth the wages of an American workman of like grade, while food and clothing cost at least one third as much as now. The artisan of the fourth century then received in "real wages" only a third as much as the artisan of to-day. To say nothing of other matters, it is hard to see how he could have kept soul and body together. His family must have known very rarely the taste of butter, eggs, or fresh meat.

694. **The peasantry** had become *serfs.* That is, they were bound to their labor on the soil, and changed masters with the land they tilled.

In the last days of the Republic, the system of great estates which had blighted Italy earlier (§§ 480, 488) cursed province after province outside Italy. Free labor disappeared before servile labor; grain culture declined; and large areas of land ceased to be tilled. To help remedy this state of affairs, the emperors introduced a new system. After successful wars, they *gave* large numbers of barbarian captives to great landlords, — thousands in a batch, — not as slaves, but as *coloni,* or serfs. The purpose was to secure *a hereditary class of agricultural laborers,* and so keep up the food supply. The coloni were really given *not to the landlord, but to the land.*

They were not personal property, as slaves were. *They were part of the real estate.* They, and their children after them, were attached to the soil, and could not be sold off it. They had some rights which slaves did not have. They could contract a legal marriage, and each had his own plot of ground, of which he could not be dispossessed so long as he paid to the landlord a fixed rent in labor and in produce.

Augustus began this system on a small scale, and it soon became a regular practice to dispose thus of vanquished tribes. This made it still more difficult for the free small-farmer to maintain himself. That class *sank* into serfs. On the other hand, the slaves *rose* into serfs, until nearly all cultivators of the soil were of this order.

This institution of coloni lasted for hundreds of years, under the name of serfdom. It helped change the ancient slave organization of labor into the modern free organization. For the slave it was an immense gain. At the moment, however, it was one more factor in killing out the old middle class and in widening the gap between the nobles and the small cultivators.[1]

But in the fourth century, the lot of the coloni, too, had become miserable. They were crushed by imperial taxes, in addition to the rent due their landlord ; and in Diocletian's time, in Gaul, they rose in desperate revolt against the upper classes, to plunder, murder, and torture — a terrible forerunner of the peasant-risings during the Middle Ages.

695. *Society was crystallizing into castes.* **Not only had the peasantry become serfs, attached from generation to generation to the same plot of ground:** *the principle of serfdom was being applied to all classes.* **The artisan was bound to his hereditary gild, and the curial and the noble each to his hereditary order. Freedom of movement seemed lost. In its industries and its social relations as well as in government, the Empire was becoming despotic and Oriental.**

696. Crushing Taxation. — The Empire was "a great tax gathering and barbarian-fighting machine." It collected taxes *in order* to fight barbarians. *But the time came when the provincials began to dread the tax-collector more than they feared the Goth.* This was partly because of the decrease in ability to pay, and partly because the complex organization cost more and more. Says Goldwin Smith: "The earth swarmed with the consuming hierarchy of extortion, so that it was said that they who received taxes were more than they who paid them." Moreover, the wealthiest classes succeeded in shifting the burden largely upon those least able to pay.

Thus, heavy as the taxation was, it yielded less and less. The revenues of the government shrank up. The empire suffered from a lack of wealth as well as from a lack of men.

---

[1] This serf system *began* on the vast estates of the emperors themselves, — where easy rental and protection made the arrangement desirable even to many free tenant farmers. Later, the system spread to big *private* estates; and it was reinforced by this practice of barbarian captives.

697. Peaceful Infusion of Barbarians.—The only measure that helped fill up the gaps in population was the introduction of barbarians from without. This took place *peacefully* on a large scale; but so far as preserving the political empire was concerned, it was a source of weakness rather than of strength.

Not only was the Roman army mostly made up of Germans: whole provinces were settled by them, *before* their kinsmen from without, in the fifth century, began in earnest to break over the Rhine. Conquered barbarians had been settled, hundreds of thousands at a time, in frontier provinces, and friendly tribes had been admitted, to make their homes in depopulated districts. Thus as slaves, soldiers, coloni, subjects, the German world had been filtering into the Roman world, *until a large part of the empire was peacefully Germanized.* Even the imperial officers were largely Germans.

This infusion of new blood helped to renew the decaying population and to check the decline of material prosperity. The Germans within the empire, in large measure, took on Roman civilization and customs; but at the same time, they kept some of their old customs and ideas and a friendly feeling for their kinsmen in the German forests. *The barrier between the empire and its assailants melted away.* This lessened the agony of the barbarian conquest, but it helped to make it possible.

698. The Government and the Money Power. — Men were not equal before the law. Not only the courts in practice, but even the written law, made vicious distinctions between rich and poor. The noble, convicted of crime, was punished more lightly than a poor man for the same offense.

Worse still were the special privileges which the government permitted to the rich for heaping up more wealth. We noted in the closing history of the Republic the pernicious alliance between the "money power" and the government. Just how far such a state of things continued under the Empire it is hard to say. But so shrewd a reformer as Diocletian believed positively that a chief factor in the ruinous cost of living to the poor was the combination of capitalists to raise prices. He speaks of "the raging avarice," "the exorbitant prices," "the unbridled desire to plunder," on the part of those who control the market; and so he issued a decree (referred to in § 693) in which he fixed the highest price which it should be lawful to ask or give for each one of some eight hundred articles of daily use, — wheat, leather, various sorts of cloth, butter, eggs, pork, beef. Such an effort was foredoomed to failure. But it is interesting as one of the few cases in which the government attempted to interfere on the side of the poor.

699. No serious attempt was made, after the early days of the Empire, **to build up a new free peasantry** by giving farms to the unemployed millions of the cities. This is strange; for such efforts to turn a dangerous weakness into a source of strength had been characteristic of the reformers who preceded the Empire, from Gracchus to Caesar (§§ 508–519, 558). The cause of the absence of such effort is probably the influence of wealth upon the ruling powers. The noble landlords who shared among themselves the wide domains of Africa, Gaul, and Spain, received gladly the free gift of thousands of coloni (§ 694) to till their lands; but they would have fought fiercely any attempt by the government to recover part of their domains to make homes for free settlers.

There is, however, another side to the question. In the days of Gracchus and of Caesar, the city mob was made up, in good part, of ex-farmers, or of their sons, who had been driven from the land against their will (§ 489). Long before Diocletian's day, the rabble of Rome or Alexandria had lost all touch with country life. Secure in free doles of grain, sleeping in gateways, perhaps, but spending their days in the splendid free public baths or in the terrible fascination of gladiatorial games or of the chariot races, they could no longer be driven to the simple life and hard labor of the farm — even if farming had continued profitable. We know that to-day, in America, hundreds of thousands of stalwart men prefer want and misery on the crowded sidewalks and under the gleaming lights of a city to the loneliness of a comfortable living in the country. So in the ancient world, it was probably too late, when the Empire came, to wean the mob from its city life.

LITERATURE OF THIS PERIOD

700. Character. — There are few works on secular subjects. Paganism was worn out. The hold of Christianity on the population was not yet firm enough. Its great minds were occupied with the defense of its doctrines, not so much against a decrepit polytheism as against the heresies which threatened it from within. It was the era of the " Fathers of the Church." These men, perfect masters of the language and equipped with all the knowledge the old classics could offer, warded off attacks, and by elucidating and explaining the Christian faith strove to unfold its hidden beauties. This period saw also the birth of Church history and Christian poetry. Many of the great names are connected with Celtic Gaul, which had been foremost in the study of classic literature during the time of the pagan empire (§ 620).

701. The chief pagan writers were : —

Ammianus, an Asiatic soldier, the author of a spirited continuation of Tacitus' history;

Eutropius, a soldier and the author of a summary of Roman history ;

Symmachus, the center of the pagan party in Rome ; he left a large collection of letters, a great number of which concern the exhibition of gladiatorial shows.

702. Prominent among the numerous Christian writers were : —

St. Ambrose, bishop of Milan, the most powerful opponent of Arianism in the West (§ 681), widely renowned for his eloquence. He also laid the foundations of ecclesiastical music and himself composed many hymns for liturgical use.

St. Athanasius, Patriarch of Alexandria, the champion of orthodoxy in the East (§ 681).

St. Augustine, born in northern Africa, the most prominent writer on the nature of Divine Grace. His famous *City of God* presents a kind of philosophy of history; he wrote it as a consolation in the disasters which had fallen upon the Roman Empire. He died during the siege of his episcopal city, Hippo, by the Vandals (§ 714).

St. Basil the Great, born in Asia Minor, educated in Constantinople and Athens, the father of Oriental monasticism. Beside many theological works he also wrote a booklet entitled *How Young Men Should Profit by the Study of the Pagan Writings*.

St. Gregory of Nazianz in Asia Minor, renowned as theologian and pulpit orator and for his efforts to create a Christian poetry. The bulk of his poems cannot be held to parallel the productions of the classic poets, but they were the best of his age, and many of them are pearls of great price.

St. Hilary of Poitiers was the champion of Catholic doctrine before St. Ambrose. He seems also to have been the author of sacred (Latin) hymns.

St. Jerome, born in what is now Bosnia. After receiving the most careful education in Rome, he became a hermit and lived for many years in a grotto at Bethlehem. Here he translated the Bible into Latin. This translation, called the *Vulgate*, is the official Bible of the Church. Many valuable books on biblical subjects embody the results of his lifelong indefatigable studies.

St. John Chrysostom, bishop of Constantinople, the most powerful pulpit orator of the Greek East.

703. Church Historians : —

Lactantius, born in northern Africa, a professor of rhetoric, author of many theological works and of an historical one, *The Deaths of the Persecutors (of Christianity)*.

Eusebius, bishop of Nicomedia, the author of the first ecclesiastical history.

Socrates, of Constantinople, a lawyer, continued the work of Eusebius.

Poets : —

Besides Sts. Gregory of Nazianz and Hilary of Poitiers the following may be mentioned : —

Ausonius of Bordeaux, Professor of Rhetoric, left many religious productions, patriotic songs, and occasional poems. One of his finest is a long description in poetic form of the river Moselle.

Paulinus of Bordeaux, died as Bishop of Nola in Italy ; his poems in many ways surpass those of Ausonius, his teacher and friend.

Sidonius and Avitus, Gallic bishops, wrote profane as well as religious poems.

Unfortunately the migration of nations fell like a frost upon this spring-time of literary activity, without, however, destroying it entirely. In Catholic Ireland especially the flame kept burning brightly, and for centuries the Green Isle was famous for the learning and hospitality of its monasteries and scholars. Here are some of the names recorded in the annals of the literature of this period of storm and stress : —

Fortunatus, an Italian poet ; many of his poems are mere flatteries to the princes on whose kindness he depended. But the general character of his works is that of seriousness. He is the author of two hymns on the Holy Cross which are still used in the liturgy of Holy Week.

Cassiodorus, became a monk after filling the highest places in the Ostro-Gothic kingdom. His own voluminous writings are less important than his efforts to preserve the works of classic and earlier Christian literature.

Pope St. Gregory the Great.

Sts. Columba, the Apostle of Scotland, and Adamnan, his successor ; Sts. Columban and his disciple Gallus, missionaries in Central Europe, all four Irishmen.

Sts. Bede, the Venerable, and Aldhelm, Anglo-Saxons.

704. Attitude of Christianity towards Pagan Literature. — The foregoing lists alone would show conclusively that there was no opposition in principle to the study of the ancient classical writers. All the great lights of Christian literature, theologians as well as poets, had been trained in their school and that long after the fall of paganism. As a matter of fact the young Christians studied the same books as their pagan contemporaries. It was felt as a very severe blow when Julian the Apostate forbade them to either study or teach the classics. That there was danger in this kind of schooling is evident. Some very few extremists would reject pagan writers altogether. Warnings against making them a customary reading or placing them in matters of conduct above the Christian writings, notably the Bible, were well founded. But prudent teachers could eliminate this peril. The principles propounded by St. Basil the Great in the above-mentioned treatise have ever been and still are guiding stars in this question for Catholic schools.

REVIEW EXERCISE FOR PART V. — (1) Add the dates 284, 325, 378, to the list. (2) Extend list of terms and names for fact drill. (3) Memorize characterization of the centuries of the Empire. (4) Review the growth of the Christian church. (5) Review briefly the movement in literature.

PART VI

ROMANO-TEUTONIC EUROPE

The settlement of the Teutonic tribes was not merely the introduction of a new set of ideas and institutions, . . . it was also the introduction of fresh blood and youthful mind. — GEORGE BURTON ADAMS.

Before entering upon this final portion of Ancient History, it will be well to reread carefully the summaries in §§ 4 and 322.

CHAPTER XLIII

THE TEUTONS

705. Early Home and the Different Peoples. — The Teutons came into our story first at the time of Marius (§ 523). At frequent intervals during the five centuries since that first invasion they had been beating fiercely upon the frontiers, and they had sent great swarms of their numbers, as prisoners and as peaceful colonists, to dwell within the empire. Now they were to break in as conquerors, so introducing one of the great eras in history.

The Rhine and the Danube had long separated the barbaric world from the Roman world. (See map on page 584.) In the fifth century the important groups of the Teutons, or Germans, as the Romans called them, were the Goths, Burgundians, Vandals, Alemanni, Lombards, Franks, and Saxons. The Norsemen were to appear later.

706. Stage of Civilization. — When appearing in history the Teutonic tribes were possessed of some primitive civilization and peculiar political institutions. Those nearer the empire were more advanced than the rest. They had no cities, but

582

their important villages were surrounded by palisades. Their dwellings were huts built of wood and roofed with straw or reed. They lived chiefly on the cattle they raised and by hunting and fishing. Agriculture, little encouraged by the conditions of their country, was managed by women and slaves. They had no true alphabet, no real literature. There were, however, simple ballads and epics which were transmitted orally and sung to the sound of a primitive kind of music. Handicraft did not rise high enough to be called a profession, except, perhaps, in the case of the armorer who forged the weapons. Their trade was barter. Skins or cloths rudely woven formed their clothing. But the nobler warriors were clad in chain mail and wore helmets crested with plumes, horns, dragons, and other strange devices. Linen clothes, artificially dyed, were common with women. The slaves, generally prisoners of war, were, as a rule, treated humanely and had opportunities to improve their condition.

707. Character. — Tacitus (§ 628) says of the Germans : —

"For my part, I agree with those who think that the tribes of Germany are free from all trace of intermarriage with foreign nations. All have fierce blue eyes, reddish hair, and huge bodies fit only for sudden exertion. They are not very able to endure labor that is exhausting. Heat and thirst they cannot withstand at all, though to cold and hunger their climate and soil have hardened them." — *Germania*, iv.

They possessed, however, some remarkable moral characteristics. They revered women. Their wives, mothers, and sisters used to follow them to war and spur them on to bravery. Says Tacitus : —

"Close by them (in the battle) are those dearest to them, so that in the midst of the fight they can hear the shrieks of women and the cries of children. These loved ones are to every man the most valued witnesses of his valor, and at the same time his most generous applauders. The soldier brings his wounds to mother and wife, who shrinks not from counting them, or even demanding to see them, and who provides food for the warriors and gives them encouragement." — *Germania*, vii.

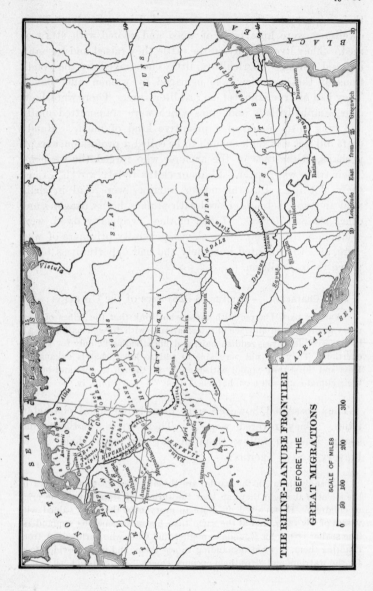

THE RHINE-DANUBE FRONTIER
BEFORE THE
GREAT MIGRATIONS

SCALE OF MILES

0   50   100   200   300

A possible captivity of their women seemed to the men more dreadful than their own. Tacitus dwells at length upon the affection and purity of their domestic relations. Life and welfare of children was religiously safeguarded.

They reverenced truth and fidelity. They possessed a proud spirit of individual liberty, a "high, stern sense of manhood and the worth of man," which was to influence later European history. Another quality is especially important. The Germans were endowed with a serious, earnest, imaginative temperament. They felt the solemn mystery of life, with its shortness of days, its sorrows, and longings. This inspired in them, not unmanly despair, but a heroism tinged with melancholy. In the *Song of Beowulf* (an old poem that has come down to us from the German forests) the chieftain goes out to an almost hopeless encounter with a terrible monster

FRONTISPIECE OF THE "GOLDEN GOSPEL." — Seventh or eighth century. In the British Museum, London.

that had been destroying his people. "Each man," exclaims the hero, "must abide the end of his life work; let him that may work, work his doomed deeds ere night come."

But there were many dark sides in their character. Their cold, damp forests had helped to make them excessive drunkards and immoderate eaters, and when not engaged in war they spent day after day in sleep or gluttony. They were desperate gamblers, too, and when other wealth was gone, they would stake even their liberty upon the throw of the dice. They also had the custom of offering to their gods human sacrifices, chiefly war prisoners.

708. Religion. — The old German religion was a rude polytheism. *Woden*, the war god, held the first place in their worship. From him the noble families all claimed descent. *Thor*, whose hurling hammer caused the thunder, was the god of storms and of the air. *Freya* was the deity of joy and fruitfulness.

These Teutonic gods live still in our names for the days of the week. Woden's day, Thor's day, and Freya's day are easily recognized in their modern dress. Tuesday and Saturday take their names from two obscure gods, Tiw and Saetere ; while the remaining two days are the Moon's day and the Sun's day.

709. Government. — Tacitus shows the Germans, organized in three political units, — village, canton, and tribe. The village was originally no doubt the home of a clan. The village and the tribe each had its popular Assembly with its chief. The tribal chief, or king, was surrounded by his council of smaller chiefs.[1]

" In the election of kings they have regard to birth ; in that of generals to valor. Their kings have not an absolute or unlimited power ; and their generals command less through the force of authority than of example. If they are daring, adventurous, and conspicuous in action, they procure obedience from the admiration they inspire." — *Germania*, vii.

" On affairs of smaller moment, the chiefs consult ; on those of greater importance, the whole community ; yet with this circumstance, that what is referred to the decision of the people is first discussed by the chiefs. They assemble, unless upon some sudden emergency, on stated days, either at the new or full moon. When they all think fit, they sit down armed. Silence is proclaimed by the priests, who have on this occasion a coercive power. Then the king, or chief, and such others as are conspicuous for age, birth, military renown, or eloquence, are heard ; they gain attention rather from *their ability to persuade, than their authority to command*. If a proposal displease, the assembly reject it by an inarticulate murmur ; if it prove agreeable, they clash their javelins ;

---

[1] Compare with the early Greek organization, §§ 102–107. See the passage in Davis, II, No. 121.

for the most honorable expression of assent among them is the sound of arms. — *Ib.* xi, xii.

710. The " Companions." — One peculiar institution must be noted. Every great chief was surrounded by a band of " companions," who lived in his household, ate at his table, and fought at his side. To them the chief gave food, weapons, and plunder: for the honor and safety of their " lord " they devoted their energies and lives. This institution existed among the Celts also, from whom the Germans may have adopted it.[1] The element of *personal loyalty* in this relation of " companion " and lord was to influence the development of later European feudalism.

711. The Charm of the South. — The sunny South, with the wonders and riches of its strange civilization, fascinated these northerners with a potent spell. For five hundred years they had been striving to enter in and possess it. The pressure of fiercer barbarians behind them and of their own increasing population had sometimes caused them to burst in for brief periods of plunder. Always hitherto they had been thwarted by some Marius, Caesar, Aurelius, Aurelian, Diocletian, or Julian. About the year 400, in the exhaustion of the empire, they began at last to come in to stay.[2]

For Further Reading. — Tacitus, *Germania*, already quoted repeatedly in these pages.

---

[1] See Caesar, *Gallic War*, book I, chs. 2 ff.

[2] For reasons of a practical nature this textbook, like most of the present day, divides history into Ancient and Modern. An objection to this division is that it obscures the position of Christ as the center and turning point of the history of mankind. The coming of a new religion, of new leading races, of a new danger (Mohammedanism), and a new empire evidently indicate a new time, which no less evidently begins with the first of these events. Hence Ancient Times should be considered to end there. The period following Ancient History is then fitly divided into Modern History (strictly speaking), beginning with the so-called Reformation, A.D. 1517, and Medieval Times, or the Middle Ages, between this and Ancient History. The present book occasionally uses Medieval and Middle Ages descriptively to designate the same period.

CHAPTER XLIV

THE WANDERING OF THE PEOPLES, 376–565 A.D.

How can a man draw a picture of that which has no shape; or tell the order of absolute disorder? It is all . . . like the working of an ant-heap; like the insects devouring each other in a drop of water. Teuton tribes, Slavonic tribes, Tartar tribes, Roman generals, empresses, bishops, courtiers, adventurers, appear for a moment out of the crowd, — dim phantoms . . . and then vanish. . . . — CHARLES KINGSLEY.

THE TEUTONS BREAK OVER THE BARRIERS

A. THE DANUBE (376–378 A.D.)

712. The West Goths: Adrianople. — The event which we now recognize as the first step in the victory of the Teutons seemed at the time only a continuation of an old policy of the Empire. Many tribes had been admitted within the boundaries as allies and had proven faithful defenders of the frontiers. In 376, such a measure was repeated on a vast scale.

The story has been told briefly in § 679. The whole people of the West Goths (*Visigoths*) appeared on the Danube, fleeing from the more terrible Huns — wild, nomadic horsemen from Tartary. Valens, emperor of the East, granted the prayers of the fugitives, allowed them to cross the Danube, and gave them lands south of the river. They were to give up their arms, while Roman agents were to supply them food until the harvest. These agents embezzled the imperial funds and furnished vile and insufficient food, while at the same time, for bribes, they allowed the barbarians to keep their arms.[1]

The Goths rose and marched on Constantinople. At *Adrianople* (378 A.D.) Valens was defeated and slain. *This*

---

[1] In much the same way, American " Indian Agents " have provoked more than one Indian war in our history.

battle marks the beginning of the Teutonic conquest. The Goths ravaged the land up to the walls of the capital, but they could not storm a great city. The new emperor, Theodosius the Great, finally pacified them, and they remained in the Danubian provinces, peaceful settlers, for nearly twenty years.

713. Alaric. — In 395, Theodosius died, and at once masses of the Goths rose under an ambitious young chieftain, *Alaric*, whom they soon made their king. Alaric led his host into Greece. For a heavy ransom, he spared Athens, but he sacked Corinth, Argos, and Sparta. He was trapped in the Peloponnesus by the gigantic Vandal, *Stilicho*, a general of Honorius, emperor of the West (§ 680); but finally the Goth bought or maneuvered his way out, with his plunder.

Arcadius, the terrified emperor of the East, then gave Alaric a commission as "imperial lieutenant" in Illyria. "There he staid, somewhere about the head of the Adriatic, poised like an eagle in mid-air, watching Rome on one side and Byzant on the other, uncertain for a while on which quarry he should swoop." In 402, he made up his mind for Rome. But Stilicho, "the Roman shield," beat him off in two battles; and he drew back for a few years more into Illyria.

714. The Sack of Rome, 410 A.D. — Meanwhile Stilicho turned upon and destroyed a more savage horde of two hundred thousand wild Germans, who had poured down through the Alps under *Radogast* and were besieging Florence. Soon afterward Honorius suspected Stilicho of plotting to seize the throne, and had him murdered. The deed was signal enough for Alaric to try Italy once more. The weak Honorius hid himself in his impregnable fortress of Ravenna, defended by its marshes, and left the Goths free to work their will. Alaric captured Rome; and then for five days and nights that proud city was given up to sack (410 A.D.) — just 800 years after its capture by the Gauls.

The civilized world had believed Rome "the Eternal City," and was thrown into unspeakable consternation by its fall (Davis' *Readings*, II, No. 122). The pagans explained it as a punishment for the desertion of the old gods. This view was important enough so that St. Augustine (§ 702) wrote his *City of God* to refute it and to show that the true "Eternal City" was not of this world. (Extracts from this work are given in Robinson's *Readings*, ch. iii. See also Davis' *Readings*, II, No. 123, for the feeling of the world for Rome even after her overthrow.)

715. The Visigothic Kingdom in Spain. — Alaric then led his host south, intending to cross to Africa by way of Sicily; but he died[1] on the way, and was succeeded by his brother *Ataulf* (Adolph). Alaric had not been a mere destructive barbarian. He had great respect for Roman civilization and the Roman name, and when he captured Rome he ordered (an order not well obeyed) that the lives of the citizens should be spared and the treasures of the temples be left unmolested. Ataulf felt even more strongly the spell of Roman civilization. Said he:—

"It was at first my wish to destroy the Roman name, and erect in its place a Gothic empire, taking to myself the place and the powers of Caesar Augustus. But when experience taught me that the untamable barbarism of the Goths would not suffer them to live beneath the sway of law, . . . I chose the glory of renewing and maintaining by Gothic strength the fame of Rome, desiring to go down to posterity as the restorer of that Roman power which it was beyond my ability to replace."

Meantime other Teutonic tribes had broken across the Rhine and were ravaging Gaul and Spain (§§ 716 ff). Ataulf married the sister of the Emperor Honorius and accepted a commission as his lieutenant to conquer these new invaders. He led his Goths out of Italy (which was what Honorius cared most for), conquered the Vandals who had seized Spain, and set up a Gothic kingdom there *(414–419 A.D.). This was the first permanent Teutonic state within the limits of the old empire.*

The Visigothic kingdom at first included much also of south Gaul; but that territory was to be lost in less than a century to the Franks (§ 742). The kingdom in Spain lasted three hundred years, to the Mohammedan conquest (§ 773), and, centuries later, its fragments grew together again into the Spain of modern times.

---

[1] Special report : story of Alaric's burial (Davis' *Readings*, II, No. 120).

B. The Rhine

716. The Bursting of the Barrier. — For nearly forty years after the departure of the West Goths, Italy had peace; but meantime the rest of the West was lost. Even before the sack of Rome, the Rhine frontier had given way. Clouds of Germans had long been massing on that river. Some of the Roman troops there were withdrawn to strengthen Italy against Alaric's expected coming; and, in 406, the barbarians forced a passage. Then, with little opposition, they spread themselves over Gaul and Spain. The leading peoples of the invasion were the *Burgundians* and the *Vandals*.

717. The Burgundians settled in southeastern Gaul, where their name has always remained. A little later, under their king, *Gundobald*, they produced the *earliest written code of Teutonic law*. Like the Goths, too, they soon came to regard themselves, in a vague way, as living under the authority of the Empire. A Burgundian king, thanking the emperor for the title Patrician, writes: —

"My people is yours and to rule them delights me less than to serve you. . . . Our ancestors have always preferred what an emperor gave to all their fathers could bequeath. In ruling our nation, we hold ourselves but your lieutenants. You, whose divinely appointed sway no barrier bounds, whose beams shine from the Bosphorus into distant Gaul, employ us to administer the remoter regions of your empire ; your world is our Fatherland."

718. The Vandals settled first in Spain ; but in 414 (§ 715), they were attacked there by the West Goths. The struggle was long and stern ; but, in 427, the Vandals withdrew, *crossing into Africa*. There, after ten years of fighting, they set up a new Teutonic kingdom with its capital at Carthage.

These Vandals were the most untamable of all the Teutonic peoples, and the word "Vandalism" has become a synonym for wanton destructiveness. Seated at Carthage, they became pirates and terrorized the Mediterranean. They ravaged much of Sicily, and, *in 455*, under their king *Geiseric*, they invaded

Italy and sacked Rome in a way that made Alaric's capture seem merciful. For fourteen days the barbarians ravaged the ancient capital, loading their ships with the spoils which Rome had plundered from all the world. Ancient Carthage was avenged, and Scipio's foreboding (§ 462) had come true.

To the infinite loss of the world, much of this plunder was ingulfed in the Mediterranean in a storm which destroyed a large part of the fleet on its way back to Africa. The Vandal kingdom lasted about a century longer, until it was overthrown by Belisarius, general of the Emperor Justinian (§ 736). At that time Africa was again reunited to the Eastern Empire.

719. Franks had long had homes on both sides of the lower Rhine, from Cologne to the sea. They had been "allies" of Rome; but now they began to add to their territory by spreading themselves slowly westward over north Gaul. In the end they proved the most important of all the Teutonic invaders, but their real advance was not to begin until toward the close of the century (§§ 739 ff.).

Meantime, in *northwestern* Gaul, a semblance of Roman authority was kept up by Roman generals, who were really independent kings.

720. The Angles and Saxons in Britain. — In 408, the Roman legions were withdrawn from Britain to defend Italy against Alaric, and, to the dismay of the inhabitants, that island was abondoned by the imperial government. For many years, in the latter part of Roman rule, fierce Saxon pirates had been cruelly harassing the eastern coasts, — swooping down in their swift barks to burn, slay, and plunder, then sacrificing to Woden on the shore a tenth of their captives, and vanishing as quickly as they came.[1]

The civilized, peaceful Britons were now left to defend themselves against these terrible German marauders as well as against the untamed Celts beyond the northern wall. In despair, they finally called in the German raiders to beat off

---

[1] The subsequent conquest of Britain will be found treated at greater length in Guggenberger, *Hist. of the Christian Era*, Vol. I, §§ 91 ff.

the other foe, and these dangerous protectors soon began to seize the land for themselves.

The chief invading tribes were the *Jutes* from the Danish peninsula (Jutland) and the *Saxons* and *Angles* (English) from its base. The Jutes made the first permanent settlement, about the middle of the century (449 A.D.), in southeastern Britain. The Saxons occupied the southern shore, and the Angles the eastern, carving out numerous petty states in a long series of cruel campaigns. Gradually these little units were welded into larger kingdoms, until there appeared seven prominent Teutonic states : *Kent,* the kingdom of the Jutes ; *Sussex, Essex,* and *Wessex* (kingdoms of the South Saxons, East Saxons, and West Saxons) ; and the English kingdoms of *East Anglia, Northumbria,* and *Mercia.* But it took the Germans a century and a half (until about 600) to confine the Britons to the western peninsulas of Wales and Cornwall.

721. The Civilizers of the Invaders. — The Teutonic invaders were to renew the political and civic life of the peoples of Europe and to invigorate it with a Christian spirit. But Christianity, as well as the higher material and intellectual civilization, they had still to receive. This task, a work of centuries, fell to the subdued populations of the Empire, now simply called Romans. Foremost among these civilizers were the Romanized *Celts* in Gaul (§ 620, note).

"Gaul far more than Italy seemed called to be the protectress of ancient civilization. It has to its credit the glory of having for ages maintained the high standard of ancient culture for the benefit of mankind." — Grisar, *History,* V. III, § 455.

About this time another nation begins to be spoken of, the *Slavs,* who followed in the wake of the Teutons. Under this name we now comprise the Poles, Bohemians, Slavonians, and others (see § 735). Their turn to deserve the gratitude of Europe will come in later centuries. But behind the Teutons and Slavs there appeared about A.D. 400 a confused mass of tribes of an entirely different stock, called *Turanians.* The fiercest among them, the Huns, were now to break into the Roman Empire.

722. The Huns and the Rallying of the West. — While the Teutons were busy setting up kingdoms in the crumbling empire, they and the Romans were threatened for a moment with common ruin. *Attila,* king of the Huns, had built up a vast military power, reaching from central Asia into central Europe. It was his boast that grass never grew again where his horse's hoof had trod. Now, in the middle of the fifth century, his terrible hordes rolled resistlessly into Gaul.

Happily the peoples of the West realized their danger and laid aside all rivalries to meet it. Theodoric, the hero-king of the Visigoths, brought up his host from Spain to fight under the Roman banner. Burgundian and Frank rallied from the corners of Gaul. And *Aëtius,* "the Last of the Romans," [1] marshaled all these allies and the last great Roman army of the West [2] against the countless Hunnish swarms which were reinforced by Tartar, Slav, Finn, and even by tributary German peoples.

723. Chalons. — The fate of the world hung trembling in the balance, while the great "battle of the nations" was fought out at *Chalons (451 A.D.).* United though they were, the forces of civilization seemed insignificant before the innumerable hosts of Asiatics. Theodoric fell gallantly, sword in hand. But at last the victory was won by the generalship of Aëtius. (An ancient account is given in Davis' *Readings,* II, 126.) Attila is said to have lost three hundred thousand men (greatly exaggerated numbers, no doubt); and with spent force his invasion rolled away to Italy and the East.

"It was the perpetual question of history, the struggle told long ago by Herodotus, the struggle between Europe and Asia, the struggle between cosmos and chaos — the struggle between Aëtius and Attila. For Aëtius was the man who now stood in the breach, and sounded the Roman trumpet to call the nations to do battle for the hopes of humanity and

---

[1] Despite his Romanized name, Aëtius was a German. Much of his youth had been spent among the Huns. Davis' *Readings,* II, 125, gives a Goth's account of Attila.

[2] The first union of the Western races against "the yellow peril."

defend the cause of reason against the champions of brute force. The menace of that monstrous host which was preparing to pass the Rhine was to exterminate the civilization that had grown up for centuries . . . and to paralyze the beginnings of Teutonic life. . . . — BURY, *Later Roman Empire*, I, 176.

724. Attila and Leo. — Attila turned upon Rome; but Pope St. Leo I journeyed to the camp, and by his intercession turned the Hun from his prey.[1] There were facts and conditions which assisted the great pope; one ancient writer hints that Attila's army was wasted under Italian fever; and no doubt it was harassed by the forces of Aëtius hanging upon its rear. Yet contemporaries saw in this victory of the helpless priest over a powerful king, who was still exasperated to the utmost by his defeat, an indubitable miracle.

At all events, Attila withdrew from Italy and died shortly after. Then his empire fell to pieces, and the Teutons of Germany regained their freedom. The remnants of the terrible Huns disappeared entirely from history.

One curious result followed Attila's invasion of Italy. To escape the Huns, some of the ancient Veneti (§ 332) of northeast Italy took refuge among swampy islands at the head of the Adriatic, and so began a settlement (or gave new strength to an old one) destined to grow into the great republic of Venice.

ITALY IN THE FIFTH AND SIXTH CENTURIES

725. The " Empire in the West " had become limited to Italy. Early in the fifth century, as we have seen, Africa, Gaul, Spain, and Britain were abandoned to the Germans. But at the capital at Ravenna, amid its impenetrable swamps, the line of " emperors in the West " lasted from the division of the Empire between the sons of Theodosius (§ 680) until Romulus Augustulus, in 476 (§ 728). During these eighty years, the real power was held by German generals whose ability alone

---

[1] Robinson's *Readings*, I, 49–51, gives two ancient accounts.

supported the tottering throne. Until 455, however, this fact was much less clear than it was after that date.

726. Summary: Story of Italy, 395–455. — The reign of *Honorius* (395–423), son of Theodosius the Great, has been referred to several times in the account of the Invasions. His great general *Stilicho the Vandal*, who had long held Alaric in check and who destroyed the hordes of Radogast (§§ 713, 714), was at last murdered by Honorius, lest he should grow too powerful. Then Alaric's Goths ravaged Italy and sacked Rome (410 A.D.). At the same time Britain was abandoned, and soon Spain, with most of Gaul, was lost to Burgundians, Franks, Vandals, and Goths (§§ 715, 718). But through the regard of Alaric's successor for Roman civilization, Italy was freed from her invaders, and for forty years rested in comparative peace.

On the death of Honorius, Theodosius II, Emperor in the East, gave the western throne to *Valentinian III*, son of a daughter of Theodosius the Great. Valentinian, a weak and wicked prince, reigned from 425 to 455. Such part of the Empire as was saved owed its preservation to Aëtius, the imperial general who for many years upheld Roman authority in much of Gaul against the German peoples, and who finally united these Germans to repulse Attila at Chalons. Aëtius expected to marry his son to the daughter of the emperor, and so secure the throne for his family; but Valentinian, jealous of his great protector, murdered him. Soon afterward Valentinian was himself murdered by a Roman senator *Maximus*, whose home he had outraged.

Maximus seized the throne and compelled Eudoxia, the widow of his victim, to marry him. Eudoxia invited Geiseric, king of the Vandals, to avenge her. The Vandals captured Rome (§ 718), and Maximus was slain, after a three months' reign.

727. Rikimer and Orestes (456–476). — After the Vandal raid, power in Italy fell to *Count Rikimer*, a German general, who in sixteen years (456–472) set up and deposed four puppet emperors. That is, *Rikimer did successfully what Honorius and Valentinian had suspected Stilicho and Aëtius of planning to do.*

Then *Orestes*, another general of the Empire, advanced a step beyond the policy of Rikimer. He deposed the reigning prince and set *his own son* upon the throne, while he himself ruled as the real power for four years, until he was overthrown and slain by *Odovaker* (Odoacer), yet another German officer in the imperial service.

728. Odovaker advanced another step in the attack upon the Empire in the West. He dethroned the boy, *Romulus Augustus the Little*, the son of Orestes (476 A.D.), and sent him to live in luxurious imprisonment in a villa near Naples. Odovaker then ruled *without even the form of an Emperor in Italy*. He did not, however, dare call himself king of Italy. Instead, he claimed to represent the distant emperor at Constantinople. At his command, the Senate of Rome sent to *Zeno* (then emperor in the East) the diadem and royal robes, urging that the West did not need a separate emperor. They asked, therefore, that Zeno receive the "diocese" of Italy as part of his dominion, and intrust its government to Odovaker as his lieutenant.[1]

Thus, in name, Italy became a province of the Greek Empire,[2] and, after 476, *there was no emperor in the West for more than three hundred years*. Odovaker's power really rested upon the support of German tribes who made up the Roman army in the peninsula. Of one of these tribes (the Heruli) he was king. But with the native Italians his authority, in theory, came from his position as the representative of the emperor at Constantinople.

Odovaker tried to reconcile his German and his Roman subjects. He gathered about him Roman philosophers and statesmen, established good order, and ruled firmly for many years, until he was overthrown by a powerful German people whose king was to carry his work still further (§ 730).

The year 476 is sometimes said to have seen the "Fall of the Empire." The act of Odovaker in that year, however, is simply a continuation of the policy of Aëtius, Rikimer, and Orestes, and that policy was to be carried still further by Theodoric (§ 731). Probably the *name* of the boy-emperor who lost the throne in 476 has had much to do with exaggerating the importance of the date. It was very tempting to say that the history of Rome and of the Empire came to an end with a ruler who bore the name of the founder of the city and the founder of the Empire. The date, however, has no more real significance than 378, 410, or 493.

---

[1] Cf. like commissions to Goths, Burgundians, and Franks (§§ 713, 717, 754).
[2] For this name, see § 734.

729. The Ostrogoths before they entered Italy. — When the West Goths sought refuge south of the Danube in 376 (§ 712), an *eastern* division of the same race had submitted to the Huns. On the death of Attila, these East Goths (Ostrogoths) recovered their independence. Soon afterward they forced their way into the provinces south of the Danube. There they dwelt for thirty years, sometimes as allies of the Empire, sometimes as enemies.

Their young king, *Theodoric*,[1] was brought up at the imperial court as a hostage. He had felt the charm of Roman civilization and adopted its culture; but, with it all, he remained a typical Teutonic hero, — of gigantic stature and romantic temper, a matchless warrior, impetuous in strife and wise in counsel, — the kingliest figure of all the centuries of the invasions.

730. The Conquest of Italy. — In 489, Theodoric asked leave from Zeno to reconquer Italy for the Empire. Both Theodoric and Odovaker had been growing too powerful to please the emperor, who would have been glad to destroy either barbarian by the other. Accordingly, with magnificent ceremonial he appointed Theodoric "patrician," and gave the desired commission

Odovaker made a gallant resistance for four years. Theodoric beat him at Verona in a great battle, and then besieged him in the fortress of Ravenna. Odovaker finally surrendered on terms, but soon after was murdered at a banquet, on some suspicion, by Theodoric's own hand, — the one sad blot on the great Goth's fame.

731. "Theodoric the Civilizer," 493–526 A.D. — Then began a Gothic kingdom in Italy, like the Teutonic states in Spain and Burgundy, and one that deserved a better fate than was to befall it. The Ostrogoths had come in *as a nation*, with women and children. They took a third of the lands of Italy, but all the rights of the Roman population were respected scrupulously. Goth and Roman lived in harmony side by side, *each under his own law.* Cities were rebuilt and new ones

---

[1] For this Theodoric, see Davis' *Readings*, II, 127. He must not be confused with Theodoric the West Goth, § 722. Students will enjoy Hodgkin's *Theodoric the Goth*.

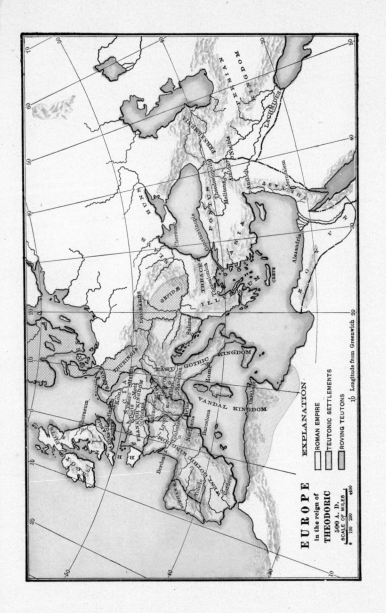

EUROPE

in the reign of

THEODORIC

500 A. D.

SCALE OF MILES

100   200   400

EXPLANATION

ROMAN EMPIRE

TEUTONIC SETTLEMENTS

ROVING TEUTONS

10   Longitude from Greenwich   20

founded, with a new period of architectural splendor. The land was subdivided into small estates. Agriculture revived, and Italy once more raised her own food. Theodoric's long

CHURCH OF SAN VITALE AT RAVENNA (time of Theodoric).

reign was peaceful, prosperous, and happy, and the peninsula began to recover her former greatness.

732. The " Empire " of Theodoric extended, indeed, far beyond Italy. He organized an alliance reaching over all the Teutonic states of the West. His wife was a Frankish princess; the Burgundian and Visigothic kings were his sons-in-law; his sister was married to the king of the Vandals. All these peoples recognized a certain preëminence in "Theodoric the Great." It seemed as though he were about to reunite the West into a great Teutonic empire, and, by three centuries, anticipate Charles the Great (§§ 785 ff.).

733. Weak Points. — After all, however, the Goths were strangers, ruling a Roman population vastly larger than themselves. More serious still, they were Arians. Theodoric had given perfect freedom to the Catholics and showed great respect to the popes. But the measures of the emperor against the Arians induced him to make reprisals in Italy. In his last years he became morbidly suspicious, and some of his truest friends, for instance, the great philosopher Boëthius, were cruelly executed. Pope John I died in chains.

A strong successor perhaps could yet have maintained the state; but Theodoric left only a daughter. The Goths at once fell into factions among themselves; and soon the kingdom was attacked and destroyed by the Empire (§ 736), to whose story we must turn for a moment.

THE EMPIRE AT CONSTANTINOPLE

734. The "Greek" Empire. — The Latin half of the empire had now crumbled away. There was left the empire east of the Adriatic. This part had always been essentially Greek in culture (§ 475). It called itself Roman for the next ten centuries; but we commonly speak of it as the *Greek Empire* or the *Byzantine Empire*. Separated from the West, it rapidly grew more and more Oriental in character. It preserved Greek

A GOLD COIN OF THEODOSIUS II (§§ 726, 737). Its distinctive character is called *Byzantine*, and is found in the art of the Eastern Empire after this date.

learning, and warded off Persian and Arabian conquest; but
for several centuries it did not greatly influence western Europe
except through the work of Justinian (§ 736).[1]

735. Slav Invasions. — When Theodoric led his Goths into
Italy, he left the line of the Danube open to the Slavs (§ 721).
That people had been filtering into the East, as the Teutons
had into the West, as slaves, coloni, and mercenaries. Now,
in 493, in a period of weak rulers, came their first real invasion.
Then, for a generation, successive hordes poured in, penetrating
as far as Greece. Even the neighborhood of Constantinople
was saved only by a Long Wall which protected the narrow
tongue of land, seventy-eight miles across, on which the capital
stood. Happily, before it was too late, another strong emperor arose.

736. Justinian the Great (527–565 A.D.) renewed the old
frontier of the Danube, saved Europe from a threatened Persian
conquest, and then turned to restore the imperial power in the
West.

He reconquered Africa, the Mediterranean islands, and part
of Spain; and he caught eagerly at the conditions in Italy,
after the death of Theodoric, to regain that land and the ancient
Roman capital. His generals, *Belisarius* and *Narses*, were victorious there also, but only after a dreadful twenty years' war
which destroyed at once the Gothic race and the rising greatness
of the peninsula. Rome itself was sacked once more (by the
Gothic king, Totila, 546 A.D.), and left for eleven days absolutely
uninhabited.

737. The Justinian Code. — Justinian is best remembered for
his work in bringing about the codification of the Roman law.
In the course of centuries that law had become an intolerable
maze. Julius Caesar had planned to codify it, and the need
had grown vastly more pressing since his time. A beginning
of the work had been made by *Theodosius II*, Emperor of the
East, and the *Theodosian Code* was published in 438.[2] Now, a

---

[1] On the Greek Empire, see Davis' *Readings*, II, Nos. 128–130.

[2] Extracts are given in Robinson's *Readings*, ch. ii.

century later, under Justinian, the great task was completed. A commission of able lawyers put the whole body of the law into a new form, marvelously compact, clear, and orderly.

This benefited not only the empire: it made easier the preservation of Roman law and its adoption by the nations of Europe in after times (cf. § 762). The reconquest of Italy by Justinian established the Code in that land. Thence, in later centuries, it spread over the West, and became the foundation of all modern legal study in continental Europe, and the basis of nearly all codes of law now in existence.

Says Ihne (*Early Rome*, 2), "Every one of us is benefited directly or indirectly by this legacy of the Roman people — a legacy as valuable as the literary and artistic models which we owe to the great writers and sculptors of Greece." And Woodrow Wilson declares (*The State*, 158) that Roman Law "has furnished Europe with many, *if not most*, of her principles of private right." [1]

738. Italy divided between the Empire and the Lombards. — When the East Goths moved into Italy, the Lombards, from beyond the Danube, had crossed that river and occupied the Balkan districts which the Goths had vacated. In 568, this new German people moved on again, — this time into Italy, most of which they soon conquered. Their chief kingdom was in the Po valley (which ever since has kept the name Lombardy), while Lombard " dukedoms " were scattered over other parts of the peninsula. The Empire retained (1) the Exarchate of Ravenna on the Adriatic, (2) Rome, with a little surrounding territory on the west coast, and (3) the extreme south. This south was to remain Greek for centuries, — the first and the last part of Italy to be Greek.

Thus the middle land, for which Roman and Teuton had struggled through two centuries, was at last divided between them, and

---

[1] English and American law is always regarded, properly, as having a very distinct origin; but Roman law profoundly affected legal development even in England and so in the United States, while the law of Louisiana came very directly from it through the French code. Wilson's *The State*, 142–161, gives an excellent account of the growth of Roman Law.

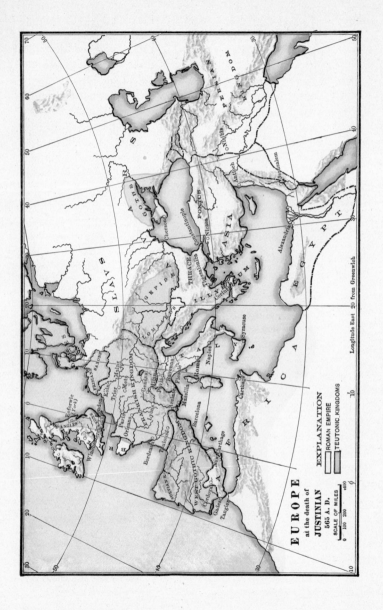

EUROPE
at the death of
JUSTINIAN
565 A. D.

SCALE OF MILES
0   100   200   300   400

EXPLANATION

ROMAN EMPIRE
TEUTONIC KINGDOMS

Longitude East 20 from Greenwich

shattered into fragments in the process (map after page 632).
Probably no other land suffered as much in the two centuries
of invasions as this beautiful peninsula, which had so long been
mistress of the Mediterranean world.

"Taking one's stand at Rome, and looking toward the north, what
does one see for nearly one hundred years ? Wave after wave rising out
of the north, the land of night and wonder and the terrible unknown
. . . and they dash against the Alps, and roll over through the mountain
passes, into the fertile plains below. Then . . . you discover that the
waves are living men, women, and children, horses, dogs, and cattle, all
rushing headlong into that great whirlpool of Italy. And yet the gulf is
never full. The earth drinks up the blood; the bones decay into the fruitful soil ; the very names and memories of whole tribes are washed away.
And the result of an immigration which may be counted by hundreds of
thousands is—that all the land is waste." — KINGSLEY, *Roman and
Teuton*, 58.

THE FRANKS

739. Preëminence among the Teutonic Conquerors. — The early
conquests of the Franks in North Gaul have been referred to
(§ 719). Their real advance began a little before the year 500,
— almost at the time of the rise of the East Goths. This was
some eighty years later than the making of Vandal, Burgundian, and Visigothic kingdoms, and as much earlier than the
Lombard kingdom.

To the Franks fell the work of consolidating the Teutonic
states into a mighty empire. Their final success was due, in
the main, to two causes.

a. They did not, like the other conquering nations, give up
their homes to *migrate* to distant lands. They merely *expanded* from their original abodes. Hence in the districts
bordering on the latter the population became completely
Teutonic or nearly so. Although this applies only to a part
of their dominion it greatly contributed to the stability of the
whole. (See § 764.)

b. They treated the old inhabitants with great consideration.
When they adopted Christianity, it was the Catholic religion
instead of Arianism. This gained for their rulers the good-

will and aid of bishops and popes, and still more reconciled with them the subjected populations.

740. Clovis ; Early Conquests. — Until nearly 500, the Franks were pagans. Nor were they a nation : they were split into petty divisions, without a common king. The founder of their greatness was *Clovis* (Chlodwig, Ludwig, Louis). In 481, at the age of fifteen, he became king of a tribe near the mouth of the Rhine. In 486, he attacked the Roman possessions in north Gaul, and, after a victory at *Soissons*, added them to his kingdom. Ten years later he conquered the Alemanni, who had invaded Gaul, and made tributary their territory beyond the Rhine. Tradition says the battle was fought at Zülpich.

741. The Conversion of Clovis. — The real importance of the battle of Zülpich lies in this — that it was the *occasion for the conversion of Clovis*. He had inherited a leaning towards Christianity from his father. His wife, *Clotilda*, was a Burgundian princess, but, unlike most of her nation, she was a devout Catholic. In the crisis of the battle Clovis had vowed to serve the God of Clotilda if He would grant victory. In consequence, the king and three thousand of his warriors were baptized.

This baptism of the Frankish king was a momentous step. By his conversion to Catholicity Clovis won the hearty support of the Church authorities, while the rule of the Arian Visigoths in Southern Gaul was hated. The Frankish kingdom now and in the future enjoyed the blessing of perfect religious unity, the best means to fill the conquered population with confidence in their conquerors.

Clovis meant to rule as a Christian king. He treated the Roman population on the same footing as his Franks, and left the bishops undisturbed in the execution of their office. He ever preserved an unswerving devotion to the saintly Clotilda, whose example and encouragement he followed in practicing a far-reaching charity towards the unfortunate, and great liberality towards ecclesiastical institutions. In politics, however, he did not free himself from pagan methods.

742. Later Conquests by Clovis and his Sons. — A domestic quarrel in the royal family of Burgundy gave him the pretext for making this fair kingdom tributary. A later war with the Visigoths, who were actually persecuting the Catholics, he officially proclaimed to be a struggle against heretics. He conquered most of their provinces north of the Pyrennes. Before the end of his reign he got rid of the kings of the other Frankish tribes and thus consolidated the whole people and country under his sole rule. (Davis' *Readings*, II, No. 132.) The sons of Clovis completed the subjugation of Burgundy, and added Bavaria and Thuringia, as tributaries, to the Frankish state. *The last two districts lay on the German side of the Rhine, well beyond the borders of the old Roman world.*

743. Empire of the Franks in the Seventh Century. — In fifty years, mainly through the cool intellect and indomitable energy of one ruler, a little Teutonic tribe mastered the great Frankish state. That state included nearly the whole of modern France, the Netherlands, Switzerland, and Germany almost to the Elbe (except for the lands of the heathen Saxons toward the mouth of that river).

Such territory to-day would make the greatest power in Europe. In the sixth and seventh centuries its preëminence was even more marked. The Gothic power in Spain was weakened by quarrels between Arian and Catholic; Italy was torn to shreds; Britain was in chaos (§ 745); non-Frankish Germany was filled with savage, unorganized tribes. *The only real rivals of the Frankish state were the Greek Empire and a new Mohammedan power* which was just rising in Arabia (§§ 770 ff.) and which was soon to contest Europe with both Greek and Frank.

744. The Kingdom after Clovis. — The family of Clovis is known, from his grandfather *Merovig*, as *Merovingian*. It kept the throne for two centuries after Clovis' death. The nation, like the rulers, did not at once become thoroughly Christianized. Only gradually did the Church, and especially the monasteries, succeed in taming its wild passions. Criminals and saints often lived under the same roof. There are found, on the one hand, cold-blooded murders and unrestrained licentiousness; on the other, noble lives of simple faith, humility, purity, and penance.

Clovis divided the kingdom among his four sons. The fragments were reunited under one of these sons, by methods similar to those of Clovis himself. Then it was again divided; and so on for long periods. The Franks themselves spread very little south of the Loire. North and South Gaul remained distinct from each other in blood and character (§§ 739, 764). But in spite of all these divisions the unity of the Frankish rule was preserved, chiefly by the coöperation of the kings in their foreign relations and by the unity of religion and hierarchy.

GROWTH OF THE TEUTONIC STATES IN BRITAIN[1]

745. Slowness of the Teutonic Conquest. — Great provinces like Gaul or Spain fell to the Vandals or Franks after one or two battles with the Roman armies. The natives themselves made almost no resistance in the field. But, as we have seen, in Britain, where there were no Roman armies, the Teutonic invaders in 150 years of incessant warfare conquered only half the island.

Causes for this delay are to be found both in the nature of the invasion and in the condition of the island.

a. The Saxons at home were living in petty tribes, *under no common government*, and therefore they could make no great organized attack. *Coming by sea*, too, they necessarily came only in small bands. Moreover, they were still *pagans*, and, unlike the Franks, they were *untouched by Roman civilization*. Therefore they spread ruthless destruction and provoked a more desperate resistance.

b. Britain was less completely Romanized than were the continental provinces: there was *more of forest and marsh*, and a *less extensive network of Roman roads*. Hence the natives found it easier to make repeated stands. The Britons, too, had not so completely laid aside military habits as had the Gauls.

---

[1] Review § 720.

NORTH SEA

BRITONS
ANGLES
SAXONS
JUTES

(Köln)
Cologne

KINGDOM OF THE FRANKS

Rheims
Mainz
BRITTANY
Paris
Orleans
Loire R.
ALAMA-
(till 496

BURGUN-
DIANS
(443-534)
St. Lyons

WEST GOTHS

Bordeaux

Narbonne
CANTABRIA

SUEVI
(415-535)

Douro R.

KINGDOM OF THE WEST GOTHS
(415-711)
Tarraco

Cordoba

(Vandals)

(Vandals)

M E D I T E R

A T L A N T I C   O C E A N

V A N D A L S
(429-534)

Longitude West 15 10 from Greenwich 5 0 5 Longitude

55
50
45
40
35

10 5 0 5

After 507 the Kingdom of the West Goths in Gau

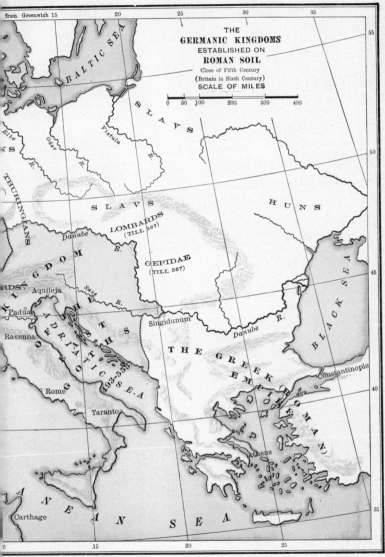

THE
GERMANIC KINGDOMS
ESTABLISHED ON
ROMAN SOIL
Close of Fifth Century
(Britain in Sixth Century)
SCALE OF MILES

0   50 100   200.   300   400

BALTIC SEA

S L A V S

Elbe R.

Oder R.

Vistula R.

THURINGIANS

S L A V S

HUNS

LOMBARDS
(TILL 567)

Danube R.

GEPIDAE
(TILL 567)

RDS'

Aquileja

Padua

OSTROGOTHS
493-553

Save R.

Singidunum

Danube R.

BLACK SEA

Ravenna

ADRIATIC SEA

Rome

Taranto

THE GREEK
EMPIRE (ROMAN)

Constantinople

Carthage

N E A N   S E A

Athens

limited to a small southern strip (Septimania)

746. England under the Saxons. — Because the conquest was so slow, it was thorough. Elsewhere the invaders were soon absorbed by the larger native populations. *England alone, of all the Roman provinces seized by the Teutons, became strictly a Teutonic country.* In the eastern half of the island, in particular, Roman institutions, the Roman language, Christianity, even names, for the most part, vanished. The Romanized natives, Celts, were slain or enslaved, or crowded into the western peninsulas of the island, chiefly in Wales. Large numbers fled across the Channel to Armorica, which since is called Brittany, or, in French, Bretagne.

747. Conversion. — About the year 600, Christianity began to win its way among these heathen conquerors. In the north, the early missionaries came mainly from the Celts of Wales and Ireland. The chief apostle of England, however, is St. Augustine, a Benedictine monk, sent with forty companions by Pope Gregory the Great. In 597 he arrived in England.[1] The differences between the Roman missionaries and the Celts were settled in the *Council of Whitby* in Northumbria in 664 A.D.

748. Three political results followed the conversion to Christianity : —

Warfare with the native Britons became milder and more like ordinary wars between rival states.

The ecclesiastical union of the island helped to create the later political union. The different states had a common church council before they had one king and one political Assembly.

The adoption of the same form of Christianity and the same church government as that on the Continent brought the island back into the general current of European thought, civilization, and politics.

The *Exercise* suggested on page 620 may be taken up here.

---

[1] On the conversion of England, see J. M. Stone, *The Church in English History*, chapters I–VII.

CHAPTER XLV

THE STATE OF WESTERN EUROPE, 400–800 A.D.

749. Plan of Treatment. — We have traced the movements of peoples and the growth of new states during the two centuries of invasions. During the next two centuries (600–800) the political story has to do with four great movements : (1) the continued *growth of the Frankish state*, until it included most of civilized Western Europe ; (2) the *rise of the Mohammedans* in Asia and Africa, and their repulse from Europe by the Greek Empire on the East and by the Franks on the West ; (3) the general recognition of the spiritual supremacy of the Holy See by the Western nations including the rulers, and the acquisition by the popes of a temporal kingdom, which made them independent of the secular powers, and (4) the *rise of the Empire of Charlemagne*, out of the alliance of the papacy and the Franks.

These several movements will be treated in the next chapters. But first, in order to understand them, we interrupt the story to survey briefly the condition into which the invasions plunged Western Europe, — (1) the chaos and misery ; (2) the survival of some of the Roman civilization ; and (3) *the new institutions* which were growing up. Such a survey is the subject of this chapter.

The period we have to treat is often called the *Dark Ages* on account of the great decline of learning and civilization in the whole West. Unenlightened non-Catholics sometimes ascribe this sad condition unhesitatingly to the influence of the Church. We shall see that its causes were far different. Nay, whatever was saved of ancient progress and whatever grew again out of the ruins of the splendid past is almost exclusively due to the uplifting activity of Christianity and its institutions.

750. The Loss to Civilization. — After all allowances are made, the invasions of the fifth and sixth centuries remain the most terrible catastrophe that ever befell so great a civilized society. Now many of the most flourishing cities were destroyed. Treves, in Gaul, was sacked five times, Rome, as we have seen, three times. The treasures of art, including libraries, were dispersed or lost, many of the fine buildings fell under the battering ram or in conflagrations. Whole districts became deserted, inhabited by wolves and bears. The greatest was the ruin of Italy under the many successive invasions.

751. Additional Causes of Decline. — Roman civilization, as we have noticed, had been falling away for two centuries. The two hundred years of barbaric invasions added tremendously to the decay. There was no tranquil leisure, no security, no opportunity for study. The old schools and their teachers were gone; the traditions of refined and literary life were fast disappearing. The new ruling class, formed by the invaders, was grossly ignorant; few of the nobles could write their name. They did not offer splendid patronage to men of letters. As a result of the breaking up of the old unity of the empire, the language of every-day speech grew fast away from the literary language. The language of learning, classic Latin, rapidly became a " dead " tongue. It could be acquired only by special study and was practically known to the clergy only. Even they frequently knew very little of it. In the mouth of the people it was more and more corrupted and occasionally mixed with Teutonic words. Thus dialects sprang up in the various former provinces of the Empire, which in the course of several centuries changed into French, Italian, Spanish, etc. This diversity of language considerably furthered the general decay.

At the same time the old Roman civilization, in many obscure ways, did survive.

752. Causes of the Survival of Roman Civilization. — *The barbarian conquests had been accomplished by small numbers.* The invasions did not greatly change the race-character of the population in Western Europe (outside of Britain). The forces which occupied the western Roman world in the fifth century were small. The highest estimate for the whole Burgundian nation is eighty thousand. The Visigoths hardly exceeded thirty thousand warriors, and Clovis annexed Roman Gaul with less than six thousand men.

The barbarians felt a wholesome reverence for the Roman Empire and for all connected with it. Clovis was delighted when the emperor at Constantinople sent him an appointment as "consul" and as a lieutenant of the Empire. The Germans were awed by the marvelous devices, the massive structures, the stately pomp, of the civilization they had conquered.[1]

The idea of the Roman Empire as the one legitimate government of the world survived. We can see *now* that the Western Empire had passed away before the year 500. But men of that day did not see it. For them the Dominion of the "Eternal City" was not dead. In their opinion it could not die. (The population of Gaul, Spain, and Italy looked upon the Teutonic rulers as the representatives of the emperor.)

The Influence of the Old Populations. — The Germans already within the Empire in the year 400 had been largely Romanized. The new invaders settled among populations ten, twenty, or fifty times their own numbers. At first the Teutons were the rulers and the bulk of the large landlords. They formed the government and the aristocratic forces in *rural* society. But the towns, so far as they survived at all, with their varied industries, remained Roman. For a long time, too, the old population furnished most of the clergy. From them, also, came the secretaries of the conquering lords and many confidential officers. Gradually these various forces secured the adoption of many customs of the old civilization by the conquerors. (See § 721.)

753. The Church and the Barbarians. — It was the Church above all that raised the new nations. True, many of her clergy sorely lacked the purity of morals and singleness of purpose required by their exalted station. Bishops and other dignitaries often acted more like worldly-minded lords. The preachers at times were themselves insufficiently instructed. Yet the danger is that the student will overrate these deplorable facts. In spite of all, the Church was the salt that kept the world sweet in those centuries of trouble and disorder.

---

[1] On the survival of classical life in Rome see Grisar, *History of Rome and the Popes in the Middle Ages*, Vol. I, pp. 130 ff.

The Church at all times demanded a certain degree of education in her ministers. She provided for some kind of schools, chiefly, though not exclusively, through the monasteries. She furnished wise and prudent counselors to the kings of the new realms. Saints there were at all times, and beside them, other bishops, priests, religious laymen and laywomen more than ordinarily inspired with zeal for true virtue and righteousness

TOMB OF THEODORIC AT RAVENNA. — The most famous surviving Gothic monument.

in themselves and their fellowmen. The Church, as a whole, protected the weak and stood for peace, education, industry, and right living. Moreover, the Church had its own government, which preserved the old forms and habits and the principles of the Roman law.[1]

---

[1] Concerning the conditions of Gaul in particular see Metlake, *The Life and Writings of Saint Columban*, pp. 42 ff.

754. The Preaching of the Church. — The Church of those centuries is sometimes accused by Protestant writers of putting *all* stress upon forms and of neglecting totally the duty of man to man. The charge is bitterly unjust. Many sermons of the seventh century place peculiar emphasis upon good works. "It is not enough," says the good Bishop St. Eloy to his flock, in a fervent exhortation, — "It is not enough, most dearly beloved, for you to have received the name of Christians if you do not do Christian works. . . . Come, therefore, frequently to church; humbly seek the patronage of the saints; keep the Lord's day in reverence of the resurrection, without any servile work; celebrate the festivals of the saints with devout feeling; love your neighbors as yourselves; what you would desire to be done to you by others, that do you to others; what you would not have done to you, do to no one; before all things have charity, for charity covereth a multitude of sins; be hospitable, humble, casting your care upon God, for He careth for you; visit the sick; seek out the captives; receive strangers; feed the hungry; clothe the naked; set at naught soothsayers and magicians; let your weights and measures be fair, your balance just, your bushel and your pint honest. . . ."

755. Monasticism — Its Origin. — There have never been wanting in the Church those who desired to accept the invitation addressed by Christ to the rich young man: "If thou wilt be perfect, go, sell all thou hast and give it to the poor, and come, follow me" (*Matt. xix, 21*). But the conditions of the first centuries did not permit the establishment of convents and other religious houses as we know them now. Men and women often led a life of virginity and self-abnegation in the homes of their relatives. For this we have the testimony not only of Christian writers but even of the pagan physician Galen (§ 628). In the third century many Christians of both sexes withdrew into the solitude of forests and deserts, to live exclusively for God and the welfare of their souls. St. Paul of Egypt is considered the first to have chosen this life of the *hermits*. But many preferred to live *in communities*, where they could have the advantage of mutual encouragement and the guidance of a superior.

756. Spread of Monasticism. — Both modes of religious life spread rapidly from Egypt, where they were extensively practiced, over the whole Orient. Europe, too, was soon covered with monasteries and, to a less degree, with hermitages. When St. Martin, bishop of Tours, the great propagator of *monasticism*, died, two thousand monks followed his mortal remains to the grave. The conversion of Ireland by St. Patrick (§ 686) did a great deal to popularize monasticism. Not only was the Isle of Saints thickly settled with monasteries of men and women, but Irish institutions rose in Scotland and even in what is now France, Switzerland, southern Germany, and northern Italy.

MONASTERY OF ST. BENEDICT AT SUBIACO.— Erected at the Grotto in which the Saint spent the first three years of his monastic life. It is situated in the middle of a rugged hillside, above the ruins of a villa of Emperor Nero. Later on, the monastery of *Monte Cassino* became his chief foundation. (See Cath. Enc. under *Subiaco*.)

757. "Rules." — Prayer and work, consisting chiefly in manual labor and the copying of books, and the practice of penance and abnegation were the principal occupations of the monks and nuns. In the way of penance, however, the Oriental monks always went farther than the Europeans. In the East, *St. Basil's Rule* was famous and became in the course of time generally adopted. It is still observed in the Basilean Order. In the West the *Rule of St. Benedict*[1] finally took the

---

[1] Davis' *Readings*, II, 137, gives extracts from the "Rule of St. Benedict." Read Munro and Sellery, *Medieval Civilization*, ch. ix, on the "Economic Services of the Monasteries."

place of the large variety of monastic regulations formerly in use. It was recommended by practical wisdom and great

THE "MONOGRAM PAGE" OF THE BOOK OF KELLS. — The book of Kells is an Irish manuscript containing the four Gospels and some other minor works. It dates from about 700 A.D. It was long preserved in the Cathedral of Kells and is now in the library of Trinity College (Prot.), Dublin. "No words can describe the beauty and the extreme splendor of the richly colored initial letters." (Cath. Enc.) This page, the most famous, shows the monogram of Christ (see legend on p. 652). Hence its name. The X appears above, three of its lines being elegantly curved. The P and an additional I are seen below.

moderation. For several hundred years the Benedictine Order was the only one in this part of Christendom. It had no general superior. An *Abbot* or *Abbess* governed each house independently of all the rest, the unity of the Order being kept up solely by the observance of the same Rule.

758. Influence of the Monasteries. (1) Civilization. — Though existing in the first place for the spiritual welfare of the religious, who took the three vows of Poverty, Chastity, and Obedience, the monasteries became great benefactors of all the people. In the beginning most of the members were laymen. The monastic community would settle in some uncultivated spot, donated by rulers or rich citizens, and by the work of their hands change it into well-tilled fields and gardens.

By word and example the monks preached the dignity of manual labor. They taught agriculture, or showed the farmers how to improve their methods. They were the teachers of the children, assisted the poor and helpless, and harbored the way-farer. For centuries the monasteries were the almshouses, inns, asylums, hospitals, and schools. Under their protecting walls new settlements arose, and many a city owes its origin to the labor of the monks. The presence of the men of God was a safeguard against oppression by unscrupulous nobles. The monks lovingly copied and often splendidly illuminated books, both spiritual and secular, and thus preserved for us the treasures of earlier ages. — Similarly the surroundings of the nuns' convents changed their aspect. The nuns educated the girls, especially the daughters of the nobility. They also supported the spiritual labors of the priests by their handi-work. They collected alms for the missionaries, followed them into foreign missions and undertook the care of converted women and children.

759. (2) **Missions.** — It was not the express purpose of the monasticism of those days to promote the spiritual welfare of others by priestly functions. Yet not only were the lives of the religious a most powerful sermon, but the results of their actual teaching and preaching are almost incredible. Irish monks, led by St. Columba, converted Scotland. Others set-tled in central Europe, where the final conversion and general Christian life of the population is greatly due to their efforts. Foremost among them is St. Columban and his disciples. The Benedictine Order became the greatest factor in the Christian-ization of the Teutonic and Slavonic nations. Sts. Augustine and Boniface (§ 747 and § 776) drew their inspiration from the solitude of Benedictine monasteries, and in turn spread their new foundations broadcast in the territories converted by them. A very large number of bishops, popes, and other men eminent for learning and sanctity proceeded from the ranks of the monks. It may truly be said that monasticism was the chief means of the Church in the conversion and civilization of Europe.

" Had it not been for the monks and monasteries, the barbarian deluge might have swept away utterly the traces of Roman civilization.

The monk was the pioneer of civilization and Christianity in England, Germany, Poland, Bohemia, Sweden, Denmark. With the incessant din of arms around him, it was the monk in his cloister, even in the remote fastnesses, for instance on Mount Athos, who by preserving and transcribing ancient manuscripts, both Christian and pagan, as well as by recording his observations of contemporaneous events, was handing down the torch of knowledge unquenched to future generations, and hoarding up stores of erudition for the researches of a more enlightened age. The first musicians, painters, farmers, statesmen, in Europe after the downfall of Imperial Rome under the onslaught of the barbarians, were monks.'' Extracts from I. G. Smith, *Christian Monasticism* (Protestant).

760. Development of Teutonic Law. — When the barbarians entered the Empire, their law was unwritten custom. Much of it continued so, but under the influence of Roman ideas, the principal tribes on the continent soon began to put parts of their law in the form of *written codes* (cf. 717). These codes throw interesting sidelights upon the times. (See Davis' *Readings*, II, No. 133.) Three points may be noted here.

a. "Law was personal." That is, a man carried his law with him wherever he went. It was felt that a Roman, a Goth, a Burgundian, even though all were members of the Frankish state, should each be judged, not by Frankish law, but by the law of his own people. In modern civilized countries, law is *territorial*, not *personal*. That is, all persons in a given country come under the same law, — the law of the land.

b. The forms of trial. There were two kinds.

The accused and accuser swore solemnly to their statements. Each was backed by his *compurgators*, — not witnesses, but persons who swore they believed that their man was telling the truth. This form of trial was *compurgation*. The value of a man as a compurgator depended upon his rank; a noble was worth several freemen. The number called for depended also upon the crime. According to one code, three compurgators of a given rank could free a man accused of murdering a serf; it took seven, if he were accused of killing a freeman; and eleven, if a noble.

Sometimes the trial was by *ordeal*. The ordeal was based

on the erroneous assumption that God will rather work an evident miracle than allow an innocent man to be punished. To clear himself of a charge, the accused would, for instance, offer to plunge his arm into boiling water, or carry red-hot iron a certain distance, or walk over glowing plowshares. If his flesh was found uninjured when examined some days later, he was declared not guilty. The idea had struck so deep roots in the popular mind, that the Church, though never approving of it, took it into her own hands. To prevent violence and fraud, she surrounded the proceedings with impressive sacred ceremonies. It required several centuries to do away finally with the barbarous custom.[1]

The nobles preferred the ordeal of the single combat, supposing that God would assist the arms of the innocent party. A relic of this ordeal is the duel, which happily is becoming rarer in our times. The Church inflicts the severest ecclesiastical penalties on duelists.

c. *Offenses were atoned for by money payments.* Warriors were too valuable to be lightly sacrificed, and punishment by imprisonment was not in keeping with Teutonic custom. Practically all crimes had a money penalty, varying from a small amount for cutting off the joint of the little finger, to the *wer-geld* (man-money), or payment for a man's life. It is significant that the fine for cutting off a man's right arm was about the same as for killing him outright. The wer-geld varied with the rank of the victim.

761. New Political Institutions. — The conquest modified the political institutions of the conquerors in many ways. Three changes call for special attention.

a. *The Teutonic kings became more absolute.* (1) They secured large shares of confiscated land, so that they could

---

[1] Such tests were sometimes made by deputy; hence our phrase, "to go through fire and water" for a friend. The byword, "he is in hot water," comes also from these trials; and so, too, the later test of witchcraft by throwing suspected old women into a pond, to sink or float. See **Davis'** *Readings*, II, Nos. 138, 139 (the latter on "ordeals").

reward their supporters and build up a strong personal following. (2) Their authority grew by custom, since, in the confusion of the times, all sorts of matters were necessarily left to their decision. (3) The Roman idea of absolute power in the head of the state had its influence. From these three factors it came to pass that the former war chiefs became real sovereigns.

b. The old nobility of blood gave way to a new nobility of office or service. The higher ranks came in part from the old class of "companions" of the king (§ 710), who were now rewarded with grants of land and intrusted with important powers as rulers (counts and dukes).

c. The popular assemblies decreased in importance as the power of the kings and nobles grew. Such assemblies, however, did not at this time altogether disappear. They survived in England as occasional *Folk-moots*, and under the Frankish kings as *Mayfield* assemblies. (See § 799 e.)

762. Summary. — Three forces shaped the history of the following centuries, — Christianity, the Roman Empire, the Teutonic nations.

Christianity, among other important contributions, furnished : —

    a. A religion which satisfied the human intellect as well as the human will and heart.

    b. The correct notion of human liberty and life, thus rescuing the rights of slaves and children and women.

    c. Security for the future of the human race by sanctifying matrimony.

    d. The correct notion of the dignity of the lowly and their occupations.

    e. A spotless ideal of virtue, the God-man Jesus Christ and His immaculate mother Mary.

    f. A world-wide organization which had already given proof of its own indestructibility, and which was strong enough to foster in its bosom all the rising institutions.

    g. Above all, it restored the worship of the One True God, "Who made heaven and earth."

The Roman Empire : —

(1) *The Population.* The bulk of the population during and after the Teutonic invasions remained ethnically much the same as before. In the West, which concerns us much more than the East, it was chiefly the Romanized Celts of Gaul and northern Italy, that come into consideration.

This population contributed : —

a. The intellectual and material civilization of ancient Greece, together with the Oriental inheritance, but all this modified by the Roman genius.

b. A universal language with its literary treasures, which even after losing its hold on the common people was to remain the vehicle of educated thought for the next thousand years.

(2) *The Political Organization* contributed : —

a. The idea and machinery of centralized government.

b. Municipal institutions.

c. Roman law.

d. The idea of a ONE lasting secular authority as the secular center and head of the civilized world.

The Teutons contributed : —

a. Themselves (cf. theme sentence on page 582).

b. A new sense of the value of the *individual* as opposed to that of the state. This idea was extended, rectified, and hallowed by Christianity. See p. 618, *b* and *d.*

c. *Loyalty to a lord,* as contrasted with loyalty to the state.

d. A new chance for democracy — in the popular assemblies of different grades, some of which, in England, were to develop *representative* features.[1]

e. A new impetus to the development of law. Teutonic law was crude and adapted to simple conditions. Yet it

---

[1] It is not correct to say that the Teutons gave us representative government. *What they did was to give another chance to develop it.* The earlier peoples had lost their chances. Some peculiar features in later English history were to develop these Teutonic assemblies in that island into representative bodies.

contained possibility of growth. It exercised a wholesome influence on the later codification of the Roman law which formed the basis of legislation in after centuries.

763. This *mingling* of forces has been felt ever since in European history. Oriental civilization quickly became uniform; society crystallized; development ceased (§§ 80–81). European civilization began with diversity and freedom. But after some centuries, the Roman Empire had begun to take on Oriental uniformity; society there, too, had crystallized (§ 695), and progress apparently had ceased. The *mingling* of the new elements contributed by the Teutons with the older elements, and both controlled by Christianity, has prevented later European society from becoming stagnant.

———

EXERCISE. — (1) Trace each barbarian people from the crossing of the barriers to the last mention in this period. (2) Trace the history of Gaul, Italy, and Spain, through the period, noting for each land what peoples affected its further development. (In both exercises, the device of *catchwords* may be used with advantage; and students may be encouraged to prepare tables, showing, in separate columns, the peoples, events, leaders, dates, etc.) (3) List battles, with leaders and dates, for rapid "fact-drills." (4) The field is a good one for exercises calling for historical imagination (see page 241).

CHAPTER XLVI

WESTERN EUROPE, 600–768[1]

THE FRANKS TO CHARLES MARTEL

764. Neustria and Austrasia. — Among the parts of the Frankish kingdom which often figured as separate states, two were eminent, *Neustria and Austrasia*. Austrasia, which contained the old homes of the Franks and the royal house, was almost compactly German, but Neustria, which consisted chiefly of the early conquests of Clovis, and was largely Gallic in population, possessed his capital, and held a certain prestige over the rest. The south of Gaul had remained almost completely Roman, *i.e.* Celtic. The Burgundian invaders of the Rhone valley and the Visigoths in Aquitaine around the Garonne had altered the population very little.

The family contests among the rulers of the sub-kingdoms (§ 743) finally became a struggle for supremacy between these two states, Neustria and Austrasia. It was plain that the other parts must fall to the victor.

765. The Mayors of the Palace. — The later Merovingian kings earned the name of "*Do-nothings.*" Real power was exercised in each sub-kingdom by a *mayor of the palace.* Originally this officer was a chief domestic, the head of the royal household; but, one by one, he had withdrawn all the powers of government from the indolent kings. At first the office of mayor was filled by the king's appointment. As it grew more important, the nobles sometimes claimed the right to elect the holder; *and in Austrasia the position finally became hereditary.* Once a year, the long-haired king himself

[1] Review § 744.

was carried forth in stately procession on his ox-cart, to be shown to the Assembly of the Mayfield. The rest of the time he lived, on some obscure estate, in indolence and pleasures that brought him to an early grave.

766. Pippin of Heristal. — Much of the seventh century was filled with anarchy and civil war. The Frankish state seemed about to fall to pieces. Indeed, Bavaria and Thuringia (purely German) and Aquitaine (the most purely Roman province) did break away into states practically independent, under their native *dukes.*

But finally, at the battle of *Testry* (687 A.D.), the Austrasians, under their mayor, *Pippin of Heristal,* established their supremacy. Austrasia at this moment had no separate king, and Pippin might now have set up an independent kingdom there; but instead he chose wisely to rule both kingdoms as mayor of Neustria, appointing a trusted friend mayor of Austrasia.

In appearance, Austrasia remained the less dignified state, but really it had given to the realm of the Franks a new line of rulers and a new infusion of German blood. *Testry stands for a second Teutonic conquest* of the more Romanized part of the Frankish state, and for a reunion of the two halves of the kingdom. Some of the great border dukedoms still remained almost independent; but *Pippin is rightly regarded as the second founder of the Empire of the Franks.*

767. Charles Martel, Sole Mayor. — Pippin's son, Charles, went farther. He concentrated in his single person the offices of mayor of Austrasia, of Neustria, and of Burgundy, and brought back to subjection the great dukedoms of Bavaria and Thuringia. He established firm order, too, among the unruly chiefs of the German frontier, and partially restored Frankish authority over Aquitaine, which was now making a gallant fight for independence.

The crushing blows Charles dealt his rivals in these struggles won him the title of the Hammer (*Martel*), which he was soon to justify in a more critical conflict that saved Europe from

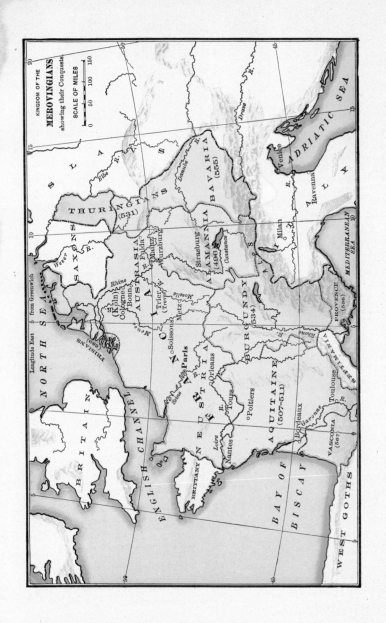

KINGDOM OF THE
MEROVINGIANS
showing their Conquests

SCALE OF MILES
0   50   100   160

NORTH SEA

SLAVS

Elbe R.

THURINGIANS
(531)

SAXONS

Weser R.

BAVARIA
(555)

Danube R.

Drave R.

ADRIATIC SEA

Venice

Ravenna

ITALY

MEDITERRANEAN SEA

Rhine

Cologne
(Köln)
Bonn

AUSTRASIA

Trier
(Treves)

Würzburg
Fulda
R. Main

Strasburg

ALAMANNIA
(496)

Constance

BURGUNDY
(534)

Milan

PROVENCE
(536)

FRISIANS

Longitude East 5 from Greenwich

Metz

Moselle R.

Meuse R.

Soissons

Paris

NEUSTRIA

Orleans

Seine R.

Marne R.

ENGLISH CHANNEL

BRITAIN

Tours

Poitiers

AQUITAINE
(507-511)

Loire R.

Nantes

BRITTANY

Rhone R.

Saone R.

Bordeaux

Garonne R.

Toulouse

VASCONIA
(507)

SEPTIMANIA

BAY OF BISCAY

WEST GOTHS

Mohammedanism (§ 773). *Except for Pippin and Martel, there would have been no Christian power able to withstand the Arab onslaught.* The victory of Testry and the pounding by the "Hammer of the Franks" came none too soon.

For Further Reading. — Davis' *Readings*, II, No. 134; Hodgkin's *Charles the Great*, 8–45.

THE MOHAMMEDAN PERIL

768. Arabia before Mohammed. — About a century after Clovis built up the empire of the Franks, a mighty power arose in Arabia, — a region until then beyond the pale of history. The best of the Arabian tribes were related to the Jews and the old Assyrians, but on the whole the peninsula contained a mongrel population. A few tribes near the Red Sea had acquired some mechanical arts and some wealth, but the greater number were poor and ignorant. All were weak, disunited, and idolatrous. The inspiring force that was to fuse them into a world-conquering nation was the fiery enthusiasm of *Mohammed*.

769. Mohammed was born in A.D. 570 at Mecca. After the early death of his parents his uncle took care of him. He is described as a man of retiring disposition, inclined to religious practices and subject to epileptic fits. When twenty-five he became wealthy by marriage with his employer, a rich widow. Until forty he continued to live the life of an influential merchant. He traveled much and picked up bits of information on Christianity and Judaism. Every year he withdrew for some time into the desert, where he devoted himself to pious meditations, which, he thought, often grew into religious trances. Finally he claimed to have had an apparition of the Archangel Gabriel, who announced to him that he was *the great prophet foretold by Moses.* This was the beginning of his new religion. At first, however, he seems to have been a visionary rather than an impostor.

Mohammedanism. — In comparison with the confusion and degradation of the Arabic religions, Mohammed's system represented a partial progress. Its best features he had gathered from Christian and Jewish sources, with which he had become acquainted on his business trips. The chief article of his "creed" is that "There is One God, 'Allah,' and Mohammed is His Prophet." The service of Allah is *Islam*, and those who profess it call themselves *Moslem*. They deny the Blessed Trinity, and hold that Moses and Christ were minor prophets sent to prepare the world for the coming of Mohammed. Prayer five times a day, a pilgrimage to Mecca once during lifetime, fasting during the entire month Ramadan, and almsgiving are enjoined. And faithful Mohammedans rigidly submit to these laws. But strangely in contrast with this emphasis on good works is their "fatalism," the doctrine that nobody can change the fate once destined for him or for anything else. The true Moslem will go to a heaven of sensual pleasures, where each of them will be waited upon by at least 80,000 slaves. There is a terrible hell for the bad. Polygamy is allowed; the husband may divorce his wives for almost any reason, but a wife cannot leave her husband. The Prophet himself, after the death of his first wife, married several. A sure way to paradise is war against the "infidels" (non-Mohammedans) ; "the sword is the key to heaven." Islam permits revenge, and confines what might be called its charity to Moslems. Friday is the sacred weekday. Mohammed's teachings were collected, by his first successor, in a book called the *Koran*, the Mohammedan Bible. It is divided into 114 *Suras*, or chapters, without any system or connection. Its numerous contradictions are one of the causes of the rise of many sects in Mohammedanism.

Mohammed's closest intimates accepted him at once; but beyond them, in the first twelve years of his preaching, he made few converts. Especially were his claims jeered by his townsfolk of Mecca, the chief city of Arabia. The priests of the old religion roused the people there against him, and finally he barely escaped with life from his home.

770. From the Hegira to the Death of Mohammed, 622–632 A.D. — This flight of the prophet from Mecca is *the Hegira,* the point from which the Mohammedan world reckons time as Christendom does from the birth of Christ. The first year of the Mohammedan era corresponds to our year 622 A.D. (The Mohammedan year, however, has only 354 days.)

From this event dates a change in Mohammed's policy. He now made converts rapidly by means of the sword, and soon captured Mecca, which became the sacred city of the faith. His fierce warriors were almost irresistible. He himself was

unscrupulous in the selection of means, as long as they served
his ends. By the time of his death he ruled over all Arabia
as prophet and king, supreme in all matters, civil, military,
and religious. This character descended to his successors, the
Caliphs, and has been claimed by the chief ruler of the Mohammedan world ever since.

771. The Ninety Years of Conquest. — Mohammed was bold
enough to address, from his deathbed, an invitation to the

THE MOSQUE OF OMAR — a famous Mohammedan temple at Jerusalem on the
site of the Temple of Solomon.   Present condition.

mightiest rulers of the world, the Greek emperor and the
king of Persia, to embrace his new faith, and to threaten
warlike measures if the invitation were not heeded. His
successors, at the head of a united Arabia, began a career of
conquest. In 638 they took Jerusalem and tore Palestine and
Syria from the weak empire. Four years later they destroyed
the Persian kingdom. They attacked and subjected Egypt,
and by 700 A.D. the dominion of the Caliphs extended from the

Black Sea through Northern Africa to the Atlantic Ocean. Thus Europe was threatened from east and west.

The conquest of Christian territory did not mean that the entire population was at once forced to apostatize. If the Christians preferred to retain their religion, they had to pay an extra tribute, and as a matter of fact were very frequently subject to vexations and even cruel persecutions.

772. Repulse in the East. — In 717 the Mohammedans appeared with a numerous force before Constantinople. Happily a line of incapable, intriguing emperors had given way to Leo III, the Isaurian, an uneducated but energetic ruler and an able general, though at the same time imbued with the Byzantine spirit of meddling with matters of ecclesiastical doctrine and discipline, and without any respect for the conscience or the pockets of his subjects.

Leo had only five months after his accession in which to restore order, but helped by an unusually severe winter and the preparations made by his predecessor he beat the Asiatics back after a twelve months' siege. *This formidable menace to Europe wore itself away on the walls of the city of Constantine.*

Arabian chroniclers themselves say that only thirty thousand survived of a host of one hundred and eighty thousand well-appointed warriors who began the siege. A chief weapon of the defense was the newly invented Greek fire, which was afterward to be used with terrible effect by the Mohammedans themselves. Six centuries later, Western Europe was still ignorant of its secret, and an old crusader who first saw it in a night battle described it as follows : " Its nature was in this wise, that it rushed forward as large round as a cask of verjuice, and the tail of the fire which issued from it was as big as a large-sized spear. It made such a noise in coming that it seemed as if it were a thunderbolt from heaven, and it looked like a dragon flying through the air. It cast such a brilliant light that in the camp we could see as clearly as if it were noonday." — JOIN-VILLE, *St. Louis.*

773. Repulse in the West. — At nearly the same time, however, the Arabs entered Spain, and were soon masters of the kingdom, except for a few remote mountain fastnesses. Then, crossing the Pyrenees, the Mohammedan flood spread over

Gaul, even to the Loire. Now, indeed, it "seemed that the crescent was about to round to the full." But the danger united the Frankish state. The duke of Aquitaine (who had long led a revolt against Frankish supremacy) fled to Charles Martel for aid; and in 732, in the plains near *Tours*, the "Hammer of the Franks" with his close array of mailed Austrasian infantry met the Arab host. From dawn to dark, on a Saturday in October, the gallant, turbaned horsemen of the Saracens hurled themselves in vain against that stern wall of iron. That night the surviving Arabs stole in silent flight from their camp. They kept some hold upon a fringe of Aquitaine for a while, but Gaul was saved.

The battle of Tours, just one hundred years after Mohammed's death, is the high-water mark of the Saracen invasion. Only a few years afterward, the Mohammedan world, like Christendom, split into rival empires. The Caliph of the East built, for his capital, Bagdad on the Tigris, the richest and greatest city in the world for centuries. The Caliphate of the West established its capital at Cordova in Spain. The two states were bitter rivals, and, with this disunion, the critical danger to Western civilization for the time passed away. *The repulses at Constantinople and at Tours rank with Marathon, Salamis, Metaurus, and Chalons, in the long struggle between Asia and Europe.*

774. Mohammedan Civilization. — After the caliphs had established themselves in royal splendor in Bagdad and Cordova, the Arabs began to show love for refinement. In fact, both these cities became centers of art and literature. In sculpture they could not accomplish much, because the Koran strictly prohibits any picture or statue; hence their ornamentation consists chiefly in *Arabesques, i.e.* fancifully interlaced lines, curved and straight. But many of their buildings are imposing. Famous are the Alhambra of Granada and the former mosque, now cathedral, of Cordova, a vast building of nineteen naves.

Their literature is less important. Its most noted production is a collection of fairy stories, the *Thousand-and-one Nights*. In spite of the prohibition of the Koran they studied the Greek philosophers, which Christian Syrians had translated into Arabic. It is in the Arabic translation that the books of

THE DAMASCUS GATE AT JERUSALEM — part of the Mohammedan wall about the city. The " minarets " on the battlements and the "pointed arch " are characteristic of Saracenic architecture.

Aristotle (§ 316) became first known in Western Europe. But the original works of the Arabian philosophers are of little value.

They transmitted to us our " Arabic " numbers, which they had received from India. They studied and in some few points improved the mathematical works of the Greeks. They have also given us many of our astronomical terms.

Yet the genius of the Arabic nation is on the whole not creative. In later times political leadership fell to races like the Turks,[1] much less capable of civilization. · Polygamy,

---

[1] The term *Saracen*, sometimes applied to any Mohammedan power, belongs strictly to the Arabs. In North Africa the Arabs mingled with the Berbers of *Mauritania*, and the race became known as *Moors* (afterward

slavery, and the degradation of woman were other obstacles to civilization. And since the Prophet's teachings were final, conditions crystallized into a changeless system opposed to all improvement. At its best, Mohammedan civilization was marked by an Oriental character. It was despotic, uniform, stagnant, sure to be outrun by that of the Western world.

FOR FURTHER READING. — Davis' *Readings*, II, Nos. 140–143. Thomas W. Allies, *Peter's Rock in Mohammed's Flood*, Chapter IV.

THE ALLIANCE OF THE PAPACY AND THE FRANKS

THE NEW KING OF THE FRANKS

775. Death of Charles Martel. — Shortly after the victory at Tours the Do-nothing king died. Charles Martel did not venture to take the title of king, but neither did he place any Merovingian on the throne. With the consent of the nobles the office of Mayor was divided between his sons, Pippin "the Short" and Karlman. But these, less secure than their victorious father, again raised a Merovingian king and ruled in his name. Soon, however, Karlman retired to a monastery, leaving Pippin the Short sole Mayor of the entire kingdom.

776. St. Boniface. — It was during the time of Charles Martel, that St. Boniface,[1] the Anglo-Saxon monk, began the systematic conversion of the eastern part of the Frankish kingdom. Christianity had been planted there in many localities, notably in the districts near the Alps, by zealous Irishmen and Franks. But their efforts were more or less sporadic. There were no bishops to provide priests for vacant stations and combat corruption, ignorance, and heresies. Wide regions, moreover, had never heard the voice of the Gospel at all. St.

---

dominant in Spain). The *Turks*, who now for almost a thousand years have been the leading Mohammedan people, came in later from Northern Asia and are allied to the Tartars.

[1] This name which means benefactor was given him by the pope. His Saxon name was Winfrid.

Boniface under incredible hardships converted the numerous heathens. In constant intercourse with Rome by visits and letters, he established bishoprics with himself as archbishop. This made him the Apostle of Germany. As Papal Delegate for all the countries north of the Alps he at last undertook, chiefly by a long series of Councils, a reformation of the Frankish Church in morals, discipline, and doctrine. Charles Martel and much more Karlman and Pippin gave him their powerful protection.

During the seventh century the intercourse between Rome and the Frankish kingdom was reduced to a minimum. St. Boniface for nearly forty years referred everything of moment to Rome, conducted his affairs according to instructions from Rome, and emphasized in all his transactions with rulers and nobles the absolute necessity of keeping in close touch with the center of Christian unity. This brought about a complete change. The whole kingdom recognized most vividly the position and power of the Successor of St. Peter, the common Father of Christendom.

777. The New King. — Pippin the Short meanwhile thought of setting aside the nominal king and assuming the royal dignity himself. Such a step would enable him to rule with greater power and efficiency. Nor was it beyond the competency of the nation to remove an unfit ruler. This was a strictly domestic affair; but an embassy crossed the Alps to far-off Rome to lay the matter before the Holy Father. Pope Zachary answered, it was better that he should be king who was actually performing the king's duties. Thereupon Pippin the Short was unanimously chosen king by the Franks. St. Boniface, by order of the Pope, anointed the first king of the Carolingian line,[1] A.D. 752. Childeric, the last Merovingian king, ended his days in a monastery. " An important revolution of the greatest benefit for Church and State, one of

---

[1] This family is named not after its ancestor but after its greatest member, Charles the Great or Charlemagne, Pippin's son. *Carolus* is the Latin for Charles. Sometimes, however, the family is styled " the Pippinides."

the most momentous events in history, was thus brought about
without the slightest disorder." [1]

THE PAPAL STATES

778. Rome and the Popes. — As we have seen, the Empire
retained in the center of Italy only small districts, with two
capitals, Ravenna in the northeast and Rome in the southwest
(§ 738).   In both territories, especially in that of Rome, the
influence of the popes was constantly growing.   The far-off
emperor did little for their inhabitants.   The old capital of
the world was now looked down upon as an unimportant provincial town.   In Constantinople one court revolution and
family intrigue followed another.   The few energetic emperors
had their hands full with the defense of the frontiers against
the Persians and their successors, the Arabs.   There was,
besides, the ever increasing tendency of the Caesars on the
Bosphorus to meddle with religious affairs.   The patriarchs
of New Rome, partly prompted by their own ambition, partly
urged on by the emperors, claimed greater power than was due
to them (§ 685).   Fortunately the several schisms caused by
these conditions were short-lived ; it was not until much later
(1043) that the East permanently tore itself away from the
unity of Christendom.   Yet the estrangement beween the two
parts of the Christian world was growing, and the decrease of
the knowledge of Greek in Italy and of Latin in the East
greatly tended to widen the breach.

But the more the people of Rome saw themselves neglected
and despised by the imperial government, the closer were they
drawn to the actual ruler of their little " state " (§ 685).   This
district was more and more looked upon as the property of
St. Peter and his successors.

The climax was capped when Leo the Isaurian published a
decree prohibiting the veneration of sacred images.   In the

---

[1] Mann, *The Lives of the Popes in the Early Middle Ages*, Vol. I, part II,
p. 273.

East, this resulted in the wholesale destruction of thousands of masterpieces of art and the cruel persecution of the defenders of the orthodox doctrine. In Italy the decree, together with a ruinous tax, roused such indignation that the people offered armed resistance, and only the intervention of the pope prevented the election of an Italian emperor.

779. The Lombard Danger. — Meanwhile the Roman and Ravennese territory was suffering from ever-repeated attacks of the Lombards. This Teutonic nation, even after becoming Catholic, retained much of its primitive ferocity. The conquest of a city by them always meant ruin for the inhabitants. The emperor should have been the active defender of his subjects in Italy; but he confined himself severely to the writing of encouraging letters and to intrusting the popes with the defense of the country by arms or by going as ambassadors to the Lombard court. If the helpless territories were not swallowed up by A.D. 750, it was exclusively due to the popes.[1] Once, indeed, Leo the Isaurian dispatched an army to Italy, but it was merely to extort enormous taxes and destroy the sacred images in the churches. When it met with the well-deserved resistance, it seized the property of the Apostolic See in southern Italy and Sicily.

780. Popes Loyal to Emperors. — Yet, though the popes were the real rulers and were so considered by the people, they always acknowledged themselves subjects of the emperor. As late as 741, a treaty negotiated by them with the Lombards was signed in the emperor's name. The popes rebuked heretical emperors fearlessly in religious matters, but not one pope broke his civil allegiance to the worst of them as long as there was still hope of bringing them to the realization of their duty. The pope certainly would have violated no right, had he renounced an allegiance which had long been forfeited by indolent, careless, and incapable emperors.

---

[1] Davis' *Readings*, No. 144.

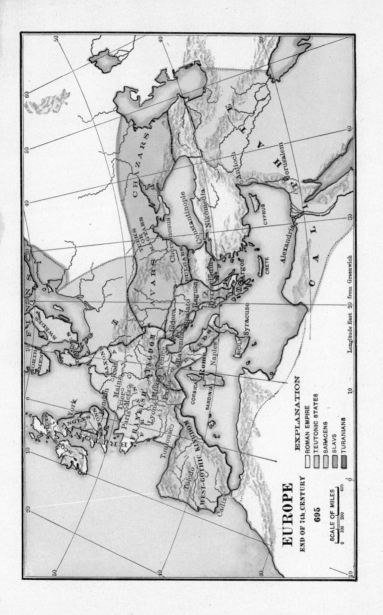

EUROPE

END OF 7th CENTURY

695

SCALE OF MILES
0   100   200   400

EXPLANATION

- ROMAN EMPIRE
- TEUTONIC STATES
- SARACENS
- SLAVS
- TURANIANS

Longitude East 20 from Greenwich

CHAZARS

BULGARS

AVARS

CALIPH

FRISIANS

SAXONS

ANGLES

FRANKISH KINGDOM

WEST-GOTHIC KINGDOM

Constantinople

Nikomedia

Alexandria

Jerusalem

Antioch

CYPRUS

CRETE

SICILY

SARDINIA

CORSICA

Rome

Naples

Syracuse

Ravenna

Argos

Ragusa

Chersonesus

Toledo

Cadiz

Toulouse

Paris

Mainz

Metz

Lyon

Milan

York

781. Foundation of the Papal States. — About A.D. 750 the attacks of the Lombards were renewed with increased violence. Letter upon letter went to Constantinople, and as

OUTER VIEW OF ST. PAUL'S GATE, ROME. — The pyramid, about 120 feet high and built before 12 B.C., is the tomb of one Cajus Sestius. When constructing his famous walls (§ 646) Emperor Aurelian embodied it in the line of fortifications. The large gate flanked by two towers (*Porta Ostiensis*) is part of Aurelian's work. It was remodeled under Honorius (§ 680). The smaller opening in Aurelian's wall to the left is of medieval origin. In the foreground appears the ancient pavement of the *Via Ostiensis* (road to Ostia). On this road St. Paul was conducted to his execution, the place of which is marked by the abbey of *Tre Fontane* (Three Fountains). Halfway between it and the city on the same road rises the splendid Basilica of St.-Paul-Outside-the-Walls, which contains St. Paul's remains. Both the gate and the road now bear the Apostle's name.

usual nothing came back but letters or messengers offering words of encouragement with neither money nor army. Under these circumstances, Pope Stephen III finally resolved to apply for aid to the new king of the Franks, Pippin the Short. He himself made the journey across the Alps and was received with the greatest honor by the nation and their monarch. In a solemn assembly king and nobles swore that they would not fight against the Lombards, hitherto their friends, to reconquer territory either for themselves or for the emperor whose claims had lapsed, but they were ready to vindicate with their swords the rights of the Church, St. Peter, and the Holy See.

The Franks crossed the Alps, and the Lombard king, Aistulf, promised to give up his conquests. Pippin might have kept these provinces for himself. He was able to defend and take care of them. But such was not his intention. He "restored them to St. Peter and his successors, to be possessed by them forever." But as soon as the Franks were beyond the Alps, Aistulf broke his word, laid siege to the very city of Rome, and devastated the surrounding country with fire and sword, not even sparing the churches and the catacombs. Promptly the Franks returned; and this time the cities and districts, including the territory of Ravenna, were actually taken possession of by Frankish envoys in the name of the pope, A.D. 756. To the Byzantine ambassadors who urged him to make the conquered provinces over to the empire, Pippin gave the noble answer: "It is not to please men that I have so often engaged in battle. It is only for love of Blessed Peter, and to obtain pardon for my sins. No amount of treasure can move me to take back what I have once offered to Blessed Peter."[1] Pope Stephen III, now real sovereign, gave Pippin the title of Patrician of the Romans, which made him the protector of the newly founded papal monarchy.

782. Popes either Princes or Prisoners. — In Rome, as a matter of fact, the popes had ever been either persecuted and prisoners or the most prominent personages. Though at all times desirable, a full sovereignty was less needed for them as long as nearly the whole Church was confined to the Roman Empire. It would be different in the times to come. "By a special dispensation of Divine Providence," says Pope Pius IX, in 1871, "the civil sovereignty came to the Roman Pontiff.

---

[1] Mann, Vol. I, Part II, p. 312.

If he were subject to another monarch's rule, he could never, in performing the duties of his Apostolic office, keep himself free from the influence of his sovereign, who might even fall away from the faith or wage war with another power." No nation will turn with full confidence to a pope who has to reckon with the political and commercial views, plans, and interests of another nation's head and government. Without the existence of the Papal States, the Crusades would have been an impossibility. They are for the Church what the District of Columbia is for the United States. They are not the private property of the popes, no more than the White House is the property of the President or the parochial residences the property of our parish priests.

783. Subsequent History. — On the whole, the Papal States, also called the States of the Church, have remained the same in extent as founded by Pippin the Short. They were often lost, for short periods, but always returned to the Head of the Church, sometimes as a result of unexpected combinations of affairs. Since 1870 they are lost again. The pope is in a most unworthy position. Yet the very shadow of independence in the government of the Church which is left to him is an effect of the generous donation of the first Carolingian king.

784. Meaning of Temporal Sovereignty. — Persons not well informed sometimes understand by the "temporal sovereignty" of the popes that peculiar position which the popes held in the Middle Ages as heads of the entire Christian commonwealth, in virtue of which they occasionally went so far as even to *depose emperors or kings. But this was no sovereignty at all.* By virtue of this position the popes never claimed any of the rights of kings or rulers in the realms concerned; they never, for instance, claimed that they could make purely commercial laws for the Christain countries, or that they, if the matter was purely temporal, could accept an appeal from a king's decision. In many cases it was simply the same power as that which they had over every other individual member in the Church, the right to see that the laws of God were obeyed, and to *inflict suitable punishment* in case of flagrant immorality and tyranny or other transgressions. Excommunication, for instance, was inflicted not only on Philip I, king of France, for adultery, but also by St. Paul on a man in Corinth for a similar crime. The power to act thus was part of the universal care for the spiritual welfare of all Christians, rulers as well as subjects. (The power of the popes to depose unworthy rulers was not seriously questioned in the Middle Ages.) But all this was no temporal sovereignty.

Temporal sovereignty is the supreme legislative, judicial, and executive power in a state, whether held by a monarch or a republican magistrate; that is to say, the power to make laws which bind all the subjects, to decide cases referring to temporal matters without the interference of a higher authority, to levy and dispose of revenues for the maintenance of public order and the furthering of temporal welfare. This was the power the popes held over the territories granted to them by Pippin the Short. Our United States Congress holds the same power over the District of Columbia.

FURTHER READING: Davis' *Readings*, Vol. II, No. 145; Thos. N. Allies, *Peter's Rock in Mohammed's Flood*, Chapter VIII, pp. 420 ff.

CHAPTER XLVII

THE EMPIRE OF CHARLEMAGNE

THE STORY

785. Charlemagne the Man. — In 768, Pippin, king of the Franks, was succeeded by his son Karl. This prince is known in history as *Charlemagne*, or Charles the Great (Carolus Magnus).[1] He was one of the most remarkable men that ever lived, and his work has profoundly influenced all later history. His friend and secretary, Einhard, describes him as a full-blooded German, — an Austrasian Frank, — with yellow hair, fair skin, and large, keen, blue eyes. He was unusually tall, but exceedingly well proportioned and graceful, so that his great height did not at first strike the observer. His appearance was always manly and stately, and his countenance commonly was open and cheerful; but, when roused to anger, his eyes blazed with a fire that few men cared to stand before.

Riding, hunting, and swimming were his favorite sports, but he delighted in all forms of bodily exercise, and through most of his life he was amazingly strong and active. He was simple in habits, and very temperate in eating and drinking. He was fond of the old German customs, and usually wore the ordinary dress of a Frankish noble, with sword at his side and a blue cloak flung over his shoulders; but he was also fond of the Roman culture, and strove to preserve and extend it among his people.

---

[1] The French form "Charlemagne" has won general acceptance, but the student must not think of Charles (Karl) as a Frenchman, or even as "king of France." He was "king of the Franks," and in history he was the predecessor of the later German kings rather than of French kings.

He spoke readily in Latin as well as in his native German; and he understood Greek when it was spoken.   Late in life he learned to write, but was never able to do much more than sign his name.   For the times, however, he was an educated man.   At table, he liked to have some one read to him, and he was particularly fond of history. He called scholarly

SILVER COIN OF CHARLEMAGNE.

The obverse side shows plainly the Latin form of his name.

men about him from distant countries and delighted in their conversation, and he did much to encourage learning.   After his death, legend magnified and mystified his fame, until he became the great hero of medieval story.[1]

786. The Frankish state at the accession of Charlemagne had much the same area as in the time of the sons of Clovis; but meantime it had been more thoroughly united and had been absorbing more of the old Roman culture, so that it was now ready to advance once more.

The realm was still in peril, it is true, from Mohammedanism on one side, and, yet more, from barbarism on the other. The first Carolingians — the two Pippins and the Hammer — had checked the invasion.   Now, under this vigorous new prince, the Franks took the aggressive and rolled back the peril on both sides.

787. Wars of Charlemagne. — This long reign of nearly fifty years (768–814) was filled with ceaseless border warfare, oftentimes two or more great campaigns to a season.   At first glimpse, therefore, Charlemagne stands forth a warlike figure, like Caesar and Alexander.   Like them he supported by arms

---

[1] Baldwin's *Story of Roland* gives some legends of Charlemagne's court. Davis' *Readings*, II, No. 146, gives Einhard's description.

tion. The *Saracens* were easily thrust back to the Ebro, so that a strip of north Spain became a Frankish mark.[1] The last *Lombard* king, Desiderius, quarreled with the pope. After fruitless negotiation, Charles marched into Italy, confirmed Pippin's grant to the pope, conquered the kingdom of Lombardy, sent Desiderius to a monastery, and with the partial consent of the nation proclaimed himself *king of the Lombards.*[2] *Bavaria,* always uncertain in its allegiance (§ 766), rebelled. Charlemagne subdued it thoroughly, sending its duke into a monastery and incorporating it into the Frankish state.

790. Political Union. — Thus all the surviving Germanic peoples on the continent of Europe, Lombards, Burgundians, Bavarians, Allemannians, Saxons, Frisians, Franks, and part of the Visigoths were united in one Christian state. The population, except in the Northeast, was overwhelmingly Roman, notably Celto-Roman, while the rule was in Teutonic hands. This unity seems to have been the aim of Charlemagne.[3] More than this he did not wish. He might easily have seized more of Spain or the provinces of the Greek Empire in south Italy. With rare moderation he even returned freely some Adriatic provinces that had voluntarily submitted to him. For mere conquest, such realms would have been vastly more attractive than the bleak Saxon-land, but it seems plain that Charles did not want conquests made for conquest's sake. He made only such acquisitions as the safety of his states or the interest of Christianity demanded. Nor did

---

[1] The defeat of Charlemagne's rear guard, on the return, by the wild tribesmen of the Pyrenees, in the pass of Roncesvalles, gave rise to the legend of the death of the hero Roland in battle with Saracens there. The details are fable, but the *Song of Roland* was the most famous poem of the early Middle Ages.

[2] Note the distinction : *Lombardy* first remained a separate kingdom though under the Frankish king ; after an attempt at rebellion Lombardy like *Bavaria* became part of the kingdom of the Franks, with no separate government.

[3] Charlemagne is said to be the first secular ruler who employed the Christian Era (§ 591, note) when dating documents.

the extension of the area of civilized life.   But very unlike them, he conceived of no civilization except that imparted by Christianity.   In fact the protection and spread of Christianity he considered as his chief aim and vocation from the beginning of his long reign.   He did not war for glory or gain.   The greater part of his time and efforts was .given to interior organization and government.   Charles was not so much a fighter as a statesman and ruler

788. The Winning of the Saxon Lands, 772–804. — The most desperate struggle was with the heathen Saxons, who still held the wilderness between the Rhine and the Elbe, near the North Sea.[1]   They were constantly harassing the Frankish dominions by devastating raids.   Missionaries never penetrated into the land.   For Charles the war against them was a necessity.   But it proved a desperate enterprise.   Nine times, after they seemed subdued, the Saxons shook off his yoke, massacred the Frankish garrisons, and returned to the abominations of paganism with its human sacrifices.   Unfortunately, Charles' methods are not above reproach.   Contrary to the demands of Christianity he forced the Saxons to be baptized, and once he massacred forty-five hundred men after they had been condemned by their own chiefs.   The genuine conversion of the Saxon leader Widukind meant a great step toward final submission.

The Saxon wars were the most fruitful of the whole century. Charles succeeded, where, eight hundred years previously, Augustus had failed, and he succeeded in a much nobler sense. The country became covered with churches and monasteries and the schools inseparable from them.   The establishment of bishoprics completed the work begun for Germany by St. Boniface.   The Saxons became fervent Christians and proved loyal subjects of their stern conqueror.

789. Spain, Italy, Bavaria. — Other foes engaged the attention the great king would have preferred to give to reconstruc-

---

[1] At present the name of Saxony is chiefly applied to other districts.

he wish to incorporate inharmonious elements into his kingdom.

It is notable also that the small Teutonic states outside his realms, — in Denmark and in England, — recognized some vague overlordship in the ruler of the continent.

791. Wars against the Slavs. — Beyond the German territory there stretched away indefinitely the Slavs and Avars, who from time to time hurled themselves against the barriers of civilization, as in old Roman days. In the closing part of his reign, Charlemagne attacked barbarism in its own strongholds. These long wars were really *defensive* in character. The Germans had now become the champions of European civilization. Gradually the first line of the people beyond the Elbe and Danube (including modern Bohemia and Moravia) was reduced to tributary kingdoms. Charles made no attempt, however, really to incorporate these conquests into his state, or to force Christianity upon them. *They were intended to serve as buffers against their untamed brethren farther east.*

The most famous event in the life of Charlemagne was the reëstablishment of the Roman Empire in the West. To this we will now direct our attention.

792. Revival of the " Roman Empire " in the West. — In the West of Europe the imperial power was dead. Yet the idea of an emperor was not forgotten. The nations, Teutonic as well as Roman, desired to see an emperor rise again who would combine imperial power with an imperial title, who would, according to the notion cherished since Constantine, be *a defender of the Church, a protector of right and justice.* There was now a ruler who lacked nothing of all the requisites but the title. Some exchange of thought on this subject had evidently taken place between the pope and Charlemagne, at least in some general way. A renewal of this sacred dignity was of advantage to both. The magic of the name would enormously increase the king's authority over the many nationalities of his realm, and the pope would gain a greater claim to the active assistance of the Frankish monarch. But the pope was the only one who, according to the spirit of the time, could take the initiative. An emperor sanctioned and crowned by the Head of all Christendom would meet with a general and unbounded enthusiasm.

793. Coronation of Charlemagne. — In A.D. 799 a band of Roman nobles, probably relying on the support of a Lombard and Byzantine faction in Italy, attacked Pope St. Leo III in a procession, and only with great difficulty could he save himself by flight. Like Stephen III he went in person across the Alps, and obtained from the king the promise of his assistance.

The following year saw Charlemagne in Rome, where he took vigorous measures for the future safety of the Holy Father. Then, on Christmas, when Charles was kneeling in St. Peter's Church to hear Mass, the pope unexpectedly approached him, placed a golden crown upon his head, and greeted him with the words, "Long life and victory to Charles, the most pious Augustus, crowned of God, the great and peace-giving EMPEROR OF THE ROMANS."

MEDALLION OF STS. PETER AND PAUL. — Second or third century. From Cath. Encyclopedia.

The cry was repeated in the church and reëchoed by the crowds outside. Christmas Day of the year 800 is one of the most memorable dates in the history of Europe. It is the birthday of the HOLY ROMAN EMPIRE.

794. Meaning of the Empire. — It makes little difference whether people considered the emperor as the successor of the deposed Romulus Augustulus (§ 728) or of the heretical tyrants of the East who had forfeited their rights. Everybody saw in him the legitimate heir of Constantine the Great, at any rate for the West. The coronation was no threat against Byzantium, but an emphatic statement of the indubitable fact that the Eastern emperors could no longer lay claim to the allegiance of the West. The West now acted for itself. By his tact Charlemagne soon overcame the sensitiveness of the Byzantine rulers, and before long was addressed by them as "emperor and king."

795. Territory of the Empire. — By his elevation the emperor gained neither any new territory nor the right of interfering in the interior affairs of any other state. Nor did he become the sovereign of the Papal States; on the contrary, it was one of the obligations of his office to guarantee these possessions to the incumbent of the Holy See. Neither did his position make him a subject of the pope in temporal matters. But the new dignity endowed him with a moral power which no feat of arms or successful conquest could have given him. Over other Christian princes, should there be any, the emperor would possess a primacy of honor, and the right of summoning them to his assistance in any enterprise undertaken for the welfare of the Church. Papacy and empire were to stand side by side, each supreme in its own sphere, the emperor being ever ready to support with physical force the spiritual government of the pope and to defend all the interests of the Church of God on earth.

The great act of A.D. 800 in St. Peter's Basilica was the beginning of that intimate union between Church and State, which in spite of many shortcomings must ever be considered as the nearest realization of the true ideal relation between the two which the world has ever known. The Papacy and the Holy Roman Empire were the two centers around which moved events of the greatest importance in European history.

All these attributes of the imperial dignity were rather acknowledged instinctively by the contemporaries of Charlemagne than formally expressed. The very designation of "Holy Roman Empire" was coined later. In our days the title emperor, as used by many rulers, is considered little more honorable than that of king. The medieval emperor, however, stood essentially higher than any other ruler; he was endowed with a sacred character; only one prince might rightfully call himself emperor, and he only after being crowned by the head of the Church in Rome.

796. The Empire of Charlemagne contrasted with the Byzantine Empire and that of Constantine the Great. — (1) All three empires may justly be called *Roman*, though not in exactly the same sense and degree. There can be no doubt about that of

Constantine. The Byzantine empire was Roman, because it was the empire of Constantine shrunk to a few provinces, whom its rulers succeeded in an unbroken line. The Western empire was Roman. The coronation of Charlemagne simply revived the ancient imperial power in the West. Moreover, Rome was the source of each emperor's power and prestige. It was the Roman pope who initiated him into his dignity by the solemn coronation. The emperor was the protector of the Roman Pontiff, the guarantor of his temporal possessions and defender of the whole Catholic Church.

(2) During the lifetime of Constantine *the city of Rome* ceased to be the seat of the central government, which was transferred to the Bosphorus. No emperor ever again resided in Rome (§ 674). But the city at least belonged to the empire and was still the queen of all its cities. Not so with the empire of Charlemagne. Rome did not belong to his empire, except as far as he had the duty and right of protection over it. But the place where the emperor happened to reside was now the center of the Western empire, in fact, some city north of the Alps. Theoretically, any Christian ruler might be crowned emperor, and the capital would change with the domains under his sovereignty. The medieval states, however, had no capitals in our sense of the word.

(3) *As to territorial extent*, Constantine's empire embraced the whole Mediterranean world; that of the Byzantines was more limited. Charlemagne practically controlled the whole West of the continent of Christian Europe, including wide areas which had never before been under Roman rule. This was not the case with later emperors, whose sovereignty extended over only a part of the realm of the great Charles. But every emperor held the supremacy of honor among all the other Christian princes. This privilege made the Western empire, in theory at least, a world empire, which would increase with every progress of Christianity. More than any other institution did this empire represent the ideal political unity of Christendom.

(4) All three empires considered themselves as the secular *guardians of Christianity;* but the coronation in the capital of the Christian world and by the supreme head of the Church, which expressed this position most solemnly, was the privilege of the Western emperor alone.

(5) The Eastern empire still served as the storehouse of the old *civilization.* No doubt there was a long period of time when no city stood higher than Constantinople in material and intellectual culture. But the empire declined constantly in extent as well as in interior strength. The despotism of its rulers throttled individual activity, crushed the active interest of the citizens in the common welfare, and forced the Church, the chief factor of civilization, into slavish subjection and unproductive stagnancy. The Western empire saved less of ancient civilization, but it possessed more active forces. Conditions were such as never to allow a destruction of personal liberty and ambition. Nor was the Church fettered as in the East. For several centuries this empire served as protector of the papacy and as a bulwark of Christianity and civilization against the pagan tribes, and as base of the evangelizing enterprises in northern and eastern countries. One cause of its later decline, though by no means the only one, was the hostile attitude of several emperors towards the very popes whom they were pledged to support.

The Eastern empire existed until A.D. 1453, when the last insignificant remnant of it was subjected by the Turks in the conquest of Constantinople. The territory of Charlemagne's empire became divided into several parts, the largest of which developed into what are now France and Germany. The imperial dignity eventually went to the ruler of the latter country. After a thousand years little was left of its prestige but the title. The last monarch who wore the crown of Charlemagne abdicated the dignity in A.D. 1806, in the turmoil caused by the French revolution. He was the grandfather of Emperor Francis Joseph of Austria. The German Empire of to-day is a new creation.

797. The Great Powers in 800 A.D. — Thus at the close of Ancient History the world is divided chiefly among four Great Powers — the two

Christian Empires and the two rival Mohammedan Caliphates.[1] *The only one of the four states that was to stand finally for progress was the Western Empire,* with its fringes in the Teutonic states of Scandinavia and England.

SOCIETY AND GOVERNMENT

798. Economic Conditions. — We must not think that the prosperity of the old empire had been restored with the old dignity. To accomplish that was to be the work of centuries more. In comparison with the old empire the West, in 800, was rather ignorant and poor. There was much barbarism in the most civilized society. Roads had fallen into neglect, and there was little communication between one district and another. Money was not abundant. Trade hardly existed. Almost the only industry was agriculture.

Perhaps this condition is best realized by looking at the revenues of Charlemagne himself. Great and powerful as he was, he was always pinched for money. There were no taxes, as we understand the word, — partly because there was no money to pay them with, and little produce. Payment was made *by service in person.* The common freemen paid by serving in the ranks in war; the nobles paid by serving there, with their followers, and also by serving, without salary, as officers in the administration. The treasury received some fines, and it was enriched somewhat by the " gifts " which were expected from the wealthy men of the realm; but its chief support came *from the produce of the royal farms* scattered through the kingdom. Charlemagne took the most minute care that these lands should be well tilled, and that each should pay him every egg and vegetable due. For the management of his estates he drew up regulations, from which we learn much about the conditions of the times. (Davis' *Readings*, II, No. 149.)

---

[1] The Caliph Haroun al Raschid at Bagdad, the hero of the *Arabian Nights*, was Charlemagne's contemporary. In an exchange of courtesies, the Saracen sent to the Frankish king a white elephant and a curious water clock that struck the hours.

799. Five features of the government deserve attention, —
the administration by *counts;* the watching of the counts by

THRONE OF CHARLEMAGNE AT AACHEN.

the *missi dominici ;* the *king's own marvelous activity ;* the
issuing of *capitularies ;* and *Mayfields.*

a. Under the Merovingians, large fragments of the kingdom fell under the rule of dukes, who became almost inde-

pendent sovereigns and who usually passed on their authority
to their sons.   Pippin began to replace these hereditary dukes

CATHEDRAL OF AACHEN — the Carolingian part (Octagon. The rear
part where the altar is seen is of later date).

with appointed *counts*, more closely dependent upon the royal
will.   This practice was extended by Charlemagne.

Except on the frontier, no one count was given a large dis-
rict; therefore the number of these officers was very great.

On the frontiers, to watch the outside barbarians, the imperial officers were given large territories ("marks") and were known as *margraves*.[1] To the counts and margraves was intrusted all ordinary business of government for their districts. They maintained order, administered justice, levied troops, and in all ways represented the king to the people.

b. Like the old dukes, the counts tended to become identified with their localities as independent rulers, and to transmit their power to their sons. To oppose this tendency directly in those times was hardly possible. So, to keep the counts in order, Charlemagne introduced a new set of officers known as *missi dominici* ("king's messengers"). The empire was divided into districts, each containing the governments of several counts, and to each such district each year there was sent a pair of these commissioners, to examine the administration and to act, for the year, as the king's self, — overseeing the work of local counts, correcting injustice, holding popular assemblies, and reporting all to the king.[2] The commissioners were moved from one circuit to another, year after year, so that they should not establish too intimate relations with one set of counts. Usually, too, the pair of *missi* were made up of one layman and one bishop, so that the two might be the more ready to check each other.

c. This simple system worked wonderfully well in Charlemagne's lifetime, largely because of his own marvelous activity. Despite the terrible conditions of the roads, and the other hardships of travel in those times, the king was constantly on the move, journeying from end to end of his vast dominions and attending unweariedly to its wants. No commercial traveler of to-day travels more faithfully, and none dreams of meeting such hardships.

---

[1] The title of count has nothing to do with counting. It is derived from the Latin word *comes*, which means companion. This was the appellation of certain officials in the later Roman Empire. The German word for it is *Graf*, the ancient form of which appears in margrave (Markgraf).

[2] Cf. § 76. See Charlemagne's instructions to the *missi*, in Robinson's *Readings*, I, 139–143.

d. With the help of his chief advisers, the king drew up collections of laws to suit the needs of the people. These collections are known as *capitularies.*

e. Mayfields. To keep in closer touch with popular feeling in all parts of the kingdom, Charlemagne made use of the old Teutonic assemblies in fall and spring. All freemen could attend and speak. Sometimes, especially when war was to be decided upon, this "Mayfield" gathering comprised the bulk of the men of the Frankish nation. At other times it was made up only of the great nobles and churchmen.

To these assemblies the capitularies were read; but the assembly was not itself a legislature. *Lawmaking was in the hands of the king.* At the most, the assemblies could only bring to bear upon him the force of public opinion.

800. Education. — Attention has been called (§ 785) to Charlemagne's interest in learning. The difficulties in building up a better education were almost beyond our comprehension. *There seemed no place to begin.* Not only the nobles, but even many of the better clergy were densely ignorant. The only tools to work with were poor.

Charlemagne did much. He secured more learned men, domestic and foreign. Anglo-Saxon, Irish, and Italian scholars received every kind of encouragement. In those days scholarship was almost exclusively represented by the clergy. Charles brought about the opening of schools in monasteries and at the seats of bishops; and he urged that these schools should not only train the clergy, but that they should teach all children to read, even those of serfs. Some of the schools established or revived at this time, as at Tours and Orleans, acquired much fame. Charlemagne also established a famous "School of the Palace" for the young nobles of the court at Aachen; and the scholar *Alcuin* was induced to come from England to direct it. The emperor himself, when time permitted, studied at the tasks of the boys.

With great zeal, too, he strove to secure a true copying of valuable manuscripts, and especially a correction of errors that had crept into existing books through careless copying.

801. The Place of Charlemagne's Empire in History. — In the early part of the eighth century there were four great forces contending for Western Europe, — the Greek Empire, the Saracens, the Franks, and the Papacy. By the year 800, the Carolingians had excluded two, while the other two had entered into the close alliance represented by the revived Roman Empire.

For centuries more, this Roman Empire was to be one of the most important institutions in Europe. Barbarism and anarchy were again to break in, after the death of the great Charles; but the imperial idea to which he had given new life and new meaning was to be for ages the inspiration of the best minds as they strove against the forces of anarchy in behalf of order, peace, and progress.

802. The Place of Charlemagne. — For his lifetime, Charlemagne restored order to Europe. It is true he was ahead of his age; and, after his death, his great design in many respects broke to pieces. It is true, too, that he built upon the work of his father and grandfather. But he towers above them, and above all other men for centuries, easily the greatest figure of a thousand years.

He stands for five great movements. He expanded the area of Christianity and of civilization, created one great Romano-Teutonic state, revived the Roman Empire in the West for the outward form of this state, reorganized civil society, brought about a revival of learning, and in various ways assisted in securing for the Papacy the independent position which it needs to develop its divine resources. Looking at this work as a whole, we may say he wrought wisely to combine the best elements into a new Christian civilization. *In his Empire the various streams of influence that we have traced in Ancient History (§ 4) were at last fused in one great current, — and Modern History was begun.*

FOR FURTHER READING. — Einhard's contemporary *Life of Charlemagne*; Thos. N. Allies, *Peter's Rock in Mohammed's Flood*, Chapter IX, esp. pp. 497 ff.

EXERCISES ON PART VI

1. Topical and "catchword" reviews: (*a*) *The Church* (see Part V also); (*b*) *The Franks;* (*c*) *The Empire.*

2. *Dates* to be added for events subsequent to the Teutonic invasions: 378, 410, 476, 622, 732, 800.

What events connected with the invasions, can the student locate, in order, between 378 and 476 ? What events in the history of the empire between 476 and 732 ? (Similar tests for other periods.)

3. *Battles.* Add to previous lists chief battles for the period 378–800.

ANCIENT MONOGRAMS OF JESUS CHRIST.

No. 1 consists of the two first Greek letters of the name of Christ. X in Greek is our Ch, and P is a Greek R. Constantine placed this symbol upon the Labarum, the standard of his army. (See § 673.) In No. 2 the lines of the X have been turned so as to form a cross, and one of them becomes identical with the vertical stroke of the P. The center letter in No. 3 is a Greek E, so that there are here the three first letters of the name of Jesus. In later centuries the devotion of the several Christian nations has put its own interpretation upon these three letters. No. 4 shows the first and the last letter of the Greek alphablet, "Alpha" and "Omega." It was suggested by the text, "I am the Alpha and the Omega, the beginning and the end." Apoc. I, 8.

BOOKLIST

HOLY SCRIPTURE

Copies of the whole Bible (Catholic or so-called Douay Edition) are for sale at low prices. But the following partial editions in handy little volumes are much more practical for students' libraries.

#* **Coppens, Charles, S.J.**, *Choice Morsels from the Bread of Life. Or: Select Readings from the Old Testament.* B. Herder, St. Louis. $0.60.

#* *New Testament.* Benziger Brothers, New York. Or:

#* *The Four Gospels and the Acts of the Apostles.* Benziger Brothers. $0.25.

#* **Ecker, James, D.D.**, *The Catholic School Bible.* B. Herder. $0.45.

Though intended for elementary schools, this book fully deserves a place in a high school library on account of the copious information which its many pictures, maps, remarks, and explanatory chapters are calculated to impart.

#* **Messmer, S. G., Archbishop**, *Outlines of Bible Knowledge.* With 70 illustrations and several maps. B. Herder. $1.80.

An excellent reference book for the libraries of high schools and colleges.

EVOLUTION

Cortie, Aloysius, S.J., *The Ages of the Sun: An Argument against Darwinism.* B. Herder, St. Louis. $0.10.

Proctor, A. E., *Science and the Evolution of Man.* B. Herder, St. Louis. $0.05.

\# **Muckermann, S.J.**, *Attitude of Catholics towards Darwinism aud Evolution.* With four plates. B. Herder, St. Louis. $0.75.

\# **Wasmann, Eric, S.J.**, *Modern Biology and the Theory of Evolution.* The Berlin discussion of the Problem of Evolution in 1907. B. Herder, St. Louis. $ 4.50.

\# **Houck, Frederick, Rev.**, *Our Palace Wonderful. Or: Man's Place in the Visible Creation.* D. P. Hansen & Sons, Chicago. $1.

> Many chapters of this work will serve as illustrative reading.

EARLIEST TIMES OF MANKIND — RELIGION — CIVILIZATION

\# *Lectures on the History of Religions* (Catholic Truth Society Publications). Five volumes. B. Herder, St. Louis. $3.

> Volumes I and II are especially useful.

\# * **Hull, Ernest, S.J.**, *Archaic Religions.* B. Herder. $0.30.

\# **Devas, Charles Stanton**, *Key to the World's Progress.* Longmans, Green & Co., New York. $1.60 ; popular edition, $0.20.

> A brilliant philosophy of history. The first chapters are a lucid discussion of the nature of civilization, somewhat different, though, from the way followed in this book.

\# * **Hull, Ernest, S.J.**, *Civilization and Culture.* B. Herder. $0.30.

Joly, N., *Man before Metal.* Appleton. $1.75.

Starr, F., *Some First Steps in Human Progress.* Flood and Vincent, Meadville, Pa. $1.

ORIENTAL HISTORY

Baikie, James, *Story of the Pharaohs* (illustrated). Macmillan, New York. $2.

* **Davis, William Stearns**, *Readings in Ancient History.* Allyn and Bacon, Boston. Two volumes : " Greece and the East " and " Rome and the West." Each $1.

> The first volume contains sixty pages of "source material" on Oriental history, with valuable introductions. See suggestions on page 10 of this text.

Ebers, M. George, *Uarda* (novel). Thos. Crowell & Co., New York.

Jackson, A. V. W., *Zoroaster.* Macmillan. $1.50.

Sayce, A. H., *Assyria, Its Princes, Priests, and People.* Revell, Chicago. $1.

JEWISH HISTORY

The Bible. See above.

\# **Gigot, Francis E.**, *Outlines of Jewish History from Abraham to Our Lord.* Benziger Brothers, New York. $1.75.

\# —— *Outlines of New Testament History.* Benziger Brothers. $1.75.

Morrison, W. D., *The Jews under Roman Rule.* Putnam's Sons, New York. $1.50.

CIVILIZATION IN ANCIENT CRETE

Baikie, James, *Sea Kings of Crete* (handsomely illustrated). Macmillan. $2.

Hawes and Hawes, *Crete, the Forerunner of Greece.* Harper, New York.

GREEK HISTORY

Source Material.

* **Davis, William Stearns**, *Readings in Ancient History.* This work is described in the list for Oriental history above. It is particularly valuable for Greek history, and should be the first library material purchased on that subject. The use of it, however, will certainly lead many students to wish to know more of certain ancient authors quoted in it; and the small list below ought to be accessible.

Aristotle, *On the Constitution of Athens;* translated by Kenyon. Macmillan. $1.

> This is the least readable of the books mentioned in this list; but it can be used in parts, under a teacher's direction.

Herodotus, Rawlinson's translation, edited by Grant; two volumes. Scribner. $3.50.

—— Macaulay's translation, two volumes. Macmillan. $4.50.

Homer's Iliad, translated by Lang, Leaf, and Myers. Macmillan. $0.80.

Homer's Odyssey, translated by Butcher and Lang. Macmillan. $0.80. Translated by Palmer. Houghton. $0.75.

Plutarch, *Lives;* translated by Clough; Everyman's Library (Dutton, New York); three volumes, each $0.75.

Thucydides, *History of the Peloponnesian War.* Jowett's translation; Clarendon Press, Oxford; four volumes. $3.50. Or the same edited in one volume and published by Lothrop, Boston. $2.50.

Everyman's Library (Dutton, New York) gives several volumes of these classics at cheaper rates. Constant additions are made to the Library. Herodotus and Thucydides can be obtained also in less desirable translations, but much cheaper, in Harper's Classical Library.

Modern Works.

* Bury, J. B., *History of Greece to the Death of Alexander*. Macmillan. $1.90.

Cox, G. W., *The Athenian Empire* (Epochs Series). Longmans. $1.

—— *Greeks and Persians* (Epochs Series). Longmans. $1.

Gulick, Chas. B., *Life of the Ancient Greeks* (illustrated). Appleton. $1.40.

Mahaffy, J. P., *Alexander's Empire*. Putnam, New York. $1.50.

—— *Old Greek Life* (Primer). American Book Co. $0.35.

ROMAN HISTORY

Source Material.

* Davis, William Stearns, *Readings in Ancient History*, as for Greek History above.

Munro, D. C., *Source Book in Roman History*. Heath. $1.

Tacitus. Two volumes. Macmillan. $2.

Modern Works.

Beesly, A. H., *The Gracchi, Marius and Sulla*. Longmans. $1.

Bury, J. B., *The Roman Empire to 180 A.D.* American Book Company. $1.50.

Fowler, Warde, *Cæsar*. Putnam. $1.50.

* How and Leigh, *History of Rome to the Death of Cæsar*. Longmans. $2.

\# Muenchgesang, R., *In Quest of Truth*. Glimpses of Roman Scenes (Fiction) (see p. 531). B. Herder. $0.80.

\# Joy, John C., S.J., *The Emperor Marcus Aurelius*. A study in ideals. B. Herder. $0.35.

Ihne, William, *Early Rome*. Longmans. $1.

* Pelham, H. F., *Outlines of Roman History*. Putnam. $1.75.

Platner, Samuel B., *The Topography and Monuments of Ancient Rome*. Allyn and Bacon, Boston. $3.00.

A lucidly written work. Very useful.

Smith, R. B., *Rome and Carthage.* Longmans. $1.

\# **Guggenberger, Anthony, S.J.,** *A General History of the Christian Era.* Three volumes. Volume one, "The Papacy and the Empire." B. Herder. $1.50 per volume.

The period from Christ to Charlemagne is covered by the first part of this volume. It furnishes copious information on many points.

CHRISTIANITY

\#* *The New Testament.* See above under *Scripture.*

\#* **Gigot, F. E.,** *Outlines of New Testament History.* Benziger Brothers. $1.75.

\# **Fouard, Constant,** *The Christ, the Son of God.* Longmans, Green & Co. Two volumes. $2.50. Cheap edition without notes and appendix, $0.25.

—— *St. Peter and the First Years of Christianity.* Longmans, Green & Co. $1.25.

These three works have copious descriptions of the religious, political and moral conditions of the Jews and Romans.

\# **Shahan, Thomas J., Rt. Rev.,** *The Beginnings of Christianity.* Benziger Brothers. $2.

Lectures on various topics of this period.

\#* **Barnes, Arthur S.,** *The Early Church in the Light of the Monuments.* Longmans, Green & Co. $1.50.

A very interesting book; chiefly on the catacombs.

\# **Wiseman, Nicholas (Cardinal),** *Fabiola, Or: The Church of the Catacombs.* Benziger Brothers. Prices from $0.50 to $1.50.

The classical novel on the early Church.

\# **Rampolla (Cardinal),** *Life of Saint Melania.* B. Herder. $1.90.

The greater part of this book has the character of a source, because it is the reproduction of writings of the Saint's own time.

\# **Allies, T. W.,** *Monastic Life from the Fathers of the Desert to Charlemagne.*

\# **Riguet,** *Life of St. Patrick.* B. Herder. $1.

\# **Brou, S.J.,** *Life of St. Augustine of Canterbury.* B. Herder. $1.50.

\# **Willibald,** *Life of St. Boniface.* Translated into English by George W. Robinson. Harvard University Press. $1.15.

Written, in Latin, three years after the Saint's death.

Most of the books enumerated under Christianity contain copious information on various topics of contemporary secular life and might as well be mentioned under other headings of this booklist.

Teutonic Period

* **Davis, William Stearns,** *Readings.* See above.

\# **Grisar, Hartmann, S.J.,** *History of Rome and the Popes in the Middle Ages.* B. Herder, St. Louis. Three volumes, each $4.50.

This splendid work is richly illustrated with pictures and maps. The narrative begins in A.D. 394.

\# **Einhard,** *Life of Charlemagne.* Translated by Turner. Harper's Classics. $0.50.

Einhard (Eginhard) was a personal friend of the great emperor.

\# **Guggenberger, Anthony,** *A General History of the Christian Era.* See above.

It would be impossible to enumerate ALL the good and recommendable books on this subject. But this list, it is hoped, will be of some service in making selections for a students' historical library.

One publication, however, is still to be mentioned. It is too bulky and expensive for many schools, but it may be accessible in public or private libraries.

The Catholic Encyclopedia. An international work of reference on the Constitution, Doctrine, Discipline, and History of the Catholic Church. Encyclopedia Press, New York. Sixteen volumes.

Its numerous articles on subjects of history make it the foremost Catholic historical publication.

The following work, too, contains a great amount of desirable information on historical subjects and on questions closely connected with history. It is well worth its cost.

Addis and Arnold, *A Catholic Dictionary containing some account of the Doctrine, Discipline, Rites, Ceremonies, Councils, and Religious Orders of the Catholic Church.* Revised, with additions, by T. B. Scannell, D.D. Ninth Edition, 1917. B. Herder, St. Louis. $6.50.

Questions to accompany this textbook have been prepared by the author. Loyola University Press, Chicago, Ill. 5 cents the copy; reduction on quantities.

INDEX

Pronunciation, except for the more familiar names and terms, is indicated by accentuation and division into syllables. As a rule, the simpler diacritical marks of Webster's *International Dictionary* are used. The soft aspirated guttural *g* of the German is represented by G, the guttural *ch* by *ċh*, and the French *n* by *ṅ*; italics are used to mark silent letters; $\overline{ae}$ and $\overline{oe} = \bar{e}$; $\overline{ei} = \bar{\imath}$; $\overline{eu} = \bar{u}$; $\bar{y} = \bar{\imath}$; $\breve{y} = \breve{\imath}$. In French words with an accent on the final syllable, that accent only is marked; but it should be understood that in such words the syllables as a rule receive nearly equal stress.

The index may be utilized for reviews upon "cross-topics," or topics that call for an arrangement different from that of the text. The most important subjects for such review are indicated in black italic.

The references are to sections.

Aachen (äċh′en), 796, *a*. Map after p. 640.

Abraham, ancestor of Hebrew race, 58.

Absolute monarchy, in Egypt, 11; in Assyria, 43; character of Oriental, 80; in Cretan period, 97; modified in Homeric Greece, 105; reappears in the tyrants, 126 (see *Pisistratus*); after Alexander in Graeco-Oriental world, 280, 304, note; in early Rome, 346, 349; of Caesar, 557; of Augustus, 570, 592; of Diocletian and the later Empire, 669–671; growth toward, in Teutonic states, 761; Mohammedan, 774; of Charlemagne, 799.

Ab-ys-sĭn′i-a, 6; Abyssinians in Egypt, 6, 10. Map, p. 16.

Academy, at Athens, 182.

Ac-ar-nā′ni-a, 195. Map after p. 98.

Ac′cad, 37, 38. Map after p. 12.

A-ċhāē′a, part of Athenian league, 199. Maps after pp. 98, 102, 202.

A-ċhaea, Greece becomes province of, 311.

A-ċhaean culture, 98, 100–112; economic side of, 108–110; clan and tribe, 100–102; government, 105–107; overthrown by Dorians, 113.

A-chaean League, 296–311; origin, 300; constitution, 301; first expansion beyond Achaea, 303; and Aratus, 304; and Lydiadas, 305; and Athens and Argos, 306; and Sparta, 307–310; fall, 311, 471.

A-ċhaeans, mythical origin of, 116, *b*. See *Achaean culture.*

A-chae′us, fabled ancestor of Achaeans, 116, *b*.

A-chil′leș, 110, 112.

A-crŏp′o-lis, the central hill-fort about which grew Greek and Latin cities, 103, 333 *d*.

Acropolis of Athens, 138, 148, 177; in Age of Pericles, 218–219; plan, p. 213; view, pp. 214, 215; "restoration," p. 225.

Ac′ti-um, battle of, 567.

Ad′rĭ-an-ō′ple, battle of, 679, 712. Map after p. 554.

Adriatic Sea, map after p. 136.

Ae′dĭles, 396.

"**Ae-ġē′an culture,**" 95 ff.

Ae-ġē′an Sea, 73, 84, 85, *d*, 95, 114, 120, 121, 122, 163, 166, 167, 189, 190,

1

191, 192, 193, 194, 202, 207, and else-
where. Maps after pp. 86, 88, 98.
Ae-gī'na, at war with Athens, 166,
200; gains prize of merit at Salamis,
180. Map after p. 102.
Ae-gos-pŏt'a-mi, battle of, 251;
Conon at, 259. Map after p. 250.
Ae-mil'i-ā'nus, 644, note.
Ae-ne'as, 544.
Ae-o'li-ans, 116, b.
Ae'o-lus, 116, b.
Aequians (ē'kwĭ-ans), 409. Map,
p. 311.
Aeschylus (ĕs'ki-lus), 222; on Sala-
mis, 179.
A-ē'ti-us, 722.
Ae-tō'li-an League, 299, 310. Map,
after p. 287.
Af-ghan-is-tän', in Persian Empire,
73; and Alexander, 279. Map after
p. 88.
Africa, early civilizations in, 6; cir-
cumnavigation of, 32; Phoenician
sailors on coast of, 34, 56; Greek
colonies in, 122; under Roman Em-
pire, 610; Diocese of, 666; Vandal
kingdom in, 718; reconquered by
Justinian, 736; Mohammedan con-
quest, 771. See Egypt, Carthage.
Ag-a-mĕm'non, king of Mycenae,
87, 107.
"Age of Cicero," 625.
"Age of Pericles," 193–240.
"Age of Tyrants," 126.
A-gĕs-i-lā'us, king of Sparta, 258.
A'gis, reforming king of Sparta, 307.
Ag'o-ra, in Athens. Map, p. 206,
with description.
Agrarian laws, Solon's, 141, 142;
Agis' and Cleomenes', 307–309; Licinian, 370, 371; of the Gracchi,
507–520; of Caesar, 558.
A-grĭc'o-la, 584.
Agriculture, plants, 3, c; in Egypt,
17, 18; Babylonian, 44, 51; in Ho-
meric Greece, 110; in Sparta, 129;
in Age of Pericles, 237, 238; early
Roman, 340, 357, 358; Roman, about
200 B.C., 408, 409; after Punic Wars,
488–490; under the Empire, 610, 611;
in later Empire, 694, 698, 699; re-

vived in Italy under Theodoric, 731;
primitive, in Empire of Charle-
magne, 798. See Peasantry.
A-grĭp'pa, 622.
A-hü'rä Mäz'dä, 78.
Aistulf (īs'tulf), 781.
Aix (äks), battle of, 524.
Aix-La-Chapelle, other name for
Aachen.
Ăl'ăr-ic, 713–715.
Alba Longa, 337, 339. Map, p. 311.
Al-cāē'us, 155.
Al'chem-y, 774.
Al-ci-bī'a-dēş, 248.
Alcuin (al'kwĭn), 800.
Alemanni (ä-lä-män'nē), 679, and
map, p. 584.
Alexander Se-ve'rus, 643.
Alexander the Great, 276–286;
youth and character, 276; acces-
sion and restoration of order, 277;
invades Asia as Champion of Hellas,
278 ff.; Persian campaigns, 278; in
the far East, 279; results of work,
280 ff.; significance of, 286; routes
of march, map after p. 270.
Alexandria, name of many Greek
cities in Asia after Alexander, 280–
282. Map after p. 270.
Alexandria in Egypt, founded, 278;
glory of, 293, 312 ff.; library at, 319;
and lighthouse, 320. Map after p.
270.
Alexandrian Age, the, 312–327.
Allia, battle of, 375. Map, p. 311.
"Allies" (socii), the Italian, 391–
394; after Punic Wars, 497; "Social
War," for citizenship, 526; admitted
to Roman citizenship, 527.
Alphabet, growth, 3, e; germs of, in
Egyptian hieroglyphs, 22; and Phoe-
nicians, 56; and Cretan writing, 93
and especially 96; late use in Greece,
114.
Ambrose, of Milan, 680, 683, 702.
Am-mi-ā'nus, 701.
Am-phĭc'ti-on-ies, 119, 121.
Am-phic'ty-on-ic League, the, 119.
Am-phi-thē'a-ter, Etruscan origin
of sports of, 331; games in, see
Gladiatorial games; buildings, 622.

Am′ten, statue of, p. 22.

An-ăb′ā-sis, 257.

An-ăc′re-on, 146, 155.

An-ax-ag′o-ras, 225, 227.

An-ax-i-man′der, 156.

An-ax-ĭm′i-nēs̱, 156.

Ancestor worship, Egyptian, 24; Greek, 99, 100, 101; Roman, 341, 570.

Ancient History, 4; field of, map on p. 9.

An′cus Mar′ti-us, 335.

Angles, the, in Britain, 720. Map after p. 606.

Animal worship, 24.

Anio River, 362. Map, p. 311.

An-tal′ci-das, Peace of, 260.

Antioch, 312; under Roman Empire, 611. Map after p. 378.

An-tī′o-chus, of Syria, 464, 465.

Antiochus the Great, 467.

An′tō-nines, the, 585–591.

An-to-nī′nus, Marcus Aurelius, 589; quotations from Thoughts of, 638.

Antoninus Pius, 588.

Antonius, Marcus ("Mark Antony"), 563–567.

Antony, Mark, see Antonius.

A-pĕl′lēs̱, 314.

Apennines, the, 326. Map after p. 308.

Aph-ro-dī′tē, 111.

Apŏl′lo, 100, 111. See Delphic Oracle.

Apologists, Christian, 659.

Apostles of Jesus Christ, 573.

Ap′pi-an, 628.

Appian Way, the, 395. See Roman Roads, and map, p. 354.

Appius Claudius, the decemvir, 362, 364.

Appius Claudius, censor, 382, 395, 399, 402.

Aqua Sextiae (ä′kwä sĕx′tĭ-ae), battle of, 524.

A′que-ducts, of Pisistratus, 146; in Graeco-Oriental cities, 282; in cities of Roman Empire, 610.

Aquitaine (ä-kwĭ-tān′), 764. Map after p. 622.

A-rā′bi-a, maps after p. 12, on p. 45, and after pp. 52, 232, 270; Arabians in Egypt, 10, 32; and Egyptian trade, 19; modern, in Chaldea, 35; language, 36. See Mohammedanism.

Arabic notation, 774.

A-rā′tus, general of Achaean League, 245–250; character and services, 246; enmity to Lydiadas, 247; betrayal of Corinth, 250.

Ar-bē′la, battle of, 278, c. Map after p. 270.

Ar-cā′di-a, 261, 265. Map after p. 102.

Arcadius, 680.

Arch, Egyptian, 22; Etruscan, 331; Roman, 414, 621; triumphal, 622.

Archbishops, 573.

Ar-chi-mē′dēs, 320, 446.

Architecture, in Egypt, 22; in Chaldea and Assyria, 52; Persian borrowed, 74; Oriental contrasted with European, 80; in Greece, orders of, 154; in Athens of Pericles, 218–220; early Roman, 338, 340, 414; later Republic, 411, 484–485; Early Empire, 621–622; early Christian, 623.

Ar′chi-trāve, in Doric order of architecture, 154.

Ar′chŏn, at Athens, 134, 135, 144, 152; king-archon, 134.

Ar-e-ŏp′a-gus, 135, 142.

A′rēs, 111.

Ar-ġi-nū′sae, 248. Map after p. 250.

Ar-ġīves, see Argos.

Ar′go-lis, 91. Map after p. 102.

Ar′gos, persistence of kingship in, 124; hostile to Sparta, 127; crippled by Sparta, 161; friendly to Persia, 172; allied to Athens against Sparta, 199; joins League against Sparta, 259; joins Achaean League, 305. Maps after pp. 98, 102.

Ā′ri-an heresy, 683.

A-ri-o-vīs′tus, 547.

Ar-is-tär′chus, 320.

Ar-is-tī′dēs, Athenian leader, 170; proposes plan for Delian League, 191.

Aristocracy, definition, 85; return to Dorian Greece, 120; in Sparta, 128; in Achaean League, 301; in early Rome, 344, 347, 356; in later Republic, 397, 400, 401, 484; in Roman Empire, 690, 691, 698; among the Germans, 709; in new Teutonic states, 761.

Ar-is-tŏph'a-nēṣ, 148, 221.

Ar'is-tot-le, quoted on Athenian history, 136, 146; place in philosophy, 316, 317, note; tutor of Alexander the Great, 276; *Natural History* of, 285; proofs of sphericity of the earth, 320.

Arithmetic, Egyptian, 23; Chaldean, 49; Roman, 619.

Ā'ri-us, 683.

Ar-mē'ni-a, and Phoenician commerce, 55; a Roman province, 606. Map after p. 12, etc.

Army, Egyptian, 12; Achaean, 113; Dorian, 113; Spartan, 130; citizen armies based on wealth at Athens, 137; Theban phalanx, 263; Macedonian, 273; Roman, reformed by Servius, 347, 348; under the Republic, 403–406; under Early Empire, 601–603; agency in unifying the Empire socially, 406, 603; reforms of Diocletian, 667; in fourth century, 687; Teutonic, 709, 710.

Ar'ri-a, 632.

Art, pre-diluvian, 1; prehistoric, p. xviii; Egyptian, 21; Babylonian, 51, 52; Persian, borrowed, 74; Oriental, 80; Cretan, 96; no Spartan, 130; Greek, of 6th century, 154, 157; in age of Pericles, 217–222; in Alexandrian Age, 312, 314; Greek influence on Roman, 487; Roman, 407; in Augustan Age, 621 ff.

Ar-tax-erx'ēṣ, king of Persia, 257, 260.

Ar'te-mis, 111.

Ar-te-mĭs'i-um, battle of, 176. Map after p. 102.

Ā'ryans, 2.

Asia, see Oriental *Culture* and *Geography*.

Asia, Province of, 472, 510.

Asia Minor, Assyrians in, 41; under Croesus, 70; Persia, 172; Hellenizing of the coast, 121; Persian Wars,

163–164, 189 ff.; Greek cities betrayed to Persia by Sparta, 250, 260; Agesilaus in, 258; Alexander in, 278; Gauls in, 290; part of Graeco-Oriental world, 287 ff.; Lycian Confederacy, 301; Roman province, 510; and Saracens, 772.

As-pā'si-a, 230, *b*.

Assembly, Homeric folk-moot, 107; Spartan, 128; in cities of Delian League, 191, 194; Achaean League, 300, 301. See *Athenian, Roman, Teutonic,* and *Mayfield*.

As'sur-Nat'sir-Pal, king of Assyria, inscription of, 41.

As-syr'i-a, 35; Semitic, 36; Empire, 40; fall, 41; contribution to government, 40; religion and morality, 41, 53; society and culture, 44–52; cuneiform writing, 47; art, 52; Roman province, 606. Maps after pp. 12 and 86.

As-tär'te, 57.

Astrology, Chaldean, 49.

Astronomy, Egyptian, 23; Chaldean, 49; Greek, 156, 320; Saracenic, 774.

Ā'taulf, 715.

Ā'ten, 24.

Ath-an-ā'si-us, 683, 702.

A-thē'nē, 111; statues on the Acropolis of Athens, 218, 219, 220.

Athenian Assembly, under Eupatrid rule, 135; constitution of classes, 137; after Solon, 142, *b*, 144, 145, 149; after Clisthenes, 151–152; of Pericles, 210.

Athenian colonization, see *Cleruchs*.

Athenian "Generals," 152, 209.

Athenian juries, 211; payment of, 212.

Athenian oratory, 223.

Athenian political capacity, 213, 214, 229.

Athenian senate, after Solon, 142, *a*; after Clisthenes, 152, 210. See *Areopagus*.

Athenian state pay, 212.

Athens, legendary founding, 103, 132; type of Ionic cities, 120; metropolis of Ionia, 121; oligarchy replaces old kingship, 134–137; progress toward democracy, to Solon, 137–139; Solon's reforms, 140–143; factions, 145; tyrants, 145–148; under Pisistratus, 146; Clisthenes' reforms, 149–153; and democracy, 152, 153; leader in culture after 600, 146 ff.; condition at Persian attack, 161; part in Ionian revolt, 164, 165; Persian heralds, 167; Marathon, 167, 168; from Marathon to Thermopylae, 169, 170; internal factions crushed, 169; a naval power, 170; at battle of Artemisium, 176; abandoned to Persians, 177; battle of Salamis, 178, 179; receives offers from Persians, 181; building of walls, 184, 185; commerce, 185, 186; proposes League of Plataea, 187; glory from Persian War, 188; assumes leadership of Asiatic Greeks, 190; Confederacy of Delos, 191–194; Athenian Empire, 195 ff.; jealousy between Sparta and, 196; greatest extent, 199; activity, 200; power, 204; population, 205; colonies, 206; revenue, 207; government, 208–211; "juries," 211; state pay, 212; Athenian political ability, 213, 229; verdict on the empire, 214; leaders and parties, 215; Pericles, 216; intellectual and artistic development, 217–232; theater money, 222; tribute by Pericles, 229; faults in, 230, 231; life in Age of Pericles, 233–240; houses, 233; family, 236; industries, 237; banquets, 239; education, 240; and Peloponnesian War, 241–251; plague in, 244; rule of the Four Hundred, 249; the "Thirty," 255; regains freedom, 256; in new league against Sparta, 259; and Peace of Antalcidas, 260; and Spartan treachery, 261; shelters Theban democrats, 262; saves Sparta, 266; and Macedon, 272, 274, 277; and Achaean League, 305; home of philosophy in Hellenistic Age, 315, 316; and learning, 312, 320; "ally" of Rome, 464; welcomes Mithridates, 532; intellectual center under Roman Empire, 619; sacked by Goths, 648; spared by Alaric, 713. Maps after pp. 98, 102, and on pp. 184, 193, 206.

A′thos, Mount, 166; canal of, 171. Maps after pp. 98, 102, etc.

At′ti-ca, products, 85; consolidated, 103, 132. See *Athens*. Maps after pp. 98, 102, and on p. 184.

Attic comedy, 221.

At′til-a, 722, 723, 724.

Augurs, 342, 343.

Augustan Age, the, 569.

Au′gus-tīne, Saint, one of the "Church Fathers", 702; the apostle of England, 747.

Augustus, 568–570, 575, 605. See *Octavius*.

Augustus, a title for Roman Emperors, 593.

Aurelian, emperor, 646.

Au-rē′li-us, Marcus, see *Antoninus*.

Ausonius of Bordeaux, 703.

Aus′pĭc-ēs, 331, note 342.

Aus-trā′si-a, 764, 765. Map after p. 622.

Autun (ō-tŭn′), 620.

Avars, 721, 791. Map after p. 640.

Ǎ′vĕn-tīne, the, map, p. 317.

Avitus, poet, 703.

Bā′al, 57.

Babel, tower of, 1, 2, 36.

Babylon, geography, 34, 35; one of the early city-states, 38; First Empire of, 39; Second, 42; society and culture, 43–53; law and property, 45; special privilege of rich in law, 46; cuneiform script, 5, 47; literature, 48; science, 49; legends of creation and deluge, 50; industry and art, 51–52; religion and morals, 53. Maps after pp. 12, 86, 88, etc.

Bactria, or Bǎc′tri-ǎn′a, 279. Map after p. 88.

Bag′dad, map after p. 630.

Baltic Sea, and Phoenicians, 54.

Banking, in Roman Empire, 614.

Banquet, place of, in Greek life, 239.

Barbarian invasions, in Egypt, 10, 31; in Euphrates lands, 36, 38, 41; Scythians (and Persia), 75; Gauls (and

Graeco-Oriental world), 290; into Italy, 330, 375; Cimbri and Teutones, 523; and Caesar, 547, 548; on frontiers of Roman Empire, 605, 607; from Aurelius to Aurelian, 648; peaceful infusion, 697; successful in fourth century, 712 ff. (see *Germans*); Huns repulsed, 721–724; and Charlemagne, 788–791.

"Barbarians" (to the Greeks), 116 *a*.

Barbarism, term explained, p. xvii.

"Barrack Emperors," 639 ff.

Barter, trade by, 19, 70.

Basil, Saint, 702.

Basilica, 623.

Bavaria, 766, 789. Map after p. 622.

Běl-i-sā'ri-us, 736.

Benedict, Saint, "rule" of, 757.

Ben-e-věn'tum, battle of, 381. Map after p. 308.

Beowulf (bě'o-wulf or bā'o-wulf), song of, 707.

Berbers, 10.

Bible, nature of, p. xv, § 2; dates given in it, 1; facsimile of Latin Bible, pp. xiv, 585, 614; New Testament, 627, 702. Greek translation (Old Testament), 319; translated into Latin, 702.

Bishops, 573.

Bi-thȳn'i-a, map after p. 270.

Black Sea, and Phoenicians, 55; Greek colonies on, 122. Map after p. 86.

Bō-a-di-ce'a, 609.

Boe-ō'tĭ-a, cities of, and Thebes, 132; early poets of, 155; under Athenian control, 199; falls away from Athens, 201. See *Thebes* and *Plataea*. Maps after pp. 98, 102, etc.

Bohemians, 721.

Bokhara (boch-ä'ra), 77.

Boniface, Saint, Apostle of the Germans, 776, 777.

Bordeaux (bôr-dō'), map after p. 598.

Bräs'i-das, 247.

Brěn'nus, 375, note.

Britain, Phoenician sailors in, 56; Caesar in, 547; Roman conquest of Southern, 578, 584, 606; Hadrian's Wall in, 587, 607; diocese of, 666;

abandoned by Roman Empire, 606, 720; Teutonic invasions, 720; gradual conquest, a Teutonic state, 745, 746; conversion to Christianity, 747; political results of conversion, 748.

Bronze, explained, 2, note; used in Egypt, 10; in Chaldea (see); in Crete, 96; displaced in Greece by Achaeans, 98, 99.

Brū'tus, Lucius Junius, first consul of Rome, 350, note.

Brutus, Marcus, the Republican, 561, 566.

Burgundians, 705; in Gaul, 716, 717; at Chalons, 722; numbers, 752; Arians, 742; conquered by Clovis, 742. Maps, p. 584 and after p. 606.

Burgundy, 764. Map after p. 622.

By'zăn-tīne Empire, 734–738, 796. See *Roman Empire in the East.*

By-zăn'ti-um, 122; a free city in the Graeco-Oriental world, 288, 674. Map after p. 136.

Cā'diz (Gades), founded by Phoenicians, 56. Map after p. 136.

Cae-'li-an Hill, the, 338. Map, p. 317.

Caesar, Caius Julius, 544; appears as leader, 544–547; in Gaul, 547, 548; rupture with Pompey, 549; five years' rule, 550–561; hope of subject nations, 551; crosses Rubicon, 553; campaign in Italy, 553, in Spain and Greece, 554; in Asia, Egypt, Africa, and Spain, 555; constructive work, 556–560; form of his monarchy, 557; murder, 561; character, 544, 562.

"Caesar," a title, 593, 663.

Cain, 1.

Cal'e-dō'ni-a, 584.

Calendar, Egyptian, 23; Caesar's, 558.

Cal-Ig'ū-la, 577.

Caliphs, 770 ff.

Căl-lĭc'rā-tēṣ, 218.

Cam-pā'ni-a, map after p. 308.

Cam'pus Mar'ti-us, 413. Map, p. 317.

Canaan. See *Palestine*.

Canal from Nile to Red Sea, 28; and Neco, 32; restored by Ptolemies, 293. Map, p. 16.

Căn'nae, battle of, 442. Map after p. 308.

Capital, in architecture, 154.

Căp'i-tō-līne, the, 338. Map, p. 317.

Că-pĭt'ū-lā-ries, 799, *d*.

Cap-pä-dō'ci-ans, 77. Map after p. 88.

Căp'ū-a, 443, 450, 558. Map after p. 308.

Car-a-căl'la, 642.

Cā'ri-ans, 64. Map after p. 88.

Căr-o-lin'gĭ-ans, name explained, 777, note.

Carpentry, tools in ancient Crete, 96.

Carthage, Phoenician colony, 56, 160; and Greeks in Sicily, 160, 181; held in check by Athenian name, 204; and Rome, 417–421; Punic Wars, 421–429, 431, 436 ff., 459–462; rebuilt by Caesar, 538; Vandal capital, 718. Map after p. 136.

Cassius (cash'i-us), and Caesar, 561.

Cassius, Spurius, 362, 373, note.

Catacombs, 660.

Cat'i-līne, 545.

Cato, Marcus Portius, 459, 506, 624.

Cato the Younger, 543, 555.

Ca-tul'lus, 625.

Caudine Forks, battle of, 380.

Cavemen, pictures by, p. xviii.

Celsus, 659.

Celts, origin of, 2; inroad into Eastern Europe, 290; in intellectual life, 620, note, 700–703; civilizers of new nations, 721, 762. See *Gauls, Ireland*.

Censors, at Rome, 368.

Centralization in Government, term explained, 671 and note.

Centuries, Assembly of, see *Roman Assembly*.

Cē'rēs, 111.

Cĕr-y̆-nē'a, 299. Map after p. 102.

Chaer-o-nē'a, battle of, 274. Map, p. 265.

Chăl'cis, map after p. 102.

Chăl-dē'a, convenient but not strictly proper name for Euphrates district, 35, note. Map after p. 12. See *Babylon*.

Chalons (shä-lōn'), battle of, 723. Map after p. 588.

Champollion (shŏn-pŏl-yōn), 5.

Charlemagne (shärl'e-mān), 785. See *Empire of Charlemagne*.

Charles Mar-tel', 767, 773.

Charles the Great, see *Charlemagne*.

Charms, Chaldean, 49.

Che'ops, 21, 27. See *Khufu*.

Cher-so-nē'sus, 169. Map after p. 136.

Chiefs, Council of, Homeric, 106; origin of Spartan senate, 128; of Athenian Areopagus, 135; Roman, 346; German, 709, 710.

China, Chinese, origin, 2; early civilization, why not studied, 4.

Chĭn'vät Bridge, the, 78.

Chĭ'os, 195. Map after p. 98.

Christ, birth, life, crucifixion, 571.

Christianity, foundation of, 571, 572; organism, 573; propagation among Jews, 650; among pagans, 651, 652; advantages of, 653; how the world was prepared for it, 654–656; persecutions of, 657–660; Nero's persecution, 579, 659; edict of Galerius, 672; and Constantine, 673–676; edict of Milan, 673, 676; and Theodosius, 680; attitude toward pagan learning, 704; and barbarians, 749, 753–759. See *Heresies, Papacy*.

Chry̆-sŏs'tom, John, 702.

Church, see *Christianity*.

Cicero, 543, 565, 625.

Ci-lĭc'ia, 77. Map after p. 88.

Cilician pirates, 541.

Cĭm'brī, the, 523, 524.

Cī'mon, 192, 197, 198.

Cĭn-cĭn-nā'tus, 373, note.

Cĭn'na, 530, 531.

Circus, Roman, 630.

Cĭs-al'pine Gaul, (Gal'li-a Cis'al-pī'na), 326. Map after p. 308.

Citizenship, Spartan, 129; Athenian, 150, 151, 256; Roman, about 200 B.C., 383–388 ff.; attempt to extend to all

Italy, 518, 527; secured by Italians in Social War, 528; and Caesar's extensions, 560, 616; later extensions, 616.

City-states, in old Egypt, 11; in Euphrates valley, 37; in Phoenicia, 55, 57; in Hellas, 103; the limit of Greek political ideals, 104; decline and fall, 268, 275; Roman, see *Rome.*

Civilization, description and division, p. xvii; prediluvian, 1; decay, 1; elementary features, 3; early centers, 6, 7; Persian, 74, 76; characteristics of Oriental, 79–81; Oriental and European (influence of geography), 82–86; Cretan, 93–97; Athenian and Greek, 146, 154–157, 232–240. Graeco–Oriental, 280–285, 312–321; Italian, 326–333; Roman, 407–416, 469, 480–505, 608–638, 687–704; decline of Roman civilization, 750, 751; causes of survival, 752; the Church and Roman civilization, 753, 754, 762; monasticism, 758; Mohammedan, 774; under Charlemagne, 798, 800.

Civil service, term defined, extent at Athens, 212 and note.

Ci-vī′lis, 609.

Clan, in Homeric Greece, 100 ff.; in Athens, 149 ff.; Roman, 345; German, 709.

Claud′i-an, poet, 617.

Claudius, Emperor, 587.

Claudius II, 645.

Cla-zŏm′e-nae, 260. Map after p. 136.

Clement of Alexandria, 659.

Clē-om′e-nēs, reformer at Sparta, 308-310.

Clē′on, Athenian leader, 247.

Clē-o-pā′tra, 34, 555, 567.

Clēr′uchs, 148, 205, 206.

Clīs′thē-nēs, 147–153.

Clo-āc′a Măx′i-ma, the, 338.

Clo-t/il′da, 741.

Clovis, 740–742.

Cnī-dus, battle of, 259. Map after p. 250.

Col′chis, 56. Map after p. 136.

Cŏl-i-sē′um, 622.

Col′line Gate, battle of, 533. Map, p. 317.

Cologne (kō-lōn′), map after p. 498.

Cō-lō′ni, see *Serfdom.*

Colonization, Phoenician, 56; Greek, 121, 122; New Athenian plan, 148, 205, 206; in Graeco-Oriental world, 280–282; Roman, 384, 389.

Column, in Egyptian architecture, 21; Greek, 154.

Commerce, early routes of, 7; Egyptian, 19; Euphrates states, 38, 51; Phoenician, 54-56; and invention of coinage, 19, 70; early Cretan, 95; and Greek geography, 85, a; in Homeric Greece, 110; Athenian, and Pisistratus, 146; growth in Athens, 148, 257; in Graeco-Oriental world, 284; Roman, about 200 B.C., 408; under Empire, 612, 613.

Com-mō′dus, 590.

"Companions" (German institution), 710.

Com-pur-gā′tion, trial by, 760.

Cō′non, 259.

Con′stans, 677.

Constantine the Great, 673 ff.

Constantine II, 677.

Constantine IV, 772.

Constantine VI, 792.

Constantinople, foundation of, 674. Map after p. 554.

Con-stăn′ti-us, 672.

Constantius II, 677.

Consular Tribunes, 367.

Consuls, 350–352.

Cooking, in ancient Crete, 96; in Greece, 234.

Cŏr-cȳ′ra, 174, 242. Maps after pp. 98, 102, etc.

Cor-dō′va, map after p. 640.

Cō-rĭn′na, 155.

Cŏr′inth, and Periander, 126; Pan-Hellenic Congress at, 172; jealous of Athens, 184, 200, 241; and Peloponnesian War, 241, 242; jealous of Sparta, 259; Congress of, under Philip, 275; and Achaean Confederacy, 310; destroyed by Rome, 471; rebuilt by Caesar, 558; sacked by Goths, 713. Maps after pp. 98, etc.

Corinthian order of architecture, 154.

Cornelia, mother of the Gracchi, 507, 514.

Crassus, 538.

Creation, 1; in Babylonian legend, 50.

Cretan civilization, 93–97.

Crĭt′i-as, 255.

Cri′to, friend of Socrates, 227.

Croe̅′sus, 70, 73, 163.

Culture (stage of civilization), 10.

Cu-nax′a, battle of, 257.

Cū-nē′i-form script, 5, 47.

Curia, the Roman, 345.

Cū′ri-als, 691.

Curio, and Caesar, 562.

Curio, Manius, 409.

Curule officers, 396, 397.

Cylinder seals, Babylonian, 51.

Cȳ′lon, 138.

Cȳnic philosophy, 317.

Cy-nos-cĕph′a-lae, battle of, 464. Map after p. 378.

Cy-rē′nē, 122. Map after p. 136.

Cyrus the Great, 72, 163.

Cyrus the Younger, 257.

Dā′cia, 586, 606. Map after p. 498.

Damascus, map after p. 12.

Danube, frontier finally crossed by Teutons, 712–714.

Dā-rī′us Cod-o-măn′nus, 278.

Darius the Organizer, 75, 76, 77, 78.

"Dark Ages," term explained, 749.

Dates, Table of, to 500 B.C., 158; for Greek history, p. 295; Roman and Greek, 396–398; Roman, 465, 569; Teutonic, 636.

David, king of the Hebrews, 62.

Debt, laws about, in Athens, 136, 141.

Dĕc′arch-ies, under Spartan protection, 253.

De-cĕm′virs, 364.

Dē′cius, 644, persecutor of Christians, 659.

Dē′dan, 55.

Delos, Confederacy of, 191–194.

Delos, plan of house from, and de-

scription, 233; island of, map after p. 98.

Delphi, 118; repulse of Gauls from, 290. Maps after pp. 98, 102.

Delphic Oracle, 118, 174, 177.

Deluge, cause, extent, 1; in Babylonian legend, 50.

Demagogues, Athenian, 209.

Dēmes, in Attica, 151.

De-mŏc′rĭ-tus, philosopher, 225.

Democracy, definition of, 85, note; germs of, in Homeric Greece, 107; tyrants pave way for, 126; Greek conception of, 128; Athens a democracy, 142, 152, 208–214; Athens mother of Ionian democracy, 195; attempted overthrow in Athens, 249, 255; in Greece overthrown by Sparta, 253; in Thebes, 268; lack in Achaean League, 301; in Republican Rome, in form, 396–402; among Teutons, 709.

Dē-mŏs′thē-nēs̱, Athenian general, 247.

Demos′thenes, Athenian orator, 223, 272.

Dĕ-si-dē′ri-us, 789.

Diana, 111.

Dictator (Roman), 354.

Dioceses (civil), 665; table of, 666.

Di-ō-clē′ti-an, 661–671; persecutor of Christians, 659, 662; edict regarding prices, 693, 698.

Di-o-dō′rus, 626.

Di-ŏg′e-nēs̱, the cynic, 317.

Di-o-nȳ′si-ŭs, historian, 334, 626.

Di-o-nȳ′sus, god of the vintage and the drama, 146, 221; theater of, at Athens, 222, 223.

Divination, Chaldean, 49; Etruscan, 331, note; Roman, 342, 343.

"Do Nothing Kings," 765.

Domestic animals, 3, b; in Egypt, 18.

Domitian, 584, 607.

"Donation of Pippin," 781.

Dō′ri-ans, 113; and Ionians, 120; mythical origin of, 116, b; in Peloponnesus, 127–130.

Doric order (in architecture), 154.

Dorus, fabled ancestor of Dorians, 116, b.

Dra'co, 139.

Drainage system, at Knossos, 93.

Drama, Greek, 146, 153, 221, 222; of Graeco-Oriental world, 282, 313; Roman, 624 ff.

Dress, Egyptian, see illustrations, pp. 22 ff.; Assyrian, p. 68; Persian, p. 87; Cretan, 96; Greek, 236; Roman, 412.

Dru'sus, rival of Gracchus, 517.

Drusus, champion of Italians, 526.

Duel, 760.

Dȳ'arch-y, 592.

Ebro, the, map after p. 378.

Ec-bät'ä-na, map after p. 86.

Eclectics, 317.

Economic conditions, definition of term, 136; in Egypt, 12–21; in Chaldea and Assyria, 44–46, 51; in Cretan civilization, 97; in Homeric Greece, 108–110; in Sparta, 129; in Athens at 600 B.C., 136; Solon's reforms, 141; in age of Pericles, 237; reaction of Oriental conquests on European Greece, 284; in late Sparta, 306; attempts at reform by Agis and Cleomenes, 307, 308; early Roman, 340, 408–410; after Punic Wars, 480–484, 488; reforms of the Gracchi, 506–518; overthrown, 519; Caesar's attempts at reform, 558; in early Empire, 609–611, 613, 614, 631; distribution of wealth in Roman Empire, 629, 689–694; decline in 3d century, 649, 650; more serious in 4th century, 687–699; in Charlemagne's Empire, 798.

Education and learning, in Egypt, 24; in Chaldea, 47–49; in Persia, 78; in Sparta, 139; importance of Greek theater for, 222, 223; in Athens (typical of Greece), 240; early Roman, 413; under Empire, 619, 620; decline in 4th century, 703–704; in "Dark Ages," 751; and Monasteries, 758; and Charlemagne, 800.

E-gē'ri-a, 335.

Egypt, early history rediscovered, 5; home of early culture, 6; geography of, 8, 9; people, 10; growth of city-states into a kingdom, 11; social classes, 12, 13; life of the wealthy, 14; life of the poor, 15; position of woman, 16; irrigation, 17; agriculture, 18; trade, 19; industrial arts, 20; fine arts, 21; pyramids, 21; literature and hieroglyphs, 22; science, 23; religion, 24; idea of future life, 25; morals, 26; story of the Pharaohs, 27–33; under the Ptolemies, 293; Alexandrian Age, 312–320; and Rome, 463, 464, 466; and Roman Empire, 619, 620.

El'bĕ, the, map after p. 498.

Elections, in Sparta, 128; in Athens, 142, 152, 210; in Achaean League, 301, 302.

Elgin marbles, 219.

Elis, 117. Map after p. 102.

E-lȳs'ī-um, 112.

Embalming, Egyptian, 25.

Em-pĕd'ō-clēṣ, philosopher, 225.

Empire, defined, 37, close.

Empire of Charlemagne, preparation for, by early Franks, 744, 764–767, 782–784, 786; by wars of Charlemagne, 787, 788, 789; revival of "Roman Empire," 792–793; meaning of, 794; territory of, 795; compared with Empire of Constantine and the "Greek Empire," 796; Teutonic character, 790; society and government, 798, 799; place in history, 801–802. Map after p. 640.

England, see *Britain*.

En'ni-us, 624.

E-pam-i-nŏn'das, 264–267.

Eph'e-sus, 122, 156. Maps after pp. 98, 102, etc.

Eph-i-al'tēṣ, Athenian statesman, 197, 198.

Ephialtes, "Judas of Greece," 176.

Ephors, Spartan, 128, 129.

Epic Age, in Greece, 155.

Ep'ic-te'tus, 630.

Ep-i-cū'rus and Ep-i-cu-rē'ans, 317.

E-pī'rus, 85. Map after p. 98.

Equites (ĕk'wi-tēz), 347, 480–484.

Era, Christian, 591, note.

Er-a-tŏs'the-nēs, keeper of the Alexandrian library, 320.

E-rech-thē'um, 218.

E-rē'tri-a, 164, 167. Map after p. 102.

E-sar-hăd'don, 40.

Es'quī-līne, the, map, p. 317.

E-thī-ō'pī-a, 9, 28, 30, 31. Map, p. 16.

E-trū'ri-a, map after p. 308.

Etruscans, 331, 338.

Eu-boē'a, 122. Maps after pp. 98, 102.

Eu'clid, 320.

Eu-dŏx'i-a, 726.

Eu-pā'trids, at Athens, 135–142.

Eu-phrā'tēs, early home of civilization, 6; "soul of the land," 34. Maps after pp. 12, 86, etc., and on p. 55.

Eu-rīp'i-dēs, Greek tragedian, 221.

Europe, contrasted with Asia, 82; typified by Greece, 84 ff.

Eu-rȳm'e-don, battle of the, 192.

Eu-sē'bi-us, 702.

Eu-trŏ'pi-us, 701.

Explorations, in the east, 5; at Troy, 90; at Mycenae, 91; in Crete, 93.

Ex'ärch, title of high officers, as governors, under the Greek Empire.

Ex'ärch-ate, territory ruled by an exarch. Perhaps the most frequently mentioned is the Exarchate named after the city of Rä-věn'na, 738, 779, 781. Map, p. 632.

Ezechiel, describing the grandeur of Tyre, 55.

Fā'bi-an policy, 441.

Fā'bi-us (Q. Fabius Maximus), 441.

Fabius Pictor, 334, 624.

Factories, in Athens, 237; in cities of Roman Empire, 611.

"Fathers of the Church," 700.

Fire-making, and prehistoric man, 3.

Flām-i-nī'nus, 464.

Flā'vi-an Caesars, the, 580 ff.

Flā'vi-us, democratic aedile, 397, note, 402.

Fŏ'rum, at Rome, 338. Map, p. 529.

Franks, the, 705, 719; preëminence among Teutonic conquerors, 739; Clovis and his empire, 740–742;

Frankish empire of the 7th century, 743, 744, 764–767; and the early Carolingians, 767, 773, 775–777; Empire of Charlemagne (which see). Maps after pp. 584, 588, 606, etc.

Freya, 708.

Frieze (frēz), in architecture, 154.

Fulminea Legio, the Thundering Legion, 589.

Gā'dēs, see Cadiz.

Ga-lā'ti-a, 290.

Gäl'bä, 580.

Gā'len, 628.

Ga-lē'ri-us, 672; edict of toleration, 672.

Gauls, see Celts; in Cisalpine Gaul, 332; sack Rome, 375; conquered by Caesar, 547, admitted to citizenship, 560.

Gei'ser-ic, 718.

Gē'lon, of Syracuse, 160.

Ge-mel'lus, 612.

"General," political administrator at Athens, 152, 209; in Achaean League, 300.

Gens, pl. gentes, see: Clan.

Ge-nū'ci-us, 362, 363.

Geography, and history, in Egypt, 6, 9, 11; in Euphrates regions, 6, 34; contrasts between Europe and Asia, 82, 84; Greece, typical of Europe, 85, 86; influence of Mediterranean, 83; of Rome and Italy, 326–329, 333.

Geometry, Egyptian, 24; Babylonian, 49; later Greek, 390.

Germans, origin, 2; early invasions, see Barbarian invasions; early homes, 705; stage of culture, 706; character, 707; religion, 708; government, 709, 710. See Alemanni, Burgundians, Goths, etc.

Gessen, 59.

Gibraltar, Straits of, 54, note. Map after p. 136.

Gilds, Roman, 408, 693.

Gladiators, 486, 630.

Gnostics, 682.

Gor-di-ā'nus I, 644, note.

Gordianus II, 644, note.

Gordianus III, 644, note.

Gŏr'gĭ-as, sophist, 225.
Gō'shen, 59.
Goths, see *Ostrogoths* and *Visigoths*.
Government, class rule selfish, 125.
See *Monarchy, Oligarchy, Democracy*.
Gräc'chus, Caius, 513–520.
Gracchus, Tiberius, 506–512.
Graeco-Oriental world, the, 280–327; mingling of East and West, 280; Hellenism the active element in, 281; Greek cities in (the many Alexandrias), 282; reaction upon European Hellas, 283–286; Wars of the Succession, 287; third century B.C. in, 288; resemblance to modern Europe, 289; Gallic invasion, 290; decline, 291; some separate states, 292–295; Achaean League (which see); society and culture, 312–321.
Gra-nī'cus, battle of the, 278. Map after p. 270.
Grā'ti-an, 672.
Greek Church, the, 778.
"Greek Empire," the, 734–738.
Greek federations, age of, 297; Aetolian, 298; Achaean, 299–311; Lycian, 301; Olynthiac, 261. See *Peloponnesian League, Confederacy of Delos, Rhodes*.
Greek fire, 772.
Greek life, in Homeric Age, 108–110; in Age of Pericles, 233–240. See *Sparta*.
Greek philosophy, "Ionic" (sixth century), 156; in Age of Pericles, 225–227; in Alexandrian Age, 315–318.
Greek religion, 198, 100–102, 111–112, 231.
Greeks, the, invasions into Egypt about 1350 B.C., 31; and geography, 82–86; rediscovery of prehistoric Greece, 87–93; Cretan culture, 94–97; Achaean culture (Homeric), 98–112; clan and tribe, 100–103; the city-state, 103, 104; government in Homeric Age, 105–107; simple society, 108; manners harsh, 109; occupations, 110; Dorian conquest, 113; Phoenician influence, 114; gap

in our knowledge, from 1100 to 600, 115; unity of feeling attained, 116–119; expansion by colonization, 121–123; disappearance of Homeric kingship, 124; "Age of Tyrants," 126; rise of Sparta to military headship, see *Sparta*; rise of democracy in Athens, see *Athens*; art and philosophy at 600, 154–157; Persian Wars (which see); Athenian leadership, see *Athens*; Spartan leadership, see *Sparta*; Theban leadership, 264–267; art, literature, and philosophy, in Age of Pericles, 217–232; life and industries, 233–240; Macedonian conquest, 269–275; failure of city-state, 268, 275; in the Orient, after Alexander, 280–282; reaction from the Orient, 283–285; political situation in third century, 296; Achaean League (which see); Alexandrian Age, 312–321; civilization compared with Roman, 324, 325; geography of, compared with Italian, 328, 329; Magna Graecia falls to Rome, 381; Greek cities friendly to Rome, 463, 464, 465; Roman "allies" defended by Rome against Antiochus, 465; petty quarrels among, and revulsion of feeling toward Rome, 470; rearrangements by Rome, and a Roman province, 471; diocese, 666; Alaric in Greece, 713.
Greeks in Italy, 122, 321: conquest by Rome, 381; influence on Rome, 413–416. See *Magna Graecia*.
Gregory I, the Great, Pope, 747.
Gregory of Nazianz, 702.
Grotefend, 5.
Gun'do-bald, 717.

Hadrian, Emperor, 587.
Hadrian's Wall, 587, 607. Map after p. 554.
Hal-i-car-năs'sus, 224. Map after p. 98.
Hă'lys River, 70. Map after p. 86.
Ha-mil'car Barca, 427, 431, 436, 437.
Hă'mites, 2.
Ham-mu-rä'bi, king of Babylon, 39; code of, 45, 46.

Hanging Gardens of Babylon, 52.
Hăn′ni-bal, 437–455, 459.
Här′mosts, Spartan, 253.
Hä-roun′ al Raschid, 797, note.
Hasdrubal, the Barcide, 447, 452, 453.
Hebrews, mission, 4, 58, 67; age of patriarchs, 58; Egyptian captivity, 31, 59; settlement in Palestine, 60; the Judges, 61; Kings, Saul, David, Solomon, 62; division, 63; kingdom of Israel suppressed, 40, 64; kingdom of Juda, 65; repulse of Sennacherib, 40; destruction of Jerusalem and Babylonian captivity, 66; restoration, 67; priesthood, prophets, 68; Alexander visits Jerusalem, 278, c; Jews in Alexandria, 319; "Jews of the Dispersion," 467; Maccabees and Rome, 467; a dependent state under Herod, 467; finally a province, 582; destruction and dispersion, 582.
Hector, Trojan hero, 109.
Hē-ġī′ra, the, 769, 770.
Helen of Troy, 87.
Helena, St., 676.
Hĕl′las, 84.
Hĕl′len, mythical ancestor of Hellenes, 84, 116, b.
Hel-lē′nēṣ, 84.
Hellenism and Hellenistic, terms explained, 275.
Hĕl′les-pont, the, 166, 171. Maps after pp. 98, 102, 136, etc.
Hĕl′ots, 98, 197.
Hŏl-vē′ti-ĭ, 547.
Hephaestus (he-fĕs′tus), 111.
Hē′ra, 111.
Her-a-clēī′tus, 156.
Her-ät′, 282.
Her-cū-lā′ne-um, 583. Map, p. 488.
Her′cū-lēs, 111, note.
Heresies, older, 682; penalties for, 684. See Arianism.
Hermann, 605.
Her′mēṣ, 111.
Hermits, 759.
Herod, 467, 582.
He-rŏd′o-tus, in Egypt, 21; place in literature, 224.
Her-ū-li, the, 728.

Hē′si-od, 155.
Hes′ti-a, 111.
Hī′ē-ro II, 423, 429.
Hī′er-o-glўphs, Egyptian, 22; on the Rosetta stone, 5.
Hilary, St., of Poitiers, 702.
Hĭm′e-ra, battle of, 181. Map after p. 136.
Hindoos, see India.
Hip-pär′ehus, son of Pisistratus, 147.
Hipparchus, the scientist, 320.
Hip′pi-as, son of Pisistratus, 147, 167.
History, sources of, p. xiii; divisions, 4, 802.
Hĭt′tītes, 7; and Egyptians, 31. Maps, pp. 55, 77.
"Holy Roman Empire," see Empire of Charlemagne (esp. 795, 796).
Homeric Age, the, see Achaean civilization.
Ho-mĕr′ic poems, 87.
Hō-no′ri-us, 680.
Hŏp′lītes, and political power, 137.
Horace, 626; quoted, 489.
Ho-rā′ti-us, 350, note.
Hŏr-tĕn′si-an Law, the, 399.
Hŏs-til′i-us, Tŭl′lus, 335.
Houses, Egyptian, 14, 15; in Euphrates valley, 52; in primitive Aegean civilization, 94; in age of Pericles, 233; early Roman, 340; Roman about 200 B.C., 411; after Punic Wars, 485.
Huns, 721–724.
Hyk′sos, 29, 30, 59.
Hy-mĕt′tus, 146. Map, p. 184.
Hy-pĕr′bō-lus, 247.
Hy′pha-sis River, 279. Map after p. 270.

I-a-pўġ′i-ans, 332. Map, p. 310.
Ic-tī′nus, 218.
Idolatry, possible origin of, 2, 53.
Il′i-ad, 87.
Il′i-um, 87. See Troy.
Illyria, 270, 277, 432. Map after p. 98
Im′brōs, 260. Map after p. 98.
Immortality, belief in, among Egyptians, 25; Babylonians, 53; Per-

sians, 78; Greeks, 112, 231; Socrates on, 227.

Im-per-ā′tor, title adopted by Caesar, 537; by Augustus, 569; by later emperors, 593.

India, early civilization in, why not studied, 4; and Persian Empire, 73; and Alexander the Great, 279.

Indus, the, 73. Map after p. 88.

Industries, in Egypt, 18–20; in Euphrates states, 51; among the Persians, 74; in Crete, 96; in Homeric Greece, 110; in Age of Pericles, 237; early Roman, 340; about 200 B.C., 408, 409; after Punic Wars — growth of capitalism and decline of free industries, 480–483, 488–492; in Early Empire, 611–613; in later Empire, 649, 687–695; in Empire of Charlemagne, 798.

Ion, fabled ancestor of Ionians, 116, *b*.

I-ō′nĭ-a, Phoenicians in, 55; colonized by Greeks, 121; early center of art and philosophy, 154–157; Persian conquest of, 163; revolt, 164, 165; Persian War in, after Plataea, 188, 189 ff.; (see *Confederacy of Delos*); betrayed to Persia by Sparta, 250, 260. Map after p. 98.

Ionians, Greek "race," origin of, 116, *b*; driven out of Peloponnesus, 113, 121; contrasted with Dorians, 120; (see *Ionia*).

Ionic order of architecture, 154.

Iran (ē-rän′), Plateau of, 40, 41, 71, 72. Map after p. 12.

Ireland, Conversion, 686; monasticism, 756; influence on Europe, 686, 759; Irish manuscript, p. 614. See *Celts*.

Irene, Empress, 792.

Iron, used before Deluge, 1; iron age, 2; not found in Egypt before 800 B.C., 20; known to Achaeans, 98.

Irrigation, in Egypt, possible cause of political union, 11; description of, 17; the work of the "Middle Kingdom," 28; in Babylonia, 35.

Is′ē-as, patriot-tyrant, 299.

Is-kan′dar, 281, note.

I-sŏc′rā-teš, 225.

Israel, Kingdom of, 64, 65. See *Hebrews*. Map, p. 77.

Is′sus, battle of, 278. Map after p. 270.

Italy, map after p. 302. Greek colonies in, see *Magna Graecia*; meaning of name in ancient times, 326; geography, 326–329; peoples, 330–332; in fifth and sixth centuries after Christ, 725–733. See *Rome*, *Goths*, *Lombards*.

Ith′a-ca, maps after pp. 98, 102.

I-ū′lus 544.

Jacob, 58, 59.

Ja-nĭc′ū-lum, Mount, 339. Map, p. 305.

Jā′nus, 341.

Javan, 55.

Jax-är′tēš River, 73. Map after p. 88.

Jeremias, bewailing the fate of Jerusalem, 66.

Jer-o-bō′am, 63.

Jē-rōme′, Saint, 702.

Jerusalem, made the capital by David, 62; besieged by Sennacherib, 40; destroyed by Nabuchodonosor, 42, 66; rebuilt, 67; destroyed by Titus, 582; patriarchate of, 682; becomes a Mohammedan possession, 777. Maps after pp. 12, 84, etc., and on p. 77.

Jesus Christ, birth and death of, 571; doctrine, 572; Church of, 573. See also *Christianity*.

Jews, see *Hebrews*.

Joseph, son of Jacob, 59.

Josue, 60.

Jō′vi-an, 679.

Juda, Kingdom of, 64 ff. Map on p. 77. See *Hebrews*.

Judea, southern part of Palestine.

Judges, of Hebrews, 61.

Jŭg′e-ra, 370.

Ju-gur′tha, 521, 522.

Julian the Apostate, 678.

Julian Caesars, the, 591 ff.

Jū-li-ā′nus, 640.

Jū′no, 111.

Jū′pi-ter, 111.

Jury, Athenian, 211; pay for, 212.
Jŭs-tĭn'i-an, 736–738; code of, 737.
Jūtes, in Britain, 720. Map after p. 606.
Jū'vĕ-nal, 628; quoted, 484.

Kăn-da-här', 281, note.
Karl'mann, 782.
Kär'nak, map, p. 16.
Kells, book of, ill. p. 614.
Khū'fū, see *Cheops.*
King-priest, in Athens, 134; in Rome, 350.
Kingship, see *Absolute monarchy.* Greek, in Homeric Age, 105; in early Rome, 346; Teutonic, 709; in new Teutonic kingdoms, 761.
Kitchen utensils, in ancient Crete, 96. Illustration on p. 117.
Kĭt'i-on, 55.
Knossos, Palace of, 93, 96; fall, 97. See *Cretan civilization.* Map after p. 12.
Kō-rän', the, 769.

Labarum, 673.
Labor, see *Agriculture, Industries.*
Lac-e-dae-mō'ni-ans, see *Sparta.*
La-cō'ni-a, Spartan supremacy in, 127; classes in, 129. Map after p. 102.
Lac-tăn'ti-us, 703.
Landholding, in Egypt, 12; in Chaldea, 44; in Sparta, 129; Cleomenes' reforms in, 306-308; in early Athens, 136; Solon's reforms concerning, 141; in Age of Pericles, 237, 238; in early Rome, 341, 357, 359, 361; Licinian laws, 370; grants to poor citizens, 409; land engrossed by the wealthy after Punic Wars, 480–492; attempts at reform, the Gracchi's, 507–519; Caesar's, 558; monopoly of, under Empire, 611, 694, 699; serfdom, 698.
Language, race and, 2; Semitic, 36; unity of Greek, 116, *a;* in Graeco-Oriental world, 281, 282; Latin in the West, 475; Greek in the East, *ib.;* growth of Romance tongues, 751.

Lateran Palace, 685.
Latin colonies, 360.
Latins, 331.
Latin War of 338 B.C., 379.
Lā'ti-um, 337. Map after p. 308.
Laws, Babylonian, 45, 46; of "Lycurgus," 30; of Draco, 139; of Solon, 141-143; in early Rome, unwritten, 356; the "Twelve Tables," 362, 364; "plebiscites," 365; Licinian, 370, 371; Hortensian, 399; of the Gracchi, 507–519; of Caesar, 558; sources of, under Empire, 593, 669; influenced by Christianity, 637, note, 654; Christianized by Constantine, 684; Justinian's Code, 737; Teutonic, 717, 731, 760.
Lay'ard, 47.
Leaders of the People, in Athens, 209.
Lebanon Mountains, map on p. 77.
Legion, the Roman, 403.
Lem'nos, 260. Maps after pp. 98, 102.
Leo I, the Great, Pope, and Attila, 724.
Leo III, Pope, and Charlemagne, 793.
Leo III, the I-sau'ri-an, emperor, saves Constantinople, 772; prohibits veneration of images, 778, 779.
Le-ŏn'i-das, 176.
Le-o-tўch'i-dēs, 189.
Lĕp'i-dus, 564, 565.
Lĕs'bos, 155, 195. Map after p. 98.
Leuctra, battle of, 263. Map after p. 102.
Libations, in Greek worship, 101.
Libraries, Babylonian, 47, 48; in Graeco-Oriental world, 282; at Alexandria, 319.
Li-cĭn'i-an laws, the, 370.
Li-cĭn'i-us, Emperor, 673.
Lĭ-gū'ri-ans, map, p. 310, and after p. 308.
Lĭ'ris, the, map after p. 308.
Literature, Egyptian, 22; Chaldean, 48-50; spread over Syria, 38; Hebrew, 68; Oriental contrasted with European, 80; early Greek Epic Age, 87, 155; in Athens of Pisistratus, 146; Lyric Age, 155; drama,

146, 155, 221–222, 313; the Age of Pericles, 221–224; Alexandrian Age, 312–313; Roman about 200 B.C., 414; before Cicero, 624; Age of Cicero, 625; Augustan Age, 626; 1st century after Augustus, 627; 2d century, 628; 4th century, 700–703; and the Church, 704; during barbarian invasions, 703; and monks, 758.

Lĭv′i-us An-dro-nĭ′cus, 624.

Livy, 334, 362, 626.

Lŏ′cris, map after p. 102.

Loire (lwär), map after p. 588.

Lombards, 738, 779, 789.

Long Walls of Athens, 199 (plan, p. 193); demolished, 254.

"Lost Tribes" of Israel, 64

Lot, in elections, 142.

Louvre (lo͞ovr), art museum in modern Paris.

Lū′can, 627.

Lu-cre′ti-us, 625.

Lўc′i-an Confederacy, 301.

Ly-cŭr-gus, 127, 130.

Lyd′i-a, map after p. 86.

Ly-dĭ′a-das, 304, 309.

Lyons, map after p. 598.

Lyric Age, the, 155.

Lỹ-san′der, 247, 251.

Mac′ca-bees, the, 467.

Mac-e-dō′nĭa, map after p. 98; subject to Persia in 500, 165; under Theban influence, 266; and Philip II, 269–270; expansion by Philip, 270–271; army, 273; conquest of Greece, 274–275; under Alexander, see *Alexander;* after Wars of the Succession, one of three Great Powers, 287, 294; decline, 291; and Achaean League, 296, 310; and Rome, 449, 463–471.

Macedonian Army, 273.

Macedonian Wars, First, 463; Second, 464; Third, 470.

Maē-cē′nas, 569, note.

Maē′li-us, Spū′ri-us, 362.

Magi (Persian), 78.

Magic, Chaldean, 49.

Magna Graecia, 122. Map after p. 136.

Mag-nē′sia, battle of, 465. Map after p. 378.

Mam′er-tines, 422.

Man-i-chaē′ans, 682.

Man-ti-nē′a, broken up into villages by Sparta, 261; restored, 265; battle of, 267. Map after p. 262.

Manufactures, see *Industrial arts, Factories.*

Măr′a-thon, battle of, 167; importance, 167. Maps after p. 98.

Mar-cel′lus, 448.

March of the Ten Thousand, 257.

Mar-dō′nĭ-us, 166, 167, 181, 182.

Mā′ri-us, 522, 523.

Marriage, established in paradise, 1; Greek, 100; in age of Pericles, 235; in early Rome, 345; under empire, 632; among Teutons, 707; in Mohammedanism, 769. See *Woman.*

Mars, 111, 341. Mar′ti-al, 631.

Mas-sĭl′i-a, 122. Map after p. 136.

Mas-si-nis′sa, 459.

Mastaba, 21.

Max-im′i-an, 663.

Mayfields, 761, c, 799, e.

Mayors of the Palace, 765.

Mecca, 769. Map, p. 498.

Mēdes, origin, 2; empire, 41, 71, 72. See *Persia.*

Mē′di-a, see *Medes.* Map on p. 55.

Medieval history, 711, note.

Med-i-ter-rā′ne-an Sea, importance of, 83.

Meg-a-lŏp′o-lis, 265, 304. Maps after pp. 102, 262.

Měg′a-ra, captures Salamis from Athenians, 140; Athenian alliance, 199; treachery of, 201; commercial interests, 241; enters Achaean League, 304. Maps after pp. 102, 202.

Meg′a-ris, map after p. 102.

Měm′phis, 11. Map, p. 16.

Me-năn′der, 313.

Men-e-lā′us, 87, 92.

Mē′nēṣ, king of Egypt, 11, 27.

Mercenaries, War of the, 431.

Me-ro-vĭn′ġi-ans, name explained, 744; Empire of, 742–744, 766, 767.

Mē′sheck, 55.

Mes-o-po-tā′mi-a, 35. Map after p. 12.

Mes-sā′na, map after p. 372.

Mes-sē′nē, 265. Map after p. 262.

Mes-sē′ni-a, 127, 196. Map after p. 102.

Me-tau′rus, battle of the, 453. Map after p. 302.

Met′o-pē, 154.

Metropolis, of a Greek colony, 123.

Met-ro-pŏl′i-tan, see *Archbishops*.

" Middle Ages," 711, note.

Mi-lan′, map after p. 308. Edict of, 673.

Mi-lē′tus, map after pp. 98, 102.

Mil-tī′a-dēş, 167, 169.

Mil′vi-an Bridge, battle of the, 673.

Mī′nōs, of Crete, 93.

Mīs′si Do-mĭn′i-ci, 799, *b*.

Mith-ri-dā′teş the Great, 528, 532, 542.

*M*nĕs′i-clēş, 218.

Mo-hăm′med, 768–770.

Mo-hăm′me-dăn-ism, history of, 768–774; term explained, 769.

Monarchy, definition of, 85, note.

Mo-năs′ti-cism, origin of, 755; spread, 756; rules, 757; influence on civilization, 758; missionary work, 759.

Money, no coinage in ancient Egypt, 19; nor in Euphrates states, 70; coinage in Lydia, 70; at Sparta, 130; Solon's, at Athens, 143; abundant in Greece after Alexander, 284; early Roman, 410; under Empire, drain to Orient, 613; lack in later Empire, 688; imperial government and the Money Power, 698; lack in Middle Ages, 798.

Moors, 774, note.

Morality, Egyptian, 24–26; Chaldean and Assyrian, 36, 41, 45, 46, 53; Persian, 78; Greek, 86, 226, 227, 231; Roman, about 200 B.C., 411, 415–416; after Punic Wars, 480, 484; under the Empire, 630–638; Teutonic, 707. See *Ten Commandments*.

Moses, 60.

Mount Athos, 166, 177. Map after p. 98.

Mŭn′da, battle of, 556.

Municipal government, under the Empire, 597.

Municipia (Roman), 385.

Museum (mū-sē′um), Plato's, at Athens, 319; Ptolemy's, at Alexandria, 319.

Mўc′a-le, battle of, 189. Map after p. 98.

My-cē′nae, 91. Map after p. 98.

Mycenaean culture, term explained, 94.

Myths, Greek, 111; Roman, 341.

Nabuchodonosor, 42, 66; prayer of, 58.

Nahum, on fall of Assyria, 41.

Năr-bŏnn*e*′, 620. Map after p. 598.

Năr′sēş, 736.

Nature worship, Egyptian, 24; Chaldean, 53; Greek, 98, 111; Roman, 341; Teutonic, 708.

Nau-păc′tus, 195. Map after p. 102.

Nau-sĭc′a-a, 108.

Navy, growth of Athenian, 170, 176, 178, 186; skill with, 242, 246 (see *Trireme*); Roman, 424, 425.

Năx′os, 195. Maps after pp. 98, 102, 202.

Ne-ăp′o-lis (Naples), 195. Map after p. 308.

Ne-ar′chus, 285; route of, map after p. 270.

Nē′co, king of Egypt, 32.

Neo-Platonists, 659.

Neo-Pythagoreans, 659.

Nē′pos, 625.

Nero, Claudius, consul, 453.

Nero, Emperor, 579.

Nĕr′va, 585.

Neus′tri-a, 764. Map after p. 622.

New Stone Age, 2.

Ni-cæ′a, Council of, 684. Map after p. 598.

Ni-cēn*e*′ Creed, the, 684.

Nĭc′i-as, 247, 248.

Nic-o-mē′di-a. Map after p. 554.

Nile, 9. Map, p. 16.

Nineveh, 37, 40, 41; palace of, described, 52; commerce of, 51. Map after p. 12.

Noe, 1.

Nor-thŭm′bri-a. Map after p. 640.

Nū′ma, 335; and gilds, 408.

Obelisk, 21.

Oc-tā′vi-us, deposed by Gracchus, 509.

Octavius Caesar, 564–567. See *Augustus*.

O-dē′um, 218.

O-do-ā′cer, see *Odovaker*.

O-do-vä′ker, 728.

O-dỹs′seus, 87, 92, 107, 108, 110, 112.

Od′ys-sey, 87.

Oe-nō′phy-ta, battle of, 200. Map after p. 250.

Oligarchy, definition of, 85, note; origin in Greece, 124; overthrown by tyrants, 125; in Athens, 135–139; overthrow in Athens, 141–142; struggle with democracy in Greece, 159; set up by Sparta in subject cities, 253; in Thebes (see *Thebes*); in early Rome, 344 ff.

O-lỹm′pi-a, 117. Map after p. 102.

Olympiad, 116.

Olympias, 276.

Olympic games, 116.

Olympus, 111. Map after p. 98.

O-lỹn′thi-ac Confederacy, 261, 297.

Olynthus, 122. Map after p. 98.

Oral Traditions, a source of history, p. xiii.

Oratory, in Greece and Athens, 223.

Ordeal, Trial by, 760.

O-rĕs′tēs, 728.

Oriental history, introductory to Greek history, 4; summary, 79–81.

Or′i-ġen, 659.

O-rĭg′i-nēs, of Cato, 624.

Orleans. Map after p. 588.

Os′ti-a, 339. Map on p. 311.

Ostracism, 153; of oligarchic leaders at Athens, 169; of Aristides, 170; of Cimon, 198.

Os′tro-goths, 729–734.

Otho, 580.

Ovid, 626.

Oxus River, 279. Map after p. 88.

Paē′tus, 632.

Pagans, term explained, 680, note.

Painting, Egyptian, 21; Greek, 154, 314.

Pal′a-tīne Hill, map, p. 311.

Palestine (Ca′na-an), 60. Map, p. 77.

Pallas Athene, see *Athene*.

Pal-mȳ′ra, map after p. 498.

Pam-phỹl′i-a, 192. Map after p. 136.

Pan-Hellenic Confederation, proposed by Athens, 187, 188.

Pan′the-on, 622.

Papacy, foundation, 573; beginnings in Rome, 651; wider recognition, 673, 685; donations to Popes, 685. Missionary enterprises, 686. See *Leo I, Leo III, Peter, St., Papal States*.

Papal States, events preparing the way for, 673, 674, 685, 778–780; foundation, 781, 782; subsequent history, 783; meaning, 784.

Pa-pĭn′i-an, 643.

Papȳ′rus, 5.

Parishes, 573.

Pā′rŏs, 169. Map after p. 98.

Par-rhā′si-us, 314.

Parsees, 78.

Par′the-non, 219, 220. See plan of Acropolis, p. 213, and illustrations, pp. 214–217.

Par′thi-ans, 278, 549, 648.

"Partnership Emperors," 663 ff., 679.

Patriarch, in the Church organization, 573.

Patriarchs, Hebrew, 58.

Pā-trĭ′cians, 344; organization, 345; government, 346; struggles with plebeians, 356–371.

Patrick, St., 686.

Paul, Apostle to the Gentiles, 651.

Pau-sā′ni-as, king of Sparta, 190.

Pausanias, historian, 628.

Peace of Antal′cidas, 260.

Peasantry, Egyptian, 15, 18; Chaldean, 44; Greek, in Age of Pericles, 237; Roman, early, 340, 408–412; after Punic Wars, 480, 488–491; in later Empire, 694, 699.

Pediments, in architecture, 154.

Pe-lŏp'i-das, 262.

Pel-o-pon-ne'si-an League, 162.

Peloponnesian War, 241-251.

Pel-o-pon-ne'sus, map, p. 169.

Pen-tĕl'i-cus, 167. Map, p. 180.

Per'ga-mos, 295, 312. Map after p. 378.

Per-i-ăn'der, 126.

Per'i-clēṣ, 197, 198, 199, 200, 202 ff.

Peripatĕt'ics, 317, note.

Persecutions of the Christians, causes, 657; court trials, 658; history, 659, 660; under Nero, 579; under Marcus Aurelius, 589; under Decius and Diocletian, 659; with the weapons of intellect, 659.

Pĕr-sĕp'ō-lis, 74. Map after p. 88.

Per'seus, of Macedonia, 470.

Persian Empire, rise, 71, 72; extent, 73; services to the world, 74; and Scythians, 75; government, 76; postroads, 77; religion and morals, 78. *Persian Wars*, see below; End of empire, see *Alexander the Great*. New Persian kingdom, 648.

Persian Wars, 159-183, 187-193, 200-202, 258-260; the antagonists, 159-161; conquest of Ionia, 163; revolt of Ionia, and Athenian aid, 164; first two attacks on Greece, 165-167; relation of Ionian revolt to Persian attack, 165; first expedition, Mount Athos, 166; second expedition, Marathon, 167; from Marathon to Thermopylae in Athens, 168-170; the third attack, 171-183; Persian preparation, 171; Greek preparation, 172; Greek lines of defense and plan of campaign, 173, 174; loss of Thessaly, 175; Thermopylae, loss of Central Greece, 176; strategy of Themistocles, 178; battle of Salamis, 179; temptation of Athens, 181; Plataea, 182; meaning of Greek victory, 183; league of Plataea, 187; war to free Ionia, 189-192; peace, 202; war revived in Asia, 258-259; peace of Antalcidas, 260.

Per'ti-nax, 640.

Peter, St., position of, 573; arrival in Rome, 651; death, 659.

Phaed'rus, 232.

Phalanx, Theban, 263; Macedonian, 273; compared with legion, 403; conquered by legion, 464.

Pha-le'rum, 185. Map, p. 193.

Phā'raohs, of Egypt, 12.

Phā'rōs, lighthouse on, 320.

Phär-sā'lus, battle of, 554. Map after p. 498.

Phĭd'i-as, 220.

Phi-dĭp'pi-dēṣ, 167.

Philip II, king of Macedonia, 270; aims and methods, 271; army, 273; invades Greece, 274; assassinated, 276.

Philip V, of Macedonia, 294, 445, 463, 464.

Phi-lĭp'pi, battle of, 566. Map after p. 498.

Phi-lip'pics, of Demosthenes, 272.

Phi-lĭp'pus, 644, note.

Phi-lĭs'tines, 61. Map, p. 77.

Phil-o-poe'men, 311.

Philosophy, see *Greek Philosophy;* of Marcus Aurelius, 638; and Christianity, 656.

Phō'cis, maps after pp. 98, 102.

Phoe-ni'cians, 54-57; influence on Greece, 114. Map, p. 77.

Phor'mi-o, 246.

Phryg'i-a, maps after pp. 86, 88.

Physical Geography, as a factor in historical development, 6, 7, 9, 10, 11, 23, 34, 35, 52, 54, 58, 82, 83, 84, 85, 86, 120, 133, 327-329, 333.

Pillars of Hercules, 56. Map after p. 136.

Pĭn'dar, 155, 277.

Pip'pin of Hĕr'is-tal, 766.

Pippin the Short, 775, 777, 781, 782.

Pi-rae'us, 185. Map, p. 193.

Pis-Is'trā-tus, 146.

Plague, at Athens, 244; in Roman world, 649.

"Plain," the, the party in Athens, 145.

Pla-tae'a, aids Athens at Marathon, 167; battle of, 182, 183; League of, 187. Maps after pp. 98, 102, etc.

Plato, 315, 319. Neo-Platonists, 659.

Plau'tus, 624.
Plebeians, Roman, 344.
Pleb'i-scītes, 365.
Pliny the Younger, 598, 630, 657.
Plōtī'nus, 651.
Plutarch, 130; quoted frequently.
Pnyx, 210. Map, p. 206.
Pōl'e-march, 134.
Poles, 721.
Political, term explained, 104, note.
Pōl'li-o, 635.
Po-lȳb'i-us, 628; quoted frequently.
Polytheism, origin, 2, 53.
Pom-pē'ii, 583. Map, p. 498.
Pompey the Great, 537-555, 582.
Pon'ti-fex Max'i-mus, 557, 593.
Pontiffs, Roman, 342.
Pon'tus, map after p. 544.
Pope, origin of name, 686, note.
Pŏr'phȳr-ȳ, 651.
Pŏr-sen'na, 350, note.
Po-seī'don, 111.
Post roads, Persian, 77. Map after p. 88. See *Roman roads*.
Pottery, significance of, in culture, 10; wheel a Babylonian invention, 51; in Cretan civilization, 95, 96. Many illustrations of, and of Greek painting on, see list, pp. vii ff.
Prāē-nĕs'te, map, p. 311.
Praetor, 372.
Prae-tō'ri-ans, 568, note 4.
Prax-it'e-lēs, 220.
Pre-fect'ure, in Italy, 390; model for provincial government, 435; a division of the Empire, 665; table of, 666. Map, after p. 554.
Prehistoric (term), 2; time in Egypt, 10; in Greece, 87-97; in Italy, 337 ff.
Priests, of Egypt, 12; of Hebrews, 62, 68; of Persians, 78; in early Greece and Rome, see *King-priest;* Christian, 573.
Princeps, title of, 568, 592.
Prō'con-sul, 406.
Prophets, Hebrew, 68.
Prop-ȳ-laē'a, of Acropolis, 218, and illustration, p. 215.
Pro-tĕc'tō-rāte, term explained, 293.
Provincial government, Roman, 435, 498-503; and Caesar, 559, 560;

under Empire, 599, 608-610, 616-617, 665-668.
*P*sam-mĕt'i-chus, Pharaoh, 32.
*P*tolemy I, of Egypt, 293.
*P*tolemy II (Philadelphus), 33, 293, 319, 320.
*P*tolemy III, 228 note, 293.
*P*tolemy, geographer, 628.
Pul, see *Tiglath-Pileser II.*
Punic Wars, see *Carthage.*
Punjab, the, map, pp. 88 and 292.
Pȳd'na, battle of, 470. Map after p. 372.
Pȳramids, Egyptian, 21.
Pȳr'rhus, 381.
Py-thăg'o-ras, 156; Neo-Pythagoreans, 659.

Quäd'i, the, 649.
Quäd-rīv'i-um, the, 619.
Quaestors, 396.
Quin-til'i-an, 627.
Quĭr'i-nal, the, map, p. 311.

Răd'o-gast, 726.
Rä-mē'sēs II, 30.
Rä-vĕn'na, map after p. 632; see *Exarchate.*
Rawlinson, 5.
Records, as source of history, p. xiv.
Redeemer, promise of, 1, 2; Hebrews and the Redeemer, 4, 58, 67.
Re-gĭl'lus, Lake, 350, note.
Rĕg'u-lus, 425-426.
Re-hō-bō'am, 64.
Relics, as source of history, p. xiv.
Relief sculpture, definition of, p. 19, note; specimens of Egyptian, Assyrian, Greek, and Roman, in illustrations, *passim.*
Religion, decay of, 2; Egyptian, 24-26; Chaldean, 53; Assyrian, 45, 53; Phoenician, 57; Hebrew, see *Hebrews;* Persian, 78; Oriental, 80; in Greece, 98, 100-102, 111, 112, 118, 119, 227, 231, 232 (see *Greek Philosophy*); Roman, 341-343; Teutonic, 707, 708. See *Christianity.*
Representative government, not a feature even of the Greek federations, 301; none in Rome, 384; not

in the provincial assemblies of the Empire, 599; to grow out of Teutonic Assemblies, 762.

Rex sā-crō'rum, 350.

R*h*ē'ği-um, 195. Map after p. 136.

Rhine frontier finally crossed by Teutons, 716–724.

R*h*ōd*e*s, maps after pp. 94, 132. Confederacy of, 288; center of Hellenistic culture, 312; and Rome, 473. Map after p. 136.

Rĭk'i-mer, 727.

Ro'bo-am, 63.

Roland, Song of, 789, note.

Roman Assemblies, patrician (curiate), 346; by centuries, 347, 348, 398, 399; by Tribes, 365, 386, 398, 399; decline after | Punic Wars, 494; in Early Empire, 596.

Roman camp, 404. Plan of, p. 361.

Romance languages, 751 and note.

Roman colonies, 384, 389. Map, p. 354.

Roman Empire, conditions leading to, see *Rome;* despotism a medicine for, 551, 552; civil war, Caesar and Pompey, 553–556; work of Caesar, 556–559; form of Caesar's government, 557; Julius to Octavius, 563–568; Augustus, 568–570; coming of Christianity, 571–573; the empire in the first two centuries, 574 ff.; story of, 575–591; character of government (principate), 592–595; local government, 596–599; imperial defense, 600–607; boundaries, 605–606; two centuries of peace and prosperity, 608–610; cities, 610–611; forms of industry, 611; commerce, 612, 613; travel, 612; banking and panics, 614; taxation and roads, 615; the world Romanized, 616, 617, 618; education, 619, 620; architecture, 621–623; literature, 624–628; morals, 629–638; "barrack emperors" of 3d century, 639–649; general decline of 3d century, 747–749; barbarian attacks, 748; decline of population, 649; slavery as a cause of decline, 650; decay in literature, 651; rise of Christianity (which see),

650–660; Diocletian's reorganization, 661 ff.; Constantine and victory of Christianity, 672–676; Constantine to Theodosius, 677–680; the Church of the 4th century, 681–686; society in the 4th century, 687–697; government and the "money" power," 698–699; decay in literature and science, 700–704. See *Germans, Barbarian Invasions, Roman Empire in the West, Roman Empire in the East.*

Roman Empire in the East, partition (administrative) by Diocletian, 663; final separation from the West, 680; West Goths in, 712–713; nominal rule over Italy under Zeno, 728; East Goths in, 729; left alone, as a "Greek Empire," 734; Slavs in, 735; revival under Justinian, reconquests of Africa and Italy, 736–737; Justinian Code, 737; loss of Italy, except the South and the exarchate, 738; decay and new revival in eighth century, repulse of Mohammedans by Constantine IV and by Leo III, 722; relation to the Empire of Charlemagne, 796.

Roman Empire in the West, separation from the East, 680; crumbles away — causes, 687–699 (see *Germans*); end of, 728; idea survives, 752; contributions to Europe, 762; revival by Charlemagne, 785–796. See *Empire of Charlemagne.*

Roman family, 345.

Roman Law, early, unwritten, 356; Twelve Tables, 362, 364; "plebiscites," 365; codification begun by Caesar, 558; sources of imperial, 593, 669; and Christianity, 655, 637, note; gentler spirit in first and second centuries, 636, 637; further development by great jurists in third century, 651; Justinian's codification, 737.

Roman life, early, 340, 341, 345; about 200 B.C., 407–416; after Punic Wars, 484–492; in Early Empire, 608–618; 630–636; decline in 3d and 4th centuries, 647–651, 687–699.

Roman names, 454, note.

Roman roads, 395, 615, 655. Maps, p. 348 and (for Empire) after p. 498.

Roman Senate, origin, 346; of 200 B.C., 400; decline after Punic Wars, 495; in early Empire, 592–593, 594; disappears except as city council after Diocletian, 669.

Rome (history), place in history, 322–324; contrasted with Greece, 325; geography, 333; legendary history, 334–335; conclusions, as to regal, 337–354; growth, 338–339; early home life, 340; religion, 341–343; classes, 344 ff.; patrician organization and government, 345–346; plebeians make way into Assembly of Centuries (which see), 347–348; life king replaced by consuls, 349–350; class struggles in early Republic, 357–370; first secession of plebs, and tribunes, 362, 363; characteristics of contest, 362, 369; Twelve Tables (Decemvirs), 362–364; Assembly of Tribes and plebiscites, 365; social fusion, 366; plebeians admitted to consulship, 367–372 (see *Licinian Rogations*); unification of Italy, 373 ff.; progress before 367 B.C., 373–375; sacked by Gauls, 375; advance to 266 B.C. (Italy united), 376–381; Rome champion of Lowland civilization against barbarians of the Highlands and the Gauls, 377; acquires Central Italy, 378–380; Samnite wars, 380; Pyrrhic, 381; Italy under Rome, 382 ff.; Roman state, extent, 383; rights of citizens, 383, 386–387, 394; subjects, 388–391, 393; policy toward subjects, 394; roads, 395; perfected Republican constitution, 396 ff.; democratic theory and aristocratic practice, 397, 401; army, 403–406; Roman life in its noblest age, 407–416; Greek influence, 416; winning of the West, 417 ff.; First Punic War, 417 ff.; strength of parties, 423; Rome becomes sea power, 424–425; wins Sicily, 429; between Punic Wars seizes Sardinia, 430–431; Adriatic a Roman sea, 432;

conquest of Cisalpine Gaul, 433; provincial system begun, 435; Second Punic War, 436 ff.; Hannibal in Italy, 439; Cannae, 442; fidelity of Latins and Italians, 443; grandeur in disaster, 444; Hannibal at the gates, 449; invasion of Africa and victory, 454; Rome mistress of the West, 455; Rome in Spain, 456–457; Third Punic War, 459 ff.; destroys Carthage, wins Africa, 462; Rome in the East, 463 ff.; First Macedonian War, 463; Second, 464; Syrian War, 465; protectorates become provinces, 466–469; sole Great Power, 474; two halves of Roman world, 475; new strife of classes, 476 ff.; industrial and moral decline after Punic wars, 480–483; decay of yeomanry, 480, 488–492; a new capitalism, 481; trade monopolies, 482; "money power" and the government, 483; rise of luxury, 484; a proletariat, 492; decay of the constitution, 493–495; the evils in Italy, 496–497; evils in the provinces, 498–503; slavery, 504,505; Cato's and Scipio's attempts at reform, 506; the Gracchi, 507–519; work overthrown, 519; new character of Roman history, biographical, 520; Jugurthine War, 521–522; Marius saves from Cimbri, 523–524; disorders and Social War, 525–527; Italy enters Roman state, 527; Marius and Sulla, 528 ff.; Marian massacres, 530; Sulla in East, 532; return, civil war, 533; Sullan massacres, 534; restores senatorial rule, 535; Pompey and Caesar, 537 ff.; Pompey's leadership, 538–542; expansion in East, 542; new leaders, 543; Catiline, 545; rise of Caesar, 544–549; expansion in West, 547–549; founding the Empire, 549 ff. See *Roman Empire.*

Rome, city under the Empire, fire, 579; government, 596; industries, 611, 614; sacked by West Goths, 714; by Vandals, 718, 726; by East Goths, 736. See *Papacy.*

Rŏm'ū-lus, 335.

Romulus Au-gŭs'tu-lus, 726.
Roncesvalles (rŏns-väl'), 789, note.
    Map after p. 640.
Ro-sĕt'ta stone, 5.
Rubicon, 543. Map after p. 308.

Sā'bīnes, 338. Map after p. 308.
Sa-gŭn'tum, 438. Map after p. 378.
Sā'is, map, p. 16.
Săl'a-mis, Athenian war for, 140;
    battle of, 178–180; significance of,
    183. Map after p. 98, and on p. 180.
Săl'lust, 625.
Sălmănăs'sar, 40, note, 64.
Sa-mā'ri-a and Samaritans, 40, 64.
    Map, p. 77.
Săm'nītes, map after p. 302.
Sā'mos, 156, 195. Maps after pp. 98,
    102, etc.
Samuel, 62.
Sā'por, 644.
Sappho (säf'o), 155.
Saracens, 774, note.
Sardinia, map after p. 136.
Săr'dis, 70; burned in Ionian Revolt,
    164. Maps after pp. 86, 88.
Săr'gon the Elder, 38.
Săr'gon, of Assyria, 40, 64.
Săs-săn'i-dae, the, 648.
Satraps, introduced by Assyrians,
    40; adopted by Persia, 76.
Saturn, 341.
Saul, 62.
Savağery, term explained, p. xvii.
Saxons, in Britain (map after p. 606).
    See Britain. Saxons on the conti-
    nent, 788. Map after p. 640.
Schliemann (shlē'män), life of, 89;
    discoveries of, 90, 91; importance,
    92.
Schools, in Age of Pericles, 240; in
    Roman Republic, 413; in Empire,
    620; in Empire of Charlemagne,
    800.
Science, Egyptian, 23; Chaldean, 49;
    early Greek, related to philosophy,
    156; in the Age of Pericles still
    bound up with philosophy, 225; lack
    of method of experiment, 230; Alex-
    andrian Age, 320; Roman, under the
    Republic, 414.

Scipio (P. Cornelius Scipio Africa-
    nus), 447, 454.
Scipio Africanus the Younger,
    462, 465, note, 493; fails at reform,
    506.
Scipio Asiaticus, 465, note.
Sculpture, Egyptian, 21; Chaldean,
    52; Assyrian, 52; Oriental con-
    trasted with European, 80; Greek,
    154, 218–220; in Graeco-Oriental
    world, 314. See Relief sculpture.
Scȳ'ros, 260. Maps after pp. 98, 102.
Scȳth'i-ans, in Assyria, 41; repulsed
    by Persians, 75.
Se-gĕs'ta, 195. Map after p. 136.
Se-leu'ci-dae, rulers of the family of
    Seleucus.
Se-leu'cus, general of Alexander,
    and king of Syria, 292.
Sĕm'ītes, 2, 58.
Semitic languages, 36.
Sen-năch'e-rib, 40.
Sĕp'tu-a-ğint, 319.
Serfdom, in Roman Empire, 694, 699.
Sĕr-tō'ri-us, 530, 531, 539.
Sĕr'vi-us Tul'li-us, 335.
Se-vē'rus, Alexander, 643.
Se-vē'rus, Sĕp-tĭm'i-us, 741.
Shaft, use in architecture, 154.
" Shaking off of Burdens," 141.
" Shore," the, party in Athens, 145.
Sicily, Greek colonies in, 122; Car-
    thaginian War in, 159, 160; Athe-
    nian disaster in, 248; and the Punic
    Wars, 422, 427, 429, 446.
Sicyon (sĭsh'i-on) and Aratus, 302.
    Maps after pp. 98, 102, etc.
Sī'don, 55. Map after p. 12.
Sidonius, poet, 703.
Si-mŏn'i-dēs, 155.
Sinai, Mount, 60. Map, p. 76.
Skeptics, 317.
Slavery, Egyptian, 15; Greek, in
    Sparta, 129; in Athens, 205, 230,
    237; Roman, under Republic after
    Punic Wars, 504, 505; under Em-
    pire, 633, 634, 637; a cause of decline
    of population, 649. See Serfdom.
Slavonians, 721.
Slăvs, origin of, 2; 721, 735, 791.
Social War, the, 526, 527.

Sŏc′rā-tēs, the Athenian, the man, 226; teachings, 225; on immortality, 227.

Socrates, of Constantinople, 703.

Sog-di-ā′na, map after p. 86.

Soissons (swä-sōn′), battle of, 740. Map after p. 622.

Solomon, 62, 76, note.

Sō′lon, and a priest of Saïs, 23; and overthrow of Eupatrids, 140–144.

Sŏph′ists, 225.

Sŏph′o-clēs, 221.

Spain, 55, Carthaginians in, see Carthage; Romans in, 447, 454, 539, 555; Visigoths in, 715; Mohammedans in, 773; Charlemagne in, 789.

Sparta, leading Dorian city, 120; kings in, 128; early history, 127; government, 128; classes of people in Laconia, 129; "Spartan training," 130; and Persian Wars, 161, 162, 164, 167, 172 ff.; delays and losses thereby, 167, 175, 176, 181; strife with Athens, 196–201; Messenian revolt, 197; Peloponnesian War, 241–251; supremacy in Greece, 253–263; Leuctra, 263; and Thebes, 265–267; decay and need of social reform, 306; Agis and Cleomenes, 307–308; and Achaean League, 309; sacked by Goths, 648, 713. Maps after pp. 98, 102, etc.

Spär′tä-cus, 505.

Sphinx, 21.

State, definition, 11, note.

Stephen III, pope, and Pippin, 781.

Stĭl′i-eho, 726.

Stoics, 317.

Stone Age, 2; in Aegean islands, 95.

Strā′bo, 628.

Strässburg, battle of, Julian's, 678; Clovis', 740, 741. Map after p. 588.

Strŏm′bo-lĭ, 733.

Sul′la, 522, 526, 528–536.

Sul-pĭ′ci-us, 528, 529.

Susa, map after p. 88.

Syracuse, 248. Map after p. 136

Sym′mä-ehus, 701.

Syria, 7. Map after p. 12, and on p. 55. Kingdom of Syria (in Graeco-Roman world), 291; Romans' conquest, 465 ff.; and the Jews, 467.

Tacitus, historian, 627; quoted frequently; on Teutons, 707, 709.

Tăl′mud, the, 68, note.

Tăn′a-gra, battle of, 200. Map after p. 102.

Ta-rĕn′tum, 122. Map after p. 136.

Tar′quin the First, 335.

Tarquin the Proud, 335.

Tar-quĭn′i-us (Lū′ci-us Tarquinius Col-la-tī′nus), 350.

Tär′shish, see Tartessus.

Tar′tar-us, 112.

Tar-tĕs′sus, same as Tarshish or Tarsis, 55.

Taurus Mountains. Maps, pp. 45, 55.

Taxation, Egyptian, 12, 15; Athenian, 195; Roman, 500; imperial, 615; in later Empire, 691, 696; in Empire of Charlemagne, 798.

Tel′lus, 341.

Tĕm′pe, Vale of, 174. Map after p. 98.

Temple of Solomon, 62.

Ten Commandments, 60.

Ten Thousand Greeks, march of the, 257.

Terence, 624.

Ter′mĭ-nus, god of bounds, 341.

Tĕr-tŭl′li-an, 659.

Tĕs′try, battle of, 766.

Teu′to-berg, battle of, 577, 605.

Teu-tō′nes, 523, 524.

Teutonic Assembly, 709; affected by conquests, 761, c.

Teutonic contributions to Europe, 762.

Teutonic kingship, 761.

Teutonic Law, 700.

Teutons, see Germans.

Thā′lēs, 156, 164.

Thăp′sus, battle of, 555.

Thā′sos, 196. Map after p. 98.

Theaters, Greek, 222; of Dionysus at Athens, 223; Pericles' policy as to, 223; Roman, 631.

Thēbes, in Egypt, 11. Map on p. 16.

Thebes, in Greece, limited leadership in Boeotia, 132; at war with Athens,

161; refuses to attend Congress at Corinth, 161; welcomes Xerxes, 176; war with Sparta, 259; Democracy in, 262; Leuctra, 263; supremacy, 264–267; Epaminondas, 264; overthrow, 267; destroyed by Alexander, 277. Maps after pp. 98, 102, etc.

The-mĭs'to-clēs, 170, 177, 178, 180, 184, 185, 186, 197.

The-ŏc'ri-tus, 313.

The-ŏd'o-ric, East Goth, 729–733.

Theodoric, Visigoth, 722, 723.

The-o-dō'si-an Code, the, 737.

The-o-dō'si-us I, 680.

Theodosius II, 726.

The-ŏg'o-ny, 155.

Ther-mŏp'y-lae, 173, 174; battle of, 176, 177. Maps after pp. 98, 102.

Ther-sī'tēs, 107.

Thē'seus, 100, 111, note.

Thĕs'pis, 146, 155, 221.

Thessaly, map after p. 98.

Thĕs-sä-lo-nī'ca, map after p. 598.

Thirty Years' Truce, the, between Athens and Sparta, 202.

Thŏr', 708.

Thrace, part of Persian Empire, 73, 165; colonized by Chalcis, 122; changing bounds, 122, note; Athenian colonies in, 148. Maps after pp. 88, 136.

Thrasybulus (thras-i-bōo'lus), 256.

Thucydides (thoo-cĭd'i-dēz), 224; quoted, 129, 184, 299.

Thū-rĭn'ġi-a, map after p. 622.

Thutmosis III (thōo-mō'sis), 30.

Tiber, commerce of early, 333. Map after p. 136.

Ti-bē'ri-us, 576, 594, 614.

Ti-cī'nus, battle of, 440. Map after p. 308.

Tĭg'lath-Pi-lē'ser I, 40.

Tiglath-Pileser II, 40.

Tigris-Euphrates states, 34–53; Alexander in, 278.

Tigris River, 34. Maps after pp. 12, 86, etc.

Tī'tus, 583.

To-gär'mah, 55.

Tō'tem-ism, Egyptian, 24.

Tŏt'i-lä, 736.

Tou-louse', 620. Map after p. 588.

Tours (tŏŏr), battle of, 773. Map after p. 622.

Trā'jan, 586, 598; persecutor of Christians, 659.

Tras-i-mē'ne, battle of, 440. Map after p. 308.

Trē'bi-a, battle of, 440. Map after p. 308.

Treves, see Trier.

Trib-ū-nic'i-an power, the, 557.

Tributary state, defined, 11, note.

Trier (Treves), 618, 750. Map after p. 598.

Trī'glyph, 155.

Trī'rēme, 200, note.

Trī-ŭm'vi-răte, First, 540 ff.; Second, 565 ff.

Trĭv'i-um, the, 619.

Troy, story of siege of, 87; excavations at, 90. Map after p. 136.

Tū'bal, 55.

Tu-rā'ni-ans, 721.

Turks, 774.

"Twelve Tables," laws of the, 362, 364; Roman textbook, 413.

"Twilight of the Gods," 707.

Tyrants, Greek, 125, 126; in Athens, 146, 147; set up by Persia in Ionia, 164; set up by Macedonia, 296; in early Rome, 349, 350.

Tyre, 55, 57; siege of, 277. Maps after pp. 12, 136.

Tўr-rhĕn'i-an Sea, map after p. 302.

Tyr-tae'us, 155.

Ul'pi-an, 632, 637, 643.

Universities, origin, 319; in Alexandrian Age, 319; in Roman Empire, 619.

Ur, in Chaldea, 37, 38, 58. Map after p. 12.

U'ti-ca, founded by Phoenicians, 56; capital of Roman Africa, 390. Map after p. 136.

Vā'lens, 679; and Visigoths, 713.

Va-lĕn-tĭn'i-an I, 679.

Valentinian II, 679.

Valentinian III, 726.

Va-lē′ri-an, Emperor, 644.
Va-lē′ri-us, M., 362.
Va-lē′ri-us, Pub-lĭc′o-la, 352.
Vandals, 715, 716, 718.
Väph′i-o cups, the, illustration on p. 113.
Varro, consul, 488.
Varro, historian, 625.
Vä′rus, 605.
Ve′ii, 374. Map, p. 311.
Ve-ne′ti, map, p. 308.
Venice, founded, 724.
Vē′nus, 111, 341.
Ves-pā-si-an (Flä′vi-us Ves-pā-si-ā′-nus), 580, 587.
Věs′ta, 341.
Vestal Virgins, 341.
Virgil, 626.
Virginia, story of, 362.
Vir-i-ā′thus, 456.
Vis′i-goths, 679, 712–714; in Spain, 715.
Vi-těl′li-us, 580.
Vŏl′scĭ-ans, 331. Map, p. 311.
Vulcan, 111.
Vŭl′gāte, the, 2.

Wars of the Succession, 287.
Wergeld (věr′gĕlt), 760.
Wheat, prehistoric cultivation, 3, c; native to Euphrates district, 55. See Agriculture.
Whĭt′by, 747. Map after p. 640.

Wingless Victory, temple of, 218; illustration, p. 159.
Wō′den, 708.
Woman, creation of, 1; position of, in Egypt, 16; in Chaldea and Assyria, 45; in the court of King Minos, 96; in early Greece, 230; in Sparta, 130; in Athens, 230, 233, 235, 238, 239; in early Rome, 345; in Roman Empire, 632, 638; among the Teutons, 707; in Mohammedanism, 769.
"Works and Days," of Hesiod, 155.
Writing, stages in invention, 3, d. See Alphabet, Hieroglyphs, Cuneiform.

Xe-nōph′a-nēs, 156
Xĕn′o-phon, 224, 257.
Xerx′ēs, 169, 171, 178, 181.
Xuthus (zōō′thus), 116, b.

York, map after p. 554.

Zā′ma, battle of, 454. Map after p. 370.
Zend A-věs′ta, 78.
Ze′no, Emperor, 728.
Zeno the Stoic, 317.
Ze-nō′bi-a, 646.
Zeus, 111.
Zeux′is, 314.
Zo-ro-ăs′ter, 78.